P9-CDV-586

SEARCH AND SEIZURE

SEARCH & SEIZURE

Constitutional and Common Law

Polyvios G. Polyviou
Sometime Fellow of Lincoln College, Oxford

Duckworth

To Georgia and Clio

First published in 1982 by
Gerald Duckworth & Co. Ltd.
The Old Piano Factory
43 Gloucester Crescent, London NW1

ISBN 0 7156 1592 0 (cased)

British Library Cataloguing in Publication Data
Polyviou, Polyvios G.
Search and seizure: constitutional and common law.
1. Searches and seizures — Law and legislation — England
2. Searches and seizures — Law and legislation — United States.
I. Title
344.202'418 KD4839

ISBN 0-7156-1592-0

Printed in Great Britain
by Ebenezer Baylis & Son Ltd
The Trinity Press, Worcester, and London

Contents

Preface

The privacy of a man's home and the security and integrity of his person and property have long been recognised as basic human rights, enjoying both an impressive history and a firm footing in most constitutional documents and international instruments. But much as these rights are valued they cannot be absolute. All legal systems must and do allow official power in various circumstances and on satisfaction of certain conditions to encroach upon rights of privacy and security in the interests of law enforcement, either to investigate an alleged offence or to apprehend a lawbreaker or to search for and seize evidence of crime. The interests at stake are compelling. On the one hand the security and privacy of a person's home and possessions should not be invaded except for compelling reasons. On the other hand society, represented by its organised institutions, also has an undeniable and equally powerful interest in effectively investigating crime and punishing wrongdoers. The task of balancing these conflicting interests is a matter of great importance and of considerable difficulty; but it must be attempted, and so far as possible, for the health of civil liberty and law enforcement alike, satisfactorily performed. The subject-matter of this book is the Anglo-American law of search and seizure, namely attempted definitions by American constitutional law and by the common law observed in England and the principal Commonwealth jurisdictions of the circumstances when official invasions of privacy and security can legitimately take place in an effort to accomplish the last of the objectives set out above, namely the discovery and seizure of evidence of crime.

My purpose is twofold: first to give a more or less accurate picture of the law of search and seizure (principally in the United States, but also in Great Britain and the Commonwealth), and secondly to investigate the particular ways in which the Fourth Amendment from which the law of search and seizure derives in the United States has received, in the past fifteen years or so, incredible—some would say ridiculous—expansion at the hands of the Supreme Court. In other words, I intend my book to be both a book on criminal procedure and a monograph on constitutional law, with particular emphasis on the development, uses and abuses of constitutional doctrine.

The law of search and seizure must answer three basic questions. Has there been a search or seizure? If there has, is it legal? If it is not, what are the consequences? In their answers to these questions American law and English law diverge significantly. In particular, remarkable developments in connection with the first and third issues, namely threshold applicability of search and seizure safeguards on the one hand and enforcement of these safeguards on the other, mean that the law of search and seizure in the United States has expanded to an extent that would be unthinkable in a common law regime that does not rest on a constitutional foundation (indeed not any foundation but one with the distinctive features of the American one) and is currently of supreme importance, being in effect the main rubric for the control of official investigative activities aimed at the gathering of information against a suspect otherwise than by interrogation. In contrast both to what will be seen to be nothing short of a doctrinal revolution and to continuous, even though sometimes strained, efforts to refer almost every question to first principles—both these phenomena being facilitated on the one hand by the vagueness and open-ended nature of the constitutional provision and on the other by the aggressive way in which American courts have discharged the tasks of judicial review and constitutional adjudication under the Fourth Amendment—English law presents a chaotic and intellectually underdeveloped state. Almost every important question is open to considerable doubt and even basic principles, if indeed there are any, are not settled. This confusion and doctrinal poverty are, to a somewhat lesser extent, also shared by the main Commonwealth jurisdictions I consider, namely Australia, New Zealand and Canada.

But comparison between the American and Commonwealth approaches and regimes is still interesting and instructive not only because of the shared concepts and terminology but also because the two systems derive from a common origin, the great case of *Entick v. Carrington*. The dramatic event of course which transformed American law was the adoption of the Fourth Amendment, which effectively converted part of criminal procedure into constitutional law. No similar event has occurred either in England or the Commonwealth jurisdictions we shall consider, which generally means that search and seizure law has not been constitutionalised but basically remains common law.[1] But at the same time significant elements of American doctrine can be traced back to the common law—and this by virtue of the adoption of a loose standard, that only 'unreasonable searches' are prohibited — and often English and Commonwealth judges when deciding search and seizure cases are aware that they are dealing with important issues regarding the liberty of the subject—a 'constitutional' element can therefore be said to be present, occasionally at least, in English and Commonwealth search and seizure cases. A comparison between American and English doctrines is not therefore out of place. But of course one cannot ignore the immeasurably greater (not to say overwhelming) mass of American materials, which means that a direct comparison cannot work. In this book I therefore discuss the two models, the constitutional (by which I refer to the interpretation of the Fourth Amendment) and the common law (by which I refer to English and Commonwealth doctrines) separately, all the more so since by far the greatest part of my book is devoted to the Fourth Amendment. But there are a common historical Introduction, a single chapter on Enforcement, where I pay particular attention to exclusionary doctrines, and a final section of Concluding Comments where I attempt to draw some comparisons.

[1] Of course Canada, Australia and New Zealand have written Constitutions (the British North America Act 1867, the Commonwealth of Australia Constitution Act 1900 and the New Zealand Constitution (Amendment) Act 1947 respectively) but these make no provision for fundamental rights (and therefore do not enshrine a right of security from arbitrary search and seizure, in contrast to the United States Constitution). Canada of course does have a Bill of Rights, but this is basically an enactment setting out the rights of citizens at common law.

1. Historical Background

(a) England

Entick v. Carrington[1] is the source of the Anglo-American law of search and seizure.[2] Developments before then can be sketched out briefly. Very little information is available about early practices in the area of what we now know as search and seizure, but it is probable that during the early administration of the criminal law officials routinely took any action that was considered necessary; this, one assumes, would be done on the strength of the authority they possessed, the written warrant being a later development.[3] At the beginning of the fourteenth century we have the first instances of legislation authorising searches and seizures, one of the first examples being an act passed in 1335 providing that innkeepers in passage ports were to search guests for imported money.[4] During the next century and a half similar powers were given to certain organised trades and other associations as a means of enforcing their regulations and charters, one prominent case being a statute passed in 1511 giving the authorities of cities, towns and boroughs 'full power and authority' to search for and (in the event of discovery) destroy adulterated oils.[5]

A new chapter is inaugurated with the use of broad search and seizure powers to enforce laws relating to the licensing of books and printing and the suppression of religious freedom and seditious libel.[6] Not long after the introduction of printing into England a system of state censorship was introduced, making it compulsory for all publications to receive a licence, and it was for the purpose of enforcing this pervasive licensing system that broad powers of search and seizure were conferred on those entrusted with its superintendence and execution.[7] During this period the main responsibility for enforcement belonged to the Stationers' Company, a private organisation

[1] (1765) 19 State Tr. 1030.

[2] See N. Lasson, *The History and Development of the Fourth Amendment to the United States Constitution* (1937) (hereinafter cited as Lasson); J. Landynski, *Search and Seizure and the Supreme Court* (1966) (hereinafter cited as Landynski); Raynard, 'Freedom from Unreasonable Search and Seizure – A Second Class Constitutional Right?', 25 *Ind. L.J.* 259 (1950) (hereinafter cited as Raynard).

[3] Lasson, at 22. Efforts to derive a right of privacy from Magna Carta have not been successful. For Coke's efforts to derive this from Art. 39, see his *Institutes of the Laws of England* (1671).

[4] 9 Edw. III, St. II, Ch. 11 (1335); see Lasson, 23; Raynard, 264.

[5] 3 Henry VIII, Ch. 14 (1511); Lasson, 24; Raynard, 264.

[6] See generally Siebert, *Freedom of the Press in England: 1476–1776* (1952); as was well observed by Stewart J. in *Stanford v. Texas*, 379 U.S. 476, 482, the history of the Anglo-American law of search and seizure is 'largely a history of conflict between the Crown and the press'.

[7] Landynski, 20–1; Lasson, 23–9; *Stanford v. Texas*, 379 U.S. 476, 482.

which was given monopoly privileges over printing in exchange for undertaking to detect violations of the licensing laws and apprehend those responsible, and in pursuance of this purpose the members of the company were authorised 'to make search wherever it shall please them in any place . . . and to seize, take hold, burn . . . those books and things . . . printed contrary to the form of any statute, act or proclamation'.[1] In the second part of the sixteenth century the Star Chamber passed two famous decrees further strengthening the licensing system. The first of these expanded the authority of the Company by giving its wardens power to inspect all books and papers brought into the country, to search any place where they suspected a violation of the printing laws to have taken or be taking place, and to seize any books or papers printed contrary to the licensing regulations. The second decree took note of widespread evasion of the printing laws, made provision for stricter censorship and conferred even more sweeping powers of search and seizure.[2] During this period seditious libel and similar 'offences' also came under the jurisdiction of the Courts of Star Chamber and High Commission, and wide powers to search for and arrest suspected offenders and to seize evidence were given to officials. The warrants conferring these powers appear to have been quite general. 'Persons and places were not necessarily specified, seizure of papers and effects was indiscriminate, everything was left to the discretion of the bearer of the warrant'.[3] During the first part of the seventeenth century general warrants were in much use. These were now widely employed to enforce laws in regulation of religion — a famous example being the circulars issued from the Court of High Commission in 1634 directing all peace officers to search every room of any house where they suspected non-conformist services to be held, to arrest all persons to be found there and to seize all unlicensed books[4] — and to search for documentary evidence that might reveal treason or sedition, a striking illustration being the order from the Privy Council directing a messenger to search for and seize 'seditious and dangerous papers' belonging to Sir Edward Coke as the great lawyer lay dying.[5] This repressive period reached its culmination with an even stricter ordinance issued by the Star Chamber in 1637 which conferred even wider powers of search and seizure, including the express provision this time that a search could take place at any time of day or night.[6]

Starting with the abolition of the Star Chamber, certain hopeful developments took place in 1640 and the following years. One was a resolution by the House of Commons that the issuing and execution of general warrants against members of Parliament in 1629 had been breaches of privilege for which those responsible were to be punished; another was a

[1] E. Arber, *A Transcript of the Registers of the Company of Stationers of London, 1554–1640* (1875); see Landynski, 21.

[2] Lasson, 24–5.

[3] Ibid., at 26.

[4] Ibid., at 28 n. 55.

[5] Landynski, 23; Lasson, 31.

[6] Lasson, 32.

growing legislative awareness of the undesirability of general warrants, evidenced among other things by the impeachment of the Earl of Strafford partly on the ground that he had granted to subordinates a general warrant of arrest.[1] But these hopeful signs did not prove lasting. In 1662 a number of statutes were passed authorising resort to powers of search and seizure as drastic as any that had previously been employed at the direction of the Star Chamber. The most important was the Licensing Act.[2] This was aimed at 'preventing abuses in printing seditious, treasonable, and unlicensed books and pamphlets' and at 'regulating . . . printing and printing presses'; prohibited the printing of many types of books and pamphlets; required the licensing of books; and gave the King's Secretaries of State almost unlimited power to issue search warrants in connection with any books that had not been licensed. The Licensing Act expired in 1679 when Charles II refused to summon Parliament. But Chief Justice Scroggs advised Charles II that despite the failure to reenact the Act seditious libel was a common law offence, that books and papers containing such libels could therefore still be seized, and indeed that to write, print or publish any book, pamphlet or other matter without a licence from the Crown was illegal. This enabled the King to issue a proclamation suppressing seditious libel and forbidding unlicensed printing, and this proclamation was in turn relied upon by Scroggs C.J. and other judges in issuing general warrants of arrest and search.[3] But that legislative opinion was once more adopting a disapproving attitude towards general warrants is shown by the fact that only a year later Scroggs C.J. himself was impeached, one of the articles of impeachment being that he had issued 'general warrants for attaching the persons and seizing the goods of his majesty's subjects, not named or described particularly in the said warrants'. After the Revolution of 1688 there were further unmistakable signs that the legislature was becoming aware that general warrants represented an oppressive and undesirable exercise of state power and that they should not as a rule be used. Examples are the abolition of a tax shortly after the Revolution, partly because its enforcement would have necessitated objectionable general searches which would constitute 'a badge of slavery upon the whole people, exposing every man's house to be entered into and searched by persons unknown to him';[4] the withdrawal of a tax bill proposed by Walpole in 1733 because of its allegedly extensive search provisions even though under its terms only those places registered as storehouses were to be liable to inspection on the authority of general warrants;[5] and William Pitt's famous parliamentary denunciation in 1763 of the cider tax and its provisions on enforcement which included powers of search and seizure.[6]

An important point to notice is that during the same period, mainly the

[1] Ibid., 32–3.

[2] 13 and 14 Charles II, Ch. 33 (1662).

[3] Lasson, 38; Landynski, 24–5; but the Licensing Act was reenacted in 1685, finally expiring in 1695.

[4] 1 Wm. and M., Ch. 10; see Lasson, 39.

[5] Lasson, 40–1.

[6] Ibid., 41–2.

seventeenth century, when both Parliament and the Crown were using the general warrant and writs of assistance to sanction serious invasions of personal freedom and security 'the common law was at work developing its protection'.[1] Particularly important in this development was the influence of Sir Matthew Hale.[2] Hale disagreed with Coke that under the common law no warrant could be issued. In his view warrants could be granted in criminal cases because of 'necessity'. But their issue should satisfy certain requirements. They were 'judicial acts' and could only be granted upon 'examination of the fact'; therefore before a justice could grant a warrant he was to receive information upon oath from the prosecutor or the witness, both as to the felony which had allegedly been committed and as to 'the causes of his suspicion', for it was only if this was done that he would be a competent judge of whether it was proper to authorise the arrest or search. Warrants, Hale also said, were not to be granted unless the complainant had 'probable cause' to suspect the allegedly stolen goods to be 'in such a house or place' and unless he showed the reasons for 'such suspicion'. And a warrant, when issued, should satisfy certain particularity requirements; in particular it should specify the name or description of the person or persons to be arrested, and it should not have a blank space to be 'filled up with the name of the party to be taken' later, for this was 'void in law'; this also meant that 'a warrant to apprehend all persons suspected and bring them before him' (i.e. the justice) was void and 'was not a sufficient justification in false imprisonment'. On the basis of these principles Hale expressed the view that warrants to search any suspected place for stolen goods were unlawful and that the only permissible search warrants were those which related to a particular place and were only issued after a demonstration of probable cause to the satisfaction of the magistrate. He knew that objectionable general search warrants had been granted in the past, but he now took them to be 'dormant' because they made 'the party to be in effect the judge'; therefore 'searches made by pretence of such general warrants give no more power to the officer or party than what they may do by law without them.' Similarly, as regards warrants of arrest against a person 'to answer such matters as shall be objected', these warrants too, Hale thought, were illegal, even though some older precedents existed in their favour.[3]

We can see from Hale that the basic doctrines which now form the backbone of the Anglo-American law of search and seizure—namely that the issuing of warrants, whether of arrest or search, is a judicial task which must only be discharged on the basis of sufficient information about the matters alleged by the complainant allowing the appropriate judicial officer to reach correct determinations, that warrants are only proper if they are granted on the basis not of mere suspicion but of probable cause concerning both the

[1] Raynard, 267.

[2] His work is *The History of the Pleas of the Crown*, prepared during the middle of the seventeenth century. It was first published in 1736, and the first American edition appeared in 1847.

[3] For consideration of Hale's views, see Lasson, 35–7; Landynski, 26–7; Raynard, 267.

commission of an offence and the suspect's alleged complicity in it and if they meet certain requirements of specificity and particularity whether as regards the person to be apprehended in the case of warrants of arrest or as regards the premises to be entered and the goods to be seized in the case of search warrants – are already sketched out with admirable clarity and precision. But for the most part, as the continued use of general warrants throughout the seventeenth century shows, 'these salutary rules of the common law exercised but little influence'[1] upon Parliament and the Crown. Indeed, despite the legislative signs after the 1688 Revolution referred to above as evidencing growing disapproval of general warrants and notwithstanding the failure to reenact the Licensing Act, the practice which had apparently grown under that Act of the Secretary of State issuing general warrants directing Crown officers both to arrest persons without either adequate evidence of their guilt or sufficient identification, and to search for and seize papers in cases of seditious libel and the like, continued well into the eighteenth century, surprisingly without much question.[2] But tension between the older jurisprudence which had favoured prerogative at the expense of liberty and the philosophy of the common law aiming at the legal consolidation of rights which had already gained basic political recognition persisted and was bound to surface sooner or later.[3]

Finally the conflict between these two incompatible 'ideologies',[4] on the one hand the ideology of the Crown deriving from the decrees of the Star Chamber and based on the continued permissibility of extensive executive action in the interests of public order and on the other the ideology of the common law premised on a developing consensus among lawyers that warrants for arrest and search should be controlled by strict procedural safeguards, came to a head and was unequivocally resolved in a series of great cases during the 1760s.[5] These cases dealt with the legality first of general warrants of arrest and secondly of warrants for the search and seizure of papers. The first issue arose out of the publication of the North Briton, a series of pamphlets criticising the government. When No. 45 of the series appeared, the government decided to punish those responsible. Lord Halifax, one of the Secretaries of State, issued a warrant directing four messengers to search for the authors, printers and publishers, to apprehend and seize them together with their papers, and to bring them before him. This was a warrant that was quite 'general as to the persons to be arrested and the places to be searched and the papers to be seized'.[6] 'Armed with this roving commission,

[1] Lasson, 37.

[2] II May's *Constitutional History of England: 1760–1860*, 124 (1912).

[3] May, supra, 124–5; Lasson, 42–3.

[4] Raynard, 268.

[5] These cases, known collectively as the General Warrant cases, are: *Huckle v. Money*, 2 Wils. K.B. 206 (1763); *Leach v. Money* (1765) 19 State Tr. 1001; *Wilkes v. Wood* (1765) 19 State Tr. 1153; *Wilkes v. Lord Halifax* (1765) 19 State Tr. 1406; and *Entick v. Carrington* (1765) 19 State Tr. 1030. See also May, supra, 124–9; W. S. Holdsworth, *A History of English Law*, vol. 10, 659–72 (1938).

[6] Lasson, 43.

the messengers, '(who) were (not) triflers in their work',[1] arrested no fewer than forty-nine persons in the next three days. Actions for trespass and false imprisonment were brought against the messengers. The defendants pleaded the general warrant as their justification, but this was held to be illegal. For Chief Justice Pratt '(t)o enter a man's house by virtue of a nameless warrant in order to procure evidence (was) worse that the Spanish Inquisition', a law 'under which no Englishman would wish to live an hour'.[2] The reason why general warrants neither naming nor describing the persons against whom they were directed were illegal was clearly set out by Lord Mansfield.[3] In some cases particular Acts of Parliament had given authority to apprehend under general warrants, as in the case of warrants to take into custody loose, idle and disorderly persons. But here there was no Act of Parliament justifying what had been done. It would therefore have to stand, if at all, upon 'principles of common law'. Reason and convenience did not justify the power claimed, because it was not proper 'that the receiving or judging of the information should be left to the discretion of the officer'; it was the magistrate himself who ought to judge and give specific directions to the executing officer. Nor did common law authorities justify general warrants. Both Hale and all others had held uncertain warrants to be void, and there was no case or book to the contrary. Could usage perhaps provide the necessary legal sanction for the general warrants in issue? Lord Mansfield thought not. A usage, to grow into a law, had to be a general usage, *communiter usitata et approbata*, and one which after long observance it would be mischievous to overturn. In contrast, what was claimed in support of the practice of issuing general warrants was only the usage of a particular office, and one that was contrary to the usage of all other justices and conservators of the peace.[4] General warrants were therefore contrary to the common law and unless authorised by statute illegal.

The second issue, namely the validity of a warrant issued by the Secretary of State to seize the papers of a person accused of a seditious libel, was dealt with in the seminal case of *Entick v. Carrington.*[5] Entick had written an unlicensed book, *The Monitor or British Freeholder*, which was regarded by the government as a seditious libel. In accordance with the practice of continuing the enforcement of the book-licensing act, although it had not been reenacted, Lord Halifax, as Secretary of State, issued a warrant directing four King's messengers, including Carrington, to search for John Entick, to seize him 'together with his books and papers', and to bring them before the Secretary of State for examination. In execution of this warrant the messengers apprehended Entick in his house and seized the books and papers in his bureau, writing-desk and drawers. Entick brought an action of trespass against the messengers for the seizure of his papers. This case, it must be noticed, is different from the earlier ones as the warrant specified the name of

[1] May, supra, 125.
[2] See *Huckle v. Money*, 2 Wils. K.B. 206 (1763).
[3] *Leach v. Money* (1765) 19 State Tr. 1001, 1026–7.
[4] Ibid., at 1026–7.
[5] (1765) 19 State Tr. 1030.

the person against whom it was directed. As regards the person, therefore, it was not a general warrant. But as regards the papers to be seized it was a general warrant, not specifying any particular papers to be seized but giving authority to the messengers to take any or all of his books and papers, according to their discretion. Lord Camden, in his masterly and memorable judgment, dealt with a number of issues, but the question to which he devoted the most attention was the legality of a search warrant for papers.[1] He had no doubt that this issue was of fundamental importance, for 'if this point should be determined in favour of the jurisdiction, the secret cabinets and bureaus of every subject in this kingdom will be thrown open to the search and inspection of a messenger, whenever the secretary of state shall think fit to charge, or even suspect, a person to be the author, printer, or publisher of a seditious libel'. The power claimed, Lord Camden went on, was an extraordinary one. A person's house would be 'rifled', and 'his most valuable papers' would be taken out of his possession before the paper, for which he was charged, was found to be criminal by any competent jurisdiction, and before he was convicted either of writing, publishing or of being otherwise concerned in the production of the offending publication. 'If honestly exerted', what the Secretary of State claimed was a power to seize the papers of a man who was charged upon oath to be the author or publisher of a seditious libel; 'if oppressively', it was a power to seize the papers of any man, described in the warrant, though he was quite innocent. Further, the power that was claimed was one that would be executed against a person before he was heard or even summoned; both the information and the informants would be unknown; and it would be executed by messengers in the presence or absence of the suspect as they saw fit, and without a witness to give evidence as to what had passed at the time, so that when the papers were taken the party injured would be left 'without proof'. Such was the power, and 'one should naturally expect that the law to warrant it should be clear in proportion as the power is exorbitant'. It was therefore for those who claimed the power to ransack a person's home and seize his papers, in this instance the defendants, to show the legal authority for their challenged entry, search and seizure. If that could not be done it would be a trespass. The basic principle was set forth by Lord Camden in ringing tones.[2]

> By the laws of England, every invasion of private property, be it ever so minute, is a trespass. No man can set his foot upon my ground without my licence, but he is liable to an action, though the damage be nothing; which is proved by every declaration in trespass, where the defendant is called upon to answer for bruising the grass and even treading upon the soil. If he admits the fact, he is bound to shew by way of justification, that some positive law has empowered or excused him. The justification

[1] See Holdsworth, supra, 5 n. 5, 667–72.

[2] Lord Camden, who previously had been Chief Justice Pratt, prefaced the passage that follows with the remarks that '(t)he great end, for which men entered into society, was to secure their property' and that 'th(is) right is preserved sacred and incommunicable in all instances where it has not been taken away or abridged by some public law for the good of the whole'.

> is submitted to the judges, who are to look into the books; and see if such a justification can be maintained by the text of the statute law, or by the principles of common law. If no such excuse can be found or produced, the silence of the books is an authority against the defendant, and the plaintiff must have judgment.

What were now the arguments given in support of the executive practice of issuing search warrants for papers in cases of seditious libel? They were four: that such warrants had been issued frequently since the Revolution; that they resembled warrants for the search of stolen goods; that such warrants had been executed without resistance upon many printers, booksellers and authors who had quietly submitted to the authority; and that the disputed power was 'essential to government, and the only means of quieting clamours and sedition'. These four arguments were rejected by Lord Camden, as follows: As regards the alleged practice, its origin was in the activities of the Star Chamber, the Licensing Act had expired, there was no support for it in the common law, and if the practice of issuing such search warrants had begun since the Revolution it had begun 'too late to be law now'; nor was the argument that there had been a general submission to such warrants a valid one since 'it would be strange doctrine to assert that all the people of this land are bound to acknowledge that to be universal law, which a few criminal booksellers have been afraid to dispute'. The suggestion that there was a resemblance between warrants for the search and seizure of papers and warrants for the search and seizure of stolen goods was equally unfounded. The difference, Lord Camden observed, was 'apparent'. In the case of searching for stolen goods one was only permitted to seize one's own goods which would then be placed in the hands of a public officer until the proceedings against the suspected felon came to an end; but in cases like the one before the court a person's own property would be seized before and without conviction, and he would have no power to reclaim his goods even after acquittal. But even if there was some similarity this was immaterial. The case of warrants for stolen goods was the only one of its kind, and therefore even if the two cases resembled each other more than they did, a new type of search warrant could only be brought about by parliamentary enactment. Finally, with respect to the argument of state necessity, or that a distinction should be drawn between state offences and others, 'the common law', in Lord Camden's proud phrase, 'does not understand that kind of reasoning, nor do our books take notice of any such distinctions'. Since therefore the defendants had failed to point to any law or other lawful authority by which the warrant to seize and carry away the plaintiff's papers could be supported the search warrant itself was illegal and void and the challenged seizure illegal and a trespass.

Following *Entick v. Carrington* the question of general warrants was discussed in Parliament. Their legality was no longer defended even by the law officers of the Crown, and in due course the House of Commons passed two resolutions condemning their use.[1] The first condemned their employ-

[1] Lasson, 48–50.

ment in cases of libel, and the second condemned their use generally.[1]

Entick v. Carrington is undoubtedly 'the central case in English constitutional law'.[2] Of course some of its specific holdings, for instance that the Secretary of State had no right to arrest except in cases of high treason, are nowadays only of historical interest; the legal and political context in which it was decided was radically different from what it is today, which in turn has resulted both in some of its language extolling the sanctity of property being characterised as rather archaic and incongruous[3] and in its relevance as an aid in the interpretation of modern statutes being questioned;[4] more importantly, as we shall see later, Lord Camden's marked unwillingness to discover lawful authority not clearly spelled out in existing law sanctioning invasions of private property in the interests of law enforcement has not been shared, at least to the same extent, by his contemporary brethren.[5] But the central principles that *Entick v. Carrington* stands for are still of undoubted validity and continuing importance. These are: every official interference with individual liberty and security is unlawful unless justified by some existing and specific statutory or common law rule; any search of private property will similarly be a trespass and illegal unless some recognised lawful authority for it can be produced; in general, coercion should only be brought to bear on individuals and their property at the instance of regular judicial officers acting in accordance with established and known rules of law, and not by executive officers acting at their discretion; and finally it is the law, whether common law or statute, and not a plea of public interest or an allegation of state necessity that will justify acts normally illegal.[6]

(b) America

In America the history of the law of search and seizure is the history of the Fourth Amendment of the Federal Constitution.[7] This reads as follows:

> The right of the people to be secure in their persons, houses, papers, and effects, against unreasonable searches and seizures, shall not be violated, and no warrants shall issue, but upon probable cause, supported by Oath or affirmation, and particularly describing the place to be searched, and the persons or things to be seized.

Discussion of the Fourth Amendment's historical background can be divided,

[1] See XVI Hansard's *Parliamentary History of England*, 207 et seq.

[2] Keir and Lawson, *Cases in Constitutional Law* 307 (1967). The learned authors said that *Entick v. Carrington* is 'perhaps' the most important case.

[3] See *Chic Fashions (West Wales) Ltd. v. Jones* [1968] 2 Q.B. 299, 319, per Salmon, L.J.

[4] See *I.R.C. v. Rossminster Ltd.* (1980) 1 All E.R. 80.

[5] See particularly *Elias v. Pasmore* (1934) 2 K.B. 164 ; *Chic Fashions (West Wales) Ltd. v. Jones* [1969] 2 Q.B. 299; *Ghani v. Jones* (1970) 1 Q.B. 693.

[6] See Holdsworth, supra, 5 n. 5, 667; R.F.V. Heuston, *Essays in Constitutional Law*, 97 (1961).

[7] See Lasson, 51 et seq.; Raynard, 269 et seq.; Landynski, 30 et seq.

for convenience, into two parts: first the use in the Colonies of the writs of assistance and the controversy that this gave rise to, and secondly the debate, such as it was, that preceded the adoption and final ratification of the Amendment.

The writs of assistance were general search warrants which were used by customs officers to search for and seize goods imported in violation of the British tax laws.[1] These writs, so called because they commanded all officers and subjects of the Crown to assist in their execution, derived from two statutes passed during the second half of the seventeenth century.[2] They were much more sweeping in nature and considerably more arbitrary in character than the English general warrants discussed above, because the latter not only related to a particular offence, for instance seditious libel, but would also lose their legal force after execution. But the 'hated'[3] writs of assistance employed in the Colonies, mainly Massachusetts, were not connected with any particular offence but simply gave customs officials blanket authority to search where they pleased for smuggled goods; in other words, the authorised officials and their assistants were empowered to search any place where they suspected smuggled goods to be and to break open any receptacle or package they saw fit. What was more, this authority was not only almost absolute in terms of scope but also continuous in terms of time; writs of assistance once given did not have to be returned after execution but continued in force during the lifetime of the reigning sovereign. These writs of assistance were rigorously enforced, and not surprisingly their oppressive use led to much dissatisfaction and in the later stages agitation. The decisive test of their legality came in 1761. King George II died in October 1760. His death meant that the writs of assistance that had been granted during his reign would soon expire and would have to be renewed. A number of Boston merchants opposed the issuance of new writs, and obtained the services of James Otis to represent them. Otis denounced the writs of assistance as 'the worst instrument of arbitrary power, the most destructive of English liberty, and the fundamental principles of law, that ever was found in an English law book', because they placed 'the liberty of every man in the hands of every petty officer.'[4] He put forward two arguments why new writs should not be granted.[5] First he argued that general warrants and writs of assistance were not known to the common law, which only allowed special warrants, and then only in cases of 'great public necessity', 'upon process and oath' and after the

[1] *Stanford v. Texas*, 379 U.S. 476, 481. The Supreme Court has reviewed the history of the Fourth Amendment on a number of occasions; see particularly *Boyd v. United States*, 116 U.S. 616; *Stanford v. Texas*, 379 U.S. 476; *Marcus v. Search Warrant*, 367 U.S. 717; *Frank v. Maryland*, 359 U.S. 360.

[2] 13 and 14 Charles II, Ch. 11 (1662); 7 and 8 Charles II, Ch. 22 (1696); see Raynard, 269–70.

[3] *Stanford v. Texas*, 379 U.S. 476, 481.

[4] John Adams was in court during the argument, and it is to his recollection and subsequent description that we mainly owe what we know about the speech of John Otis; see Adams, *Life and Works of John Adams*, vol. 2, 523–7; see also *Boyd v. United States*, 116 U.S. 616 (1886).

[5] Lasson, 59–60; Landynski, 34–5.

showing of 'good grounds of suspicion'. The original Act of 1662 should therefore be construed in a similar manner, as only authorising special writs. But even if the Act did authorise general writs, then, Otis argued, it was contrary to Magna Carta and of no force, on the reasoning of Coke in *Dr Bonham's Case* that 'An act against the Constitution is void'. The court was apparently almost persuaded, but decided to ask for further information from England. When this was received it heard further argument and finally decided in favour of the customs officers, granting the first of these new writs to Charles Paxton in December. But even though he lost his case, there is general agreement that Otis's denunciation of the writs of assistance in 1761 in Boston was 'perhaps the most prominent event which inaugurated the resistance of the colonies to the oppressions of the mother country'.[1] 'Then and there,' said John Adams, 'was the first scene of opposition to the arbitrary claims of Great Britain. Then and there the child Independence was born. In fifteen years, namely in 1776, he grew to manhood, and declared himself free'.[2]

In view of these developments it is somewhat surprising that the Declaration of Independence made no explicit reference to the issuance and use by the Crown of writs of assistance. But between 1776 and 1787 almost every State adopted some type of provision extending protection from arbitrary search and seizure. The first provision was that adopted by Virginia in its Declaration of Rights.[3] This was restricted to a condemnation of general warrants which were characterised as 'grievous and oppressive'. Later formulations of the guarantee from arbitrary search are broader in scope, in that they not only seek to outlaw general warrants and writs of assistance but also appear to confer a substantive right to be protected from certain types of search and seizure. The first example of this more elaborate type of provision is s.10 of the Pennsylvania Declaration of Rights.[4] This first declares that 'the people have a right to hold themselves, their houses, papers, and possessions free from search and seizure', and then prohibits the issuing of general warrants, which are characterised as 'contrary to that right', namely the right initially conferred. Even more comprehensive, and closely approximating to the Fourth Amendment itself, is Article 10 of the Massachusetts Declaration of Rights, adopted in 1780.[5] This proclaims first, that 'every subject has a right to be secure from all unreasonable searches and seizures of his person, his house, his papers, and all his possessions', and secondly, that general warrants are contrary to this right and should no longer be issued. Against this background, and given the importance the people themselves attached to protection from oppressive practices and governmental abuses similar to those under the writs of assistance, it is strange that the Constitutional Convention which met in Philadelphia in 1787 omitted any Bill or Declaration of Rights.

[1] *Boyd v. United States*, 116 U.S. 616, 625.

[2] *Works of John Adams*, vol. 10, 247–8; see also *Boyd v. United States*, 116 U.S. 616, 625; and *Stanford v. Texas*, 379 U.S. 476, 482.

[3] In 1776; see Lasson, 79.

[4] In 1776; see Lasson, 80–1.

[5] See Lasson, 82.

A number of reasons have been suggested to explain this omission.[1] One view is that the framers did not realise either the strong popular feeling for the inclusion in the Constitution of a declaration of protected rights or the importance of the subject. Another is that the framers thought that the bills of rights adopted by the States would be enough, and that in any case there would be no danger from the federal government, since that was only to enjoy specific and enumerated powers of which authority over civil rights was not one. Whatever the true reason for the failure to include in the constitutional document a bill of rights, this omission soon became one of the most controversial topics in the extensive debates both in the country and in the state conventions preceding the ratification of the Constitution.[2] In Virginia some urged rejection of the Constitution on the ground that it did not contain a provision forbidding arbitrary search and seizure; other States strongly urged the adoption of a bill of rights, including a search and seizure provision; almost everywhere there were forceful arguments that it was not enough that the federal government had been given no express power in the area and that it was therefore essential for the 'liberties of the people' to be spelled out clearly in the Constitution itself; and President Washington himself in his first inaugural address urged the need for some constitutional revision so that 'the characteristic rights of freemen' would be better protected.

The lead in steering the amendments that would incorporate a bill of rights into the Constitution was assumed by Madison. One of his proposals concerned a search and seizure provision. This, apparently only directed against general warrants, read as follows:

> The rights of the people to be secured in their persons, their houses, their papers, and their other property, from all unreasonable searches and seizures, shall not be violated by warrants issued without probable cause, supported by oath or affirmation, or not particularly describing the places to be searched, or the persons or things to be seized.

In August 1789 the House of Representatives, sitting as a Committee of the Whole, considered the proposed amendments. The search and seizure provision that came before it was as follows:

> The right of the people to be secured in their persons, houses, papers, and effects, shall not be violated by warrants issuing without probable cause, supported by oath or affirmation, and not particularly describing the place to be searched, and the persons or things to be seized.

It was first recommended that two errors should be corrected: first that the word *secured* should become *secure*, and secondly that the phrase 'unreasonable searches and seizures', omitted from Madison's proposals,

[1] Lasson, 85–6.
[2] See Lasson, 88–97; Landynski, 40–1.

should be included. The proposal, in other words, was that the Amendment should protect 'The right of the people to be secure in their persons, houses, papers and effects, against unreasonable searches and seizures'. This proposal was accepted. Then the following exchange took place, as reported by the congressional report.

> Mr. Benson objected to the words 'by warrants issuing'. This declaratory provision was good as far as it went, but he thought it was not sufficient; he therefore proposed to alter it so as to read 'and no warrant shall issue'.
>
> The question was put on this motion, and lost by a considerable majority.[1]

The text of the Amendment should therefore have been what was placed before the House in August 1789 as modified by the correction of the two errors in the first part of the proposal. In this way the Amendment would only have protected the right to be free from unreasonable searches and seizures from general warrants, namely warrants not issued in accordance with its specificity requirements, and would not have conferred an independent right of freedom from unreasonable searches and seizures, distinct from the specification of the particularity standards to which valid warrants were to conform. And yet the Fourth Amendment as it exists today is what Benson proposed and what was clearly rejected. Not only does it provide for the procedure leading to the issuing of search warrants and for their contents when issued, but it also embodies and confers a right broader than the guarantee that a person's security should not be violated by general warrants—the right to be secure from unreasonable searches and seizures irrespective of the presence or absence of a warrant. It is impossible to answer with any certainty the question why it is Benson's version which was not carried that today forms the Fourth Amendment. One suggested possibility[2] is that since Benson was the chairman of the committee which had been appointed to arrange the amendments as passed he must have ignored the version which had been adopted and again put forward his own, this time as if it had been approved by the House. Whatever the truth of the matter, the alteration was not noticed, and Benson's version was ultimately passed by the Senate and the House and ratified by the States.[3] As we have seen, this, as it now appears in the Constitution, contains two different clauses, the first protecting the right of the people to be secure from unreasonable searches and seizures, and the second providing that warrants should not be issued except in accordance with the procedural safeguards of oath or affirmation, probable cause, and particularity. What the relationship between these two clauses is—not surprisingly, given the lack of any discussion by the framers in the debates preceding adoption—has caused very great difficulty. This will be discussed extensively at a later stage.

[1] Annals of Congress, 1st Congress, 1st Session, at 783.
[2] Lasson, 101–3.
[3] In 1791.

(c) *Boyd v. United States*

For almost a century after its adoption the Fourth Amendment hardly ever came before the Supreme Court. Two early cases deserve brief mention. In the first[1] it was confirmed that the Fourth Amendment applied only to criminal proceedings and not to civil proceedings for the recovery of debt; in the other[2] it was held that letters and packages in the mail could not be opened without a search warrant. The first important case on the interpretation of the Fourth Amendment to come before the Court was *Boyd v. United States*, in 1886.[3] This case has been much criticised,[4] indeed it may no longer be correctly decided,[5] but it has had a profound and undeniable impact on the subsequent development of the American law of search and seizure. What was in issue in *Boyd* was a statute providing that in forfeiture proceedings under the customs revenue law a court could order a defendant to produce documents allegedly containing proof of guilt and that failure to comply with the order would be regarded as an admission of the allegations and charges against the defendant. Boyd complied with a court order directing him to produce an invoice under protest, arguing that both the court order and the statute under which it had been issued were unconstitutional. The Supreme Court unanimously agreed that the statute offended the privilege against self-incrimination embodied in the Fifth Amendment and was therefore unconstitutional. But seven members of the Court also expressed the view that the statute also violated the Fourth Amendment in that it authorised unreasonable searches and seizures.[6] It was not necessary, the majority decided, that there should be a forcible entry upon premises or an actual search for papers before there could be search and seizure within the meaning of the Fourth Amendment. A compulsory production of a person's private books and papers to be used against him in a criminal or penal proceeding or for a forfeiture was also within the spirit and scope of the Fourth Amendment (i.e. it was a search), basically because the purpose and result of a compulsory production of papers would be the same as the purpose and result of more typical searches and seizures, and the same applied to a provision that did not order a compulsory production of papers but which had the effect of making their non-production an admission of the charges the papers would allegedly prove. But—and this was the second stage of the Court's inquiry—granted that a *search and seizure* were involved in what the challenged statute authorised, were they *unreasonable* within the meaning of the Fourth Amendment? At this point the Court turned its attention to the privilege against self-incrimination. The seizure or

[1] *Murray v. Hoboken Land Company*, 18 How. 272, 15 L. ed. 372 (1855).

[2] *In re Jackson*, 96 U.S. 727, 24 L. ed. 77 (1877).

[3] 116 U.S. 616 (1886).

[4] 8 Wigmore, *Evidence* § 2264 (1940).

[5] See particularly *Couch v. United States*, 409 U.S. 322 (1973); *Fisher v. United States*, 425 U.S. 391 (1976); *Andresen v. Maryland*, 427 U.S. 463 (1976).

[6] Miller J., whom Waite, C. J. joined, could find no search or seizure in what the statute had authorised. The Fourth Amendment was therefore inapplicable, and the only constitutional provision that was relevant was the Fifth Amendment.

compulsory production of a man's private papers to be used in evidence against him was equivalent to compelling him to be a witness against himself; it was therefore within the prohibition of the Fifth Amendment. But what was the relevance of the Fifth Amendment's privilege against self-incrimination in an inquiry about the reasonableness or unreasonableness of a search (which the majority had already located)? It was relevant because the Court regarded the two Amendments as intimately related. They threw much light upon one another. In particular when the thing forbidden by the Fifth Amendment, namely compelling a man to be a witness against himself, was the object of a search and seizure of his private papers, it was an 'unreasonable search and seizure' which was within the prohibition of the Fourth Amendment.

A number of important themes emerge from *Boyd*. First, Justice Bradley, delivering the majority opinion, expressed the view that the Fourth Amendment did not only forbid forcible entries and actual searches and seizures but rather embodied broad rights to personal freedom and security. The argument for this was simple. *Entick v. Carrington* had recognised such a broad right, and Lord Camden's judgment in this case was foremost in the minds of those who drafted the Fourth Amendment. *Entick v. Carrington* and its principles were therefore part of the Fourth Amendment. But what exactly were these principles, and what was the right enshrined in the constitutional guarantee from unreasonable searches and seizures? Justice Bradley's observations on this have been quoted many times, and have had great influence on subsequent Fourth Amendment jurisprudence.

> The principles laid down in this opinion (*Entick*) affect the very essence of constitutional liberty and security. They reach farther than the concrete form of the case then before the court, with its adventitious circumstances; they apply to all invasions on the part of the government and its employees of the sanctity of a man's home and the privacies of life. It is not the breaking of his doors, and the rummaging of his drawers, that constitutes the essence of the offence; but it is the invasion of his indefeasible right of personal security, personal liberty and private property, where that right has never been forfeited by his conviction of some public offence, — it is the invasion of this sacred right which underlies and constitutes the essence of Lord Camden's judgment. Breaking into a house and opening boxes and drawers are circumstances of aggravation; but any forcible and compulsory extortion of a man's own testimony or of his private papers to be used as evidence to convict him of crime or to forfeit his goods, is within the condemnation of that judgment. In this regard the Fourth and Fifth Amendments run almost into each other.

It can be seen that, partly because of the sweeping language of his opinion, Justice Bradley does not delineate even in a rough manner the parameters of the fundamental right he is recognising. Nor does he give a criterion for recognising a search when this is not obvious.[1] These questions would be left

[1] 'Note, The Life and Times of *Boyd v. United States* (1886–1976)', 76 *Mich. L. Rev.* 184, 188 (1977).

to subsequent cases and future judges. But if a test can be extracted from his judgment it is that 'any measure, regardless of its form, which accomplishes the same result'[1] as a conventional search will come within the ambit of the Fourth Amendment and be evaluated according to its standards.

The last sentence from the passage quoted above takes one to the second theme of *Boyd*, the close connection that allegedly exists between the Fourth and Fifth Amendments. Here again Justice Bradley relied on some statements by Lord Camden in *Entick v. Carrington* apparently linking the right against unlawful searches with the privilege against self-incrimination and condemning the warrants in issue there not only because of their generality but also because their effect was to authorise a search for and a seizure of *evidence*, as opposed to, say, stolen goods where the property did not belong to the subject of the search.[2] Obviously building on these statements, Justice Bradley developed the thesis that there was an 'intimate relation' between the two Amendments, not only in terms of history but also in terms of the help they afforded in each other's interpretation. In giving its opinion the Court did not spend much time developing this reciprocal relationship, nor in investigating its implications. It only observed that the 'unreasonable searches and seizures' condemned by the Fourth Amendment were almost always made for the purpose of compelling a man to give evidence against himself, which was prohibited by the Fifth; and compelling a man 'in a criminal case to be a witness against himself' in turn cast light on what was an 'unreasonable search and seizure' within the meaning of the Fourth Amendment. On the basis of this 'similarity' the majority expressed itself unable to perceive that the seizure of a man's private books and papers to be used in evidence against him was substantially different from compelling him to be a witness against himself. Such a seizure was therefore unconstitutional. The Court's merging of the guarantee from unreasonable searches with the privilege against self-incrimination has been convincingly criticised.[3] As regards history, the two principles are only connected in that both were used in the struggle for political liberty and in the development of a body of procedural safeguards. But their particular political and legal pedigrees are very different.[4] Nor are the functions performed by them (as traditionally understood) any closer. The purpose of the privilege is to protect a person from any incriminating disclosure sought by legal process from him as a witness. The most obvious example of this is when testimonial compulsion is brought to bear upon a person for the purpose of extracting from his lips an admission of guilt. But another, more controversial, instance of its application is when testimonial compulsion is employed against an individual to make him produce existing documents or even chattels. For even though the documents or chattels are not oral in form and are already in existence at the time the process is used 'still there is a testimonial disclosure implicit in their production',[5] this being

[1] Fraenkel, 'Concerning Searches and Seizures', 34 *Harv. L. Rev.* 361, 367 (1921).
[2] 19 State Tr. 1030, 1073.
[3] 8 Wigmore, *Evidence* § 2264 (McNaughton rev. 1961).
[4] Ibid.
[5] Ibid.

the witness's assurance that what is produced is what was demanded. In other words, as soon as a process or an act of compulsion is seen ultimately to depend upon the witness's own testimonial responsibility, his 'moral responsibility for truthtelling', as Wigmore puts it[1], the privilege against self-incrimination can be invoked. This of course is what happened in *Boyd*, and this case should therefore have been decided solely on the basis of the Fifth Amendment. But this formulation of the privilege means that documents or other articles obtained otherwise than through the use of testimonial compulsion directed against the witness himself cannot be brought within its orbit. The principal example of this is the obtaining of articles by search and seizure, independently of any testimonial process and without calling upon the party affected to incriminate himself.[2] The privilege against self-incrimination cannot therefore be violated by searches and seizures. 'In short, the principles of the Fourth and Fifth Amendments are complementary to each other; what the one covers, the other leaves untouched'.[3] On the basis of this delineation of the ambits of the two provisions the holding of *Boyd* that the Fourth Amendment applies to an order against the defendant himself to produce incriminating documents was wrong.[4] The other implication of *Boyd's* elaboration of a close and cooperative relationship between the constitutional protections from unreasonable searches and from compulsory self-incrimination is that the seizure of books and the like is apparently absolutely prohibited, whether under the Fifth Amendment or under the Fourth or more correctly as a result of their joint operation.[5] For if the seizure of a man's private papers to be used against him in evidence is, as the Court says, for all purposes the same as attempting to force him to incriminate himself, the privilege should also forbid the search and seizure of a person's books and papers when their aim is to obtain information from them that will be used to incriminate him, irrespective of the presence or absence of a warrant. In other words, under the principles of *Boyd* not only is the provision protecting from unreasonable searches made to cover what is properly the subject-matter of the privilege against self-incrimination, that is orders against the defendant for the disclosure of incriminating information or the production of documents, but also the Fifth Amendment is in effect engrafted on to the Fourth even in the latter's undisputed area of operation, and this by its principles being allowed to determine—and in the result preclude—the

[1] Ibid.

[2] Ibid.

[3] 8 Wigmore, *Evidence* § 2264 (1940).

[4] An even more restrictive formulation of the privilege against self-incrimination would only apply it where the compelled act *itself* constitutes an incriminating communication, so that where the government knows that documents which it wishes to claim are in existence and in the defendant's hands a subpoena to obtain them is not a violation of the privilege because the act of production would not be testimonial (or sufficiently testimonial) in nature; see 'Note', supra, 15 n.1, at 208, and *Fisher v. United States*, 425 U.S. 391 (1976) and *Andresen v. Maryland*, 427 U.S. 463 (1976). In other words, *Boyd* is wrong even under the Fifth Amendment.

[5] This was settled in *Gouled v. United States*, 255 U.S. 298 (1921), now overruled by *Warden v. Hayden*, 387 U.S. 294 (1967).

reasonableness of searches and seizures even in the absence of testimonial compulsion. But what is the difference between warrants for the seizure of stolen goods and the like and warrants for the seizure of incriminating documents? The answer of the *Boyd* majority is that in the case of stolen goods, contraband and the like the person subjected to the search is not entitled to their possession since the government or the claimant can set up a superior right; in contrast, an individual's private books and papers cannot be claimed either by the government or by another claimant under a superior proprietary or possessory right.[1] One can therefore see that ultimately the holding of *Boyd*, via the privilege against self-incrimination, is based, much like *Entick v. Carrington* itself, on property considerations. In 'th(is) respect, the doctrine contained the seeds of its own destruction'.[2]

The third theme of *Boyd* has proved more durable. This is that the guarantee from unreasonable searches and seizures, like the other provisions embodying fundamental personal rights, should be construed broadly. After observing that it did not matter that the proceeding which had been challenged before them was free from many of the aggravating characteristics of 'actual' searches and seizures, since this too contained 'their substance and essence' and brought about 'their substantial purpose', Justice Bradley eloquently sketched out the approach that courts should follow in cases under the Fourth Amendment in words that have been repeated endlessly:

> It may be that (what happened) is the obnoxious thing in its mildest and least repulsive form; but illegitimate and unconstitutional practices get their first footing in that way, namely by silent approaches and slight deviations from legal modes of procedure. This can only be obviated by adhering to the rule that constitutional provisions for the security of person and property should be liberally construed. A close and literal construction of them deprives them of half their efficacy, and leads to gradual depreciation of the right, as if it consisted more in sound than in substance. It is the duty of courts to be watchful for the constitutional rights of the citizen, and guard against any stealthy encroachments thereon. Their motto should be *obsta principiis*.

Boyd has always been regarded as perhaps the most important case on the law of search and seizure—now, not so much because of its specific holding as because of the way it approached the Fourth Amendment. There have been many phases in development since them. During some, courts, in apparent defiance of *Boyd*'s admonitions, have taken a rather restrictive attitude towards the right to be secure from unreasonable searches and seizures. More frequently, the American judiciary, in accordance with its spirit, has adopted

[1] 'The search for and seizure of stolen or forfeited goods, or goods liable to duties and concealed to avoid the payment thereof, are totally different things from a search for and seizure of a man's private books and papers for the purpose of obtaining information therein contained, or of using them as evidence against him. . . . In the one case, the government is entitled to the possession of the property; in the other it is not': 116 U.S. 616, 623 (1886).

[2] 'Note', supra, 15 n. 1, at 189.

with enthusiasm what has been identified above as *Boyd's* central directive, namely that the Fourth Amendment should be read broadly—as embodying a broad right of personal security—and has struggled valiantly to work out its implications. These developments will be discussed at length in what follows.

2. What are 'Searches' and 'Seizures'?

The Fourth Amendment prohibits unreasonable searches and seizures. A search that is unreasonable is unconstitutional. The meaning of constitutional unreasonableness will be investigated later. But naturally the first and most important question is whether a search or seizure has taken place.[1] If there has been no search or seizure, the Fourth Amendment does not apply and the issue of reasonableness will not be reached; in other words, in terms of individual rights, no personal interest recognised by the Constitution has been infringed, and, in terms of the permissibility and legality of law enforcement practices, official conduct not amounting to a search or seizure does not have to be reasonable and is in effect altogether exempt from all legal control. Conversely, if a search has taken place, there has been an intrusion on constitutionally protected individual rights, and the particular form of police conduct or practice must be considered under the guarantee of immunity from unlawful search and seizure, which means that it must meet the standard of constitutional reasonableness.[2] Obviously a forcible entry into a house for the purpose of seizing tangible evidence of crime is a search in the full sense; but what about other police activities that might also be thought to jeopardise a person's rights to personal security, privacy and liberty, from early on identified as the prime purpose of the Fourth Amendment? Many examples from the cases can be found. What about electronic eavesdropping, whether by wiretapping or in other ways, resulting in the interception of private conversations; the use of other mechanical or non-mechanical devices aimed at obtaining certain other (not so restricted) types of information against persons suspected of crime; the employment of informers and other secret agents; other forms of secret non-physical surveillance and clandestine observation, whether by the unassisted senses of seeing, hearing or smelling, or by the use of instruments or aids reinforcing the naked senses; examination of the business and financial records deposited with and kept by banks and similar institutions; and many others?

Two related issues can immediately be seen to be crucial. To begin with, to say that official activities such as the above which are directed towards the obtaining of restricted information are not searches is to say that they can be

[1] See generally 1 W. LaFave, *Search and Seizure* 220–435 (1978); Amsterdam, 'Perspectives on the Fourth Amendment', 58 *Minn. L. Rev.* 349 (1974); 'Note, From Private Places to Personal Privacy: A Post-Katz Study of Fourth Amendment Protection', 43 *N.Y.U.L. Rev.* 968 (hereafter referred to as 'Note') (1968).

[2] Amsterdam, supra, at 388; Dworkin, 'Fact Style Adjudication and the Fourth Amendment: The Limits of Lawyering', 48 *Ind. L.J.* 329, 335 (1973); Kitch, 'Katz v. United States: The Limits of the Fourth Amendment', 1968 *Sup. Ct. Rev.* 133.

engaged in by the police at their unfettered discretion, without any constraint and outside any judicial control, however attenuated, obviously at considerable cost both to individual liberty and society's collective sense of security; to say that all police investigative practices without exception are searches means that Fourth Amendment principles will almost certainly be extended 'to improbable and unwarranted lengths' and that 'the genuine liberties protected by the Fourth Amendment' may suffer by being made 'bedfellows with spurious liberties improvised by farfetched analogies'.[1] In terms of the coverage of search and seizure law as an abstract matter one's instinctive reaction is to look for the middle ground between on the one hand the strict constructionist extreme—that since the Amendment was adopted in view of specific historical evils, mainly forcible entries and indiscriminate rummaging under general warrants and writs of assistance, it *should* extend to nothing else, constitutional searches being therefore confined to trespassory invasions and other such quests for physical evidence—and on the other the activist extreme—that the purpose of the Fourth Amendment is not to proscribe the evils and abuses that were uppermost in the minds of those responsible for its enactment but to protect personal and societal security and liberty in the broadest sense and to the fullest extent, and that therefore every governmental information-gathering activity endangering privacy and liberty, however subtle and indirect, constitutes a search and should therefore only be allowed if it is consistent with applicable Fourth Amendment safeguards.[2] But, as a matter of substantive coverage, where exactly is this middle line to be drawn? The second issue relates to the *precise* source of Fourth Amendment principles. For it is not enough for a line between those law enforcement practices that should be regulated and those that should not to commend itself as reasonable and proper either to scholars or to courts. In terms of Fourth Amendment law distinctions between what is constitutionally controlled and what can be engaged in by the police at their discretion, and between what individual desires to freedom from unsolicited intrusion and observation will be accorded judicial protection as opposed to those whose safeguarding will be relegated to what at best can only be fragile official self-restraint, must have a legitimate base in something beyond the doctrinal vulnerability of ad hoc and ultimately subjective determinations either that certain law enforcement methods are undesirable or that it is 'unfair' to expose citizens to certain risks. But where, then, is the meaning of the Fourth Amendment to be distilled from?[3] If one looks to history, there is the danger that the Amendment will be confined to the specific (or similar) abuses that gave rise to its enactment in the first place. Conversely, if one abandons the quest for the (literal) original understanding and views the Fourth Amendment broadly and expansively, not as containing a set of restrictions on certain types of official conduct but as embodying nothing less than 'the very essence of constitutional liberty and security',[4] the constitutional

[1] *On Lee v. United States,* 343 U.S. 747, 754 (1951).
[2] Amsterdam, supra: Kitch, supra.
[3] See Amsterdam, supra.
[4] *Boyd v. United States*, 116 U.S. 616, 627–30 (1886).

prohibition could easily be triggered by every non-consensual governmental effort to obtain information because every unsolicited investigative activity 'must, of necessity, intrude to some degree upon the security of those investigated',[1] a reading that would place considerable if not unbearable strain on the internal structure of the Amendment. Should perhaps an intermediate model be attempted, embodying the values and purposes of the framers but attempting to transpose them, give them concrete form and apply them to modern conditions?[2] Despite a great number of cases and volumes of critical commentary fundamental questions regarding the Amendment's coverage remain; this is likely always to be so; for, as will also inescapably emerge, the twin questions of the scope and meaning of the concepts of 'search' and 'seizure' and of the principles through which the constitutional prescriptions will be judicially applied ultimately depend neither on linguistic considerations nor on voyages of historical discovery but on one's (conscious or unconscious) choice of basic approach to the Fourth Amendment, the constitutional scheme as a whole, and the role of judicial review.

But whatever the considerations that ultimately determine the matter the question that must be asked and answered is: What are searches and seizures? In *Boyd v. United States,*[3] it will be remembered, the Supreme Court, invalidating a federal law under the Fourth Amendment even though the challenged procedure 'was hardly a search or seizure in any linguistically evident sense',[4] used broad language. The Amendment, the majority said, embodied nothing less than fundamental rights of personal security and personal liberty and prohibited not only forcible entries and physical searches but also all official 'invasions' of 'the sanctity of a man's home and the privacies of life'.[5] But both the broad approach of *Boyd* and its implications were ignored in *Olmstead v. United States*[6] where the Supreme Court held that telephone wiretapping was not a search or seizure and therefore did not come within the Fourth Amendment. Chief Justice Taft read the Amendment's purpose restrictively and by reference to its specific historical origins, as being 'to prevent the use of governmental force to search a man's house, his person, his papers, and his effects, and to prevent their seizure against his will', and expressed the view that it was to be construed 'in the light of what was deemed an unreasonable search and seizure when it was adopted'. It followed that the Amendment did not forbid telephone wiretapping. 'There was no searching', because 'there was no entry of the houses or offices of the defendants', and 'there was no seizure', because the evidence had been secured 'by the use of the sense of hearing and that only'. Two lines of reasoning run through the Court's opinion.[7] First, the Fourth

[1] Kitch, supra, at 134.

[2] See generally Amsterdam, supra; 'Note', supra, 20 n. 1; La Fave, supra.

[3] 116 U.S. 616 (1886).

[4] Amsterdam, supra, at 364.

[5] See above, Chapter 1, at 14–19.

[6] 277 U.S. 438 (1928).

[7] See *United States v. White*, 401 U.S. 745, 748 (1971); *Katz v. United States*, 389 U.S. 347, 364 (1967), per Black, J. dissenting; 'Note', supra, 20 n. 1, at 971–2.

Amendment can only be violated by a seizure of 'tangible material effects'; words cannot be seized, and therefore 'hearing or sight' are not forbidden by the constitutional prohibition. Secondly, the Fourth Amendment can only come into operation when there is 'an actual physical invasion of (the defendants') house or curtilage for the purpose of making a seizure'; here there had been no such physical invasion or entry since the insertion of the wires had been made 'without trespass upon any property of the defendants'. In dissent Justice Brandeis delivered his most memorable opinion.[1] His great contribution, it has been pointed out,[2] was the drawing of a distinction between the interest the Fourth Amendment is intended to protect and particular forms of invasion of that interest. As to the latter, when the Fourth Amendment was adopted, he observed, force, violence, breaking and entry were the only means by which the government could disturb a man's privacy and obtain incriminating evidence against him; but 'subtler and more far-reaching means of invading privacy ha(d) become available to the government', discovery and invention had made it possible for the government 'by means far more effective than stretching upon the rack' to obtain disclosure of private communications, and indeed 'the progress of science in furnishing the government with means of espionage (was) not likely to stop with wiretapping'. To Lord Camden far slighter intrusions seemed 'subversive of all the comforts of society'. Could it be that the Constitution afforded no protection against such gross encroachments upon privacy and security as had been made possible by modern technology? He could not agree. It was instead necessary to seek 'the principle underlying the Fourth Amendment' and give it 'effect'. For Justice Brandeis the purpose of those who framed the Amendment was 'to secure conditions favourable to the pursuit of happiness'; recognising 'the significance of man's spiritual nature, of his feelings and of his intellect', they sought 'to protect Americans in their beliefs, their thoughts, their emotions and their sensations'; they therefore conferred as against the government, principally by the Fourth Amendment, 'the right to be let alone—the most comprehensive of rights and the right most valued by civilised men'. And both the Amendment's purpose and the right it conferred were to be effectuated by an equally expansive principle. 'To protect that right every *unjustifiable intrusion* by the government *upon the privacy of the individual*, whatever the means employed, must be deemed a violation of the Fourth Amendment.' With regard to the specific issue

[1] 277 U.S. at 471. Holmes, Butler and Stone, JJ. also dissented. Holmes, J., while he did not deny it, was not prepared to say that 'the penumbra of the 4th and 5th Amendments covers the defendant' although he agreed that 'courts are apt to err by sticking too closely to the words of a law where those words import a policy that goes beyond them'. But he agreed with the second argument of Brandeis, J. that the government should not use evidence obtained by means of a criminal act (ibid., at 470). Butler, J. thought that wiretapping involved a search and seizure ('Tapping the wires and listening in by the officers literally constituted a search for evidence', ibid., at 487); and Stone, J. agreed with the opinions of Holmes, Brandeis and Butler, JJ.

[2] See Beaney, 'The Constitutional Right to Privacy in the Supreme Court', 1962 *Sup. Ct. Rev.* 212; J. Landynski, 'Search and Seizure and the Supreme Court' 203–5 (1966); 'Note', supra, 20 n. 1; King, 'Electronic Surveillance and Constitutional Rights: Some Recent Developments and Observations', 33 *Geo. Wash. L. Rev.* 240 (1964).

before them Justice Brandeis had no doubt that telephone wiretapping fell within the Amendment; whenever a telephone line was tapped 'the privacy' of the persons at both ends of the line was 'invaded' and all conversations between them on any subject could be overheard; and as techniques of espionage writs of assistance and general warrants were but 'puny instruments of tyranny and oppression when compared with wire tapping'. But the Brandeis dissent did not carry the day, and in the years that followed it was the majority's subordination of the Fourth Amendment to tangible considerations, evidenced both by the requirement that there be a physical entry and by the doctrine that only tangible items could be seized, that prevailed.[1]

Olmstead has been extensively criticised. The chief objections levelled at its 'physical trespass' and 'material effects' doctrines are the following.

1. The 'trespass' and 'tangible evidence' limitations are not necessitated even by a literal reading of the Fourth Amendment. 'In every-day talk, as of 1789 or now, a man "searches" when he looks or listens.'[2] Looking around a room and listening to the sounds are therefore forms of searching, and similarly intercepting conversations is a form of seizing.[3] *Boyd* itself, whose authority was not impeached in *Olmstead*, detects a search and seizure in a requirement that a defendant should produce documents, and if *subpoenas duces tecum* and 'the orderly process of a court's procedure'[4] are to be controlled by the Fourth Amendment, there is no reason why it should, in other contexts, be restricted to physical entries and the detention of tangible evidence.[5]

2. As enduring constitutional doctrine, confinement of Fourth Amendment protection to instances of the seizure of the tangible fruits of actual trespasses cannot be supported. Since the function of a Constitution is not only to address the specific grievances giving rise to its adoption but also *and primarily* to continue the effective protection of the personal and societal interests animating the Framers and ultimately underlying its provisions, clauses guaranteeing individual liberty must be recognised as having 'a similar capacity of adaptation to a changing world',[6] judicial review and the scope of its remedies should not be limited to the suppression of the particular evils uppermost in the minds of those responsible for the initial drafting, and therefore the Fourth Amendment should not be tied either to a predefined type of abuse or to the technology of a bygone era but should rather be viewed as affording meaningful vindication of basic rights to security, privacy and freedom from unjustifiable governmental intrusion.[7]

3. The *Olmstead* 'trespass' and 'material effects' doctrines seem to be based on the notion of property, namely that the primary function of the Fourth

[1] King, supra; Landynski, supra.
[2] *United States v. On Lee*, 193 F. 2d 306, 313, per Frank, J. dissenting.
[3] *Lopez v. United States*, 373 U.S. 427, 459 (1963), per Brennan, J. dissenting.
[4] *Olmstead v. United States*, 277 U.S. 438, 478 (1928), per Brandeis, J. dissenting.
[5] See Brandeis, J.'s dissent in *Olmstead*, supra; Amsterdam, supra, at 361–7.
[6] *Olmstead v. United States*, 277 U.S. 438, 473 (1928), per Brandeis, J. dissenting.
[7] See Amsterdam, supra, 396–400; Brandeis, J.'s dissent in *Olmstead*, supra; Brennan, J.'s disssent in *Lopez*, supra.

Amendment is to protect private property from trespasses and other physical encroachments. But much authority, principally *Boyd*, supports the broader proposition that the gist of the Fourth Amendment is the entrenchment of a comprehensive right of personal privacy, the safeguarding of personal and collective security from arbitrary official intrusion, and protection of individual liberty in a much wider sense than that entailed by private property.[1]

According to these objections, mainly the last two, any acceptable constitutional analysis of the Fourth Amendment, both of its purpose and of any mediating decisional principles through which it is to be applied, should have as their starting point and emphasise the interest to be protected, however this is formulated, and not any particular means of violating it.[2]

Whatever its shortcomings as constitutional doctrine *Olmstead*'s interpretation of the Fourth Amendment as limited to the tangible discoveries of physical trespasses enjoyed one important advantage, that it provided a clear-cut and easy to apply decisional yardstick assuring a considerable measure of certainty and predictability in judicial determinations. The other undeniable consideration was that rejection of the requirement of a physical invasion as a prerequisite to the applicability of the Fourth Amendment would necessitate the development of another test or principle aimed at the elaboration both of a coherent organising framework and of a set of workable guidelines for judicial decision. 'When an old rule is discarded, the generation of new principles is inevitable and necessary in order to obtain rational, consistent, and at least somewhat predictable results.'[3] The first attempt to escape from the fetters of *Olmstead* took the form of the tentative emergence of a set of propositions emphasising the privacy of places and seeking to demarcate certain areas as protected enclaves within which the individual would be protected and thus enjoy immunity both from physical intrusions directed towards the seizure of tangible items and from non-trespassory surveillance, eavesdropping and other efforts at the gathering of private information.[4] This, conveniently called the doctrine of constitutionally protected areas, was never fully articulated, but, drawing on many hints from the cases, its main components can be set out as follows: Fourth Amendment protection can be invoked when the petitioner at the time of the intrusion was in a place accepted by society as an area where considerable privacy and a large measure of security from governmental intrusion should be enjoyed. The principal and most obvious example of such a place was the private home. But 'the physical scope of Fourth Amendment protection'[5] extended well beyond. Thus, a business office was a protected

[1] See *Lopez v. United States*, 373 U.S. 427, 460 (1963), per Brennan, J. dissenting; *Camara v. Municipal Court*, 387 U.S. 523 (1967); *Warden v. Hayden*, 387 U.S. 294 (1967).

[2] Amsterdam, supra, at 365. [3] 'Note', supra, at 968.

[4] See 'Note', supra, 20 n. 1, at 969–71; 'Note, A Reconsideration of the Katz Expectation of Privacy Test', 76 *Mich. L. Rev.* 154, 171–83 (1977); Dutile, 'Some Observations on the Supreme Court's Use of Property Concepts in Resolving Fourth Amendment Problems', 21 *Cath. U. L. Rev.* 1 (1971).

[5] *Lanza v. New York*, 370 U.S. 139, 143 (1962).

area,[1] and so were apartments[2] and hotel rooms;[3] similarly privately owned vehicles and occupied taxicabs could not be subjected to unreasonable searches.[4] But 'open fields'[5] were outside the Amendment's protective cover, and so were other places not sharing any of the usual characteristics of homes, offices, hotel rooms and automobiles; if for instance a place was one which was either open and accessible to the public or normally subject to a large measure of surveillance and observation, no constitutional immunity from unreasonable searches and seizures could be claimed.[6] The cases formulated no test but rather seemed to ask whether the area occupied by the defendant was endowed with sufficient 'attributes of (the) privacy of a home'.[7] Two things must be emphasised: if the area was held to be a constitutionally protected one, whether because of ownership, personal dominion, or possession of the requisite measure of control, protection from unreasonable searches would attach as soon as there was a legally sufficient governmental intrusion, and after 1960, as will be seen below, it made no difference that the intrusion resulted not in the seizure of tangible items but in the interception of conversations, for example by surreptitious electronic eavesdropping.[8] Secondly, the developed doctrine of constitutionally protected areas, unlike *Olmstead*'s trespass rule, was based not on property but on considerations of privacy; certain places, in other words, would be protected from official intrusion not because the petitioner had the requisite proprietary or possessory interest but because he had a sufficient and socially recognisable interest in keeping them private.[9] In this sense the protected areas doctrine, as will be seen below, still figures prominently in Fourth Amendment adjudication even though theoretically it has been displaced by the now dominant *Katz* 'expectation of privacy' test.

In *Katz v. United States,*[10] generally accepted as marking the beginning of a new chapter of Fourth Amendment jurisprudence,[11] government agents intercepted the contents of the defendant's end of telephone conversations by attaching an electronic listening and recording device to the outside of a public telephone booth from which the incriminating calls had been placed. The Supreme Court, by a majority of seven to one,[12] could not accept the government's argument that a 'search' could only occur when there had been

[1] *Gouled v. United States*, 255 U.S. 298.

[2] *Jones v. United States*, 362 U.S. 257.

[3] *Lustig v. United States*, 338 U.S. 74; *United States v. Jeffers*, 342 U.S. 48.

[4] *Terrones Rios v. United States*, 364 U.S. 253.

[5] *Hester v. United States*, 265 U.S. 57.

[6] See 'Note', 82 *Harv. L. Rev.* 187, 190; 'Note', supra, 20 n. 1, at 971; 'Note', 76 *Mich. L. Rev.* 154, 180 (1977); see also *Silverman v. United States*, 365 U.S. 505, 511 n. 4 (1961) (quoting with approval *United States v. On Lee*, 193 F. 2d 306, 315–16 (1951), per Frank, J. dissenting).

[7] *Lanza v. New York*, 370 U.S. 139, 143 (1962).

[8] See *Silverman v. United States*, 365 U.S. 505, 509 (1961).

[9] 'Note', 76 *Mich. L. Rev.* 154, 180 (1977).

[10] 389 U.S. 347 (1967).

[11] La Fave, supra, at 228; *Smith v. Maryland*, 99 S. Ct. 2577 (1979).

[12] Black, J. dissented because he could not agree that electronic eavesdropping constituted a 'search' or 'seizure'. Marshall, J. did not participate.

a 'physical intrusion' into a 'constitutionally protected area', rejecting both *Olmstead's* trespass doctrine and the concept of 'constitutionally protected areas'. 'The Fourth Amendment', Justice Stewart observed in his opinion for the Court, 'protects people, not places'. What a person knowingly exposed to the public, even in his own home or office, was outside Fourth Amendment protection; but 'what he seeks to preserve as private, even in an area accessible to the public, may be constitutionally protected'. In the case before them '(t)he government's activities in electronically listening to and recording the petitioner's words violated the *privacy upon which he justifiably relied* while using the telephone booth' and '*thus* constituted a search and seizure within the meaning of the Fourth Amendment'; and since no warrant had been obtained, the challenged electronic surveillance was unconstitutional and its results would be suppressed.

Obviously, and of course not surprisingly, Justice Stewart's opinion in *Katz* suffers from much uncertainty and ambiguity. To begin with, the comment that the Fourth Amendment protects 'people, not places' cannot mean either that places now enjoy no protection or that the Amendment's coverage can invariably or even usually be drawn independently of areas and places;[1] what the Court's opinion rather meant was, first that property interests should not determine the extent of Fourth Amendment protection, and secondly that the constitutional immunity from unreasonable searches and seizures should not depend on the physical penetration of an enclosed place. More importantly, not much light is thrown on the test of 'justifiable reliance on privacy'. What was the real reason Katz was protected from electronic surveillance? Was it because of his own attitude or because the police had behaved improperly? In terms of theory, does the definition of a 'search' turn upon the behaviour and circumstances of the person subjected to the intrusion or upon the conduct of the searcher?[2] The Court simply says that what a person seeks to preserve as private '*may*' be accorded constitutional protection, and observes that '(o)ne who occupies (a telephone booth), shuts the door behind him, and pays the toll that permits him to place a call is surely entitled to assume that the words he utters into the mouthpiece will not be broadcast to the world'. This emphasis on the defendant's actions to ensure privacy might suggest that the primary focus in determining the presence of 'justifiable reliance on privacy' is on subjective considerations, mainly the behaviour of the petitioner and the expectations of freedom from detection he actually entertains; but the Court also speaks of Katz as being *entitled to assume* that his communications will be protected, and elsewhere it mentions 'the vital role that the public telephone has come to play in private communication',[3] suggesting that Fourth Amendment coverage is fundamentally fixed not by an inquiry into what precautions aimed at preserving privacy were taken but by an analysis calculated to determine whether constitutional protection *should* be granted, in other words what expectations to freedom from surveillance and detection

[1] 'Note', supra, 20 n. 1, at 976; 'Note', 82 *Harv. L. Rev.* 187–92; see also Harlan, J.'s concurring opinion in *Katz*, 389 U.S. at 360.

[2] Dworkin, supra, 20 n. 2, at 335.

[3] *Katz v. United States*, 389 U.S. at 352.

it is *right* to credit the defendant with.[1] But equally clearly the possible primacy of normative considerations cannot mean that the defendant's actions should be disregarded. An attempt to answer some of these questions was made by Justice Harlan who joined the Stewart opinion but chose to add a few remarks in order to explain and make clearer what he took to be the Court's holding. In his view the Fourth Amendment could be invoked if a person had 'a constitutionally protected reasonable expectation of privacy';[2] this in turn depended on the satisfaction of two conditions, 'first that a person have exhibited an actual (subjective) expectation of privacy, and, second, that the expectation be one that society is prepared to recognise as "reasonable" '.[3] It is Justice Harlan's *Katz* concurrence and his 'reasonable expectation of privacy' test that have commanded the attention of most courts and exerted the greater influence in subsequent judicial attempts to determine when a 'search' has taken place and when therefore governmental action must be subjected to the Fourth Amendment.

As can be seen, both the Stewart and Harlan approaches contain a subjective and an objective element, but even though the latter is now stressed more and more at the expense of the former, both must be addressed in turn. It is clear that a wholly, or even primarily, subjective approach to *Katz*'s tests of justifiable reliance and reasonable expectation of privacy will not do as an acceptable basis for judicial interpretations of the scope of the Fourth Amendment.[4] To say that before a person can be protected from official intrusion he must entertain an actual or subjective expectation of privacy means that the applicability of the Fourth Amendment might ultimately depend not on a principled theory concerning either what practices the government should not engage in or what claims to constitutional protection each person must be recognised as having but on governmental conditioning of individuals *not* to expect privacy, for instance by announcing that unrestricted electronic surveillance would now be engaged in or that there would in future be inspection of letters going through the post;[5] and the Supreme Court has now indicated that, despite the continued use of subjective terminology, subjective considerations cannot in many circumstances provide 'an adequate index'[6] of constitutional protection, particularly where the government has attempted to diminish expectations of privacy by means of 'influences alien to well-recognised Fourth Amendment freedoms'.[7] Conversely there are cases where a person entertains a strong subjective expectation of privacy, for instance that he is not being observed or that his incriminating statements are not being overheard, but where it is abundantly obvious that he will not be protected. Thus '(a) burglar plying his

[1] See 'Note', supra; 'Note', 82 *Harv. L. Rev.* 187, 191.
[2] 389 U.S. at 360.
[3] 389 U.S. at 361.
[4] Amsterdam, supra, 20 n. 1, at 384; Dworkin, supra, 20 n. 2, at 335–7; La Fave, supra, at 229–30.
[5] Amsterdam, supra, at 384.
[6] *Smith v. Maryland*, 99 S.Ct. 2577 (1979).
[7] Ibid.

trade in a summer cabin during the off season may have a thoroughly justified subjective expectation of privacy, but it is not one which the law recognises as legitimate'[1] and it will not therefore be enforced; similarly, 'if two narcotic peddlers were to rely on the privacy of a desolate corner of Central Park in the middle of the night to carry out an illegal transaction, this would be a reasonable expectation of privacy', in that there would be virtually no risk of discovery and they would therefore not be unreasonable in discounting the possibility of detection, but 'if by extraordinary good luck a patrolman were to illuminate the desolate spot with his flashlight, the criminals would be unable to suppress the officer's testimony as a violation of their rights under the Fourth Amendment',[2] because again the actual expectation of not being discovered is not one that 'society is prepared to recognise as "reasonable"';[3] subjective reasonableness, in other words, cannot be equated with constitutional justifiability. The principal inquiry into justifiable reliance and reasonable expectations of privacy must therefore be a 'normative'[4] one. But despite the ultimate primacy of objective and normative considerations, and the inadequacy of the 'actual (subjective) expectation of privacy formulation'[5] as a charter of Fourth Amendment protection, a distinction must still be drawn between, on the one hand, a requirement that the petitioner should be able to demonstrate that he entertained (or even exhibited) a subjective anticipation of privacy, which is not insisted upon as a pre-condition to the applicability of the Fourth Amendment, and on the other the doctrine that a positive assumption of risk or reckless disregard as to whether privacy is maintained has the effect of defeating claims to constitutionally enforceable privacy, it being well established, as both Justices Stewart and Harlan emphasised in *Katz*, that objects, activities or statements knowingly exposed to the plain view of outsiders are not protected 'because no intention to keep them (private) has been exhibited'.[6] In this sense, knowing exposure to the public, whether it is indifference to detection or an actual expectation of discovery, seems to be 'a form of estoppel which prevents a defendant from claiming privacy after the fact when his earlier actions indicate open indifference to the fact that he is being or may be observed'.[7] But this will not often be the case.

But whatever the best way of formulating the subjective element and organising the requirements that must be satisfied before *Katz* can operate, there is little doubt that 'it is not enough that an individual desired or anticipated that he would be free from governmental intrusion';[8] rather the application of the Fourth Amendment depends on whether the person in-

[1] *Rakas v. Illinois*, 439 U.S. 128, 143 n. 12 (1978).
[2] 'Note', 43 *N.Y.U.L. Rev.* 968, 983 (1968).
[3] *Katz v. United States*, 389 U.S. 347, 361, per Harlan, J. concurring.
[4] *Smith v. Maryland*, 99 S.Ct. 2577, 2580 n. 5 (1979).
[5] 1 W. La Fave, *Search and Seizure* 15 (Pocket Part, 1980).
[6] Harlan, J. concurring in *Katz v. United States*, 389 U.S. at 361.
[7] 'Note', 82 *Harv. L. Rev.* 187, 192 (1968).
[8] *Rakas v. Illinois*, 439 U.S. 128, 151 (1978), per Powell, J. concurring.

voking its protection can claim a 'reasonable',[1] 'justifiable'[2] or 'legitimate'[3] expectation of privacy that has been invaded by governmental action. 'Only *legitimate* expectations of privacy', recent Supreme Court decisions declare with increasing emphasis, 'are protected by the Constitution';[4] in other words, only those expectations of privacy will be enforced which '*deserve*'[5] Fourth Amendment protection by virtue of the social recognition they command. It follows that it is judicial determinations as to what expectations of privacy are socially reasonable and legitimate or should be accorded constitutional recognition or can justifiably be relied on that provide the key to the delineation both of the reach of the Fourth Amendment and of the scope of a person's right to be protected from unreasonable searches and seizures.[6] How are these made? An answer which some give is that the reasonableness of an expectation and therefore its protection from official investigatory action depend upon the totality of the circumstances of each situation,[7] in particular on the actions of the person asserting reliance on privacy, for instance whether he took normal precautions to maintain privacy, the way he has used a place or location, and many others. But this, similarly to the totally subjective approach, does not answer the threshold question of justifiability, social or constitutional, but at most the subsidiary question, already dealt with, of whether the particular defendant was reasonable in expecting privacy or should instead be taken to have waived his Fourth Amendment protection, for instance by the assumption of the risk of detection. What, then, are the sources from which the necessary justification and legitimation, designating only some expectations of privacy as socially reasonable while refusing to extend protection to others, emanate? The answer, now confirmed by many cases, must be that the necessary social legitimation derives from outside the Fourth Amendment,[8] and since it is not to be extracted from the subjective anticipations of suspects, or from the precautions they took to avoid detection, or from the totality of the circumstances, the required justifiability must be sought in the 'habits of life',[9] in the prevalent social and political standards, in the accepted customs and values of past and present.[10] In social terms it has been well pointed out that privacy is 'a creature of life in a human community and not the

[1] See *Katz v. United States,* 389 U.S. 347, 361 (1967), per Harlan, J. concurring; *Terry v. Ohio*, 392 U.S. 1, 9 (1968); *Mancusi v. DeForte*, 392 U.S. 364, 368 (1968).

[2] *Katz v. United States*, 389 U.S. 347, 353 (1967); *United States v. White*, 401 U.S. 745, 748–9 (1971).

[3] See *United States v. Chadwick*, 433 U.S. 1, 7, 11 (1977); *Smith v. Maryland*, 99 S.Ct. 2577, 2580 (1979).

[4] *Rakas v. Illinois*, 439 U.S. 128, 151 (1978), per Powell, J. concurring.

[5] Ibid.

[6] La Fave, supra, at 230–4.

[7] See Powell, J.'s concurring opinion in *Rakas v. Illinois*, 439 U.S. 128 at 152–5; Dworkin, supra, at 334–7.

[8] *Rakas v. Illinois,* 439 U.S. 128, 143 n. 12 (1978), per Rehnquist, J.; La Fave, supra, at 231–4; Amsterdam, supra, at 403.

[9] Gross, 'The Concept of Privacy', 42 *N.Y.U.L. Rev.* 34, 36 (1967); La Fave, supra, at 232.

[10] See Harlan, J. dissenting in *United States v. White*, 401 U.S. 745, 786 (1971).

contrivance of a legal system concerned with its protection';[1] that it is 'society and culture' that ultimately dictate 'what sorts of privacy one may reasonably expect';[2] and that the criteria for reasonable expectations must therefore be found in 'the flow of life', 'the customs and sensibilities' of the people generally, and the overall structure of organised society.[3] In similar fashion, in constitutional terms, applications of *Katz* and determinations of what expectations of privacy are reasonable and justifiable must necessarily rest both on 'contemporary norms of social conduct and (on) the imperatives of a viable democratic society',[4] as reflected in the Constitution.[5] More fully, what measure of privacy and personal security *should* the individual be assured, or what risks is it not only unfair but also dangerous to impose on him (and the citizenry in general) in the absence of a warrant? And if the language of expectations and risks is used, this must be done cautiously, for expectations and risks should neither be located nor attributed 'without examining the desirability of saddling them upon society'.[6] As this type of analysis was succinctly put by Justice Powell in a recent case, 'the scope of the (Fourth) Amendment must be determined by the scope of privacy that a free people legitimately may expect'.[7]

In truth, in deciding what expectations of privacy are socially legitimate and deserving of Fourth Amendment protection, American courts as a general matter, and however they may present their rulings, concentrate not so much on the justifiability of the expectations of the complainant as on the impact of a particular *type of investigative activity* on the individual's (and society's) 'sense of security balanced against the utility of the conduct as a technique of law enforcement'.[8] Therefore governmental intrusions and any other law enforcement practices which 'significantly jeopardise the sense of security which is the paramount concern of Fourth Amendment liberties'[9] must be held to be searches, which means that in their case the presence of a judicial warrant will normally be insisted upon, neither self-restraint on the part of officials nor overall reasonableness satisfying constitutional standards. The issue here in other words is not what expectations particular individuals entertained, or whether the particular police practice was necessary. 'Rather the matter must be viewed from a much broader perspective.'[10] Would allowing the police regularly to engage in the particular practice in question, totally unregulated by judicial superintendence, endanger or compromise society's collective sense of security by 'the amount of privacy and freedom remaining to citizens' being diminished 'to a compass inconsistent with the aims of a free and open society'?[11] What judges should therefore ask

[1] Gross, supra, at 36.
[2] 'Note', 6 *U. Mich. J. L.* Rev. 154, 179–80 (1972); La Fave, supra, at 232.
[3] 'Note', supra; La Fave, supra, at 232.
[4] *United States v. Vilhotti*, 323 F. Supp. 425 (1971).
[5] Harlan, J. dissenting in *United States v. White*, 401 U.S. 745, 786 (1971).
[6] Ibid.
[7] *Rakas v. Illinois*, 439 U.S. 128, 151 (1978), per Powell, J. concurring.
[8] Harlan, J. dissenting in *United States v. White*, supra, at 786.
[9] Ibid.
[10] La Fave, supra, at 233.
[11] Amsterdam, supra, at 403.

themselves, it has been authoritatively declared,[1] is whether a particular practice or method, legally uncontrolled and limited only by official forbearance and self-discipline, is a tolerable technique of law enforcement given 'the values and goals of our political system' or cannot but undermine 'that confidence and sense of security' that are characteristic and essential features of a free society. If the answer is that the latter is the case then the practice in question amounts to a search within the Fourth Amendment, and therefore 'has no place' otherwise than in pursuance of accepted constitutional processes. One thing is clear. Whichever is the better way of approaching the issue of delimiting the scope of the Fourth Amendment, the relevant determinations can only be made in the light of the perceived demands of the overall system of government as reflected in the Constitution. Different kinds of political regime presuppose, and in turn allow, different patterns of privacy, individual and collective security, and freedom from governmental intrusion,[2] and ultimately definitions of 'searches' and 'seizures' depend on society's, or the judiciary's, view of where the elusive line between protected privacy and subjection to uncontrolled official investigative activity should be drawn.

We shall now consider certain cases where the issue of whether a 'search' has taken place has caused difficulty.

(a) Seizures and searches of persons and tangible effects

The Fourth Amendment prohibits unreasonable searches and seizures of persons, houses, papers, and effects. Seizures and searches must be addressed separately. Seizures of persons include all *intrusions* upon personal security, whether these take the form of arrests, investigatory detentions, or any other official restraints of the liberty of the person.[3] It was in *Terry v. Ohio*[4] that the Supreme Court finally laid to rest the notion that the Fourth Amendment did not come into play as a limitation upon police conduct if the officers stopped short of a 'technical arrest' or a 'full-blown search', by recognising first that when a law enforcement officer 'stops' a person and restrains his freedom to go away he thereby 'seizes' that person, and secondly that when the officer then 'frisks' the person stopped by examining the outer surfaces of his clothing in an effort to find weapons a 'search' has taken place; both the 'stop' and the 'frisk' are therefore subject to the Fourth Amendment, and will only be upheld if reasonable. But if there has been no 'seizure' (or search) the Fourth Amendment does not apply. 'Obviously,' the Court observed in *Terry*, 'not all personal intercourse between policemen and citizens involves "seizures" of persons'; only when the officer had 'in some way' restrained a person's liberty would it be held that a 'seizure', bringing into operation Fourth Amendment safeguards, had occurred.[5] Not surprisingly, where the

[1] Harlan, J. dissenting in *United States v. White*, 401 U.S. 745, 785–90 (1971). Subsequent quotations, unless otherwise indicated, come from this judgment.

[2] See A. Westin, *Privacy and Freedom* 23 (1967).

[3] *Davis v. Mississippi*, 394 U.S. 721 (1969).

[4] 392 U.S. 1, 19 (1968).

[5] Ibid., at 19 n. 16; see 3 W. La Fave, *Search and Seizure* 46–57 (1978).

line should be drawn between official *restraint* and *voluntary* personal intercourse is far from clear, and ultimately depends upon all the circumstances of a situation. But some themes have emerged. A police officer who merely approaches a person and asks a question is neither seizing that person nor intruding upon his security to an extent sufficient to bring the Fourth Amendment into play.[1] 'There is nothing in the Constitution which prevents a policeman from addressing questions to anyone on the streets.'[2] What if an officer, instead of merely putting a question, either asks or calls out to a person to stop so that he can talk to him or ask him a question?[3] Apparently it all depends on the precise facts. If the conduct of the police officer in calling out to someone to stop so that he can ask him some questions gives rise to a reasonable inference of an actual or intended detention, the request or command is a 'seizure'; but if the call to stop communicates no intention to detain, but only serves as an appropriate means under the circumstances of advising a person of the officer's desire to talk to him, it will not amount to a 'seizure' and will therefore be outside the Amendment.[4]

As the many cases show, there is no agreement on the surely fundamental issue of the formulation of the test that will determine whether a 'seizure' has taken place or not.[5] For some the test is not what the defendant himself thought, but what a reasonable man, innocent of any crime, would have thought had he been in the defendant's shoes. So certain investigatory encounters do not constitute either arrests or seizures even though the person stopped may have thought that he was under some sort of restraint, *provided* that a reasonable man would have interpreted the official action not as a forcible encroachment on his freedom but merely as a way of attracting his attention. A good example is *United States v. Burrell*[6] where an officer followed the defendant, approached him from the rear as he walked, placed his hand on his elbow, and said, 'Hold it, Sir, could I speak with you a second?' The defendant's immediate reply was 'It's registered, it's registered', upon which the officer conducted a search which brought to light a pistol. Did the officer's initial action, the placing of the hand on the elbow, amount to a seizure? The court took the view that it did not. Although to a guilty mind the touching of the elbow coupled with the simultaneous request to speak with the defendant might have appeared as the expression of an intent either to effect an arrest or bring about a forcible stop, 'the normal reaction

[1] *People v. Howlett*, 274 N.E. 2d 885 (1971); *People v. King*, 139 Cal. Rptr. 926 (1977).

[2] *Terry v. Ohio*, 392 U.S. 1, 34 (1968), per White, J. concurring; see also Remington, 'The Law Relating to "On the Street" Detention, Questioning and Frisking of Suspected Persons and Police Arrest Privileges in General', 51 *J. Crim. L., C. & P.S.* 386, 389 (1960); La Fave, ' "Street Encounters" and the Constitution', 67 *Mich. L. Rev.* 40 (1968–69).

[3] See *People v. Howlett*, 274 N.E. 2d 885 (1971); *People v. King*, 139 Cal. Rptr. 926 (1977).

[4] *People v. King*, 139 Cal. Rptr. 926, 927 (1977); but see *People v. De Bour*, 352 N.E. 2d 562 (1976) which refuses to accept the position that in the absence of a forcible stop all constitutional considerations disappear.

[5] La Fave, supra, at 50–5.

[6] 286 A. 2d 845 (1972).

of a reasonable, innocent person' would have been different; to him the touching of the elbow and the request merely amounted to the transmission of a desire to speak; no official intrusion had therefore taken place, and there was no need for the officer's action to be supported by probable cause or reasonable suspicion. For others this is not satisfactory, principally because constitutional safeguards are intended to protect the innocent and the guilty alike; the best approach therefore is a subjective one, whether that is the *suspect*, and not the reasonable man, *feels* free to walk away after he has been asked a question or been approached by the police.[1] But again it has been convincingly argued that if this is the test then 'virtually all police-citizen encounters must in fact be deemed to involve a Fourth Amendment seizure'[2] because in the great number of cases it is a fiction to suppose that a person who has been accosted by the police and is being questioned feels free to walk away. Another possibility is a modified version of the first approach put forward above, based on a combination of the objective test with a presumption that a police-citizen encounter normally involves a seizure; a street encounter is therefore a seizure unless a reasonable person would believe that he was still free to go, a showing by the defendant that he *felt* himself constrained imposing a burden on the State to rebut this by a showing that the reasonable person would have formed a different view.[3] It is impossible to reconcile all the statements in the cases, but an objective test of some sort comes closer to explaining the actual results.[4] The short test appears to be that if the conduct of the police, verbal or physical, is what would *generally* be interpreted as a means of communication or of attracting someone's attention—and one that ordinary citizens would also usually employ—there is no seizure; but if official behaviour goes beyond this, courts will not hesitate before holding that the actions of the police come within and must therefore be justified under the Fourth Amendment.[5]

But if, on the correct interpretation of the facts, the individual's freedom to walk away has been interfered with either by physical restraint or by sufficient show of authority,[6] if there has been 'an element of command, authority, force, threat, coercion, physical stopping or restraint',[7] there has been a seizure of the person (or of a vehicle), however limited the purpose of the stop and however brief the resulting detention or intrusion. Examples abound. The Fourth Amendment has therefore been applied to strictly limited investigative stops, even though these usually took less than a minute and involved nothing more than a 'brief question or two',[8] to a police signal—by means of a flashing red light—that a driver should stop his vehicle,[9] to an

[1] See *State v. Evans*, 517 P. 2d 1225, 1229 (1974).

[2] La Fave, supra, at 50; see also *People v. Jordan*, 357 N.E. 2d 159, 162 (1976).

[3] See La Fave, supra, at 52–3; *State v. Tsukiyama*, 525 P. 2d 1099 (1974).

[4] *State v. Tsukiyama*, 525 P. 2d 1099, 1102 (1974).

[5] See also A.L.I., *A Model Code of Pre-Arraignment Procedure* 258 (Proposed Official Draft, 1975); La Fave, supra, at 53.

[6] *Terry v. Ohio*, 392 U.S. 1, 19 n. 16.

[7] *State v. Tsukiyama*, 525 P. 2d 1099, 1105 (1974).

[8] See *United States v. Brignoni-Ponce*, 422 U.S. 873 (1975).

[9] See *Carpenter v. Sigler*, 419 F. 2d 169 (1969); *United States v. Harflinger*, 436 F.

order that the suspect should roll down the window of his car,[1] to the routine stops of vehicles either to check drivers' licences and proper vehicle registration[2] or to determine the presence of illegal aliens,[3] etc. But a subpoena to compel a person to appear before a grand jury has been held not to constitute a 'seizure'[4] even though the summons may be inconvenient or burdensome, not only because there seems to be a general duty to appear and give evidence before the grand jury[5] but also because '(t)he compulsion exerted by a grand jury subpoena differs from the seizure effected by an arrest or even an investigative "stop" in more than civic obligation';[6] thus a subpoena is served in the same manner as other forms of legal process, involves no stigma whatever, and remains at all times under judicial supervision, unlike arrests and investigative stops, which are normally effected with force or the threat of it and often in demeaning circumstances.[7]

Searches of persons or tangible effects have been defined either as forcible or intrusive involuntary examinations or inspections of what would otherwise be closed to public view for the purpose of collecting information,[8] or, more broadly, as intrusions on personal security by agents of the public that are sufficiently significant to amount to cognizable invasions of an individual's reasonable expectations of privacy as to his person or material effects.[9] Even though after *Katz v. United States*[10] there can obviously be a search without any physical intrusion either into the person (the body and clothing) or into any other enclosure (whether of land or of other material things), it is naturally easier to establish that there has been conduct within the Fourth Amendment if there has been some physical invasion or contact with something within the Amendment's protective cover. Searches of the person therefore include rummaging through a person's pockets or clothing,[11] patting down one's outer clothing without going into the pockets or other inner recesses,[12] extracting an individual's blood by means of a hypodermic needle,[13] taking scrapings from beneath his fingernails,[14] clipping a few

---

2d 928 (1970); see also *United States v. Nicholas*, 448 F. 2d 622 (1971), where it was held that when police officers stationed themselves on either side of the defendant's car and flashed their badges there had been a sufficient show of authority to amount to a 'seizure'.

[1] *Adams v. Williams*, 407 U.S. 143, 146 n. 1 (1972).

[2] *Delaware v. Prouse*, 99 S.Ct. 1391 (1979).

[3] *United States v. Martinez-Fuerte*, 428 U.S. 543 (1976).

[4] *United States v. Dionisio*, 93 S.Ct. 764 (1973).

[5] *Branzburg v. Hayes*, 408 U.S. 665, 682.

[6] *United States v. Dionisio*, 93 S.Ct. 764, 769 (1973).

[7] *United States v. Doe (Schwartz)*, 457 F. 2d 895, 898.

[8] *State v. Ashby*, 345 So. 2d 225, 227 (1971).

[9] *Elson v. State*, 337 So. 2d 959, 963 (1976); *Huffer v. State*, 344 So. 2d 1332 (1977); *State v. Oliver*, 368 So. 2d 1331, 1335 (1979).

[10] 389 U.S. 347 (1967).

[11] *Sibron v. New York*, 392 U.S. 40 (1968).

[12] *Terry v. Ohio*, 392 U.S. 1 (1968).

[13] *Schmerber v. California*, 384 U.S. 757 (1966).

[14] *Cupp v. Murphy*, 412 U.S. 291 (1973).

hairs from the defendant's head,[1] performing a gun residue test on a suspect's hands and wiping sample residue from them,[2] administering a benzidine test upon the defendant which showed the presence of blood on his penis shortly after an alleged sexual assault,[3] or any other 'physical touching of an individual's body or clothing that causes hidden objects or matters to be revealed'.[4] As a general matter it would therefore appear that the *obtaining* of *physical evidence* from the person of the accused involves conduct within the Fourth Amendment at two *distinct* levels—there is first the seizure of the person necessary to bring him into the custody of the authorities and then there is the subsequent search for and seizure of the evidence.[5]

At the other extreme it is well established, as *Katz* also confirms, that physical characteristics constantly exposed to the public do not enjoy Fourth Amendment protection,[6] and therefore their observation and (visual) examination have been held to be outside the ambit of constitutional safeguards.[7] This reasoning has been applied to a man's facial features, his handwriting, and the physical characteristics of his voice, its tone and manner, as opposed to the content of his conversation. Since no person can have a reasonable expectation that his facial and vocal features and his handwriting will be protected from others, courts will refuse to construct 'a wall of privacy' around those characteristics which are 'open for all to see or hear';[8] and since there is no initial right to constitutional protection the required disclosure of a person's voice or the compelled execution of handwriting or voice exemplars will similarly be held not to intrude upon Fourth Amendment interests.[9]

[1] *United States v. D'Amico*, 408 F. 2d 331 (1969).

[2] *State v. Howell*, 524 S.W. 2d 11, 17 (1975).

[3] *United States v. Smith*, 470 F. 2d 377 (1972).

[4] *State v. Oliver*, 368 So. 2d 1331, 1335 (1979). A difficult, and as yet unresolved, problem is that of fingerprinting. Is fingerprinting a search or seizure within the Fourth Amendment? Different views have been taken on this. Some would hold that it involves a search (see *United States v. Kenaan*, 496 F. 2d 181, 182 (1974)), basing their view on *Davis v. Mississippi*, 394 U.S. 721 (1969). But *Davis* dealt with another issue, namely with whether *detention* for fingerprinting was within the Amendment, and indeed there are remarks in the Court's opinion ('(f)ingerprinting involves none of the probing into an individual's private life and thoughts that marks an interrogation or search') which suggest that fingerprinting involves neither a search nor a seizure; and in *Dionisio*, supra, the Court drew a distinction between the initial dragnet detentions in *Davis* which were held to be constitutionally impermissible and 'th(e) fingerprinting itself'; see also *Commonwealth v. DeWitt*, 314 A. 2d 27 (1973), where fingerprints were said to be similar to exposed physical characteristics the examination of which does not come within the Fourth Amendment.

[5] See *United States v. Dionisio*, 93 S.Ct. 764, 769 (1973); *State v. Sharpe*, 200 S.E. 2d 44, 47 (1973).

[6] See *Katz v. United States*, 389 U.S. 347 (1967).

[7] *United States v. Dionisio*, 93 S.Ct. 764, 771 (1973).

[8] *United States v. Doe (Schwatz)*, 457 F. 2d 895, 898–9.

[9] *United States v. Dionisio*, 93 S.Ct. 764, 772 (1973). It has been argued persuasively that though the decisions in *Dionisio*, supra, and *United States v. Mara*, 93 S.Ct. 774 (1973) – that grand jury orders compelling the furnishing of voice and handwriting samples – are correct, these should have been based not on the theory of 'exposed physical characteristics' but on the ground that the *only* constitutional

What about the administration of scientific or medical tests that yield evidence but involve neither intrusions beneath the surface of the body nor any kind of physical contact? The cases seem to fall into two categories. There are those which deal with the use of X-rays and the device known as the magnetometer, which is employed to detect the presence of weapons and the like in airport security systems. Here courts have invariably detected a search within the Fourth Amendment; thus in *United States v. Allen*[1] it was held that use of X-rays comes within the Fourth Amendment (particularly since it could not be said that examination by means of X-rays involved a lesser invasion than that represented by the taking of blood, which was certainly a search and seizure), and in *United States v. Epperson*[2] the court had little doubt that use of the magnetometer was a search, since the very purpose of this device was to search for metal and disclose its presence in areas where there is a normal expectation of privacy. Much greater difficulty has been encountered with the second type of case which deals with another police technique, use of an ultraviolet lamp to examine the defendant's hands in order to determine whether he has used a certain item.[3] The cases take different positions. In *Commonwealth v. DeWitt*[4] the court thought that examination of the suspect's hands by means of ultraviolet light did not amount to a search, principally because there was 'no reasonable expectation of privacy as to the presence of foreign matter on (his) hands', the foreign matter being comparable to physical characteristics which were constantly exposed to the public.[5] But in *United States v. Kenaan*[6] a similar inspection was held to come within the Fourth Amendment as it was thought to involve 'the kind of governmental intrusion into one's private domain' that should be controlled by the Fourth Amendment. Three possibilities appear open: The first is to prefer *Kenaan* to *DeWitt*, and to propound the general principle that 'a detailed inspection, by special instrument, of one's skin' is a search within the Fourth Amendment.[7] The second is to prefer the *DeWitt*

---

safeguard applicable in cases where the evidence can only be procured *by the will* of the subject is the privilege against self-incrimination, and not the search and seizure provision. *Dionisio* and *Mara*, in other words, are not like *Schmerber*, supra, and *Cupp v. Murphy*, supra, involving the *involuntary* seizure of blood samples and scrapings from underneath the suspect's fingernails, but only raise the question 'whether the coercion of the defendant's will, by order of the grand jury to force him to produce speech or writing specimens, is . . . barred by the privilege against self-incrimination' (*Model Code*, supra, at 499).

[1] 337 F. Sipp. 1041 (1972).

[2] 454 F. 2d 769 (1972).

[3] The problem here usually arises as follows. The police first treat a certain item, for instance narcotics, with fluorescent grease or other some similar substance; they then shine ultraviolet light over the defendant's hands in order to determine whether he handled the incriminating object; if his hands glow when subjected to the ultraviolet light it means that he has touched the object.

[4] 314 A. 2d 27 (1973).

[5] To the same effect are *United States v. Richardson*, 388 F. 2d 842 (1968), and *United States v. Millen*, 338 F. Supp. 747 (1972).

[6] 496 F. 2d 181 (1974).

[7] Ibid., at 182; see also *State v. Howell*, 524 S.W. 2d 11, 17 (1975).

approach, and to draw a distinction between equipment, such as the magnetometer, which is used to detect the presence of 'some object which is covered and thus not subject to direct viewing', and means which are used 'to disclose the presence of something which is not concealed in the sense of being covered or enclosed, but which cannot be perceived by the naked eye'.[1] The third possibility is to draw no sharp line between types of technical equipment but to deal with each case not involving physical contact on its own facts.[2]

(b) Administrative inspections

Most search and seizure cases come from the criminal context, namely where the governmental intrusion in issue was initiated for the purpose of discovering evidence of crime. A search 'ordinarily implies an examination of an individual or of his property (in order) to discover contraband or evidence of some violation of the law, to be used in prosecution of a criminal action'.[3] But what if the intrusion complained of was not actuated by the desire to locate and seize evidence of crime but was instead undertaken in pursuance of some administrative or municipal code, for instance to ascertain the physical condition of a house or business premises and to determine whether this complies with applicable health or safety regulations? In other words, should the *purpose* of an intrusion or examination be material in determining whether there has been a *search* within the Fourth Amendment? One line of argument is that a search is '(a) quest for evidence of crime',[4] that the basic purpose of the constitutional safeguard is to control official intrusions aimed at obtaining evidence to be used in criminal proceedings, and that therefore inspections under municipal ordinances and the like are not within Fourth Amendment coverage.[5] This reasoning has now been rejected. Three points are usually made in refutation of the view that administrative inspections are not 'searches' within the Amendment. To begin with, a distinction between an 'inspection' and a 'search' has 'no basis in semantics, in constitutional history, or in reason'.[6] In either case what is sought is information, and to say that the framers of the Fourth Amendment meant to control invasion of their homes only if government officials were *looking for something*, and not when they were *merely looking*, would be to attribute to them 'a degree of irrationality not otherwise visible in their dealings with potential tyranny'.[7]

[1] La Fave, supra, at 262 and 264.

[2] Thus, as was observed in *DeWitt*, supra, at 31, the examination in issue was 'both limited and controlled', it involved no 'personal indignities or physical discomfort', and was neither 'annoying, frightening, or humiliating'. In other circumstances, it was suggested, an examination by ultraviolet light might well amount to a search.

[3] *United States v. Johnson*, 431 F. 2d 441, 445 (1970), per Godbold, J. dissenting.

[4] *Marshall v. United States*, 422 F. 2d 185, 189 (1970).

[5] A similar approach was adopted by Frankfurter, J. in *Frank v. Maryland*, 359 U.S. 360 (1959). It is not at all clear whether Frankfurter, J. at 365, took the view that administrative inspections were not searches or whether he thought that they were reasonable even in the absence of a warrant.

[6] *District of Columbia v. Little*, 178 F. 2d 13, 18 (1949), per Prettyman, J.

[7] Ibid.

Secondly, the basic purpose of the Fourth Amendment is not protection from official entries aimed at the discovery of incriminating evidence but general protection of the right to privacy and security in one's home.[1] This means that all official entries into the home must be regulated by the Fourth Amendment, whatever their purpose or motivation; as Justice Harlan has put it, 'the Constitution protects the privacy of the home against *all* unreasonable intrusion of *whatever* character', and therefore 'searches' for Fourth Amendment purposes must be defined as all and any 'invasions on the part of the government and its employees of the sanctity of a man's home'.[2] Finally, a restriction of the Fourth Amendment to the criminal law context would not only go contrary to the venerable concept that a man's home is his castle[3] but would also bring about the anomalous result that only suspected criminals would be protected by the constitutional safeguards.[4] Nor is it correct to argue that the Fourth Amendment is premised upon and limited by the provision of the Fifth Amendment regarding self-incrimination so that only if the latter is found to be applicable can constitutional protection from unreasonable searches and seizures be invoked. 'Th(is) argument,' Judge Prettyman has said, 'is wholly without merit, preposterous in fact';[5] for whatever might be the exact relationship between the privilege against self-incrimination and the provision protecting from unconstitutional searches it had nowhere been suggested that the Fifth Amendment operated to limit the Fourth (as opposed to complementing it). The basic premise of the Fourth Amendment, in other words, is not to extend some type of protection from incrimination but to protect a man's right to the privacy of his home. It is therefore nothing short of 'a fantastic absurdity'[6] to arrive at the conclusion that a man suspected of crime has a right to protection from illegal searches of his home but that a man not suspected of crime has no such protection.

This second view, that the Fourth Amendment covers all governmental intrusions on personal security and therefore all official entries into the home, is supported by *Camara v. Municipal Court*[7] where the Supreme Court, emphasising that 'the basic purpose of th(e) Amendment . . . is to safeguard the privacy and security of individuals against arbitrary invasions by governmental officials', held that 'searches' included not only searches for criminal evidence but also administrative inspections to enforce fire, health, housing or similar regulatory codes. Since such administrative inspections were significant intrusions upon the interests in privacy and security protected by the Fourth Amendment they were searches and would only be upheld if

[1] *Wolf v. Colorado*, 338 U.S. 25, 27.

[2] *Poe v. Ullman*, 367 U.S. 497, 550–1 (1961) (dissenting opinion); see also *Terry v. Ohio*, 392 U.S. 1, 18 n. 15 (1968); *Katz v. United States*, 389 U.S. 347, 352 (1967).

[3] See *Wyman v. James*, 400 U.S. 309, 339 (1971), per Marshall, J. dissenting.

[4] See *Camara v. Municipal Court*, 387 U.S. 523, 530 (1967); *District of Columbia v. Little*, 178 F. 2d 13, 17 (1949).

[5] *District of Columbia v. Little*, 178 F. 2d at 16, per Prettyman, J.

[6] Ibid., at 17. See also the dissenting opinion of Douglas, J. in *Frank v. Maryland*, 359 U.S. 360, at 375–80.

[7] 387 U.S. 523 (1967).

found to be reasonable. On this view 'search' within the Fourth Amendment refers to any intrusion by governmental officers upon an individual's person, property or privacy for the purpose either of seizing tangible objects or of obtaining information by inspection or surveillance.[1] But such broad and inclusive definitions have been somewhat shaken by a post-*Camara* case, *Wyman v. James*,[2] where a majority of the Supreme Court held that a social caseworker's visit to the home of a recipient of welfare assistance did not consititute a 'search' within the Fourth Amendment. This, Justice Blackmun said, was due to two factors, first the rehabilitative aspects of the visit and secondly the fact that refusal to allow a requested visit would result not in the imposition of a criminal penalty but only in the termination of the particular welfare benefits. This reasoning has been convincingly criticised.[3] To begin with, it is questionable whether it is correct to characterise the welfare home visit as exclusively rehabilitative; such visits also seek to find out whether welfare assistance is being used properly, and in this sense they are unmistakably investigative. Secondly, if attention is directed to a comparison of sanctions, there is little doubt that termination of welfare benefits is at least as serious a sanction as imposition of a criminal penalty. Finally, even assuming that the home visit is primarily rehabilitative, it still does not follow that it is not a search; the two propositions emerging from *Camara* are that the governmental purpose behind a particular type of intrusion is irrelevant to the question of whether it is a 'search' and that the governing criterion in defining 'searches' is whether a particular intrusion is a significant imposition on personal privacy and security; from this point of view the home visit in *Wyman v. James* is certainly a 'search' because *all governmental entries into the home* are potentially severe intrusions upon individual and family privacy; both administrative inspections and welfare visits therefore should come within the Fourth Amendment and be evaluated by reference to its safeguards.[4]

(c) Electronic eavesdropping[5]

The holding of *Olmstead*, it will be remembered, was that the search and seizure provisions did not come into play unless there had been either a seizure of 'tangible material effects' or 'an actual physical invasion' of a house or its

[1] A.L.I., *Model Code of Pre-Arraignment Procedure* 121 (Proposed Official Draft, 1975).

[2] 400 U.S. 309 (1971).

[3] 'Note', 85 *Harv. L. Rev.* 258 (1971); see also Marshall, J.'s dissenting opinion in *Wyman v. James*, 400 U.S. 309, 338 (1971).

[4] Burger, C. J. and Black, Harlan and Stewart, JJ. agreed with Blackmun, J. that the home visit was not a search and with his alternative ground for decision that even if the home visit was a search it was reasonable even though there was no warrant. Douglas, Brennan and Marshall, JJ. dissented; and White, J. only agreed with the second ground.

[5] See generally Wright, 3 *Federal Practice and Procedure* 42–59 (1969); King, 'Electronic Surveillance and Constitutional Rights: Some Recent Developments and Observations', 33 *Geo. Wash. L. Rev.* 240 (1964); J. Landynski, *Search and Seizure*

curtilage.[1] This principle, the trespass doctrine, as has been seen, remained substantially undisturbed until the 1960s and was only officially pronounced dead in *Katz v. United States*.[2]

The doctrine that electronic surveillance not involving a physical intrusion into a protected area, whether by wiretapping or by the use of other devices, does not violate constitutional rights to be free from unreasonable searches and seizures is illustrated by *Goldman v. United States*[3] where federal agents obtained evidence of incriminating conversations by placing a device known as the 'detectaphone' *against* the wall separating the defendant's premises and the adjoining office to which they had gained access. It was held that *Olmstead* should neither be distinguished nor overruled, that no physical trespass had taken place with regard to the installation of the listening device, and that the use of the detectaphone in the circumstances of the case to listen to conversations in an adjoining room between persons suspected of crime involved no violation of the Fourth Amendment. But even before its overruling *Olmstead* did not apply where electronic eavesdropping had only been made possible by means of 'an unauthorised physical encroachment'[4] upon a constitutionally protected area. In *Silverman v. United States*[5] police officers, suspecting the defendant of conducting gambling operations at a particular location, obtained permission to enter the adjoining house. Using a 'spike mike', an electronic listening device consisting of a microphone, amplifier and earphones connected to a foot-long spike which was inserted into the party wall and against the defendant's heating system, the police were able to overhear incriminating conversations. The Supreme Court held the evidence inadmissible. In *Olmstead*, it was pointed out, there had been no physical invasion of any sort of the petitioner's house or office; here, by contrast, the incriminating conversations had been overheard only by means of an unauthorised usurpation of part of the petitioner's premises, namely the heating system which was an integral part of the area occupied by the defendant. Nor was it necessary to decide whether there had been a technical trespass under local-property law relating to party walls, the Court observed, since Fourth Amendment rights were not 'inevitably measurable in terms of

---

and the Supreme Court 198–244 (1966); Schwartz, 'The Legitimation of Electronic Eavesdropping: The Politics of "Law and Order"', 67 *Mich. L. Rev.* 455 (1969); S. Dash, R. Schwartz & R. Knowlton, *The Eavesdroppers* (1959); 'Comment, Eavesdropping, Informers, and the Right of Privacy: A Judicial Tightrope', 52 *Cornell L.Q.* 975 (1967); Kamisar, 'The Wiretapping—Eavesdropping Problem: A Professor's View', 44 *Minn. L. Rev.* 891 (1960); 'Note, From Private Places to Personal Privacy: A Post-Katz Study of Fourth Amendment Protection', 43 *N.U.Y.L Rev.* 968 (1968); Scoular, 'Wiretapping and Eavesdropping Constitutional Development from Olmstead to Katz', 12 *St. Louis L.J.* 513 (1968). It must be noted that the terms electronic eavesdropping and electronic surveillance are used interchangeably in this account.

[1] *Olmstead v. United States*, 277 U.S. 438, 466 (1928).

[2] 389 U.S. 347 (1967).

[3] 316 U.S. 129 (1942).

[4] *Silverman v. United States*, 365 U.S. 505, 510 (1961).

[5] Ibid.

ancient niceties of tort or real property law'; it was enough that officers had without warrant and without consent 'physically entrench(ed)' into a man's office or house. It is difficult to reconcile *Goldman* and *Silverman* in terms of any viable theory of Fourth Amendment rights,[1] particularly if one disclaims interest in the subtleties and trivialities of local trespass law, as *Silverman* proclaims. If the Fourth Amendment secures 'the right of a man to retreat into his own home and there be free from unreasonable governmental intrusion',[2] what principled distinction can there be between an electronic device placed on the outside wall of a house, declared to be permissible in *Goldman*, and an electronic device that has penetrated a wall, declared to be constitutionally impermissible in *Silverman*? The invasion of privacy and the governmental intrusion into personal security are as great in one case as in the other,[3] irrespective of the fortuitous circumstance of the exact location of the eavesdropping device.

An important point about *Silverman* of course is its implicit assumption that it is not only tangible or material effects that are barred from admission into evidence by the exclusionary rule as having been obtained by means of an unlawful invasion of protected interests but also verbal statements and conversations. Another way of stating this is to say that one may have a seizure not only of material items but also of words, incriminating statements and conversations.[4] But when verbal communications are brought within the coverage of the constitutional protection from unreasonable seizures and once the judiciary, mainly because of a determination not to allow fundamental rights to become outdated by technological developments,[5] refuse 'to crowd the Fourth Amendment into the mold of local property law',[6] the only support for the position that electronic eavesdropping unaccompanied by some kind of physical penetration involves no constitutionally cognizable search is some version of the trespass rationale, serious dissatisfaction with which both as constitutional exposition and as analytically tenable doctrine was being expressed more and more openly.[7] That it could not be long before the Supreme Court in its interpretation of the search and seizure provisions discarded property distinctions 'without sound policy justification in the

[1] Wright, supra, 40 n. 5, at 47–8.

[2] *Silverman v. United States*, supra, at 511, per Stewart, J.

[3] Ibid., at 513, per Douglas, J. concurring.

[4] See also *Wong Sun v. United States*, 371 U.S. 471, 485 (1963); *United States v. White*, 401 U.S. 745, 775 (1971), per Harlan, J. dissenting.

[5] See *United States v. Stone*, 232 F. Supp. 396, 399 (1964); the dissenting opinion of Brandeis, J. in *Olmstead v. United States*, 277 U.S. 438 (1928); and the dissenting opinion of Brennan, J. in *Lopez v. United States*, 373 U.S. 427, 466 (1963).

[6] *Lopez v. United States*, 373 U.S. 427, 460 (1963), per Brennan, J. dissenting.

[7] Wiretapping, as opposed to other forms of electronic eavesdropping, was dealt with by statute, s.605 of the Federal Communications Act of 1934 which prohibited the interception and publication of telephone, telegraph, or radio communications (see Wright, supra, 40 n. 5, at 44–5). Only a criminal sanction was provided in the statute itself but the Supreme Court, construing § 605 generously, developed the doctrine that evidence obtained by wiretapping is not admissible in court: see *Nardone v. United States*, 302 U.S. 379 (1937); see Wright, supra, at 45.

realm of values protected by the Fourth Amendment'[1] was becoming increasingly clear throughout the early 1960s not only by the outright rejection of what were thought to be securely entrenched rules based on fictional and procedural considerations ultimately deriving from property concepts[2] but also by the noticeable trend espoused by more and more judges of emphasising in decision after decision that the principal purpose of the Fourth Amendment was the protection of individual privacy and security, not property.[3] Unequivocal notice that the demise of *Olmstead* and its progeny was imminent was given in *Berger v. New York.*[4] Here the Supreme Court considered the constitutionality of a state statute allowing judicial officers to issue in appropriate cases and after satisfaction of the standard of reasonable cause orders authorising electronic eavesdropping involving trespassory intrusions. The majority opinion made two principal points: it first took note of 'the fantastic advances' in the field of electronic surveillance which by making it possible to eavesdrop 'on anyone in almost any given situation' constituted 'a great danger to the privacy of the individual'[5] and a very serious threat to liberty, and secondly had little doubt that the employment of eavesdropping devices, particularly if used indiscriminately and without the most exacting judicial supervision, raised grave questions under the constitutional provision extending protection from unreasonable searches and seizures. The Fourth Amendment, the Court's opinion concluded, did not have the effect of making the precincts of the home or office sanctuaries which the law could never reach; but it did prescribe constitutional standards that had to be complied with before 'official invasion(s)' into protected areas or interests could be permitted.[6] In *Berger* the eavesdropping statute, as construed, was declared to be unconstitutional, and even though *Olmstead* and its trespass doctrine were not explicitly overruled, there was little doubt that electronic surveillance, whether made possible by trespassory invasions of protected areas or not, was now fully within the purview of the Fourth Amendment.

Against this background of steady constitutional development[7] — *centring* on the significant perception that the Fourth Amendment is essentially intended to protect not from particular forms of intrusion (particularly if these are framed in terms of trespasses or physical invasions) but from all types of official investigatory action that threaten either individual privacy or the

[1] *United States v. White*, 401 U.S. 745, 778 (1971): per Harlan, J. dissenting.

[2] See *Warden v. Hayden*, 387 U.S. 294 (1967); see also *Chapman v. United States*, 365 U.S. 610; *Jones v. United States*, 362 U.S. 257; *United States v. Jeffers*, 342 U.S. 48.

[3] See *Camara v. Municipal Court*, 387 U.S. 523 (1967); *Warden v. Hayden*, supra, n. 2, at 304; *Lewis v. United States*, 385 U.S. 206 (1966); *Hoffa v. United States*, 385 U.S. 293 (1966); the first comprehensive exposition of the argument that electronic surveillance comes within the Fourth Amendment is the dissenting opinion of Brennan, J. in *Lopez*, 373 U.S., at 446–71.

[4] 388 U.S. 41 (1967).

[5] Ibid., at 47 and 62.

[6] Ibid., at 64.

[7] This is brilliantly sketched out in the dissenting opinion of Harlan, J. in *White*, supra, at 780 et seq.

related sense of security, and *assisted* in part by the new found flexibility of the warrant machinery as a result of which it was no longer always necessary to insist on the existence of probable cause in the usual sense before authorising a search[1] and which in this way helped allay the fears of those who in the wake of *Berger* predicted that it would not be possible in the context of electronic surveillance to devise warrants with the exacting specificity normally required under the Fourth Amendment—*Katz's* formal dispatch both of *Olmstead* and of the notion that the constitutional prohibition of unreasonable searches and seizures could only apply if there had been a prior physical intrusion into a constitutionally protected area came as no surprise. *Katz*,[2] it will be remembered, dealt with the attachment of an electronic listening and recording device to the outside of a public telephone booth from which the defendant had made a number of calls. In declaring the recordings inadmissible in the absence of a warrant authorising the surveillance the Supreme Court held that *Olmstead* and *Goldman* should be overruled and the trespass doctrine there enunciated rejected, that the absence of a physical intrusion into the telephone booth was constitutionally immaterial, that the government's activities in electronically listening to and recording the defendant's words had violated the privacy upon which he had justifiably relied, and that accordingly the warrantless employment in the circumstances before them of an electronic device constituted an unconstitutional search and seizure.[3]

What are the limits of *Katz* in this area?[4] In particular, does it reach all kinds of electronic eavesdropping? To begin with, it is quite clear that it makes no difference whether the electronic eavesdropping is accomplished by means of wiretaps involving connection to telephone lines and interception of telephonic communications, or by means of sophisticated electronic devices known as 'bugs', of the type involved in *Silverman* and *Katz*.[5] A more difficult case is presented when one party to the monitored conversation knows of the government's eavesdropping activities,[6] for instance where an informer who is collaborating with the police equips himself with an electronic device intended to record or transmit the defendant's incriminating conversations,

[1] See particularly *Camara v. Municipal Court*, 387 U.S. 523 (1967).

[2] 389 U.S. 347 (1967).

[3] Wiretapping and electronic eavesdropping are now dealt with by Title III of the Omnibus Crime Control and Safe Streets Act of 1968 which regulates the interception of wire or oral communications, interception being defined as the acquisition of the contents of any wire or oral communication 'through the use of any electronic, mechanical, or other device' (18 U.S.C.A. § 2510(4)); see Wright, supra, 40 n. 5, at 54–9. The present account only deals with constitutional developments under the Fourth Amendment.

[4] See Kitch, '*Katz v. United States*: The Limits of the Fourth Amendment', 1968 *Sup. Ct. Rev.* 133.

[5] For a discussion of the various types of electronic eavesdropping, see *Berger v. New York*, 388 U.S. 41, 46 et seq. (1967).

[6] The best treatment of electronic surveillance with the consent of one of the parties is Greenawalt, 'The Consent Problem in Wiretapping and Eavesdropping: Surreptitious Monitoring with the Consent of a Participant in a Conversation', 68 *Colum. L. Rev.* 189 (1968).

as contrasted with the fact situation in *Katz*, where of course conversations had been listened to and recorded without the consent or knowledge of either party. Two types of case must further be distinguished within the broad rubric of what can be called consensual electronic eavesdropping, participant recording and participant monitoring. The former refers to the use of an electronic device by a participant in a conversation which only records the conversation, whereas participant monitoring refers to the use of an electronic device by a participant which simultaneously transmits the exchange to a third party. One view is that the two should be sharply distinguished in terms of the inroads they normally entail on privacy and security, and further that this distinction should be reflected in adjudication under the Fourth Amendment. On this argument participant monitoring is particularly offensive since it inevitably involves simultaneous and automatic transmission of all that is said to third parties, whereas participant recording merely preserves the conversation in a more reliable form without simultaneously divulging its contents to third parties; further, it may be that what is recorded will never be played again and in this way never reach third parties, but even if subsequent disclosures are made this will be not by way of simultaneous transmission (which at the relevant time is beyond the effective control of either party) but rather because the equipped or 'bugged' participant has decided after listening to the recordings to share what was said with others. For these reasons it is argued that participant recording is analogous to the doctrine of misplaced confidence (according to which if a 'friend' in a case without any element of electronic surveillance decides to reveal incriminating conversations to the police there is no question of the courts coming to the complainant's help) and should therefore not be brought within the Fourth Amendment, unlike participant monitoring.[1] Another view, much more widely held, is that the precise nature of the monitoring does not much matter, for two main reasons: first, while it is true that participant recording does not involve a simultaneous transmission to third parties, it does result in a permanent record of the conversation, which makes the practice equally objectionable; and secondly in most cases the recording is in fact played for third parties, which thus makes the invasion of privacy at least as intrusive as that entailed by simultaneous transmission.[2]

In any case two broad views have been taken with regard to the constitutionality of the use of electronic devices by a participant. The view[3] that participant eavesdropping, whether monitoring or recording, involves no search or seizure and therefore falls outside the constitutional guarantee relies heavily on the notion of assumption of risk, already touched upon in our discussion of the subjective component of *Katz*, and can be put forward as follows: As will also appear shortly, law enforcement agencies have authority to use police informers; a police agent or informer who conceals his identity and intentions can repeat what was said to him by the defendant, mainly because one who communicates directly with another assumes the risk that

[1] *People v. Hall*, 276 N.W. 2d 897, 901 (1979), per Danhof, C.J., dissenting.
[2] *People v. Hall*, supra, at 898; and Greenawalt, supra, 44 n. 6, at 225 n. 180.
[3] See *United States v. White*, 401 U.S. 745 (1971).

the person he is holding the conversation with may divulge what is being said to others; it *should* now make no difference if the police informer *instead* of reporting and divulging his conversations with the defendant to others without the aid of electronic devices *either* simultaneously records them with electronic equipment he is carrying on his person *or* simultaneously transmits them either to recording equipment located elsewhere or to other police officers monitoring the transmitting frequency. As it has been put by Justice White, if the conduct and revelations of an agent operating without electronic equipment do not invade the defendant's constitutionally justifiable expectations of privacy neither *should either* a simultaneous recording of the same conversations made by the agent *or* a simultaneous transmission of the incriminating exchanges to third parties.[1] If the defendant, in other words, must be taken to risk the trustworthiness of the person he is talking to, in the sense that the law will refuse to protect him from a 'trusted' accomplice turning prosecution witness, he should also be deemed to assume the risk that the same person is either recording or transmitting the conversations which are later offered in evidence against him. This first view of the use of electronic devices by a participant is supported by three Supreme Court cases. The first deals with participant recording and the other two with participant monitoring. In *Lopez v. United States*[2] the defendant attempted to offer a bribe to an internal revenue agent investigating tax violations. The agent reported the matter to his superiors who instructed him 'to play along' and equipped him with a pocket recorder, which recorded further incriminating statements made by Lopez at another meeting a few days later. The agent testified about the conversation with the defendant, and the recording was also admitted into evidence. The Supreme Court first rejected the argument that the agent should not have been permitted to testify about his conversation with the defendant, since any other holding would effectively mean that a private offer of a bribe would be a constitutionally protected communication, an untenable conclusion. Since the agent could properly testify about his conversation with Lopez, why should the most reliable evidence of this admissible conversation be excluded? Indeed, the majority opinion continued, the instant case involved 'no "eavesdropping" whatever in any proper sense of that term'. The tape recording had been made by a participant in the conversation and the government had not used an electronic device 'to listen in on conversations it could not otherwise have heard'. The defendant had taken a risk in offering the bribe, and this included 'the risk that the offer would be accurately reproduced in court, whether by faultless memory or mechanical recording'. The use of electronic devices for simultaneous transmission of a conversation to third parties has been considered in two Supreme Court cases, *On Lee v. United States*[3] and *United States v. White.*[4] In *On Lee* government agents enlisted the services of a former friend and employee of the defendant, who was suspected of trading

[1] Ibid., at 751.
[2] 373 U.S. 427 (1963).
[3] 343 U.S. 747 (1952).
[4] 401 U.S. 745 (1971).

in narcotics. The 'friend' was equipped with a transmitting device which enabled agents standing outside the defendant's laundry to overhear a number of incriminating admissions he made. The basic reason the majority offered for holding evidence of the monitored conversations admissible was the fact that no trespass had been committed. This part of *On Lee*'s holding cannot of course survive *Katz*. But the Court's opinion also noted that even if the principles of *Olmstead* and *Goldman* were rejected the defendant in *On Lee* would still fail since in the latter case, unlike the earlier ones, the eavesdropping that was objected to had taken place 'with the connivance of one of the parties'. The defendant was talking indiscreetly with one he trusted and he was overheard, and it was immaterial that this had been accomplished with aid from a listening device rather than by the naked ear. This risk analysis has now been adopted by *United States v. White*[1] where, on very similar facts, four members of the Court refused to detect in *Katz* any indication that *On Lee*'s second ground should no longer be regarded as correct. One contemplating illegal activities, Justice White observed, should realise that his companions might be cooperating with the police. If he sufficiently doubts their trustworthiness their association would probably end. 'But if he has no doubts, or allays them, or risks what doubt he has, the risk is his', and it was immaterial whether the informer was equipped with a transmitter or not. Electronic surveillance where one of the parties to an incriminating conversation was a police informer did not therefore involve any violation of Fourth Amendment rights.

The view that the principles of *Katz* govern all uses of electronic devices intercepting communications, whether or not a participant in the recorded or monitored conversation is collaborating at the material time with the authorities, and that the warrant requirement applies and must be complied with not only in cases of third-party electronic monitoring, as in *On Lee* and in *White*, but also in cases of electronic recording by a government agent of a face-to-face conversation with a suspect, as in *Lopez*, can be developed as follows:[2] The correct approach, as has been seen from our general discussion of *Katz*, is not to focus on the expectations, anticipations and risks entertained or assumed by a particular individual but rather to investigate the more general impact of a given practice on 'the sense of security that is the true concern of the Fourth Amendment's protection of privacy'.[3] In this

[1] Ibid. White, J. announced the judgment of the Court, and his opinion was joined by Burger, C.J., Stewart (the author of the Court's opinion in *Katz*) and Blackmun, J.J. Black, J. concurred on the broader ground put forward in his *Katz* dissent, namely that electronic eavesdropping does not constitute a 'search' or 'seizure' within the Fourth Amendment. Douglas, Brennan, Harlan and Marshall, JJ. took the view that any kind of warrantless electronic surveillance violates the Fourth Amendment. At times it is not clear whether the opinion of White, J. proceeded on the basis that electronic surveillance carried on with the consent of a participant was not a search within the Fourth Amendment, or whether such activities must be upheld under 'fluid concepts of reasonableness' (*White*, supra, at 753).

[2] See the dissenting opinion of Harlan, J. in *United States v. White*, 401 U.S. 745, 768 (1971).

[3] Ibid., at 788 n. 24.

respect a rule of law that permits official monitoring or recording of private conversations provided only that a willing assistant is found may well have serious social consequences; the main one of these is the following: free communication—that is so often characterised by exaggeration, falsehood, impetuosity and frivolity, but which despite its light-hearted character performs important social and political functions, for instance by liberating daily life and by allowing frank exchanges in the context of small groups that in turn are instrumental to the development of individual and other relationships in a free society[1]—would certainly be inhibited if the frequency of third-party eavesdropping were or became such that there developed a widespread suspicion that much informal conversation, far from enjoying substantial confidentiality, was being transmitted and recorded. As to the main argument of *Lopez*, *On Lee* and *White*, namely that it makes no difference whether secrets are revealed by the unaided repetition of an unequipped informer or by the use of an electronic device, this ignores the vital difference between electronic surveillance—whether accomplished by means of third-party monitoring and recording or not—which ensures full and accurate disclosure of all that is said free of the possibility of error and oversight that inheres in human reporting, and other more traditional police methods, for instance the use of unequipped informers and ordinary non-electronic eavesdropping. Since therefore the impact of widespread third-party eavesdropping is such as to threaten important social and political values, principally the confidence, spontaneity and related sense of security that are so heavily dependent on the possibility of limited and confidential communication and which in turn help support the concept of a pluralistic society and important elements of the democratic system, it should not be allowed unless a search warrant has been obtained authorising the monitoring or recording of the conversations that it is proposed to adduce in evidence.

This line of reasoning was adopted by four members of the Supreme Court in *White* and by a number of state courts.[2] For them the difficult question of participant electronic eavesdropping cannot be solved by mechanical application either of a risk analysis or of the doctrine of misplaced trust; permissive formulations allowing government officials to record and/or monitor at their unrestricted discretion the private conversations of all those with whom either they or their agents come into contact would seriously and impermissibly impair essential individual and societal rights to privacy and

[1] Ibid., at 787 et seq.; see also Greenawalt, supra, 44 n. 6, at 217, and Schwartz, 'On Current Proposals to Legalize Wire Tapping', 103 *U.Pa. L. Rev.* 157, 162 (1954).

[2] See particularly *People v. Beavers*, 227 N.W. 2d 511 (1975) and *People v. Hall*, 276 N.W. 2d 897 (1979). Harlan, J. in *White* confined his dissenting views to the problem presented by the actual facts, namely simultaneous electronic monitoring, which means that he did not have to discuss directly the question of the continued authority of *Lopez*, the majority opinion of which he had indeed authored. But he admitted that his approach in *Lopez* was at variance with his general approach in *White* (see *White*, supra, at 788 n. 24), even though factual distinctions might *still* be made between *Lopez* where 'a known government agent' had used a recording device and other cases.

security; and therefore all forms of electronic eavesdropping, whether of the nonconsensual kind employed in *Katz* or of the type dealt with in *Lopez* and *White*, should not be engaged in unless the appropriate authorities both have probable cause and have submitted their evidence to the detached determination of a neutral and independent magistrate.

(d) Non-electronic surveillance

(i) Observation

It is often said that as a general matter mere observation does not constitute a search,[1] both because '(a) search implies a prying into hidden places for that which is concealed and it is not a search to observe that which is open to view',[2] and because of the needs of law enforcement which, it is said, demand that traditional investigative activities should not be forbidden.[3] Many courts have therefore taken the view that even though '(p)eering through a window or a crack in a door or a keyhole is not in the abstract genteel behaviour', the Fourth Amendment cannot be taken to provide general protection against 'all conduct unworthy of a good neighbour'.[4] The Fourth Amendment therefore does not itself draw the blinds the occupants could have drawn but did not.[5] But, as will be seen, it is an over-simplification to say that observation as such never violates constitutional rights, or that it is always permissible to look in through windows and doors. For even though it is occasionally asserted that there is a difference of constitutional dimensions between electronic eavesdropping, involving the use of mechanical devices, and unaided surreptitious surveillance, only involving the use of some of man's five senses,[6] it is unlikely, as others have noticed, that *Katz* can or should be applied in so mechanical a fashion. If *Katz*[7] holds, first that the Fourth Amendment protects people, not places, secondly that what a person knowingly exposes to the public cannot claim protection, but thirdly that what he seeks to preserve as private, even in an area accessible to the public, may be constitutionally protected,[8] it should not be impossible to bring at least some forms of visual surveillance within the coverage of the Fourth Amendment. Accordingly

[1] See 68 *Am. Jur.* 2d, *Searches and Seizures* § 23.

[2] *State v. Hanawahine*, 50 Haw. 461, 433 P. 2d 149 (1968).

[3] *State v. Smith*, 37 N.J. 481, 181 A. 2d 761 (1962), cert. denied, 374 U.S. 835 (1963).

[4] Ibid.

[5] Ibid.; see also A.L.I., *A Model Code of Pre-arraignment Procedure* 497–8 (1975) where it is pointed out, first, that keeping watch over premises, looking in through windows and doors, and similar activities are 'permissible under the civil and criminal laws of most jurisdictions', secondly, that they are 'traditional police practices and may generally be engaged in with impunity by private persons', and thirdly, that if the Fourth Amendment could be violated by such actions 'the principle of *Katz* (would) be extended to improbable and unwarranted lengths'.

[6] See *Lopez v. United States*, 373 U.S. 427, 465–6 (1963), per Brennan, J. dissenting.

[7] 389 U.S. 347 (1967).

[8] Ibid., at 351.

many recent cases reject the alleged 'constitutional' distinction between 'electronic' eavesdropping and 'simple' surveillance, and adopt the general principle that *any* governmental intrusion into an individual's reasonable expectations of privacy is a 'search' within the Fourth Amendment,[1] whether it takes the traditional form of a physical search or only consists of a surreptitious auditory[2] or visual[3] invasion, whether electronic or non-electronic.

The many cases are not easy to summarise or reconcile, constitutional doctrine is still in the formative stages of early development, but in the attempt to develop workable criteria to determine when justifiable expectations of privacy have been violated by visual intrusions three factors are mainly considered,[4] the nature of the area or place involved, the precautions if any taken by the defendant to ensure his privacy, and the position of the officer who conducted the observation. These three criteria are interrelated, but it is helpful to consider them separately.

The first question is whether the defendant has shown a prima facie reasonable expectation of privacy with regard to a particular area or location. While it is true that *Katz* rejected the notion that the Fourth Amendment protects areas or zones, application of the 'reasonable expectation of privacy' test usually requires reference to a place.[5] The home, it goes without saying, is covered by legitimate expectations of privacy, but Fourth Amendment protection extends beyond. A distinction which is traditionally made here is between the 'curtilage' of a home which basically enjoys the same protection and the essentially unprotected 'open fields'.[6] Curtilage refers to the ground, buildings and areas immediately surrounding and adjacent to the house, formerly usually enclosed.[7] More simply, the 'curtilage' denotes such area as is necessary and convenient to a dwelling and is habitually used for family purposes.[8] Whether the place searched is within the curtilage depends on all the facts, mainly its proximity or annexation to the dwelling, its inclusion within the general enclosure surrounding the home, and its use and enjoyment as an adjunct to the domestic economy of the family.[9] In contrast, open areas around the house are not included within the prohibition of the Fourth Amendment, which means that evidence about them can be obtained and relevant testimony received independently of constitutional safeguards.

[1] See *Lorenzana v. Superior Court,* 108 Cal. Rptr. 585 (1973); *People v. Sneed,* 108 Cal. Rptr. 146 (1973); *People v. Edwards,* 80 Cal. Rptr. 633 (1969)

[2] *Katz v. United States*, 389 U.S. 347 (1967) (electronic intrusion); *United States v. Case*, 435 F. 2d 766 (1970) (non-electronic).

[3] *People v. Triggs,* 106 Cal. Rptr. 408 (1973); *People v. Sneed,* 108 Cal Rptr. 146 (1973).

[4] See generally *State v. Kender*, 588 P. 2d 447 (1979); *State v. Stachler*, 570 P. 2d 1323 (1977); *Lorenzana v. Superior Court,* 108 Cal.Rptr. 585 (1973).

[5] See the concurring opinion of Harlan, J. in *Katz*, supra.

[6] See *Wattenburg v. United States*, 388 F. 2d 853, 857 (1968).

[7] See *Rosencranz v. United States*, 356 F. 2d 310, 313 (1966).

[8] *United States v. Potts*, 297 F. 2d 68, 69 (1961).

[9] See *McDowell v. United States*, 383 F. 2d 599, 603 (1967); *Care v. United States,* 231 F. 2d 22, 25 (1956); *People v. Sneed,* 108 Cal. Rptr. (1973).

The 'open fields' exception owes its origin to *Hester v. United States.*[1] Here federal revenue agents without a warrant observed the defendant and his companion either throw away or drop jugs of illegally distilled whisky in an open field. The Supreme Court held that their testimony was admissible even if there had been a trespass. The basic reason for this was that it was the defendant's own acts, and those of his associates, which had disclosed the incriminating items, and there could be no seizure in the sense of the Fourth Amendment when there had only been an examination of what had been abandoned. But even if the examination of the vessels had taken place upon private land the position could be no different. '(I)t is enough to say that the special protection accorded by the Fourth Amendment to the people in their "persons, houses, papers, and effects", is not extended to the open fields.' The distinction between the latter and the house, Justice Holmes concluded, was as old as the common law.[2] The 'open fields' doctrine of *Hester* has been applied on numerous occasions, and has, for instance, been used to justify the seizure of items in fields clearly separated from the defendant's buildings,[3] the search of a cave used as a distillery in a field across the road and more than a block from the defendant's home,[4] the search of an abandoned farm leading to the discovery of a concealed suitcase containing the proceeds of a robbery,[5] the search of a field owned by the defendant's mother and posted with 'no trespassing' signs put up by his stepfather,[6] and a health inspector's action in entering the outdoor premises of a business without either a warrant or the owner's consent and there conducting visual pollution tests of smoke being emitted from the chimneys.[7] Some courts have recently taken the view that in the wake of *Katz* neither the curtilage concept nor the open fields doctrine are appropriate in ascertaining the extent of the constitutional protection from unreasonable searches and seizures.[8] Their reasoning proceeds as follows: The Fourth Amendment guarantees not enjoyment of property but personal security from arbitrary official intrusions;[9] consistently with this its protection consists not in a proscription of trespasses but in a prohibition of unreasonable searches and seizures,[10] and in accordance with *Katz* its application should therefore be determined not by property

[1] 265 U.S. 57 (1926).

[2] For a critical appraisal, see Mascolo, 'The Role of Abandonment in the Law of Search and Seizure: An Application of Misdirected Emphasis', 20 *Buff. L. Rev.* 399, 408 (1971).

[3] *McDowell v. United States,* supra.

[4] *Care v. United States,* supra.

[5] *United States v. Brown*, 473 F. 2d 952 (1973).

[6] *Commonwealth v. Janek*, 363 A. 2d 1299 (1976).

[7] *Air Pollution Variance Board v. Western Alfalfa*, 416 U.S. 861 (1974).

[8] See *People v. Edwards,* 80 Cal. Rptr. 633; *People v. Sneed,* 108 Cal. Rptr. 146; *Phelan v. Superior Court,* 151 Cal. Rptr. 599 (1979); *State v. Kender,* 588 P. 2d 477 (1979); *Wattenburg v. United States,* 388 F. 2d 853, 857 (1968).

[9] As the Supreme Court put it in *Katz*, 'the Fourth Amendment protects people, not places'.

[10] See *People v. Terry,* 77 Cal. Rptr. 460 (1969); *People v. Edwards,* 80 Cal. Rptr. 633 (1969); *People v. Fly* 110 Cal. Rptr. 158 (1973); *Phelan v. Superior Court,* 151 Cal. Rptr. 599 (1979).

concepts,[1] whether that of constitutionally protected areas or the ancillary ones of curtilage and open fields, but by whether '(the complainant) has exhibited a reasonable expectation of privacy, and, if so, whether that expectation has been violated by unreasonable governmental intrusion'.[2] Good examples of this broader approach are *People v. Edwards*,[3] where it was held that a trash can within a few feet of the back door of the defendants' home was within the coverage of the Fourth Amendment, and *Phelan v. Superior Court*,[4] where it was held that the petitioners' subjective expectation of privacy with regard to the cultivation of their marijuana garden was objectively reasonable in that the garden was located in an isolated ravine on privately owned property and was protected by trees and by a fence covered with branches. According to these and other cases the problem of whether testimony based on observation offends the Fourth Amendment can arise in countless situations and cannot be solved by the application of 'fixed mechanical rules',[5] such as the 'open fields' doctrine, the curtilage concept, the doctrine of 'looking through an open window', and others. The test should rather be whether there has been an unconstitutional invasion of privacy, which in the area of unaided surveillance has been developed in greater detail as follows: First, the complainant must have exhibited a subjective expectation of privacy; secondly, this expectation must be objectively reasonable; and thirdly this expectation must have been violated by an unreasonable governmental intrusion.[6] This is sometimes described more compendiously as the test of overall reasonableness.[7] But other opinions take the view that the 'open fields' doctrine of *Hester* retains its vitality as an independent rule and can still be used for the decision of search and seizure cases altogether apart from *Katz*.[8] An intermediate possibility is that the 'open fields' doctrine is not a separate and independent principle resting on real property considerations and resulting in the automatic exclusion of whole areas from the ambit of constitutional protection but rather a subsidiary rule that is fully consistent with the teaching of *Katz* and which holds, first that where an object or activity is open and visible to members of the public observations, interceptions and seizures are beyond the Fourth Amendment,[9] and secondly that if despite a technical trespass any invasion of privacy that has been

[1] *People v. Edwards*, supra; see also *Terry v. Ohio*, 392 U.S. 1 (1968); *Katz v. United States*, 389 U.S. 347 (1967); *Brett v. United States*, 412 F. 2d 401, 406 (1969); *Camara v. Municipal Court*, 387 U.S. 523.

[2] *People v. Edwards*, supra, at 635; see also *People v. Sneed*, 108 Cal. Rptr. 146, and *Phelan v. Superior Court*, 151 Cal. Rptr. 599.

[3] 80 Cal. Rptr. 633 (1969).

[4] 151 Cal. Rptr. 599 (1979).

[5] *People v. Sneed*, 108 Cal. Rptr. 146, 149 (1973).

[6] Ibid.; see also *Phelan v. Superior Court*, supra.

[7] See *People v. Edwards*, supra; *People v. Sneed*, supra; *Phelan v. Superior Court*, supra.

[8] See *United States v. Brown*, 473 F. 2d 952, 954 (1973); *Commonwealth v. Janek*, 363 A. 2d 1299 (1976); *Air Pollution Variance Board v. Western Alfalfa*, 416 U.S. 861, 865 (1974).

[9] *State v. Stachler*, 570 P. 2d 1323, 1326 (1977).

occasioned is at most 'abstract and theoretical'[1] there will again be no constitutional violation.

The second important element courts normally look to in determining whether the defendant can legitimately complain of testimony based on official observation is whether he took any precautions to prevent visual surveillance.[2] In general, 'an internal uncommunicated need for privacy'[3] does not qualify for Fourth Amendment protection. The defendant must have sufficiently demonstrated an expectation of privacy from surveillance, for instance by erecting a fence, by placing up screens, or by taking other reasonable steps intended to protect a garden or other area from the observation of outsiders.[4] But it is not necessary to take measures that result in total concealment before a constitutionally justifiable expectation of privacy can arise. 'Only reasonable efforts to secure privacy under all the circumstances are required',[5] or otherwise there would be 'a regression into an Orwellian society in which a citizen, in order to preserve a modicum of privacy, would be compelled to encase himself in a light-tight, air-proof box'.[6] In this respect it must be noticed that it is perfectly possible to manifest or entertain a reasonable expectation of privacy from a particular point of observation or with regard to a particular class or category of persons but not from or with regard to others. To put it somewhat differently, the mere fact that a person may have consented to observation from some sources and by some persons does not necessarily mean that he must thereby be regarded as foregoing or waiving his Fourth Amendment protection as to intrusions from all sources and by all persons, particularly government agents.[7] It was thus held in *People v. Triggs*[8] that a person in an open-stalled public rest room has a reasonable expectation of privacy from clandestine observation by police officers from a concealed position, though he could have no such expectation of privacy from observation through the open door, whether made by members of the public or the police. Similarly, it was held in one case[9] that the fact that a hotel guest must be taken to expect that a maid will come into his room to clean up does not mean that he should also expect that a hotel clerk will lead the police on a search of his room, and in another case[10] the argument that the complainant should have anticipated the occasional presence of cattlemen and hikers on his unfenced garden was treated as

[1] *Air Pollution Variance Board v. Western Alfalfa*, 416 U.S. 861, 865 (1974).

[2] See *State v. Kender*, 588 P. 2d 447, 450 (1979).

[3] *Dean v. Superior Court*, 110 Cal. Rptr. 585, 589 (1973).

[4] See *Phelan v. Superior Court*, supra; *State v. Kender*, supra; *Dean v. Superior Court*, supra.

[5] *Phelan v. Superior Court*, supra.

[6] *Lorenzana v. Superior Court*, 108 Cal. Rptr. 585, 593 (1973).

[7] See *People v. Edwards*, 80 Cal. Rptr. 633 (1969); *People v. Krivda*, 96 Cal. Rptr. 62, 69 (1971); *People v. Sneed*, 108 Cal. Rptr. 146 (1973).

[8] 106 Cal. Rptr. 408 (1973).

[9] *People v. McGrew*, 82 Cal. Rptr. 473, 478 (1969), overruled on other grounds in *People v. McKinnon*, 103 Cal. Rptr. 897; see also *Krauss v. Superior Court*, 96 Cal. Rptr. 455 (1971), and *People v. Sneed*, supra, at 150.

[10] *Phelan v. Superior Court*, supra, at 606.

irrelevant when what was in issue was the presence of police officers conducting a deliberate search for marijuana. One of the most interesting examples of this selective waiver of otherwise legitimate expectations of privacy is *People v. Sneed*[1] where it was held that a police helicopter flight at an altitude of about twenty-five feet over the backyard of a house rented by the defendant in search of marijuana plants which were not visible from the road constituted a serious governmental intrusion into the defendant's privacy and therefore amounted to a search. The defendant, of course, the court noted, had no reasonable expectation of privacy either from the observation of his neighbours and others similarly placed or from airplanes and helicopters flying 'at legal and reasonable heights', but this did not mean that he did not have the right to be free from police observation by helicopter from the air at twenty or twenty-five feet. *Sneed* can be contrasted with *State v. Stachler,*[2] where it was held that the defendant who grew marijuana in his backyard did not have any reasonable expectation of privacy from aerial observation since in this case there was no showing that the helicopter was flying at an unreasonably low altitude or had engaged in prolonged aerial surveillance or had used highly sophisticated viewing devices; on the contrary, there was much evidence that there were many helicopter and other flights over the area, so that any actual expectation of privacy that the defendant may have entertained was inconsistent with the habits and rational anticipations of others living in the area.[3]

A third important factor to consider in determining whether official observation or surveillance involves a violation of a constitutionally justifiable expectation of privacy is the position of the law enforcement officer. A number of cases establish that observation of things in plain sight made by an officer from a place where he has a right to be does not amount to a search in the constitutional sense. In *People v. Berutko*[4] police officers went to a common passageway running outside the defendant's apartment and from there observed contraband through an opening in the curtains which the defendant had drawn. The court noted that at no point had the officers strayed from common areas available to the other tenants of the building as well as to any other persons lawfully admitted to the premises either by the tenants or the management. Rather, the instant case simply involved 'observation by an officer from a place where he had a right to be' and through an opening which the defendant himself had provided through his arrangement of the drapes covering his window. Similarly, a number of other cases[5] establish that if evidence is in open view from an area of common use, for instance if it is visible from the street or from the driveway to which all with legitimate business are impliedly invited, it may be seized without a warrant, but that if evidence is only discovered as a result of an encroachment

[1] 108 Cal. Rptr. 146 (1973).

[2] 570 P. 2d 1323 (1977).

[3] See also *Dean v. Superior Court,* Cal. Rptr. 585 (1973).

[4] 77 Cal. Rptr. 217 (1969).

[5] See *Lorenzana v. Superior Court,* 108 Cal. Rptr. 585 (1973) and the other cases cited there (at 590 n. 4).

or intrusion into a constitutionally protected area, that is an area within the defendant's legitimate expectations of privacy, it cannot be so seized. It follows that when a police officer has gained access to a place to which he has not been expressly or impliedly invited, the intrusion is unlawful and the fruits of any observation that is only made possible by it will not be allowed into evidence. It was therefore held in *People v. Cagle*[1] that there had been an unconstitutional search where police officers looked through the defendant's bathroom window which was at the rear of the house, far from all normal access routes; and in *Lorenzana v. Superior Court*[2] it was held that there had been a violation of justifiable expectations of privacy where officers stood upon private property exhibiting no invitation to public use and looked into the defendant's home. Indeed, after much litigation on the intractable problems posed by police observation into protected areas, mainly homes, from the outside, the Supreme Court of California[3] has distilled the following specific propositions from the broad principles of *Katz*: The resident of a house has the right to rely on the privacy both of his home and of the immediately surrounding area unless either his residence or his activities have been exposed to the intrusion complained of, whether by high visibility or by the existence of public pathways or other invitations to the general public to enter upon the property; it follows that searches and observation conducted without a warrant from non-common portions of the property surrounding one's residence are invariably unconstitutional; but in exceptional cases a simple trespass does not foreclose a reasonable search,[4] and naturally, as both *Katz* and many other cases show, the absence of a trespass does not save an otherwise unreasonable one. Some of these rules, it can readily be seen, even though dressed in the currently fashionable garb of justifiable expectations of privacy and despite emphatic protestations that one should not rely on generalisations such as protected areas and the like, are not very different from the allegedly discredited notions of 'curtilage' and 'open fields', and surely the chief lesson of the developments sketched out above, particularly where unaided non-electronic surveillance is concerned, is that it is difficult to settle the issue of the extent of Fourth Amendment protection without much reference to, if not outright reliance on, 'places' and 'areas'.[5]

(ii) Overheard conversations

The general trend of authorities both before and since *Katz* is that the overhearing of conversations by the unaided ear does not of itself constitute a search and therefore does not come within the Fourth Amendment.[6] It is thus

[1] 98 Cal. Rptr. 348 (1971).

[2] 108 Cal. Rptr. 585 (1973).

[3] See *Lorenzana*, supra, at 591–4.

[4] See *Phelan v. Superior Court*, 151 Cal. Rptr. 599 (1979); *People v. Edwards*, supra; *People v. Sneed*, supra.

[5] See the concurring opinion of Harlan, J. in *Katz v. United States*, 389 U.S. 347 (1967); but see *Dean v. Superior Court*, 110 Cal. Rptr. 585 (1973), and *People v. Edwards*, supra.

[6] See particularly *United States v. Llanes*, 398 F. 2d 880 (1968); *United States v. Fisch*, 474 F. 2d 1071 (1973); *United States v. McLeod*, 493 F. 2d 1186 (1974);

said that *Katz* involved electronic eavesdropping and not the overhearing of conversations; that, as Justice Stewart himself observed in *Katz*, what a person knowingly exposes to the public, even in his own home, is not entitled to Fourth Amendment protection; and that 'conversations carried on in a tone of voice quite audible to a person standing outside the home are conversations knowingly exposed to the public'.[1] But even though some of the cases seem to adopt the inflexible position that ordinary eavesdropping can *never* come within the constitutional guarantee both because the risk of being overheard is said to be inherent in human society[2] and because any other holding might result in the making of many fine distinctions based on audibility and the like,[3] many of them involve rather obvious fact situations, for instance where no precautions at all were taken or where the conversations in question were clearly audible to people in public places. Other courts have been reluctant to adopt the position that overheard conversations can always be admitted in evidence, whatever the circumstances. It was therefore said in one case[4] that '(o)ne who intends a conversation or transaction to be private *and* takes reasonable steps to keep it private is protected from government intrusion', and in another[5] it was held that evidence gathered by government agents as a result of a surreptitious overhearing of the defendant's conversations which were carried on behind closed doors, the officers themselves being stationed in a hallway which was found not to be a public place, was inadmissible since it had been obtained by an unconstitutional search. The cases are not easy to reconcile, but two things are clear: if there has been a trespass or other intrusion into a constitutionally protected area evidence of overheard conversations will be suppressed; but where there has been no improper intrusion, and the only complaint is that there has been an invasion of privacy by the naked ear, the defendant will have to show the reasonableness of his reliance, mainly by convincing evidence that the place where the conversations took place is acknowledged as a protected or private one and that he took every reasonable precaution to prevent or frustrate eavesdropping.[6]

United States v. Perry, 339 F. Supp. 209 (1972); *State v. Moses*, 367 So. 2d 800 (1979); *Ponce v. Craven*, 409 F. 2d 621 (1969).

[1] *United States v. Llanes*, supra, at 884.

[2] See *Lopez v. United States*, 373 U.S. 427, 465 (1963), per Brennan, J. dissenting; and *Hoffa v. United States*, 385 U.S. 293 (1966).

[3] See *People v. Guerra*, 98 Cal. Rptr. 627 (1971), where the court refused to draw 'a constitutional line between the whisper and the shout', and *United States v. Fisch*, supra, 55 n. 6, at 1077, where the court again refused to divide either 'the listening room into privileged or burdened areas' or 'the conversation into degrees of audibility'.

[4] *United States v. Hadden*, 397 F. 2d 460 (1968).

[5] *United States v. Case*, 435 F. 2d 766 (1970).

[6] See *United States v. Fisch*, supra, 55 n. 6, at 1077, where the test is said to be one of overall reasonableness, and *United States v. Perry*, 339 F. Supp. 209, 213 (1972).

(e) Informers and secret agents.[1]

The employment of secret agents and informers, even though supported by consistent historical usage, is, not infrequently, fraught with serious danger, and thus presents important and difficult problems. Even though it has been maintained[2] that it cannot be said either that every use of informers and undercover agents is proper or, alternatively, that no such use is, but that the true position is that in this area, as in every other, courts should strive to strike a balance not unlike the one that has emerged with regard to electronic eavesdropping—one, that is, that will safeguard essential rights without at the same time depriving the police of the use of reasonable investigative techniques—a more accurate description of existing law and practice is that the testimony of secret agents and informers is invariably admitted,[3] even though they may have been hired by the government for the specific purpose of gathering information, and despite the fact that the surveillance took place on protected premises.

What are the arguments for and against the use of informers and secret agents? There is little doubt that important individual and societal interests would be threatened by the widespread use of informers. To begin with, it is undeniable, as historical experience proves only too well, both that rights to personal privacy are invaded not only by physical entries and tangible seizures but also by official investigatory action that results in individuals becoming objects of all-encompassing surveillance, and that 'the indefeasible right of personal security'[4] would be worth very little if there was protection only from obvious and crude police intrusions but none from officers' using stealth, fraud and deception in order to insinuate themselves into private enclaves and there in effect purloin words spoken in confidence.[5] For these reasons immunity from surveillance and observation has appeared to many quite as important as more conventional types of personal freedom. Indeed, true freedom can easily be seen to be incompatible with a system of official espionage. 'Men may be without restraints upon their liberty; they may pass

[1] See generally Kitch, '*Katz v. United States*: The Limits of the Fourth Amendment', 1968 *Sup. Ct. Rev.* 133; Donnelly, 'Judicial Control of Informants, Spies, Stool Pigeons and Agents Provocateurs', 60 *Yale L.J.* 1091 (1951); 'Note', 73 *Harv. L. Rev.* 1333, 1338–9 (1960); 'Comment, Judicial Control of Secret Agents', 76 *Yale L.J.* 994 (1967); Greenawalt, 'The Right of Privacy', in *The Rights of Americans – What They Are, What They Should Be,* 299, 315–16 (N. Dorsen ed. 1970); Bergstrom, 'The Applicability of the "New" Fourth Amendment to Investigations by Secret Agents – A Proposed Delineation of the Emerging Fourth Amendment Right to Privacy', 45 *Wash. L. Rev.* 785 (1970).

[2] *Hoffa v. United States*, 385 U.S. 293, 315 (1966), per Warren, C.J. dissenting.

[3] See Greenawalt, supra, n.1, at 315; but see *Massiah v. United States*, 377 U.S. 201 (1964), where it was held that under the Sixth Amendment, guaranteeing the right to assistance of counsel, the defendant's incriminating statements, elicited by a co-defendant working for the government after he had been indicted and in the absence of his counsel, were not admissible at his trial.

[4] *Boyd v. United States*, 116 U.S. 616, 630, per Bradley, J.

[5] See *Lopez v. United States*, 373 U.S. 427, 470 (1963), per Brennan, J. dissenting.

to and from at pleasure; but if their steps are tracked by spies and informers, their words noted down for crimination, who shall say that they are free?'[1] Two related things have also been particularly stressed. First, one of the most cherished and jealously guarded freedoms, liberty of communication, would be severely curtailed if it was widely suspected that confidential conversations were listened to by spies and informers and taken down for possible use in criminal proceedings. Free speech, after all, is undermined not only by the existence of illiberal and unnecessary restraints on what may be said but also by an atmosphere of fear that results in people being afraid to speak without inhibition in what they might otherwise have regarded as the secure privacy of home and office. The second consideration is the demonstrable and widely shared feeling, born no doubt of historical experience, that the widespread employment of informers and spies will cause lasting damage to the open and fair administration of justice. The law, it is often said, ought not to be open to the just charge of having been dictated by 'the odious doctrine',[2] as Justice Brandeis called it, that the end justifies reprehensible means, and the unrestrained use of informers and agents provocateurs has not surprisingly seemed to many not only indicative of just such a philosophy but also more characteristic of tyranny and alien systems of bondage than of systems based on respect for the rule of law. The methods of the State, as Justice Frankfurter once put it,[3] must be such as to command respect, and at least some uses of informers do not, both in their undoubted tendency to undermine the integrity of the normal processes of the law and in their well-documented potential for being turned into the methods of a police state.

But undesirable though the use of informers may be from an ideal point of view, and despite the general realisation that substantial individual and societal interests will seriously suffer by their widespread and uncontrolled employment, informers are at times a necessary technique of law enforcement, particularly with regard to the enforcement of certain laws where it is all but impossible to obtain evidence save by the use of decoys.[4] Two further considerations that must be taken into account in any attempt at devising a workable system of regulation in this area are these: first, informers are and may be used in a great number of situations and their employment may assume innumerable forms, ranging from the passive non-revelation of identity to considerably more serious forms of deception, including the active penetration of a constitutionally protected area or even the entrapment of a weak and vulnerable victim. A single solution, in the form of a rule either permitting or disallowing all uses of informers, cannot be satisfactory; the law must instead attempt to distinguish between those deceits, persuasions and stratagems which on general policy grounds are acceptable and should therefore be permissible, and those which are not. The

[1] E. May, *Constitutional History of England* 275 (1863).

[2] See *Olmstead v. United States*, 277 U.S. 438, 471, 485 (1928), per Brandeis, J., dissenting.

[3] *On Lee v. United States,* 343 U.S. 747, 758–61 (1952).

[4] See *Lewis v. United States*, 385 U.S. 206, 210 n. 6 (1966), per Warren, C.J.; see also *Model Penal Code* § 2.10, comment, at 16 (Tent. Draft No. 9, 1959).

second point is that even though the use of informers may raise important legal and constitutional problems, these are not necessarily Fourth Amendment ones. In many of the cases involving the use of a secret agent the real question is (or should be) not whether there has been a violation of the Fourth Amendment, which after all only forbids unreasonable searches and seizures, but whether the tactics the police used involved that type of unfairness that is offensive either to some other constitutional and legal provision or to more general considerations pertaining to the integrity of the judicial process.[1] At the same time, since the central purpose of the Fourth Amendment is the protection of individual privacy and security, since it is generally accepted that secret agents and informers impair the sense of security both of those who fear their use and perhaps of society in general,[2] and since people are generally credited with justifiable expectations of privacy against the surreptitious monitoring of their confidential conversations, should not at least some uses of secret agents and police spies, particularly when there has been an encroachment upon either a protected area or a private relationship, be held to involve a search and seizure in the constitutional sense? The short answer is that the Supreme Court has traditionally assumed that if someone willingly divulges information to other persons he takes the risk that they may prove to be government agents and that they may turn over to the authorities any incriminating evidence thus obtained, and it has yet to hold that the testimony of a police informer should be suppressed as having been obtained by an unconstitutional search. But a number of unclear hints have also been dropped that certain uses of informers may after all involve violations of the Fourth Amendment. The position is by no means clear, and there is much room both for speculation and for the future development of constitutional doctrine curtailing some uses of secret agents.

The issue of the applicability of the Fourth Amendment to informers and secret agents has been considered by the Supreme Court in two cases, *Lewis v. United States*[3] and *Hoffa v. United States*.[4] In the former a federal narcotics agent, by misrepresenting his identity and stating his willingness to buy narcotics, was invited into the defendant's home where on two occasions sales of narcotics took place, the agent during neither of his visits seeing, hearing or taking anything not contemplated by the defendant. The Court had no difficulty in holding that the Fourth Amendment was not violated by the admission into evidence of the agent's testimony and of the narcotics he had

[1] Other matters that are occasionally canvassed in this connection are the Fifth Amendment (protection from compulsory self-incrimination), the Sixth Amendment (right to assistance of counsel; see *Massiah v. United States,* supra, 57 n. 3), the doctrine of entrapment, the Due Process Clause, the exercise of judicial supervisory powers over the administration of criminal justice where 'the waters of justice (have been) polluted', see *Mesarosh v. United States*, 352 U.S. 1, 14 (1956). See generally *Hoffa v. United States*, 352 U.S. 293 (1966). Such claims have invariably failed, with the exception of *Massiah,* supra.

[2] Greenawalt, supra, at 315.

[3] 385 U.S. 206 (1966).

[4] 385 U.S. 293 (1966).

allegedly purchased. Chief Justice Warren's opinion made the following points: This was a simple case of the police employing a stratagem or deception to obtain evidence, and a holding that what had happened was constitutionally prohibited would have come close to a rule that all uses of secret agents were unconstitutional, an untenable proposition in view of the demonstrable necessity for some undercover activity in the enforcement of narcotics laws; the fact that the officer had entered the defendant's home did not compel a different conclusion because even though the home was traditionally accorded the full range of Fourth Amendment protections this was not so when it had in effect been converted into a commercial centre to which outsiders were invited for the purpose of concluding illegal transactions; finally the police pretence in the instant case had resulted in 'no breach of privacy' since it had involved no design on the part of the authorities 'to observe or hear what was happening in the privacy of a home' but had only encouraged the suspect to say things which he was willing and anxious to say to anyone interested in buying narcotics.[1] The implication of Chief Justice Warren's opinion is that *if* the police deception had resulted in a breach of privacy there *may* well have been a search within the meaning of the Fourth Amendment, but the Court neither defines the concept of 'breach of privacy' nor provides any information about the circumstances in which official deception resulting in the penetration of a home or other protected area will amount to an unconstitutional intrusion. There was a lone dissent from Justice Douglas. In his view entering another's home in disguise to obtain evidence was a search that should bring into play the safeguards of the Fourth Amendment; therefore when the agent had reason to believe that the defendant possessed narcotics a search warrant should have been obtained. Justice Douglas did not deny that a householder who admitted a government agent knowing him to be such waived any right of privacy he may have had; he also thought that one who invited or admitted 'an old "friend" ' took the risk that the friend would disclose confidences to the police; but it was different, he concluded, when government played an ignoble role by 'planting' an agent in one's home or by using 'fraud and deception' in getting him there.

In *Hoffa* the defendant was being tried for misusing union funds. Partin, a union official, was at this time in prison awaiting trial on a number of charges; following discussions with law enforcement agents who told him that Hoffa might attempt to tamper with the jury and asked him to obtain and give them any evidence of wrongdoing he discovered in connection with Hoffa's activities, Partin was released from jail and joined Hoffa's entourage; on several occasions during the time that followed Partin, who was accepted by the Court as being at all relevant times a government informer, overheard a number of incriminating statements made by Hoffa and his friends in his hotel suite and passed the information to police officers, as a result of which the defendant was prosecuted for attempting to bribe members of the jury at his earlier trial; later, the informer's wife received payments from government

[1] This statement appeared in the government's brief in *Lewis,* supra, but was apparently adopted by Warren, C.J. in his opinion for the Court, at 212.

funds, and the charges against Partin were either dropped or not actively pursued. The defence contention was that Partin's failure to disclose his role as a government informer vitiated the consent that Hoffa had given to his repeated entries into the hotel suite, and that by listening to Hoffa's statements Partin had conducted an illegal 'search' for verbal evidence. The Supreme Court did not doubt that a hotel room could be the object of Fourth Amendment protection, or that conversations as well as tangible objects could be seized. But Hoffa's argument none the less involved a 'misapprehension of the fundamental nature and scope' of the Fourth Amendment. What the Fourth Amendment protected was the security a man relied upon when he placed himself or his property within a constitutionally protected area, not a person's misplaced confidences. In the instant case Partin had not entered the hotel suite 'by force or by stealth' but 'by invitation', he was not 'a surreptitious eavesdropper', and every conversation which he heard had either been directed to him personally or knowingly carried on in his presence. 'The petitioner, in a word, was not relying on the security of the hotel room; he was relying upon his misplaced confidence that Partin would not reveal his wrongdoing.' The informer's testimony was therefore admissible. But the Court's opinion pointedly mentioned in 'an enigmatic footnote'[1] that it was not considering the question of the Fourth Amendment's applicability if Partin had been a stranger to the defendant.

Lewis and *Hoffa* would have been easy cases under *Olmstead*. There is no trespass, and intangible conversations cannot be seized in the same way as material objects. But once the decisive criterion is not whether there has been a physical intrusion but either whether legitimate expectations of privacy have been infringed or whether the particular practice may have an adverse impact upon society's sense of security, the case for the application of the Fourth Amendment is by no means weak. Equally clearly, neither the notion of privacy, as used by the Court in *Lewis*, nor the doctrinaire concepts and language of risk and misplaced confidence of *Hoffa* can provide much satisfaction. Thus, if some simple version of privacy is the test, even *Lewis*, traditionally assumed to be an easy case, is by no means free of difficulty. Thus, to the Court's argument that the officer was invited one can reply that the invitation was procured by deception, to the majority's silence on the issue of search one can deny that there is much difference between attaching a recording device to a wall and planting a secret agent in someone's home, the argument that a government agent in the same manner as a private person may accept an invitation to do business and enter private premises for 'the very purposes contemplated by the occupant' may be countered by the observation that the *Lewis* agent entered not in order to do business with the defendant but in order to obtain evidence against him,[2] and to the fear that prohibition of the deception practised in *Lewis* will unduly hamper the government in apprehending criminals one can repeat Justice Douglas's point that suppression of the evidence in question would not mean that wrongdoers could erect impenetrable barriers around their activities since any protected

[1] Kitch, supra, at 150.
[2] Ibid., at 145; see also Bergstrom, supra, at 801, 806.

area, including a home, can always be invaded by legitimate police entries and searches authorised by judicial warrants.[1] In the light of *Katz* the holding of *Lewis* can be formulated in one of two ways: first, when you deal with or pass information to another person you take the risk that he has already deceived you as to his identity or intentions or that he may subsequently betray you; secondly, the Fourth Amendment does not apply when, whatever a man's subjective hopes and expectations, the information that has been gathered had not been kept private but had knowingly been exposed to the public or a significant section of it; for even though the concept of limited communication and the related right to open up one's privacies to limited classes of people are important components of Fourth Amendment freedoms, and even though the agent in *Lewis* was not a member of the class of persons to whom the defendant *intended* to disclose information,[2] on the facts as found by the Court the defendant had converted his home into a commercial centre by inviting in anyone willing to deal with him.[3] If a different perspective is adopted, and the material issue in *Lewis* and similar cases is framed not in terms of the individual's expectations or assumption of risks but in terms of an overall evaluation of the type of deception practised by government agents, surely the conclusion must still be that the deception in *Lewis* was not a serious one. True, it involved an affirmative misrepresentation of identity, as opposed to the passive failure to reveal one's true identity, but there was no general exploratory quest intended to secure evidence of wrongdoing but only a limited and specific encounter precisely tailored to a particular investigation; while the incriminating statements and transactions took place in the defendant's home the location was fortuitous, in the sense that they could have taken place anywhere and it was not more likely that they would occur at home than elsewhere;[4] and finally the other circumstances leading to and surrounding the deception involved no additional aggravating or offensive factors, for instance exploitation of a relationship of trust. In terms of the nature of police conduct one may thus explain *Lewis* either as a case where the ethical and social mischief assumed to inhere in official undercover activity was balanced against and eventually found to be outweighed by countervailing arguments justifying the need for the challenged deception as the only way whereby evidence of a serious offence could be discovered, or more broadly as a holding that use of a false identity as an instrument of crime detection is generally permissible provided that the agent obtains no information not similarly exposed to the other members of his adopted class.[5]

But any ambiguities lurking in the Court's opinion in *Lewis* and possible difficulties with determining the limits of its holding do not mean that the distinction drawn by Justice Douglas between 'an old "friend" ', in which case

[1] See *Osborn v. United States*, 385 U.S. 323 (1966).

[2] Bergstrom, supra, at 806.

[3] This was the narrow ground on which Brennan and Fortas, JJ. joined the majority of the Court in *Lewis*, supra.

[4] Comment, supra, at 1011.

[5] Bergstrom, supra, at 801.

one takes the risk that the friend will disclose the private information to the police, and a secret agent, who is planted there by the government and against whom the defendant must be protected, fares any better, particularly when tested against the notions of risk and misplaced confidence. In what sense does one take, or must be assumed to take, the risk that an old friend will divulge confidences to the government but not that a new acquaintance or the person he is dealing with for the first time is at the relevant time co-operating with the authorities? In terms of normal expectations and the assumption of risks it is more likely that the reverse is the case. In any case, why is the invasion of privacy and security more serious in one case than in the other? Indeed it appears to be an oversimplification to regard 'informer' cases as capable of being accommodated into only two categories, 'friends' and 'plants'. At least three *broad* situations can be distinguished. The first and universally acknowledged to be the simplest is the case where a friend of the accused on his own initiative and without any contact with the government decides to inform on him and no further incriminating conversations take place. In the second the government have prevailed upon someone, either a friend of the accused, as in *Hoffa*, or a stranger, as in *Lewis*, to work or cooperate with them in obtaining incriminating evidence against the suspect; he does so, and engages the defendant in conversation, the deception not amounting to entrapment. A third and intermediate situation arises when the 'friend' or accomplice decides to turn informer but neither offers his services to the government nor is enlisted by them; after the evidence in the form of incriminating remarks made by the accused has been 'collected' by the friend it is passed on to the government. These cases and any additional variations within them that can be devised can be approached either in terms of expectations and risks or in terms of a set of judgments concerning the overall propriety of types of police undercover activity; both approaches, however imperfectly, seem to be involved in the cases, and the two can of course be combined by means of a formula incorporating elements of both, for instance that one risks (or must be taken to risk) certain types of police deception but not others. The issues and problems are many and complex; but they are not necessarily or primarily Fourth Amendment ones.[1] It cannot of course be denied either that the reality to which the accused is exposed in the first case, when prior to the incriminating conversations there had been neither governmental approach nor decision to turn informer, is radically different from that facing him in the second type of situation, when the apparent friend is in fact a secret agent collecting information against him, or that possible distinctions can be made between different uses of informers, whether one uses as his starting point some notion of privacy or a concept of the general impropriety and unfairness of certain police practices, or that arguments concerning the need for some type of regulation, whether legal or constitutional, are substantially more compelling in the case of some than of

[1] The principal issue is whether the Fourth Amendment should primarily be viewed as a protection of the interests of individual citizens or as 'a regulation of governmental conduct': see Amsterdam, 'Perspectives on the Fourth Amendment', 58 *Minn. L. Rev.* 349, 367 (1974).

others. But equally clearly it is neither justifiable nor sensible to attempt to derive from the generalities of the Fourth Amendment detailed codes regulating governmental uses of informers; what is more, Fourth Amendment analysis of informer situations couched in terms of risk or based on the doctrine of misplaced confidence does not provide much satisfaction.

This can be seen in *Hoffa*. The basis of the Court's opinion was that Hoffa when making incriminating statements was relying not on the security of his hotel suite but on his misplaced confidence that Partin would not reveal evidence of his wrongdoing. But why could it not be said that the defendant was relying not only on his friend not divulging any confidential information either communicated to or overheard by him but also on the security, namely the freedom from official intrusion, of his hotel suite, an area normally considered to be free from governmental surveillance?[1] And if some kind of legitimate expectation of privacy is the test, could it be said that Hoffa was unreasonable in assuming that those of his conversations that were carried on in the privacy of his hotel suite would be free from governmental interception unauthorised by legal processes? Further, if one compares *Hoffa* with *Lewis* the following 'aggravating' circumstances will be noticed.[2] First, in *Hoffa*, unlike *Lewis*, a constitutionally protected area, a hotel suite, was actively and intentionally penetrated, and it was certainly not accidental or fortuitous that most of the incriminating conversations had taken place there. Indeed Hoffa must have talked freely not so much because of his misplaced confidence in his friends as because of what turned out to be a mistaken belief that there had been no governmental infiltration of his hotel room. A second element, again absent in *Lewis* and insufficiently noticed in *Hoffa*, is the exploitation of a relationship of trust, namely that the only way in which the government was enabled to obtain the information it was seeking in the latter case was by 'using' Hoffa's friendship with Partin. Some have protested at what they have seen as judicial adoption of a formula allowing the government 'to use son against father, nephew against uncle, friend against friend' and 'to undermine the sanctity of the most private and confidential of all conversations',[3] and have argued that since expectations of privacy and a sense of security are among the legitimate objects of Fourth Amendment protection communications to close friends and relatives should be protected either in the context of the constitutional protection from unreasonable searches and seizures or in the course of judicial supervision over the administration of criminal justice.[4] But not only was the Court not impressed with these considerations but it also indicated, citing *Lewis*, that it was reserving the question of a secret agent not originally a friend of the suspect who by the use of deception had insinuated himself into the presence of the suspect. What is the exact implication of this? Is the Court actually suggesting

[1] Kitch, supra, at 150–2.

[2] See Comment, supra, 57 n. 1, at 1012–13; 'The Supreme Court, 1966 Term', 81 *Harv. L. Rev.* 69, 191–4 (1967).

[3] *Osborn v. United States*, 385 U.S. 323, 347 (1966), per Douglas, J. dissenting.

[4] See Comment, supra, 57 n. 1, at 1013, and the dissenting opinion of Warren, C.J. in *Hoffa v. United States*, 385 U.S. 293, 313 (1966).

that *Lewis* is a more difficult case than *Hoffa*? But this is unlikely since, with the exception of Justice Douglas, there was general agreement that *Lewis* was a simple case. Rather, the distinction seems to be between a case such as *Hoffa* where the secret agent had been a friend of the defendant before the decision to turn informer and a case where the 'friend' turns out to have been a government agent all along, the argument apparently being either that 'although one has to take the risk that one's friends will become informers one does not have to take the risk that one's friends will be government plants'[1] or alternatively that, where the undercover activity in question envisages a secret agent first obtaining the suspect's friendship and then using this 'friendship' to inform on him, the deception attributable to the police is much greater. In contrast, *Lewis* is simpler because there the agent did not engage in active steps in order to gain the suspect's confidence but only concluded one single transaction with him, involving neither intimacy nor friendship. But perhaps the main difference between *Lewis* and *Hoffa* is that the circumstances leading to the deception and the gathering of the incriminating information in the latter case were striking. Not only did the government resort to dubious and offensive methods in making possible Partin's infiltration of Hoffa's hotel room, but also the informer's consequential intrusion into the defendant's privacy was broad and unlimited. Again, unlike *Lewis*, where the government agent misrepresented his identity in order to obtain evidence of specific criminal activity which was already taking place, the informer in *Hoffa* was employed so that he would engage in more or less general surveillance and in order to gather information about crimes that *might* be committed in the future.[2] Partin, in other words, became 'the equivalent of a bugging device which moved with Hoffa wherever he went'[3] and which indiscriminately and without any limitation intercepted his private conversations. But the Supreme Court, as has been seen, refused to regard these differences between *Lewis* and *Hoffa* as material, or to draw any distinctions in terms of the Fourth Amendment between different types of informers and the situations in which they have operated, or to propound any doctrine other than that the misplaced belief of wrongdoers concerning the non-revelation of their confidences will not be protected.

But since some questions still remain open one is justified in considering basic principle. In terms of the applicability of the Fourth Amendment to informer situations two broad approaches appear open. The one that is supported by the cases is to deny that use of informers involves a search or seizure in the constitutional sense on the broad basis that each party to a conversation takes the risk of divulgence either by the other parties or by those he has willingly admitted to his presence. Additional support for this view may be derived from the related considerations that the Fourth Amendment must not be overswollen with cases; that once informers are brought within

[1] Kitch, supra, at 150.

[2] *Hoffa v. United States,* supra, 64 n. 4, at 321, per Warren, C.J. dissenting; see also Comment, supra, 57 n. 1, at 1011 et seq.; 'The Supreme Court, 1966 Term', 81 *Harv. L. Rev.* 69, 196.

[3] *Hoffa,* supra, at 319.

the Amendment it will be necessary to make minute and subtle distinctions so as not to endanger the admissibility of other types of evidence resulting from the incautious disclosure of confidences to supposed friends; that the central issue here is not solely or principally invasion of privacy but whether government officers, consistently with the integrity of the judicial process, should be allowed to resort to the tactics they used; and that therefore alternative methods of control outside the Fourth Amendment should be developed to curb police abuses in the use of secret agents. The second view is to say that the search and seizure provisions are as a general matter applicable because practices involving the use of informers and secret agents impair society's sense of security, except for cases where for instance an obvious risk is taken by offering a bribe to a known government agent,[1] or where rights to privacy are waived by opening a previously protected area to commercial transactions,[2] or where a friend who is not at the time a government agent turns informer and reports to the police. But in cases where an informer is 'planted', a warrant must be obtained, but perhaps even then only if a constitutionally protected areas has been invaded otherwise than fortuitously. Further distinctions can be made on this basis, especially if a flexible view is taken of reasonableness and an effort is made to correlate the permissible degree of official intrusiveness to the kind of evidence or justification that must support the police deception in issue. It has therefore been proposed,[3] first that deliberate penetration of a constitutionally protected area is fully covered by the Fourth Amendment, should therefore be judicially controlled, and should only be allowed where probable cause supporting the particular intrusion exists; secondly, that the use as a police spy of a person enjoying a close relationship of trust with the suspect should also be judicially controlled, again by the application of probable cause standards; and thirdly, that other types of active solicitation to crime, not covered by the preceding two categories and typified by the use of a police agent to buy narcotics on a street corner, should only be resorted to when some such standard as reasonable suspicion, falling somewhat below traditional probable cause formulations but still capable of providing justification for the official attempt to ensnare an unsuspecting individual, has been or can be satisfied.

At present it seems highly unlikely that this second view will be taken. For the time being, and as at present composed, the Supreme Court will almost certainly continue assuming that a party to a conversation takes or more accurately must be saddled with the risk of disclosure by those to whom he has confided information or who listened to it otherwise than by surreptitious eavesdropping, whether they always were, or only subsequently became, government agents. But if practices involving the use of secret agents become much more prevalent, and abhorrent, than they now are, and if the currently held view, that uncontrolled non-electronic surveillance via the medium of undercover methods is a tolerable technique of law enforcement, is re-examined in view both of a fuller appreciation of the underlying values of the

[1] *Lopez v. United States,* 373 U.S. 427 (1963).
[2] *Lewis v. United States*, 385 U.S. 206 (1966).
[3] Comment, supra, at 1015 et seq.

democratic system and of a fresh appraisal of its likely impact upon the individual's and society's sense of security that is now regarded as the real concern of the Fourth Amendment, the Supreme Court may be reluctant to impose on individual citizens and society alike the undoubted risks and dangers inherent in at least some of the more intrusive uses of undercover agents and in unrestrained police spying, at least without the protection of the warrant requirement.[1]

(f) Compilation and disclosure of financial and other records

One of the most usual features of our age is the collection of an enormous amount of information by agencies such as banks and the like.[2] Is access to them by government officers controlled by the Fourth Amendment? This question primarily depends on whether a reasonable expectation of privacy exists with regard to bank records and similar financial documents, and was dealt with by the Supreme Court in two important recent cases.[3] In *California Bankers Association v. Shultz*[4] the Supreme Court upheld certain provisions of the Bank Secrecy Act 1970 which required financial institutions to maintain numerous records, including records of their customers' identities, copies of checks and similar instruments, and statements showing all transactions in each account.[5] It was argued that the Act was unconstitutional because when a bank made and kept records under governmental compulsion it acted as a government agent and thereby engaged

[1] See generally the dissenting opinion of Harlan, J. in *United States v. White*, 401 U.S. 745, 768, 786–91 (1971), and Greenawalt, supra, at 315.

[2] See 1 La Fave, *Search and Seizure* 409–17 (1978); 'Note, Government Access to Bank Records', 83 *Yale L.J.* 1439 (1974) (hereinafter referred to as 'Note'); 'Comment, A Bank Customer has no Reasonable Expectation of Privacy of Bank Records: *United States v. Miller*', 14 *San Diego L. Rev.* 414 (1974).

[3] In a group of cases it has been held that the records of telephone and gas companies relating to things like names and addresses (of the subscriber) and (in the case of telephone companies) the number of the calling and receiving telephones were not within any reasonable expectation of privacy, since it would be unreasonable to assume that information relating to these matters was regarded by the individual as immune to disclosure: see *People v. Elder*, 134 Cal. Rptr. 212 (1976), *United States v. Baxter*, 492 F. 2d 150 (1973), *United States v. Fithian*, 452 F. 2d 505 (1971). But, as *Baxter*, at 167, makes clear, even though '(t)elephone subscribers are fully aware that records will be made of their toll calls', this only means that it is 'the fact that a conversation took place' that is not protected; 'the content of telephone conversation(s)' enjoys full Fourth Amendment protection, as *Katz*, 389 U.S. 347 (1967), itself shows.

[4] 416 U.S. 21 (1974).

[5] The Bank Secrecy Act 1970 also contained certain reporting requirements, namely requirements that certain transactions should be not only recorded but also reported. The reporting requirements applicable to foreign financial dealings were upheld as constitutional, since they were well within the power of Congress to legislate with respect to foreign commerce. The crucial question of the constitutionality of the regulations for the reporting by financial institutions of domestic financial transactions was not reached since the depositor plaintiffs were found to lack standing to challenge the domestic reporting provisions.

in a 'seizure' of its customers' records. The Court accepted that in compiling customers' records and in collecting the required information the banks were acting under governmental compulsion, but it was held that the mere *maintenance* of such records without any requirement that they be disclosed to the government did not constitute either a search or seizure within the Fourth Amendment. The main reason for this holding was that the records which the Act required a bank to keep pertained to 'transactions to which the bank itself was a party', the fact that a large number of banks voluntarily kept similar records before being 'an indication' that 'the records were thought useful to the bank in the conduct of its own business, as well as in reflecting transactions of its customers'.[1] This reasoning is not very clear, and does not appear to address 'the underlying question',[2] namely whether bank customers have a reasonable expectation of privacy in 'the documentary details of the financial transactions reflected in their bank accounts'.[3] On one view compulsory requirements that routine banking transactions be recorded pose serious threats to socially justifiable expectations of privacy, both because information given to banks is normally intended to be confidential, and because collected information can easily be divulged—indeed there is no point in requiring the collection of certain types of information unless it is intended at a later stage to obtain and make use of them; this does not of course mean that the acquisition of information, whether by the government directly or by private agencies under governmental compulsion, is flatly prohibited, but only that record-keeping requirements should be brought under, and assessed in terms of, the constitutional guarantee against unreasonable searches and seizures.[4] The Court's answer to this seems to be either that once information has been divulged to another no cognisable expectation of privacy remains or that there can be no initial expectation of privacy with regard to banking records; on either interpretation depositors have no Fourth Amendment rights in banking records and similar sources of information collected but not yet disclosed to others.[5]

But what if the issue is not the required *maintenance* of bank customers' records but *access* to them by government agencies? Are records of an individual's accounts with his bank completely outside the protection of the

[1] 416 U.S. 21, 52 (1974).

[2] Note, 88 *Harv. L. Rev.* 188, 191 (1974).

[3] *California Bankers Association*, 416 U.S. 21, 82 (1974), per Douglas, J. dissenting.

[4] 'Note', 88 *Harv. L. Rev.* 188, 191–3 (1974); see also Douglas, J.'s dissent in *California Bankers Association*, supra.

[5] But it does not appear that a majority in *California Bankers Association* was willing to go as far as this. Thus, Douglas, Brennan and Marshall JJ. dissented, and two of those who constituted the majority, Powell and Blackmun, JJ., seemed to have little doubt that at some point *domestic* reporting requirements would have to be assessed within the Fourth Amendment. Powell J. observed that, whatever the language of the Act, its provisions had been narrowed by regulations only requiring the reporting of transactions exceeding $10,000, and it was only from this perspective that the legislative provisions infringed no constitutional right. If it was not for these restrictive regulations Powell, J. would obviously have held that 'legitimate expectations of privacy (were) implicate(d)' (416 U.S. at 79).

Fourth Amendment? If, according to *Boyd v. United States*,[1] 'a compulsory *production* of a man's private papers is within the scope of the Fourth Amendment', is there any reason why banking records should not be similarly protected? This question came before the Supreme Court in *United States v. Miller*[2] where a subpoena was issued to two banks to obtain records maintained pursuant to the record-keeping requirement upheld in *California Bankers Association*; the requested material, consisting mainly of microfilms of checks, deposit slips and other records, was duly produced, and the defendant was convicted of illegal distilling operations; should the evidence have been suppressed as having been obtained by means of an illegal search and seizure? The Supreme Court, in a much criticised[3] opinion, held that the defendant possessed no Fourth Amendment interest in the bank records that could be vindicated by a challange to the subpoenas, and that the defendant had rightly been convicted. Two principal points were made by the majority. To begin with, the subpoenaed documents did not fall within 'a protected zone of privacy'; they were not the defendant's 'private papers'; unlike the claimant in *Boyd* the defendant could assert 'neither ownership nor possession'; in fact, the materials in issue were the business records of the banks. Secondly, even if one directed one's attention to the *original* records (checks and deposit slips) rather than to the microfilm *copies* actually viewed and obtained by means of the subpoena, there was still no legitimate expectation of privacy in their contents; the checks were not confidential communications but negotiable instruments to be used in commercial transactions; and all other documents obtained, including financial statements and deposit slips, contained only information *voluntarily* conveyed to the banks and exposed to their employees; in short, the depositor took the *risk*, in revealing his affairs to another, that the information would be conveyed by that person to the government. *Miller* therefore holds that depositors have no Fourth Amendment interest in their banking records, which presumably means that the government can obtain unrestricted access to them.[4]

Miller does not fit in comfortably either with *Katz v. United States*[5] or with the doctrinal shift from property to privacy.[6] It is thus undeniable that '(f)inancial transactions can reveal much about a person's activities,

[1] 116 U.S. 612, 622 (1886).

[2] 425 U.S. 435 (1976).

[3] See La Fave, supra, 67 n. 2, at 411–17. La Fave calls the *Miller* decision 'pernicious', and characterizes its reasoning as 'woefully inadequate'.

[4] The *Miller* Court emphasised that the case before it, unlike *Burrows v. Superior Court*, 529 P. 2d 590 (1974), involved access to banking records by means of 'legal process' in the form of a subpoena. It might therefore have been different if the banks had provided the information in issue 'in response to an informal oral request' (529 P. 2d, at 593). But the Court in *Miller* also states that the Fourth Amendment issue does not turn on whether the subpoenas were defective (at 441 n. 2), and there are other statements in the opinion asserting unequivocally that 'no Fourth Amendment interests of the depositor are implicated' in situations such as the one in *Miller* (at 444, per Powell, J.).

[5] 389 U.S. 347 (1967).

[6] See *Warden v. Hayden*, 387 U.S. 294 (1967).

associations, and beliefs';[1] '(i)n a sense', as Justice Douglas has succinctly put it, 'a person is defined by the checks he writes', since by examining an individual's banking records one can compile 'a fairly accurate account of his religion, ideology, opinions, and interests'.[2] Both the tests of *Katz*[3] and *White*[4] appear therefore to be satisfied: there is first a subjective expectation of privacy, as it is abundantly clear that the customer of a bank expects that documents such as checks and deposit slips which he transmits to the bank in the course of his personal affairs or business operations will remain private and confidential, and secondly this expectation is reasonable and socially justifiable—the overwhelming majority of banks and customers would profess it (by regarding information in the possession of banking institutions as strictly confidential) and the availability of unrestricted access to private banking records would present considerable potential for abuse;[5] as this was put by the California Supreme Court in *Burrows v. Superior Court*,[6] where in a similar factual situation a conclusion contrary to that of the Supreme Court in *Miller* was reached, '(t)o permit a police officer (unrestricted) access to these records . . . and to allow the evidence to be used in any subsequent criminal prosecution . . . opens the door to a vast and unlimited range of very real abuses of police power'.

What about the Court's argument in *Miller*, relying on *Hoffa v. United States*[7] and *Lopez v. United States*,[8] that in the banking situation there has been voluntary exposure to the public, so that Fourth Amendment protection can no longer be invoked whatever may have been the position previously? The majority thought that the bank customer voluntarily relinquishes information to the bank and that by doing so he takes the risk of subsequent disclosure to third parties, including the government. But this characterisation of the situation hardly appears adequate. For a start, unlike the situation in *Hoffa* and *Lopez*, the disclosure by individuals and business firms of their financial affairs to a bank is not voluntary in any realistic sense since 'it is impossible to participate in the economic life of contemporary society without maintaining a bank account'.[9] Secondly, the majority's application of *Hoffa*'s assumption of risk doctrine appears particularly misplaced in the context of the relationship between bank and customer; it is

[1] *California Bankers Association v. Schultz*, 416 U.S. 21, 78–9 (1974), per Powell, J. concurring.

[2] Ibid., at 85, per Douglas, J. dissenting.

[3] 389 U.S. 347 (1967); see particularly Harlan, J.'s concurring opinion in *Katz*.

[4] 401 U.S. 745, 751 (1971).

[5] It is noteworthy, as pointed out in 'Note', 83 *Yale L.J.* 1439, 1464–5, that banks are under a legal duty to maintain the secrecy of their depositors' transactions, and that the depositor has certain common law rights with regard to the control of information relating to his banking records. *Miller* leads to 'the anomalous conclusion' ('Note', supra, at 1464–5) that, while safeguarded against all others, the depositor's privacy enjoys no meaningful protection when 'the prying eye belongs to the government' (ibid.).

[6] 529 P. 2d 590 (1974).

[7] 385 U.S. 293, 302 (1966).

[8] 373 U.S. 427 (1963).

[9] *Burrows v. Superior Court*, 529 P. 2d 590, 593–6 (1974).

of course true that there has been no 'seizure' by the bank which is a party to the transaction, but '(s)urely this is irrelevant to the question of whether a government search or seizure is involved';[1] the fact that one has given private papers to the bank for a strictly limited purpose, within the context of a confidential relationship, does not (and should not) mean that one has waived all rights to the privacy and non-disclosure of the papers; and therefore a more accurate description of the bank-customer relationship appears to be that, like the user of the pay phone in *Katz* who was held 'entitled to assume that the words he utter(ed) into the mouthpiece (would) not be broadcast to the world'[2] despite the fact that he was at that very time communicating his thoughts to a third party, the customer, having written or deposited a check, has a reasonable expectation that his check will be examined only for internal bank purposes—and not be recorded and revealed to the government so that criminal proceedings can be initiated against him.[3] It is indeed difficult to avoid the conclusion that personal *information* contained in banking records and similar financial documents should be entitled to a measure of protection not only from other individuals and private entities but also from government agencies.[4] *Miller*, partly through reliance on property considerations[5] and partly through insensitive application of a rigid 'misplaced confidence' doctrine, has brought about a 'highly questionable'[6] gap in Fourth Amendment coverage.

(g) Other methods of surveillance

Numerous other investigative techniques are now available to law enforcement officers, and their use raises complex and difficult questions concerning the applicability of the Fourth Amendment. Three such methods will be considered here, 'beepers', 'pen registers', and 'mail covers'.[7]

(i) Beepers

A beeper is an electronic tracking device. It is a small radio transmitter that broadcasts only a signal; it does not record or transmit either conversations or

[1] *California Bankers Association v. Schultz*, 416 U.S. 21, 95 (1974), per Marshall, J. dissenting.

[2] 389 U.S., at 352.

[3] *California Bankers Association*, 416 U.S., at 96, per Marshall, J. dissenting.

[4] A holding that the Fourth Amendment is applicable would not of course mean that banking information would be totally inaccessible to government agencies conducting legitimate investigations. It would only mean that such information would only be obtainable by means of the procedures set out in the Constitution (see Douglas, J.'s dissent in *California Bankers Association*, supra, at 82). Applicability of the Fourth Amendment would simply mean that a seizure of a customer's bank records could only be made after satisfaction of the warrant and probable cause requirements (see Marshall, J.'s dissent in *United States v. Miller*, 425 U.S., at 456).

[5] This was how Powell, J. in *Miller* distinguished *Boyd*. It is as if the *Miller* Court is prepared to recognize as legitimate and socially justifiable *only* those expectations of privacy which take the form of *proprietary* or *possessory* relationships.

[6] 'Note', supra, at 1465.

[7] See 1 La Fave, *Search and Seizure* 400–9, 417–32 (1978).

sounds. A beeper is attached to a moving thing, and by means of following by another device the signals it emits law enforcement officers are able to determine the beeper's location (and therefore the suspect's location as well). Is use of a beeper for the purpose of following the suspect's movements or the location of some item a search within the Fourth Amendment? If it is, the search must be reasonable before it can be upheld. If it is not, it can be engaged in by the police and others in their unfettered discretion, and there will be no occasion to reach issues of reasonableness and probable cause.

'It is self-evident that an electronic beeper is a device that has great potential as a law enforcement tool and even greater potential for . . . intrusion upon legitimate expectations of privacy',[1] but as yet no consistent judicial policy with regard to beepers and Fourth Amendment rights has emerged.[2] Courts have not been sure to what extent constitutional protection should adjust to technological advances,[3] and have been impressed, not to say baffled, by the complexity of this issue, by the great number of settings in which it may arise, and by the persuasiveness of the conflicting arguments.[4] The major thrust of the argument that use of a beeper is not a search is that, functionally, the beeper only facilitates (ordinary) visual surveillance which, except for unusual cases, is not within the Fourth Amendment.[5] Thus, it is a well established proposition that permissible techniques of surveillance include more than the five senses of police officers and their unaided physical abilities. Binoculars,[6] dogs that track and sniff out contraband,[7] searchlights,[8] fluorescent lamps[9] and other such investigative aids have not usually been held to involve a search, and the beeper, it is now said, is analogous to them, it being only '(a) sophisticated device'[10] that assists in an unaided surveillance. *Katz*, on this argument, is readily distinguishable because there law enforcement officers had used electronic means to listen to and record the defendant's *words*; in contrast, when what is monitored is *public movement and location* there is no encroachment upon reasonable

[1] *United States v. Bailey*, 465 F. Supp. 1138 (1979).

[2] Most courts have permitted the warrantless use of electronic beepers, but their reasons for so doing have varied. Some have taken the view that use of beepers involves no search; others have disagreed with this, regarding monitoring by means of electronic beepers as conduct falling within the Fourth Amendment, but have then upheld the warrantless installation and use of such tracking devices either under various standard exceptions to the warrant requirement (for instance the automobile exception) or on the basis of a specially developed principle allowing use of beepers in order to track down contraband (see *United States v. Emery*, 541 F. 2d 887 (1976)). There is as yet no Supreme Court decision on the matter (see generally 'Note, Tracking *Katz*: Beepers, Privacy and the Fourth Amendment', 86 *Yale L.J.* 1461 (1977)).

[3] *United States v. Bruneau*, 594 F. 2d 1190, 1196 (1979).

[4] Ibid.

[5] *United States v. Hufford*, 539 F. 2d 32 (1976); *United States v. Dubrofsky*, 581 F. 2d 208 (1978).

[6] *Hodges v. United States*, 243 F. 2d 281 (1957).

[7] *United States v. Bronstein*, 521 F. 2d 459, 461–3 (1975).

[8] *United States v. Lee*, 274 U.S. 559 (1927).

[9] *Commonwealth v. DeWitt*, 314 A. 2d 27 (1973).

[10] *United States v. Hufford*, 539 F. 2d 32, 34 (1976).

expectations of privacy because one who exposes his movements to observation must take the risk that such movements may be followed not only by the unaided eye but also by electronic devices. '(This) device,' as one court put it,[1] 'only augments that which *can* be done by visual surveillance *alone*'; if the police had more agents and more automobiles at their disposal they could easily have followed the suspect's movements without use of a beeper; and it should make no constitutional difference that shortage of resources has necessitated resort to electronic devices as an aid to ordinary surveillance. If therefore there has been no constitutional violation during the *attachment or installation* of a beeper,[2] its use *to monitor* the movements of either an individual or some other item involves no conduct falling within the Fourth Amendment.

The opposing line of argument proceeds as follows:[3] It is true that what one exposes to public view may be observed or seized by the police;[4] it is also true that one cannot expect that one's movements, particularly along the public highway,[5] will remain secret, and that a person has no constitutionally recognised right to assume that law enforcement officers will not *enhance* their ability to see or follow him by using various artificial means such as binoculars or even radar, or by observation from the air.[6] But use of a beeper to monitor the movements of a vehicle or the whereabouts of some other item involves something more than *magnification* of the observer's senses.[7] 'True,' one court has observed, 'when an individual gets into his car and drives away

[1] Ibid.

[2] It should be pointed out that, particularly in the case of vehicles, one must distinguish between *attachment* of the device and *monitoring* through the device. (Occasionally attachment and monitoring are not dealt with separately: compare *United States v. Hufford*, 539 F. 2d 32, 33–4 (1976), with *United States v. French*, 414 F. Supp. 800, 803 (1976), *United States v. Frazier*, 538 F. 2d 1322 (1976), and *United States v. Holmes*, 521 F. 2d 859 (1975)). If the beeper was attached in the course of an invasion of a constitutionally protected area, for instance a garage, there will obviously be a violation of the Fourth Amendment (see *Hufford*, 539 F. 2d 32 (1976)). But what if the beeper was attached to the exterior of the car when this was parked in a public space? Even here many courts have detected no violation of constitutionally protected privacy because any trespass that may be involved is regarded as so minimal as to be of no consequence (see *United States v. Moore*, 562 F. 2d 106, 111 (1977), *United States v. Frazier*, 538 F. 2d 1322, 1326 (1976), and *Cardwell v. Lewis*, 417 U.S. 583 (1974), where the Supreme Court held that there had been no Fourth Amendment violation where the police removed paint scrapings from the outside of a parked car).

[3] See *United States v. Bobisink*, 415 F. Supp. 1334 (1976); *United States v. Holmes*, 521 F. 2d 859 (1975); *United States v. Moore*, 562 F. 2d 106 (1977).

[4] *Katz v. United States*, 389 U.S. 347, 351 (1967).

[5] See *Cardwell v. Lewis*, 417 U.S. 583, 590 (1974).

[6] See *United States v. Moore*, 562 F. 2d 106, 112 (1977).

[7] Ibid.; see also *United States v. Bobisink*, 415 F. Supp. 1334, 1339 (1976). One possible distinction between on the one hand searchlights (*United States v. Lee*, 274 U.S. 559 (1927)), dogs (*United States v. Solis*, 536 F. 2d 880 (1976)) and binoculars (*Fullbright v. United States*, 392 F. 2d 432 (1968), and on the other electronic beepers is that binoculars, tracking dogs and search lights are not 'sophisticated modern mechanical or electronic devices' (*Solis*, 536 F. 2d at 882) whereas electronic beepers are. Another possible distinction, mentioned by Mansfield, J. in his

he can anticipate that he might be observed by someone following him. But it is something else *entirely* to have one's whereabouts monitored continuously by an undisclosed bug.'[1] Similarly, the installation of a signalling device upon one's possessions allowing government officers to confirm their precise location goes far beyond any ordinary powers of observation or detection which they may be presumed to have and which citizens should reasonably expect. As another court has put it, when a beeper has been attached, whether by use of stealth or by means of trespass, the vehicle or other object has been transformed into 'a messenger' in the service of those seeking to keep a record of its movements and location,[2] and this can hardly be said to fall within an individual's usual anticipation. 'It offends common sense to suggest that such a continuous electronic surveillance would not violate any reasonable expectation of privacy'.[3] Nor, this argument goes, is *Katz* irrelevant. *Katz* and subsequent cases not only extend the Fourth Amendment to the interception and recording of oral statements and private communications, but also extend general protection from all and any violations of reasonable expectations of privacy—the privacy, in other words, on which the defendant justifiably relied. It could now be argued that citizens have a reasonable expectation of privacy not only in the content of their conversations but also in their movements,[4] and that the possibility of being followed about in public by government agents does not mean that one must anticipate (in other words, be saddled with the danger) that one's every movement will be continuously (and indiscriminately) monitored by a secret transmitter. 'Certainly the average reasonable citizen, with his reasonable expectation of privacy, would take little solace in the fact that, while his every movement was recorded, his conversations were not'.[5] Nor does the public nature of the defendant's activity mean that he can expect no constitutional protection at all. Here an analogy can be drawn with *Katz* itelf: while the telephone booth itself was *public*, the defendant was held to be entitled to keep out the 'uninvited ear'; similarly, while moving about in public makes one vulnerable to observation and visual surveillance, the individual should still be able to keep out the 'uninvited monitoring device'.[6] This second view therefore denies that there is any rational basis for distinguishing between on the one hand the installation of a 'beeper' on either a car or some other lawfully possessed item in order to trace and follow the movements of an individual, and on the other the placing of an electronic device on the outside

---

concurring opinion in *United States v. Bronstein*, 521 F. 2d 459 (1975), is that certain devices, such as binoculars and searchlights, only *aid* the senses whereas others, such as electronic beepers, replace them (at 464).

[1] *United States v. Bobisink*, 415 F. Supp. 1334 (1976).

[2] *United States v. Moore*, 562 F. 2d 106, 112 (1977).

[3] *United States v. Bobisink*, 415 F. Suppl 1334 (1976).

[4] 'Surely a person's movements constitute an area where he should be able to have some expectation of privacy': *United States v. Bobisink*, 415 F. Supp. 1334 (1976).

[5] Ibid., at 1339.

[6] See *United States v. Moore*, 562 F. 2d 106, 112 (1977).

of a telephone booth in order to overhear and record conversations;[1] in both cases the government searches for and gathers information not generally available, and in so doing invades an individual's right of personal security and violates the privacy upon which he should be able to rely; it follows that use of beepers and similar electronic tracking devices constitutes a search and should only be upheld if it satisfies applicable standards of reasonableness.[2]

The many cases from state and lower federal courts take very different positions on the use of beepers.[3] It remains to be seen how the Supreme Court deals with the problem when it eventually comes before it.

(ii) Pen registers

A pen register is a device that is installed at the premises of the telephone

[1] *United States v. Holmes*, 521 F. 2d 859 (1975), aff'd en banc by an equally divided court, 537 F. 2d 227 (1976).

[2] This conclusion would not necessarily mean that the government would need a warrant before it could instal such devices. It may be that in a given situation an exception to the warrant requirement would apply. In that case, particularly where a moving vehicle was involved, installation and monitoring would be constitutional on the basis of probable cause. But see 'Note', 86 *Yale L.J.* 1461, at 1503, where it is argued that it is necessary to establish special beeper warrant procedures similar to those authorized in *Berger v. New York*, 388 U.S. 41 (1967) for electronic eavesdropping (but see La Fave, supra, 71 n. 7, at 432).

[3] Broadly speaking, the cases fall into two categories, those where a beeper has been used to follow a vehicle and those where it was used for some other purpose, for instance to keep track of a *particular* object (mainly narcotics or other contraband). As regards vehicular surveillance, *United States v. Hufford*, 539 F. 2d 32 (1976), followed by many other cases, holds that when a person drives along the public road he does not have a reasonable expectation of privacy, principally because his movements have been exposed to public view. This is rejected in *United States v. Holmes*, 521 F. 2d 859 (1975), in *United States v. Bobisink*, 415 F. Supp. 1334 (1976), and in *United States v. Moore*, 562 F. 2d 106 (1977) (the appeal from *Bobisink*), on the ground that '(a) person has a right to expect that when he drives his car into the street the police will not attach an electronic surveillance device to the car in order to track him' (*Holmes*, at 866). The other category of cases deals with the placing of beepers in contraband, stolen goods and the like. This has normally been upheld on the ground that the presence of illegality eliminates any legitimate expectation of privacy that might otherwise have existed (see *United States v. Emery*, 541 F. 2d 887 (1976); *United States v. Bishop*, 530 F. 2d 1156 (1976); *United States v. Perez*, 526 F. 2d 859, 863 (1976)). In such cases moreover the view is taken that since the purpose of the beeper is to monitor contraband it makes no difference that the installation of the electronic device has also resulted in some surveillance over an individual (see *United States v. French*, 414 F. Supp. 800, 803 (1976), where the court, rejecting the defendant's contention that his privacy of movement was unconstitutionally invaded, emphasised that the beeper had been aimed 'not at keeping track of (the defendant) or the truck as such' but at 'tracking marijuana'; see also *United States v. Emery*, 541 F. 2d 887, 889–90 (1976), where a beeper had been used to track a parcel of drugs and where a concurrent tracking of persons was not considered significant). But this reasoning has not been applied to other goods whose possession is legal (*United States v. Moore*, 562 F. 2d 106 (1977); see also *United States v. Holmes*, 521 F. 2d 859 (1975), where it was held both that the installation of a beeper to private property was a search and that monitoring movements by means of an electronic device involved a constitutionally cognisable invasion of legitimate expectations of privacy).

company and records the *numbers* dialled from the telephone at an individual's home. It does not overhear oral communications and does not indicate whether calls are actually completed. Is the installation of a pen register a search within the Fourth Amendment? The Supreme Court, in *Smith v. Maryland,*[1] answered this question in the negative. Application of the Fourth Amendment, Justice Blackmun observed in delivering the majority opinion, depended on the presence of a legitimate expectation of privacy that had been invaded by governmental action, an inquiry that in turn embraced the two questions set forth in Justice Harlan's concurring opinion in *Katz*, first whether the individual had exhibited an actual (subjective) expectation of privacy and secondly whether his expectation was one that society was prepared to recognise as reasonable. With regard to the first, the Court doubted whether people in general entertained any actual expectation of privacy with regard to the numbers they dialled; all telephone users surely realised that they conveyed phone numbers to the telephone company, since it was only through telephone company equipment that calls could be completed, and similarly all subscribers could realise that phone companies had facilities for making more or less permanent records of dialled numbers, since it was only by collecting information about all calls dialled that telephone bills could be compiled. But even if the defendant did entertain some subjective expectation that the phone numbers he dialled would remain private, the Court did not think that this expectation was one that society should be prepared to recognise as reasonable. The reason for this was that, as many cases had held, there could be no legitimate expectation of privacy in information an individual voluntarily turned over to third parties.[2] As in *Miller*,[3] where it was held that a bank depositor had no constitutionally recognisable expectation of privacy in financial information voluntarily conveyed to banks, so here too the defendant could claim no legitimate expectation of privacy since '(he had) voluntarily conveyed numerical information to the telephone company and "exposed" that information to its equipment in the ordinary course of business'. In so doing the defendant assumed the risk that the telephone company would reveal to the police the numbers he had dialled. Three members of the Court dissented.[4] Justice

[1] 99 S.Ct. 2577 (1979).

[2] The issues of exposure to third parties and of assumption of risk are normally considered under the first part of Harlan, J.'s *Katz* concurrence, namely whether an individual has exhibited an actual expectation of privacy. But here the Court considers them under the second part, whether an expectation of privacy (that the individual has manifested) is 'legitimate'. In so doing, the Court gives its sanction to a strict rule (which it builds into the concept of 'legitimacy' of expectations) that when an individual has voluntarily conveyed information to a third party he no longer maintains a constitutionally protected interest in it. It should also be noted that Blackmun, J., in his majority opinion, does not touch upon the question of whether it is *necessary or desirable*, in terms either of individual privacy or of society's collective sense of security, that there *should* be constitutional protection with regard to the information in issue. The majority, in other words, completely ignores the 'normative' aspects of the *Katz* inquiry.

[3] *United States v. Miller*, 425 U.S. 435 (1976).

[4] Brennan, J. joined the dissenting opinions of both Stewart and Marshall, JJ.

Stewart, the author of the *Katz* opinion, did not agree with the majority's sharp distinction between the *content* of telephone calls and information about the *numbers* dialled; the latter too was 'an internal part of the telephonic communication' that *Katz* had held to be entitled to constitutional protection, and it was simply not enough to say that there was no legitimate expectation of privacy in the numbers dialled because the caller 'assume(d) the risk' that the telephone company would disclose them to the police. Justice Marshall protested against the majority's 'assumption of risk' analysis. To begin with, even assuming that individuals knew (or should assume) that a phone company collected information about numbers dialled from a private telephone for internal reasons, it did not follow that they also expected (or should be regarded as expecting) this information to be made available either to the public in general or to the government in particular. 'Privacy is not a discrete commodity, possessed absolutely or not at all'.[1] Therefore those who disclosed certain facts to a bank[2] or the telephone company for a limited business purpose did not have to assume that this information would be released to other persons for other purposes.[3] More fundamentally, Justice Marshall, following Justice Harlan's dissent in *United States v. White*,[4] did not think that risks of disclosure and publicity should be imposed without examining the desirability of saddling them upon society; the central question was what risks '(an individual) should be forced to assume in a free and open society';[5] and this could only be answered by evaluating not only the *nature* of the investigative practice in question but also its *likely impact* on the *basic values* underlying the Fourth Amendment. From this perspective he had no doubt that unrestricted and widespread pen register surveillance of private telephones was 'an extensive intrusion' that seriously jeopardised individual privacy and society's sense of security;[6] use of pen registers should not therefore be insulated from independent judicial review by means of the warrant process.

Powell, J. took no part in the consideration of this case.

[1] *Smith v. Maryland*, 99 S.Ct. 2577, 2585 (1979), per Marshall, J. dissenting.

[2] But of course *United States v. Miller*, 425 U.S. 435, does not support Marshall, J.'s statement with regard to banks.

[3] Another consideration that was stressed by Marshall, J., in *Smith v Maryland* and which had also been emphasised by the dissenters in *Miller*, supra, and *California Bankers Association v. Shultz*, 416 US. 21 (1974), is that the doctrine of assumption of risk should not apply where there was no realistic choice. In the third-party consensual surveillance cases the defendant presumably had exercised some discretion in deciding who should enjoy his confidential communications (see *Lopez v. United States*, 373 U.S. 427 (1963); *Hoffa v. United States*, 385 U.S. 293 (1966); *United States v. White*, 401 US. 745 (1971)). But this is not so in the context of telephone conversations; as *Katz* acknowledges, the telephone has come to play 'a vital role . . . in private communication' and '(a) telephone call simply cannot be made without the use of telephone company property' (per Stewart, J. dissenting, in *Smith v. Maryland*, supra, at 2583).

[4] 401 U.S., at 786.

[5] *Smith v. Maryland*, 99 S.Ct. 2577, 2585 (1979), per Marshall, J. dissenting.

[6] As Marshall, J. noted, privacy in placing calls was of value not only to those engaged in criminal activity; many individuals, including members of unpopular

(iii) Mail covers

Similar to the pen register is the *mail cover.*[1] A mail cover is a procedure by which the United States Postal Service at the request of some governmental agency segregates all mail sent to a particular addressee (the suspect) and records all information which appears on its outside cover. Such information includes the name of the addressee, the postmark, the name and address of the sender (if they appear), and the class of mail. The letters themselves are not opened, and their contents are not read. After inspection, the mail itself is promptly delivered to the addressee, and the Postal Service furnishes the information only to the requesting agency.[2] The mail cover collects much useful information in connection with the investigation of certain types of crime, but it is also open to abuse, and, particularly when used in combination with other investigative techniques, 'makes the suspect's life an open book to investigators'.[3] Is the mail cover a search within the Fourth Amendment? Before 1967 the constitutionality of mail covers was uniformly sustained[4] but no clear reason was ever given. After *Katz* the crucial question is seen to be whether 'an individual has a reasonable expectation of privacy which would prevent the government from inspecting information contained on the outside of mail addressed to him'.[5] But even now the invariable judicial attitude, but not without forceful disagreement from some,[6] is that the mail cover is not a search.[7] The basic reason given is that there can be no justifiable expectation of privacy in information that has been exposed to the public. In the same way that *Miller*[8] holds that a bank customer has no legitimate expectation of privacy in the contents of his checks and deposit slips because '(they) contain only information voluntarily conveyed to the banks and exposed to their employees', so here too the information that is collected and passed on to the government is 'voluntarily conveyed to the

---

political organisations and journalists with confidential sources, might legitimately wish to prevent disclosure of their private sources; and therefore allowing the government unrestricted access to telephone records might impede 'certain forms of political affiliation and journalistic endeavour' that were important features of 'a truly free society'.

[1] La Fave, *Search and Seizure* 400–3 (1978); 'Note', 4 *Colum. J.L. & Soc. Prob.* 165 (1968).

[2] Under applicable postal regulations a mail cover can be instituted in the interest of (a) protecting national security, (b) locating a fugitive, or (c) obtaining evidence of the commission or attempted commission of a crime (which must be a felony). Thirty days is the maximum period for which a mail cover may be requested initially in cases other than those involving national security or breach of postal regulations, but the period may be extended by renewal of the request. But 120 days is ordinarily the maximum.

[3] *United States v. Choate*, 576 F. 2d 165, 187 (1978), per Hufstedler, J. dissenting.

[4] See *Lustiger v. United States*, 386 F. 2d 132, 139 (1967).

[5] *United States v. Choate*, 576 F. 2d 165, 175 (1978).

[6] See La Fave, supra, n. 1; and the dissenting opinion of Hufstedler, J. in *Choate*, supra.

[7] *United States v. Choate*, 576 F. 2d 165 (1978).

[8] 425 U.S. 435 (1976).

Postal Service and exposed to its employees or others in the ordinary course of passage of letters and packages from the senders to the defendant'.[1] Nor does it make a difference that the information may have been revealed on the assumption that it would be used only for a limited purpose and that the confidence placed in the third party (here the Postal Service) would not be betrayed. While the Supreme Court has not as yet passed on the constitutionality of the mail cover, its decision in *Smith v. Maryland*[2] upholding the pen register makes it probable that it will refuse to characterise the mail cover as a search.

(h) Abandonment

If property has been abandoned it may be searched and seized by the police without a warrant and irrespective of whether there was at the material time probable cause.[3] Abandoned property falls outside the coverage of the Fourth Amendment because abandonment brings to an end previously existing rights to and expectations of privacy. In other words, since protection from unconstitutional searches only extends to reasonable expectations of privacy, no issue of search is presented in cases where abandonment has demonstrated that expectations of privacy and the interest to be free from governmental intrusion have come to an end.[4] Once the owner of personal property has brought his right of privacy to an end by abandoning the property it becomes bona vacantia, there is nothing unlawful in a governmental appropriation of it, and its seizure is constitutional.[5] Abandonment in the law of search and seizure must not be confused with abandonment in the law of property. In the law of property the question, as it normally arises, is whether an owner of property has voluntarily, intentionally and unconditionally relinquished his title, claim or interest in it so that another person, having acquired possession, may successfully assert his superior interest.[6] In constitutional law, particularly in the area of search and seizure, 'the issue is not abandonment in the strict property-right sense, but whether the person prejudiced by the search had voluntarily discarded, left behind, or otherwise relinquished his interest in the property in question so that he could no longer retain a reasonable expectation of privacy with regard to it at the time of the search'.[7] In essence what is abandoned in the law of search and seizure is not necessarily the defendant's property, but rather his

[1] *United States v. Choate*, 576 F. 2d 165, 175 (1978).

[2] 99 S.Ct. 2577 (1979).

[3] See Mascolo, 'The Role of Abandonment in the Law of Search and Seizure: An Application of Misdirected Emphasis', 20 *Buff. L. Rev.* 399 (1971).

[4] *State v. Brown*, 341 N.E. 2d 325, 326 (1975).

[5] *Abel v. United States*, 362 U.S. 217, 241 (1960); see also *Corngold v. United States*, 367 F. 2d 1, 7 (1966); *State v. Taylor*, 347 So. 2d 172, 180 (1977); *United States v. Gibson*, 421 F. 2d 662 (1970).

[6] See Mascolo, supra, n.3, at 401–2; *City of St. Paul v. Vaughn*, 237 N.W. 2d 365, 370 (1975).

[7] *United States v. Colbert*, 474 F. 2d 174, 176 (1973); see also *United States v. Boswell*, 347 A. 2d 270, 274 (1975).

reasonable expectations of privacy therein.[1] In many cases of course the property will have been abandoned in the property sense as well,[2] but the fact that before property can be deemed to be abandoned for purposes of search and seizure the defendant must be found to have finally relinquished his constitutionally cognisable expectations of privacy in the discarded items has two implications: first, a determination of abandonment is not a question as to the applicability of local property law and concepts but ultimately one of federal constitutional law; and secondly, since abandonment has the drastic effect of bringing to an end what by definition were justifiable expectations of privacy, before it can be inferred '(one) must take into consideration not only the property law concept of abandonment but also the issue of waiver of a basic constitutional protection'.[3]

How is abandonment proved? Two often-repeated propositions can be set out with apparent simplicity. The first is that since a finding of abandonment entails loss of constitutional rights to privacy and security, and since an individual who abandons property exposes himself to what would otherwise be unreasonable official intrusions, the burden of proving abandonment rests on the one asserting it, normally the government, and is not easy to discharge, an allegation of abandonment must be made to appear affirmatively and 'by clear, unequivocal and decisive evidence',[4] and an intention to abandon will not ordinarily be presumed, particularly if the conduct of the owner can be explained consistently with a continued claim.[5] The second is that the question of whether property together with any related constitutional interest in privacy has been abandoned is a factual one.[6] In determining whether property has in fact been abandoned, as opposed for instance to being temporarily discarded or placed in the custody of a carrier,[7] all facts and circumstances must be considered and weighed. Primary attention must be focused on the behaviour of the person alleged to have abandoned the property. 'Abandonment is an ultimate fact or conclusion based generally upon a combination of act and intent. How did the person who was supposed to have abandoned the property act, that is, what did he do, and, secondly, what was his intention?'[8] For most courts the critical factor is intent. 'Abandonment,' it is often said, 'is primarily a question of intent',[9] but naturally intent can in general only be *inferred* from 'words spoken, acts done, and other objective facts'.[10] All relevant circumstances existing at the

[1] *City of St. Paul v. Vaughn*, 237 N.W. 2d 365, 371 (1975).

[2] See *Abel v. United States*, 362 U.S. 217 (1960); *Friedman v. United States*, 347 F. 2d 697 (1965).

[3] Mascolo, supra, at 401.

[4] *Linscomb v. Goodyear Tire & Rubber Co.*, 199 F. 2d 431, 435 (1952); *Friedman v. United States*, 347 F. 2d 697, 704 (1965); *Peyton v. United States*, 275 A. 2d 229, 230 (1971); *United States v. Boswell*, 347 A. 2d 270, 274 (1975).

[5] Ibid.

[6] *State v. Brown*, 341 N.E. 2d 325, 326 (1975).

[7] See *Corngold v. United States*, 367 F. 2d 1, 7 (1966).

[8] *Friedman v. United States*, 347 F. 2d 697, 704 (1965).

[9] *United States v. Colbert*, 474 F. 2d 174, 176 (1973).

[10] Ibid.; see also *Friedman v. United States*, 347 F. 2d 697, 704 (1965).

time of the alleged abandonment must be considered, and if from the totality of the evidence 'an intent to abandon is reasonably inferable',[1] justiciable expectations of privacy will be held to have been relinquished and constitutional protection from unreasonable searches and seizures will be inapplicable. These principles are illustrated by many examples. The basic case is again *Hester v. United States*[2] where, it will be remembered, the principle of abandonment was in part relied upon by the Supreme Court in holding admissible in evidence the whisky contents of certain containers discarded by the defendant when he was pursued by revenue officers. '(T)here was no seizure in the sense of the law', Justice Holmes said, 'when the officers examined the contents of each (container) after it had been abandoned'. Many other cases deal with similar situations, namely with the dropping, throwing away or leaving behind of articles by a person pursued or approached by police officers.[3] In *United States v. Colbert*[4] the defendants were walking down a street carrying briefcases. They were stopped by police officers for questioning. As the officers approached, the defendants put the briefcases on the sidewalk and on being asked about their contents denied that they owned the briefcases or that they had knowledge of them. The defendants began to walk again but were arrested and placed in a patrol car, and again denied any connection with or knowledge of the briefcases. An officer returned to the briefcases and discovered a pair of shotguns for the possession of which the defendants were subsequently convicted. It was held that the facts, mainly the physical act of setting the briefcases down, the verbal disclaimers and the act of walking away, constituted conclusive evidence of an intent to abandon. It followed that there had been an abandonment of the briefcases which had deprived the defendants of standing to complain of the subsequent search and seizure. In *United States v. Edwards*[5] the defendant, pursued by police in an automobile chase, failed to negotiate a turn, stopped the automobile, and ran away leaving the lights on and the engine running. The police conducted a warrantless search of the car and seized contraband. It was held that the defendant had no standing to question the legality of the search as he had abandoned the car, thus forfeiting 'any reasonable expectation to a continuation of his personal right against having his car searched'. Similarly, in *United States v. Smith*[6] the defendant and another man were observed in a public toilet stall behaving suspiciously. A police officer ordered them to come out, and as the two of them emerged a pouch containing articles usually employed for the injection of narcotics was dropped on the floor. It was held that the pouch on being

[1] *United States v. Boswell*, 347 A. 2d 270, 274 (1975); see also *Friedman*, supra, and *City of St. Paul v. Vaughn*, supra, at 370.

[2] 265 U.S. 57 (1924).

[3] A number of cases also deal with the abandonment, and search, of hotel rooms. The main example is *Abel v. United States*, 362 U.S. 217 (1960); see also *Feguer v. United States*, 302 F. 2d 214 (1962) and *Parman v. United States*, 399 F. 2d 559 (1968).

[4] 474 F. 2d 174 (1973).

[5] 441 F. 2d 749 (1971).

[6] 293 A. 2d 856 (1972).

knowingly dropped became abandoned property and could be examined and seized by the officers. And in *Brown v. United States*[1] the seizure of a shopping bag which the defendant dropped as the police were approaching was held to be not 'a "seizure" in the fourth amendment sense, but merely a retrieval of abandoned property'.

It is often said that an abandonment of property must be voluntary, purposeful and *complete*, but since it is fundamental doctrine that the subtle distinctions of private property law are not to be applied to the determination of search and seizure issues,[2] which in turn means that the crucial issue is not whether there has been complete abandonment in the strict property-law sense but whether it can *fairly and reasonably* be said that the defendant has given up reasonable expectations of privacy with regard to the property or article he has discarded,[3] it generally makes no difference whether or not the defendant intended to return and retrieve what has now been seized by the police. A striking example is *United States v. Brown*[4] where the defendant buried on an abandoned farm a suitcase containing the loot from a bank robbery. The police searched the farm without a warrant and recovered the suitcase. The act of leaving the suitcase buried in an open field was construed as an abandonment of it by the defendant, and it was therefore held that the officers were justified in opening it without first obtaining a warrant. Similarly, in *Smith v. United States,*[5] where the appellant threw away a revolver as he was being pursued by a police officer and the defence contended that he had not abandoned it but intended to return and reclaim it, the court regarded the question of his precise intent as irrelevant. 'By removing this article from his coat pocket and tossing it into the street, he had obviously given up its possession by leaving it in a public place where it might have been discovered and picked up by any passerby', and even though 'such temporary surrender of possession' was unlikely to be viewed as tantamount to loss of title if the owner brought a civil action against the finder, it was in the circumstances of the case enough to constitute abandonment which made invocation of the Fourth Amendment impossible. There is of course something artificial about explaining these cases in terms of an intent to abandon. It can thus hardly be said that the defendant in *Edwards*[6] intended to abandon his property rights in a valuable car or that the accused in *Brown*[7] intended to abandon the loot he had taken such pains to conceal in the unoccupied field. On the basis of these and other cases it has therefore been argued that emphasis on intent is misplaced, and that the proper test for abandonment in the context of search and seizure is neither 'whether all

[1] 261 A. 2d 834 (1970).

[2] See *Jones v. United States*, 362 U.S. 257 (1960); *United States v. Edwards*, 441 F. 2d 749 (1971); *City of St. Paul v. Vaughn,* 237 N.W. 2d 365 (1975).

[3] *United States v. Colbert*, 474 F. 2d 174, 176 (1973); *Smith v. United States*, 292 A. 2d 150, 151 (1972).

[4] 473 F. 2d 952 (1973).

[5] 292 A. 2d 150 (1972).

[6] 441 F. 2d 749 (1971).

[7] 743 F. 2d 952 (1973).

formal property rights have been relinquished'[1] nor whether the defendant had in any meaningful sense intended to abandon his property but rather whether, applying the Fourth Amendment not in 'a hypertechnical manner'[2] but with ordinary common sense, the defendant *should* be regarded by virtue of his own voluntary behaviour in relinquishing even though for a short while 'his possession and control of the property'[3] as having divested himself of his right not to have the property or article he has discarded subjected to searches and seizures, thus forfeiting any Fourth Amendment protection he may previously have enjoyed concerning the security of such property.[4]

An element that has been closely examined in determining whether there has been voluntary abandonment is police behaviour.[5] The reason for this is that if there has been police impropriety as a result of which property has been discarded there will be no voluntary abandonment. The Fourth Amendment will therefore still apply, which in turn means that a warrantless search or seizure of personal property will normally be unconstitutional. In *Fletcher v. Wainwright*[6] police officers in the course of investigating a theft of jewels, without either a warrant or probable cause to arrest, attempted to gain admission to a hotel room by kicking down the door, upon which one of the occupants threw stolen jewelry out of the window. It was held that since the initial entry was improper and the items had been thrown out of the window 'as a direct result of that illegality' the police were not entitled to the fruits of their seizure. The property, in other words, had not been abandoned, and the Fourth Amendment applied. But other courts have been willing to infer voluntary abandonment despite *some* police impropriety. It has therefore been held that a person's otherwise voluntary abandonment of property will not be tainted or made involuntary by a prior illegal police stop; only when the police begin to conduct an illegal search will a subsequent abandonment of property be held to be an involuntary one.[7] The many cases are difficult to reconcile and much depends on the precise facts of each situation, but three propositions on which most would agree are the following: first, an abandonment of property must be voluntary and must not have been prompted or caused by an illegal action; secondly, it may be that despite some illegal act the discarding of the property can still be construed not as the product of the prior impropriety but as a voluntary abandonment,

[1] *United States v. Wilson*, 472 F. 2d 901, 902 (1973).

[2] *United States v. Edwards*, 441 F. 2d 749, 753 (1971).

[3] *United States v. Boswell*, 347 A. 2d 270, 278 (1975), per Pair, J. dissenting.

[4] It is surprising that not many courts have applied a 'risk analysis' to the issue of abandonment, particularly in those cases where property has been discarded in the course of police pursuit. It might thus be said that if someone abandons or discards property, particularly in a public place, he accepts the risk that the pursuing officers will conduct a search, whatever his real intentions may be (see *United States v. Edwards*, 441 F. 2d 749, 753 (1971)).

[5] Mascolo, supra, at 406–7.

[6] 399 F. 2d 62 (1968); see also *Capitoli v. Wainwright*, 426 F. 2d 868 (1970) and *Hobson v. United States*, 226 F. 2d 890 (1955).

[7] See *Freyre v. State*, 362 So. 2d 989, 991 (1978), and *State v. Oliver*, 368 So. 2d 1331, 1335 (1979).

principally because the nexus between the lawless conduct and the subsequent discovery and seizure of the challenged evidence has become 'so attenuated as to dissipate the taint';[1] and thirdly the onus in such cases of proving that the connection between any police impropriety and the ultimate seizure of the evidence is so remote that it can be disregarded rests on the police.[2]

But in the area of abandonment too the governing criterion at the end of the day is neither the presence or absence of police illegality prior to what is alleged to be an act of abandonment, nor satisfaction of some subsidiary test, but rather whether the defendant should still be accorded at least some degree of immunity from official investigatory action[3] with regard to the discarded item. After *Katz*, here as in other areas the question is whether at the material time a reasonable expectation of privacy exists, and occasionally this concept is manipulated with what strikes some as sensitive refinement and others as unrealistic exactitude.[4] Good examples are *Work v. United States*[5] and *People v. Edwards*[6] in both of which it was held that an examination of the contents of a garbage can near the house was improper. The placing of incriminating evidence in the trash can, it was concluded, was not an abandonment of it, except as regards those persons expressly or impliedly authorised to remove its contents, for instance trashmen. In terms of the doctrine of abandonment the issue can be said to be whether one can abandon property vis-à-vis some people but not vis-à-vis others. Some have maintained that such decisions, by recognising a constitutional right of privacy in the contents of a garbage can, distort the Fourth Amendment; that protection for privacy should not be extended to artificial limits, nor be made to depend on minute distinctions and subtleties; and that the very act of placing an article or package in a garbage can is a socially recognisable act of abandonment that should be accepted as such and not then be qualified depending on who it was who examined its contents and seized the incriminating evidence.[7] The argument that abandonment can indeed be 'selective', adopted in *Work* and *Edwards*, is the one that has been mentioned at a number of points above and which in general has had a mixed reception (but not much success at the level of the Supreme Court as recent cases like *United States v. Miller* and *Smith v. Maryland* demonstrate), namely that since the central criterion governing the applicability of the Fourth Amendment is whether the defendant can be credited with a reasonable expectation of privacy with regard to the particular intrusion complained of,

[1] See *Wong Sun v United States*, 371 U.S. 471 (1963); *Fletcher v. Wainwright*, 399 F. 2d, 62, 64 (1968).

[2] *Freyre v. State*, supra, 83 n.7; see also *People v. Baldwin*, 250 N.E. 2d 62, 63 (1969).

[3] Mascolo, supra, at 408.

[4] See *State v. Nittolo*, 317 So. 2d 748 (1975), and *Mattier v. State*, 301 So. 2d 105 (1974).

[5] 243 F. 2d 660 (1957).

[6] 80 Cal, Rptr. 633 (1969).

[7] See *Work v. United States*, supra, at 663 et seq., per Burger, J., dissenting; La Fave, 'Search and Seizure: "The Course of True Law . . . Has Not . . . Run Smooth" ', 1966 *U. Ill. L. F.* 255, 335 n.480.

it is perfectly possible to exhibit a justifiable expectation of security only as to some categories of people and not as to others. As the California Supreme Court observed in *Edwards*, one can ascribe many reasons why houseowners would not want the things they throw away examined by neighbours and others since '(h)alf truths leading to rumour and gossip may readily flow from an attempt to "read" the contents of another's trash'.[1] A privately owned trash can should not therefore be subjected to searches and examinations by unauthorised persons, whether neighbours or police officers, unless of course the requirements of the Fourth Amendment have been satisfied.

(i) Concluding comments

The following concluding comments can now be made:

Privacy, as has been seen, is a term that has been used extensively in discussions of the coverage of the Fourth Amendment. But much usage has produced no clarity. For if there is one thing almost all are agreed about it is that privacy is pehaps the most vague, amorphous and confusing of concepts, used by different people to mean different things and connoting a great number and variety of 'rights' and 'interests', only some of which are related.[2] Some have used privacy broadly and in an open-ended manner as a synonym for personal autonomy, integrity and freedom. Others have used privacy to describe the freedom (whether legally recognised or not) of an individual to repel uninvited intrusions, physical or other, into his private domain. But the most influential approach is to use privacy in an 'informational' sense, as connoting the interest in retaining control over information about oneself;[3] privacy is thus defined as 'the claim of individuals, groups, or institutions to determine for themselves when, how, and to what extent information about them is communicated to others'[4] or as 'control over knowledge about oneself'.[5] The last two senses, privacy as freedom from intrusion and privacy as the interest in the non-disclosure of information about oneself, are of course closely connected because usually intrusion and involuntary loss of private information go together, in the sense that the latter is generally only obtainable by means of the former, whether the intrusion takes the form of a physical invasion of someone's private realm or only manifests itself in more

[1] 80 Cal. Rptr. 633, 638 (1969), per Burke, J.

[2] See Douse, 6 *J.L.R.* 154 (1972); A. Westin, *Privacy and Freedom* (1967); Fried, 'Privacy,' 77 *Yale L.J.* 475 (1968); Gross, 'The Concept of Privacy', 42 *N.Y.U.L. Rev.* 34 (1967); *Nomos XIII: Privacy (Yearbook of the American Society for Political and Legal Philosophy*, J. Pennock and J. Chapman eds. 1971) (hereinafter referred to as *Nomos XIII*); Brandeis and Warren, 'The Right to Privacy,' 4 *Harv. L. Rev.* 193 (1890).

[3] Douse, supra, n.2, at 163–70; Beaney, 'The Right to Privacy and American Law', 31 *Law and Contemp. Prob.* 253, 254 (1966); S. Stromholm, *Rights of Privacy and Rights of Personality: A Comparative Survey* (1967); Van den Haag, 'On Privacy', *Nomos XIII,* supra, at 149 et seq.; Fried, supra, n.2, at 477–8; Bloustein, 'Privacy as an Aspect of Human Dignity: An Answer to Dean Prosser', 39 *N.Y.U.L. Rev.* 962 (1964); M. Ernst and A. Schwartz, *Privacy: The Right to be Let Alone* (1968).

[4] A. Westin, *Privacy and Freedom* 7 (1967).

[5] Fried, 'Privacy', 77 *Yale L.J.* 475, 483 (1968).

subtle ways, for instance by surveillance;[1] but normally the chief complaint in a privacy context relates not to unwelcome intrusion but to the loss of restricted information about oneself, and in any case when one considers the law of search and seizure it is official activities directed towards or resulting in the obtaining of (usually incriminating) information that the relevant legal controls seek to regulate. In this sense the Fourth Amendment and the resulting constitutional law aim to accommodate important but conflicting governmental and individual interests, on the one hand the government's interest to collect what is felt to be necessary evidence and on the other the individual's need to maintain effective control over the appropriation and involuntary dissemination of information about himself.[2]

In terms of the Fourth Amendment a number of different ways in which the notion of privacy has been used must be sharply distinguished. First, on occasion privacy is used in a purely descriptive (and conclusory) sense, particularly to denote the kind of official conduct that comes within the Amendment's proscriptions, as where it is said that by protecting against unreasonable searches and seizures the Fourth Amendment protects against invasions of privacy or that practices and procedures that violate privacy are constitutionally prohibited;[3] invasions of privacy in this sense are those official intrusions and appropriations that have been declared by the relevant jurisprudence to constitute infringements of the right enshrined in the Fourth Amendment. Secondly, the concept of privacy is often invoked in attempts either to proclaim the purpose of the Fourth Amendment, as where it is said that its role is 'to protect against invasions of privacy'[4] and to safeguard personal privacy, or to express one of the principal features or cardinal virtues underlying the guarantee against unreasonable searches and seizures, for instance where it is said that the Fourth Amendment embodies nothing less than a fundamental spiritual and intellectual concept, namely that only by valuing the privacy of home and person and only by protecting the individual in the privacy of his life, beliefs, emotions and sensations will conditions favourable to the pursuit of happiness be secured.[5] Thirdly, the concept, or some version, of privacy, suitably refined, may be used as a decisional test, as a judicial instrument, in other words, determining the applicability of the Fourth Amendment by giving more concrete guidance (than that which can be extracted from the constitutional text) as to when searches and seizures—that is to say, the fact situations on proof of which the constitutional guarantees come into operation—have taken place. Needless to say it is this last sense which is the most significant from the standpoint of the constitutional lawyer.

The constitutional position of privacy, in the context of the law of search

[1] Douse, supra, at 169.

[2] Greenawalt, 'The Right of Privacy', in *The Rights of Americans*, 299–300 (N. Dorsen ed. 1971).

[3] See *United States v. Lefkowitz*, 285 U.S. 452, 464 (1932); *Nardone v. United States*, 302 U.S. 379, 383 (1937); *Wolf v. Colorado*, 338 U.S. 25, 27 (1949).

[4] *Warden v. Hayden*, 387 U.S. 294, 305 (1967).

[5] See the dissent of Brandeis, J., in *Olmstead v. United States*, 277 U.S. 438, 478 (1928); J. Landynski, *Search and Seizure and the Supreme Court* 47 (1966).

and seizure, can be set out in the form of three propositions, as follows. First, the Fourth Amendment cannot be translated into a general constitutional 'right to privacy';[1] nor does it embody any broad right to be let alone. Instead the Amendment only protects 'individual privacy against certain kinds of governmental intrusion',[2] unreasonable searches and seizures. But secondly, as has been seen, in the definition of the latter the Supreme Court has invariably adopted a particular version of privacy interests, the 'justifiable reliance'[3] on or 'reasonable expectation'[4] of privacy test. But equally clearly the concept and terminology of privacy are not dictated either by the constitutional text or by irresistible implication from it. Conceivably 'privacy' may not have figured at all in Fourth Amendment law. Thus it appears quite *possible* that the principal objective of the constitutional provision against unreasonable searches and seizures is the protection of the individual's right of personal security,[5] and that the yardstick for delimiting Fourth Amendment coverage is the existence of a 'reasonable' or socially 'justifiable' expectation of '*freedom* from governmental intrusion'[6]. Alternatively, even if it is maintained that the basic value animating the core of the Fourth Amendment is that of 'privacy', it has often been pointed out that while certain aspects of individual privacy are within its compass 'its protections go further and often have nothing to do with privacy at all',[7] unless of course one defines constitutional privacy either in an all-inclusive definitional sense or as a synonym for those notions and ideals specifically embodied in the constitutional safeguard from illegal searches. Yet another formulation attempting to combine the 'privacy' and 'security' or 'freedom from intrusion' perspectives is to say that the interest protected by the Fourth Amendment is freedom from 'unreasonable governmental intrusions' into the privacy of persons, homes and effects,[8] or that 'the core values the Fourth Amendment protects are privacy interests',[9] the principal of *which* is freedom from unreasonable governmental intrusions aimed at the obtaining of information. But whatever the possibilities or varieties of terminology, current theory has it that the *values* of the Fourth Amendment are to be channelled by the *Katz* 'privacy' or 'reliance' *test,* as developed in subsequent cases[10]. The final point is that even though one must clearly distinguish between general concepts of privacy and security from specific judicial tests (almost always now couched in the language of 'reasonable' or 'justifiable' expectations of privacy and freedom from governmental intrusion elaborated in *Katz* and more recent

[1] *Katz v. United States*, 389 U.S. 347, 350–1 (1967).

[2] Ibid.

[3] See *Katz v. United States*, 389 U.S. 347, 353 (1967).

[4] Ibid, at 361, per Harlan, J., concurring.

[5] See *Boyd v. United States*, 116 U.S. 616, 630 (1886).

[6] See *Combs v. United States*, 408 U.S. 224, 227 (1972); *Mancusi v. DeForte*, 392 U.S. 364, 368 (1968); *Rakas v. Illinois*, 439 U.S. 128 (1978).

[7] *Katz v. United States*, 389 U.S. 347, 350 (1967).

[8] See *United States v. Chadwick*, 433 U.S. 1, 7 (1977).

[9] *United States v. Chadwick*, 433 U.S. 1, 9 n.4 (1977).

[10] See particularly *United States v. White*, 401 U.S. 745 (1971); *Rakas v. Illinois*, 439 U.S. 128 (1978); *Smith v. Maryland*, 99 S.Ct. 2577 (1979).

cases) prevalent notions of privacy and security—that is to say, widely held views as to how much privacy and security from official intrusion and information-gathering people need and must be assured in the interests of social welfare and democratic government—have an inevitable, even though not usually immediate and perhaps not always perceptible, impact on judicial determinations of the reach of the Fourth Amendment.[1] Deeply felt social or political needs after all have a way of working themselves into the constitutional fabric.

One of the main problems lurking in any attempt to construct a coherent framework of Fourth Amendment law is the tension between what can be called the atomistic and regulatory perspectives.[2] Should the Fourth Amendment be viewed from an individual perspective, emphasising protection of individual interests and focusing upon the delineation of protected 'atomistic spheres',[3] or from the limitation perspective, emphasising control of governmental conduct and ultimately aiming at the elaboration of a regulatory charter demanding of government agencies adherence to procedures, whenever possible predetermined, that respect and do no jeopardise society's collective sense of security? More fully, the individual perspective requires of courts the identification, demarcation and protection of individual interests, and in terms of a *Katz*-based definition of the operative concepts of searches and seizures asks of them to articulate the individual's justifiable expectations of privacy, in this way sketching the parameters of the right or rights embodied in the Amendment. The limitation perspective regards the lawful exercise of governmental power as the paramount objective of the law of search and seizure, views the conditioning of the legality of intrusive police practices upon individual expectations as inherently dangerous and as ultimately subversive of individual freedom, and puts forward a conception of the Fourth Amendment as 'a general command to government to respect the collective security of the people in their persons, houses, papers and effects, against unreasonable searches and seizures',[4] a command that should be translated not into narrow rules of criminal procedure but into a set of doctrines 'regulating police practices broadly, generally and directly'.[5] Uncertainty about the dominant perspective can be traced to the text of the Fourth Amendment itself. What is protected is the 'right . . . to be . . . secure . . . against unreasonable searches and seizures'; a substantive right appears to be

[1] See the dissenting opinion of Harlan, J. in *United States v. White*, supra, and the concurring opinion of Powell, J. in *Rakas v. Illinois*, supra.

[2] See Bacigal, 'Some Observations and Proposals on the Nature of the Fourth Amendment', 46 *Geo. Wash. L. Rev.* 529 (1978); Amsterdam, 'Perspectives on the Fourth Amendment,' 58 *Minn. L. Rev.* 349, 367 (1974); La Fave, ' "Case-by-Case Adjudication" versus "Standardized Procedures": The Robinson Dilemma', 1974 *Sup. Ct. Rev.* 127; Weinreb, 'Generalities of the Fourth Amendment', 42 *U. Chi. L. Rev.* 47 (1974); Dworkin, 'Fact Style Adjudication and the Fourth Amendment: The Limits of Lawyering', 48 *Ind. L. J.* 329 (1973).

[3] Amsterdam, supra, at 367.

[4] Ibid., at 372.

[5] Ibid.

conferred, but this is defined negatively, in terms of what must not take place, unreasonable searches and seizures indicating the types of behaviour the government must not engage in. What is the better reading of the Amendment—one that looks upon it as safeguarding an affirmative right of some sort or one that forbids certain kinds of governmental conduct?[1] It is of course true that if courts take either the individual perspective or the regulatory one as the sole charter of Fourth Amendment adjudication to the exclusion of the other, and if moreover this is applied with the kind of rigorous logical consistency one does not usually come across in constitutional law, important consequences (and differences from existing patterns of authority) will result.[2] But this has not happened, and even though, in terms of terminology, the main level at which the Supreme Court has operated is the individual one, and despite the fact that many of the operative concepts of Fourth Amendment law such as standing are premised on the atomistic perspective,[3] in the main the individual and regulatory views have been used conjunctively and their results can be found intertwined in the cases.[4] This compromise has already been discussed in our treatment of *Katz* and its progeny and can now be set out as follows. What the Fourth Amendment recognises is the right to be secure from unreasonable searches and seizures. Unreasonable searches and seizures are what the government must avoid engaging in. But searches and seizures do not describe objectively identifiable categories of governmental behaviour or specific official wrongs (as was more or less the case when searches denoted trespassory entries, and seizures detentions of tangible items), but are to be defined in terms of the reliance on and expectations of privacy of individuals, which in turn cannot be determined without considering the nature of the particular governmental

[1] See Douse, supra, 85 n.2, at 156; Hufstedler, 'The Directions and Misdirections of a Constitutional Right of Privacy', 26 *Record of N.Y.C.B.A.* 546, 549–50 (1971); 'Note, From Private Places to Personal Privacy: A Post-Katz Study of Fourth Amendment Protection', 43 *N.Y.U.L. Rev.* 968 (1968).

[2] See Bacigal, supra, 88 n. 2, at 530–1, 560–1. To take one of the most obvious examples, the *purpose* of the search is irrelevant from the individual perspective, since an invasion of privacy remains the same irrespective of official motivation. Administrative inspections are therefore searches even though they are normally prompted by benign motives and not by the intent to initiate criminal proceedings. The individual perspective is exemplified by *Camara v. Municipal Court,* 387 U.S. 523 (1967). Official purpose, however, is of great importance from the limitation perspective. 'From the limitation perspective . . . acceptability of the search depends on the legitimacy of the government's official purpose and motive' (Bacigal, supra, at 530). Only quests for criminal evidence should therefore be termed 'searches', the limitation perspective maintains; routine inspections prompted by health, safety or welfare considerations are not 'searches', or, at most, should only be evaluated in terms of overall reasonableness (see *Frank v. Maryland,* 359 U.S. 360 (1959), where the Fourth Amendment was viewed as primarily extending to quests for criminal evidence, and *Wyman v. James,* 400 U.S. 309 (1971), where a warrantless caseworker's home visit was held to be lawful because the investigatory technique there utilised was 'a gentle means, of limited extent and of practical and considerate application').

[3] See Amsterdam, supra, at 367.

[4] See Bacigal, supra, at 531.

practice used in the gathering of incriminating information against the defendant and its broad impact on society's collective sense of security. It has thus been seen that whether expectations of privacy are legitimate within the language of *Katz* and subsequent cases depends neither on the subjective anticipations of privacy or freedom from intrusion entertained by an individual nor on the risks he assumes or must be presumed to have accepted, but on the expectations of privacy he *should be credited with* and on the risks of involuntary disclosure and surveillance *he must be saddled with* and thus *forced to assume* in a free and open society. What the constitutional prohibition of unreasonable searches and seizures demands of the judiciary is nothing less than the related prescriptive tasks of delineating the parameters of the individual's sphere of security from unjustifiable governmental intrusion and of prohibiting certain official practices as fundamentally inconsistent with the type of political system the Constitution exemplifies. This means, and in turn has the effect, that in defining the reach of the individual's Fourth Amendment rights and in examining the desirability of forcing society to accept certain risks courts must not only bear in mind the need to foster a sense of individual and collective security without which there can be no political freedom but must also examine and evaluate the character of particular official investigative practice with reference to basic constitutional (and societal) values. And this task, as has been seen, is normally performed by a general judicial policy, given respectable form by the reasonable expectations of privacy test, of regarding official intrusions that endanger individual and collective security and privacy to a significant extent as searches, which means that before they can be held to be valid the requirements of the Fourth Amendment must be satisfied.[1]

Another major source of difficulty is that the coverage of the Fourth Amendment does not depend only on the judiciary's perception of the undesirability of certain police practices or the justifiability of saddling individuals with certain risks; it is also closely connected first with the relationship between the two parts of the Amendment, namely the clause outlawing unreasonable searches and the provision about warrants, and secondly with the requirement of probable cause.[2] The traditional understanding, as will be seen later, is that, subject to certain carefully drawn exceptions, a search can only be constitutional if it is performed under the authority of a properly issued warrant; its general reasonableness, assessed in the light of all the surrounding circumstances, is not enough. Further, again with certain exceptions, a search, whether with or without a warrant, can only be constitutional if it is preceded and supported by probable cause, namely reason to believe that the proposed investigation will uncover a specific incriminatory item in a particular place. The dilemma can now be seen clearly.[3] The more one expands the coverage of the Fourth Amendment, the more difficult it becomes to insist on the traditional safeguards of a

[1] See Harlan, J. dissenting in *United States v. White,* 401 U.S. 745 (1971); *Rakas v. Illinois,* 439 U.S. 128 (1978); *Smith v. Maryland,* 99 S.Ct 2577 (1979).

[2] See Amsterdam, supra, particularly at 395–7.

[3] Ibid., at 395.

judicial warrant and the antecedent presence of probable cause. If for instance a 'search' in the constitutional sense is defined as any governmental activity designed to or resulting in the involuntary obtaining and disclosure of information that the complainant wishes to keep private it will either become impossible to conduct many types of governmental investigation which almost all would consider necessary, or the traditional internal structure of the Fourth Amendment based as it is on the essential procedural requirements of a showing of probable cause and the obtaining of a warrant will have to be watered down to the point of extinction.[1] If, that is, a 'search' is defined in very expansive terms but it is sought to allay fears that law enforcement will be unduly hampered by the flexible and pragmatic interpretation of the Amendment's operative terms, mainly probable cause, a number of different levels of Fourth Amendment doctrine will have to be developed;[2] these too, almost certainly, will eventually be qualified by numerous and subtle rules and qualifications and in the process the Fourth Amendment will be converted into a chaotic and confusing body of law assuring neither satisfactory protection for the citizen nor predictability of judicial results.[3] But if conversely one seeks to avoid the dangers of compromising the historically hallowed structure of the Fourth Amendment and its chief supporting pillars, prior authorization by a judicial officer and satisfaction of the requirement of undiluted probable cause, by rigorously insisting on the maintenance of 'the traditional monolithic model',[4] one will inevitably have to exempt altogether from constitutional scrutiny '(p)olice practices that cry for some form of constitutional control but not the control of a warrant or a probable cause requirement',[5] for instance brief stops for the purpose of limited 'weapons searches'. It will be seen below how the Supreme Court has resolved this dilemma.[6] Here it suffices to point out that both the issue of the Fourth Amendment's coverage and attempted definitions of what constitutes a 'search' or 'seizure' cannot be divorced from the consideration that to refuse to describe a particular police practice or other official method of obtaining information as a search is to put it outside the scope of the constitutional command and beyond the reach of judicial superintendence, whether by means of the warrant process or simply by the demand that it be conducted in a reasonable manner and only on the basis of some adequate ground supporting the particular exertion of official activity.

To summarise, the scope of the Fourth Amendment depends on the one hand on normative judicial determinations as to what risks concerning the dissemination of restricted information it is proper to saddle society with and what official practices it is possible to allow the police to engage in outside any judicial regulation without the resulting diminution of privacy and loss of

[1] See Kitch, '*Katz v. United States*: The Limits of the Fourth Amendment', 1968 *Sup. Ct. Rev.* 133, 134; Greenawalt, 'The Right of Privacy', in *The Rights of Americans* 304–6 (N. Dorsen ed. 1971).

[2] Amsterdam, supra, at 393–4.

[3] Ibid., at 394.

[4] Ibid., at 395.

[5] Ibid.

[6] See 231–48.

security reaching the point where 'the aims of a free and open society'[1] are irrevocably compromised, and on the other on the particular theory one has developed regarding both the relationship of the Amendment's parts and the flexibility with which its operative concepts, principally the demand for reasonableness and the requirement of probable cause, can (or should) be read. It is therefore hardly surprising, first that no 'bright line'[2] can be drawn either between the protected and the unprotected (individual ad societal interests) or between the permissible and the impermissible (police practices), and secondly that this line is bound to shift with changing views both within

[1] Amsterdam, supra, at 403.

[2] *Rakas v. Illinois*, 439 U.S. 128, 168 (1978), per White, J. dissenting. In *Rakas*, where it was held that passengers do not normally have a legitimate expectation of privacy in the glove compartment or in the area under the seat, Rehnquist, J., after stating that legitimation of expectations of privacy must have a source outside the Fourth Amendment, indicated that the necessary legitimation was to be effected 'either by reference to concepts of real or personal property law or (by reference) to understandings that are recognised and permitted by society' (ibid., at 143 n.12). 'One of the main rights attaching to property is the right to exclude others', Rehnquist, J. observed, and this meant that 'one who owns or lawfully possesses or controls property will in all likelihood have a legitimate expectation of privacy by virtue of this right to exclude'. *Katz*, Rehnquist, J. admitted, had rejected the idea that Fourth Amendment protection depends upon a common-law interest in real or personal property, but 'the Court has not altogether abandoned use of property concepts in determining the presence or absence of the privacy interests protected by that Amendment'. It has been observed ('Note', 93 *Harv. L. Rev.* 171, 178 (1979)) that the *Rakas* majority has 'revived the centrality of property and possession by explicitly investing only the owner/possessor with a clear "legitimate expectation"'. This is true, for even though Rehnquist, J. acknowledges that as a result of *Katz* and subsequent cases concepts of property no longer exclusively determine the presence of constitutionally recognised privacy interests, the *Rakas* majority demarcates two areas of Fourth Amendment protection, 'the area marked out by property concepts' ('Note', supra, at 178), and cases where 'understandings that are recognised and permitted by society' have been shown to exist. (For a similar analysis, see below, at 363–8.) No guidance is offered by the majority that would help one to distinguish legitimate from non-legitimate expectations of privacy. Powell, J. in his concurring opinion in *Rakas* did set forth certain criteria, emerging from previous cases, to be used in determining the legitimacy of privacy expectations, mainly whether normal precautions were taken, how the location was used, the fact that expectations of privacy with regard to automobiles are weaker than in the case of houses, and the additional factor that a distinction has been recognised in some cases between the rights of passengers and the rights of an individual who has exclusive control of an automobile or of its locked compartments. But Powell, J., too recognises that these four indicia are not exclusive, and that '(t)he range of variables in the fact situations of search and seizure is almost infinite' (439 U.S. at 156). The dissenters in *Rakas* would focus on 'legitimate presence' during the search. White, J., dissenting, thought that legitimate presence in a private place should be sufficient to give rise to a legitimate expectation of privacy, viewed *Rakas* as indistinguishable from cases where individuals in taxis, apartments and the like had been allowed to challenge searches, and expressed the view that what the Court was worried about was the exclusionary doctrine (which it seems that it was, see 439 U.S. at 152 n.1, per Powell, J. concurring). In his view, the issue of that rule's continued validity should be faced directly 'instead of distorting other doctrines in an attempt to reach what are perceived as the correct results in specific cases' (per White, J. at 157).

the judiciary and among society at large concerning on the one hand the legitimate needs of law enforcement and on the other the measure of privacy and security from official surveillance and intrusion that individuals need and must be secured consistently with a plurastic society and the democratic system of government as reflected in the Constitution.[1]

[1] Harlan, J. dissenting in *United States v. White*, 401 U.S. 745 (1971).

3. Search Warrants

'The bulwark of Fourth Amendment protection is the Warrant Clause'.[1] A warrant is simply an authorisation from a judicial officer which allows the police to embark upon a search or to effect a seizure, and the Warrant Clause sets out both what must be done to obtain a warrant and what a valid warrant must contain.[2] The place of the warrant requirement in the overall constitutional scheme and its relevance in determination of constitutional reasonableness will be considered extensively below.[3] But there is general agreement as to its functions.[4] These are two. First, the warrant represents an independent and unbiased assurance that a search will not proceed without there being probable cause to believe not only that a crime has been committed but also that specified persons, places or effects have been involved and are therefore legitimate targets of intrusive investigation. The second type of protection secured by the warrant requirement is that judicial superintendence helps ensure that searches and other invasions of personal security will be as limited as possible.[5] Here the evil that it is attempted to suppress is the unlimited exploratory rummaging permitted by the 'general warrants' abhorred by the colonists,[6] and the warrant accomplishes this second objective of narrowly limiting permitted intrusions to the circumstances justifying their initial authorisation by requiring a 'particular description' of any place to be searched or things to be seized (and by therefore prohibiting any further intrusion).

The basic principles governing the issuance of search warrants are the following. First, warrants supporting entries, searches and seizures must be based on probable cause, namely reasonable grounds to believe that specific 'things' connected with criminal activity are located on the premises to which entry is sought; secondly, determinations of probable cause—that is to say, assessments of the sufficiency of evidence that seizable items will be found in the place to be searched—must be made by neutral and detached magistrates, invariably judicial officers; and thirdly search warrants, since they too can be used as potent instruments of oppression,[7] must conform to strict standards of specificity and particularity making general searches

[1] *Franks v. Delaware*, 98 S.Ct. 2674, 2681 (1978), per Blackmun, J.

[2] The Warrant Clause provides that 'no Warrants shall issue, but upon probable cause, supported by Oath or affirmation, and particularly describing the place to be searched, and the persons or things to be seized.'

[3] See, below, at 131 et seq.

[4] See *Coolidge v. New Hampshire*, 403 U.S. 443, 467 (1971), per Stewart, J.

[5] See *Coolidge v. New Hampshire*, supra, at 467.

[6] See *Stanford v. Texas*, 379 U.S. 476, 481 (1965).

[7] *People v. Wiedeman*, 154 N.E. 432 (1926).

impossible and aiming to prevent the seizure of one thing under a warrant describing another.[1] These three issues, namely review by a neutral magistrate, existence of probable cause, and the requirement of 'particular description', together with issues of seizability and execution, will be discussed in turn.

(a) Neutral and detached magistrates

It is fundamental Fourth Amendment doctrine that a search warrant can only be issued by persons who are 'judicial officers' or 'neutral and detached magistrates'.[2] The basic reason for this is that the protection intended to be secured by the Fourth Amendment only becomes meaningful if the determinations of probable cause on which invasions of privacy and intrusions into personal security are to be grounded are drawn not by law enforcement officers or others entrusted with the tasks of investigating crime and apprehending criminals[3] but by persons who can be trusted to reach neutral, unbiased and trustworthy determinations that the conditions insisted upon before a search can be undertaken have been met. Thus, an issuing magistrate, the Supreme Court has held, must meet two tests: he must be neutral and detached—that is to say, must be someone independent of the police and the prosecution—and he must be capable of determining whether probable cause exists for the requested search.[4] More particularly, the following propositions emerge from the cases. First, prosecutors and law enforcement officers are obviously not neutral and detached magistrates and therefore cannot issue search warrants. Thus in *Coolidge v. New Hampshire*[5] it was held that a search warrant issued by the state attorney-general 'who was actively in charge of the investigation and later was to be chief prosecutor at the trial' was invalid even though the attorney-general, under state law, was authorised as a justice of the peace to issue warrants. The Court took the view that 'there could hardly be a more appropriate setting than (the one before them) for a per se rule of disqualification rather than a case-by-case evaluation of all the circumstances' since 'prosecutors and policemen simply cannot be asked to maintain the requisite neutrality with regard to their own investigations'. Does the *Coolidge* ruling extend to all employees of the executive branch or those invested with executive responsibilities, or should its rule of per se disqualification be confined to cases where the issuing officer, as in *Coolidge* itself, was involved in the investigation or prosecution of the defendant? Some would limit it in this way,[6] but the predominant view is that possession or exercise of executive power automatically disqualifies one from being a neutral and detached magistrate even though the employee of the

[1] *Marron v. United States*, 275 U.S. 192, 196 (1927).

[2] Terms such as 'judicial officer', 'magistrate', and 'independent judicial officer' have been used interchangeably, and it has been noted that these variations in terminology are not significant (see *Shadwick v. Tampa*, 407 U.S. 345, 349 (1972)).

[3] See *Johnson v. United States*, 333 U.S. 10, 14 (1948).

[4] *Shadwick v. Tampa*, 407 U.S. 345, 350 (1972).

[5] 403 U.S. 443, 449–53 (1971).

[6] *State v. Hill*, 564 P. 2d 841, 843 (1977).

executive branch issuing the warrant was not working on the particular case at the time.[1]

But even though the terms 'judicial officer' and 'magistrate' imply some connection with the judicial branch it has never been held that only lawyers or judges can grant warrants irrespective of the judicial system or the type of warrant involved, and in *Shadwick v. Tampa*[2] the Supreme Court held that at least on the facts before them, involving warrants of arrest for violations of municipal ordinances, court clerks qualified as neutral and detached magistrates. There had been no showing whatever of partiality or bias, the record showed no connection with any law enforcement activity or authority which might distort the independence judgment the Fourth Amendment required, and there had been no demonstration that the clerks lacked capacity to determine probable cause or that the task of issuing warrants of the type involved was too difficult for them to accomplish.[3] The Court, as can be seen, was careful to limit its ruling to arrest warrants and it has been argued that different considerations might apply in the considerably more complex area of search and seizure where a layman might have greater difficulty in making the sophisticated judgments required;[4] as against this it has been observed that applications for search warrants invariably turn upon factual issues, that there is nothing inherent in the process of determining probable cause that puts it beyond the capacity of lay persons, and that 'holders of a law degree have no corner on common sense, the standard according to which affidavits for search warrants are to be tested and interpreted'.[5] On this view neutrality and capacity to make the probable-cause determinations required are all that is demanded.

Finally, it goes without saying that the presence of a direct personal interest, for instance the possibility of pecuniary profit, in the outcome of applications for search warrants negates the necessary detachment and neutrality. This was held to be the case in *Connally v. Georgia*[6] where the issuing justice of the peace was unsalaried but received a fee of $5 when a search warrant was issued but not when the warrant was denied. The justice's financial welfare therefore was enhanced only by positive and not by negative action, and this clearly brought about a situation which offered 'a possible temptation to the average man as a judge or which might lead him not to hold the balance nice, clear and true between the State and the accused'.

[1] *Hawkins v. State*, 203 S.E. 2d 622, 623 (1973).

[2] 407 U.S. 345 (1972).

[3] It should be noted that even though the Court did not determine the question whether a State could vest warrant authority in someone entirely outside 'the sphere of the judicial branch', the tenor of Powell, J's opinion suggests that before someone can qualify as a 'magistrate' capable of issuing warrants he should be connected with the judicial branch. What the Court wished to reject was the per se invalidation of a state or local warrant system on the ground that the issuing magistrate is not a lawyer or a judge.

[4] See *People v. Escamille,* 135 Cal. Rptr. 446 (1976).

[5] *People v. Mack*, 136 Cal. Rptr. 283 (1977).

[6] 429 U.S. 245 (1977).

(b) Probable cause

Search warrants can only be issued on the basis of probable cause.[1] But the necessity of a showing of probable cause is not confined to the issuing of search warrants, it being well established that probable cause must also be demonstrated both before arrest warrants can be issued and before warrantless searches or arrests can be held valid.[2] Naturally probable cause for arrest and probable cause for search cannot be completely equated since '(e)ach requires probabilities as to somewhat different facts and circumstances';[3] thus in the case of arrest probable cause means evidence or information of a certain degree of probative value warranting a reasonable belief that a crime of a given type has been committed and that a particular person is responsible for it,[4] whereas what justifies search warrants, or warrantless searches, is a sufficient showing that incriminating items, namely items reasonably believed to be connected with criminal behaviour, are located on the property to which entry is sought; a search warrant, in other words, unlike a warrant for arrest, is issued to enter and search premises or other property, and seize the evidence sought, does not require a showing that the occupant is guilty of any offence[5] and need only be supported by probable cause to believe that the items sought will be found in the place to be searched and that these are seizable by being adequately connected with criminal behaviour.[6]

Probable cause, defining the point at which the individual's interest in privacy must yield to the governmental interest in investigating criminal behaviour by searching for incriminating items,[7] is thus a fundamental concept of criminal procedure, in effect amounting to 'the best compromise that has been found for accommodating (two) often opposing interests'[8], on the one hand the interest of the citizen to be protected from unreasonable intrusions upon his privacy and security and on the other the interest of the community to be adequately protected by efficient law enforcement. 'Requiring more would unduly hamper law enforcement. To allow less would be to leave lawabiding citizens at the mercy of the officers' whim or caprice'.[9] But despite its importance probable cause remains an elusive concept, and

[1] See 1 W. LaFave, *Search and Seizure* 436–716 (1978).

[2] *Giordenello v. United States*, 357 U.S. 480, 485–6 (1958); *Aguilar v. Texas*, 378 U.S. 108 (1964).

[3] La Fave, 'Search and Seizure: "The Course of True Law . . . Has Not . . . Run Smooth" ', 1966 *U. Ill. Law Forum* 255, 260–1; see also *Zurcher v. Stanford Daily*, 436 U.S. 547, 556 (1978).

[4] La Fave, supra, at 260–1.

[5] T. Taylor, *Two Studies in Constitutional Interpretation* 48–9 (1969); see also *Zurcher v. Stanford Daily*, 436 U.S. 547 (1978); Amsterdam, 'Perspectives on the Fourth Amendment,' 58 *Minn. L. Rev.* 349, 358 (1974); 'Comment', 28 *U. Chi. L. Rev.* 664, 687 (1961).

[6] *Zurcher v. Stanford Daily*, 436 U.S. 547, 556 (1978).

[7] Greenawalt, 'The Right of Privacy', in *The Rights of Americans* 303 (N. Dorsen ed. 1971).

[8] *Brinegar v. United States*, 338 U.S. 160, 176 (1949).

[9] Ibid.

one that is difficult both to analyse and to reduce to more specific and manageable propositions. Often this results in platitudes with which it is difficult to disagree but which throw little light on what is required, as where it is said that 'when the State's reason to believe incriminating evidence will be found becomes sufficiently great the invasion of privacy becomes justified and a warrant to search and seize will issue'[1] or that '(t)he rule of probable cause is a practical, non-technical conception'[2] and must be approached as such. The process of elucidation best begins with stating what probable cause is not.

On the one hand it is clear that 'the term "probable cause" means less than evidence which would justify condemnation';[3] that the standard of probable cause is not the prima facie showing of criminal activity, but only its probability;[4] and that since there is a large difference between guilt and probable cause, as well as between the tribunals which determine them, there is 'a like difference in the quanta and modes of proof required to establish them',[5] which means not only that considerably less evidence is required for the issuance of an arrest or search warrant than for conviction, but also that legally unimpeachable findings of probable cause can rest upon evidence, for instance hearsay, which is not legally admissible at the criminal trial itself.[6] On the other hand it is equally clear that, whatever may have been the position previously, probable cause has come to mean more than bare suspicion,[7] the very purpose of the constitutional requirement being the impermissibility of search warrants being issued on loose and vague allegations, unsupported by any objective factual foundation. Probable cause is thus often contrasted in the cases with 'mere suspicion', official 'whim or caprice', 'mere rumour', or states of mind like personal intuition and unarticulable subjective feeling.[8] Probable cause then falls in between bare and unsubstantiated suspicion on the one hand and proof or even a prima facie showing of guilt on the other but not surprisingly it is simply not possible to say 'at precisely what point between th(ese) extremes probable cause is to be located'[9] or what (mathematically measured) quantum of evidence must be adduced before probable cause justifying a requested intrusion will be held to have been established. The central point of all explanations of probable cause appears to be 'a reasonable ground for belief'[10] that the search for which a

[1] *Fisher v. United States*, 425 U.S. 391, 400 (1976).

[2] *Brinegar v. United States*, 338 U.S. 160, 176 (1949).

[3] *Locke v. United States*, 7 Cranch 339, 348,3L. ed. 364, 367.

[4] See *Spinelli v. United States*, 393 U.S. 410, 419 (1969); see also *Beck v. Ohio*, 379 U.S. 89, 96 (1964).

[5] *Brinegar v. United States*, 338 U.S. 160, 173; see also *United States v. Ventresca*, 380 U.S. 102, 108 (1965).

[6] *Jones v. United States*, 362 U.S. at 272; *Aguilar v. Texas*, 378 U.S. at 114; *United States v. Ventresca*, 380 U.S. at 108.

[7] *Brinegar v. United States*, supra, at 175.

[8] See A.L.I., *Model Code of Pre-Arraignment Procedure* 293 n.12 (1975).

[9] La Fave, supra, at 476.

[10] *McCarthy v. De Armit*, 99 Pa. 63, 69, quoted with approval in *Carroll v. United States*, 267 U.S. 132, 161 (1925), and *Brinegar v. United States*, 338 U.S. 160, 175 (1949).

warrant is sought, or on the basis of which a warrantless search has been undertaken, will uncover seizable items providing evidence of crime. Perhaps the most often quoted definition is that probable cause exists if the facts and circumstances either within the officers' personal knowledge or of which they had trustworthy information are sufficient in themselves 'to warrant a man of reasonable caution in the (particular) belief'.[1] Probable cause in other words can be equated with reasonable cause, and denotes a substantial, concrete and objective basis in fact supporting the officers' belief that a given state of affairs justifying official action exists.[2]

Analysis of probable cause in terms of 'reasonable grounds to believe' raises two difficult problems:[3] first, does probable cause only exist if the factual basis on which the warrant is sought is more probable than not, and secondly, is probable cause a fixed or a variable concept? As regards the first issue, some commentators have taken the view that probable cause can only be present if the existence of the fact which it is sought to establish is more probable (i.e. likely to exist) than its absence 'since it would be strange to speak of someone believing something he thinks is less probable than not'.[4] On this view if for instance the evidence shows only a 33⅓ per cent chance that a seizable object will be found in a particular place the application for a search warrant must be rejected because the degree of probability is less than 50 per cent. But the Supreme Court has never required either (in the case of arrest) that guilt should be more probable-than-not or (in the case of search and seizure) that it should be more-probable-than-not that the seizable items will be found where they are thought to be. Its general attitude is summed up well by what was said in *Brinegar v. United States*: 'In dealing with probable cause we deal with probabilities. These are not technical; they are the factual and practical considerations of everyday life on which reasonable and prudent men, not legal technicians, act.'[5] Accordingly, the overwhelming majority of courts and commentators have taken the view that the more-probable-than-not standard is far too strict; that mathematical tests, whether based on the more-probable-than-not standard or any other fixed degree of probability, are unsuitable; and that it is enough if the officer's belief in the existence of the relevant facts is reasonable and substantial, going beyond mere suspicion, and resting on an objective and concrete factual basis that is capable both of articulation by the officer himself and of consideration and ultimate

[1] *Carroll v. United States*, supra, at 162.

[2] The *Model Code*, supra, prefers the formulation of 'reasonable cause' to 'probable cause' since the latter might be thought to carry the implication that guilt must be more probable than not. It is pointed out that in earlier times the word 'probable' only meant 'that which was capable of being proved or worthy of belief' and was not linked to 'more recent notions of probabilities measured mathematically'. It is therefore thought inappropriate to use the word 'probable' in a modern statute even though of course 'probable cause' is the term used in the Fourth Amendment.

[3] Greenawalt, supra, at 303.

[4] Ibid.; see also La Fave, ' "Street Encounters" and the Constitution: *Terry, Sibron, Peters,* and Beyond,' 67 *Mich. L. Rev.* 29, 73–5 (1968); for clarification, see La Fave, supra, at 476–93.

[5] *Brinegar v. United States*, supra, 338 U.S. at 175.

evaluation by the issuing magistrate.[1]

The second problem, whether probable cause is a fixed or variable concept, is considerably more difficult. The phrases 'probable cause', 'reasonable cause' and 'reasonable grounds' to believe (that the specific things to be searched for are to be found on the property to which entry is sought) suggest that probable cause is not a matter of degree varying either with the type of crime under investigation or with any other particular circumstance, but a fixed and objective standard; the requirement of probable cause cannot therefore be found satisfied in some cases by a lesser quantum of evidence than what would be insisted on in others. On this view probable cause is the prerequisite for any legitimate intrusion into a person's security; without it the exercise of police power is arbitrary;[2] and to dilute it in some cases in the interests of law enforcement would be 'to water down constitutional guarantees and give the police the upper hand'.[3] An alternative theory asserts that since probable cause performs the essential role of mediating between opposing personal and societal interests it should not always be approached in the same way; that the requirement of probable cause should not invariably demand the same amount of evidence irrespective of the nature of the suspected crime or the degree of intrusiveness of the particular invasion of privacy; and that a sliding scale approach, determining the reasonableness—and hence the constitutionality—of each official investigative action by balancing, on the one hand, the governmental interest invoked in support of the intrusion (including the degree of suspicion entertained by the police) against, on the other, the endangered personal interest (including the severity of the particular invasion), is better calculated to capture the spirit of the Fourth Amendment and effect a sensible compromise between essential protection for the citizen and the legitimate claims of law enforcement than 'the present monolithic model'[4] which insists on the production of the same quantum of evidence before action falling within the boundaries of the Fourth Amendment can be held to be lawful.[5] This problem is also dealt with elsewhere. Here three points must be made. To begin with, whatever the deficiencies of monolithic systems insisting on the same quantum of evidence and the same degree of probability irrespective of the circumstances of the individual case, sliding scale approaches and graduated models would produce incredible complication,[6] would result in the dilution of traditional safeguards, and would inevitably reduce Fourth Amendment protections to the prescription that the legality of searches and seizures should depend not on conformity with objective and constant criteria but on overall reasonableness; there might in other words be the demise of an independent

[1] Model Code, supra, at 293, 294–6.

[2] See 'Brief for the N.A.A.C.P. Legal Defence and Educational Fund, Inc. as Amicus Curiae' at 56–7, *Terry v. Ohio*, 392 U.S. 1 (1968), quoted in Amsterdam, 'Perspectives on the Fourth Amendment', 58 *Minn. L. Rev.* 349, 393–5 (1974).

[3] *Terry v. Ohio*, 392 U.S. 1, 39 (1968), per Douglas, J. dissenting.

[4] Amsterdam, supra, n.2, at 393–4.

[5] See Barrett, 'Personal Rights, Property Rights and the Fourth Amendment', 1960 *Sup. Ct. Rev.* 46, 63; see also 1 W. La Fave, *Search and Seizure* 450–9 (1978).

[6] See Amsterdam, supra, at 393–4.

probable cause doctrine and reversion to currently discredited notions allowing liberal departures from the warrant process in the name of overall reasonableness, ultimately the reasonableness of any particular intrusion determining whether probable cause existed.[1] Broad balancing approaches, accompanied by the general recognition of the variability of the requirement of probable cause, are therefore most unlikely to carry the day. The second point, however, recognises that in at least two areas, that of administrative inspections and that of the 'stop-and-frisk' cases, to be discussed in greater detail elsewhere, invasions of Fourth Amendment rights can proceed on less stringent standards of probable cause, not entailing reasonable cause to believe that the 'evidence' ultimately to be seized will be uncovered by the particular intrusion.[2] In the former the Supreme Court decided[3] that the warrant requirement of the Fourth Amendment does apply to administrative inspections, which as we have seen are entries under health and safety regulations, but that probable cause for the issuance of 'administrative' warrants exists not only, as orthodox theory would have it, when available information reasonably supports the conclusion that conditions within a specific building constitute a violation of a particular provision, but also when reasonable legislative or administrative standards (based upon such things as the passage of time or the condition of the entire area) for conducting an area-wide inspection are satisfied with respect to a particular building. This dilution of traditional probable cause was explicitly premised on a balancing of 'the need to search against the invasion which the search entails'.[4] More fully, the two factors in the area of administrative inspections which were thought to warrant the adoption of a less exacting probable cause standard were, first, the compelling public interest demanding that reasonable municipal health and safety standards be enforced, it being highly improbable that adherence to traditional probable cause concepts would achieve acceptable results, and, secondly, the relatively minor invasion of privacy usually entailed by administrative entries.[5] 'Reasonableness,' the Supreme Court emphasised, was 'the ultimate standard'.[6] If 'a valid public interest justifie(d) the intrusion contemplated', then there would be 'probable cause to issue a suitably restricted search warrant'.[7] The Supreme Court used similar balancing reasoning in the 'stop-and-frisk cases' where the issue was whether police officers could stop a person and subject him to a limited search for weapons in the absence of probable cause for a full arrest. It was decided[8] that, even though 'stop and frisk' practices are within and therefore have to be consistent with the Fourth Amendment, probable cause as traditionally understood is not necessary and therefore does not have to be present before

[1] Ibid.; see also Greenawalt, 'The Right of Privacy,' in *The Rights of Americans* 305–6 (N. Dorsen ed. 1971).

[2] See Greenawalt, supra; La Fave, supra, at 450–1.

[3] *Camara v. Municipal Court*, 387 U.S. 523 (1967).

[4] Ibid., at 537.

[5] Ibid.

[6] Ibid., at 538.

[7] Ibid., at 539.

[8] *Terry v. Ohio*, 392 U.S. 1 (1968).

brief police seizures and limited searches for weapons can be held to be reasonable, and therefore constitutional. Instead such limited official intrusions will be upheld where a police officer observes conduct which leads him reasonably to conclude that 'criminal activity may be afoot'[1] and that the individual confronting him is armed and dangerous. In these two areas, it can be seen, traditional probable cause has been relaxed, partly because of the state interests at stake militating in favour of speedy governmental action and partly because 'the practices at issue were somewhat unique and clearly distinguishable from the typical arrest or search in that they involved a lesser intrusion into freedom and privacy'.[2] As a general matter it therefore appears unlikely that the *Camara—Terry* balancing approach will be carried over into cases involving criminal investigations aimed at securing convictions. But even here there are occasional hints that probable cause standards may vary depending either on the type of crime at issue or on the degree of intrusion.[3] As regards the former there are judicial pronouncements to the effect that the seriousness of the offence should be taken into account and in certain cases allowed to legitimise police action in the absence of traditional probable cause. Thus in *United States v. Soyka*[4] Judge Friendly was not at all averse to straightforward recognition that the gravity of the suspected crime should be a factor bearing on the validity of decisions to arrest or search, in *People v. Sirhan*,[5] involving a search of Sirhan's room after the assassination of Senator Kennedy, 'the mere possibility' of evidence of a conspiracy to assassinate prominent political leaders was held to justify a search unsupported by either a warrant or conventional probable cause, and elsewhere it is candidly acknowledged that absence of probable cause will not jeopardise the legality of official action undertaken in the interests of preserving life or averting other serious consequences.[6] But even these cases and pronouncements do not necessarily support a relaxation of probable cause standards when a serious offence is being investigated. A more plausible explanation of the scanty materials, and an approach that will do considerably less damage to the accepted structure of Fourth Amendment law, is to justify such 'emergency' types of police action geared to the prevention of serious consequences not in terms of a theory varying the necessary quantum of evidence depending on the seriousness of the suspected offence but on the basis of their 'utility . . . for purposes other than securing a conviction'.[7] In other words, emergency police action taken in the interests of protecting the community and necessitated by the exigencies of a particular situation is valid even in the absence of probable cause. Here it can indeed be said either that probable cause standards must be relaxed or that the official intrusion complained of must only be tested against the broad constitutional mandate of reasonableness, which naturally makes it essential to focus upon the

[1] Ibid., at 40.
[2] La Fave, supra, at 450.
[3] See *Brinegar v. United States*, 338 U.S. 160 (1949), per Jackson, J. dissenting.
[4] 394 F. 2d 443 (1968), in a dissenting opinion.
[5] 497 P. 2d 1121 (1972).
[6] See section on 'Emergency Entries and Searches', at 188–200.
[7] *United States v. Soyka*, 394 F. 2d 443, 452 (1968), per Friendly, J. dissenting.

governmental or societal interest invoked in justification. But where what is in issue is police action directed against a particular individual and aiming at his eventual apprehension and conviction fixed probable cause standards, demanding in terms of theory the same quantum of evidence and degree of probability, must be met, whether the suspected offence is murder or some minor violation. In the area of search and seizure this means first that any entry to secure evidence of crime against either the possessor of the premises or some other person must be capable of justification in terms of probable cause, and secondly that what probable cause connotes is reasonable cause to believe that the specific 'things' to be searched for and seized are located on the particular property.[1]

The converse situation to a relaxation of probable cause in view of the gravity of the suspected crime is its stiffening in cases where the official action that is sought to justify is especially intrusive. It has thus been argued that even though a given quantum of evidence reaching on a notional mathematical scale a certain degree of probability would be enough to meet the requirements of the Fourth Amendment where a conventional search or seizure is involved, greater justification, that is over and above what would suffice for an ordinary demonstration of probable cause, is constitutionally necessary where the governmental search or other intrusion entails a peculiarly severe impairment of the citizen's privacy;[2] influential calls have therefore been made that, at least in certain contexts, the showing of justification should match the degree of intrusion *and* that this should be reflected in the explicit recognition that a higher standard of probable cause is required in the case of certain particularly intrusive police activities, as where what is in issue is a search during the night or a method of obtaining evidence that is open to serious abuse, for instance eavesdropping or penetration beneath the body's surface.[3] But others have objected to any suggestion that probable cause is a matter of degree,[4] even though it is clear that to increase the required quantum of evidence necessary to support probable cause in a small number of select and well-delineated areas would not bring about either the chaotic and undesirable results to which across-the-board sliding-scale approaches would inevitably lead or the resuscitation of discredited theories of overall reasonableness.

To summarise, as a general matter, probable cause appears to be a fixed concept; this is justifiable not only because sliding-scale versions would produce multiple gradations and innumerable categories but also because the very flexibility of balancing tests usually ends by fatally compromising the predictability and deterrence of orthodox models; probable cause therefore requires the same quantum of evidence concerning the relevant conclusion, here the location of seizable evidence of crime, and does not vary either with the nature of the crime or with any other particular factor, even though

[1] See *Zurcher v. Standard Daily*, 436 U.S. 547, 556 (1978).

[2] La Fave, supra, at 452–4.

[3] See *Berger v. New York*, 388 U.S. 41 (1967), per Stewart, J. concurring; *Gooding v. United States*, 416 U.S. 430 (1974), per Marshall, J. dissenting.

[4] See *United States v. Falcone*, 505 F. 2d 478 (1974).

naturally all facts and circumstances must be taken into account in making probable cause determinations; but in two areas, that of administrative inspections and in 'stop and frisk' cases, traditional probable cause has been supplanted by more lenient standards geared to overall reasonableness, and, similarly, where there is a pressing need for immediate action, even full-scale searches may be made in the absence of probable cause; finally, in certain very exceptional cases the degree of intrusion entailed by the search may be held to demand not only reasonable grounds to believe in the existence and discoverability of incriminating evidence, but also a very clear showing 'that in fact such evidence will be found'.[1]

(c) Applications for search warrants

A search warrant can only be issued on the basis of an application requesting the magistrate's permission to enter and search premises, and seize specific evidence of crime. An application for a search warrant is invariably made by a law enforcement officer, and normally takes the form of an affidavit the purpose of which is to set before the magistrate facts and circumstances tending to show or from which it may be inferred that the things to be seized are connected with criminal activity and that these can be found at the place or on the person to be searched.

The affidavit on the basis of which a search warrant is sought is clearly of central importance to the scheme of the Fourth Amendment, and on many occasions the Supreme Court has dealt with what affidavits must contain before they can support findings of probable cause. Two broad propositions dominate the cases. First, affidavits for search warrants, 'normally drafted by non-lawyers in the midst and haste of a criminal investigation', must be tested and interpreted not in a legalistic but 'in a commonsense and realistic fashion';[2] and in assessing the sufficiency of affidavits and determining probable cause issuing magistrates should neither confine themselves by 'niggardly limitations or by restrictions on their common sense'[3] nor insist on '(t)technical requirements of elaborate specificity once exacted under common law pleadings'[4]; for there is a very real danger that '(a) grudging or negative attitude by reviewing courts towards (applications for search) warrants will tend to discourage police officers from submitting their evidence to a judicial officer before acting',[5] which in turn will encourage warrantless searches. But, secondly, since the very purpose of the warrant requirement is to interpose the meaningful scrutiny of a disinterested judicial officer between the police and the citizen, probable cause cannot be made out by affidavits which are purely conclusory, merely stating the applicant's suspicion or belief that probable cause exists without setting forth and detailing some of the 'underlying circumstances' upon which that suspicion or belief is based;[6] this

[1] *Schmerber v. California*, 384 U.S. 757 (1966); see La Fave, supra, at 454.
[2] *United States v. Ventresca*, 380 U.S. 102, 108 (1965).
[3] *Spinelli v. United States*, 393 U.S. 410, 419 (1969).
[4] *United States v. Ventresca*, supra, 380 U.S. at 108.
[5] Ibid.
[6] *Aguilar v. Texas*, 378 U.S. 108, 114 (1964).

means that an affidavit on the basis of which a search warrant is requested must contain at least some of the facts and circumstances upon which the affiant's belief that particular incriminating items can be found in the place which it is sought to enter is based and by which it is reasonably supported; for unless sufficient material demonstrating seizability and location is put before the issuing court enabling it to reach independent probable cause determinations the magistrate will be unable to perform his neutral and detached function and will serve 'merely as a rubber stamp for the police'.[1] Two good examples of the basic principle that it is the magistrate himself and not the police who must decide whether the basis for issuing warrants exists are *Nathanson v. United States*[2] and *Giordenello v. United States.*[3] In the former a warrant issued on the basis of a sworn allegation that the affiant 'has cause to suspect and does believe' that certain property was in a specified location was held to be contrary to the Fourth Amendment as the affidavit 'went upon a mere affirmation of suspicion and belief without any statement of adequate supporting facts'; mere affirmation or belief or suspicion was not enough, the Court declared, and probable cause had to be inferred 'from facts or circumstances presented' to the magistrate. In *Giordenello* the affiant had sworn that the defendant on or about a given date had received and concealed narcotics in violation of federal law. Inferences as to probable cause had to be drawn by judicial officers, the Court repeated, and the purpose of a complaint or affidavit was to enable the appropriate magistrate to determine whether the 'probable cause' required to support the warrant existed. 'The (magistrate) must judge for himself the persuasiveness of the facts relied on by a complaining officer and should not accept without question the complainant's mere conclusion.' In the light of these principles the warrant was invalid because it did not provide 'any basis' for a judicial determination that probable cause existed.

Particularly difficult problems are caused by the inclusion in the affidavit of hearsay evidence, when, that is, the person applying for the search warrant seeks to rely on tips from informers.[4] The broad principle that has been accepted is that hearsay may be included in the affidavit and indeed form the basis for the issuance of the search warrant 'so long as there (is) a substantial basis for crediting the hearsay'.[5] This rather cryptic statement has been 'explained' by the Supreme Court on a number of occasions. In *Aguilar v. Texas*[6] the warrant was based on an affidavit stating that the affiants had

[1] *United States v. Ventresca*, 380 U.S. 102, 109 (1965).

[2] 290 U.S. 41 (1933).

[3] 357 U.S. 480 (1958).

[4] It is now settled that the informant's identity need not be disclosed where a warrant for arrest or search is being requested (see *Aguilar v. Texas*, supra, 378 U.S. 108, at 114). Nor, it was decided in *McCray v. Illinois*, 386 U.S. 300 (1967), does a different principle apply where what is in issue is the legality of a warrantless search or arrest. 'The Fourth Amendment is served if a judicial mind passes upon the existence of probable cause' (*State v. Burnett*, 201 A. 2d 39, 45 (1964)); but on a motion to suppress the judge may, in his discretion, order disclosure if this is needed in the interests of justice (see 'Note', 81 *Harv. L. Rev.* 196–200).

[5] *Jones v. United States*, 362 U.S. 257, 272 (1960).

[6] 378 U.S. 108 (1964).

received 'reliable information from a creditable person' to the effect that narcotics were being illegally kept at the defendant's premises. The affidavit was held by a majority to be insufficient to establish probable cause; indeed the vice in the impugned complaint was 'at least as great as in *Nathanson* and *Giordenello'*, for here the 'mere conclusion' that the defendant possessed narcotics was not even that of the affiant himself but that of an unidentified informant. The Court did not doubt that an affidavit could be based on hearsay information, not reflecting the direct personal observations of the affiant, but it was essential that the magistrate should be informed of 'some of the underlying circumstances from which the informant concluded that the narcotics were where he claimed they were' *and* of 'some of the underlying circumstances from which the officer concluded that the informant . . . was "credible" or his information "reliable" '.[1] Thus a complaint including or based on hearsay can only provide a foundation for the neutral judgment that resort to the criminal process is justified if it includes information of two distinct types: first, information which, if true, would show that the criminal evidence that is sought is indeed where it is said to be, and secondly, information relating to the credibility of the real source of the incriminating testimony and tending to establish the reliability of the informant.[2] *Aguilar's* 'two-pronged test'[3] was elaborated and applied in *Spinelli v. United States*[4] where a search warrant had been granted on the basis of an affidavit alleging among other things that a 'reliable informant' had informed the police that the defendant was involved in illegal gambling operations. It was held that probable cause had not been shown for the issuance of the warrant since *Aguilar's* two standards had not been satisfied, the affidavit neither containing any reason in support of the conclusion that the informant was 'reliable' nor sufficiently stating the underlying circumstances from which the informant had concluded that the defendant was engaged in illegal gambling activities. The central point of Justice Harlan's *Spinelli* opinion was the rejection of a 'totality of circumstances' approach, under which an informant's tip must be evaluated as a whole; 'a more precise analysis' was necessary, the majority observed; under this evaluation of the content of the tip—whether, that is, this would, *if* true, provide a sufficient basis for probable cause—and assessment of the reliability of the information—namely the trustworthiness of the particular informer as indicated by independent corroborative evidence—were analytically distinct; both *Aguilar's* requirements had to be satisfied, which meant that one could not argue from satisfaction with the contents of the tip to the conclusion that the information itself was trustworthy since, however detailed the tip, there would still be a possibility that the information might be fabricated; hence the *Aguilar—Spinelli* requirement that there should be independent evidence before the magistrate going to the credibility of the informant. This strict approach has been weakened by *United States v. Harris*,[5] which seems to

[1] Ibid., at 114.
[2] See *Jaben v. United States*, 381 U.S. 214 (1965).
[3] *Spinelli v. United States*, 393 U.S. 410, 413 (1969).
[4] 393 U.S. 410 (1969).
[5] 403 U.S. 573 (1971), noted in 43 *U. Colo. L. Rev.* 357 (1972); see also 85 *Harv.*

mark a return to the older (and looser) 'substantial basis' approach used before *Aguilar* and *Spinelli*. In *Harris* a warrant had been issued on the basis of an affidavit stating that the informant, 'a prudent person', had told the affiant, a federal tax investigator, that he had often bought illegally distilled whiskey at Harris's house. Some further detail from the informer's personal observation was given in the affidavit about the defendant's activities. There was no indication that the informer had given reliable information before and there was no other evidence of his trustworthiness as a source of information, but the tax investigator's affidavit asserted that Harris had a reputation as a person dealing in illegal whiskey, observed that others had supplied information about his activities, and reported that some illegal whiskey had been found in a house under his control within the previous four years. It was argued that the warrant had been issued illegally since the tax investigator's affidavit contained no evidence concerning the issue of the informer's reliability, and there is little doubt that *Spinelli*'s strict analysis would suggest that even though the informer's tip satisfied the first *Aguilar* test—since his description of the defendant's criminal activity, if true, provided a factual basis for a finding of probable cause—no independent evidence as to the informer's credibility had been placed before the magistrate enabling him to decide whether the information was indeed true. But by a majority of 5 to 4 the Supreme Court decided that the affidavit provided enough information for a determination of probable cause and that therefore the warrant had been lawfully issued. Chief Justice Burger did not think that *Aguilar* and *Spinelli* had questioned the 'substantial basis' approach of earlier cases, and suggested that the affidavit had to be considered as a whole to see whether it could support a finding of probable cause; nor could the contents of the tip and the issue of credibility be rigidly separated, since, according to the majority, a detailed allegation by the informant of criminal activity might of itself (at least when, as in the instant case, it was coupled with the investigator's own knowledge of the suspect's reputation) not only provide a sufficient factual basis to satisfy the first of *Aguilar*'s tests but also corroborate the reliability of the informer and the trustworthiness of his information, satisfying in this way *Aguilar*'s second test as well. Under this 'flexible'[1] approach the two *Aguilar* tests merge, and the *Spinelli* requirement that evidence distinct from the allegation or description of criminal activity and showing the informant's reliability should be put before the magistrate no longer plays an independent role in the assessment of the sufficiency of affidavits.[2] The test now seems to be 'whether the information given by the informant, taken in the light of the totality of circumstances, can reasonably be said to be reliable'.[3]

L. Rev. 53 (1971).

[1] *United States ex rel. Saiken v. Bensinger*, 489 F. 2d 865, 867 (1973).

[2] Four members of the Court in *Harris* also thought that the informer's admissions of crime carried 'their own indicia of credibility' and were themselves 'sufficient' to support a finding of probable cause; for criticism of this, see 43 *U. Colo. L. Rev.* 357, 366 (1972), and 'Note', 85 *Harv. L. Rev.* 53, 60 (1971).

[3] *United States v. Fiorella*, 468 F. 2d 688, 691 (1972); *United States v. Carmichael*, 489 F. 2d 983, 991 (1973).

(d) Particularity and specificity requirements

If the judicial officer is satisfied on the basis of the affidavit that probable cause exists he will issue a search warrant authorising the search and seizure requested. It is 'elemental'[1] doctrine that only those warrants which describe with particularity the place to be searched and the items to be seized are constitutional. The Fourth Amendment itself provides that no warrants should be issued except those 'particularly describing the place to be searched, and the persons or things to be seized', and it has been declared[2] that these 'precise and clear' words reflected the determination of those responsible for the Bill of Rights that there should be security 'from intrusion and seizure by officers acting under the unbridled authority of a general warrant'. The principle of particularity, insisting that descriptions of places, persons and effects in warrants should be such as to leave the executing officer with no doubt or discretion as to the premises he is to search or the items he is to seize,[3] is closely connected with the standard of probable cause, since, as has been seen, before probable cause justifying an official intrusion can be held to exist there must be found to be grounds supporting reasonable belief, not only that there has been some legal violation, but also that seizable property connected with such a violation is located on certain premises or on some other property which can be unmistakably identified so as to be capable of detailed specification.[4] Before standards of specificity are discussed two preliminary points must be made. First, in addition to an adequate description of any premises to be searched or items to be seized, a warrant must be addressed to, thereby authorising its execution by, an officer competent to execute search warrants, and must specify the grounds on which it was issued and the identity of the applicant and any other persons whose affidavits were submitted to the magistrate and on the basis of which probable cause was established;[5] in this connection it has been held that a warrant applied for and given on the basis of a fictitious name is void since '(w)hen the affiant is cloaked in secrecy there is no one who can be held responsible'[6] and the aggrieved party cannot then probe and challenge the validity of the search. Secondly, it may be that the vice of inadequate description in the warrant can be cured by a sufficiently detailed description of the premises or property in issue in the complaint or affidavit, provided this is incorporated in the warrant itself.[7] For the affidavit is not a part of the warrant,[8] and therefore a description in a detached affidavit, however

[1] *People v. Royse*, 477 P. 2d 380, 381 (1970) per Hodges, J.

[2] *Stanford v. State of Texas*, 379 U.S. 476, 481 (1965).

[3] *Marron v. United States*, 275 U.S. 192, 196 (1927); *Coolidge v. New Hampshire*, 403 U.S. 443, 467 (1971); *People v. Martens*, 170 N.E. 275, 276; *People v. Smith*, 169 N.E. 2d 777, 780; *People v. Staes*, 235 N.E. 2d 882, 885.

[4] *Lowrey v. United States*, 161 F. 2d 30 (1947); *Zurcher v. Stanford Daily*, 436 U.S. 547, 556 (1978).

[5] A.L.I., *Model Code of Pre-Arraignment Procedure* § SS 220.2 (Proposed Official Draft, 1975).

[6] *United States ex rel. Pugh v. Pate*, 401 F. 2d 6 (1968); *King v. United States*, 282 F. 2d 398 (1960); see also *Model Code*, supra, n.5, at 512.

[7] *People v. Staes*, 235 N.E. 2d 882, 885 (1968).

[8] *Hampton v. State*, 252 S.W. 1007; *Minton v. State*, 212 S.W. 2d 373.

detailed, cannot, without more, be used to aid an insufficient description in the warrant;[1] but if the affidavit is attached to the warrant, and the warrant either expressly adopts the description in the affidavit or even merely refers to it, the description in the affidavit is incorporated in the warrant 'by proper reference'[2] and the warrant is then valid.

Perhaps the most important part of a search warrant is the description of the place to be searched. It is difficult to set out detailed rules since each case, it has often been repeated, must be decided on its own facts and circumstances, but it is clear that the guiding principle is that while technical or complete accuracy is not insisted upon the description of the premises to be searched must be such that 'the officer with the search warrant can with reasonable effort ascertain and identify the place intended'.[3] In other words, the description of the premises requires no more than 'practical accuracy',[4] the test being not whether the description is completely accurate in every detail but rather 'whether it furnishes a sufficient basis for identification of the property so that it is recognisable from other adjoining and neighbouring properties'.[5] Whatever the preferable formulation of the specificity requirement, the essential point is that the description of the place should be such that unnecessary or unauthorised invasions of privacy are prevented and the executing officer is not allowed to use arbitrary or discretionary judgment, but only 'reasonable effort', as to what premises he is to search.[6] Particularly difficult problems are raised where an apartment house or other multiple-occupancy structure is searched.[7] It is settled doctrine that in terms of the Fourth Amendment 'searching two or more apartments in the same building is no different (to) searching two or more completely separate houses'.[8] Probable cause must therefore be shown for searching each apartment or sub-unit. If such probable cause is shown, and there is a search warrant for the apartment house or building in question, some hold that there is no reason for requiring a separate warrant for each resident since a single warrant can cover different apartments or sub-units in a single building.[9] But the general rule is that a search warrant must specify which sub-unit is to be searched where sub-units or multiple units exist.[10] An

[1] *People v. Staes*, supra, at 885; *O'Brien v. State*, 14 S.W. 2d 51.

[2] *United States v. Womack*, 509 F. 2d 368, 382 (1974); *People v. Staes*, supra, at 885; *Bloom v. State*, 283 So 2d 134.

[3] *Steele v. United States*, 267 U.S. 498, 503 (1924); *State v. Daniels*, 217 A. 2d 610, 614 (1966). The particularity requirement is discussed exhaustively in Mascolo, 'Specificity Requirements for Warrants under the Fourth Amendment: Defining the Zone of Privacy', 73 *Dick. L. Rev.* 1 (1968).

[4] *United States v. Santore*, 290 F. 2d 51 (1960); see also *United States v. Falcone*, 109 F. 2d 579, 582 (1940); *Townsend v. United States*, 253 F. 2d 461 (1958).

[5] *State v. Daniels*, 217 A. 2d 610, 615 (1966).

[6] *Steele v. United States*, 267 U.S. 498, 503 (1924); *Fine v. United States*, 207 F. 2d 324 (1953); *State v. Daniels*, 217 A. 2d 610, 614 (1966).

[7] 68 Am. Jur. 2d, *Searches and Seizures* § 77.

[8] *United States v. Hinton*, 219 F. 2d 324, 325–6 (1955).

[9] Ibid.

[10] *Tynan v. United States*, 297 F. 177 (1924); *People v. Franks*, 221 N.W. 2d 441, 443 (1974).

exception to the requirement that a search warrant which fails to specify a sub-unit is constitutionally defective has been recognised where the multiple-unit character of the premises is neither externally apparent nor known to the officer applying for or executing the warrant.[1] Thus, in *Owens v. Scafati,*[2] a search warrant was held to have described the premises to be searched with sufficient particularity despite its failure to recognise the dwelling's multi-unit character since there had been no showing that the police officers knew or should have known either from its physical appearance or from any other circumstance that the place in question was 'a multiple dwelling house'; and in another case[3] a search made under the authority of a warrant describing the place to be searched as '130 W. 74th Street, Basement Apt., N.Y.' was held valid even though there were a number of apartments in the building since it would have been impossible to discover this until after the search had taken place. But since the 'test is whether (the officers) should have known that the building was not a one-family house'[4] good faith on the part of the police in applying for and obtaining a warrant neither confined to the sub-unit in question nor supported by probable cause as to the remainder of the building will not be enough when they should have known better, as in *United States v. Esters*[5] where it was found that the officers who had made reasonable observation of the premises should have known that the structure searched was a two-family dwelling.

What about mistakes in the warrant? Since search warrants must not be read in 'a hypertechnical manner'[6] minor errors will be excused if the description of the premises is otherwise sufficient;[7] but if an error is not minor but goes to the substance of the warrant then the warrant cannot stand. If therefore the description of the place to be searched is in all essential respects adequate, and would have sufficed to support a valid search without reference to the number on the apartment door, the incorrect designation of the number will be held to be mere 'surplusage', not invalidating the search warrant;[8] but where a place has an established street address, and this is the only method of description used, only the correct address will suffice, and a 'wrong address' search warrant will involve failure to comply with minimum specificity standards.[9] It is also clear that in cases of errors which are not minor and would normally invalidate a warrant the executing police officer is not allowed to correct the deficiency prior to the intrusion. 'Since only a

[1] *Delly v. State*, 352 A. 2d 331, 333 (1976).

[2] 273 F. Supp. 428 (1967).

[3] *United States v. Ramos*, 282 F. Supp. 354 (1968).

[4] *United States v Esters*, 336 F. Supp. 214 (1972); see also *United States v. Santore*, 290 F. 2d 51 (1960); *State v. Chisholm*, 499 P. 2d 81 (1972); *Delly v. State*, supra.

[5] 336 F. Supp. 214 (1972); see also *People v. Franks*, 221 N.W. 2d 441, 444 (1974).

[6] *State v. Gillin*, 541 P. 2d 1150, 1151–2 (1975).

[7] *State ex rel. Flournoy v. Wren*, 498 P. 2d 444, 453 (1972); *State v. Gillin*, supra.

[8] *State v. Gallo*, 279 So. 2d 71, 72 (1973).

[9] *People v. Royse*, 477 P. 2d 380, 381–2 (1970).

judicial officer may issue a search warrant, it necessarily follows that only a judicial officer may alter, modify or correct the warrant.'[1] A modification of the apartment number in a search warrant by the executing officer is therefore improper and invalidates the warrant. But apparently in determining whether a description of premises in a search warrant is sufficiently detailed to satisfy constitutional standards of specificity the executing officer's prior knowledge, particularly where the executing officer was also the applicant on the basis of whose affidavit the magistrate issued the warrant in the first place, may be relevant and may be taken into account. It has therefore been held that where an error in the description of premises is innocent and technical, and there is additional descriptive language which is enough for a reasonably certain identification of the place in question, the personal knowledge of the executing officer as to the place intended to be searched is an element to be considered in determining whether the designation of the premises is sufficient.[2] But of course this does not mean that the officer's personal knowledge can cure a significantly deficient description.

Similar principles have been developed and applied in the case of descriptions in search warrants of persons[3] and vehicles.[4] Thus, even though there is not much authority on this subject since most cases deal with the search of places and the seizure of things, and not of persons, there is little doubt that a warrant for the search of a person must describe the person to be searched with the degree of specificity and accuracy insisted upon in the case of premises.[5] This means that where a search warrant is issued for the purpose of conducting a personal search the individual against whom the warrant is directed should be particularly described so that the executing officer will know for whom the warrant is intended.[6] If the name of the person is known it should be stated in the warrant.[7] If it is not known a reasonably accurate description of the person intended to be searched will suffice.[8] Otherwise the warrant will be declared invalid. It was therefore held in one case[9] that a warrant simply naming the person to be searched as 'John Doe' did not conform to the required specificity standards since if such a warrant were upheld the executing officer would be able to search anyone he wished. But if the direction to search 'John Doe' is followed by the detailed physical description of the defendant, coupled with the precise location at which he can be found, the warrant will be held to be valid as sufficiently particularised.[10] In the case of vehicles too the test is not absolute accuracy but

[1] Ibid.; see also *Hernandez v. People*, 385 P. 2d 996.
[2] See 68 Am. Jur. 2d, *Searches and Seizures* § 74; *State v. Walsh*, 199 S.E. 2d 38 (1973); *State v. Daniels*, 217 A. 2d 610, 615 (1966).
[3] See 'Annotation', 49 *A.L.R.* 2d 1209.
[4] See 'Annotation', 47 *A.L.R.* 2d 1444.
[5] *People v. Staes*, 235 N.E. 2d 882, 885 (1968).
[6] *Garrett v. State*, 270 P. 2d 1101 (1954).
[7] *Denmark v. State*, 108 P. 2d 550 (1940); 'Annotation', supra, n.3, at 1211.
[8] 'Annotation', supra, n.3.
[9] *People v. Staes*, 235 N.E. 2d 882 (1968).
[10] *United States v. Ferrone*, 438 F. 2d 381 (1971).

whether the description in the search warrant is sufficient to enable the officer to find and identify the vehicle with reasonable certainty.[1] Vehicular search warrants held to be constitutional normally describe the car to be searched by licence number, or by a combination of licence number and make of the car, or by a description of the make of the car.[2] The name of the operator of the car may also aid in its identification, as when a warrant authorising the search of '(an) automobile, make and licence number unknown, but believed to be Buick or Oakland, and operated by' the defendant and another person was upheld.[3]

Search warrants must, as the language of the Fourth Amendment makes clear, particularly describe the things to be seized. This is intended first to make general searches impossible and secondly to prevent the seizure of one thing under a warrant describing another.[4] As with the part of the warrant authorising entry and search of premises, so here too the purpose of the specificity requirement is to deprive the executing officer of arbitrary discretion and to confine his power to the more or less precise tasks of locating, identifying and seizing the property mentioned in the warrant; and as with the other types of case discussed above sufficient particularity and not complete accuracy is the test. Thus, a minute and detailed description of the property to be seized is not required, but the property must still be described in such a way that the officer making the search will not seize the wrong property.[5] A search warrant describing the items to be seized as an 'undetermined amount of United States currency' and 'weapons' was therefore held[6] to be constitutionally defective in that both descriptions were so vague as to vest the executing officers with broad discretion as to what they could seize. In contrast, and emphasising that the particularity requirement is 'a rule of reason'[7] mandating 'a common-sense interpretation, free from nit-picking',[8] it was held in one case that the evidence to be seized was adequately specified where it was described as 'specimen of head hair sample of the person' of the defendant[9] and in another that the seizure of a record book belonging to a firearms dealer under a warrant authorising the seizure of 'business records relating to purchase and sale of firearms' was proper since the warrant was not 'overly broad'.[10] It should also be noted that statements which would otherwise be considered to be fatally general will not be held to invalidate a search warrant if they can be given a sufficiently specific interpretation as a result of the particularity of the preceding sentences and the limiting impact of the overall context. A good example is *Andresen v.*

[1] 'Annotation', supra, at 111, n.4.
[2] *Bowling v. State*, 408 S.W. 2d 660 (1966); *State v. Olsen*, 445 P. 2d 926 (1968).
[3] *Wilkerson v. Commonwealth*, 255 S.W. 76 (1923).
[4] *Marron v. United States*, 275 U.S. 192 (1927).
[5] *People v. Prall*, 145 N.E. 610, 612 (1924).
[6] *People v. Holmes*, 312 N.E. 2d 248 (1974).
[7] *United States v. Scherer*, 523 F. 2d 371, 376 (1975).
[8] *Commonwealth v. Deren*, 337 A. 2d 600, 604 (1975).
[9] Ibid.
[10] *United States v. Scherer*, supra.

Maryland[1] where the Supreme Court dealt with warrants authorising the search of the business offices of an individual suspected of false pretences in connection with his real estate activities. Each warrant, at the end of an exhaustive list of particularly described documents, included the phrase 'together with other fruits, instrumentalities and evidence of crime at this (time) unknown', but the Court took the view that the challenged phrase was not a separate sentence but should be read as referring to the particular crime of false pretences being investigated. The warrants, accordingly, did not authorise the executing officers to conduct a search for evidence of other crimes, but only to search for and seize evidence relevant to the particular crime of false pretences, and were therefore valid.

An important principle that enjoys firm recognition is that the constitutional requirement that warrants must particularly describe 'the things to be seized' is to be accorded 'the most scrupulous exactitude'[2] when the 'things' are books, papers or related items. This is because a lesser standard would endanger the First Amendment protecting freedom of speech. It was therefore held in *Stanford v. State of Texas*[3] that a warrant authorising the seizure of 'books, records, pamphlets, cards, receipts, lists, memoranda, pictures, recordings and other written instruments concerning the Communist Party of Texas and (its) operations' was invalid, the Court remarking that '(t)he indiscriminate sweep of th(is) language (was) constitutionally intolerable' when what was in issue was 'literary material'.[4] But this principle, it must be noted, only applies where the basis of the challenged seizure is the content of the seized articles or the ideas they contain. Thus normal standards of particularity apply where the books the seizure of which is authorised are records of unlawful activities or contraband, for instance stolen goods.[5]

(e) Seizable items

The basic principle that is now accepted is that a search warrant may be issued for (a) the fruits of crime and contraband, (b) things used or intended to be used in the commission of crime, such as weapons, and (c) items of

[1] 427 U.S. 463 (1976).

[2] *Stanford v. Texas*, 379 U.S. 476, 485 (1965); see also *Marcus v. Search Warrant*, 367 U.S. 717; *A Quantity of Books v. Kansas*, 378 U.S. 205.

[3] 379 U.S. 476 (1965).

[4] Ibid., at 468.

[5] Ibid., at 485 n.16. For consideration of special problems regarding the question whether the procedures leading to the issuing and execution of search warrants authorising the seizure of books and the like were adequate in view of the need to protect First Amendment freedoms and avoid the suppression of constitutionally protected publications, see *Marcus v. Search Warrant*, 367 U.S. 717; *A Quantity of Books v. Kansas*, 378 U.S. 205 (1964); *Freedman v. Maryland*, 380 U.S. 51 (1965); *Blount v. Rizzi*, 400 U.S. 410 (1971); *Heller v. New York*, 413 U.S. 483 (1973); 'Note, The Prior Adversary Hearings', 46 *N.Y.U.L. Rev.* 80 (1971); 'Note, Prior Adversary Proceedings on the Obscenity Question', 70 *Colum. L. Rev.* 1403 (1970); and A.L.I., *Model Code of Pre-Arraignment Procedure* 517–20 (Proposed Official Draft, 1975).

evidentiary significance concerning the alleged offence in connection with which the search warrant is being sought.[1] But this was not always the position, since for a long time it was thought that the Fourth Amendment prohibited the seizure of mere evidence.[2] The distinction between the seizure of items of evidential value only, that was prohibited whether under the authority of warrants or not, and the seizure of instumentalities, fruits of crime or contraband, that could be effected either under properly issued warrants or in case an exception to the warrant process could be established, was developed in *Gouled v. United States,*[3] where the Supreme Court derived from *Boyd v. United States*[4] the proposition that search warrants may be resorted to 'only when a primary right to such search and seizure may be found in the interest which the public or the complainant may have in the property to be seized, or in the right to the possession of it, or when a valid exercise of the police power renders possession of the property by the accused unlawful and provides that it may be taken', only when, that is, the property that is sought is an instrumentality or fruit of crime, or contraband. As to these three categories a defendant has no proprietary or possessory right since the fruits of crime belong to the victim, weapons or other things used or intended to be used in furtherance of crime become the property of the State under an expansion of the ancient concept of deodand, and there can be no private right in what the law proclaims to be contraband. Thus when the State searches for and seizes such items it is pursuing and vindicating a proprietary or possessory right either of its own or of the victim of crime.[5] No such justification can be invoked when mere evidence is being sought. Search warrants, the *Gouled* Court therefore declared, could not be used as a means of gaining access to a man's house or office 'solely for the purpose of making search to secure evidence to be used against him in a criminal or penal proceeding'; and to permit mere evidence to be used against the defendant would in effect be to compel him 'to become a witness against himself'.[6]

The rule that mere evidence could not be seized, whether under a warrant or otherwise, was condemned from the very beginning. It was thus pointed out that nothing in the language of the Fourth Amendment supported the alleged distinction between mere evidence on the one hand and instrumentalities, fruits of crime of contraband on the other; that even though 'the rationale for this curious doctrine ha(d) never been satisfactorily

[1] See A.L.I., *Model Code of Pre-Arraignment Procedure*, 502–7 (Proposed Official Draft, 1975).

[2] See 'Note, Search and Seizure in the Supreme Court: Shadows on the Fourth Amendment', 28 *Univ. Chi. L. Rev.* 664 (1961); 'Note, Limitations on Seizures of "Evidentiary" Objects: A Rule in Search of a Reason', 20 *Univ. Chi. L. Rev.* 319 (1953); Maguire, *Evidence of Guilt* 182 (1959); 8 Wigmore, *Evidence* §§ 2184a and 2264 (McNaughton rev. 1961).

[3] 255 U.S. 298 (1921).

[4] 116 U.S. 616 (1886).

[5] See *State of New Jersey v. Bisaccia*, 213 A. 2d 185 (1965); *People v. Thayer*, 408 P. 2d 780 (1966).

[6] 255 U.S. at 309 and 311.

articulated'[1] it was almost certainly property concepts, particularly the theory that the sovereign may search for and seize only those objects which it is illegal to possess or to which he may assert a claim because they have been wrongfully obtained or used, that had fathered the *Gouled* rule and that these were unrelated both to the basic purpose of the Amendment which was to protect not property interests but personal rights to privacy and security (since obviously these would be disturbed not only by evidentiary searches but also by quests directed to the discovery of instrumentalities, fruits of crime or contraband and since the mere evidence rule whatever the protestations to the contrary could not prevent or limit exploratory searches) and to 'the real issues of individual privacy and law enforcement';[2] and that, again despite some of the opinions invoked in its support, the *Gouled* limitation could not plausibly be inferred from the Fifth Amendment protecting from compulsory self-incrimination since the mere evidence rule, although often invoked in cases involving the seizure of papers, was not limited to papers but purported to prohibit the seizure of any object that was merely evidential,[3] and since in any event, even in the case of self-incriminatory papers or writings, the privilege against self-incrimination does not prohibit their seizure but only efforts to obtain them by subpoena (for only in this second case would their production amount to an admission on the part of the defendant as to genuineness).[4]

Gouled was finally overruled in *Warden v. Hayden*[5] involving the hot pursuit of a fleeing felon and the warrantless seizure of items of clothing. The Supreme Court rejected the notion that property interests controlled the right of the government to search and seize, affirmed that the principal purpose of the Fourth Amendment was the protection of privacy and personal security rather than property, declared its determination to discard fictional and procedural barriers ultimately resting on property concepts, pointed out that the rationale most frequently suggested for the mere evidence rule, namely that it prevents exploratory searches since 'limitations upon the fruit to be gathered tend to limit the quest itself,[6] was not truly served by the *Gouled* doctrine and that in any case efficaciousness in promoting the cause of privacy could not suffice as a justification since many other arbitrary expedients also tending to protect privacy that might be devised would

[1] *People v. Thayer*, 408 P. 2d 780, 781 (1966), per Traynor, C.J.

[2] Ibid,; see also *State v. Bisaccia*, supra.

[3] Since the *Gouled* rule protected not private papers but mere evidence, private papers that were instruments of crime, for instance a spy's code books (*Abel v. United States*, 362 U.S. 217 (1960)) were subject to seizure.

[4] See Maguire, *Evidence of Guilt* 23 (1959); Meltzer, 'Required Records, the McCarran Act, and the Privilege Against Self-Incrimination', 18 *U.Chi. L. Rev.* 687, 700 (1951); 8 Wigmore, *Evidence* § 2184a (McNaughton rev. 1961).

[5] 387 U.S. 294 (1967). The *Gouled* principle had already been abandoned in a number of jurisdictions (see particularly *State v. Bisaccia*, supra, 114 n. 5, and *People v. Thayer*, supra, 114 n. 5), and had been ignored by the Supreme Court in *Schmerber v. California*, 384 U.S. 757 (1966) allowing the involuntary extraction of a blood sample in order to determine the presence of alcohol.

[6] *United States v. Poller*, 43 F. 2d 911, 914 (1930), per Learned Hand, J.

obviously be unsupportable, and expressed the view that even though the rejection of the mere evidence rule would naturally enlarge the area of permissible search privacy and security would still be jealously protected since legitimate police intrusions could only take place after satisfaction of the probable cause and particularity requirements of the Fourth Amendment, in the case of mere evidence probable cause meaning reason to believe that the evidence sought or seized will aid either in a particular apprehension or conviction, or in the investigation of a particular crime. But the *Hayden* Court did not rule out the possibility that there could still be some limit on the permissible objects of search and seizure, whether derived from the Fourth Amendment or from its interaction with the Fifth. Thus, Justice Brennan noted that the items of clothing involved in *Hayden* were not 'testimonial' or 'communicative' in nature and that as a result their introduction in evidence did not compel the defendant to become a witness against himself; it was not necessary therefore to consider whether there were 'items of evidential value whose very nature precludes them from being the object of a reasonable search and seizure'.[1]

One view, expressed both before and after *Warden v. Hayden*, is that there are such items which cannot legitimately be seized whether under a warrant or otherwise, and that a legitimate distinction can be drawn whether 'in terms of the underlying value the Fourth Amendment seeks to protect'[2] or in terms of an alleged close relationship between the Fourth and Fifth Amendments between tangible evidentiary items which can lawfully be seized and items of testimonial value, principally private papers, for instance 'a diary containing incriminating entries', which cannot.[3] On this view the Fourth and Fifth Amendments are interrelated, the traditional distinction drawn by Wigmore[4] between taking papers from a defendant by search and seizure and obtaining them from him by force of process, for instance by subpoena, is 'more shadow than substance'[5] since in either case the defendant is 'the unwilling source of the evidence and the Fifth Amendment forbids that he shall be compelled to be a witness against himself in a criminal case',[6] and therefore what cannot be obtained from the defendant without infringing the privilege against self-incrimination should likewise be outside governmental powers of search and seizure under the Fourth Amendment, whether by warrant or otherwise. A more limited theory would reject any ambitious doctrine that the Fourth Amendment protects broadly against the seizure of things whose compulsory production would be forbidden by the Fifth Amendment and would attempt to develop a distinct 'class of papers so intimately confidential and so much a part of personhood that they ought to enjoy a superlative privacy and be protected from seizure (even) upon an adequately grounded warrant'.[7] For

[1] 387 U.S. at 302–3.

[2] *State v. Bisaccia*, 213 A. 2d 185, 191 (1965), per Weintraub, C.J.

[3] *Hayden v. Warden*, 363 F. 2d 647, 657–8 (1966), per Haynsworth, C.J.

[4] 8 Wigmore, *Evidence* § 2264 at 379–80 (McNaughton rev. 1961).

[5] *Hill v. Philpott*, 445 F. 2d 144, 149 (1971).

[6] *Gouled v. United States*, 255 U.S. 298, 306 (1921).

[7] *Hill v. Philpott*, 445 F. 2d 144, 150 (1971), per Fairchild, J. dissenting; see *United States v. Bennett*, 409 F. 2d 888 (1969), where Friendly, J. suggested 'that an

policy reasons, in other words, mainly because '(a)n area of complete freedom for personal conversation and writing, so long as there is no furtherance of crime involved, preserves important First Amendment values'[1] and because seizure of private papers such as letters and diaries is felt to be a peculiarly severe impairment of privacy running 'perilously close to the ban on self-incrimination',[2] it has been suggested that private documents serving no purpose in the furtherance of any criminal enterprise but being admissions pure and simple should not be permitted objects of search or subjects of seizure.[3] But any exception for private papers to be immunised from powers of search and seizure would still not cover documents sought for reasons other than their testimonial content, for instance when it is sought to obtain handwriting samples.

A view more in accord with tradtional theory concerning the historical origins and functions of the Fourth and Fifth Amendments is that the boundaries of the protection demarcated by the self-incrimination clause are radically different from the parameters of the right to be secure from unreasonable searches and seizures in that the former only comes into operation if compulsion is applied against the defendant so as in effect to force him to give testimony that 'the articles produced are the ones demanded',[4] which is clearly not the case with seizures not involving the cooperative participation of the defendant, where, that is, proof of authenticity is only obtained by means of the testimony of other persons and without any employment of the accused's oath or testimonial responsibility;[5] that proposed limitations geared to testimonial or communicative contents are only relevant to the Fifth Amendment and utterly irrelevant to determinations about what may be seized under the Fourth Amendment; that in any event doctrines based on testimonial character are not very effective in protecting privacy since documents or private papers that are instrumentalities of crime have never been protected against seizure either under a search warrant or in connection with a reasonable search incident to a lawful arrest, which of course means that such documents must be read before it can be decided whether they are indeed instrumentalities of crime so that limitations on the nature of what may be seized do not necessarily narrow the search; and that therefore documents or papers, whether private or not, do not as such enjoy special sanctity in terms of what may be seized under the Fourth Amendment.

This orthodox theory, that the Fourth and Fifth Amendments cover radically different areas, that the Fifth cannot be invoked unless compulsion has been applied to the will of the defendant forcing him to incriminate

---

approach geared to the objective of the Fourth Amendment to secure privacy would seem more promising than one based on the testimonial character of what is seized'.

[1] *Model Code of Pre-Arraignment Procedure*, supra, at 505.

[2] Ibid.

[3] Ibid.

[4] 8 Wigmore, *Evidence* § 2264 at 379–80 (McNaughton rev. 1961).

[5] Ibid.; see *United States v. Bennett*, 409 F. 2d 888, 896 (1969).

himself, and that there are no evidential items whose testimonial character or contents preclude a valid search and seizure, seems now to have been adopted by the Supreme Court in *Andresen v. Maryland*,[1] a case involving the seizure under search warrants of specified business documents regarding a fraudulent sale of land. The Court admitted that in some earlier cases there were broad statements implying that the Fifth Amendment's self-incrimination clause applied not only to the compelled production of papers under a subpoena but also to the search for and seizure of a person's private papers, but did not regard them as accurate. The correct principle was that stated by Justice Holmes, that 'a party is privileged from producing the evidence but not from its production',[2] which of course means that the protection extended by the privilege against self-incrimination 'adheres to the person, not to information that may incriminate him'.[3] Thus, although an individual is protected by the Fifth Amendment from complying with a subpoena ordering the production of personal records in his possession because 'the very act of production may constitute a compulsory authentication of incriminating information',[4] that same material enjoys no similar immunity from an otherwise legitimate seizure since the individual against whom the search is directed is not required to aid in the production or verification of incriminating evidence. Even though *Andresen* dealt with business records, the tenor of the Court's opinion makes it most unlikely that the Fifth Amendment can ever be successfully invoked to prevent the seizure of papers, however confidential or intimate. But is it still possible that the seizure of some types of evidence, principally private papers, is prohibited by the Fourth Amendment?[5] Some have pointed out that *Andresen* did not deal with the Fourth Amendment question, and that it might still be possible that certain highly private papers should be held to be immune from search and seizure.[6] But this is highly improbable given both the conceptual clarity and traditional appeal of the orthodox theory set out above and the difficulty of developing sufficiently particularised and adequately principled categories within the framework of the Fourth Amendment forbidding certain types of seizure.[7] The logical implication of the overruling of *Gouled* is that any relevant evidence is within the reach of an otherwise lawful search and seizure, and that therefore '(n)o zone of privacy now exists that the government cannot enter (once the necessary conditions have of course been satisfied) to take an individual's property for the purpose

[1] 427 U.S. 463 (1976).

[2] *Johnson v. United States*, 228 U.S. 457, 458 (1913).

[3] *Couch v. United States*, 409 U.S. 322, 328 (1973).

[4] *Andresen v. Maryland*, 427 U.S. 463, 477 (1976); *Fisher v. United States*, 425 U.S. 391 (1976).

[5] See 1 W. La Fave, *Search and Seizure* 395–9 (1978).

[6] Ibid.; see also 'Note', 67 *J. Crim. L. & C.* 389, 396 (1976); *Hayden v. Warden*, 363 F. 2d 647 (1966); *Couch v. United States*, 409 U.S. 322 (1973), per Marshall, J., dissenting; T. Taylor, *Two Studies in Constitutional Interpretation* 70 (1969).

[7] But of course even if the Fourth Amendment is not interpreted to preclude the seizure and use in evidence of certain private documents it may still be desirable to develop a statutory prohibition upon their seizure (see La Fave supra, at 397, and *Model Code of Pre-Arraignment Procedure*, supra, § 210.3(2)).

of obtaining incriminating information'.[1]

Granted that mere evidence is not beyond governmental reach, 'to what extent is the government's means of acquiring such evidence limited by the constitutionally protected expectation of privacy of persons not suspected of criminal activity?'[2] This problem arose in an acute form in *Zurcher v. Stanford Daily*[3] where the police, acting under a warrant, searched the offices of the respondent, a student newspaper that had published articles and photographs of a clash between demonstrators and police, seeking to obtain photographs of demonstrators suspected of injuring a number of policemen. The basic question was what protection third parties not suspected of crime enjoyed under the Fourth Amendment. More specifically, were law enforcement agents required to explore the subpoena duces tecum alternative before seeking to obtain search warrants against third parties for materials in their possession? The District Court answered this in the affirmative,[4] holding that third parties are entitled to greater Fourth Amendment protection than suspects, that a warrant to search for criminal evidence reasonably believed to be located on the premises of a third party should not be issued except where the magistrate has before him an affidavit establishing proper cause to believe that the materials in question will be destroyed or that a subpoena duces tecum is otherwise impractical, and that therefore in third-party situations recovery of the objects or evidence sought should normally be effected by means of a subpoena. The Supreme Court disagreed, refused to read into the Fourth Amendment new limitations on the use of the warrant process, and affirmed what it regarded as orthodox doctrine. The critical element in a reasonable search, the Court declared, is not that the owner of the property which it is sought to enter and search is supected of crime but that there is reasonable cause to believe that the specific 'things' to be searched for and seized are located there. The Fourth Amendment therefore does not forbid the issuing of warrants to search property on which there is probable cause to believe that fruits, instrumentalities or evidence of crime can be found merely because the owner or possessor is not himself suspected of complicity in the crime being investigated; and once the government demonstrates probable cause to believe that incriminating evidence will be found at certain premises an invasion of privacy becomes justified and a warrant to search and seize can be issued even though the place to be searched is occupied by an innocent person.

(f) Execution of search warrants

Execution of search warrants raises many problems. Three of the most difficult will now be discussed. The first two concern the manner in which and the time when warrants can be executed, and the third relates to what can be seized under a validly issued warrant.

[1] 'Note', 76 *Mich. L. Rev.* 184, 211 (1977); see LaFave, supra, at 394.

[2] Kamisar, LaFave, Israel, *Modern Criminal Procedure* 226 (1974).

[3] 436 U.S. 547 (1978).

[4] *Stanford Daily v. Zurcher*, 353 F. Supp. 124 (1972), noted in 86 *Harv. L. Rev.* 1317 (1973).

(i) Manner of execution

Before an officer can execute a search warrant, and before therefore attempting an entry, he must give notice of his authority and purpose to the person to be searched or the person in apparent control of the premises to be entered.[1] Both the common law requirement—that the police officer executing the warrant must 'signify the cause of his coming and make a request to open the doors'[2]—and the constitutional standard—that prior to entry the police must announce their presence, authority and purpose[3]—have a similar twofold purpose, first to protect privacy and security by preventing police entry of the house without reasonable warning, and secondly to preclude violent resistance to unexplained intrusions, in this way reducing the possibility of danger to both officer and citizen which might result from misunderstanding and misinterpretation of the purpose of the entry.[4] For these reasons, but of course mainly because of its intimate relationship with fundamental rights to security from unlawful official intrusion,[5] numerous decisions in both the federal and state courts have recognised, as have the English courts, that the requirement of prior notice is not only 'deeply rooted in (the Anglo-American) heritage'[6] but also 'of the essence of the substantive protections which safeguard individual liberty'.[7] At the same time in almost all States there are exceptions to this so-called 'knock and announce' doctrine since it is generally recognised that rigid insistence on strict compliance with 'knock and wait' rules in the execution of search warrants, no matter what the circumstances, would hamper the orderly enforcement of criminal law and endanger compelling societal interests,[8] whether by exposing the executing officer to serious danger or by resulting in the destruction of the evidence or by jeopardising in other ways the safe execution of the warrant.[9] It is therefore broadly agreed that forcible entry without prior announcement of identity or purpose and a demand for admittance may be justified when 'exigent and necessitous circumstances exist',[10] but there is much uncertainty

[1] See A.L.I., *Model Code of Pre-Arraignment Procedure* 513–16 (Proposed Official Draft, 1975); 68 Am. Jur. 2d, *Searches and Seizures*, § 91; Wright, *Federal Practice and Procedure: Criminal* § 671; 'Note', 55 *Minn. L. Rev.* 871 (1971).

[2] *Semayne's Case,* 77 Eng. Rep. 194, 195 (1603); see also *Launock v. Brown*, 2 B. & Ald 592, 593–4, 106 Eng. Rep. 482, 483 (1819).

[3] *Ker v. California*, 374 U.S. 23 (1963); see also *Sabbath v. United States*, 391 U.S. 585 (1968); *Miller v. United States*, 357 U.S. 301 (1958).

[4] *Tatman v. State*, 320 A. 2d 750 (1974).

[5] *People v. Rosales*, 437 P. 2d 489, 492 (1968); but see *State v. Gassner*, 488 P. 2d 822, 824 (1971), where, in the absence of *Ker*, it would have been concluded that 'the announcement requirement is never of constitutional proportions'; see also Sonnenreich & Ebner, 'No-Knock & Nonsense, An Alleged Constitutional Problem', 44 *St. John's L. Rev.* 626, 646–7 (1970).

[6] *Miller v. United States*, 357 U.S. 301, 313–14 (1958).

[7] *Ker v. California*, 374 U.S. 23, 49 (1963), per Brennan, J. dissenting.

[8] *State v. Young*, 455 P. 2d 595, 598 (1969); *State v. Beason*, 534 P. 2d 44, 47 (1975).

[9] See *People v. Maddox*, 294 P. 2d 6 (1956); *People v. Carrillo*, 412 P. 2d 377 (1966); *People v. Gilbert*, 408 P. 2d 365 (1965).

[10] *State v. Young*, 455 P. 2d, at 598.

about both the identity of these exceptions and their reach.[1]

'No-knock' laws allowing in certain circumstances unannounced police entry into private houses are formulated in numerous ways,[2] and while it is clear that no-knock entries can in principle be constitutional,[3] many basic issues have not as yet been settled and much debate on when the notice requirement can constitutionally be disregarded by the executing officer continues. As a general matter non-compliance with generally applicable prior notice rules is excused when there are reasonable grounds to believe that insistence on prior announcement would increase the danger to the life and limb of the executing officer or other persons, frustrate an arrest, or permit the destruction or disposal of the evidence sought.[4] The peril to life and limb exception applies when it can be shown that without an immediate and unannounced entry the executing officer will be exposed to danger,[5] for instance when at the moment of entry he knows that the suspect is armed with a weapon which he has used in the past to resist arrest. Much greater difficulty attends the destruction of evidence exception. The main problem is this: Should the exception only come into operation when the destruction of the evidence sought is actually being attempted within the premises which it is proposed to enter, or is the ready destructibility of the evidence—the fact, in other words, that the property sought is usually easily and quickly destroyed—enough? In *Ker v. California*[6] police officers followed the defendant whom they had probable cause to suspect of possessing narcotics. While they were following him by car the defendant made a U-turn in the road and disappeared. The officers, without securing a search warrant, obtained a passkey from the building manager and entered the defendant's apartment, without prior notice; narcotics were discovered in plain view. The Supreme Court, by a narrow majority,[7] held that the officers' method of entry was not unreasonable and therefore not inconsistent with constitutional standards. Justice Clark, delivering the Court's opinion, did not doubt either that California's exception to the notice requirement where exigent circumstances were present was constitutional or that the necessary justification to excuse the officers' failure to give notice on the facts before them was 'uniquely present', both because of the officers' belief that the defendant was in possession of narcotics 'which could be quickly and easily destroyed' and because of his 'furtive conduct in eluding them shortly before the arrest' which provided support for the belief that he may well have been

[1] 'Note', 55 *Minn. L. Rev.* 871 (1971).

[2] *Model Code of Pre-Arraignment Procedure* 513–16 (1975).

[3] *Ker v. California*, 374 U.S. 23 (1963).

[4] See *People v. Gastelo*, 432 P. 2d 706 (1967); *People v. Rosales*, 437 P. 2d 489 (1968).

[5] See *Read v. Case*, 4 Conn. 166 (1822); *Ker v. California*, 374 U.S. 23, 54–5 (1963); *People v. Maddox*, 294 P. 2d 6, 9 (1956).

[6] 374 U.S. 23 (1963), discussed in 'Note', 55 *Minn. L. Rev.* 871, 882 et seq. (1971).

[7] Black, Stewart and White, JJ. joined Clark, J.'s opinion. Harlan, J. concurred only in the result. Warren, C. J. and Douglas and Goldberg, JJ. agreed with Brennan, J.'s dissent.

expecting the police. For these reasons the officers' method of entry was not unreasonable under the Fourth Amendment. Justice Brennan dissented on the ground that despite the possible existence of probable cause for a person's arrest the Fourth Amendment would still be violated by an unannounced police intrusion into a private home, with or without a warrant, except where the persons within already knew of the officers' authority and purpose, or where the officers were justified in the belief that persons within were in imminent peril of bodily harm, or where those within, made aware of the presence of someone outside, were then engaged in activity which warranted the officers in the belief that an escape or the destruction of evidence was being attempted. Since on the record before them the defendant was completely unaware of the officers' presence and there was absolutely no activity within the apartment capable of supporting the belief that anyone within was attempting to destroy evidence 'the minimal conditions' for the application of the destruction of evidence exception were, on Justice Brennan's view, simply not present.

Ker is not an easy case to interpret since Justice Clark in his majority opinion did not devote much time to the unannounced entry issue; and even though *Ker* certainly holds that it is constitutionally permissible to make an unannounced entry 'when it was likely that evidence would otherwise be destroyed',[1] much doubt remains about the proper scope of the destruction of evidence exception. Three types of situation, and three possible approaches, figure in the cases. To begin with, there are cases where the executing officers have reasonable cause to believe that persons within are engaged in the actual destruction of evidence, or that once their presence is known the destruction of evidence will be attempted, or that specific preparations for the destruction of evidence in the event of police entry have been made and can easily be put into operation.[2] Here, it is generally agreed, since '(t)here is no constitutional right to time in which to dispose of evidence',[3] compliance with applicable knock-and-notice provisions is excused 'not because of a blanket rule based on the type of crime involved but because the particular circumstances of the case give rise to a reasonable belief that immediate action is necessary to prevent the destruction of physical evidence'.[4] If, for example, the police have reliable information that the small quantity of narcotics they wish to seize is kept near a toilet so that it can easily be disposed of, or if when the police approach they hear indications that evidence is being destroyed, of if officers observe persons within a house in possession of easily disposable narcotics or other such evidence, notice in the form of an announcement and request for entry can be dispensed with.[5] Secondly, there are cases where no specific showing is made that unless immediate unannounced action is taken evidence will be destroyed, and where therefore non-compliance with the

[1] *State v. Gassner*, 488 P. 2d 822, 826 (1971), per Schwab, C. J.

[2] Ibid., at 826.

[3] *State v. Mitchell*, 487 P. 2d 1156, 1161 (1971), per Schwab, C. J.

[4] *State v. Harris*, 530 P. 2d 646, 654 (1975), adopting *People v. De Santiago*, 453 P. 2d 353, 359 (1969).

[5] See *State v. Gassner*, supra.

relevant notice requirement can only be excused on the basis of a theory that a blanket 'no-knock' policy is automatically permissible in certain situations, principally those involving narcotics, where the material evidence is, by its very nature, readily destructible.[1] The view that unannounced entry to execute a search warrant is always reasonable in narcotics cases on the ground that those involved in narcotics violations are normally on the alert to destroy the easily disposable evidence at the first sign of an officer's presence was supported by some early authorities but was decisively rejected by the California courts in a line of cases beginning with *People v. Gastelo*[2] where it was held that the requirement of prior notice of authority and purpose before forcing entry could only be departed from on the basis of the officer's reasonable and good faith belief that compliance would actualy permit the destruction of evidence. Such a belief must be based on the specific facts of the particular case and cannot be justified by a general assumption either that certain classes of persons are more likely than others to destroy evidence or that all cases involving easily disposable evidence are within the exceptions to the notice and demand requirement.[3] 'Under the Fourth Amendment a *specific* showing must always be made to justify *any* kind of police action tending to disturb the security of the people in their homes.'[4] Unannounced forcible entry, on the *Gastelo* reasoning, is a very serious disturbance of personal security and cannot be justified on a blanket basis. 'Just as the police must have sufficiently particular reason to enter at all, so must they have some particular reason to enter in the manner chosen.'[5] A third group of cases[6] refuse to adopt a blanket exception for narcotics or any other type of case, since then the destruction of evidence exception could well come close to consuming the general rule itself,[7] but are equally not persuaded that the strict *Gastelo* standard, which requires a particularised showing of imminent peril to the evidence on the specific facts of each case, is constitutionally required as an integral part of the Fourth Amendment, whether generally or by *Ker v. California*. Instead they attempt to develop an intermediate position[8] which is believed to be consistent with the notice requirement and yet makes adequate allowance for the practicalities of law enforcement. This holds that if before making a search the police have probable cause to believe that there is a small, readily disposable amount of evidence at the premises to be searched (or do not know the amount), and they *also* reasonably believe that there is a likelihood that the evidence might be destroyed if prior notice is given, then they may enter without requesting permission. But these two

[1] See *People v. De Lago*, 213 N.E. 2d 659 (1965); *Henson v. State*, 204 A. 2d 516 (1964).

[2] 432 P. 2d 706 (1967); see also *People v. Rosales*, 437 P. 2d 489 (1968); *People v. Marquez*, 77 Cal. Rptr. 967 (1969); *People v. De Santiago*, 453 P. 2d 353 (1969).

[3] *Rosales*, supra.

[4] *Gastelo*, supra, at 708.

[5] Ibid.

[6] *State v. Mitchell*, 487 P. 2d 1156 (1971); *State v. Gassner*, 488 P. 2d 822 (1971).

[7] See *Commonwealth v. McCloskey*, 272 A. 2d 271 (1970); *State v. Gassner*, 488 P. 2d 822, 827 (1971); *Gastelo*, supra.

[8] *State v. Gassner*, 488 P. 2d 822, 827–8 (1971), per Schwab, C. J.

conditions constitute 'the minimum showing'[1] necessary to invoke the destruction-of-evidence exception to the constitutional requirement that prior announcement be given.

(ii) Time of execution

Warrants are normally issued under state statutes which invariably provide that they must be served and executed within a given time, usually ten days.[2] Failure to execute a warrant within the specified period makes it void.[3] Can searches under the authority of warrants be conducted at night time? There is general agreement that night-time entries and searches involve a particularly severe impairment of the values underlying the Fourth Amendment,[4] (i)t (being) difficult to imagine a more severe invasion of privacy than the night-time intrusion into a private home',[5] and it has therefore been strongly argued[6] that as a matter of constitutional law searches conducted in the middle of the night should require a considerably more persuasive justification than ordinary daytime searches. On this view it is (or should be) Fourth Amendment doctrine that 'increasingly severe standards of probable cause are necessary to justify increasingly intrusive searches', and in some situations, the night-time search of a private home being one of the most obvious, this principle should require the showing of additional justification for a challenged invasion over and above that of the existence of probable cause.[7]

The constitutional question has not been resolved, as in most cases the matter of the timeof execution is governed by detailed statutory provisions. These assume a number of different forms;[8] in some jurisdictions 'the aversion to night time searches (felt) throughout the ages'[9] has not resulted in any special safeguards, i.e. there is no provision restricting, in the absence of unusual circumstances, the execution of warrants to daytime hours; indeed in some there is explicit statutory authorisation permitting execution at any time; but in other jurisdictions a search warrant can only be executed during daytime unless the warrant itself directs execution at night time,[10] and in most

[1] Ibid., at 828.

[2] See A.L.I., *Model Code of the Pre-Arraignment Procedure* 512–13 (Proposed Official Draft, 1975); 68 Am. Jur. 2d, *Searches & Seizures* § 110; Wright, *Federal Practice & Procedure: Criminal*, § 671.

[3] Wright, supra, § 671; Rule 41(c) Fed. Rules, as amended on Oct. 1, 1972, provides that the warrant shall command the officer to search within a specified period of time not exceeding 10 days. But this is merely the 'outer limit' (see Kamisar, La Fave and Israel, *Modern Criminal Procedure* 260 (4th ed. 1974)). If by the time the warrant is served, even within the ten days, probable cause no longer exists, the search is apparently illegal.

[4] See *People v. Watson*, 142 Cal. Rptr. 245 (1977), and Marshall, J.'s dissent in *Gooding v. United States*, 416 U.S. 430, 461 (1974).

[5] *Jones v. United States*, 357 U.S. 493, 498 (1958), per Harlan, J.

[6] By Marshall, J. in *Gooding v. United States*, supra, n.3, at 464 et seq.

[7] Ibid.

[8] See *Model Code*, supra, at 512.

[9] *State v. Wilson*, 540 P. 2d 1268, 1269 (1975), per Hathaway, J.

[10] See, for instance, California's Penal Code § 1533 (West Supp. 1971).

cases a warrant so stating can only be obtained on satisfaction of requirements additional to a showing of probable cause, normally either when 'the affidavits are positive that the property is on the person or in the place to be searched' or where 'good cause' or 'reasonable cause' has been shown.[1] As can be seen, even though in both types of regime a night-time search can only be directed on the basis of a demonstration of 'some reason thereof in addition to what would normally be probable cause for issuing the warrant in the first place',[2] the nature of the showing is different in the two cases. In the former, it is apparently enough if the affidavits contain positive evidence that the property is on the premises; if a reasonable inference can be drawn that this indeed is so the warrant can direct 'that it be served at any time', as in *Gooding v. United States*[3] where it was held, first that such a provision required no special showing for the need of a night-time search other than a showing that the contraband was likely to be on the property or person to be searched at the time, and secondly that such a showing had been made where an affidavit submitted by a police officer suggested that there was a continuing traffic of drugs from the suspect's apartment, a purchase through an informer confirming that drugs were available. It is more difficult to interpret the requirement of 'good cause' or 'reasonable cause' upon a showing of which the magistrates may insert a direction in a search warrant authorizing its execution at any time of the day or night, and in the absence of which the warrant can only be executed during the day.[4] Some cases adopt what has been called 'a broad and rather loose interpretation'.[5] On this a statute requiring 'good cause' invests the issuing magistrate with 'a broader discretion to direct a night time search'[6] than under a requirement that the affidavits be positive as to the location of the evidence; and in some cases 'good cause' for issuing a warrant that could be served during the night was principally if not exclusively based on the nature of the contraband, as in *Solis v. Superior Court*[7] where a night-time search of known heroin dealers was upheld even though the affidavits supporting the search warrant contained no specific facts necessitating a night-time intrusion, it being apparently enough that 'heroin is the most dangerous of the illicit drugs' and that 'heroin pushers are as active at night as during the day and probably more so'.[8] More recent pronouncements take a different view by transferring the reasoning of *People v. Gastelo*[9] from the manner of search to its timing. In the same way that *Gastelo* rejected the notion that forcible entries can be authorised by a blanket rule based on the type of crime or evidence involved it has been

[1] The first form is exemplified by Rule 41(c) Fed. Rules of Crim. Proc., before its amendment on Oct. 1, 1972. The second form is that of the current Rule 41(c).

[2] *Galena v. Municipal Court for Oakland—Piedmont Judicial District*, 47 Cal. Rptr. 88 (1965), per Sullivan, J.

[3] 416 U.S. 430 (1974).

[4] *State v. Wilson*, 540 P. 2d 1268 (1975).

[5] *People v. Watson*, 142 Cal. Rptr. 245, 246 (1977), per Franson, J.

[6] *Galena v. Municipal Court*, supra, at 95, per Sullivan, J.

[7] 408 P. 2d 945 (1966).

[8] Ibid., at 946.

[9] 432 P. 2d 706 (1967).

strongly argued[1] that since execution at night of a search warrant is a more serious invasion of the security of a man's home than day-time execution the magistrate's exercise of discretion in authorising the former cannot be based solely on the nature of the evidence to be seized or the type of crime involved, but must rest on more specific reasons deriving from the actual circumstances of the particular case why the severe intrusion entailed by a night-time search should be sanctioned. On this more exacting interpretation of the 'good cause' requirement the affidavits put before the magistrate must contain specific facts which show 'a necessity for service of the warrant at night rather than between the hours of 7 a.m. and 10 p.m.'.[2] In practice this apparently means that the magistrate, before authorising a night search, must be informed of facts from which it may reasonably be concluded that the evidence to be seized will not be in the place to be searched during the day.[3]

(iii) What may be seized?

One of the most fundamental principles of the law of search and seizure is that the scope of a search must be strictly tied to, and circumscribed by, the reasons and circumstances justifying its inception.[4] This principle, 'by (which) the Fourth Amendment protects the individual against unfettered discretion',[5] applies with equal force both to warrantless searches and to searches authorised by and undertaken under warrants, and its two most obvious consequences in the particular case of warrants are, first that the scope of the search must be such as is authorised by the warrant and is reasonably necessary to discover the things specified, and, secondly, that once the things so specified are discovered the search must proceed no further. But what if in the course of an otherwise valid search the officers come across things not specified in the warrant but which they reasonably suspect to be connected with, and to afford evidence of, criminal behaviour? Can these unspecified things also be taken into police possession, or should only those items particularly specified in the warrant be subject to seizure?[6] Some courts, taking the view that the scope of permissible search and seizure should be inflexibly tied to the authorisation of the warrant and that nothing should be left to the discretion of the executing officer, have followed the uncompromising severity of an early dictum in *Marron v. United States*,[7] that '(t)he requirement that warrants shall particularly describe the things to be seized makes general searches under them impossible and prevents the seizure

[1] *People v. Watson*, 142 Cal. Rptr. 245, 247 (1977), per Franson, J.

[2] Ibid., at 248.

[3] See, as reinterpreted by Franson, J. in *Watson*, supra, *People v. Grant*, 81 Cal. Rptr. 812; *People v. Govea*, 45 Cal. Rptr. 253; *People v. Mardian*, 121 Cal. Rptr. 269; *Galena v. Municipal Court*, 47 Cal. Rptr. 88.

[4] *Terry v. Ohio*, 392 U.S. 1; *Chimel v. California*, 395 U.S. 752; *Coolidge v. New Hampshire*, 403 U.S. 443.

[5] *People v. Hill*, 117 Cal. Rptr. 393, 417 (1974).

[6] See La Fave, 'Search and Seizure: "The Course of True Law . . . Has Not . . . Run Smooth', 1966 *U. Ill. L. F.* 255, 274–7; A.L.I., *Model Code of Pre-Arraignment Procedure* § SS 220.3 (Proposed Official Draft, 1975).

[7] 275 U.S. 192 (1927).

of one thing under a warrant describing another', and have disallowed the reception into evidence of seized items not named in the warrant, even if this is contraband, at least if there were 'no exigent circumstances requiring an immediate response'.[1] On this view to permit the seizure of unauthorised items in the course of a lawful search would eliminate the constitutional requirement of 'particualrity' and would open, in practice if not by logical necessity, the door to general searches. This strict theory is felt by some to be even more necessary after the rejection of the 'mere evidence' rule since now that the seizure of purely evidentiary items is possible authorised searches for particular items can all the more easily be used as devices for gaining access to premises for general exploratory searches for evidence.[2]

But the overwhelming majority of state and federal courts have never interpreted the *Marron* dictum literally,[3] nor have they insisted that seizure of incriminating items not mentioned in the warrant is never possible, but have adopted the position, first that generally only those things described in the search warrant may be seized, but secondly that when officers in the course of a bona fide effort to execute a valid search warrant discover articles which, though not included in the warrant, are reasonably identifiable as contraband or as fruits or instrumentalities of crime or as evidence tending to establish the commision of an offence, 'they may seize them whether they are initially in plain sight or come into plain sight subsequently, as a result of the officers' efforts'.[4] The main argument for this is common sense, namely that 'when an article subject to lawful seizure properly comes into an officer's possession in the course of a lawful search it would be entirely without reason to say that he must return it because it was not one of the things it was his business to look for';[5] but this 'permissive' doctrine is invariably qualified by strong emphasis on the 'limiting' principle that before such 'unauthorised' seizure can be upheld there should be both probable cause connecting the particular item with criminal behaviour and proof that the discovery was inadvertent and in the course of an otherwise legitimate search.[6] It should also be noted that even though some formulations of this doctrine, namely that items not specified in the warrant but reasonably believed to be subject to seizure as sufficiently connected with a criminal offence may be taken into police custody when discovered inadvertantly, limit the seizable objects to contraband or instrumentalities of crime,[7] after *Warden v. Hayden*[8] no distinction can properly be drawn between contraband or instrumentalities

[1] *People v. Baker*, 244 N.E. 2d 232, 237 (1968); see *United States v. Coots*, 196 F. Supp. 775 (1961); see La Fave, supra, at 274.

[2] See *People v. Baker*, 244 N.E. 2d 232 (1968).

[3] See, e.g., *United States v. Alloway*, 397 F. 2d 105 (1968); *People v. Hall*, 204 N.E. 2d 824 (1965); La Fave, supra, at 274–5.

[4] *Skelton v. Superior Court*, 460 P. 2d 485, at 494.

[5] *Abel v. United States*, 362 U.S. 217, 238 (1960); *People v. Hall*, 204 N.E. 2d 824, 827 (1965).

[6] *People v. Hill*, 117 Cal. Rptr, 393 (1974); *People v. Miller*, 131 Cal. Rptr. 863 (1976).

[7] See *Skelton v. Superior Court*, supra, 460 P. 2d, at 494.

[8] 387 U.S. 294 (1967).

on the one hand and mere evidence on the other.[1] But the possibility that mere evidence outside the confines of the warrant can now be seized poses a serious danger of indiscriminate evidentiary quests and unlimited seizures, and the need has been felt for the development of a distinct rule, derivable from traditional concepts of probable cause, which 'accomodates the Fourth Amendment's requirement of specificity and the government's legitimate interest in solving crime'.[2] As the Supreme Court put it in *Warden v. Hayden* itself, '(t)here must . . . be a nexus—automatically provided in the case of fruits, instrumentalities or contraband—between the item to be seized and criminal behaviour'. Thus, in the case of 'mere evidence', probable cause must be examined in terms of cause to believe that the evidence not named in the warrant which it is sought to seize 'will aid in a particular apprehension or conviction'.[3] Clearly the 'nexus' rule, which can be viewed as an exception to the specificity requirement of the warrant clause and the adoption of which was prompted by the perceived need to achieve a 'realistic balancing of the requirements of effective law enforcement and the necessity to protect the privacy of the citizen from unwarranted governmental intrusion',[4] is not satisfied by the seizure of items on the ground that they 'might reveal something'.[5] Mere speculation or even suspicion is insufficient. The police officers who seize an unnamed article must rather be aware *at the moment of seizure* of specific and articulable facts from which a link between the item to be seized and criminal behaviour can reasonably be inferred. But it is not necessary that the seized article should be capable by itself of forming the source of probable cause. All events and circumstances at the time and place of the arrest or search can be considered in assessing the existence of probable cause, and the officer is allowed to take into account the entire situation with which he is confronted, including not only the intrinsic qualities of the object itself but also any other circumstances attending its discovery.[6]

The proposition that even though the scope of a search should be strictly circumscribed by the reasons making possible its initial authorisation the seizure of incriminating items is not so limited has received support from the Supreme Court's formulation of the 'plain view' doctrine in *Coolidge v. New Hampshire*.[7] This asserts that during an otherwise lawful search of premises, whether under a warrant or not, evidence sufficiently connected with criminal behaviour falling into plain view may be seized. A valid search therefore does not exceed its allowable scope or limits merely because of the seizure of incriminating items coming within the plain view of police officers who have the right to be in the position from where the observation and discovery become possible. An example of the applicability of the 'plain view' doctrine, Justice Stewart said in *Coolidge*, is 'the situation in which the police

[1] *People v. Hill*, 117 Cal. Rptr. 393, 416 (1974).
[2] Ibid., at 417.
[3] 387 U.S. 294, 307.
[4] *Skelton v. Superior Court*, supra, 460 P. 2d, at 494.
[5] *People v. Hill*, supra, at 417.
[6] *People v. Miller*, 131 Cal. Rptr. 863, 865–6 (1976).
[7] 403 U.S. 443 (1971).

have a warrant to search a given area for specified objects, and in the course of the search come across some other article of incriminating character'.[1] The seizure of such items, it was held, was permissible since to require the police who in the course of an otherwise perfectly lawful search inadvertently came upon a piece of evidence to ignore it until they had obtained a warrant particularly describing it would often be 'a needless inconvenience and sometimes dangerous—to the evidence or to the police themselves'. But, it must be repeated, the 'plain view' doctrine as formulated in *Coolidge* is not activated by the mere fact that evidence is in 'plain view' at the moment of its seizure but only comes into operation if the police can prove both that there was a legitimate prior justification for the initial intrusion and for their being in the position from which they observed or came across the items, and that the discovery of the evidence was *inadvertent*. The reason for this formulation is that this version of the 'plain view' doctrine does not turn an initially valid and therefore limited search into a general one, 'while the inconvenience of procuring a warrant to cover an inadvertent discovery is great'.[2]

[1] Ibid., at 465.
[2] Ibid., at 469.

4. Unreasonable and Warrantless Searches

If it is found that a search within the constitutional term has taken place, it will have to be evaluated under the Fourth Amendment and will only be upheld if it is consistent with its requirements. The Amendment, as we have seen, contains two clauses, the first forbidding 'unreasonable searches and seizures' and the second requiring that warrants should only be issued on the basis of certain conditions, more particularly that they should proceed on the basis of probable cause and that they should meet certain tests of specificity. But what are 'unreasonable' searches and seizures? And what is the place and relevance of the warrant process as regards determinations of reasonableness?[1] The difficulty is that there is almost no evidence concerning the crucial issue of the relationship between the two sections of the Amendment. Grammatically, both of the two main views with regard to the reasonableness of searches are plausible.[2] On one view the second clause is an explanation of the first, so that any search without a warrant is unreasonable. Conversely, one could say that, linguistically, the two clauses are quite distinct and that therefore there is no necessary textual relationship between them, the second section only addressing those searches in fact conducted under warrants and saying nothing either about when a warrant is necessary or about what other circumstances can make a search reasonable and lawful. The historical record too does not yield much information that can cast light on how the constitutional quality of reasonableness is to be approached.[3] Some have taken it for granted that the lesson of history is 'plain', and that this is that searches are unreasonable unless authorised by a validity issued search warrant.[4] But this is not easily maintainable.[5] The history of the Amendment shows only that it was a reaction to the abuses associated with the

[1] See, generally, J. Landynski, *Search and Seizure and the Supreme Court* 42–4, 266–70 (1966); 'Comment, Search and Seizure in the Supreme Court: Shadows on the Fourth Amendment', 28 *U. Chi. L. Rev.* 664, 678–86 (1961); Landynski, 'The Supreme Court's Search for Fourth Amendment Standards: The Warrantless Search', 45 *Conn.B.J.* 2 (1971).

[2] Weinreb, 'Generalities of the Fourth Amendment', 42 *U. Chi. L. Rev.* 47 (1974).

[3] See generally N. Lasson, *The History and Development of the Fourth Amendment to the United States Constitution* 51–105 (1937); Reynard, 'Freedom from Unreasonable Search and Seizure—A Second Class Constitutional Right?', 25 *Ind. L.J.* 259, 262–77 (1950); Fraenkel, 'Concerning Searches and Seizures', 34 *Harv. L. Rev.* 361, 366, 379 (1921).

[4] See the dissenting opinions of Frankfurter, J. in *Harris v. United States*, 331 U.S. 145, 161–2 (1947) and in *United States v. Rabinowitz*, 399 U.S. 56, 70 (1950).

[5] See Taylor, *Two Studies in Constitutional Interpretation* 38–50 (1969); *Payton v. New York*, 100 S.Ct. 1371, 1397 (1980), per Rehnquist J. dissenting.

writs of assistance and general warrants, that it was concern and anxiety about the possible future recurrence of similar instances of official oppression that prompted its adoption, and that the framers, with the exception of Benson,[1] do not appear to have been motivated by anything other than a desire to outlaw the general warrant, and certainly are most unlikely to have aimed at changing the common law, whatever it may have been, with regard to other types of search, for instance those on arrest. There is therefore no historical justification, on this second view, for raising the warrant requirement to the status of the exclusive or even the predominant criterion for assessing the reasonableness, and hence the constitutionality, of searches.[2]

Consistently with this sharp divergence on the historical background of the Fourth Amendment, two broad views have been put forward on the reasonableness of searches and seizures.[3] The first is that it is only unreasonable searches that are prohibited by the Fourth Amendment, not searches without warrant or any other category; since the Constitution does not itself define what 'unreasonable' searches are and since there is (and can be) no fixed formula by reference to which it can be decided the question of reasonableness must be resolved not by any rule of thumb but on the facts and circumstances of each case; the relevant test therefore is not whether it was reasonable or possible to have procured a search warrant, but 'whether the search (itself) was resonable', a question that is to be approached flexibly and which depends on 'the total atmosphere of the (particular) case' before the court.[4] The second view is that as a general matter constitutional reasonableness for Fourth Amendment purposes depends on the presence of a validly issued warrant, in other words that a search can only be reasonable if it is preceded by a warrant issued in compliance with the warrant clause, subject to a few exceptional cases.[5] As it was put by its leading proponent, '(w)ith minor and severely confined exceptions, inferentially a part of the Amendment, every search and seizure is unreasonable when made without a magistrate's authority expressed through a validly issued warrant'.[6] It is this second view that now commands the support of the Supreme Court.[7]

[1] It seems clear that Benson intended to give the Amendment a broader scope. He observed that the provision that had been proposed was 'good as far as it went' but that 'it was not sufficient'. See Lasson, supra,130 n.3, at 101. But again there is no evidence as to what interpretation Benson intended his own proposed version to have.

[2] See Taylor, supra.

[3] See Leagre, 'The Fourth Amendment and the Law of Arrest', 54 *J. Crim. L., C. & P.S.* 393, 398–9 (1963).

[4] *United States v. Rabinowitz*, 339 U.S. 56, 63–6 (1950).

[5] See *Trupiano v. United States*, 334 U.S. 699, 705 (1948); *Chimel v. California*, 395 U.S. 752, 761 (1969); *United States v. United States District Court*, 407 U.S. 297, 317 (1972).

[6] See his dissents in *Harris v. United States*, 331 U.S. 145, 161–2 (1947), from where this extract comes, and in *United States v. Rabinowitz*, 339 U.S. 56, 70 (1950).

[7] But see the contrary statements in *Cady v. Dombrowski*, 413 U.S. 433, 439 (1973); *United States v. Edwards*, 415 U.S. 800, 807 (1974). Another view that can be maintained regarding the relationship of the two sections of the Amendment is

The basic reason for the adoption of this second view, as given in recent cases, is not that there is historical evidence supporting it but that it is only through prior judicial authorisation—rather than by way of subsequent and possibly biased evaluations of overall reasonableness in the light of the surrounding circumstances—that Fourth Amendment rights can adequately be safeguarded.[1] As the Supreme Court has put it, the prominence of the warrant requirement reflects '(the) basic constitutional doctrine that individual freedoms will best be preserved through a separation of powers and division of functions among the different branches and levels of government',[2] which in this context takes the form of a requirement that executive decisions to invade individual privacy and security should be subjected to a procedure of antecedent justification before judicial authorities. Otherwise there will be a serious risk that executive discretion will be abused. The classic statement of this position is that of Justice Jackson in *Johnson v. United States:*[3]

> The point of the Fourth Amendment, which often is not grasped by zealous officers, is not that it denies law enforcement the support of the usual inferences which reasonable men draw from evidence. Its protection consists in requiring that those inferences be drawn by a neutral and detached magistrate instead of being judged by the officer engaged in the often competitive enterprise of ferreting out crime. Any assumption that evidence sufficient to support a magistrate's disinterested determination to issue a search warrant will justify the officers in making a search without a warrant would reduce the Amendment to a nullity and leave the people's homes secure only in the discretion of police officers . . . When the right of privacy must reasonably yield to the right of search is, as a rule, to be decided by a judicial officer, not by a policeman or government enforcement agent.

This same point was made by the English courts in the course of the outlawing of the general warrant ordering the arrest of unnamed individuals whom the

---

that a search must be reasonable and that certain searches are unreasonable even if authorised by apparently valid warrants. Searches for mere evidence were therefore regarded as unreasonable even though there was a warrant: see *Gouled v. United States*, 255 U.S. 298 (1921). But *Gouled* has now been overruled (see *Warden v. Hayden*, 387 U.S. 294 (1967)), and it appears that everything can be seized under a properly drafted warrant. Another view is that even though warrants are necessary before searches can be reasonable the reasonableness clause can still enjoy an independent function because it has the effect that a search can only be constitutional if it is performed both under a warrant and *reasonably* (see *Arkansas v. Sanders*, 99 S.Ct. 2586 (1979)). In this sense, the warrant clause governs the issuance of search warrants and the reasonableness clause is addressed to their execution (see Leagre, supra, at 398 n.53).

[1] See *United States v. United States District Court*, supra; *Arkansas v. Sanders*, supra; *Coolidge v. New Hampshire*, 403 U.S. 443, 481 (1971).

[2] *United States v. United States District Court*, supra, 407 U.S., at 317.

[3] 333 U.S. 10, 14 (1948).

officers thought to be guilty of seditious libel. It was not 'fit', said Lord Mansfield, 'that the receiving or judging of the information ought to be left to the discretion of the officer'. It was the magistrate who 'ought to judge' and give 'certain directions to the officer'.[1] Similarly, the Supreme Court has noted, it is only by requiring that conclusions concerning probable cause and the scope of searches should be drawn by neutral magistrates rather than by the officers themselves who are entrusted with the tasks of law enforcement that both the risk of unreasonable assertions of executive authority will be minimised and precautions taken to ensure that the extent and intensity of otherwise legitimate searches do not exceed what is necessary in the public interest.[2] In contrast, ex post facto review based on whether the particular search was reasonable or not on all the facts and circumstances of each case is not equally effective in assuring protection for Fourth Amendment rights, for two reasons: first, an *advance* decision, particularly a judicial one, can be expected to be faithful to the cardinal principle of legality that a search or seizure must be legal or illegal at its inception instead of being judged by reference to its result, unlike subsequent review which cannot but be 'subtly influenced by the familiar shortcomings of hindsight judgment'[3]; secondly post-search review, unlike prior evaluation, cannot reach the cases which do not result in prosecution.[4] For these reasons then American courts now operate on the basis that it is only prior review by a neutral and detached magistrate that can provide both an independent check upon executive discretion and a timely means of effectuating Fourth Amendment rights. Reasonable searches are therefore those conducted under validly issued warrants, subject to certain exceptions. These will now be studied.

(a) Search incident to arrest

The main exception to the warrant requirement is that a search is valid when it is incident to a valid arrest.[5] In greater detail, when a lawful arrest is made the arresting officer may search the person arrested and the immediately surrounding area in order to disarm the suspect and thus prevent him from escaping, and in order to discover and seize either the fruits of the crime for

[1] *Leach v. Three of the King's Messengers*, 19 State Tr. 1001, 1027 (1765).

[2] See *Coolidge v. New Hampshire*, supra; *United States v. United States District Court*, supra; *Arkansas v. Sanders*, supra.

[3] *Beck v. Ohio*, 379 U.S. 89, 96 (1964); see also La Fave, 'Warrantless Searches and the Supreme Court: Further Ventures Into the "Quagmire",' 8 *Crim.L.Bull.* 9, 10–11.

[4] *United States v. United States District Court*, supra.

[5] See generally Landynski, *Search and Seizure and the Supreme Court* 98–117 (1966); A.L.I., *A Model Code of Pre-Arraignment Procedure* 521–8 (1975); 'Comment, Search and Seizure in the Supreme Court: Shadows on the Fourth Amendment', 28 *U.Chi.L. Rev.* 664, 678–86 (1961); Way, 'Increasing Scope of Search Incidental to Arrest', 1959 *Wash. U.L.Q.* 261; La Fave 'Search and Seizure: "The Course of True Law . . . Has Not . . . Run Smooth",' 1966 *U.Ill.L.F.* 255, 277–93; 68 Am.Jur. 2d, *Searches and Seizures* 691–5, 747–52; Wright, *Federal Practice and Procedure* (vol. 3), 61–71 (1969); 'Annotation', 23 L.Ed. 2d 966; Taylor, *Two Studies in Constitutional Interpretation* 39–49 (1969).

which the arrest has been made, or any instruments, things or other items which may either have been used in the commission or which may constitute evidence of the same offence. The search-incident-to-arrest exception enjoys considerable historical support,[1] and the theory invariably invoked in its justification, as is apparent from its standard formulation set out above, is the need on the one hand to disarm the suspect and deprive him of instruments by means of which he might attempt to escape, and on the other to take from him destructible evidence of the crime on the basis of which the arrest has been effected and which unless the suspect is promptly searched might no longer be available.[2]

But whatever the correct formulation or the precise parameters of the doctrine permitting warrantless searches incident to arrest, there can be no question that '(this) exception comes close to swallowing the rule'[3] demanding adherence to judicial processes before searches uncovering criminal evidence can be upheld. Thus the number of searches which are sustained under this exception far exceed the number of those where a search warrant has been obtained and it is hardly likely that this will ever change, both because '(a)rrests are bound greatly to outnumber applications for search warrants' and because 'arrests will continue to require searches'.[4] As it has therefore been observed, instead of warrantless arrest searches being exceptional, 'the reality is just the reverse'.[5]

'Few areas of the law have been as subject to shifting constitutional standards over the last fifty years as that of the search "incident to an arrest".'[6] Most of the debate has centred on two key issues: First, what is the proper (or better) historical, constitutional and textual explanation of such warrantless searches? Should they be regarded and justified as an exception to the warrant requirement, or should their legality be judged by reference to the standard of overall reasonableness? Secondly, what is the proper scope of searches incident to arrest? Should they be confined to the person of the arrestee or at least to his immediate possessions and to the area within his physical control, or should they extend beyond, and if so how far beyond? Before these difficult issues are discussed two essentially preliminary matters must be dealt with. First, the exception allowing contemporaneous warrantless searches incident to arrest only applies if there has been a valid arrest. If the arrest, whatever the reason, is constitutionally defective, the

[1] See Hale, *Pleas of the Crown* § 60–1; 1 Stephen, *History of the Criminal Law of England* 193 (1883); 1 Bishop, *New Criminal Procedure* § 210, at 152 & n.75 (2d ed. 1913); Pollock & Maitland, *The History of English Law* 582–3 (2d ed. 1903); see also *Leigh v. Cole*, 6 Cox C.C. 329 (1853); *Dillon v. O'Brien*, 16 Cox. C.C. 245 (1887); *Houghton v. Bachman*, 47 Barb. 383, 392 (1866); *Closson v. Morrison*, 47 N.H. 482 (1867).

[2] See *Preston v. United States*, 376 U.S. 364, 367 (1964); 'Note, Scope Limitations for Searches Incident to Arrest', 78 *Yale L.J.* 433 (1969); *Chimel v. California*, 395 U.S. 752 (1969).

[3] La Fave, supra, 133 n.5, at 278; see also Kaplan, 'Search and Seizure: A No Man's Land in the Criminal Law', 49 *Calif.L.Rev.* 479, 490 (1961).

[4] Taylor, supra, 133 n.5, at 49.

[5] Ibid.

[6] *Chimel v. California*, 395 U.S. 752, 770 (1969), per White, J. dissenting.

search is invalid too, and application of the exclusionary rule will result in the suppression of the evidence.[1] Further, the evidence will also be ruled inadmissible if it was not the search that was incidental to the arrest but the arrest that was incidental to the search.[2] In other words, 'an arrest may not be used as a pretext to search for evidence',[3] and if it is found that an arrest was not a bona fide one, but 'a sham or a front being used as an excuse for making a search',[4] then both the arrest itself and the ensuing search are illegal. For as it was succinctly put, since a search cannot be embarked upon without authority and since the relevant authority cannot be gained retrospectively,[5] 'a search is not to be made legal by what it turns up. In law it is good or bad when it starts and does not change character from its success.'[6] The second requirement is that a search can only be incidental to an arrest if it is substantially contemporaneous with it.[7] For since the rule allowing warrantless searches incident to arrest is based on the need to seize weapons which might be used to assault the arresting officer and to prevent the destruction of evidence of the crime, a search that is remote in terms of time from the arrest cannot be similarly justified and will not be permitted unless another of the exceptions to the warrant requirement can be invoked.[8] The same applies to searches which are remote from the arrest in terms of 'place' or location. Even before *Chimel v California*[9] overruling permissive decisions with regard to the legitimate scope of searches incident to arrest, a search of a house could not be upheld as incident to an arrest unless that arrest took place inside the house and not somewhere outside,[10] whether it was two blocks away[11] or only twenty feet away.[12] In the light of recent developments the concept of 'immediate vicinity'[13] must be given an even more restrictive connotation. This will be considered shortly.

The issue of the proper basis of the incident-to-arrest exception depends upon the relationship of the two sections of the Fourth Amendment. This has already been discussed. One possible view, while not necessarily[14] challenging the primacy of the warrant requirement as a general matter, argues that arrest-based warrantless searches should be regarded as forming a group of their own and that they should be evaluated by reference to the

[1] *Beck v. Ohio*, 379 U.S. 89 (1964); see Wright, supra, 133 n.5, at 62.

[2] Wright, supra, n.1, at 63; see also *Amador — Gonzalez v. United States*, 391 F. 2d 308 (1968).

[3] *United States v. Lefkowitz*, 285 U.S. 452, 467 (1932).

[4] *Taglavore v. United States*, 291 F. 2d 262, 265–6 (1961).

[5] *Harris v. United States*, 331 U.S. 145, 167 (1947), per Frankfurter, J. dissenting.

[6] *United States v. Di Re*, 332 U.S. 581, 595 (1948), per Jackson, J.

[7] See *Vale v. Louisiana*, 399 U.S. 30, 33–4 (1970).

[8] *Stoner v. California*, 376 U.S. 483 (1964); *Preston v. United States*, 376 U.S. 364, 367–8 (1964).

[9] 395 U.S. 752 (1969).

[10] See *Vale v. Louisiana*, 399 U.S. 30, 34 (1970).

[11] *James v. Louisiana*, 382 U.S. 36 (1965).

[12] *Shipley v. California*, 395 U.S. 818 (1969).

[13] *Shipley v. California*, supra, at 819.

[14] See generally *United States v. Rabinowitz*, 339 U.S. 56 (1950); see also *South Dakota v. Opperman*, 428 U.S. 364, 381 (1976), per Powell J. concurring.

reasonableness clause.[1] This view is no longer accepted, and here too, in tune with the currently prevalent theory regarding the relationship between the two sections of the Amendment, the present doctrinal position can be set out as follows: The fundamental rule over *the whole of search and seizure law* is that with the exception of a few carefully defined classes of cases a search is unreasonable and unconstitutional unless it has been authorised by a valid search warrant;[2] searches and seizures incident to arrest constitute one of these exceptional categories; but since all exceptions to the warrant requirement should be regarded with caution, bearing in mind the strong policy in favour of resorting to the warrant process whenever possible, the search-incident-to arrest exception should also be carefully watched, lest it be 'enthroned into the rule'.[3] Consistently with these tenets courts have recently been urged not to forget that the permissibility of arrest-based contemporaneous searches is based on necessity, more particularly to prevent assaults upon police officers and the destruction of material evidence which (by most) has been taken to mean that if the considerations that typically justify such warrantless searches are wholly absent in a particular case, and no exigent circumstances are present to excuse the failure to submit the facts to a neutral magistrate, as where the search is remote in time or place from the arrest, there will be held to have been no justification for not complying with the generally applicable warrant requirement and the particular intrusion will be declared unconstitutional.[4]

The second and more controversial issue which has provoked 'strong and fluctuating differences of view on the (Supreme) Court'[5] concerns the proper scope of arrest-based searches. Two broad views have been advanced on this, the permissive view and the strict view. The permissive view[6] is that when an arrest has been made it is permissible to search both the person of the suspect and the place where the arrest takes place, either because of an assumption that the dangers which the incident-to-arrest exception is intended to meet might still manifest themselves unless the premises in which the suspect was found are promptly searched, or because it is felt that once an arrest has been made any additional invasion of privacy stemming from an accompanying search of the relevant premises is relatively minor and can be disregarded. A variant of this is that save for the person of the arrestee there is no predetermined area that may be searched, that the reasonableness of each search is a question to be determined upon the facts of the particular case, but that in an appropriate case the entire house or premises where the arrest took place may be searched. In determining what an 'appropriate' case is it is

[1] See Taylor, supra, at 43.

[2] See *United States v. United States District Court*, 407 U.S. 297, 315 (1972); *Katz v. United States*, 389 U.S. 347, 356 (1967); *Camara v. Municipal Court*, 387 U.S. 523, 528 (1967).

[3] *United States v. Rabinowitz*, 339 U.S. 56, 80 (1950), per Frankfurter, J. dissenting.

[4] *Preston v. United States*, 376 U.S., at 367; *Chimel v. California*, supra.

[5] *Abel v. United States*, 362 U.S. 217 (1960).

[6] See *Harris v. United States*, 331 U.S. 145 (1947); *United States v. Rabinowitz*, 339 U.S. 56 (1950); 'Annotation', 23 L.Ed. 2d 966; Wright, supra, at 67.

possible that the basic permissive rule can be modified further, in two distinct directions. It might first be said that the right to conduct a search as an incident to a lawful arrest is a limited right that arises only if it was not possible to obtain a warrant in time; if it was therefore suspected that evidence was hidden on the premises and it was reasonably practicable to obtain a warrant any search beyond the person of the arrestee will be disallowed.[1] Alternatively, a search of the entire house could be upheld only if certain further subsidiary conditions were met, for instance if the search was not an exploratory one but had been directed at the discovery of specific items, if there was at the relevant time probable cause that items connected with the crime would be found at the place of arrest,[2] and if the search of the place of arrest did not exceed those limits that were appropriate to the type of investigation under way.[3]

The main problem with permissive doctrines, particularly those that appear to confer unqualified authority to search the entire premises of the arrestee, is that it is difficult to assign to them limits which are not arbitrary, or based on subjective considerations as to what is a 'reasonable' search.[4] Indeed it is difficult to see why it should be regarded as reasonable to search the entire premises when the defendant is arrested there but unreasonable when the arrest takes place in the street outside.[5] Particular objection has been taken to the *broad* view of the permissible consequences of the initial impairment of privacy, i.e. the arrest. It has thus been argued that there is no reason why further interferences with separable aspects of privacy and independent rights to property should automatically flow from the original intrusion represented by the arrest. Since the Fourth Amendment itself protects persons, houses and effects, it would be paradoxical if the mere fact of a permissible invasion of personal security, without the presence of any additional considerations such as unforeseen circumstances of necessity, could per se legitimise further intrusions into other and conceptually distinct interests accorded autonomous recognition by the Constitution.[6] As this point

[1] See *Trupiano v. United States*, 334 U.S. 699 (1948); Carrington, '*Chimel v. California*—A Police Response', 45 *Notre Dame Law* 559 (1970).

[2] See LaFave, 'Warrantless Searches and the Supreme Court: Further Ventures into the "Quagmire",' 8 *Crim. L. Bull.* 9, 12–15.

[3] See *Harris v. United States,* supra.

[4] See *Chimel v. California*, 395 U.S. 752, at 766 et seq., per Stewart, J.; *Harris v. United States*, 331 U.S., at 197, per Jackson, J. dissenting; *United States v. Rabinowitz*, 339 U.S., at 83, per Frankfurter, J. dissenting.

[5] See 'Note, Scope Limitations for Searches Incident to Arrest', 78 *Yale L.J.* 433, 435 & n.14 (1969); 'The Supreme Court, 1968 Term', 83 *Harv. L. Rev.* 7, 161–2 (1969); La Fave, supra, n.2, at 12 n.27; and *United States v. Jackson*, 149 F. Supp. 937 (D.D.C.), rev'd on other grounds, 250 F. 2d 772 (D.C. Cir. 1957).

[6] See *United States v. Rabinowitz*, 339 U.S., at 71, per Frankfurter, J. dissenting; this same point was also made well by L. Hand, C.J., in *United States v. Rabinowitz*, before this case came to the Supreme Court, at 176 F. 2d 732, 735: 'It is true that when one has been arrested in his home or his office, his privacy has already been invaded; but that interest, though lost, is altogether separate from the interest in protecting his papers from indiscriminate rummage, even though both are customarily grouped together as parts of the "right of privacy".'

was forcefully put by Justice Frankfurter, '(t)o derive from the common law right to search the person as an incident of his arrest the right of indiscriminate search of all his belongings is to disregard the fact that the Constitution protects both (from) unauthorised arrest and (from) unauthorised search'.[1] On this reasoning authority to arrest does not dispense with the requirement that in the case of searches the relevant authority should be procured independently but only confers authority—itself the product of compelling necessity—to search the person arrested and seize certain articles within his immediate physical control. Even more vulnerable is the fiction of control and the manipulation of doctrines of possession and custody often used by the proponents of permissive doctrines. For one line of argument that figures prominently in permissive formulations is that since the arresting officers, as is universally acknowledged, can search and seize incidentally to a valid arrest not only the person of the arrestee but also what is within his immediate control and possession, and since everything in the arrested person's house is or at least may be presumed to be within his exclusive possession and control, the area which can legitimately be subjected to search cannot be limited either to the person of the arrestee, or to what is in such immediate physical relation to him as to be a projection of his person, or even to the room in which the arrest took place, but should extend beyond and cover the entire premises.[2] But clearly 'immediate custody', 'immediate control', 'control', 'possession' and such phrases when used in a Fourth Amendment context, particularly that of the incident-to-arrest exception, have very different connotations from comparable phrases used in the law of property.[3] 'For some purposes, to be sure, a man's house and its contents are deemed to be in his 'possession' or 'control' even when he is miles away', but 'this mode of thought and these concepts are irrelevant to the application of the Fourth Amendment and hostile to respect for the liberties which it protects'.[4] Arguments based *exclusively* on 'control' and 'possession' can in fact only support an extended authority to search incident to lawful arrest if one unwittingly slides from one legal meaning to another, not in deference to inherent similarities or considered reasoning but as a result of succumbing to the beguiling and treacherous ambiguity of equivocal legal terminology.[5]

The strict view[6] of the permissible scope of arrest-based searches is based on three interrelated propositions, the following: First, the general requirement that a search warrant should be obtained is not lightly to be dispensed with, any exceptions to it are to be jealously and carefully drawn,

[1] *Harris v. United States*, 331 U.S. 145, at 165, per Frankfurter, J. dissenting.

[2] *Harris*, supra, at 152, per Vinson, C.J.

[3] See the dissenting opinions of Frankfurter, J. in *Harris*, at 168 ('By "immediate custody" (one does) not (mean) that figurative possession which for some legal purposes puts one in "possession" of everything in a house') and in *Rabinowitz*, at 78.

[4] *Harris*, supra, at 164, per Frankfurter, J. dissenting.

[5] *Rabinowitz*, supra, at 78–9, per Frankfurter, J. dissenting.

[6] This was forcefully put forward by Frankfurter, J. in his dissents in *Harris*, supra, and *Rabinowitz*, supra; see also the dissenting opinions of Murphy and Jackson, JJ. in *Harris*.

and the burden of showing that a particular case falls within one of them should be an onerous one.[1] Secondly, the *sole* reason why arrest-based searches need not be accompanied by warrants is the immediate need to deprive the arrested person of weapons, which he might use against those effecting the arrest, and the evidence, which he might readily destroy;[2] if these dangers on the facts of a particular case do not exist, the exception logically should not apply. Thirdly, the fact that the incident-to-arrest exception applies, in the sense that there was or may have been a danger of the destruction or concealment of evidence on the one hand or of the use of weapons on the other, does not preclude further judicial inquiry into the reasonableness of the particular search; on the contrary, it is now universally accepted that a warrantless search can only comply with the requirements of the Fourth Amendment if its scope is no broader than what is reasonably necessary to accomplish the legitimate governmental objectives that have given rise to the exception from the warrant requirement in the first place; as a result, in determining the constitutionality of a particular search the inquiry is a dual one—whether the intrusion was justified at its inception, and whether it was (and remained) reasonably related in scope to the circumstances intitially justifying the interference.[3] On this basis an arrest-based search should not go beyond the person arrested, the objects upon him or in his immediate physical control, and the limited area within his reach from which he might seize weapons or evidence.[4] In other words, the scope of arrest-based searches must be closely tied to the protective and evidentiary considerations necessitating their recognition in the first place. Two implications follow from adoption in the case of arrest-based searches of the 'scope limitation' principle, namely that all warrantless searches must be reasonably limited in extent and scope by reference to their initial and justifying purposes, and from insistence that it is the actualities of each situation rather than wholly hypothetical dangers or fictional reasoning based on concepts borrowed from the law of property that should determine constitutionality. First, if there is no possibility that the arresting officer's safety will be endangered or that material evidence will be destroyed, there should be no right to conduct a warrantless search at all; and secondly no search should in any case be more intrusive than what is necessary to recover

[1] See *Coolidge v. New Hampshire*, 403 U.S. 443, 449 (1971).

[2] See *Preston v. United States*, 376 U.S. 364, 367 (1964), where 'the rule allowing contemporaneous searches' is said to be justified, 'for example', by 'the need to seize weapons' and by 'the need to prevent the destruction of evidence', but, as it has been pointed out, '(d)espite the mysterious "for example", a thorough search of the case law reveals no other justifications for warrantless searches incident to arrest which do not collapse upon careful inspection into one of the two bases articulated in *Preston*': 'Note, Scope Limitations for Searches Incident to Arrest', 78 *Yale L.J.* 433, 434 n.12 (1969).

[3] See *Terry v. Ohio*, 392 U.S. 1, at 19–20 (1968).

[4] See *Chimel v. California*, 395 U.S. 752, at 763 (1969); see also the views of Frankfurter, J. in *Harris*, supra, and *Rabinowitz*, supra, which have been substantially adopted by the Supreme Court in *Chimel*.

any weapons and evidence that might be available.[1]

The twin attractions of strict doctrines, particularly those versions that limit the area that can be searched to that within the immediate reach of the arrestee, are that they seem true to the justifications that have obviously necessitated recognition of the incident-to-arrest exception, and that they circumscribe the limits of permissible search neither arbitrarily nor subjectively but by means of themes allegedly deriving from concern with Fourth Amendment values, subject only to irresistible qualifications necessitated by the pressing claims of law enforcement. On this view once one goes beyond the person of the arrestee and the area demarcated by the extent of his physical reach no rational line of limitation can be drawn,[2] and 'freehanded'[3] searches without the significant restraints entailed by the interposition of the unbiased judgment of a neutral magistrate will become the order of the day. The chief weaknesses of strict doctrines are practical.[4] What are the considerations that should guide reviewing courts in determining the question of the arrestee's reach? Will not the application of standards such as 'immediate area', 'immediate physical control', and 'reach of the arrestee' inevitably result in quite as much uncertainty and in as many variations in judicial emphasis as more flexible and broadly-based doctrines predicated on reasonableness?[5] Is it not easier to have some kind of hard-and-fast rule, for instance that on arrest inside a house the officers may search the whole house, provided of course that the crime for which the arrest is made is one involving material evidence that is likely to be inside the house?[6] Further, it is abundantly obvious that strict prohibition of arrest-based searches beyond the arrestee's immediate reach will result in loss of material evidence. One can easily imagine circumstances in which an arrest is effected in one part of the house and the officers suspect that evidence located in another

[1] But see *United States v. Robinson*, 94 S.Ct. 467 (1973) and other cases where a person is arrested for an offence involving no real evidence, or no evidence which may be hidden on his person, and where there is no indication that he is carrying a weapon. Strict application of the *Terry* 'scope limitation' principle might suggest that searches of the person should not be allowed in such cases; contra *Robinson*, supra.

[2] *Chimel*, supra, at 766; *Harris*, supra, at 197, per Jackson, J. dissenting; and *Rabinowitz*, at 79 et seq., per Frankfurter, J. dissenting.

[3] *Rabinowitz*, supra, at 79, per Frankfurter, J. dissenting.

[4] Carrington, supra.

[5] As is pointed out by L. Hand C.J. in *United States v. Rabinowitz*, 176 F. 2d 732 at 735, the concept of 'immediate reach' involves 'a penumbra of uncertain area', but this was inevitable since 'fixed outlines (were) impossible'.

[6] But if such a rule is adopted, what is its juridical basis? If privacy of person (violated by the arrest) and privacy of place (violated by the search) are regarded as distinct (in that the one is not regarded as automatically flowing from the other) a violation of privacy of place must be justifiable independently—in other words, it must be justifiable as an intrusion directed towards the obtaining of specific items, or otherwise it will be a fishing expedition; but if so, and the police knew or suspected about the items being there, why did they not obtain a warrant? Conversely, if these items first came to their notice after entry, is it not preferable to develop and rely on a specialised exception based on emergency rather than to use absolute rules—and ones that do much violence to the Fourth Amendment?

part is in danger of being destroyed by associates of the arrestee or by members of his family. In such cases should they stand by and in effect do nothing until a search warrant is obtained, or should the possibility of a loss of evidence result in a temporary extension of their limited right of search and seizure under the incident-to-arrest doctrine?[1] But if the latter solution is chosen, and in view of the undoubted danger that any authority to conduct more extensive searches whenever it is feared that evidence may be destroyed could well be abused to the point that once more the exception displaces the principle, should other, and if so what, limiting qualifications be insisted upon?[2]

Difficulties with both extreme permissive and strict models could well prompt serious consideration of intermediate solutions.[3] One, that combines a number of diverse elements, is to condition the legality of an arrest-based search extending beyond the person of the arrestee and the immediately surrounding area on the impracticability of obtaining a warrant. If it was practicable to obtain a search warrant, then the right to search incident to an arrest should in no case go beyond the person of the arrestee and his physical projections.[4] But if this requirement is met, if in other words it is found that it was not practicable to obtain a search warrant before the arrest, then a search for specific things which the officers reasonably believe to be on the premises should be allowed, and then again only if the officers can demonstrate a reasonable probability that weapons or evidence would either be taken, removed or destroyed while a search warrant was being obtained. A somewhat different approach that is more lenient to the arresting authority would be to elevate to the role of the decisive criterion, not whether it was practicable to obtain a warrant before the arrest, but whether the arresting officer reasonably believes that there are on the premises at the time of the arrest things connected with the offence for which the arrest is made and which are likely to be removed or destroyed before a search warrant can be obtained.

Decisional trends have fluctuated dramatically between the permissive and strict doctrines. A number of phases can be distinguished. The early cases dealt with the search of the person of the arrestee and the seizure of things in his immediate possession,[5] and it was this limited right that the Supreme

[1] This raises a problem not only of substantive law but also of organisation. Thus provision for emergency action in cases of an arrest on premises may be made either by way of a suitable formulation of the search-incident-to arrest exception or by way of the elaboration of a distinct exception to the warrant requirement predicated not on recognition of authority to search when there has been an arrest but on authority to take action in the interests of the preservation of evidence when there are circumstances of emergency. But what is clear is that a narrow and restrictive formulation of the incident-to-arrest exception goes hand-in-hand with a disinclination to recognise the legality of official 'emergency' action (see *Chimel*, supra, and *Vale v. Louisiana*, supra).

[2] See generally 'Note, Police Practices and the Threatened Destruction of Tangible Evidence', 84 *Harv. L. Rev.* 1465 (1971).

[3] See *Model Code*, supra, SS. 230.5.

[4] *Trupiano v. United States*, 334 U.S. 699 (1948).

[5] Way, supra, at 263.

Court referred to in *Weeks v. United States*[1] when it was observed that the right 'to search the person of the accused when legally arrested to discover and seize the fruits or evidences of crime' had always been recognised under English and American law and could not be disputed. Subsequent dicta affirmed that when a man was legally arrested for an offence the police could seize and retain not only what was found upon his person but also whatever was 'in his control',[2] but even though 'control' is obviously broader than 'person', there was as yet no reference to any right to search premises, or any part thereof, merely because the arrest had taken place there. But before long the search incident-to-arrest exception is cast in expanded form in *Agnello v. United States*[3] where the Supreme Court spoke, still by way of dictum, to 'the right without a search warrant contemporaneously to search persons lawfully arrested while committing crime and to search the place where the arrest is made' in order to seize weapons and evidence. Elevation of what may have been only a carelessly phrased dictum to something approaching ratio comes with *Marron v. United States*[4] where the Supreme Court held that on arresting a person in charge of a place where intoxicating liquors were being unlawfully sold the officers 'had a right without warrant contemporaneously to search the place in order to find and seize the things used to carry on the criminal enterprise'. But this broad principle appeared to be subjected to drastic revision in *Go-Bart Importing Co. v. United States*[5] and *United States v. Lefkowitz*[6] where *Marron v. United States* was explained as a case (1) where an offence involving the use of the place where the arrest had been made was actually being committed in the officers' presence, (2) where the things which had been seized were 'visible and accessible and in the offender's immediate custody',[7] and (3) where there had been no 'general search or rummaging of the place'.[8] But where there was no question either of an arrest for a crime actually being committed in the officers' presence or of the seizure of incriminating items in plain view then any search extending beyond the person and its immediate surroundings would be held to be unreasonable.[9]

But in *Harris v. United States*,[10] involving the most extensive search without warrant ever to receive the Supreme Court's approval[11] and regarded by many as the biggest step backward in the protection of privacy in the Court's

[1] 232 U.S. 383 (1914).

[2] *Carroll v. United States*, 267 U.S. 132 (1925).

[3] 269 U.S. 20 (1925).

[4] 275 U.S. 192 (1927).

[5] 282 U.S. 344 (1931).

[6] 285 U.S. 452 (1932).

[7] *Go-Bart*, 282 U.S., at 358; but, as Way, supra, at 268, points out, this limited characterisation is hardly a correct description of *Marron* since in this case the search went beyond the room in which the arrest had been made and extended to a closet.

[8] Ibid.

[9] This is how Frankfurter, J. explained *Go-Bart*, supra, and *Lefkowitz*, supra, in his dissenting opinion in *Rabinowitz*, supra, at 78.

[10] 331 U.S. 145 (1947).

[11] Landynski, supra, at 103.

history,[1] the caution and restrictive attitude of *Go-Bart* and *Lefkowitz* were thrown to the winds.[2] In *Harris* the defendant was arrested on charges of fraud and forgery. The arrest took place in the living-room of Harris' four-room apartment, but then the arresting officers conducted a thorough search, lasting about five hours, of the entire apartment. The officers stated that they were looking for specific cancelled checks alleged to have been used for forgery purposes. In the bedroom they lifted the carpets, stripped the bed linen, turned over the mattresses, and eventually, in a small desk drawer, came across a sealed envelope marked 'personal papers'. This was promptly torn open and was found to contain incriminating evidence on the basis of which Harris was convicted of a separate offence. By a majority of five to four[3] the search was upheld as incident to a lawful arrest. The starting point of the Court's opinion was that the Fourth Amendment had never been held to require that every search and seizure should be effected under the authority of a search warrant; search and seizure incident to lawful arrest was a settled practice of ancient origin, and the only question in the instant case concerned its permissible boundaries. Previous cases had recognised that a search incident to arrest could, 'under appropriate circumstances', extend beyond the person of the arrestee to the premises under his 'immediate control', and no support could be found for the suggestion that such a search could not validly extend beyond the room in which the arrest took place. *Since* Harris was 'in exclusive possession' of the entire apartment, *since* '(h)is control extended quite as much to the bedroom in which the draft cards were found as to the living-room in which he was arrested', and *since* the cancelled checks could 'easily' have been concealed in any of the four rooms of the apartment, the very extensive search that had been conducted was reasonable. But the same meticulous investigation would not have been upheld in cases where 'the nature and size of the object sought or the lack of effective control over the premises on the part of the persons arrested' required that any search 'be less extensive'. The guiding criterion was overall reasonableness, and one had to look 'to the particular circumstances of the particular case'. On the facts before them, the majority concluded, the search did not go beyond what the situation 'reasonably demanded'. But only a year later there was an abrupt departure from the doctrinal approach of *Harris* and its emphasis on loose standards of reasonableness.[4] In *Trupiano v. United States*[5] federal agents received information long before making their raid that an illegal distillery was being operated on certain property. When the agents descended on the site one of them clearly saw the still in operation. He then entered the building, placed the man in charge under arrest, and at the same time seized the illegal distillery. The arrest was held to have been valid, but a majority

[1] Way, supra, at 271.

[2] See *Chimel v. California*, supra, at 757–8, per Stewart, J.

[3] The Court's opinion was delivered by Vinson, C.J.; Frankfurter, Rutledge, Murphy and Jackson, JJ. dissented.

[4] This was because of a fundamental change of view by Douglas, J., who had agreed with the majority in *Harris* but now joined the Frankfurter group to form a narrow (5 to 4) majority in *Trupiano*.

[5] 334 U.S. 699 (1948).

also held that the contemporaneous seizure was illegal because the officers had ignored the 'cardinal rule' that 'law enforcement agents must secure and use search warrants wherever reasonably practicable'. The authority to search or seize without a warrant as an incident to a lawful arrest, the Court's opinion announced, was a 'strictly limited right' that grew out of the 'inherent necessities of the situation at the time of the arrest', and the *mere* fact that there had been a valid arrest could not *ipso facto* legalise a contemporaneous search or seizure without a warrant. In the instant case no reason had been shown why the arresting officers had not armed themselves with a search warrant, and this was enough to render the seizure unlawful. The *Trupiano* doctrine—namely, that the basic test of the constitutionality of warrantless searches and seizures is whether it was practicable at the time to secure a search warrant—was itself rejected, again within only two years, by *United States v. Rabinowitz*.[1] Here federal officers arrested the defendant in his place of business, a small one-room office, on a charge of selling and having in his possession forged and altered government stamps. They then searched, without a search warrant, the desk, safe and filing cabinets in the office for about an hour and a half, and seized a number of forged stamps which were subsequently used at the defendant's trial. A majority of the Supreme Court overruled *Trupiano*, holding, first that the relevant test was not whether it was reasonable to have obtained a search warrant but whether the search itself was reasonable, and secondly that the particular search before them was reasonable, because (1) the search and seizure were incident to a valid arrest, (2) what had been searched was a business room to which the public was invited, (3) the room was 'small' and under 'the immediate and complete control' of the defendant, (4) the search did not extend beyond the room used for unlawful purposes, and (5) the possession of the forged stamps was a crime. Even though *Rabinowitz* itself insisted that the question of whether a search was reasonable could only be decided in the context of the specific facts of each case subsequent cases interpreted its holding, and that of *Harris* too, as standing for the broad proposition that a warrantless search incident to arrest could generally extend to the whole area, usually a house or place of business, considered to be in the possession or under the control of the person arrested.[2]

The latest, but very probably not the last, turn in the odyssey of the incident-to-arrest exception came in 1969 when the Supreme Court in *Chimel v. California*,[3] involving the extensive warrantless search of the defendant's three-bedroom house following his arrest there for burglary, overruled *Harris*

[1] 339 U.S. 56 (1950). The Supreme Court's composition had changed between *Trupiano* and *Rabinowitz* by the death of two members of the Frankfurter group who had dissented in *Harris* and joined the majority in *Trupiano*, Murphy and Rutledge, JJ.; their replacements, Clark and Minton, JJ., joined those who had dissented in *Trupiano* and thus helped form a new majority for the permissive doctrine.

[2] See *Chimel v. California*, supra, at 760; 'Note', supra, 139 n.2 at 435 n.14.

[3] 395 U.S. 752 (1969); see Carrington, '*Chimel v. California*—A Police Response', 45 *Notre Dame Law* 559 (1970); 55 *Minn. L. Rev.* 1011 (1971); 'The Supreme Court, 1968 Term', 83 *Harv. L. Rev.* 7, 163 (1969).

and *Rabinowitz*, adopted an uncompromising version of the strict doctrine set out above, and held that since the search of the defendant's house went far beyond his person and the area from within which he might have obtained either a weapon or something that could have been used as evidence against him, and since there was no justification in the absence of a warrant for extending the search beyond that very limited area, both the challenged search and the resulting seizure of the incriminating items (primarily coins) were illegal. The Court's opinion puts forward and in turn rests on the following propositions: The cardinal doctrine by means of which the Fourth Amendment is to be implemented is not overall reasonableness but the general requirement that a search warrant should be obtained, which means that 'in the absence of well-recognised exceptions' a search of premises is illegal unless it is supported by a search warrant; the only justification for the incident-to-arrest exception is necessity, more particularly the need on the one hand to protect the arresting officer from any weapons that might be used against him and on the other to prevent the destruction of evidence by the arrested person; since it is equally fundamental Fourth Amendment doctrine that the scope and intensity of any search, particularly if it is a warrantless one, should be strictly tied to and ultimately determined by the circumstances rendering its initiation permissible, when an arrest is made it is reasonable for the arresting officer to search the person arrested and 'the area into which an arrestee might reach in order to grab a weapon or evidentiary items', also called 'the area within his immediate control', in order to prevent him from gaining possession either of a weapon or of destructible evidence;but it is not reasonable (because it is not necessary) to proceed further; if therefore a search undertaken in pursuance of the incident-to-arrest exception goes beyond the area of the arrestee's 'immediate control' it will be held to be unreasonable.

A number of problems with the *Chimel* standard can immediately be noticed. There are, first, the more or less inevitable problems of definition and application. What is the area within the reach of a suspect which can lawfully be searched? Is this, whatever the terminology in which it is presented, an essentially objective concept, or does it vary with the physical build and the individual characteristics of the particular arrestee? What circumstances or factors restrict the scope of the search, and which, if any, are capable of expanding it? What is the relevance of the arresting officer's knowledge of the mobility and other circumstances of the particular suspect?[1] A different type of problem arises because of the possibility that material evidence may be destroyed if the entire premises are not searched without delay. This is illustrated by the facts of *Chimel* itself. If the police had simply arrested the defendant, taken him to the police station and later returned with a search warrant, it may well be that his wife, who in all probability knew of her husband's offences, would have removed the incriminating evidence. In view of what he saw as the likelihood in such cases of the threatened destruction of evidence, Justice White, dissenting in *Chimel,*

[1] Carrington, supra, at 568–70.

proposed that warrantless searches and seizures beyond the area of immediate control should be allowed when the arresting officers have probable cause to search and 'there is a clear danger that the items for which they may reasonably search will be removed before they return with a warrant'.[1] This view denies that it wishes to challenge the currently prevalent doctrine that warrants should as a rule be insisted upon, but it maintains, first, that there is an exception in cases where there are 'exigent circumstances' and, secondly, that 'the fact of arrest supplies such an exigent circumstance', since the officers' departure to obtain a search warrant may involve 'the risk' of not recovering the fruits of the crime.[2] It may be retorted that while it is true that it may not be practicable for the arresting officers to obtain a warrant after they have made the arrest, 'this does not explain why it would not sometimes (or, perhaps, often) be possible to avoid those exigent circumstances by simply obtaining a search warrant *before* the arrest is made'.[3] In *Chimel* itself the crime for which the defendant was arrested had occurred some time before, the police apparently thought that there was no emergency because they only executed the arrest warrant after considerable delay, and despite the fact that probable cause to search for the coins obviously existed no explanation whatever was given why a search warrant had not been obtained *before* Chimel's arrest.[4] But what if exigent circumstances manifest themselves *after* entry and arrest, for instance by the police first becoming aware of the existence of evidence on the premises and of the probability of its destruction *after* the arrest was made? But, as can already be seen, the relevant question here is not about the limits of an arrest-based search but about whether there should be an independent exception justifying warrantless searches in cases where evidence is threatened with destruction, for it is only if the answer is in the affirmative that it becomes necessary, first to specify the instances in which a real need to act immediately and without first obtaining a search warrant should be held to exist, and then to decide whether even in such situations it should be incumbent upon the arresting officers, at least as a first step, not to conduct a thorough search but instead to take other less intrusive measures for safeguarding the endangered evidence.

(b) Search incident to arrest after Chimel

Whatever the difficulties with the new standards, there can be no doubt about the formulation of the governing criterion for searches incident to arrest after *Chimel*,[5] and this can be set out as follows: At the time and place of arrest the arresting officers may search *the arrestee's person* and *the area within his immediate control* in order to meet two needs, first to prevent the officers' safety from being endangered and the arrest itself frustrated, and

[1] *Chimel*, supra, at 774, per White, J., dissenting.
[2] Ibid., at 781.
[3] La Fave, supra, 137 n.2, at 14.
[4] Ibid.
[5] See 'Note, Search and Seizure since *Chimel v. California*', 55 *Minn. L. Rev.* 1011 (1971).

secondly to prevent the concealment or destruction of evidence of the crime on the basis of which the arrest has been effected. The operative test is the area within the arrestee's 'immediate control', and even though this cannot be defined with precision,[1] it refers to the area from within which the arrestee '*might gain possession*' of a weapon or destructible evidence or the area into which he '*might reach*' in order to grab a weapon or evidence.[2] The phrases 'area within immediate control' and 'area within (the arrestee's) reach' seem to be used interchangeably.[3] But even though it is generally agreed that the permissible scope of search incident to arrest has been severely narrowed by *Chimel*, there is still, not surprisingly, no uniformity in the cases but instead two broad approaches to the new standard of 'immediate control' seem to be taken. One takes an uncompromising stand on the requirements that the police, barring virtual necessity, must obtain advance judicial approval of searches and seizures through the warrant procedure and that the scope of any search must be rigidly determined by the circumstances which rendered its initiation permissible; that courts must adhere not only to the form but also to the spirit of *Chimel*; and that therefore warrantless searches incident to arrest will only be upheld by strict reference to 'the exigencies of preventing harm to the arresting officers, the escape of the suspects, or the destruction of evidence'.[4] The other, less exacting, approach reads *Chimel* more restrictively, namely as having principally been directed against routine rummaging searches, as condemning only searches remote in time or place from the arrest, and as not necessarily disapproving of an automatic search of the room or area where the arrest occurred.[5] On this second view '*Chimel* prohibited general exploratory searches incident to arrest but did not erect impenetrable barriers at every doorway'.[6]

Some recent cases interpreting *Chimel* and the main propositions emerging from them can be set out as follows. Although *Chimel* involved a search of a three-bedroom house, its holding and principle have not been limited to the prohibition of 'such massive searches'.[7] Indeed the *Chimel* Court expressly overruled *United States v. Rabinowitz*[8] which had involved the search of a single room, explicitly refused to distinguish between full-house searches and limited single-room searches, and made it clear that there could be no

[1] *United States v. Mason*, 523 F. 2d 1122, 1131 (1975), per Bazelon, C.J., concurring in part and dissenting in part.

[2] *Chimel v. California*, supra, at 763, 766.

[3] See *Chimel*, supra; see also *Taylor v. Comm.*, 577 S.W. 2d 46 (1979); *United States v. Mapp*, 476 F. 2d 67 (1973); *United States v. Shye*, 473 F. 2d 1061 (1973); *United States v. Frick*, 490 F. 2d 666 (1973).

[4] See *United States v. Shye*, 473 F. 2d 1061, 1066 (1973); *United States v. Mapp*, 476 F. 2d 67, 80 (1973); *United States v. Baca*, 417 F. 2d 103; *United States v. Mason*, 523 F. 2d 1122, 1130 (1975), per Bazelon, C.J., dissenting in part.

[5] *People v. Fitzpatrick*, 300 N.E. 2d 139, 143 (1973); see also *United States v. Frick*, 490 F. 2d 666, 673 (1973), per Goldberg, J. dissenting, cert. denied, 419 U.S. 831 (1974).

[6] *United States v. Bradley*, 455 F. 2d 1181, 1187 (1972).

[7] *United States v. Mason*, 523 F. 2d 1122, 1131, per Bazelon, C.J. dissenting in part.

[8] 339 U.S. 56 (1950).

justification either for a routine search of any room other than that in which the arrest occurred or for that matter for a search of closed or concealed areas of the room itself.[1] Consistently with this it was held in *United States v. Griffith*[2] that the search of a bathroom, a room other than that in which the prisoner had been arrested, was forbidden by *Chimel*, as was the search of a closed suitcase and other concealed and inaccessible areas in the room itself. But since the exception of search incident to arrest is justified by the need to protect the arresting officer and to prevent the destruction of evidence, and since the scope of the particular search must be delineated accordingly, *Chimel* has not been construed to mean that the area within an arrestee's immediate control must be confined to 'that precise spot which is at arm('s) length from the arrestee at the moment of his arrest'.[3] Courts have often observed that an arrestee, both at the moment of arrest and shortly thereafter, retains to a considerable extent his mobility and may thus either lunge forward or move backward or to the side and in this way bring himself within the orbit of an area from which he might grab a weapon or evidentiary items.[4] *Chimel* does not hold that the police may not seize items within this area, but it is for the State to show that the search and seizures took place in the area 'within the reach' of the arrestee, something which can usually only be done by precise evidence concerning (1) 'the location of the items with respect to the whereabouts of the arrestee', (2) the accessibility of the items, and (3) their nature.[5] Some courts have a slightly different starting point. To them it is evident that on arrest normal expectations of privacy sharply diminish,[6] that 'normal extensions of the person remain subject to search',[7] and that articles customarily carried by an arrested person fall within the ambit of his immediate control for purposes of the *Chimel* rule, whether or not the search of such an extension takes place before or after the defendant's physical removal to a room other than that in which he was arrested.[8] It is apparently enough for some if articles such as purses, wallets, jackets, hats

[1] 395 U.S. at 766 et seq.

[2] 537 F. 2d 900 (1976); see also *United States v. Mapp*, 476 F. 2d 67, 80 (1973), *United States v. Hayes*, 518 F. 2d 675 (1975) and *Taylor v. Comm.*, 577 S.W. 2d 46 (1979).

[3] *Scott v. State*, 256 A. 2d 384, 389 (1969).

[4] Ibid. This has come to be known as the 'lunge' doctrine (see Carrington, '*Chimel v. California*—A Police Response', 45 *Notre Dame Lawyer* 559, 577 (1970)); see also *Application of Kiser*, 419 F. 2d 1134, 1137 (1969), where it was held that the range of permissible search was the area within the arrestee's 'leaping range'. As was pointed out in *Scott v. State*, supra, at 388, *Chimel* itself speaks of the area within 'immediate control' as that into which he '*might*' reach in order to grab a weapon or evidentiary items.

[5] *Scott v. State*, supra, at 389.

[6] See *United States v. DeLeo*, 422 F. 2d 487 (1970).

[7] *People v. Belvin*, 80 Cal. Rptr. 382, 384 (1969).

[8] Ibid., at 384. At times seizures of items or effects carried on, used by or near the arrestee at the time of arrest are dealt with not by reference to *Chimel*'s concept of immediate control (see *Belvin*, supra, at 384) but by way of the right to search the arrestee's *person* at the time of arrest: see *United States v. Robinson*, 414 U.S. 218 (1973) and *People v. Brisendine*, 531 P. 2d 1099 (1975).

and overcoats are in the vicinity of the arrestee at the time of arrest and that they normally accompany him on his removal to some other place.[1] In accordance with this it was held in one case[2] that where the defendant was arrested when sitting on her bed the seizure by the police of her purse lying on the floor was in accordance with *Chimel*. But it is still unclear if such items can be seized even though they are not within the arrestee's immediate control, particularly if the arrested person and the articles he would normally be expected to wear or take away with him are in different rooms.[3] A related problem arises if associates of the arrestee are known to lurk either within or near the room in which he was arrested. What is the effect of this upon the area which can be searched by the police? In other words, is the ambit of the 'grabbing distance' conditioned not only by the accused's potential for assaulting the arresting officers and destroying evidence but also by the danger that apparent confederates may behave likewise? The problem arose in *United States v. Manarite*[4] where on arresting the defendant the police noticed two unidentified men standing near two tables. It was held that searches of, and seizures from, areas not within the immediate control of the arrestee but within the reach of the unidentified men were consistent with *Chimel* since 'it was entirely reasonable and absolutely necessary for the safety of the law enforcement officials to consider the two men as (the defendant's) possible agents or accomplices, in effect as extensions of (his) physical presence, constructively placing (him) within reach of the two tables'. But it should be noted that in *Chimel* itself the Supreme Court refused to expand the spatial scope of a search incident to arrest because it was possible that a third party might take the opportunity to destroy evidence,[5] and other courts have been reluctant to sanction another exception to the warrant requirement based on the need to prevent third party destruction of evidence.[6] It is not clear what are the limits of *Manarite*, but consistently with *Chimel* it could be limited in one of two ways, either by suggesting that such a warrantless search should be upheld only if there was an overwhelming and demonstrable need for immediate action,[7] or by confining its holding to situations where the search was of areas within the immediate control of people who could fairly be described as 'extensions' of the arrested person(s).[8]

The reason underlying the limited right of warrantless search incident to arrest allowed in *Chimel* is the danger that the defendant will seize a weapon

[1] It may be that before such personal items can be seized they should be 'in use' by the arrestee at the time of arrest (see *Belvin*, supra), but it is not clear what this means, in particular whether it refers to actual use or control, or whether it has some more attenuated meaning.

[2] *People v. Belvin*, 80 Cal. Rptr. 382 (1969).

[3] 'Note', supra, at 1019.

[4] 314 F. Supp. 607 (1970).

[5] Cf. White, J.'s dissenting opinion in *Chimel*, supra.

[6] See *United States v. Davis*, 423 F. 2d 974 (1970) and *Vale v. Louisiana*, 399 U.S. 30 (1970).

[7] See *Schmerber v. California*, 384 U.S. 757 (1966) and *Cupp v. Murphy*, 93 S.Ct. 2000 (1973); see also *Vale v. Louisiana*, 399 U.S. 30, 35 (1970).

[8] *United States v. Manarite*, 314 F. Supp. 607, 616 (1970).

or destructible evidence. Whether this danger exists depends upon all the circumstances of each case. But it stands to reason that what is in the arrested person's immediate control or within his reach is determined mainly by where he stands at the time of the arrest and shortly thereafter.[1] If the arrestee moves towards some other area of the room, the area that can reasonably be considered to be within his control expands. Thus in *United States v. Mason*,[2] where the arrestee requested his jacket from the closet and stepped forward to a point within three or four feet of a closet, it was held that by doing so he brought within his immediate control the area round the closet, including a partially open suitcase concealing a weapon. Of course *Chimel* does not permit the arresting officers to lead the accused from place to place and then use his presence in each location to justify expanding the scope of the warrantless search incident to the arrest.[3] Nor can a search be upheld simply because the arresting officers decide to remove the handcuffs from the defendant after placing him under effective control.[4] The principle seems to be that police officers are not allowed either to take positive action or indeed to desist from taking sound precautions if the purpose or natural result of what they have done or failed to do is to bring about a situation which enlarges the area under a defendant's control, in this way artificially expanding the scope of the warrantless search. It was thus held in one case[5] that the *Chimel* doctrine did not permit the arresting officers to order the accused to dress and then refuse to bring him his clothes, thus requiring him to move about the room in order to comply with their directions. The officers' only legitimate purpose in being in the room was to make an arrest, and they did not have the right to create a situation which gave them a pretext for searching beyond the area of the defendant's immediate control. If it is found that the accused's proximity to the area which gives rise to the challenged enlargement of the initially narrow authority to search was brought about by official action or inaction, only a compelling justification can apparently cure the presumptive violation of the strictures of *Chimel*.[6]

Another related principle is that once a suspect is under the effective control of the arresting officers the area of permissible search under *Chimel* is narrowed accordingly. There are a number of cases illustrating this point. In

[1] A frequent formulation is that the permissible scope of warrantless arrest-based searches must be determined by reference to the criterion of reasonableness (see *United States v. Robinson*, 94 S.Ct. 467, at 478 (1973), per Marshall, J. dissenting; *Scott v. State*, 256 A. 2d 384, at 389 ('the search is tested by its reasonableness') and *United States v. Davis*, 423 F. 2d 974 (1970) (('s)ince a search incident to arrest is a warrantless search, it must ultimately be defined in terms of reasonableness')). Such formulations of course do not entail a return to the currently discredited *Rabinowitz* approach. What they rather stand for is that the area of 'immediate control' cannot be demarcated either in advance or mechanically, but only on all the facts of each case and in the light of the specific dangers confronting the arresting officers.

[2] 523 F. 2d 1122 (1975).

[3] Ibid., at 1126.

[4] Ibid., at 1133.

[5] *United States v. Griffith*, 537 F. 2d 900, 904 (1976).

[6] *Griffith*, supra, and *Mason*, supra, at 1133.

United States v. Mapp[1] it was held that a closet within which the incriminating evidence was discovered was not within the arrestee's immediate control since at the relevant time there were about five or six officers in the one-bedroom apartment, certainly more than sufficient manpower to prevent the person concerned, a woman, from reaching the closet. 'Unless (she) was either an acrobat or a Houdini, (one) cannot conceive how the closet could have fallen within the area of her immediate control',[2] particularly since an armed officer stood between her and what was seized. To hold otherwise, it was observed, would in effect be to uphold a search of all the enclosed areas of the room where the arrest was made, a result expressly forbidden by *Chimel*. Similarly, it was held in *United States v. Shye*[3], where all the suspects had already been lined up against a wall and searched for weapons, that the warrantless search of an area four feet from the defendant was improper since at that time 'the officers had the situation completely under control'. But it may be different if the officers involved can point to any 'articulable reasons'[4] leading them to believe that the arrestee was an especially dangerous person against whom extraordinary protective measures were required, or that the search was *a bona fide attempt* to secure an area which they reasonably believed to be within the arrestee's immediate control.

In neither *Mapp* nor *Shye* was the suspect handcuffed, and in both the question was assumed to be one of effective control. But in a number of other cases courts have distinguished between the situation in which the suspect is handcuffed and that in which he is not, and have upheld a more extensive search before the arrestee was handcuffed.[5] Thus, in *United States v. Weaklem*[6] it was held that the seizure of cocaine from a cabinet within two to four feet of where the arrestee was lying on the floor was justified as incident to arrest even though any resistance from the defendant had by that time been apparently overcome; since he was not yet handcuffed it was still conceivable, however unlikely it may have been, that he could yet make an attempt to destroy the evidence. And in *United States v. Patterson*,[7] where the female defendant was arrested for forgery while standing in a doorway between the kitchen and the living-room, it was held that the seizure of an envelope in the kitchen was consistent with *Chimel* despite the presence of five arresting officers, one of whom was standing between the arrestee and the kitchen cabinet from which the envelope was seized; the court accepted that there were 'restraints of sorts' but was not willing to treat them as the equivalent of handcuffing in putting the surrounding area beyond the arrestee's immediate control. Even handcuffing is on occasion ignored, as in

[1] 476 F. 2d 67, 80 (1973).
[2] Ibid.
[3] 473 F. 2d 1061, 1066 (1973).
[4] *United States v. Mapp*, supra.
[5] See generally *United States v. Griffith*, 537 F. 2d 900, 904 (1976) and *United States v. Mason*, 523 F. 2d 1122, 1132 n.16 (1975), per Bazelon, C.J., dissenting in part.
[6] 517 F. 2d 70 (1975).
[7] 447 F. 2d 424 (1971), cert. denied, 404 U.S. 1064 (1972); cf. *United States v. Baca*, 417 F. 2d 103 (1969), cert. denied, 404 U.S. 979 (1971).

People v. Fitzpatrick[1] where the fact that the police had handcuffed the defendant before they conducted their search of a closet was held to be immaterial. Indeed in some cases it is assumed both that the arrested person maintains 'immediate control' of an area even after he has been arrested, handcuffed and removed from the scene,[2] and that the 'grabbing distance' authorised in *Chimel* is to be delineated objectively, and irrespective either of the arrested person's continued capacity to grab[3] or of any realistic danger of a possible destruction of material evidence. In these cases 'the physical realities' of the arrest are subordinated to 'what amounts both literally and figuratively to a yardstick test',[4] divorced from the exigencies initially giving rise to this exception from the warrant requirement and assuming something of the objective features of pre-*Chimel* tests, albeit in a more limited form. This does not appear to be consistent with the strict approach of *Chimel*, whatever one may think of its merits. And many other cases, as we have seen, regard the issue as one of 'effective control', a test that they approach not on the basis of objective assumptions about 'reach', 'control' or 'grabbing distance' but as a question concerning the particular arrestee's actual potential for using weapons against the officers or for destroying relevant evidence.

(c) Search of the person incident to arrest

In *Chimel* the Supreme Court did not doubt that there was extensive authority to search the person of the arrestee upon his valid arrest. As Justice Stewart put it, 'when an arrest is made, it is reasonable for the arresting officer to search the person arrested in order to remove any weapons that the latter might seek to use in order to resist arrest or effect his escape'. Further, the arresting officer can search for and seize 'any evidence' on the arrestee's person in order to prevent its concealment of destruction.[5] Many other similar broadly worded statements can be found testifying to the existence of an apparently unqualified authority to search the person of the arrestee in order to find and seize evidence of the crime on which he is arrested, as well as weapons which might be used against the arresting officers. But most of *these* statements are dicta, while others hint at possible limitations. What, for instance, of offences where there is no question of any evidence, and where there is absolutely no indication that the arrested person is in possession of weapons? Does a police officer have the automatic right to conduct a full search of the person incident to a lawful arrest even for the technical violation

[1] 300 N.E. 2d 139 (1973).

[2] See Kamisar, LaFave and Israel, *Modern Criminal Procedure* 275 (4th ed. 1974) and see *United States v. Wysocki*, 457 F. 2d 1155 (1972); *People v. Perry*, 266 N.E. 2d 330 (1971).

[3] *People v. Floyd*, 260 N.E. 2d 815, 817 (1970).

[4] *United States v. Frick*, 490 F. 2d 666, 673 (1973), per Goldberg, J. dissenting in part.

[5] 393 U.S., at 762–3.

of a traffic regulation?[1] It is thus obvious that as a general rule there can be no 'fruits' or 'implements' of violations of traffic regulations. If now the only legitimate objectives of an arrest-based search of the person are, first, the seizure of the fruits, instrumentalities and other evidence of the crime for which the arrest is made in order to prevent its destruction or concealment, and, secondly, the disarming of the arrestee by the prompt removal of any weapons that he might seek to use either to resist arrest or to effect his escape, it could be argued on the basis of the obvious inapplicability of the first justification that the search of a person arrested for a traffic violation is *only* legitimate if it is capable of justification as one for weapons, and that it *cannot* be so justified if there is no indication that the suspect is armed. Another related question concerns the permissible intensity of legitimate scope of arrest-based searches, particularly in the case of arrests for offences where there is absolutely no question of evidence. If the only proper justification for such searches is the removal of weapons, should the arresting officers be allowed to conduct a full search or should their intrusion, in the absence of special circumstances, be limited to a frisk of the suspect's clothing? In terms of theory, these difficult questions can be formulated as follows. Should arrest-based searches of the person be governed by a careful analysis of the applicability of the justifications *traditionally* rendering such searches reasonable, or should the many categorical statements apparently embodying an unqualified right to search the person on arrest be taken literally? Does the 'scope limitation' principle, according to which a search is unreasonable not only if it was unjustified at its inception but also if it was not exactly related in scope to the circumstances justifying the official intrusion in the first place, apply in this context as well, or should it be confined to non-arrest situations, such as protective frisks for weapons? Is case-by-case adjudication of such issues the best way to forestall violations of the Fourth Amendment, or will an absolute rule, dispensing with the vagaries of the uninstructed individual judgment of each arresting officer concerning the permissibility of each and every intrusion and instead emphasising regularity of administration and obedience to carefully prescribed standard procedures, provide a better standard both for the guidance of the police and for the more effective protection of individual rights?

Two views with regard to arrest-based searches of the person can be put forward on the basis of general considerations, the first broad and apparently unqualified and the other narrower and more restrictive. The first maintains that a custodial arrest of a suspect based on probable cause is a reasonable intrusion under the Fourth Amendment and that a full search of the person contemporaneously with, or shortly after, the arrest requires no further

[1] See generally A.L.I., *A Model Code of Pre-Arraignment Procedure* 522–4 (1975); 'Note, Search and Seizure Incidental to Arrest for Traffic Violation', 40 *Marq. L. Rev.* 610 (1965); Simeone, 'Search and Seizure Incident to Traffic Violations', 6 *St. Louis U.L.J.* 506 (1960); 'Comment, Search Incident to Arrest for Minor Traffic Violations', 11 *Am. Crim. L. Rev.* 801 (1973); 'Note, Searches of the Person Incident to Lawful Arrest', 69 *Colum. L. Rev.* 866, 871 (1969); 'Note, Scope Limitations of Searches Incident to Arrest', 78 *Yale L.J.* 433, 444 (1969).

justification, whatever the offence on which the person searched has been arrested. Two arguments are advanced in support of the formulation of the authority to search in unqualified terms, first that an individual lawfully subjected to a custodial arrest retains no significant interest in the privacy of his person,[1] and secondly that any requirement that a search for weapons should *only* be possible if the arresting officer entertains reasonable apprehensions about his safety would be difficult to administer in that its application would necessarily depend upon subjective evaluation rather than on objective yardsticks and could thus expose the police to further serious danger.[2] The narrower doctrine[3] disagrees, and demands some justification *additional* to the fact of a lawful arrest before sanctioning a full search of the arrestee's person; alternatively, it might automatically permit an intrusion less than a full search—for instance, either a search directed towards specific evidentiary items in the case of arrests for offences involving tangible evidence, or a limited frisk for weapons of all those who have been arrested and placed in police custody—but in any case insists that the scope of *any* search of the person incident to arrest must be strictly circumscribed by the justifications permitting the offical intrusion in the first place. This second approach can be set out as follows. There is no doubt that the purposes of arrest-based searches of the person are to remove from the person of the arrestee destructible evidence of the crime for which he is arrested and to disarm him. The evidentiary and protective functions of such searches must be distinguished sharply, and appropriate limitations developed accordingly. Obviously when the arrest is for a crime for which evidence exists, a warrantless intrusion directed to the discovery of the evidence the suspect is likely to carry on his person is reasonable under the 'search incident to arrest' exception. But if what allows such evidentiary searches is the reasonable fear that without them valuable evidence will be destroyed, offences in the case of which it is demonstrable that no evidence exists must be treated differently. It is thus maintained, for instance, that upon stopping a motorist for a traffic violation the police have secured the only evidence which is available. No further intrusion can therefore be justified, and it logically follows that searches *for evidence* in the case of arrests for routine traffic violations are unreasonable and therefore unconstitutional because in reality they can only be 'fishing' expeditions for possible evidence of other crimes. Different considerations, according to this second approach, become relevant when the justification invoked in support of searches of the person is the interest in the

[1] *United States v. Robinson*, 414 U.S. 218, 237 (1973), per Powell, J. concurring; contra Marshall, J. dissenting in the same case, at 257.

[2] This line of argument is developed persuasively in *United States v. Robinson*, 471 F. 2d 1082, 1115 (1972), per Wilkey, J. dissenting; see also *United States v. Robinson*, 414 U.S. 218, 235 (1975), per Rehnquist, J. and La Fave, ' "Case-By-Case Adjudication" versus "Standardised Procedures": The *Robinson* Dilemma', 1974 *Sup. Ct. Rev.* 126, 141, 162 (1975).

[3] This is developed in the dissenting opinion of Marshall, J. in *United States v. Robinson*, 414 U.S. 218 at 238 et seq. and in the opinion of J. Skelly Wright, J. in *United States v. Robinson*, 471 F. 2d 1082 (1972) in the United States Court of Appeals (D.C.C.).

safety of police officers, i.e. the disarming of suspects by the removal of weapons. It cannot obviously be assumed that certain classes of arrested persons will never be armed, and there is little doubt that routine traffic stops are often attended by considerable danger for the arresting officer. But the right to search for weapons is neither automatic nor indeed necessarily connected with the fact of arrest. What instead gives rise to the need and the consequential authority to conduct a protective search for weapons is the reasonable apprehension that the person arrested is armed and dangerous, and it is quite irrelevant whether the protective search for weapons is incident to an arrest based on probable cause or to an investigative stop based only upon reasonable suspicion under *Terry v. Ohio*.[1] Warrantless intrusions incident to arrest directed towards the finding of weapons should therefore be permissible only if and when the arresting officer is able to point to specific and articulable facts which, in common with rational inferences drawn from them, reasonably warrant his belief that the person with whom he is dealing is both armed and dangerous; and in this and in other areas where the Fourth Amendment is relevant the scope limitation principle means that a search for weapons, like any other search, must be strictly circumscribed by the exigencies which initially made it lawful, here the need to discover and remove weapons. To put it somewhat differently, the scope of any search for weapons should be made to depend on the circumstances of the specific confrontation taken as a whole and not be determined a priori by the technical niceties of the law of arrest;[2] and in no case should it be extended beyond its original and indeed only purpose of securing the safety of the officer and preventing the arrestee's escape.

On the basis of general considerations such as these many courts have concluded, first that in the absence of special circumstances a police officer has no automatic right to search either the person or the vehicle incident to a lawful arrest for the violation of a mere traffic violation, secondly that a search for weapons can only be undertaken where there exist special facts or circumstances which give the officer reasonable grounds to apprehend danger from the arrestee, and thirdly that the scope of any search that might be permitted should not go beyond what is reasonably required to discover and remove dangerous weapons. Examples abound. In *Barnes v. State*[3] the defendant was stopped and arrested by two police officers for a brake light violation. A full search of his person was then conducted, including shining a flashlight into his overcoat pocket. It was held that the search was illegal since it was not 'a legitimate search for weapons'. The contention that any search of the person of one lawfully arrested was valid was rejected, and although a limited 'pat down' for weapons would have been constitutional, a full search

[1] 392 U.S. 1 (1968). Under *Terry*, as will be seen later, the police have power *to stop* a person reasonably suspected of committing or of being about to commit a crime (even though there is no probable cause for an arrest) and *to subject him* to a limited search for weapons *if* this action is reasonable (or necessary) given the officer's need to protect himself and others nearby from attack.

[2] *People v. Superior Court of Los Angeles County (Simon)*, 496 P. 2d 1205, 1218 (1972).

[3] 130 N.W. 2d 264 (1964).

of the person was considered to be neither necessary nor reasonable. In *State v. Curtis*[1] police officers arrested the defendant for a trivial traffic violation. It was held that a search of his person was unlawful since 'the validity of a search for weapons following a traffic arrest depends on whether the officer had reasonable grounds to believe (that) a search was necessary for his own safety or to prevent an escape', a condition that had not been met here. Similarly, in *People v. Marsh,*[2] where the defendant had been arrested for speeding, it was held that a subsequent search of his person producing incriminating evidence was illegal. The court accepted that, as a *general* rule, when an individual was lawfully arrested, the arresting officer could conduct a contemporaneous search of his person for weapons or for evidence of the particular crime for which the arrest had been made. This did not cover arrests for traffic violations, and here any search had to be capable of justification as one for weapons. There was in any case something incongruous about subjecting traffic offenders to the indignity of a search for weapons, unless of course the officer who effected the arrest had good cause for believing himself to be in danger. The result of these and many other authorities[3] was nothing less than rejection of traditional formulations according to which arrest-based contemporaneous searches of the person directed towards the discovery of either evidence or of weapons were without more reasonable intrusions under the Fourth Amendment. According to them the only kind of search justified automatically by a lawful arrest is the quest for evidence, and of course only in the case of those offences where material evidence exists. In contrast, the search for weapons is a *special and independent* exception to the proscription against warrantless searches, and one that can only be activated by reasonable suspicion that the officer is in danger.

But this analysis, after considerable success at both the federal and state levels, was rejected by the Supreme Court in *United States v. Robinson*,[4] where a majority upheld a full search of the person of an individual arrested for operating a vehicle after his licence had been revoked. The Court took the view, first that the authority to search in this area derives from the fact of a lawful arrest and not from the exigencies of the particular situation or from the probability that weapons or evidence may be found on the suspect's person; secondly that there is a distinction of constitutional dimensions between, on the one hand, *Terry*-type stops, where the most intrusive search that the Fourth Amendment will allow is, at least initially, a limited frisk for weapons and, on the other, cases where a lawful custodial arrest has been

[1] 190 N.W. 2d 631 (1971).

[2] 20 N.Y. 2d 98, 228 N.E. 2d 783 (1967).

[3] See particularly *People v. Superior Court of Los Angeles County*, 496 P. 2d 1205 (1972); *People v. Zeigler*, 100 N.W. 2d 456 (1960); *United States v. Humphrey*, 409 F. 2d 1055, 1058 (1969); and *Amador-Gonzalez v. United States*, 391 F. 2d 308, 315 (1968), per Wisdom, J.

[4] 414 U.S. 218 (1973); see La Fave, supra, 154 n.2; White, 'The Fourth Amendment as a Way of Talking about People', 1974 *Sup. Ct. Rev.* 165 (1975); 'The Supreme Court, 1973 Term', 88 *Harv. L. Rev.* 41, 181 (1974); see also *Model Code*, supra, at 523.

made, since in this second type of situation the danger normally confronting the officer is far greater than in the context of fleeting confrontations between citizen and police exemplified by *Terry* and similar cases; and thirdly that it was not proper to distinguish in terms of authority to search between arrestable offences or types of custodial arrest both because they all shared a common basis that in the majority's view provided sufficient justification supporting a full contemporaneous search of the person—namely, the fact of a lawful arrest—and because a system of case by case adjudication geared to overall reasonableness and ultimately subordinating the legality of an arrest-based search not to objective and manageable criteria but to the existence on all the facts of each case of a demonstrable relationship between the particular intrusion and the perceived need for the protection of the arresting officer to which the narrower view would inexorably lead was regarded as undesirable.[1] In the majority's view it was 'the fact of the lawful arrest which establishes the authority to search', and therefore in the case of 'a lawful custodial arrest' a '*full search*' of the person was 'not only an exception to the warrant requirement of the Fourth Amendment, but also a "reasonable" search under that Amendment'. The same result was reached in *Gustafson v. Florida*[2] where the defendant was arrested for driving without a valid licence in his possession. It was argued by the petitioner that *Robinson* could be distinguished, first because in *Gustafson* the offence for which the arrest had been made was 'trivial in nature', carrying with it no mandatory minimum sentence as did the offence for which the defendant in *Robinson* had been arrested, and secondly because, again unlike *Robinson*, there were no police regulations requiring the arresting officer to take the suspect into custody or to conduct full-scale body searches upon arrest in the field. These differences were declared by the Court to be irrelevant.[3] Since, as was held in *Robinson*,

[1] The majority's rejection of the case-by-case method of Fourth Amendment adjudication was criticised by Marshall, J. in dissent (414 U.S. at 238), but even he concluded that an officer is always justified in conducting a routine pat-down search for weapons whenever he takes a suspect into custody. For an eloquent exposition of the merits of general, standardised search procedures, as compared to a system of ad hoc responses to the circumstances of each case, see *United States v. Robinson*, 471 F. 2d 1082, 1115 (1972), per Wilkey, J. dissenting.

[2] 414 U.S. 260 (1973).

[3] See La Fave, supra, 154 n.2, at 161. As the *Model Code*, supra, 153 n.1, at 523, points out, *Gustafson* appears to allow a full search of anyone stopped for a traffic offence, however minor, 'if the officer has authority to take the violator to the police station'. The Court's failure to make a distinction between cases where the arresting officer in conducting a full search is acting in pursuance of detailed police regulations and cases where there are no comparable regulations but the officer is free to arrest (and take to the station) or merely issue a ticket (as in *Gustafson*) has been particularly regretted by some. Amsterdam, 'Perspectives on the Fourth Amendment', 58 *Minn. L. Rev.* 349, 416 (1974) had said that the Supreme Court in not finding such differences material missed the chance to make 'the greatest contribution to the jurisprudence of the Fourth Amendment since James Otis argued against the writs of assistance in 1761'. It must be noticed that in *Gustafson* Stewart, J., concurring, made the potentially important point that there may be some minor offences for which a custodial arrest is constitutionally impermissible, whether or not authorised by state law; see also White, supra, at 208.

it was the fact of lawful arrest which gave rise to the authority to search, it was sufficient in *Gustafson* too that the officer had probable cause to arrest the defendant and that he lawfully effectuated the arrest, placing the arrestee in custody. Do *Robinson* and *Gustafson* then confer unqualified authority upon a police officer to stop and arrest a motorist for a traffic violation and then subject him to extensive searches of the person? It certainly appears so. One possible limitation is that *Robinson* and *Gustafson* only apply when a 'custodial arrest' has been made, a key phrase repeatedly used in the Court's opinion but nowhere defined. Even though it may be difficult to ascertain its exact parameters,[1] the *Robinson* opinion quotes police testimony defining a 'full custodial arrest' as one in which an officer 'would arrest a subject and subsequently transport him to a police facility for booking',[2] but it is not indicated whether the latter requirement is a necessary concomitant of the term. But in any case the Supreme Court in *Robinson* and *Gustafson* dealt with situations where there was a custodial arrest and by its own admission did not reach questions presented by 'routine traffic stops', i.e. where the officer simply issues a notice of violation and allows the offender to proceed, without taking him in custody to the police station. On this basis a possible distinction that can be made is between those traffic and other minor offenders who are merely cited and immediately released, and those who are arrested *and* taken to the police station. Since in the second case the arresting officer will have to take the suspect to the police station and almost certainly travel in close proximity with him, it is only reasonable that an automatic search for weapons should be permissible; but in the former situation, where the officer's intention is simply to book or cite the defendant for his violation and allow him to continue on his way, an automatic search should not be allowed, unless the officer is able to point to specific facts reasonably supporting his suspicion that the person he is dealing with is armed and dangerous. For as Chief Justice Wright explained in *People v. Superior Court (Simon)*[3], 'when it becomes necessary that an officer should confine a traffic law violator within his police vehicle, the officer risks the danger that the violator may be armed with and draw a weapon'. Since the danger is not necessarily eliminated by handcuffing the suspect, as he may still be able to use a weapon hidden on his person, a limited search for weapons should be permitted.[4] It is of course difficult to reconcile this type of reasoning with *Robinson* because the basis on

[1] See *People v. Superior Court (Simon)*, 496 P. 2d 1205 (1972); *People v. Brisendine*, 531 P. 2d 1099, 1110 n.14 (1975).

[2] 414 U.S. at 221 n.2.

[3] 496 P. 2d 1205, 1214 (1972).

[4] Ibid., at 1225. This approach classifies traffic and other 'arrests' (a term that of course depends upon state law) as follows: (a) those where the 'arrested person' is cited and immediately released; (b) those where the offender may or must be taken before a magistrate and given the option to post bond; and (c) those where a felony is involved and a full custodial arrest will take place. If a case falls into the first group the officer can only take action if this is required by his own safety; in the second type of case a limited pat-down is automatically permissible since the offender and the officer will travel together (in those cases where the violator *will* be taken before a magistrate); in the third more extensive measures may be taken *because* the danger increases.

which it proceeds is that the critical factor in such situations is not the fact of arrest, but rather the greater likelihood of danger to the officer where the traffic or other violator is to be detained for a substantial period of time. But that such an approach still holds considerable attraction for many courts is clear from *People v. Brisendine*[1] where the California Supreme Court, in construing California's search and seizure provisions,[2] refused to follow *Robinson*. Here the defendant and other campers were *arrested* for a fire ordinance violation. Before escorting them out of the prohibited area and back to the patrol car, where they would be cited for the fire ordinance violation and ordered to appear before a magistrate at some future date, the arresting officers conducted a thorough search of the persons of all the defendants. The knapsack of one of them was picked up, squeezed and, when it was decided that its outer layer was too hard for ascertaining whether it contained weapons, searched. The search uncovered a plastic bottle with a cap on it, and this was found to contain marijuana. It was held that since it was necessary for the arresting officers to be in close proximity with the defendant and his companions for a prolonged period of time a limited weapons search, consisting of a frisk or pat-down, was reasonable; this being the case, the officers were justified in investigating further when the pat-down of the defendant's knapsack proved inadequate to disclose if it contained weapons; but the subsequent intrusion into the bottle inside the sack could not be justified by the purpose of discovering weapons which had alone validated the search at its inception, and it accordingly followed that the incriminating items had been obtained by means of an unreasonable search and seizure in violation of the California Constitution. The court's opinion is based on three propositions, diametrically opposed to the categorical approach of *Robinson* and *Gustafson*. First, courts should not apply hard and fast rules for determining the reasonableness of warrantless searches. 'Rather, we must be concerned, in a case-by-case analysis, with whether the extent of the search exceeded the attainment of the objectives which justified its inception'; secondly, the sole justification for searches in the case of traffic and other offences where there is no question of any evidence is the protection of the arresting police officer and others nearby, and any intrusion must therefore be confined in scope to what is reasonably calculated to discover weapons; and thirdly, before a search for weapons can properly exceed the limited scope of a frisk or pat-down, the officer conducting the search must be able to point to specific facts reasonably supporting his apprehension or

[1] 531 P. 2d 1099 (1975).

[2] On this it was held first that California's constitutional prohibition against unreasonable searches and seizures has independent force and was not intended to mirror its federal counterpart, and secondly that citizens of California are entitled to greater protection against unreasonable searches and seizures under the California Constitution than that required by the United States Constitution. In other words, state courts are the ultimate arbiters of state law, including state constitutional provisions that are identical to the federal ones, unless of course state interpretations purport to restrict the liberties guaranteed under the federal charter (see also *State v. Kaluna (Hawaii)*, 520 P. 2d 51 (1974) and Falk, 'The State Constitution: A More Than "Adequate" Nonfederal Ground', 61 *Cal. L. Rev.* 273 (1973)).

suspicion that the suspect is armed.

As is clear from the case which has just been discussed, it is generally assumed that as regards the incident-to-arrest exception similar considerations to the ones canvassed in the case of searches of the person govern warrantless searches of personal effects carried on the person or in the immediate possession of the arrestee.[1] Since it was necessary that the sack should accompany the officers and the suspect out of the area it could be subjected to the same type of protective search as the person of the arrestee. But this was only so because it was possible that it too could contain weapons. If this was not possible, either because of its size or because of other circumstances, the California court would obviously not have upheld even a limited protective examination, as was in effect held with regard to the bottle. Presumably the same applied to the arrestee's other belongings. But the issue is neither clear nor free from difficulty, particularly if the *Robinson-Gustafson* approach is adopted. *Robinson* illustrates the problem well. There, after an initial pat-down, the arresting officer felt an object in the left breast pocket of the overcoat the suspect was wearing, but could not tell what it was. He then reached into the pocket and pulled out the object which proved to be 'a crumpled up cigarette package'. A subsequent investigation of the contents of the cigarette package revealed heroin. One possibility, consistently with the flexible approach adopted by the California Supreme Court set out above, is to draw a sharp distinction between the search of *Robinson*'s person on the one hand and the search of his 'effects', including his cigarette package, on the other. Since the officer was making a custodial arrest and it would clearly have been unreasonable to expect him to place the suspect in his car for transportation to the police station without first taking reasonable measures to ensure his safety, a protective search for weapons, in the sense of a frisk of the arrestee's person, clothing and any other possessions he was carrying with or on him and which could have included the only legitimate object of the search—weapons—was justified. But in terms of the discovery of weapons, the only justification making the search permissible in the first place, the examination of the contents of the package was unjustified, particularly after the object in the arrestee's pocket had been removed and was under the officer's control. On the *Brisendine* theory only what can fairly be explained in terms of protection for the officer or others nearby is consistent with the Fourth Amendment. The *Robinson* opinion disagrees. It refuses to break up what it regards as a single process flowing from the fact of a lawful arrest into its various constituent steps; takes the view that since a custodial arrest is a reasonable intrusion any associated search is also reasonable in that it does not significantly add to the invasion of privacy that has already occurred with the constitutionally unobjectionable arrest; and concludes by affirming that what is entailed by all custodial arrests is the authority to conduct a *full* search both of the person and apparently of any effects the suspect is carrying, irrespective of any probability that weapons or evidence would in fact be found in any of the items so inspected, and perhaps subject only to the

[1] See also 68 Am. Jur. 2d, *Searches and Seizures* § 93; see *People v. Brisendine*, 531 P. 2d 1099, 1108 (1975). See also *People v. Belvin*, 80 Cal. Rptr. 382 (1969).

general and not too demanding qualification that such incidental searches should be free of any 'extreme or patently abusive characteristics' that would independently violate the Due Process Clause.[1] The position therefore appears to be that—so far as the Supreme Court is concerned (but not necessarily state courts)—on a custodial arrest a warrantless search and seizure of items either on the person of the arrestee or within the area of his immediate control is without more reasonable, altogether apart from any calculation on the part of the arresting officer that weapons or destructible evidence may be involved. But, it must still be noted, a search of possessions seized at the time of an arrest cannot be justified as incident to that arrest if 'the search is remote in time or place from the arrest'.[2] It was therefore held in *United States v. Chadwick*[3] that once law enforcement officers had reduced the luggage of the arrestee to their exclusive control, and there was no longer any danger that the arrestee might gain access to the property to seize a weapon or to destroy evidence, a search of that property was not an incident of the arrest.

The compulsory extraction of blood for purposes of analysis, the administration of other medical tests and any intrusions into the human body, i.e. beyond the body's surface, as has been seen, plainly constitute searches[4] of 'persons' within the language of the Fourth Amendment, and their legality even in the case of arrested individuals depends not so much on the line of cases associated with the traditional right affirmed in *Robinson*—namely, the right to search the person of one who is validly arrested in order to discover and seize weapons and evidence—as on distinct principles developed in their specific context.[5] These may be set out as follows. Search warrants are normally required before tests involving intrusions into the human body can be administered, and such warrants should not be given in the absence of a clear indication that material evidence will be found. But if on the particular facts of a case the arresting officers are confronted with an emergency, in the sense that the delay necessary to obtain the warrant will result in the inevitable destruction, disappearance or loss of the evidence, then they may proceed without securing a warrant, *provided* that the tests, methods or procedures involved are reasonable, entail no meaningful risk, and have been administered in a proper environment and according to accepted medical practices. These conditions were found to have been satisfied in *Schmerber v. California*.[6] Here, after the defendant's arrest, while he was at a hospital receiving treatment for injuries suffered in a car accident, a blood sample was withdrawn from his body by a physician at the direction of a police officer acting without a search warrant, despite the arrestee's refusal to give his consent to the blood test. It was held that the

[1] 414 U.S. 218, 236 (1973), per Rehnquist, J.

[2] *Preston v. United States*, 376 U.S., at 367 (1964).

[3] 433 U.S. 1 (1977).

[4] See *Schmerber v. California*, 384 U.S. 757 (1966); *United States v. Allen*, 337 F. Supp. 1041 (1972); *United States v. Smith*, 470 F. 2d 377 (1972).

[5] See 68 Am. Jur. 2d, *Searches and Seizures* § 29; *Model Code*. supra, 153 n.1, at 143 and 525; 'Annotation', 16 L. Ed. 2d 1332; and 'Annotation', 22 L. Ed. 2d 909.

[6] 384 U.S. 757 (1966).

Constitution did not forbid minor intrusions into an individual's body under 'stringently limited conditions'. Search warrants were necessary for searches of dwellings and as a general matter no less could be required where intrusions into the human body were concerned. But given, first, the undeniable fact that delay would cause the speedy disappearance of any evidence of alcohol in the blood, secondly the high degree of probability that relevant evidence was contained in the arrestee's blood, and thirdly the absolute propriety of the means and procedures employed in the instant case in obtaining the challenged evidence of blood-alcohol content, it was concluded that the warrantless extraction of the defendant's blood was 'an appropriate incident' of his arrest. In one case[1] *Chimel*-type reasoning was applied, even though what was in issue was a severe, though brief, intrusion into bodily security and despite the fact that no arrest had at the relevant time been made. Here fingernail scrapings were taken without consent from a suspect detained in custody but not yet arrested, although there was probable cause to believe that he was guilty of his wife's murder. The Supreme Court held that the seizure of a sample of scrapings from under the suspect's fingernails was constitutionally permissible under the principles of *Chimel*. It was true that no arrest had at the time of the challenged intrusion been made, and a full *Chimel* search would not therefore have been upheld. But not only was there probable cause to believe that the defendant had committed an offence, but also testimony had been given that after he refused to give his consent to the taking of the samples he put his hands behind his back and appeared to rub them together. In these circumstances, considering 'the very limited intrusion undertaken incident to the (suspect's) detention' and 'the ready destructibility' of the evidence, the warrantless action of the police in subjecting an individual to a 'very limited search' that was 'necessary' to preserve 'highly evanescent' evidence would be held to be reasonable. One possible interpretation of this difficult case is that it announces an *independent* proposition combining elements of *Chimel* and *Schmerber*—namely, that where there is probable cause to believe both that an individual hides or carries on his person readily destructible evidence and that this evidence will be lost unless immediate action is taken, then a minor intrusion strictly commensurate with the emergency or need confronting the police will be sustained even though it was not preceded either by an arrest or by a search warrant.[2]

(d) Searches of vehicles

Automobiles present special Fourth Amendment problems, and their attempted resolution by the Supreme Court presents considerable interest.[3]

[1] *Cupp v. Murphy*, 412 U.S. 291 (1973).

[2] The *Model Code*, supra, 153 n.1, at 525, expresses the view that in *Cupp v. Murphy* 'the Court in fact applied a *Carroll* rule (allowing police to search mobile cars) to an individual who was ambulatory and could easily destroy evidence which the police had reason to believe was under his fingernails'.

[3] See generally 'Note, Warrantless Searches and Seizures of Automobiles', 87 *Harv. L. Rev.* 835 (1974); 'Annotation, Warrantless Search of Automobile', 26 L.

The many decisions are difficult both to analyse and to reconcile, for even though there has been some measure of agreement on (at least the formulation of) some 'general principles',[1] the vague language in which these are usually cast has not been translated into more detailed and precise formulas for determining concrete cases. A number of things are often repeated in the cases. It is first of all clear that automobiles are 'effects'[2] and thus within the express protection of the Fourth Amendment. But 'common sense dictates that questions involving searches of motorcars or other things readily moved cannot be treated as identical to questions arising out of searches of fixed structures like houses',[3] and what follows from this is that 'what may be an unreasonable search of a house may be reasonable in the case of a motorcar',[4] or, to put it somewhat differently, 'less stringent warrant requirements have been applied to vehicles',[5] with the result that 'warrantless examinations of automobiles have been upheld in circumstances in which a search of a home or office would not'.[6] This has been necessitated by two main considerations. There is first the mobility of automobiles which often gives rise to circumstances of necessity making strict insistence on enforcement of the warrant requirement unrealistic and on many occasions impossible;[7] for since '(a) vehicle can be quickly moved out of the locality or jurisdiction in which the warrant must be sought',[8] it stands to reason that 'the officers might be deprived of valuable evidence if required to obtain a warrant before effecting any search or seizure'.[9] One of the main problems with regard to warrantless searches of automobiles is already apparent.[10] Should the twin elements of mobility and exigency on the basis of which this justification proceeds be taken in the sense of actual mobility and actual necessity, so that warrantless examinations of vehicles should be upheld only where there was a danger, whether immediate or at the very least not improbable, that the car would be removed from the jurisdiction and

---

Ed. 2d 893; 68 Am. Jur., *Searches and Seizures* (2d ed.) § 45; American Law Institute, *Model Code of Pre-Arraignment Procedure* 550–2 (1975).

[1] *Cady v. Dombrowski*, 413 U.S. 433 (1973), per Rehnquist, J.; see also *South Dakota v. Opperman*, 428 U.S. 364, 381 (1976), per Powell, J. concurring.

[2] *Cady v. Dombrowski*, 413 U.S. 433 (1973), per Rehnquist, J.; *Brinegar v. United States*, 338 U.S. 160, 182 (1949), per Jackson, J. dissenting.

[3] *Preston v. United States*, 376 U.S. 364, 366 (1964), per Black, J.

[4] *Preston v. United States*, 376 U.S. 364, 366, 367 (1964), per Black, J.; see also *Carroll v. United States*, 267 U.S. 132 (1925); *Brinegar v. United States*, 338 U.S. 160 (1949).

[5] *Cardwell v. Lewis*, 417 U.S. 583, 589, 590 (1974), per Blackmun, J.; see also *Chambers v. Maroney*, 399 U.S. 42, 49 (1970); *Cady v. Dombrowski*, supra.

[6] *South Dakota v. Opperman*, 428 U.S. 364, 367 (1976), per Burger, C.J.

[7] See *Brinegar v. United States*, 338 U.S. 160, 182 (1949), per Jackson, J. dissenting; *South Dakota v. Opperman*, 428 U.S. 364, 367 (1976), per Burger, C.J.

[8] *Carroll v. United States*, 267 U.S. 132, 153 (1925), per Taft, C.J.; see also *Chambers v. Maroney*, 399 U.S. 42, 48 (1970); *Cady v. Dombrowski*, 413 U.S. 433 (1973).

[9] *Chambers v. Maroney*, 399 U.S. 42, 62 (1970), per Harlan, J. dissenting.

[10] See 'Note, Warrantless Searches and Seizures of Automobiles', 87 *Harv. L. Rev.* 835, 842–3 (1974).

valuable evidence destroyed, or should 'the vagrant'[1] and 'ambulatory'[2] nature of vehicles be taken in the sense of 'inherent mobility', so that warrantless searches should be sustained even in cases where the possibilities of a removal of the vehicle or of the destruction of the evidence were 'remote, if not non existent'[3]? But if mobility and the element of necessity created by it are the reasons for making another exception to the warrant requirement it would at first sight appear strange if warrantless examinations of vehicles which for some obvious reason could, or would, not be moved and in the case of which there was ample time to obtain a search warrant were upheld. The second consideration traditionally emphasised in drawing a constitutional distinction between houses and cars is that as a general matter 'the search of an automobile is far less intrusive on the rights protected by the Fourth Amendment than the search of one's person or of a building'.[4] This is because 'the expectation of privacy with respect to one's automobile is significantly (weaker) than that relating to one's home or office',[5] a conclusion that in turn is based not only on the demonstrable fact that automobiles, unlike houses, are subjected to continuous and at times demanding governmental regulation,[6] but also on the undeniable consideration that the chief function of the motorcar is transportation, not residence.[7] This second justification too cannot be pushed to what some might regard as its logical limit. For, despite 'the obviously public nature of automobile travel' which means that 'a car has little capacity for escaping public scrutiny' when travelling through public roads where its occupants and its contents are in plain view, it would surely be impermissible either to regard the exercise of a desire to be mobile as a waiver of one's right to be free of unreasonable governmental intrusion[8] or effectively to reach the conclusion that no part of the interior of an automobile enjoys meaningful constitutional protection,[9] the individual's

[1] *Cady v. Dombrowski*, 413 U.S. 433 (1973), per Rehnquist, J.

[2] Ibid.

[3] *Cady v. Dombrowski*, supra; see also *South Dakota v. Opperman*, 428 U.S. 364, 367 (1976), per Burger, C.J.; *Chambers v. Maroney*, supra; *Cooper v. California*, 386 U.S. 58 (1967).

[4] *Almeida—Sanchez v. United States*, 413 U.S. 266, 279 (1973), per Powell, J. concurring.

[5] *South Dakota v. Opperman*, 428 U.S. 364, 367 (1976), per Burger, C.J.; see also *Cardwell v. Lewis*, 417 U.S. 583, 590 (1974), per Blackmun, J.

[6] *South Dakota v. Opperman*, supra, at 368, per Burger, C.J.

[7] *Cardwell v. Lewis*, supra, at 590, per Blackmun, J. Another justification sometimes put forward as an independent ground for the 'constitutional' difference between houses and cars is 'the extensive and often noncriminal contact with automobiles' which often brings local officials in 'plain view' of evidence, fruits, or instrumentalities of crime: see *Cady v. Dombrowski*, supra. This is often put forward as one of the arguments why one's expectation of privacy is diminished with regard to automobiles as opposed to one's home: see *South Dakota v. Opperman*, supra, at 368, per Burger, C.J.

[8] *Cardwell v. Lewis*, supra, at 591, per Blackmun, J.

[9] For the proposition that the interest in the privacy of one's automobile is meaningful and at times substantial, see *United States v. Ortiz*, 422 U.S. 891, 896 (1975), where it was recognised that 'a search, even of an automobile, is a substantial invasion of privacy'; *Almeida—Sanchez v. United States*, 413 U.S. 266,

interest in the privacy of all areas of his car being 'negligible'.[1] But even though, as can be seen, the purported justifications for distinguishing between searches of automobiles and searches of houses are not always as obvious as some might think, nor (at least in some contexts) as free of doubt and ambiguity as is sometimes suggested, it is now settled consitutional doctrine that warrantless examinations of automobiles will be sustained in many circumstances which would certainly not justify the search of a home or of other private premises.[2] The many decisions illustrating such circumstances do not mean that '(t)he word automobile is a talisman in whose presence the Fourth Amendment fades away and disappears',[3] but they do demonstrate that 'for the purposes of the Fourth Amendment there is a *constitutional* difference between houses and cars'.[4] As will be seen shortly, refinement of these broad agreed generalities into workable guidelines for the disposition of individual cases has been attended both by much confusion[5] and by sharply differing approaches to the surely crucial issue of how much substantive protection from official investigative intrusions cars *should* enjoy.

A study of the many cases yields three possible approaches to the analysis of problems posed by warrantless searches of automobiles. The first is to insist on traditional orthodoxy, namely that the Fourth Amendment's prohibition against unreasonable searches and seizures is determined by the warrant clause, that therefore a warrantless search of private property is per se unreasonable under the Fourth Amendment unless it falls within one of the few specifically established and well-delineated exceptions, and that searches of automobiles are likewise governed by this general rule, which means that before a warrantless intrusion into or examination of a vehicle can be upheld it must be found to come within one of the recognised exceptions, whether of the traditional type or of the type that are exclusively associated with automobiles.[6] The second possible approach takes the fundamentally

---

269–70 (1973); *Coolidge v. New Hampshire*, 403 U.S. 443, 461 (1971); see also *Cardwell v. Lewis*, 417 U.S. 583, 591 (1974). Indeed, if the basic constitutional test in this as in other areas is one's socially recognised expectation of privacy (see *Katz v. United States*, 389 U.S. at 351; *United States v. Dionisio*, 410 U.S. at 14), then it would follow that a distinction should, at least in some contexts, be drawn between those parts of the automobile normally considered private, such as a locked glove compartment, and others: see 'Annotation', supra, 162 n.3, at 901; and, from a somewhat different context, see *Mozzetti v. Superior Court*, 484 P. 2d 84 (1971).

[1] See Szwajkowski, 'The Aftermath of *Cooper v. California*', 1968 *U. Ill. L.F.* 401, 410; see also 'Annotation', supra, 162 n.3, at 901.

[2] See *Cady v. Dombrowski*, 413 U.S. 433 (1973); *Chambers v. Maroney*, 399 U.S. 42 (1970); *Carroll v. United States*, 267 U.S. 132 (1925); and the concurring opinion of Powell, J., in *South Dakota v. Opperman*, 428 U.S. 364, 382 (1976).

[3] *Coolidge v. New Hampshire*, 403 U.S. 443, 461 (1971), per Stewart, J.

[4] *Cady v. Dombrowski*, supra, at 439, quoting *Chambers v. Maroney*, supra, at 52.

[5] See *Coolidge v. New Hampshire*, 403 U.S. 443 (1971); *Cady v. Dombrowski*, supra, at 440, per Rehnquist, J.

[6] See the dissenting opinions of Harlan, J. and Brennan, J. in *Chambers v. Maroney*, supra, and *Cady v. Dombrowski*, supra, respectively; see also *Coolidge v. New Hampshire*, supra, *Almeida—Sanchez v. United States*, 413 U.S. 266 (1973), and *Preston v. United States*, 376 U.S. 364 (1964).

opposite view that in the area of vehicular searches constitutional validity depends not on the presence of an antecedent judicial authorisation but on whether the particular search was 'unreasonable',[1] that the quality of reasonableness or unreasonableness cannot be fixed by per se rules but must instead be decided upon on the facts and circumstances of each case,[2] and that the most one can do is to derive from prior cases certain general guidelines or principles in the light of which novel fact situations are to be tested.[3] An intermediate approach, which tries to steer a middle course between on the one hand rigorous enforcement of the warrant requirement and on the other disposition of individual cases in accordance with ultimately subjective views regarding the acceptability of certain types of police conduct, is to acknowledge that while it is general Fourth Amendment doctrine that 'the definition of reasonableness turns, at least in part, on the more specific dictates of the warrant clause'[4] in the case of vehicular searches the requirement of a prior judicial authorisation cannot be insisted upon to the same extent as in other areas, with the result that, even though there is 'no general automobile exception to the warrant requirement',[5] the difference between houses and cars is of constitutional dimensions.[6]

The many cases can be grouped under three headings. There are first warrantless vehicular searches which can be justified under established exceptions to the warrant requirement. The ones most often invoked in this connection are the 'search incident to arrest' exception and the 'plain view' doctrine.[7] As regards the former, it has never been doubted that a search of an automobile, or at least of parts of it, is constitutionally valid if it can fairly be described as incident to a valid arrest.[8] But is is important to bear in mind two things. To begin with, the rule allowing contemporaneous warrantless searches as incident to lawful arrest can only be justified either by the need to seize weapons or other things with which the arrestee might assault the arresting police officers or by the need to prevent the destruction of evidence of the crime being investigated that is either in the accused's possession or under his control, and is therefore inapplicable where the search is 'remote in

[1] *Cooper v. California*, 386 U.S. 58, 61 (1967); *United States v. Rabinowitz*, 339 U.S. 56, 66 (1950).

[2] *Coolidge v. New Hampshire*, 403 U.S. at 509–10, per Black, J. concurring and dissenting.

[3] See *South Dakota v. Opperman*, 428 U.S. at 375, per Burger, C.J.

[4] *South Dakota v. Opperman*, 428 U.S. at 381, per Powell, J. concurring; see also *United States v. United States District Court*, 407 U.S. 297, 315 (1972); *Camara v. Municipal Court*, 387 U.S. 523, 528 (1967).

[5] *South Dakota v. Opperman*, supra, at 382, per Powell, J. concurring.

[6] See *Chambers v. Maroney*, supra, at 52; *Cady v. Dombrowski*, supra, at 439; *South Dakota v. Opperman*, supra, at 382.

[7] Other exceptions are the 'hot pursuit' one and the one based on consent: see generally *United States v. Mapp*, 476 F. 2d 67, 76 (1973). As regards warrantless searches based on consent, see the separate opinion of Harlan, J. in *Chambers v. Maroney*, 399 U.S. 42 (1970) and 'Annotation', supra, 162 n. 3, at 910.

[8] *Preston v. United States*, 376 U.S. 364 (1964); *Dyke v. Taylor Implement Mfg. Co.*, 391 U.S. 216 (1968); *Chambers v. Maroney*, 399 U.S. 42 (1970); and 'Annotation', supra, n.1, at 898–9.

time or place from the arrest'.[1] The principle that only a search that is 'substantially contemporaneous with the arrest'[2] can he upheld as incident to arrest is illustrated by *Preston v. United States.*[3] Here the police arrested the petitioner and two others for vagrancy after receiving a report that the three men were behaving suspiciously. The men were first searched for weapons at the scene and then taken to police headquarters. The car in which they were seating at the time of their arrest, but which had not then been searched, was towed to a garage where it was thoroughly searched without a warrant. The Supreme Court unanimously held that the incriminating evidence which was discovered was inadmissible because the warrantless search of the car was too remote in time or place to be incident to the prisoner's valid arrest. 'Once an accused is under arrest and in custody, then a search (of his automobile) made at another place, without a warrant, is simply not incident to the arrest'.[4] *Preston* has now been followed[5] in numerous decisions, both in the Supreme Court and elsewhere, and the consistent position of most courts is 'to respect the literal language of *Preston* (and) not attempt, by fine distinctions, to escape its control'.[6] Thus, in *Heffley v. Hocker*[7] the defendant had been arrested following a report that he had attempted to sell a number of weapons. The arresting officer could see several weapons through the window of the car but at the time made no attempt to seize them. The car was then driven to the police station where it was searched. The resulting evidence was held to have been illegally seized since, despite some factual differences, it was not possible to limit the rationale of *Preston.*[8] When the search of the defendant's car had been made at the police station Heffley was neither in the vehicle nor in its immediate vicinity; he was in another part of the building in police custody and therefore had no power to obtain from the interior of the vehicle either a weapon or something that could have been used as evidence

[1] *Preston v. United States*, 376 U.S. 364, 367 (1964); see also *Dyke*, supra, and *Chambers*, supra.

[2] *Stoner v. California*, 376 U.S. 483, 486 (1964).

[3] 376 U.S. 364 (1964).

[4] Ibid., at 367.

[5] It is not easy to reconcile *Preston* with subsequent cases, particularly *Cooper v. California*, supra, and *Chambers v. Maroney*, supra. It is possible (and indeed perfectly consistent with Black, J.'s opinion for the Court) to advance a broad interpretation of *Preston* and say, first, that 'a warrantless search of an automobile is per se unreasonable unless incident to a lawful arrest or unless it would be impracticable to secure a warrant *and* at the same time prevent the vehicle from being removed from the jurisdiction': *Williams v. United States*, 412 F. 2d 729, 733 (1969) and, secondly, that '(o)nce an accused is under arrest and in custody', then a warrantless search made at another place is unconstitutional. Alternatively, one might plausibly say that 'the Court has taken what might be called a second look at *Preston*' and has confined it to the 'search incident to arrest' exception (see *Williams v. United States*, 412 F. 2d 729, 734 (1969)). It is clear that this second narrower reading of *Preston* currently enjoys the support of the Supreme Court: see *Cady v. Dombrowski*, supra, where Rehnquist, J., expressed the view that *Preston* stands only for the proposition that the search challenged there could not be justified as one incident to an arrest. In other areas other principles, extrapolated from other cases, apply.

[6] *Ramon v. Cupp*, 423 F. 2d 248, 250 (1970).

[7] 420 F. 2d 881 (1969).

[8] See *Ramon v. Cupp*, 423 F. 2d 248, 250 (1970).

against him. This was 'the critical fact', and it followed that the 'justifications' for a warrantless search which were found to have been absent in *Preston* were similarly inapplicable in this case as well. The second thing to remember is that, consistently with *Chimel v. California*,[1] the extent of a vehicular warrantless search which it is attempted to justify as incident to a valid arrest under *Preston v. United States* may not go beyond the person of the accused and the area from within which he might have obtained either a weapon or readily destructible evidence that could have been used against him.[2] In other words, the scope of the search must not go beyond the exigency which brings the 'incident to arrest' exception into play,[3] and any intrusion beyond what is necessary either for the personal safety of the officers and others nearby or for the preservation of evidence that could readily be destroyed is illegitimate.[4] It remains to be seen how strictly *Chimel* is applied to vehicular searches. It is relatively clear that a full search of the car even at the time of the arrest cannot now be upheld as a search incident to arrest.[5] But what about an examination of some areas of the car, such as a glove compartment, which are within the reach of the arrestee, but from which in view of the presence of the police he is unlikely to be able to take weapons or evidence? Indeed, in terms of a strict application of the rationale of *Chimel*, once an arrested person is *out* of the car there would appear to be no justification for *any search* of its interior since nothing in the car would then be within his grasp.[6] Clearly everything depends upon the facts of each case, but the dominant trend seems to be against a narrow interpretation of *Chimel*'s operative criterion of the area within the arrestee's 'immediate control'.[7] It was thus held in one case[8] that the search of the defendant's automobile while the defendant was standing within leaping range of the guns in the back seat met the *Chimel* test.

Other often-invoked traditional exceptions to the warrant requirement in the case of automobiles are non-criminal custodial examinations, considered in the next section, and the seizure of evidence in 'plain view'.[9] As regards the latter, in should first be noticed that the *mere* observation of objects 'in plain view' within an automobile by an officer who has a right to be where he is is not a search at all and therefore falls outside the ambit of the Fourth

[1] 395 U.S. 752 (1969).

[2] See *Chimel v. California*, supra; *Preston v. United States*, supra; *Heffley v. Hocker*, 420 F. 2d 881 (1969).

[3] See *Chambers v. Maroney*, supra, at 61, 62, per Harlan, J. dissenting; see also *Chimel v. California*, 395 U.S. at 763, and *Terry v. Ohio*, 392 U.S. 1, 20 (1968).

[4] *Chambers v. Maroney*, supra, at 61, per Harlan, J. dissenting.

[5] See La Fave, 'Warrantless Searches and the Supreme Court: Further Ventures into the "Quagmire",' 8 *Crim. L. Bull.* 9, 18; see also *Application of Kiser*, 419 F. 2d 1134 (1969).

[6] See Nelson, '*Chimel v. California:* A Potential Roadblock to Vehicle Searches', 17 *U.C.L.A. L. Rev.* 629, 647; 'Annotation', supra, at 900.

[7] *Chimel v. California*, supra, at 763.

[8] *Application of Kiser*, 419 F. 2d 1134 (1969).

[9] See 'Annotation, Search and Seizure: Observation of Objects in "Plain View",' 29 L. Ed. 2d 1067.

Amendment.[1] Even a more thorough examination of an automobile's *exterior* may be held to have invaded no constitutional right to be free from unreasonable governmental intrusions.[2] provided that any invasion of privacy in which the examination has resulted is no more than 'abstract and theoretical'.[3] As regards 'seizures' (which plainly fall within the terms of the Fourth Amendment) of objects 'in plain view', the essential test of legality is whether the police officer seizing the object or item in plain view had a prior and sufficient justification for the intrusion in the course of which he inadvertently came across the incriminating piece of evidence.[4] An example is offered by *Harris v. United States*[5] where the Supreme Court upheld the warrantless seizure of an automobile registration card which had fallen within the plain view of a police officer as he was opening the door of an impounded car in order to roll up the windows and take other necessary measures 'to protect it while it was in police custody'. Since the door of the impounded vehicle had lawfully been opened the *initial* intrusion during which the card first became available was justifiable, and since the discovery was clearly *accidental*, the 'plain view' exception to the warrant requirement was applicable.

The second heading consists of a separate and perhaps sui generis exception to the warrant requirement established in *Cooper v. California*.[6] Here the accused had been arrested and charged with a narcotics offence. A car which he had used for the transportation of narcotics was seized 'as evidence' by police under California law which permitted such a car to be 'held as evidence' until forfeiture had been declared or the car ordered released. A week after the arrest of the accused and the seizure of the car the police conducted a thorough search of it and took out of a glove compartment further evidence of drugs which was then used against the accused. The Supreme Court, by a narrow majority, held that the search was not unreasonable.[7] *Cooper* is a difficult case,[8] but four possible explanations of

[1] See 'Annotation', supra, 162 n.3, at 896; see *Harris v. United States*, 390 U.S. 234 (1968); *Cardwell v. Lewis*, 417 U.S. 583 (1974).

[2] *Cardwell v. Lewis*, supra, at 589.

[3] *Cardwell v. Lewis*, supra, quoting from *Air Pollution Variance Board v. Western Alfalfa Corp.*, 416 U.S. 861, 865 (1974). At times it is not made very clear whether such unobjectionable examinations of the exterior of cars are legal because they are not searches at all or because they are not unreasonable within the terms of the Fourth Amendment (see *Cardwell v. Lewis*, supra, at 589, 591, 592.)

[4] See *Coolidge*, supra, 403 U.S. at 466; see also the dissenting opinion of Brennan, J. in *Cady v. Dombrowski*, supra.

[5] 390 U.S. 234 (1968).

[6] 386 U.S. 58 (1967).

[7] In *Cooper* there is language suggesting that the applicable test is whether the particular search was reasonable under the Fourth Amendment (386 U.S. at 61, per Black, J.). Even though this is quoted with apparent approval by Burger, C.J., delivering the Supreme Court's opinion in *South Dakota v. Opperman*, 428 U.S. at 372, in view of other cases (mainly *Coolidge*, supra) it cannot be said that this is the applicable test either over the whole area of the Fourth Amendment or in the context of vehicular searches in general.

[8] For discussions of *Cooper* and attempted reconciliations of it with other authorities, mainly *Preston*, see *People v. Sullivan*, 272 N.E. 2d 464, 470 (1971),

its holding can be advanced. The first is to confine it very much to its own facts, and derive from it the proposition that the Fourth Amendment does not prohibit the examination or search of 'a car validly held by officers for use as evidence in a forfeiture proceeding'[1] (or that 'a search in connection with the seizure of an automobile for purposes of forfeiture proceedings' need not be preceded by a warrant).[2] The second reading of *Cooper* is that the warrantless search of the car was constitutional because it was 'closely related'[3] to the reason the accused had been arrested, the reason his car had been impounded, and the reason it was being retained. In contrast, *Preston* was different precisely because the fact that the police had custody of the car was totally unrelated to the vagrancy charge for which the accused had been arrested.[4] Thirdly, it might be said that since the *Cooper* car had been seized under state law and was to be kept in custody for a considerable period of time it would have been unreasonable to hold that the police had no right, even for their own protection, to search it.[5] In other words, the kind of police custody in issue in the instant case had given the police special possessory rights, and the search could therefore be sustained as 'an integral part of their right of retention'.[6] The fourth and broadest explanation of *Cooper* is that it validates searches of automobiles on the basis of mere lawful custody by the police.[7] As will be seen later, even though the situation is by no means clear, it would appear that the most plausible explanation of *Cooper* is one which maintains first that while lawful custody of an automobile is not per se sufficient for dispensing with the warrant requirement, the reason for and nature of the particular police custody may have this effect,[8] and secondly that possession and retention of an automobile held as evidence of crime and pending forfeiture proceedings constitute such special custody.[9]

The main exception to the warrant requirement in this area, known as the 'automobile exception', traditionally sustains the search of a moving automobile where there is probable cause to support the particular search

Williams v. United States, 412 F. 2d 729 (1969), and *Mozzetti v. Superior Court*, 484 P. 2d 84 (1971).

[1] *Cooper v. California*, supra, at 62.

[2] See the dissenting opinion of Brennan, J. in *Cady v. Dombrowski*, supra.

[3] *Cooper v. California*, supra, at 61; see also *Sullivan* and *Mozzetti*, supra.

[4] *Cooper*, supra, at 61, per Black, J.

[5] Ibid., at 61, 62; see also *South Dakota v. Opperman*, 428 U.S. 364, 373 (1976), where the authority of *Cooper* was cited as support for the constitutionality of routine inventory examinations. Burger, C.J., in *Opperman* characterised the 'search' of *Cooper* as an 'inventory', but even though the search in the latter case was undertaken (and subsequently upheld) in part on the basis of custodial considerations it was different from routine inventories conducted solely for caretaking purposes since, as emphasised by Black, J., it was closely related both to the arrest of the defendant and to the reason his car had been impounded. As it was put by Burger, C.J. himself in *Opperman*, supra, the search in *Cooper* took place in 'a distinctly criminal setting' (428 U.S. at 372).

[6] *Cady v. Dombrowski*, 413 U.S. 433, 453 (1973), per Brennan, J. dissenting.

[7] For a discussion of this, see *Mozzetti v. Superior Court*, 484 P. 2d 84, 91 (1971).

[8] See *Cooper v. California*, supra, at 61, and *Mozzetti*, supra, at 91.

[9] Ibid.

and it is not practicable to obtain a warrant because the vehicle can be quickly moved out of the jurisdiction. This exception to the warrant requirement was first formulated in *Carroll v. United States*[1] where the Supreme Court upheld the admissibility in evidence of contraband liquor seized as a result of a warrantless search of a car on the highway. The basis of the Court's holding was that there was 'a necessary difference'[2] between a search of a store, house or other structure in respect of which a warrant could readily be obtained and a search of a ship, wagon or automobile for contraband goods 'where it is not practicable to secure a warrant because the vehicle can be quickly moved out of the locality or jurisdiction in which the warrant must be sought'.[3] But where the securing of a warrant was 'reasonably practicable', one had to be used.[4] Chief Justice Taft, delivering the Court's opinion, went on to observe that the search of an automobile of the type before them proceeded on a theory that was quite different from that justifying searches incident to arrest. As regards the latter, the validity of search or seizure would basically turn on the validity of the arrest. In contrast the right to search moving automobiles and the validity of consequential seizures did not depend on any right to arrest. 'They are dependent on the reasonable cause the seizing officer has for belief that the contents of the automobile offend against the law.'[5] Since on the facts before them the seizing officer was found to have had probable cause to believe that the automobile which he stopped and searched had contraband liquor which was being illegally transported, the seizure in issue and the resulting convictions were held to have been constitutional. *Carroll* dealt with the warrantless search of a moving vehicle where there was probable cause to believe that it contained contraband[6] and where it was not practicable to secure a warrant.[7] On the basis of these facts and in view of the tenor of Chief Justice

[1] 267 U.S. 132 (1925); see Landynski, *Search and Seizure and the Supreme Court* 87–98 (1966). It must be pointed out that in *Carroll* national prohibition legislation was found by the Court to have authorised warrantless searches of cars suspected of its violation. In other words, in *Carroll* the Supreme Court could only have required a warrant by holding an Act of Congress unconstitutional. Some have argued that in the absence of specific statutory authorisation warrantless searches of cars should be treated differently, i.e. warrants should in general be insisted upon. This was argued forcefully by Jackson, J., in *United States v. Di Re*, 332 U.S. 581, 585–6 (1948) and in *Brinegar v. United States*, 338 U.S. 160, 183 (1949), but his views have not prevailed.

[2] *Carroll v. United States*, 267 U.S. 132, 153 (1925).

[3] Ibid.

[4] Ibid., at 156.

[5] Ibid., at 158–9.

[6] *Carroll* involved a search for and the seizure of contraband, and one possibility would have been to limit its doctrine to searches for contraband and not extend it to general searches of vehicles for evidence of crime. This 'limitation' appears to have enjoyed the support of Harlan, J. (see *Chambers v. Maroney*, supra, at 62 n.7) but clearly does not represent the law (see also 'Note', supra, 162 n.3, at 839 n.24).

[7] In *Carroll* the search of the car *preceded* the arrest, and as is pointed out by La Fave, supra, 168 n.5, at 18 n.36, on the facts of *Carroll* 'the officers could not have arrested the occupants of the car and *then* held the vehicle while a search warrant was sought, as a warrantless misdemeanour arrest could be made only for an offence

Taft's opinion it could be thought that vehicular searches cannot be sustained under the 'automobile exception' where there is no reasonable likelihood that the car would or could be moved. On this view '(o)nly in exigent circumstances will the judgment of the police as to probable cause serve as a sufficient authorisation for a search',[1] and 'exigencies do not exist'[2] where for one reason or another the car cannot be moved away. There should be a distinction, in other words, between on the one hand a situation where an automobile is stopped on the highway and where 'the opportunity to search is fleeting' because the car is 'readily movable',[3] and on the other a situation where the circumstances are such—no alerted criminal bent on flight, no possibility of the car being moved, no possibility of confederates threatening a destruction of evidence[4]—that it is both possible and practicable to obtain a warrant and where therefore 'the meaning and purpose of the rule of *Carroll v. United States*'[5] are simply inapplicable. But although it is widely acknowledged that the original justification for the 'automobile exception' was provided by the actual mobility of automobiles stopped on the highway and the presence of circumstances of necessity making it practically impossible to insist on adherence to the warrant requirement warrantless vehicular searches have been upheld on the basis of the *Carroll* doctrine in circumstances in which there was no realistic possibility of the vehicle being removed from police custody or of evidence contained in it being destroyed.[6]

---

committed in the officer's presence (i.e. detected directly by his senses, rather than on the basis of prior information, which was the case in *Carroll*). An important point to notice is that even though one might agree that where officers have reason to believe that a vehicle travelling on a public road contains evidence of crime they should be permitted to take steps necessary 'to preserve (the) evidence and to make a search possible' (per Harlan, J. in *Chambers v. Maroney*, supra, at 62), it does not follow that 'those steps (should) include making a warrantless search of the entire vehicle on the highway' (ibid.). One might thus argue, as Harlan, J., did in *Chambers*, supra, that since 'departures from the warrant requirement (should) strictly conform to the exigency presented' and since 'the police could prevent removal of the evidence by temporarily seizing the car for the time necessary to obtain a warrant', the lesser intrusion of a temporary seizure of the car during the time necessary to obtain the search warrant should be preferred to a full warrantless search (see *United States v. Van Leeuwen*, 397 U.S. 249 (1970) where brief detention while a warrant was being obtained, as opposed to an immediate search, of suspicious packages sent through the mail was upheld as reasonable).

[1] *Chambers v. Maroney*, supra, at 51, per White, J.

[2] *Ramon v. Cupp*, 423 F. 2d 248 (1970).

[3] *Chambers v. Maroney*, supra, at 51, per White, J. Indeed this is how White, J. in *Chambers* explained *Carroll*. '*Carroll* holds a search warrant unnecessary where there is probable cause to search an automobile stopped on the highway; the car is movable, *the occupants are alerted*, and the car's contents may never be found again if a warrant must be obtained' (emphasis added) (*Chambers*, supra, at 51).

[4] *Coolidge v. New Hampshire*, 403 U.S. at 462.

[5] Ibid.

[6] See *Cady v. Dombrowski*, supra, at 441; *South Dakota v. Opperman*, supra, at 367; *Chambers v. Maroney*, supra. See *The Model Code of Pre-Arraignment Procedure*, supra, 162 n.3, at 550, where it is not thought that there is much justification in the context of vehicular searches for the revived *Trupiano* principle

In *Chamber v. Maroney*[1] it was held that where in the middle of the night and in a dark parking lot police officers stopped an automobile and arrested the occupants for robbery, their subsequent search of the automobile at the police station, after both the automobile and its occupants had been taken there, was valid on the ground that there had been probable cause to believe that articles which those conducting the search were entitled to seize were contained in it. In his opinion for the Supreme Court Justice White took as his starting point *Carroll* which he read as holding a search warrant unnecessary where there was probable cause to search an automobile *stopped on the highway*. The reason for this was that since the car might be moved by its occupants relevant evidence could disappear while a warrant was being obtained. An immediate search was therefore permissible in the interests of preserving evidence. This reading of *Carroll* does not of course dispose of *Chambers*, since in the latter case the police did not conduct 'an immediate search' but rather seized the car and took it to the police station before searching it. But this, Justice White observed, made no difference. 'The probable-cause factor still obtained at the station house *and so did the mobility of the car*.' The subsequent search of the automobile was therefore constitutional.[2]

But *Chambers*, despite its considerable extension of *Carroll*, does not sanction warrantless searches of automobiles in all cases simply on the basis of probable cause,[3] nor does it hold that the demonstrable absence of circumstances of necessity, coupled with the existence of adequate

---

that a warrant must be obtained if circumstances permit. 'Assuming that there is probable cause to search the vehicle, *and that the vehicle is mobile*, it would be artificial that courts should disallow the search on the ground that the officer should have known that he would be able to secure a warrant without losing his target' (emphasis added). For this reason the *Model Code* proposes no such requirement, but at the same time the word 'mobile' is not explained; and in the formulation of the applicable rule (see *Model Code* §§260.3) '(a)n officer who has reasonable cause to believe that a moving or readily movable vehicle . . . contains things subject to seizure . . . may search the vehicle'.

[1] 399 U.S. 42 (1970).

[2] White, J., considered whether, 'because of the preference for a magistrate's judgment', only 'the immobilisation of the car should be permitted' until a search warrant was obtained. '(A)rguably, only the "lesser" intrusion is permissible until the magistrate authorises the "greater".' But this was rejected by him since 'which is the "greater" and which the "lesser" intrusion is itself a debatable question' the answer to which was likely to depend on a variety of circumstances (*Chambers*, supra, at 51, 52). Harlan, J., in dissent, disagreed with the majority's conclusion that there was no constitutional difference between 'on the one hand seizing and holding a car before presenting the probable cause issue to a magistrate and on the other hand carrying out an immediate search without a warrant' (per White, J. at 52) since, in his view, it was clear that 'a warrantless search involves the greater sacrifice of Fourth Amendment values' (*Chambers*, supra, at 63). In his view, therefore, on facts such as the ones in *Chambers* (and indeed in *Carroll*) only the lesser intrusion of 'the simple seizure of the car' for a short period during which a search warrant is obtained should be permitted.

[3] *Chambers*, supra, at 50.

opportunity to obtain a search warrant, does not at times negative the 'automobile' exception to the warrant requirement, particularly when there was no question of the car having been stopped on the highway or in any other area open to the public[1] before the arrest of the accused or the initial seizure of the vehicle. A case in point is *Coolidge v. New Hampshire*.[2] Police officers, having concluded that they had probable cause, obtained warrants authorising them to arrest the accused for murder and to search his car. The accused was duly arrested in his house and his car which was parked in the driveway was seized and towed to the police station where it was searched and vacuumed two days later. A divided Supreme Court held that the warrant authorising the search of the automobile was invalid on the ground that it had not been issued by a neutral magistrate. The search of the defendant's car could not therefore constitutionally rest upon it. Could the 'warrantless' search be justified under the 'automobile exception'? Justice Stewart, delivering the Court's opinion,[3] thought not. Since (1) the police had known well in advance of the presence and possible relevance of the automobile and had planned all along to seize it, (2) the accused was aware that he was a suspect in the murder investigation but had been extremely co-operative throughout and there was no suggestion that he meant to flee, (3) he had already had ample opportunity to destroy any incriminating evidence, (4) the automobile was regularly parked in the driveway of his house and was not being used in any illegal activity when it was seized, and (5) there was no conceivable way in which the accused or any one else could have gained access to the car after the police arrived on his property, 'the opportunity for search was hardly "fleeting" ', there were no exigent circumstances justifying the absence of a valid warrant, and the search of the automobile was therefore illegal. In other words, whereas *Chambers* and similar cases imply or assume that potential or abstract mobility is enough in order to activate the *Carroll* rule, *Coolidge* attaches no constitutional significance to 'this sort of mobility'[4] but instead demands 'some real possibility of the car's being moved'.[5] The truth of the matter is that the various cases cannot be reconciled either by logic or by a consistent theory of Fourth Amendment rights.

To summarise, a number of possible versions of the 'automobile exception' can be formulated on the basis of the cases and of the numerous conflicting statements appearing in them. One might first adopt the position that there is a constitutional difference between houses and cars[6] and that warrantless

[1] See *Model Code*, supra, at 162.

[2] 403 U.S. 443 (1971).

[3] In this branch of his opinion Stewart, J. spoke for only four members of the Court (himself, Douglas, Brennan and Marshall, JJ.). Harlan, J. did not expressly concur in this part of the Stewart opinion even though he had dissented in *Chambers*, supra, and normally took a strong stand on Fourth Amendment issues. That the question of the practicality of obtaining a warrant is still a controversial one, see *Cardwell v. Lewis*, 417 U.S. 583, where on this question the eight Justices (Powell, J. disposing of the case on different grounds) divided evenly.

[4] *Coolidge*, supra, at 461 n.18, per Stewart, J.

[5] 'Note', supra, 162 n.3, at 842–3.

[6] See *Chambers*, supra, at 52.

searches of the latter supported by probable cause that the particular automobile contains items of evidence subject to seizure are constitutional.[1] The second formulation maintains that warrantless vehicular searches and seizures must be supported by more than probable cause before they can be upheld, that it is fundamentally because of their mobility that automobiles may be searched without a warrant upon facts not justifying a warrantless search of a house or office, but that this mobility is ever present; in other words it is an inherent characteristic of automobiles and not a question of fact to be determined in the circumstances of each case. The third version, while subscribing to the principle of *Carroll*, strongly denies that 'mystical exigencies'[2] or attenuated mobility or unsubstantiated fears about the 'potential for the car's removal'[3] can excuse the failure of the police to secure a warrant. On this view basic constitutional rules cannot be overlooked simply because the subject of a seizure is an automobile, and the *Carroll* doctrine is limited to cases where a *moving* automobile on the road presents a situation where it is not practicable to secure a warrant. But 'where there is no reasonable likelihood that the automobile would or could be moved, the *Carroll* doctrine is simply inapplicable'.[4] A possible way of reconciling *Chambers* and *Coolidge* is to say that the former stands for the specific proposition that 'police officers with probable cause to search an automobile on the scene where it was stopped could constitutionally do so later at the station house without first obtaining a warrant',[5] at least where the search takes place a reasonable time after the initial seizure which obviously must itself be justifiable,[6] whereas *Coolidge* holds that where it is practicable to obtain a warrant, and any possible necessity for conducting a warrantless search has been disproved conclusively *and* to the police officers' satisfaction, then the prima facie applicable 'automobile exception' can no longer be

[1] *Chambers* contains some hints of this, but White, J. denies it (at 50); but see Harlan, J., ibid., at 63 n.8.

[2] *Cardwell v. Lewis*, supra, at 598, per Stewart, J. dissenting.

[3] Ibid., at 595, per Blackmun, J., and at 598, per Stewart, J. dissenting.

[4] Ibid., at 598, per Stewart, J. dissenting; *Coolidge*, supra; *Preston*, 376 U.S. 364.

[5] *Texas v. White*, 423 U.S. 67, 68 (1975), per curiam; further, this is how *Chambers* is explained in *Coolidge*, supra. As Stewart, J. pointed out in the latter case, *Chambers* held only that 'where the police may stop and search an automobile under *Carroll*, then they may also seize it and search it later at the police station' (*Coolidge*, supra, at 463); this point is also made in 'Note', supra, at 845, where it is observed that '*Chambers* is *Carroll* after arrest, at the station house'; but see *Cardwell v. Lewis*, 417 U.S. 583, 595 (1974), per Blackmun, J., where the fact that in *Chambers* the car was seized after being stopped on the highway whereas in *Cardwell v. Lewis* it was seized from a public parking lot was described as of 'little, if any, legal significance'. But, as Blackmun, J. himself intimates in *Cardwell*, supra, at 593, the position would have been different if the seizure of the automobile had required entry upon private property.

[6] Another possible limitation is that the rule in *Chambers* allowing a subsequent warrantless search of a car only applies when *it is reasonable* to take the car to the station house so that it may be searched there instead of subjecting it to an immediate search at the spot of the initial seizure (see *Chambers*, supra, at 52 n.10, per White, J. and *Texas v. White*, 423 U.S. 67, 69 (1975), per Marshall, J. dissenting). But this seems to be rejected by the majority in *Texas v. White*, supra.

invoked[1] with the consequent revival of the need to obtain a valid search warrant, particularly if the car to be searched was not initially seized by being stopped on the open road but has at all relevant times been stationary—especially if it is on the defendant's land or premises so that its search and any resulting seizures require 'an entry upon private property'.[2]

(e) Custodial searches

Another difficult line of cases deals with 'inventory', 'custodial' or 'caretaking' searches.[3] These have usually considered the legality of the routine inspection of vehicles in police custody (and the fortuitous discovery and seizure of incriminating evidence) *when* the purpose of (and therefore the justification for) the initial intrusion was not to find evidence of crime or contraband to be used in subsequent criminal proceedings but rather to identify the contents of the vehicle on the assumption of police custody and catalogue them, in this way ensuring their proper care by the police and the storage bailee and protecting both from subsequent unfounded claims of loss or damage on the part of the owner of the vehicle. In this way the typical police inventory is not intended to ferret out evidence of crime but is viewed as an aid to the vehicle owner because it provides him with a detailed list of the items taken into temporary police custody and (normally) stored at the police garage. A typical case is *People v. Sullivan*.[4] A car driven by the defendant was found to be illegally parked. Later a police tow truck removed it to a Police Department storage area where it was examined by a police officer acting under state regulations requiring that an officer removing a vehile should compile a record of any valuable property found in it. A loaded gun was discovered. Was it admissible in evidence against the prisoner or had it been procured by an unlawful search? The court had no doubt that in inspecting vehicles they took into custody the police were not seeking evidence of crime but were taking precautions which any bailees of personal property would normally be expected to take for the benefit of the absent owner and as a

[1] 68 Am. Jur., *Searches and Seizures* § 45.

[2] *Cardwell v. Lewis*, supra, at 593, per Blackmun, J. Another often discussed question is 'whether or not the right of vehicular search extends to the persons of individuals occupying the vehicle' (*Model Code*, supra, 162 n.3, at 551). Some think it 'both illogical and impracticable to exempt from search the occupants themselves' and it has therefore been proposed that in the case of vehicular searches 'the officer may search the suspected occupants' (ibid., at 163), provided of course that the things sought are 'of such size and nature that they might be concealed on the person' (ibid., at 164). But the Supreme Court, in *United States v. Di Re*, 332 U.S. 581 (1948), has held that the right to search a car under *Carroll* does not extend to the occupants. 'A person, by mere presence in a suspected car, (does not) lose immunities from search of his person to which he would otherwise be entitled' (ibid., at 587, per Jackson, J.).

[3] See generally A.L.I., *Model Code of Pre-Arraignment Procedure* 528–31 (1975) (hereinafter referred to as *Model Code*); 'Note, Warrantless Searches and Seizures of Automobiles', 87 *Harv. L. Rev.* 835, 848–53 (1974); Stroud, 'The Inventory Search and the Fourth Amendment', 4 *Ind. Legal F.* 471 (1971).

[4] 272 N.E. 2d 464 (1971).

safeguard against subsequent claims of loss or damage that might be alleged against the authorities. Was this warrantless 'inventory' or 'caretaking' examination legal under the Fourth Amendment? More generally, should police inventories be preceded by judicial authorisation?[1] If not, what is the basis on which such procedures can be justified consistently with the Fourth Amendment?[2]

Three possible answers are available, and are sketched out in the numerous cases dealing with this issue: The first is that such police inventories or custodial examinations are not 'searches' as the term is used in the Constitution; they need not therefore be justified under the provisions of the Fourth Amendment. This is based on the view that a 'search' is an intrusion for the purpose of seizing things to be used in a criminal prosecution, which is precisely what inventory examinations of the type discussed here are not.[3] But this attempt to distinguish between inventories and searches has not gained much support. Similar arguments have been used as the ones advanced in the area of administrative inspections. It is thus undeniable that police inventories normally involve a substantial intrusion into the privacy of vehicle owners, and consistently with the admonition of the Supreme Court that 'the sounder course is to recognise that the Fourth Amendment governs *all* intrusions by agents of the public upon personal security',[4] most courts have refused, in this area too, either to espouse 'an overly technical definition of search'[5] or to entertain the notion that the Fourth Amendment does not come into play if the officers stop short of what some would regard as a 'full-blown search'.[6] As the matter was put in an important case, 'regardless of professed benevolent purposes and euphemistic explication',[7] an inventory search involves a thorough and wide-ranging exploration by the police of an individual's private property; and since the basic purpose of the Fourth Amendment is 'to safeguard the privacy and security of individuals against arbitrary invasions by governmental officials',[8] and since 'constitutional rights may not be evaded through the route of finely honed but non substantive distinctions',[9] police officers should not be held exempt from the

[1] Of course, as is pointed out in *Mozzetti v. Superior Court*, 484 P. 2d 84, 92 (1971), in the inventory context generally there is 'no basis upon which a magistrate might issue a search warrant', since inventory examinations, by their very nature, are general random explorations of what is searched.

[2] For a careful analysis of the various questions that arise in this context, see *South Dakota v. Opperman*, 428 U.S. 364, 376 (1976), per Powell, J. concurring.

[3] See *Haerr v. United States*, 240 F. 2d 533, 535 (1957): 'A search implies an examination of one's premises or person *with a view* to the discovery of contraband or evidence of guilt to be used in prosecution of a criminal action. The term implies exploratory investigation or quest.' See also *United States v. Blackburn*, 389 F. 2d 93, 95 (1968); *Faubion v. United States*, 424 F. 2d 437 (1970), per Hill, J. dissenting; and *People v. Norris*, 68 Cal. Rptr. 582 (1968).

[4] *Terry v. Ohio*, 392 U.S. 1 (1968).

[5] Ibid.

[6] Ibid.

[7] *Mozzetti v. Superior Court*, 484 P. 2d 84, 88 (1971).

[8] *Camara v. Municipal Court*, 387 U.S. 523 (1967).

[9] *Mozzetti*, supra, at 88.

constitutional requirements of reasonableness simply because they are not searching with the express purpose of finding evidence of crime. The conclusion therefore is that 'a search is no less a search, a seizure no less a seizure, because termed an inventory'.[1]

The second possibility, diametrically opposed to a holding that a custodial examination is not a search at all, is to hold not only that a full search is involved but also that it should be held to be unreasonable unless it has been authorised by a valid search warrant. This is supported by a number of cases. In *Mozzetti v. Superior Court*[2] the defendant, while driving her car, was injured in an accident. The police, acting under statutory authority, took the car which was blocking the road into their custody. In the course of his inventory a police officer saw a small suitcase on the back seat. This was opened, 'apparently to determine if it contained any articles of value'; a quantity of marihuana was found, and the owner was prosecuted. The court held that this was an illegal search and seizure. It was not doubted that the police, in the course of 'valid protective measures', might take note of any personal property in plain sight within the vehicle being taken into custody; any objects 'clearly visible without probing', including the suitcase in this instance, might then be listed in an inventory or other police report. But the search *into* the closed suitcase, the court decided, fell into another category. This was not incident to lawful arrest, was not based on probable cause to believe that the vehicle contained contraband, and was not justified by the peculiar nature of the police custody involved. Nor were there exigent circumstances making the search necessary. A similar conclusion was reached in *Williams v. United States*,[3] a federal case. Here the police, after arresting the defendant for vagrancy, impounded and then searched his car pursuant to a 'police policy to inventory all impounded cars'. The 'inventory' was held to be an illegal search and stolen articles found in the vehicle were not admitted into evidence. The court noted that the official reason for arrest was vagrancy, that the reason for impounding the car was that it had been abandoned and was probably stolen, and that the reason for the search was the police policy of searching all impounded cars. There was therefore 'no particular relationship between the reason for arrest, the reason for taking the car in custody, and the reason for the search'.[4] What was in issue was a policy of conducting general searches not specifically related to the reason the particular car was impounded, and such practices were unconstitutional. Three points are made in support of this approach by its proponents. There is first reliance on orthodox Fourth Amendment doctrine. Since the basic rule is that with the exception of certain well-defined cases a search can only be justified by a search warrant,[5] and since custodial examinations and

[1] *People v. Sullivan*, 272 N.E. 2d 464, 469 (1971), per Fuld, C.J. dissenting.

[2] 484 P. 2d 84 (1971).

[3] 412 F. 2d 729 (1969).

[4] Ibid., at 735; see also *People v. Sullivan*, supra, n.1, at 470, per Fuld, C.J. dissenting, and *Cooper v. California*, 386 U.S. 58, 61 (1967).

[5] See, e.g., *Chimel v. California*, 395 U.S. 752 (1969); *Terry v. Ohio*, 392 U.S. 1 (1968); *Stoner v. California*, 376 U.S. 483 (1964); and *United States v. Mapp*, 476 F. 2d 67, 76 (1973).

inventories do not fall within any of the traditional exceptions to the warrant requirement, they are unreasonable searches.[1] The second point made is that inventory examinations of the type that normally take place usually entail significant invasions of privacy and should therefore only be undertaken in pursuance of neutral judicial authorisation. 'The inventory, by its nature, involves a random search of the articles left in an automobile taken into police custody; the police are looking for nothing in particular and everything in general.'[2] This fact, which indeed is relied on by some as justifying the conclusion that inventories are not searches at all, has not implausibly been viewed by others as an additional convincing reason why 'a random police search is the precise invasion of privacy which the Fourth Amendment was intended to prohibit'.[3] A third argument in support of the view that warrants are necessary questions the very rationale on the basis of which inventory examinations are normally justified—namely, that police inventories protect the interests of vehicle owners by safeguarding their property. It has thus been observed that 'items of value left in an automobile to be stored by the police may be adequately protected merely by rolling up the windows, locking the vehicle doors and returning the keys to the owner',[4] or, if necessary, by 'moving visible items (like small suitcases) into the trunk for safekeeping'.[5] Further, in most of these cases all precautions reasonably necessary for safeguarding the vehicle owner's property have already been taken by the time the police conduct their inventories; thus, the defendant's automobile, at the time of the examination, is parked in a guarded police area and is 'under the *sole* custody and control of the police'.[6] The view has therefore been expressed that in such cases nothing further may be gained, in the interests of the safety of the vehicle owner's property, by the further tactic of a police exploration and inventory of the car's contents.[7]

The third possible approach to these vehicular caretaking searches is that they should be subjected to the broad test of reasonableness in all the circumstances of the particular case.[8] *On this view*, even though *Preston v.*

[1] See *Mozzetti*, supra, 177 n.7, at 88; *South Dakota v. Opperman*, 428 U.S. 364, 381 et seq. (1976), per Powell, J., concurring. Thus there is no arrest, so the incident-to-arrest exception does not apply, there is neither the element of mobility nor probable cause to believe that the particular vehicle contains evidence of crime, so the automobile exception does not apply, and thirdly the circumstances of the usual custodial examination do not result in the police being vested with a possessory interest in the impounded car, as where an automobile is held as evidence of crime before the institution of forfeiture proceedings. The last exception mentioned here is exemplified by *Cooper v. California*, 386 U.S. 58 (1967).

[2] *Mozzetti v. Superior Court*, supra, 484 P. 2d, at 92.

[3] Ibid.

[4] Ibid.

[5] Ibid.; but see on this point the remarks of Powell, J. concurring, in *South Dakota v. Opperman*, 428 U.S. 364, 379 (1976).

[6] *People v. Sullivan*, 272 N.E. 2d 464, 470 (1971), per Fuld, C.J. dissenting.

[7] Ibid.

[8] See *South Dakota v. Opperman*, 428 U.S. 364 (1976); *Cady v. Dombrowski*, 413 U.S. 433 (1973); *People v. Sullivan*, supra.

United States[1] and *Cooper v. California*[2] are not easy to reconcile, the former is best confined to the problems posed by warrantless searches incident to arrest. In contrast, *Cooper* stands for the broader proposition (either over the whole area of vehicular searches or at least in the context of searches of automobiles in the custody of the police) that 'any warrantless search is to be tested by its reasonableness under all the circumstances'.[3] In assessing the validity of an inventory search in a particular case one must therefore ask whether it was reasonable on all the facts.[4] Consistently with this elevation of overall reasonableness to the status of the controlling criterion in the area of custodial searches the great majority of state courts have held that thorough inspections of vehicles in police custody where the custody and the examination *were not intended to produce criminal evidence* against the owner but were merely 'incidental to proper control and protection'[5] do not constitute unreasonable searches. One typical example is *People v. Sullivan*,[6] the facts of which were given above. The inventory examination in issue, the court decided, was not an unreasonable search. It was only an incident to a routine and proper check on an unattended vehicle lawfully taken into custody. The challenged procedure was far removed from 'the processes and objectives of the criminal law', there was no direct nexus between the inspection and an intent to prosecute, and the purpose of what the police had done was to promote public safety and to facilitate the attainment of non-criminal objectives. The search was therefore reasonable.[7] Three considerations are stressed in the many state decisions[8] upholding warrantless inventory searches as reasonable: first, the element of custody which is thought by some to give the police possessory rights not only to the vehicle but also to its contents; secondly, the alleged benignity of police intent, namely that in the context of inventory searches the purposes of the police are benevolent and not connected (at that point) with the initiation of criminal proceedings; and thirdly the fact that in *Cooper v. California* the Supreme Court upheld as constitutional a search undertaken partly in pursuance of

[1] 376 U.S. 364 (1964).

[2] 386 U.S. 58 (1967).

[3] *Williams v. United States*, 412 F. 2d 729, 734 (1969); see also *United States v. Rabinowitz*, 339 U.S. 56, 66 (1950) and *Cooper v. California*, 386 U.S. 58 (1967).

[4] *Williams v. United States*, supra, n.3; *South Dakota v. Opperman*, 428 U.S. 364, 372 (1976), per Burger, C.J.; and *Coolidge v. New Hampshire*, 403 U.S., at 509–10 (1971), per Black, J. concurring and dissenting.

[5] *People v. Sullivan*, supra, 178 n.1, at 467; see also *South Dakota v. Opperman*, supra, n.4, at 371, per Burger, C.J.

[6] 272 N.E. 2d 464 (1971).

[7] See also *State v. Montague*, 438 P. 2d 571 (1968).

[8] In addition to the ones set out here, see *State v. Criscola*, 444 P. 2d 517 (1968), *People v. Clark*, 336 N.E. 2d 892 (1975), and the list contained in the opinion of Burger, C.J. in *South Dakota v. Opperman*, supra, n.4. Authority for routine inventory searches is now of course provided by *South Dakota v. Opperman*, supra, but before that it was *Cooper v. California* that was mainly relied upon. But it is still worth considering other possible solutions because state constitutional guarantees of freedom from unreasonable searches and seizures may well be interpreted more strictly than the federal provision, that is as requiring warrants.

custodial considerations. These arguments have not been found persuasive by others. On the first point it has been declared by many authorities, and assumed by most, that 'the fact that the police have custody of a prisoner's property for the purpose of protecting it while he is incarcerated does not *alone* constitute a basis for an exception to the requirement of a search warrant'.[1] This of course does not deny that property in police custody may be subject to warrantless searches 'under exceptions springing from reasons other than custody alone'[2] but only asserts that mere legal custody of an automobile by the police does not create 'some new possessory right to justify the search of that vehicle'.[3] Indeed, as was pointed out in *Cooper v. California* itself, 'lawful custody of an automobile does not of itself' exempt 'searches thereafter made of it' from applicable constitutional requirements.[4] The second argument invoked by those supporting the applicability to custodial searches of a broad criterion of reasonableness—namely, the benign motivation of those conducting the search—is contradicted by the cases on administrative searches which regard it as anomalous that the individual should only be 'fully'[5] protected by the Fourth Amendment when suspected of criminal behaviour. On this basis since 'the focus in Fourth Amendment cases today is on privacy'[6] rather than on either property rights or protection from criminal investigations, all searches of private property without proper consent, except for certain carefully defined classes of cases, should be regarded as unreasonable unless they have been authorised by valid search warrants.[7] Finally those who support the requirement of a search warrant explain *Cooper v. California* restrictively, not as sanctioning the automatic search of automobiles in police custody but as adopting the narrower proposition that the reason for and the nature of the particular custody may constitutionally justify a warrantless vehicular search,[8] holding in the particular case that custody of an automobile held as evidence of crime before and during forfeiture proceedings is such custody. Further, in *Cooper*, it will be remembered, the officers had seized the petitioner's car *because* of the crime for which he had been arrested, and the subsequent search was very closely connected[9] both with the reason for the arrest and with the reason the car had been impounded and was being detained, circumstances which are

[1] *Brett v. United States*, 412 F. 2d 401, 406 (1969).

[2] Ibid.

[3] *Mozzetti v. Superior Court*, 484 P. 2d 84, 91 (1971).

[4] 386 U.S. 58, 61 (1967).

[5] *Camara v. Municipal Court*, 387 U.S. 523, 530 (1967).

[6] *Brett v. United States*, 412 F. 2d 401, 406 (1969); see also *Katz v. United States*, 389 U.S. 347 (1967).

[7] See *Camara v. Municipal Court*, 387 U.S. 523 (1967); *Cady v. Dombrowski*, 413 U.S. 433, particularly the dissenting opinion of Brennan, J.; and *Coolidge v. New Hampshire*, 403 U.S. 443 (1971).

[8] See *Cooper v. California*, 386 U.S. 58, 61 (1967); *Mozzetti v. Superior Court*, 484 P. 2d 84, 91 (1971).

[9] *Cooper v. California*, supra; see also *People v. Sullivan*, 272 N.E. 2d 464, 470 (1971), per Fuld, C.J. dissenting, and *Williams v. United States*, 412 F. 2d 729, 734–35 (1969).

not normally present in cases of custodial examinations. Of course, the main objection to those who maintain that the relevant question in this context is 'not whether it was reasonable to procure a search warrant, but whether the search itself was reasonable'[1] is precisely that which was put forward by those who supported the warrant process in the area of searches incident to arrest in the days when broad theories of reasonableness represented established doctrine. 'To say that the search must be reasonable is to require some criterion of reason.'[2] Simply to say that the search must be reasonable is no guide, and is in any case far removed from 'considerations relevant to Fourth Amendment interests'.[3] On this view the only test of reason is that '(t)here must be a warrant to permit (a) search, barring only inherent limitations'.[4]

But whatever the possible attraction of traditional arguments supporting the need to obtain prior judicial authorisation before inventory searches of vehicles in police custody can be undertaken, the Supreme Court in *Cady v. Dombrowski*[5] and *South Dakota v. Opperman*[6] has now given its imprimatur to a reading of the Fourth Amendment which, at least in this context, maintains that 'only the general standard of "unreasonableness" (is) the guide in determining whether searches and seizures meet the standard of that Amendment'.[7] In *Cady* the defendant had a one-car accident near a small town while driving a rented car. The car was towed by the police to a garage and the defendant was arrested for drunken driving. Early the next day an officer, looking for a service revolver which the defendant (who had identified himself as a policeman) was thought to possess, made a warrantless search of the car and found in the trunk certain bloodied items which were later introduced in evidence at the accused's trial for murder. It was held that the warrantless search of the car did not violate the Fourth Amendment. The search was not unreasonable since the police had exercised legitimate and proper control over the car which constituted a hazard on the highway and the search for the revolver plausibly believed to be in the car had been actuated by concern for 'the safety of the general public who might be endangered if an intruder removed (it)'. The fact that the protection of the public might, in the abstract, have been accomplished by 'less intrusive' means did not, by itself, render the search unreasonable. The opinion of the Court is not easy to analyse, but it is clear that the majority was strongly influenced by custodial considerations. As it was put by Justice Rehnquist, 'the type of caretaking search' conducted in the instant case of 'a vehicle that was neither in the custody nor on the premises of its owner and that had been

[1] *United States v. Edwards*, 415 U.S. 800, 807 (1974), referring to *Cooper v. California*, 386 U.S. 58 (1967).

[2] *United States v. Rabinowitz*, 339 U.S. 56, 83, per Frankfurter, J. dissenting.

[3] *Chimel v. California*, 395 U.S. 752.

[4] *United States v. Rabinowitz*, 339 U.S. 56, 83, per Frankfurter, J. dissenting.

[5] 413 U.S. 433 (1973).

[6] 428 U.S. 364 (1976).

[7] *Cady v. Dombrowski*, supra, n.5, per Rehnquist, J. And in *South Dakota v. Opperman*, supra, the Court extracts from general standards of reasonableness a considerably more precise rule, namely that 'inventories pursuant to standard police procedures are reasonable' (per Burger, C.J., 428 U.S. at 372).

placed where it was by virtue of lawful police action' was not unreasonable 'solely because a warrant had not been obtained'. A possible reading of this is that once an automobile is in the lawful custody of the police, a warrantless search of it is not unreasonable provided it was not unwarranted, in the sense that the other circumstances of the case support the action of the police. *South Dakota v. Opperman* is easier to analyse, and in contrast to both *Cooper* or *Cady* provides clear support for routine inventory searches of automobiles in police custody. Here, after the defendant's car had been impounded for multiple parking violations, the police, following standard procedures, searched and compiled an inventory of the contents of the car. Marijuana was discovered in the glove compartment for the possession of which the defendant was subsequently charged. In an opinion by Chief Justice Burger, expressing the view of five members of the Court, it was held that the police inventory search, following standard police procedures,[1] was not unreasonable under the Fourth Amendment[2] since this had not been a pretext concealing an investigatory police motive and the search itself had not been unreasonable in scope.[3] An important point to notice is that it has so far

[1] This was particularly emphasised by the majority opinion because, as indicated by Burger, C.J., the existence of 'standard procedures' in the local police department is 'a factor tending to ensure that the intrusion would be limited in scope to the extent necessary to carry out the caretaking function' (428 U.S. 364, at 375). Powell, J., in his concurring opinion, made the point that 'in the criminal context' the requirement of a warrant protects the individual because it makes sure that inferences regarding probable cause are drawn by a neutral and detached magistrate instead of by a manifestly non-neutral police officer. 'Inventory searches, however, are not conducted in order to discover evidence of crime', and therefore the officer conducting the search does not make 'a discretionary determination to search based on a judgment that certain conditions are present'. Inventory searches are normally conducted in accordance with established police rules, and thus there are 'no special facts for a neutral magistrate to evaluate' (428 U.S. 364, 383–4).

[2] The view of Burger, C.J., was that whether a search was reasonable depended upon the facts and circumstances of each case, but that prior cases, mainly *Cooper v. California* (386 U.S. 58), *Cady v. Dombrowski* (413 U.S. 433), *Cardwell v. Lewis* (417 U.S. 583) and others, 'unmistakably' pointed to the conclusion that 'in following standard police procedures' when conducting inventory searches the police were not behaving unreasonably. Inventory searches are therefore, at least as a general matter, reasonable and hence constitutional.

[3] Over the protest of Marshall, J., dissenting, the Court concluded that the inventory was not unreasonable in scope. Once the policeman was lawfully inside the car to secure personal property in plain view, Burger, C.J. observed (428 U.S. 364, 376 n.10), 'it was not unreasonable to open the unlocked glove compartment, to which vandals would have had ready and unobstructed access once inside the car'. As was pointed out by Marshall, J. in dissent, 'the Court's opinion does not authorise the inspection of suitcases' and the like 'which might themselves be sealed' and which could therefore easily be secured 'without further intrusion' (428 U.S. 364 at 389 n.6), and Powell, J. in his concurring opinion, had no doubt that an 'unrestrained search of an automobile and its contents' would constitute 'a serious intrusion upon the privacy of the individual' (428 U.S. 364 at 380). It appears that the test which Burger, C.J. would apply would be whether what the police had engaged in was a genuine caretaking procedure or in truth constituted a quest for evidence, or, to put it somewhat differently, whether the search was a true inventory or merely a pretext concealing an investigatory motive (ibid., at 376).

been assumed, in common with most authorities,[1] that the only legitimate aims of custodial examinations are to protect the petitioner's personal property from loss or damage and to protect the police and storage bailee from unfounded tort claims, and that these should both determine the justifiability of the particular intrusion complained of and circumscribe its scope. Consistently with this it would be inadmissible under the rubric of custodial or inventory examinations either to engage in a search for particular evidence or to conduct the particular examination in a way that can only be explained in evidential rather than in custodial terms. That such limitations may not be strictly observed may be gleaned not only from a number of cases dealing with custodial searches of individuals[2] but perhaps from *Cady v. Dombrowski* itself where 'the sole purpose for the initial intrusion into the vehicle was to search for the gun';[3] but the position is by no means clear.[4] In sum, the clear trend of authorities with regard to the custodial examination of vehicles is that the police may search vehicles presently in their custody which have either been impounded following arrest or been detained in pursuance of adequate and proper justification under state law or other good cause for the twin purposes of protecting the property of the unavailable owner and safeguarding themselves from possible future allegations in tort,[5] provided that the particular search was reasonable in all the circumstances of the case and did not exceed the limits normally derivable from permissible custodial purposes.[6]

Similar conclusions have been drawn in the area of custodial searches of the person[7] and of personal effects[8] other than vehicles. But here many courts

[1] See, for instance, *Mozzetti v. Superior Court*, 484 P. 2d 84, 88; *People v. Sullivan*, 272 N.E. 2d 464, 465; *Model Code*, supra, at 528–31.

[2] See *United States v. Edwards*, 415 U.S. 800 (1974).

[3] This was pointed out by Brennan, J. in dissent in *Cady v. Dombrowski*, supra.

[4] *Cady* is a difficult case to analyse because it falls in between a case where the search is purely custodial, i.e. where the police are simply conducting an inventory without anything specific in mind, and an acknowledged evidentiary quest, i.e. where evidence to be used in possible criminal proceedings is sought. In *Cady* the police were actually looking for the vehicle owner's service revolver which they had reasonable grounds to believe to be in the car, but 'the sole justification for the warrantless incursion', as Burger, C.J., explained the case in *South Dakota v. Opperman*, supra, 'was that it was incident to the caretaking function of the local police to protect the community's safety'. Therefore, even though the search in *Cady* had been instituted *precisely* because the police thought that the revolver would be in the car, the search was in truth initiated for safekeeping and not evidential purposes. In *South Dakota v. Opperman* itself, supra, Burger, C.J., emphasised that in *Cady* the police had taken steps to ensure that 'their intrusion would be limited in scope to the extent necessary to carry out the caretaking function', and it therefore seems probable that he himself would insist on the observance of similar limits in custodial searches of vehicles (but it is not clear how rigorously: see Marshall, J.'s dissenting opinion, supra, at 385 n.1).

[5] In *South Dakota v. Opperman*, supra, 'the protection of the police from potential danger' is added, at 369; see also *Cooper v. California*, supra, at 61–2.

[6] See the *Model Code*, supra, at 146–7.

[7] See *United States v. Edwards*, 415 U.S. 800 (1974).

[8] See *United States v. Robbins*, 424 F. 2d 57 (1970); *Faubion v. United States*, 424 F. 2d 437 (1970).

have upheld warrantless custodial 'inventory' searches of defendants as incidental to arrest on the principle that since the police may search the person whom they arrest when they do so, it should make no difference 'whether this is done on the spot or at the jail where he is booked'.[1] Thus, in *Baskerville v. United States*[2] it was held that a lawful search had occurred where the defendant was arrested, taken into custody, and then searched by jail officers who placed his personal property in an envelope. About two weeks later the envelope was examined by other officers and was found to contain forged documents. The search was upheld as incident to a lawful arrest, and the fact that it had been made a considerable time after the arrest was treated as immaterial. Similarly, in *Cotton v. United States*[3] it was held that when a person was arrested 'his person and his clothing and the contents of his pockets were lawfully taken into police custody' and were properly subjected to thorough examination. If the search then produced any other evidence, including evidence of crimes other than that for which the prisoner was arrested, that was not something to which he could object.[4] Indeed some regard it as proper for the police to look for any evidence, so long as the arrest is not then found to have been a mere pretext for doing so.[5] Numerous other authorities treat it almost as axiomatic that 'searches and seizures that could be made on the spot at the time of arrest may legally be conducted later when the accused arrives at the place of detention';[6] that both the person and the property in his immediate possession may be searched at the station house after the arrest has occurred at another place; and that the clothing or other belongings of the prisoner may be seized on arrival at the place of detention and later subjected to laboratory analysis the results of which are then admissible in later proceedings.[7] Other courts take a more restrictive attitude and refuse to lend their authority to the proposition that 'an accused whose effects are held by the police for safekeeping has, by the single fact alone of the police custody of the property, surrendered his expectations of the privacy of those effects'.[8] Thus, in *Brett v. United States*,[9] where the defendant was

[1] *Cotton v. United States*, 371 F. 2d 385, 392 (1967). This is not easy to support if the requirement of contemporaneity applies to custodial searches of the person as well as to other searches incidental to arrest since obviously a search conducted at the police station some time after the arrest is not contemporaneous with it (see *State v. Stevens*, 132 N.W. 2d 502, 507 (1965)). For this reason other justifications are on occasion canvassed, among them the 'plain view' doctrine (where applicable), the now discredited doctrine that inventory examinations are not searches, or that there is a distinct category of 'independently justifiable' inventory searches (see the *Model Code*, supra, 176 n.3, at 529). Equally, since a warrantless custodial search of the person can only be valid if the arrest itself was valid a custodial examination is in some sense a consequence or incident of the arrest (see *Model Code*, supra, at 529 n.24).

[2] 227 F. 2d 454 (1955).

[3] 371 F. 2d 385 (1967).

[4] Ibid.; see also *Taglavore v. United States*, 291 F. 2d 262, 265.

[5] *Cotton v. United States*, supra, at 393.

[6] *United States v. Edwards*, 415 U.S. 800, 803 (1974).

[7] Ibid., at 803–5, and authorities there cited.

[8] *Brett v. United States*, 412 F. 2d 401, 406 (1969).

[9] Ibid.

arrested, searched, though not thoroughly, and then taken to jail where his clothing and effects were put in a bag for routine safekeeping, it was held that a subsequent search of his clothing which uncovered heroin three days later was unconstitutional. But it would apparently have been different had the items introduced into evidence been items seized at the time of arrest for subsequent use as evidence,[1] or if they were the result of a subsequent inspection of items so seized,[2] or if the challenged search had in effect been a later look at items which had remained in police custody after having been discovered in an earlier and admittedly valid search.[3] And in *United States v. Edwards*[4] the Supreme Court, by a narrow majority, upheld a warrantless *evidentiary* search and seizure of a defendant's clothing which took place about ten to twelve hours after his arrest. The lower court decided that although the arrest was lawful and probable cause existed to believe that the defendant's clothing would yield incriminating evidence, the warrantless seizure and search of the clothing carried out 'after the administrative process and the mechanics of the arrest' had come to an end was unconstitutional. The Supreme Court, in a difficult opinion, disagreed, both, it seems, because, contrary to the opinion of the lower court, 'the normal processes incident to arrest and custody had not been completed' when the prisoner was placed in his cell and because on all the facts the police had done 'no more' when they conducted their search than they were entitled to do 'incident to the usual custodial arrest and incarceration'. The challenged search was therefore 'a normal incident of a custodial arrest', and reasonable delay in effectuating it was immaterial. Two points can be made here with regard to 'custodial' or inventory searches of arrested individuals. The usual rationale of 'search incident to arrest' has been convincingly criticised.[5] It has been repeated many times that 'a search can be incident to an arrest *only* if it is *substantially* contemporaneous with the arrest and is confined to the immediate vicinity of the arrest',[6] or, as it was emphatically put in a related context, 'once an accused is under arrest and in custody, then a search made at another place is simply not incident to the arrest'.[7] If therefore the search takes place at the police station a considerable time after the arrest, it can hardly be said to be 'substantially contemporaneous' with it. After all, 'the mere fact of an arrest does not allow the police to engage in warrantless searches of unlimited geographic or temporal scope'.[8] The second point relates to the justification and scope of custodial searches incident to incarceration. It is quite generally accepted that the scope of a search must be strictly tied to and justified by the circumstances which rendered its initiation

[1] *United States v. Caruso*, 358 F. 2d 184 (1966).

[2] See *Brett v. United States*, supra, 185 n.8, at 405.

[3] This is how *Baskerville v. United States*, 227 F. 2d 454 (1955) was explained in *Brett*, supra, at 405.

[4] 415 U.S. 800 (1974).

[5] See the dissenting opinion of Stewart, J. in *Edwards*, supra, at 810, and the dissent of McCree, J. in *United States v. Robbins*, 424 F. 2d 57 (1970).

[6] *Stoner v. California*, 376 U.S. 483, 486 (1964).

[7] *Preston v. United States*, 376 U.S. 364, 367 (1964).

[8] *United States v. Edwards*, 415 U.S. 800, 810 (1974), per Stewart, J. dissenting.

permissible,[1] and 'the legitimate aims'[2] of warrantless custodial searches of the person are often described as, first to safeguard the property of a prisoner from loss by theft and the like during his incarceration, secondly to protect the police from unfounded charges of theft from prisoners, and thirdly to protect the lives of prisoners and others from assaults by prisoners with the use of weapons carried in.[3] In contrast, the scope and limits of warrantless searches incident to arrest are different.[4] If now the scope of a warrantless *custodial* search is to be genuinely limited to achieving the three purposes outlined above, and if it is at the same time accepted that such custodial warrantless examinations are not validated by the rule allowing searches incident to lawful arrest, evidentiary quests where the evidence sought cannot be used to harm others during imprisonment would seem to fall well outside the 'custodial' purposes normally accepted as freeing the police in this area from the need to obtain a warrant.[5] In *Edwards* itself it was conceded that the seizure of the respondent's clothing was not a matter of 'routine jail procedure' but had been undertaken solely for the purpose of searching for incriminating evidence. If therefore *Edwards* cannot be explained as involving a search incident to lawful arrest it must stand as authority for the proposition that the legal arrest of a person has the effect, 'for at least a reasonable time and to a reasonable extent', of taking 'his own privacy out of the realm of protection from police interest in weapons, means of escape, and evidence'.[6] In other words, there is now recognition of yet another 'exceptional' category of warrantless searches, namely searches and seizures of the arrested individual and of items in his possession that could be made on the spot at the time of arrest but which are conducted later, whether in pursuance of custodial or evidentiary considerations, at the place of detention. But while it should therefore be acknowledged as current doctrine that the effects in a prisoner's possession *at the place of detention* that were subject to search and seizure at the time and place of his arrest may lawfully be searched and seized without a warrant 'even though a substantial period of time has elapsed between the arrest and subsequent administrative processing, on the one hand, and the taking of the property for use as evidence, on the other',[7] there is little doubt that the presence of circumstances which render custodial searches incident to incarceration

[1] See *Terry v. Ohio*, 392 U.S. 1 (1968).

[2] *Model Code*, supra, at 530.

[3] See *Farrie v. State*, 266 N.E. 2d 212, 215 (1971), per DeBruler, J. dissenting.

[4] *Model Code*, supra, 176 n.3, at 530. The two purposes of a search incident to arrest are to remove weapons from the arrestee and to deprive him of evidence which he might destroy. The considerations in other words which have prompted recognition of this exception are both protective and evidentiary, whereas in the case of custodial searches the relevant purposes, as traditionally formulated, relate not to the obtaining of evidence but to the provision of appropriate custodial care (see *Model Code*, supra, at 140).

[5] See DeBruler, J.'s dissenting opinion in *Farrie v. State*, supra.

[6] *United States v. De Leo*, 422 F. 2d 487, 493 (1970), quoted with full approval in *Edwards*, supra, at 808.

[7] *Edwards*, supra, at 807, per White, J.

unreasonable or oppressive 'either because of their number or their manner of perpetration'[1] would cast a wholly different complexion on the matter.

(f) Emergency entries and searches

Should there be, and is there, an emergency exception to the warrant requirements?[2] Some do not favour such a development. Their view is that one must take seriously the cardinal principle governing the application of the Fourth Amendment—that searches conducted outside the judicial process without the prior approval of a judicial officer are per se unreasonable and unconstitutional 'subject only to a few specifically established and well-delineated exceptions';[3] that a generalised doctrine of emergency is not one of them; that any concept of emergency would be both difficult to define and almost certain to be abused; and that therefore one should not lightly recognise a doctrine of exigent circumstances which could potentially lead to Fourth Amendment rights becoming fatally compromised. The other view is that 'constitutional guarantees of privacy and sanctions against their transgression do not exist in a vacuum but must yield to paramount concerns for human life and the legitimate need of society to protect and preserve life';[4] that 'society (should not) be frustrated and denied reasonable protection by mechanical adherence to formalism',[5] for instance by the police being required to lay siege to an apartment waiting for a search warrant even though lives may be at stake; and that therefore '(t)he need to protect or preserve life or avoid serious injury'[6] should be regarded as justification for what would clearly be illegal in the absence of circumstances of emergency or necessity, which in constitutional terms means that even though warrants are generally required before searches can be undertaken, 'the exigencies of the (particular) situation'[7] may make the needs of law enforcement or considerations pertaining to the preservation of life or property so compelling that warrantless searches not falling within one of the traditional exceptions to the warrant requirement can still be held to be reasonable under the Fourth Amendment. As a general matter it is this second view that now prevails. In numerous contexts official 'emergency activities',[8] including warrantless entries and seizures, are now regarded as legitimate. But considerable doubt still surrounds the so-called emergency or exigency

[1] *Charles v. United States*, 278 F. 2d 386, 389, cert. denied, 364 U.S. 831 (1960), referred to with approval in *Edwards*, supra, at 808 n.9.

[2] See generally Mascolo, 'The Emergency Doctrine Exception to the Warrant Requirement under the Fourth Amendment', 22 *Buffalo L. Rev.* 419 (1972); 'Note, The Emergency Doctrine, Civil Search and Seizure, and the Fourth Amendment', 43 *Ford. L. Rev.* 571 (1975); and A.L.I., *Model Code of Pre-Arraignment Procedure* §§ 260.5 (Prop.'Off. Draft 1975).

[3] *Katz v. United States*, 389 U.S. 347, 357 (1967).

[4] *People v. Mitchell*, 347 N.E. 2d 607, 611 (1976).

[5] *Wayne v. United States*, 318 F. 2d 205, 214 (1963), per Burger, J.

[6] Ibid., at 212.

[7] *Mincey v. Arizona*, 98 S. Ct. 2408, 2414 (1978).

[8] Ibid.

doctrine; indeed it is not clear whether one is here dealing with a single exception to the warrant requirement encompassing numerous fact situations or with a number of separate and conceptually unrelated exceptions that have been recognised in diverse 'emergency situations',[1] and in any case the many cases have not as yet arranged themselves in orderly or even definable patterns.

But whatever the best way of arranging the materials, a great number of cases and dicta, from both federal and state courts, have now applied or recognised an 'exigent circumstances' doctrine. In the Supreme Court the emergency doctrine first appeared in a rather casual dictum in *Johnson v. United States*,[2] a case involving violations of narcotics laws. Justice Jackson observed that there could be 'exceptional circumstances' in which 'on balancing the need for effective law enforcement against the right of privacy' it might be contended that a magistrate's search warrant should be dispensed with; but the Supreme Court concluded that no such circumstances were present on the facts before them since '(n)o suspect was fleeing or likely to take flight', the search was 'of permanent premises, not of a movable vehicle', and '(n)o evidence or contraband was threatened with removal or destruction'. The insistence of *Johnson v. United States* on the presence of a warrant was reiterated with added emphasis in *McDonald v. United States*.[3] 'A search without a warrant,' it was stated, 'demands exceptional circumstances', and '(a)bsent some grave emergency', the Fourth Amendment required that a magistrate should determine *in advance* the propriety of an official invasion of privacy in the interests of law enforcement. Fidelity to this central constitutional principle did not allow the absence of a search warrant to be excused without a showing by those seeking exemption from the requirement of a prior judicial authorisation that 'the exigencies of the situation made that course imperative', a showing that had not been made here. But it might have been different if it could genuinely be said that the police '(were) responding to an emergency', for instance if the officers passing by the street had heard a shot and a cry for help. A case where circumstances of necessity justifying a warrantless entry were held to exist is *Warden Md. Penitentiary v. Hayden*,[4] involving the 'hot pursuit' of a fleeing suspect, where the Supreme Court took the view that the exigencies of the situation made the course there followed, in contrast to *McDonald*, both inevitable and constitutionally reasonable.

Three broad categories of cases normally considered under emergency doctrines can be distinguished. There are thus cases where the warrantless entry, search and seizure were motivated by the need to prevent the threatened or feared destruction of evidence, cases of 'hot pursuit', and other cases where the authorities were responding to miscellaneous emergency situations demanding immediate action',[5] for instance where the police have made an entry in order to help a person in need of immediate aid, or where

[1] 68 *Am.Jur.* 2d § 56.
[2] 333 U.S. 10 (1948).
[3] 335 U.S. 451 (1948).
[4] 387 U.S. 294 (1967).
[5] See *Mincey v. Arizona*, 98 S. Ct. 2408, 2413–14 (1978).

they come upon the scene of a serious crime and they make a prompt search of the area to see if there are other victims or if the culprit is still hiding on the premises,[1] or where circumstances suggesting the possibility of an unexploded bomb in an apartment have unexpectedly arisen and an immediate search is conducted,[2] or where the police look into the pockets of a man who has suddenly become unconscious in order to discover who he is,[3] or where the police force an entry in response to a cry for help or a shot or signs of violence,[4] at least if the other circumstances warrant the belief that the presence of a police officer is urgently required if serious harm is to be averted.

Emergency quests for evidence will be dealt with first. It is of course fundamental constitutional doctrine that the fact that the police entertain a reasonable belief that contraband or instrumentalities of crime or other seizable items are concealed on certain premises provides no justification for a warrantless entry and the seizure of the articles sought without a warrant.[5] '(T)he universally accepted principle is that even though the authorities have probable cause to make the search, they must still first obtain a warrant, unless one of the exceptions appl(ies)'.[6] But what if it is feared that unless immediate action is taken relevant evidence will become unavailable, whether by destruction or removal? Is there an *independent* exception to the warrant requirement, distinct from those dealing with searches incident to arrest and with searches of 'moving' or 'movable' vehicles, that allows the police to invoke a doctrine of 'exigent circumstances', more specifically a doctrine of threatened or imminent destruction, and thus excuse their failure to adhere to 'time-consuming'[7] judicial processes relating to the issuance of warrants during which the evidence that is sought might disappear? This is a question that is impossible to answer with any certainty. In terms of theory a number of solutions appear open.[8] One would be to reject any new exception addressed to the problem of the threatened destruction of evidence in view of the unquestionable dangers of police abuse. Since '(t)here is almost always a partisan who might destroy or conceal evidence',[9] recognition of an exception justifying warrantless searches whenever the police fear that unless immediate action is taken material evidence could disappear would go a long way towards seriously undermining the centrality of the warrant requirement.

[1] Ibid.

[2] *People v. Superior Court (Peebles)*, 85 Cal. Rptr. 803; see also *United States v. Melville*, 309 F. Supp. 829 (1970); *United States v. Chadwick*, 433 U.S. 1, 15 n. 9 (1977).

[3] *People v. Gomez*, 40 Cal. Rptr. 616.

[4] See generally *Wayne v. United States*, 318 F. 2d 205, 214 (1963), per Burger, J.; see also Mascolo, supra, at 427 n.33.

[5] *Agnello v. United States*, 269 U.S. 20 (1925); see generally La Fave, 'Warrantless Searches and the Supreme Court: Further Ventures Into the "Quagmire"', 8 *Crim. L. Bull.* 9, 15–17.

[6] *United States v. Brewer*, 343 F. Supp. 468, 472 (1972).

[7] *United States v. Soriano*, 482 F. 2d 469, 474 (1973).

[8] See 'Comment, Third Party Destruction of Evidence and the Warrantless Search of Premises', 1971 *U.Ill.L.F.* 111, 119–20.

[9] *United States v. Davis*, 423 F. 2d 974, 979 (1970).

Another solution would agree that there is no broad rule allowing warrantless searches and seizures whenever there is apprehension (even though reasonable) of a threatened destruction of evidence but would maintain that there is a considerably narrower authority allowing the police to enter and search when there is not merely a threat but a very substantial risk or clear danger of its loss or future unavailability, for example if there are reasonable grounds to believe that the evidence sought is at that very time being disposed of, or at the very least if its destruction is *imminent*.[1] A third solution would be to accept the existence in some circumstances of a doctrine of 'threatened destruction', however this is defined, but to insist that as a general matter this should only give the police authority to take intermediate steps short of a warrantless entry and search during the time that is required to obtain a search warrant;[2] such intermediate steps could include surveillance of the premises from the outside (but this would not prevent the destruction of disposable evidence by persons within the premises), temporary detention of the occupants of the premises (which is itself attended by serious constitutional difficulties, particularly if the officers are at the relevant time outside and detention of the occupants would therefore require a warrantless entry), or even impounding and temporarily seizing the premises themselves pending the issuance of a warrant (which would in many cases be a considerably more serious imposition on Fourth Amendment rights than an immediate warrantless search). A final solution would be to construct a specific 'threatened-destruction' exception to the warrant requirement, allowing the police limited authority to secure evidence threatened with destruction or loss but at the same time insisting on certain safeguards intended to neutralise the most pronounced dangers of 'police abuse or oppressive over-use of such an authority'.[3] Not surprisingly, a number of ways of framing such a narrowly circumscribed exception are available, varying in degrees of strictness and detail.[4] One suggested version would allow warrantless emergency searches if it had not been possible to secure the necessary warrant beforehand, in other words if probable cause to search the premises did not exist before the police arrived on the scene, and if there was probable cause to believe *both* that relevant evidence was on the premises *and*

[1] See *Schmerber v. California*, 384 U.S. 757, 770 (1966); *United States v. Jeffers*, 342 U.S. 48, 52 (1951); *MacDonald v. United States*, 335 U.S. 451, 455 (1948).

[2] See 'Comment', supra, 190 n. 8; 'Note', Police Practices and the Threatened Destruction of Tangible Evidence', 84 *Harv. L. Rev.* 1465 (1971); see *United States v. Van Leeuwen*, 397 U.S. 249 (1970), where, pending the issuance of a search warrant, suspicious packages sent through the mail were detained; the Supreme Court held that such detention in all the circumstances of the case was not unreasonable; see also *United States v. Garay*, 477 F. 2d 1306 (1973), where it was held that, while 'exigent circumstances' may have justified the warrantless detention of the defendants who were suspected of transporting marijuana and who were preparing to board an airplane, such circumstances could not validate the warrantless search of their suitcases; '(i)n short, the officers could and should have held the bags until they obtained a warrant authorising an examination of their contents'.

[3] *Model Code*, supra, at 553.

[4] 'Comment', supra, at 120–3.

that this was likely to be destroyed, for instance by associates of the arrested person (normally the occupier), unless immediate action was taken.

Cases and dicta from the Supreme Court are inconclusive but in their totality would appear to support either the second solution or something similar to the last model. *Schmerber v. California*,[1] discussed earlier, is the only non-vehicle case where the Court upheld a warrantless search solely on the ground that unless immediate action was taken the evidence would be destroyed, and even though the language used was that of 'threatened destruction'—namely, that the 'delay necessary to obtain a warrant threatened "the destruction of evidence" '—the danger to the continuing availability of the evidence was considerably more immediate than that—the alcohol was actually disappearing from the blood at the time[2] —and the case has subsequently been explained as one in which what was ultimately seized was 'in the process of destruction'.[3] *Cupp v. Murphy*[4] can also be explained in similar fashion, for as has been seen not only was the evidence of fingernail samples seized without a warrant 'highly evanescent' and readily destructible, but there was also testimony before the Court that after the accused refused to consent to the taking of samples from under his fingernails 'he put his hands behind his back and appeared to rub them together'.[5] It was therefore clear that unless immediate action was taken highly material evidence would vanish. Other cases have referred to the 'imminent'[6] destruction of evidence as the basis for an emergency exception to the warrant requirement, while other judicial pronouncements have spoken in more general terms of 'emergencies', 'exigent circumstances' and 'exceptional situations'.[7] The only Supreme Court case in which the issue arose squarely is *Vale v. Louisiana*.[8] Here the police, having warrants for Vale's arrest, were watching his mother's house from a short distance away. Shortly afterwards a car arrived, the driver did not get out but sounded the car's horn, and the accused came out and had a conversation with the driver. From Vale's behaviour the officers were convinced that a narcotics transaction was taking place. As they approached, the accused began to walk quickly back towards the house and the driver of the car, a known narcotics addict, placed something in his mouth and apparently swallowed it. Vale was arrested just outside the house and was then taken inside where the officers conducted a cursory inspection to see whether anybody else was present. A few minutes later the accused's mother and brother arrived at the house, the officers *then* proceeded with a full

[1] 384 U.S. 757 (1966).

[2] See *United States v. Brewer*, 343 F. Supp. 468, 472 (1972).

[3] See *Vale v. Louisiana*, 399 U.S. 30, 35 (1970).

[4] 412 U.S. 291 (1973).

[5] Ibid., at 296.

[6] See *United States v. Jeffers*, 342 U.S. 48, 52 (1951); *Mincey v. Arizona*, 98 S.Ct. 2408, 2414 (1978); *Michigan v. Tyler*, 436 U.S. 499, 509 (1978).

[7] See *Vale v. Louisiana*, 399 U.S. 30, 34 (1970). In *Roaden v. Kentucky*, 93 S.Ct. 2796, 2802 (1973), Burger, C.J. said that warrantless official action to preserve evidence of crime was reasonable in circumstances 'in whch police action literally must be "now or never"'.

[8] 399 U.S. 30 (1970).

search, and narcotics were found in one of the bedrooms. It was held, first that since the arrest had not taken place inside the house a search of the interior could not be upheld as incident to the arrest, and secondly that even if the officers had probable cause to conduct the search the existence of such an exceptional situation as to justify a warrantless search had not been shown. The Court's decision is not free from much difficulty,[1] but Justice Stewart appears to have made three principal points in response to the state court's conclusion that the search was 'independently supportable because it involved narcotics which are easily removed, hidden or destroyed', particularly since it could not be known whether there was anyone on the premises who could destroy the evidence. First, this rationale could not apply to the instant case 'since by their own account the arresting officers (had) satisfied themselves that no one else was in the house when they first entered the premises'; secondly, and 'entirely apart from that point', the State had not met its burden of showing that 'an exceptional situation' existed justifying a warrantless search, principally because there was no evidence that the officers were 'responding to an emergency' or that 'the goods ultimately seized were in the process of destruction'; and finally, since the officers had been able to procure warrants for Vale's arrest, there was no reason 'to suppose that it was impracticable for them to obtain a search warrant as well'. All three points can be questioned. The Court's first argument simply observes that at the time of *entry* no one else was in the house, but fails to discuss the arrival of Vale's mother and brother who almost certainly knew what was going on and had strong reasons to destroy any available evidence. If at that point the police were forced to leave the premises the readily destructible evidence of narcotics would surely have been disposed of. Did the Court perhaps assume that the police could remain in the house in order 'to maintain (the) status quo until a warrant could be obtained'?[2] But if this is so (and there is no evidence of this at all), what are the limits of a potentially very intrusive police authority to take intermediate steps involving substantial invasions of privacy and freedom of movement pending the issuance of a search warrant? As to the second point it might be argued that even though 'the process of destruction' rationale is an adequate explanation of *Schmerber* and similar cases, it is considerably stricter than previous formulations and far too crippling a restriction on the police who should (on this argument) be given power to take immediate action towards the preservation of readily destructible evidence *if* there is a real (or substantial) danger that such evidence will disappear during the time it would take to obtain a warrant, whether by destruction at the hands of third parties or otherwise. Even more questionable is the Court's intimation that *since* the officers were in possession of arrest warrants they should similarly have obtained a search warrant. The difficulty with this is that the arrest warrants related to events other than the transaction observed by the officers,[3] and in all likelihood '(p)robable cause for the search (that actually took place) arose for the first time when the police observed the

[1] See La Fave, supra, 190 n.5, at 16–17.
[2] Ibid.
[3] See Black, J.'s dissent in *Vale*, supra, at 40.

activity of Vale and (the car's driver) in and around the house'.[1] But whatever the difficulties with *Vale v. Louisiana*, it is clear authority that the Supreme Court will not lightly excuse warrantless entries and searches in the name of the preservation of evidence threatened with destruction, but will at the very least insist on the satisfaction of three conditions before the 'emergency' exception can operate in this context, first that the existence of exceptional circumstances must be shown convincingly by the police, secondly that any goods or evidentiary items ultimately seized were at the relevant time either in the process of destruction or almost certain to become unavailable during the time normally necessary to obtain a search warrant, and thirdly that a warrant could not practically have been obtained earlier.

A second category of 'emergency' cases are the 'hot pursuit' ones, in which the police have observed, or have received information about, the commission of a crime and have pursued the apparent suspect fleeing from the scene. Such cases fall in between the first and third categories. The warrantless entry and subsequent search in 'hot pursuit' situations are motivated 'solely by a desire to effect a *specific* arrest or seizure,[2] and these cases are therefore different from those discussed under the third heading where the challenged official intervention is normally prompted by humanitarian considerations or at the most by the need to conduct a *general* investigation into an unsolved crime; but they are also different from cases dealing with the threatened or imminent destruction of evidence because, even though both entail substantial invasions of privacy in a distinctly criminal setting and can therefore be called 'true criminal search(es)',[3] before the 'emergency' exception, discussed above, validating warrantless seizures of incriminating evidence so that its destruction may be averted can operate there must be probable cause to believe that the contraband or other items that are sought are on the premises; in contrast, in the context of 'hot pursuit', one only needs probable cause that the person pursued has committed some criminal act.[4] The most important 'hot pursuit' case is *Warden v. Hayden*[5] where the police pursued a robber into a house which they then searched for the suspect and for any weapons which he had used in the robbery or might use against them. The warrantless entry and search were held to be lawful since the Fourth Amendment did not require police officers 'to delay in the course of any investigation if to do so would gravely endanger their lives or the lives of others'. Speed here was essential, and 'only a thorough search of the house for persons and weapons could have insured that Hayden was the only man present and that the police had control of all weapons which could be used against them or to effect an escape'. The seizures that occurred were therefore justified because they were an integral part of 'an effort to find a suspected felon' within the house into which he had run only minutes before the police

[1] Ibid.
[2] Mascolo, supra, 188 n. 2, at 427 n. 33.
[3] 'Note', 43 *Ford. L. Rev.* 571, 583 n. 98.
[4] Ibid.
[5] 387 U.S. 294 (1967).

arrived.[1] Similarly, in *People v. Smith*,[2] where the police pursued a suspect who had just murdered two policemen, it was held that it was reasonable for the police to enter the suspect's house in search of him, since there was cause to believe that he may have been inside and 'fresh pursuit of a fleeing suspect who has committed a grave offence and remains dangerous to life and limb may constitute "exceptional circumstances" sufficient to justify a search without a warrant'; and in *Fellows v. Maryland*[3] it was held that police officers who were called to the scene of a murder and who had good reason to suspect that the perpetrator was still inside were entitled to seize bloodstained clothes they came across when they were going about searching for him. What must be shown in 'hot pursuit' cases is that the police *entered* the premises 'for the sole purpose of locating and apprehending'[4] the suspect, and that any warrantless seizures were effected either in the course of a genuine search for the fleeing felon or as part of an effort to neutralise the hazards his undetected presence (and that of possible confederates) might pose. Therefore, as a general matter, the scope of a warrantless search incident to 'hot pursuit' should be determined by the need 'to prevent the dangers that the suspect at large in the house may resist or escape',[5] and should involve no broader evidentiary quest, particularly once the suspect and any of his accomplices also on the premises have been apprehended and any weapons have been seized. But even if the suspect is not found in the house the police have entered in 'hot pursuit', it does not mean that 'they (are) compelled to close their eyes to the contents of the house',[6] especially if all they look for is evidence that would identify the suspect. But once it appears that the relevant area is vacant, containing neither the suspect nor any weapons which could be used against them, the police have no reason and therefore are not allowed to make a complete search and seize incriminating articles and other evidentiary items.[7] And it goes without saying that the 'hot pursuit' doctrine can only apply when there is a real emergency.[8] If there is no particular urgency the police must obtain a warrant before entering and conducting a search. Thus, where the warrantless entry was effected nearly two hours after a murder was committed, and the police officers were not in actual pursuit of any suspect and had no idea who or where the murderers were, and where there was no particular reason to believe that the suspects were inside the house searched, it was held that there was no emergency situation which could be characterised as one of 'hot pursuit'.[9]

Finally, many cases have dealt with numerous and strikingly diverse emergency situations that involve neither the seizure of evidence threatened

[1] Ibid., at 299.
[2] *People v. Smith*, 409 P. 2d 222 (1966).
[3] 283 A. 2d 1 (1971).
[4] Ibid., at 3.
[5] *Warden v. Hayden*, 387 U.S. 294, 299 (1967).
[6] *People v. Smith*, 409 P. 2d 222, 235 (1966).
[7] See *Fellows v. State*, 283 A. 2d 1, 3 (1971); *Gross v. State*, 201 A. 2d 808 (1964).
[8] *Fellows v. State*, 283 A. 2d 1, 3 (1971).
[9] *People v. Hill*, 528 P. 2d 1, 19 (1974).

with or in imminent danger of destruction nor pursuit of a fleeing suspect. Examples and applications of the general principle that '(n)ecessity often justifies an action which would otherwise constitute a trespass'[1] abound and are not easy to classify, but for the sake of convenience if not for analytical clarity they may be ranged under certain rough subheadings. There are first cases where the police intervention in issue had taken place 'in response to an emergency situation' and was not motivated 'by the intent to apprehend and arrest (the suspect) or to seize evidence',[2] cases in other words where there is immediate need for the assistance of the police for the protection of life or property or so that harm either to themselves or to the general public can be prevented.[3] The basic elements of the emergency exception in the context of 'humanitarian' interventions are the following. The police must have reasonable grounds to believe that 'there is an emergency at hand'[4] and 'a compelling need'[5] for prompt action in the interests of protecting life or property, for instance that 'a person within is in need of immediate aid'[6] or that emergency aid and assistance are required by someone in distress.[7] Thus in *People v. Roberts*,[8] while conducting a burglary investigation, the police went to an apartment, knocked on the door and received no response. 'They (then) heard several moans or groans that sounded as if a person in the apartment was in distress' and entered to investigate and render aid. It was held that the officers had not acted unreasonably or in violation of the defendant's constitutional rights, and that evidence discovered in plain sight after the emergency entry had been validly seized. Similarly, in *United States v. Barone*,[9] it was held that police officers upon hearing loud screams at night properly demanded entrance to the room from which the screams came; and when they were lawfully on the premises it was also proper for them to seize evidence of crime in plain view; having entered reasonably in an emergency

[1] *People v. Roberts*, 303 P. 2d 721, 723 (1956); see also *Horack v. Superior Court*, 478 P. 2d 1, 4 (1970); *People v. Smith*, 496 P. 2d 1261, 1263 (1972). But it should be borne in mind that the issue, as presented in such cases, is not one of tort (whether of trespass or of the doctrine of necessity in the law of torts) but of constitutional law, and it has pertinently been observed that 'an individual's rights under tort law differ substantially from an individual's rights under constitutional law' ('Note', 43 *Ford. L. Rev.* 571, 585 n. 106 (1975)). The most obvious result of this is that 'the need to preserve property will not in every case justify an official intrusion' (ibid.). This basically accords with the authorities, for even though many of them formulate the emergency doctrine in terms that encompass the protection of property, most of them (and certainly the important ones) deal with the preservation of life.

[2] *People v. Mitchell*, 347 N.E. 2d 607, 609 (1976).

[3] See Mascolo, supra, 188 n. 2; 'Note', 43 *Ford L. Rev.* 571 (1975); see also *United States v. Barone*, 330 F. 2d 543, 545; *Root v. Gauper*, 438 F. 2d 361, 364; *Wayne v. United States*, 318 F. 2d 205, 211–12; *State v. Hardin*, 518 P. 2d 151; *United States v. Johnson*, 467 F. 2d 630; *United States v. Melville*, 309 F. Supp. 829.

[4] *People v. Mitchell*, 347 N.E. 2d 607, 609 (1976).

[5] *Michigan v. Tyler*, 436 U.S. 499, 509 (1978).

[6] *Mincey v. Arizona*, 98 S.Ct. 2408, 2414 (1978).

[7] *Root v. Gauper*, 438 F. 2d 361, 364 (1971).

[8] 303 P. 2d 721 (1956).

[9] 330 F. 2d 543 (1964).

'they did not have to blind themselves to what was in plain sight simply because it was disconnected with the purpose for which they entered'.[1] Secondly, any entry and search that takes place must not be motivated by the intent to arrest or seize evidence. It is of course possible, and indeed usual, that some criminal activity may be responsible for the event or problem that the police are dealing with, and this is why the police in such cases are normally *also* allowed to launch a preliminary criminal investigation;[2] but still 'the protection of human life or property in imminent danger must be the motivation for the search rather than the desire to apprehend a suspect or gather evidence for use in a criminal proceeding'.[3] A good example is *People v. Mitchell*.[4] Here it was held that where a hotel maid had disappeared shortly after reporting for work one morning the 'emergency doctrine' enabled the police to make warrantless searches of hotel rooms and other protected areas in an effort to find her. Even though it was suspected that she had been kidnapped, it was found that at the time entry was made into the defendant's room, where the maid's body was discovered, the *primary* intent of the police was to locate the maid and render assistance to her. No criminal investigation had as yet been launched, because it was not known at that time whether a crime had in fact taken place, and therefore the possibility of criminal activity was not 'the primary motivation for the search of the (defendant's) room'. The final requirement before such emergency searches and any consequential seizures can be upheld is that it must be shown that the incriminating evidence that the defendant seeks to have suppressed was discovered in the course of a genuine response to the emergency situation. '(T)he emergency exception does not give (the police) carte blanche to rummage for evidence'[5] over and beyond what is necessary in order to meet the particular emergency. Not only should there be a direct relationship between the area to be searched and the emergency, but also the search should be suitably tailored to meet the particular emergency. In *People v. Mitchell*[6] it was held that the search of the defendant's room was reasonable because it was necessary for the discharge of legitimate 'emergency' police functions. A careful search of the public areas of the hotel had revealed nothing and pointed to the probability that the maid was in one of the rooms. Furthermore, the defendant's room was on the sixth floor, the very floor on which the maid was last seen, and if the police were to discharge their duty of finding the maid a search of that room was imperative and therefore proper. A case where the emergency search exceeded the permissible limits is *United States v. Goldenstein*[7] where the police validly entered the defendant's room in emergency circumstances and, on not finding him there, proceeded to search through his belongings. Evidence found in one of his suitcases was suppressed because it had not been properly seized.

[1] *People v. Roberts*, supra, 303 P. 2d 721, 723.
[2] *People v. Mitchell*, supra, 347 N.E. 2d 607, 610; Mascolo, supra, 426.
[3] *People v. Mitchell*, supra, 347 N.E. 2d 607, 610.
[4] 347 N.E. 2d 607 (1976).
[5] Ibid., at 610; see also *People v. Roberts*, 303 P. 2d 721, 723.
[6] 347 N.E. 2d 607.
[7] 456 F. 2d 1006 (1972).

A second category of miscellaneous cases (where again there is neither an intent to seize specific evidence in order to preserve it from destruction nor a situation of hot pursuit) are what might be called the 'criminal investigation' cases. These—since the two interests, namely preservation of life or property and crime detection, often coincide—are closely connected with and often shade off into the group of cases just discussed, but here the *primary* concern of the police, in contrast to the earlier category, is not simply to render assistance to persons in distress but to initiate a criminal investigation. In any case it is settled that when the police come upon the scene of a crime they may make a prompt warrantless search of the area both to see whether there are other victims and to apprehend the culprit if he is still on the premises.[1] But the fact that a crime, however grave, has been committed clearly does not mean that the Fourth Amendment is no longer applicable. On the contrary, only those warrantless searches found to have been necessitated by the exigencies of the particular situation will be so upheld. It was therefore held in *Mincey v. Arizona*[2] that a four-day warrantless search of an apartment where a shooting took place could not be justified under any 'emergency exception'. Such an extensive search, the Supreme Court unanimously declared, could hardly be rationalised 'in terms of the legitimate concerns that justify an emergency search'; thus, except for the fact that the offence under investigation was a homicide, there were no exigent circumstances, there was no indication that evidence would be lost, destroyed or removed during the time required to obtain a search warrant, and indeed there was no suggestion that a search warrant could not easily and conveniently have been obtained. '(T)he seriousness of the offence under investigation (does not of) itself create exigent circumstances of the kind that under the Fourth Amendment justify a warrantless search.' But it is possible that the implications of an offence when coupled with its undoubted gravity will allow an emergency search that both in terms of distance from the offence itself and in terms of intensity goes considerably beyond what is normally permitted. A good example is *People v. Sirhan*[3] where it was held that where the victim of a shooting was a major presidential candidate, the crime was one of enormous gravity, and the officers believed both that there might be a conspiracy to assassinate other political leaders in the country and that prompt action on their part was necessary, a search of the defendant's place of residence was reasonable and lawful, justified by the apparent emergency, even though there was no probable cause but only a possibility that evidence of conspiracy would be found and despite the fact that the search was a very thorough one.

Another category of cases where there is a compelling need for official action and no time to obtain a warrant consists of miscellaneous holdings, mainly from what could be called 'the regulatory field'.[4] Thus, a number of

[1] *Mincey v. Arizona*, 98 S.Ct. 2408, 2414 (1978).

[2] 98 S.Ct. 2408 (1978).

[3] 102 Cal. Rptr. 385 (1972). For an exposition of the view that the gravity of the offence is occasionally an appropriate factor to take into consideration, see *Brinegar v. United States*, 338 U.S. 160, 182.

[4] *Michigan v. Tyler*, 436 U.S. 499, 509 (1978).

cases have recognised the legality in emergency situations of prompt administrative inspections,[1] the warrantless seizure of unwholesome food,[2] the imposition of health quarantines,[3] compulsory vaccinations[4] and even the summary destruction of animals infected with dangerous diseases,[5] and the like. In a recent case[6] the Supreme Court had no doubt that a burning building presented 'an exigency of sufficient proportions' to render a warrantless entry reasonable. 'Indeed, it would defy reason to suppose that firemen must secure a warrant or consent before entering a burning structure to put out the blaze.'[7] And once in a building for this purpose fire-fighters may seize evidence of arson that is in plain view.

In conclusion, it must be pointed out that all emergency searches are subject to two general conditions, already briefly mentioned. First, in such cases as in any other where there is no search warrant the burden is on the State to show 'proper justification';[8] this is not easy to discharge and, it goes without saying, 'the mere fact that law enforcement may be made more efficient can never by itself justify disregard of the Fourth Amendment'.[9] But even though in justifying the particular warrantless search the police must be able to point to specific and articulable facts which reasonably warrant their intrusion, and even though 'an objective standard as to the reasonableness of the officer's belief must be applied',[10] courts must have regard both to the difficulties normally facing the police and to the need in many cases to take quick action, often on incomplete and possibly false information. '(T)he business of policemen and firemen is *to act*, not to speculate or meditate'[11] on whether a report they have received is correct, and 'people could well die in emergencies if police tried to act with the calm deliberation associated with the judicial process'.[12] For this reason the benefit of hindsight will be ignored if at the relevant time the officers *in fact* had a reasonable belief that an emergency existed.[13] Secondly, an emergency warrantless search must be strictly circumscribed by the exigencies which justify its inception; the right to enter premises in response to an emergency situation does not justify a search of the premises for some other purpose, nor can an emergency entry be used as a pretext for conducting a general search of a protected area for incriminating evidence;[14] and if the emergency has come to an end a warrant must be obtained before the authorities can continue with their search, as in

[1] *Camara v. Municipal Court*, 387 U.S. 523, 539.

[2] *North American Cold Storage Co. v. City of Chicago*, 211 U.S. 306.

[3] *Compagnie Francaise v. Board of Health*, 186 U.S. 380.

[4] *Jacobson v. Massachusetts*, 197 U.S. 11.

[5] *Kroplin v. Truax*, 165 N.E. 498.

[6] *Michigan v. Tyler*, 436 U.S. 499 (1978).

[7] Ibid., at 509.

[8] *People v. Sirhan*, 102 Cal. Rptr. 385, 402 (1972).

[9] *Mincey v. Arizona*, 98 S.Ct. 2408, 2414 (1978).

[10] *Root v. Gauper*, 438 F. 2d 361, 364 (1971).

[11] *Wayne v. United States*, 318 F. 2d 205, 212.

[12] Ibid.

[13] See *Root v. Gauper*, 438 F. 2d 361, 365; *Wayne v. United States*, 318 F. 2d 205, 212.

[14] *People v. Roberts*, 303 P. 2d 721, 723.

Michigan v. Tyler,[1] the arson case mentioned above, where, after holding both that the Fourth Amendment is not violated by the warrantless entry of firemen to extinguish a fire and that officials need no warrant to remain in a building for a reasonable time to investigate the cause of a blaze after it has been extinguished, the Supreme Court also ruled that subsequent entries 'clearly detached from the initial exigency' were invalid in the absence of either a warrant or consent.

(g) Seizure of items in 'plain view'

It is now well established that the police may legitimately seize without a warrant evidence in 'plain view'.[2] Applications of the 'plain view' doctrine have already been noted in a number of contexts, for instance where there is a warrant and in the course of the ensuing search the police come across criminal evidence not specified in it, or where the police are conducting a search or examination under another exception to the warrant requirement during which incriminating items are discovered. Thus the police may stumble upon evidence while in 'hot pursuit' of a fleeing suspect or while conducting an otherwise legal search incident to arrest or when they are engaged in a reasonable inventory inspection. In all these cases, it is now settled, the incriminating evidence falling within the 'plain view' of the police can be seized without a warrant. These cases do not so much illustrate examples of the enlargement of an initially limited authority *to search* as they exemplify a separate exception to the warrant requirement recognising a police power of *warrantless seizure*.[3] But this power, it is also clear, depends upon the presence of certain conditions. These are essentially two.[4] The first is that the police should have come across the incriminating piece of evidence during an otherwise justifiable intrusion. The 'plain view' doctrine does not itself confer authority to enter or initiate a search and cannot come into operation until a search is in progess. What it does is to supplement a prior justification by conferring in certain circumstances the power of *warrantless seizure*. The second condition is that the discovery should be accidental or inadvertent. If it was otherwise, not only would the police be tempted to secure entry on some convenient pretext and then engage in fishing expeditions for incriminating evidence, but also there would be no reason for making an exception to the warrant requirement. For if the discovery is not inadvertent it must have been anticipated, and where the police know in advance the location of the evidence and intend to seize it, there is no reason why they should not obtain a warrant. These principles are illustrated by *Coolidge v. New Hampshire*[5] involving the warrantless seizure of a car parked

[1] 436 U.S. 499 (1978).

[2] See La Fave, 'Warrantless Searches and the Supreme Court: Further Ventures Into the "Quagmire"', 8 *Crim. L. Bull.* 9, 25–6; 1 La Fave, *Search and Seizure* 240–8 (1978).

[3] See A.L.I., *Model Code of Pre-Arraignment Procedure* 553–4 (1975).

[4] See *Coolidge v. New Hampshire*, 403 U.S. 443, 467–73 (1971), per Stewart, J.

[5] Ibid.

in the suspect's driveway. The 'plain view' doctrine was held not to apply because the police knew of the automobile's location well in advance, had intended to seize it when they came upon the suspect's property, and therefore had ample opportunity to obtain a valid warrant. The discovery of the car was therefore not inadvertent, and it followed that its seizure without a warrant was unlawful.

(h) Warrantless seizure of persons[1]

The arrest of a person is 'quintessentially a seizure'.[2] It therefore comes within the Fourth Amendment and will only be upheld if it is reasonable. Should it be authorised by a warrant, like a search or other types of seizure falling within the Amendment? The answer is no. It is quite generally accepted that the warrantless arrest of a person is a reasonable seizure within the constitutional guarantee, provided it is based on probable cause and has been effected in a reasonable manner, despite the fact that there were no exigent circumstances and there was ample opportunity to obtain a warrant.[3] Two reasons have been given for the legality of warrantless arrests.[4] The first is that a constitutional rule permitting arrests only with a warrant or in emergency circumstances would severely hamper effective law enforcement. Not only is it often the case that by the time information amounting to probable cause to arrest a man has been collected the suspect will know of police interest in him and thus be likely to flee, but also on many occasions good police work may require postponing an arrest even after probable cause has been established in order to place the suspect under surveillance and thus secure other evidence necessary to prove guilt.[5] Further, most arrests take place on the street or as part of a developing confrontation when a requirement of exigent circumstances, that is that a warrant should have been obtained if there was adequate opportunity to do so, would be particularly difficult to apply.[6] The second reason that has been given for dispensing with the warrant requirement in the case of arrests is that an arrestee cannot be held for long without a neutral judicial determination that there are grounds justifying his arrest and detention.[7] Since then the issue of probable cause will be determined shortly after the arrest, in contrast to the case of most searches and seizures of property, there is no compelling need to insist that an arrest should if possible be authorised by a warrant. These reasons have not been found convincing by others.[8] It has thus been argued, relying partly on the

[1] See La Fave, 'Warrantless Searches and the Supreme Court: Further Ventures Into the "Quagmire"', 8 *Crim. L. Bull.* 9, 20–4.

[2] *United States v. Watson*, 423 U.S. 411, 428 (1976), per Powell J. concurring.

[3] La Fave, supra, n. 1, at 20.

[4] See *Chimel v. California*, 395 U.S. 752, 779 (1969), per White J. dissenting.

[5] *Watson*, supra, n. 2, at 431, per Powell J. concurring.

[6] See generally A.L.I., *Model Code of Pre-Arraignment Procedure* § 120.1 (1975), and see the commentary, 289, 303.

[7] See *Gerstein v. Pugh*, 420 U.S. 103 (1975).

[8] See particularly the dissent of Marshall, J. in *Watson*, supra, at 434.

fact that it is the standard practice of the F.B.I. to obtain a warrant before making an arrest, that a warrant requirement would not unduly burden legitimate law enforcement interests, and that even though there may be a reasonably speedy determination of the legality of a warrantless arrest subsequent review is no substitute for prior judicial evaluation. Indeed, since the Fourth Amendment speaks in the same terms about the freedom of both persons and property from unreasonable seizure, and since in most cases an arrest—normally resulting in the individual temporarily losing his right to control his person and movements—is likely to be a more serious intrusion than a search, some have taken the view that the Fourth Amendment should be applied not in a manner that emphasises property interests but so as to provide adequate protection of personal liberty from illegal arrests[1] and that therefore the same limitations should be imposed upon arrests as in the case of searches.[2] But even though '(l)ogic (m)ight) seem to dictate that arrests (should) be subject to the warrant requirement at least to the same extent as searches',[3] the Supreme Court has been impressed not only by the difficulties that law enforcement would be faced with if warrantless arrests without accompanying circumstances of necessity were held to be illegal but also by the quite general acceptance in almost all jurisdictions of the common law rule that a police officer may make a warrantless arrest if he has probable cause to believe the suspect to be a felon.[4] And only recently, for these 'historical and policy reasons',[5] it was held in *United States v. Watson*[6] that, consistently with the rule at common law, the Fourth Amendment was not violated by the warrantless felony arrest of a suspect in a public place when there was probable cause for the arrest, it being immaterial that there were no exigent circumstances and that the arresting officers could have first obtained a warrant.

Watson involved the warrantless arrest of an individual in a public place. What if the individual to be arrested is in his home so that he can only be taken by the police entering his premises? Can they proceed without a warrant? Until very recently this basic question was unresolved. The view that the police could enter a suspect's home without a warrant in order to arrest him, provided only there was probable cause to believe that he had committed a felony and was present at that time in the house, was supported by a number of arguments.[7] There was first the historical acceptance of warrantless entries to make felony arrests both at common law and in the practice of many American States.[8] A second line of argument was that the

[1] See Barrett, 'Personal Rights, Property Rights, and the Fourth Amendment', 1960 *Sup. Ct. Rev.* 46, 47.

[2] See Marshall J.'s dissent in *Watson*, supra.

[3] *Watson*, supra, at 429, per Powell, J. concurring.

[4] *Watson*, supra, at 417–26, per White, J. delivering the majority opinion.

[5] Ibid., at 432, per Powell, J. concurring.

[6] 423 U.S. 411 (1976).

[7] See the majority opinion of the New York Court of Appeals in *People v. Payton*, 380 N.E. 2d 224 (1978).

[8] Both the common law and state authority are clear, but there is not the same kind of unanimity as in the case of warrantless arrests in public places: see *Watson*, 423 U.S. at 422–3 and *Payton v. New York*, 100 S.Ct. 1371, 1387 (1980).

common law power of entry in order to place under arrest was not a blanket one but had been surrounded by carefully developed safeguards which more than made up for the absence of a warrant.[1] Thus at common law, in the absence of exigent circumstances, entries to arrest could be made only for felony; even in cases of felony the arresting officers were required to announce their presence and demand admission before they would be held entitled to enter without the consent of the occupant; entries could be made only during daytime; and it was apparently necessary that the officers entering to arrest should have reasonable grounds to believe not only that the person to be arrested had committed a crime but also that he was present in the house at the time of the proposed entry.[2] On this second argument these four restrictions on home arrests—felony, knock and announce, daytime, and stringent probable cause—constituted 'powerful and complementary protections for the privacy interests associated with the home',[3] in effect making it possible for an individual suspected of a serious crime to surrender at the front door of his home and thus preventing any further invasion of privacy involved in home arrests. In contrast, a general rule that a warrant should precede home arrests would hamper effective law enforcement quite as much as a similar requirement in the case of other arrests, and would introduce new complications, both with regard to the work of police officers who in the absence of a clear and categorical rule will have to tackle on an ad hoc basis the difficult task of deciding whether the circumstances are sufficiently exigent to justify a warrantless entry to arrest and with regard to the work of the courts, since whenever there is a warrantless home arrest there will be the possibility of litigation with respect to the existence of exigent circumstances, whether it was practicable to get a warrant, whether the suspect was about to flee, and the like.[4] The third argument in support of the legality of routine warrantless home arrests is that searches and arrests are radically different, in two distinct ways:[5] first, there is a 'substantial difference between *the intrusion* which attends an entry for the purpose of searching the premises and that which results from an entry for the purpose of making an arrest'. Thus, in the case of a search, the invasion of the householder's privacy will normally be more extensive and of greater magnitude than what might be expected to occur on an entry made exclusively for the purpose of effecting his arrest. This is because a 'search' by its nature often contemplates or involves a thorough exploration of private possessions before the items to be seized are located, and this quest usually entails the revelation to the official eye of numerous personal items and details which would otherwise be free from public scrutiny. In contrast, entry for the purpose of effecting an arrest is, as a general matter, rather different. 'While the taking into custody of the person of the householder is

[1] *Payton v. New York*, 100 S.Ct. 1371, 1395 (1980), per White, J. dissenting.
[2] Ibid.
[3] Ibid.
[4] Ibid., at 1396.
[5] See *People v. Payton*, 380 N.E. 2d at 228–9. Subsequent quotations, until otherwise indicated, come from the majority opinion of the New York Court of Appeals.

unquestionably of grave import, there is no accompanying prying into the area of expected privacy attending his possessions and affairs.' Since *personal seizure* alone does not require a warrant, the question is whether the fact of an arrest *in one's home* as contrasted to an arrest in a public place involves such an *added* intrusion into privacy that a warrant should here be demanded; and on this view since entry on the premises for making an arrest does not entail a significant intrusion on the privacy of the home there is no good reason for drawing a distinction between arrest within the home and arrest in a public place. Indeed, 'it may well be that because of the added exposure the latter may be more objectionable'. Secondly, those who uphold the legality of warrantless home arrests believe that there is a significant difference between the governmental objectives behind searches and arrests respectively. Since the community's interest in the apprehension of criminal suspects is of a 'higher order' than its interest in the recovery of evidence, and since the hazards created by the failure to apprehend far exceed the risks which may follow non-recovery, it is perfectly consistent to adopt a more lenient test for the constitutionality of arrests than of searches.

The view that a warrant is necessary to enter a home to arrest or seize a person does not necessarily dispute that there may be differences of degree between searches and arrests within the home, but argues that both types of intrusion share the same fundamental characteristic, 'the breach of the entrance to an individual's home'.[1] On this reasoning '(f)reedom from intrusion into the home or dwelling is the archetype of the privacy protection secured by the Fourth Amendment';[2] and even though a warrantless arrest in a public place, generally accepted as legal, is also a serious intrusion, '(t)o be arrested in the home involves not only the invasion attendant to all arrests but also an invasion of the sanctity of the home'. This is simply 'too substantial an invasion to allow without a warrant'[3] (which as a protection is viewed as immeasurably superior to ex post facto evaluation), except of course where exigent circumstances exist. The basic tenet of this second view is that the fundamental distinction is not between searches and arrests but between searches and seizures that take place on a man's property—his home or office—and those carried out elsewhere.[4] *Any* search or seizure carried out on a suspect's premises without a warrant is unconstitutional unless it falls within one of the established exceptions, and therefore a warrantless entry into private premises in order to arrest the occupant is similarly unreasonable, unless again one of the *same* exceptions to the warrant requirement applies.

Until recently the Supreme Court had not passed on this issue,[5] and the general assumption was that warrantless home arrests were constitutional.[6]

[1] *Payton v. New York*, 100 S.Ct. 1371, 1381 (1980).

[2] *Dorman v. United States*, 435 F. 2d 385, 389 (1970).

[3] *United States v. Reed*, 572 F. 2d 412, 423 (1978).

[4] See *Coolidge v. New Hampshire*, 403 U.S. at 474–5.

[5] See *Jones v. United States*, 357 U.S. 493, 499–500 (1958), per Harlan, J.; *Coolidge*, supra, at 480, per Stewart, J.; *Watson*, supra, at 433, per Stewart, J., concurring.

[6] But see *Accarino v. United States*, 179 F. 456 (1949), where it was states that 'a government official cannot invade a private home unless (1) a magistrate has

This has now changed. In *Payton v. New York*[1] the Court addressed the constitutional question directly, and by a majority came down in favour of the second view, namely, that the Fourth Amendment prohibits police officers from making a warrantless and non-consensual entry into a suspect's home in order to make a routine felony arrest. The Court took the view that the 'basic principle of Fourth Amendment law'[2] was that searches and seizures, whether of effects or persons, inside a home without a warrant were presumptively unreasonable. 'At the very core of the Fourth Amendment stands the right of a man to retreat into his own home and there be free from unreasonable government(al) intrusion',[3] and this meant that, except for circumstances of necessity, any official invasion of the security of a home should be subjected to prior independent scrutiny. As Justice Stevens put it, '(i)n terms that apply equally to seizures of property and to seizures of persons, the Fourth Amendment has drawn a firm line at the entrance to the house'. In the absence of exigent circumstances,[4] 'that threshold may not reasonably be crossed without a warrant'.[5]

(i) Consent searches

(i) Consent and voluntariness

Fourth Amendment rights can be waived,[6] and this means that warrantless searches which have voluntarily been consented to are constitutional, even though there was at the time no probable cause for the search.[7] Reservations have been expessed about the desirability of recognising so wide an exception to the warrant and probable cause requirements on the ground that consent searches are 'overproductive of credibility issues and susceptible to abuse',[8] but such arguments have not prevailed, and the constitutional position is now clear that '(a) search to which an individual consents meets Fourth Amendment requirements',[9] even though it may have been practicable to

---

authorized him to do so; or (2) an immediate major crisis in the performance of duty affords neither time nor opportunity to apply to a magistrate'; and see *Dorman v. United States*, 435 F. 2d 385 (1970).

[1] 100 S.Ct. 1371 (1980) reversing *People v. Payton*, supra.

[2] *Coolidge v. New Hampshire*, 403 U.S. at 474–5.

[3] *Silverman v. United States*, 365 U.S. 505, 511.

[4] 'Exigent circumstances' would appear to include (1) whether a serious offence, particularly a crime of violence, is involved; (2) whether the suspect is reasonably believed to be armed; (3) whether there is a clear showing of probable cause; (4) whether strong reason exists to believe the suspect will escape if not swiftly apprehended. See *Dorman v. United States*, 435 F. 2d 385 (1970); *Vance v. North Carolina*, 432 F. 2d 984, 990 (1970).

[5] *Payton* holds that for Fourth Amendment purposes an *arrest* warrant founded on probable cause inplicitly carries with it the limited authority to enter a house in which the suspect lives when there is reason to believe that he is inside.

[6] *Zap v. United States*, 328 U.S. 624 (1946).

[7] See 'Annotation, Validity, under Federal Constitution, of Consent to Search', 36 L. Ed. 2d 1143.

[8] A.L.I., *A Model Code of Pre-Arraignment Procedure* 532 (1975).

[9] *Katz v. United States*, 389 U.S. 347, 358 n. 22 (1967).

have obtained a search warrant. A plausible case can be made[1] that not all 'consent' cases are the same, but that three categories should instead be distinguished: first, situations where the police could not have obtained a search warrant because there was no probable cause; secondly situations where a warrant could have been obtained (in the sense that there was probable cause and that it was practicable to secure one) but was not; and thirdly cases where there was probable cause but a warrant was not obtained because it was impracticable to do so, for example where there is a confrontation between officer and suspect in the 'informal and unstructured conditions'[2] of a roadside search. It is arguable that these three situations should be subjected to different treatment, for instance by placing a much heavier burden of proving consent on the government in the first two cases[3] or alternatively by insisting that a consent search should not be allowed where it would have been easy for the police to have obtained a valid search warrant.[4] But such arguments have not appealed to the Supreme Court which has dealt with all types of consent searches on the same basis and by reference to the same body of principles.

The governing principles in this area can be stated with deceptive simplicity. Consent to a warrantless search and the waiver of Fourth Amendment rights which it entails must be 'freely and voluntarily given';[5] in other words consent can only be effective if it is voluntary; the burden of proving free consent is borne by the government and can only be discharged by clear, positive and convincing evidence;[6] waiver of the right to be free from what would otherwise be illegal searches and acquiescence in the loss of fundamental constitutional protections can neither be presumed[7] nor lightly inferred;[8] and it must clearly be shown by the government that the consent on which it relies is not contaminated by any duress or coercion, actual or implied,[9] since '(w)here there is coercion there cannot be consent'.[10] In particular, it must be demonstrated not only that the consent was not given in response to threats, force or coercion, but also that it was not granted 'only in submission to a claim of lawful authority',[11] the general principle here being that submission to law-enforcement officers who in effect represent to the defendant that they have authority to enter and search, if necessary against

[1] See Weinreb, 'Generalities of the Fourth Amendment', 42 *U. Chi. L. Rev.* 47, 57–58 (1974).

[2] See *Schneckloth v. Bustamonte*, 93 S.Ct. 2041, 2050 (1973).

[3] Weinreb, supra.

[4] See *United States v. Matlock*, 94 S.Ct. 988, 998 (1974), per Douglas, J. dissenting.

[5] *Bumper v. North Carolina*, 391 U.S. 543, 548 (1968).

[6] *United States v. Mapp*, 476 F. 2d 67, 77 (1973).

[7] *Johnson v. Zerbst*, 304 U.S. 458 (1938); *United States v. Mapp*, 476 F. 2d 67, 77 (1973).

[8] *United States v. Gaines*, 441 F. 2d 1122, 1123 (1971); *United States v. Mapp*, supra.

[9] *United States v. Wallace*, 160 F. Supp. 859 (1958); *Schneckloth v. Bustamonte*, 93 S.Ct. 2041, 2059 (1973).

[10] *Bumper v. North Carolina*, 391 U.S. 543, 550 (1968).

[11] *Schneckloth v. Bustamonte*, 93 S.Ct. 2041, 2051 (1973).

his will, is not such consent as can constitute the 'understanding and intentional waiver of the constitutional right'[1] that will be insisted upon. Thus a search conducted in reliance upon a warrant cannot later be sustained on the basis of consent if it turns out that the warrant was invalid, and the result will obviously be the same both where the intruding officers simply assert that, or behave as if, they have authority to search without any attempt to rely upon a warrant[2] and where they falsely say they have a warrant. In *Bumper v. North Carolina*[3] an elderly Negro widow allowed four white officers to search her home after they asserted they had a search warrant. The Supreme Court had little difficulty holding the alleged consent to be invalid, noting that where law enforcement officers claimed authority to search a house under a warrant they in effect announced that the occupant had no right to resist the search. The situation was 'instinct with coercion—albeit colourably lawful coercion', and 'submission to official authority under circumstances pregnant with coercion'[4] was not the understanding, intelligent and unequivocal consent that had to be established before constitutional rights could effectively be waived.

Two questions that have long troubled American courts are, first, whether it should be shown that the defendant *knew* that he had a right to refuse before his consent can be held to be valid, and, secondly, the precise relevance of custody, where, that is, the person consenting to a warrantless search was at the relevant time in the custody of the police. On the first question, whether a showing of knowledge of a right to refuse—invariably consisting in a warning of rights—should be a prerequisite to a voluntary consent, courts have differed sharply. Powerful arguments can be marshalled in support of the view that consent cannot validate a warrantless search unless it is preceded by an appropriately formulated warning of rights. It is thus first said that 'the general test'[5] of the effective waiver of constitutional rights, namely whether there has been 'an intentional relinquishment or abandonment of a *known* right or privilege',[6] should be applicable here as well as in the area of the privilege against self-incrimination and elsewhere, and that it is accordingly difficult to see how it can meaningfully be said that a citizen has waived something as precious as the constitutional guarantee of security from unreasonably searches and seizures without ever being aware (or proved to have been so) of its existence.[7] On this view since the concept of voluntary consent includes the notion of capacity to choose, and since the latter necessarily depends upon knowledge that there is a choice to be made, one cannot truly be said to have consented to what would otherwise be an

[1] *Johnson v. United States*, 333 U.S. 10, 13 (1948).

[2] Ibid. (entry demanded under colour of office); see also *Amos v. United States*, 255 U.S. 313 (1921) (statement by officers that they had come to search the premises for violations of the law).

[3] 391 U.S. 543 (1968).

[4] *United States v. Mapp*, 476 F. 2d 67, 77 (1973).

[5] Wright, *Federal Practice & Procedure* 79 (vol. 3) (1969).

[6] *Johnson v. Zerbst*, 304 U.S. 458, 464 (1938).

[7] *Schneckloth v. Bustamonte*, 93 S.Ct. 2041, 2073 (1973), per Brennan, J. dissenting.

illegal search by relinquishing the constitutional right to be free from unreasonable intrusions upon one's security without proof that he knew that he had the alternative of refusing to accede to a police request to search.[1] Another type of argument in favour of the view that consent searches should be preceded by warnings of rights is that unless courts insist on the need to advise persons of the right to withhold consent, and if the only operative criterion is the broad rubric of voluntariness rather than more concrete guidelines, the inevitable result, given the unavoidable complexities of the task of engaging in retrospective investigations of a 'consenting' person's state of mind and in view of the often-noticed 'extreme difficulty of determining from the record the extent to which the person whose consent was sought acted on the assumption that the police *had a right* to make a search',[2] will be a set of cases 'in which the courts provide a lengthy factual description followed by a conclusion',[3] in most cases that consent was voluntarily given, and with very little by way of general principle or convincing distinctions;[4] the police therefore, as with confessions and interrogation, should be put under an affirmative obligation to advise the person whose consent is requested or sought of his right to insist on the presence of a warrant.[5] This view has now been rejected by the Supreme Court in *Schneckloth v. Bustamonte*[6] where it was held that consent searches may be valid without proof that the consenting person knew that he had a right to withhold consent. Consent, in other words, *may* be voluntary even though the consenting party did not know that he had the constitutional right to refuse to allow the search. When the subject of a search was not in custody and the State attempted to justify a search on the basis of consent, the Fourth Amendment, Justice Stewart said delivering the Court's opinion, required that it should be demonstrated that the consent was in fact voluntarily given, and was not the result of duress or coercion. 'Voluntariness is a question of fact to be determined from all the circumstances, and while the subject's knowledge of a right to refuse is a factor to be taken into account, the prosecution is not required to demonstrate such knowledge as a prerequisite to establishing a voluntary consent.' It was true, the majority recognised, that to establish a waiver of constitutional rights in 'trial-type' situations, for instance the right to counsel and the privilege against self-incrimination, the State had to demonstrate an intentional abandonment of a *known* right, but the protections of the Fourth Amendment were regarded as of a wholly differ-

[1] Ibid., at 2073, per Marhall, J. dissenting.
[2] *Model Code*, supra, at 533.
[3] Weinreb, supra,
[4] Ibid.
[5] *Model Code*, supra, n. 3, 532–7.
[6] 93 S.Ct. 2041 (1973); 412 U.S. 218 (1973). The Supreme Court's 'indefensibly narrow view of voluntariness' (*Model Code*, supra, 205 n. 8, at 536) is criticized by the *Model Code*, supra, and it is there proposed not that the State must affirmatively prove that the subject of the search *knew* that he had a right to refuse consent but that a suitably formulated warning (namely that there is no obligation to consent and that anything found may be taken and used in evidence (§§ 240.2(2)) should be a prerequisite to an 'effective consent'.

ent order' since they had nothing whatever to do 'with promoting the fair ascertainment of truth at a criminal trial'; it was therefore proper to confine the standard of a 'knowing' and 'intelligent' waiver to those rights which the Constitution guaranteed in order to preserve a fair trial and not extend it to the rights conferred by the Fourth Amendment. All 'the unique facts and circumstances of each case'[1] must therefore be examined in deciding whether a particular consent was in fact voluntary or coerced, and in doing so both 'subtly coercive police questions as well as the possibly vulnerable subjective state of the person who consents'[2] must be taken into account.

What if the person who is alleged to have consented is at the relevant time in custody? In *Schneckloth v. Bustamonte* the Supreme Court took special care to confine its remarks to situations where the subject of the search was not in custody, and it has often been recognised that if the consenting person is at the relevant time under arrest and in custody a particularly heavy burden will rest on the prosecution to prove voluntariness.[3] But here too, the Supreme Court has now decided,[4] the fact of custody makes no difference in principle (even though it may be taken into account as part of the overall facts), the 'totality of circumstances' test of *Schneckloth v. Bustamonte* is the one to apply (which means that the question remains whether the arrestee's consent was his own 'essentially free and unconstrained choice' or whether at the time his 'will ha(d) been overborne and his capacity for self-determination critically impaired'),[5] and consequently absence of proof that the defendant knew that he could withhold consent, 'though it may be a factor in the overall judgment', is not to be given 'controlling significance'.[6]

(ii) Scope

What is the permissible scope of consent searches?[7] The basic principle here appears to be that '(a) consent search is reasonable only if kept within the bounds of the actual consent'.[8] For since consent is a waiver of the right to insist that a warrant should be obtained, it follows that 'the need for a warrant is waived only to the extent granted by the defendant in his consent'.[9] A defendant's consent, in other words, either by what it *expressly allows* or by its *assent* to what is explicitly requested may limit the permissible scope of a warrantless search in approximately the same way that the specifications of a warrant limit the extent of an authorised search. If therefore the consent specifies either certain areas or certain items as the only ones that can legitimately be searched or seized without a warrant, the officers must

[1] *Schneckloth v. Bustamonte*, 93 S.Ct. 2041, 2050 (1973).

[2] Ibid., at 2049.

[3] See 68 *Am. Jur.* 2d, 701–702 (1973).

[4] *United States v. Watson*, 423 U.S. 411 (1976).

[5] *Schneckloth v. Bustamonte*, 412 U.S. at 225–6, quoting from *Culombe v. Connecticut*, 367 U.S. 568, at 602.

[6] *United States v. Watson*, 423 U.S. 411, 424 (1976).

[7] See *Model Code*, supra, 205 n. 8, at 537–8; 68 *Am. Jur.* 2d, 753–4 (1973).

[8] *United States v. Dichiarinte*, 445 F. 2d 126, 129 (1971); *Honig v. United States*, 208 F. 2d 916, 919 (1953).

[9] *United States v. Dichiarinte*, 445 F. 2d 126, 129 n. 3 (1971).

regulate and confine their activities accordingly. A good example if *United States v. Dichiarinte*[1] where the evidence showed that the defendant's consent was limited to a search for narcotics; it followed that the officers only had power to conduct such a search as would be necessary to establish whether any narcotics were concealed on the premises and could not use what had been a limited consent as a licence to engage in a general exploratory search; when they therefore read through the defendant's papers to find evidence of tax evasion, as opposed to merely looking through them for narcotics, they exceeded the permissible limits fixed by the defendant's consent and were in violation of the Fourth Amendment. In the same way that a government officer is not allowed to use a precise and legal warrant 'as a ticket'[2] to get into a man's home and, once inside, to engage in unconfined searches and indiscriminate seizures, police officers cannot use a defendant's limited consent as a ticket to get inside his home and there conduct general searches.[3] But if of course government agents acting within the parameters of the defendant's consent come across contraband, fruits or instrumentalities of crime, or other evidence of criminal behaviour lying before them in plain view, they may seize them.[4]

(iii) Third-party consent searches

Normally it is the defendant himself who is asked for, and gives, his consent to a search of his own property; and since rights of security from unreasonable searches and seizures are personal to him a defendant who has given his consent freely and voluntarily cannot then complain that the search has brought to light fruits or evidence of crime.[5] But it may be that the consent the police are relying upon as justifying their warrantless intrusion has been given not by the person primarily affected, namely the person implicated by the uncovered incriminating evidence, but by some third party who has either an interest in or some measure of control over the area or property to be searched or seized, or who is in some close relation to the defendant. The question of the circumstances in which third-party consent is effective to validate warrantless searches and seizures of the defendant's property is a difficult one,[6] but, as a general matter, it is now accepted that when the prosecution seeks to justify a warrantless search by proof of voluntary consent 'it is not limited to proof that consent was given by the defendant, but may show that permission to search was obtained from a third party who possessed common authority over or other sufficient relationship to the premises or effects sought to be inspected'.[7] The right of a third party in appropriate circumstances to consent to a search of jointly controlled premises or property

[1] 445 F. 2d 126 (1971).

[2] *Stanley v. Georgia*, 394 U.S. 557, 572 (1969).

[3] *United States v. Dichiarinte*, supra, at 130.

[4] This is an application of the 'plain view' doctrine.

[5] *Silva v. State*, 344 So. 2d 559, 562 (1977).

[6] See 68 *Am. Jur.* 2d, 702–705 (1973); 'Note, Third-Party Consent Searches: An Alternative Analysis', 41 *U. Chi. L. Rev.* 121 (1973); Wright, *Federal Practice & Procedure* 86–88 (vol. 3) (1969).

[7] *United States v. Matlock*, 94 S.Ct. 988, 993 (1974).

has arisen and been judicially recognised in diverse circumstances involving both varied relationships between the consenting party and the person against whom the incriminating evidence is used and widely differing measures of third-party control over the seized items,[1] for this reason no single formula for determining whether the third party possessed an independent right to consent to a warrantless search which will serve to permit the evidence obtained thereby to be used at trial has emerged, but instead all circumstances must be considered, particularly the third party's legal and possessory rights to the items or premises searched, his relationship to the subject of the search and any other facts as they objectively appeared to the searching officers at the time.[2] Broadly speaking, the authority of a third party to consent to a search has traditionally been justified by reference either to the sufficiency of the third party's possessory interest in the searched area[3] or to the existence of an agency relationship between the consenting party and the defendant,[4] but more recently many courts have been using the currently fashionable doctrines of legitimate expectations of privacy and assumption of risk;[5] the reason therefore why joint use of or common authority over the searched items may suffice to support third-party waiver of Fourth Amendment rights is that in such circumstances 'the relationship of each person to the property demonstrates that the non-consenting user *assumed the risk* that such consent might be given',[6] or, to put it somewhat differently, in cases of joint use or authority the defendant has no reasonable expectation of privacy that the common property will not be officially inspected at the invitation of one of the co-inhabitants or co-users; in any case it is abundantly clear that power to consent to warrantless searches will not be inferred merely from a property interest the third party has in the property at stake but at the very least from compelling evidence indicating 'mutual use of the property by persons generally having joint access or control for most purposes'[7] so that it is

[1] See *Roberts v. United States*, 332 F. 2d 892 (1964), spouses; *United States v. Matlock*, 94 S.Ct. 988 (1974), cohabitants; *United States v. Airdo*, 380 F. 2d 103 (1967), mistresses and lovers; *Pasterchik v. United States*, 400 F. 2d 696 (1968), hosts and house guests; *Government of Virgin Islands v. Gereau*, 502 F. 2d 914 (1974), trespasser and owner; *Wright v. United States*, 389 F. 2d 996 (1968), roommates; *Anderson v. United States*, 399 F. 2d 753 (1968), automobile bailors and bailees; *United States v. Stone*, 401 F. 2d 32 (1969), parents and children; *United States v. Sferas*, 210 F. 2d 69 (1954), business partners; *United States v. Murphy*, 506 F. 2d 529 (1974), employer and employee; *State v. Smith*, 531 P. 2d 843, hospital patient and hospital authorities.

[2] *United States v. Phifer*, 400 F. Supp. 719 (1975).

[3] See 'Note', supra, 210 n. 6, at 128; see also *Chapman v. United States*, 365 U.S. 610 (1961).

[4] See 'Note', supra, at 129.

[5] See *United States v. Phifer*, 400 F. Supp. 719, 733 (1975); *Government of Virgin Islands v. Gereau*, 502 F. 2d 914, 926 (1974); *United States v. Sor-Lokken*, 557 F. 2d 755, 757 (1977); see also *United States v. Matlock*, supra, 94 S.Ct. at 993 n. 7.

[6] *Government of Virgin Islands v. Gereau*, supra, at 926; see also *People v. Nunn*, 304 N.E. 2d 81.

[7] *United States v. Matlock*, 94 S.Ct. 988, 993 n. 7 (1974); see also *Chapman v. United States*, 365 U.S. 610 (1961), and *Stoner v. California*, 376 U.S. 483 (1964).

reasonable to recognise that the third party has the right to permit the entry, search or seizure 'in his own right'.[1]

We shall now consider some of the most interesting problems that arise in the area of third-party consent searches. Perhaps the most usual is whether the constitutional rights of the defendant can be waived by his spouse. For some time the question of whether protection against unreasonable searches and seizures could in effect be given up by the consent of one's spouse to enter and search premises or seize other property jointly occupied or controlled by husband and wife was regarded as a 'serious' and 'close' one,[2] the Supreme Court avoided the issue in *Amos v. United States*,[3] and indeed many courts had taken the position that the wife (and of course the husband too) had 'no implied authority'[4] to license a warrantless search of his (or her) property and that therefore '(t)he mere consent of a wife, not shown to have authority from her husband for the waiver of a right of constitutional dimensions, must be rearded as a nullity'.[5] More recently the weight of authority has tilted decisively in favour of the view both that the consent of a spouse 'who possesses common authority over premises or effects is valid against the absent (defendant)',[6] *and* that wife and husband *normally* possess co-equal authority over and access to the *premises* they occupy. It was thus held in one case[7] that a spouse could consent to a search of the common home when it had been shown that each spouse exercised control and dominion over the house, and in another[8] that the accused's wife could validly consent to a search of the premises and the seizure of certain items since the wife was not only a joint proprietor of the house searched but also a joint occupant of the bedroom where the objects seized were found and since the cheques taken were from a jointly handled account in the wife's name alone. The husband too has power in cases of common authority or mutual use in effect to waive his wife's Fourth Amendment rights, as in *United States v. Patterson*[9] where it was held that the husband could consent to a warrantless search of a closet and the seizure of a revolver and a jacket used in a bank robbery and admitted in evidence against the wife since the evidence clearly indicated that he had common authority over the home, the bedroom and the closet where the incriminating items were found. A number of so-called exceptions qualify what might

[1] *United States v. Matlock*, supra, at 993 n. 7. In 'Note', supra, 210 n. 6, at 123, it is proposed that a consent search should be constitutional only where the consenting party has rights of possession and control at least equal to those of the defendant and 'an interest in consenting' sufficient to defeat, and thus render unreasonable, the defendant's expectation that 'the third party will not consent to an invasion of the defendant's privacy'. Many hints of this model can be found in the cases, including *Matlock*, supra.

[2] *Roberts v. United States*, 332 F. 2d 892, 895 (1964).

[3] 225 U.S. 313, 317 (1921).

[4] *United States v. Rykowski*, 267 F. 866, 871 (1920).

[5] *United States v. Greer*, 297 F. Supp. 1265, 1270 (1969).

[6] See *United States v. Matlock*, 94 S.Ct. 988, 993 (1974); see also *United States v. Thompson*, 421 F. 2d 373 (1970).

[7] *Yuma County Attorney v. McGuire*, 532 P. 2d 157 (1975).

[8] *People v. Chism*, 211 N.W. 2d 193 (1973).

[9] 554 F. 2d 852 (1977).

otherwise have been an effective third-party consent validating a search against a spouse. Thus, though a spouse who is a joint occupant has authority to consent to a search of jointly held premises or property if the other party is unavailable, the consenting person has no such power if the other party is present and objects, particularly if the police officers are aware that the objecting party is the one whose constitutional rights are at stake.[1] Another exception recognised by some courts is that of a consent motivated by hostility and a conscious desire to harm one's spouse by betraying him (or her) to the authorities, on the ground that when a wife intentionally acts against her husband's interests 'she would not be acting in harmony with the marital relationship from which her joint right of ownership or control is derived, but in antagonism to it'.[2] According to these authorities a spouse's right of consent is therefore spent when 'it reaches th(e) point of deliberate antagonistic intrusion on the rights of the other (party)'[3] Finally, if it is shown that by agreement or understanding the wife did not have use of or access to a particular area of the house or a particular piece of property or other item where or over which the husband enjoyed sole domain, her consent will not make admissible in evidence against him the fruits of the search.[4] But courts are generally reluctant to engage in the drawing of minute distinctions[5] and therefore do not often qualify the authority of a spouse to consent once joint dominion and control over the family home have been established, as in *State v. Gillespie*[6] where it was held that the defendant's wife had authority to consent to the search and seizure of her husband's field jacket which, even though exclusively used by him, was 'an ordinary item of (his) wearing apparel which had been left hanging in the community home in a community closet'; on the facts of the case the 'exclusive use' exception had not therefore been satisfied.

What should again be emphasised is that even though many judicial pronouncements are cast in terms of relationships—some relationships, it is thus said, do not confer the relevant authority on the consenting party, sons, for instance, being unable to consent for their fathers[7]—and even though such an analysis may be convenient as a starting point—primarily in that proof of certain relationships seems to cast a burden on the defendant to

[1] *Silva v. State*, 344 So. 2d 559 (1977).

[2] *United States ex rel. Cabey v. Mazurkiewicz*, 431 F. 2d 839, 843 (1970).

[3] Ibid.; see also *Silva v. State*, 344 So. 2d 559, 561 (1977).

[4] *Commonwealth v. Sebastian*, 500 S.W. 2d 417, 419 (1973); *Yuma County Attorney v. McGuire*, 532 P. 2d 157, 158 (1975).

[5] For the general attitude of the Supreme Court, see generally *Frazier v. Cupp*, 394 U.S. 731, 749 (1969), where the Court 'dismissed rather quickly' the contention that the consent of the defendant's cousin to a search of the bag which was jointly used by both men was only effective as to one compartment within the bag and ineffective as to the others. The Court was unwilling to engage in 'metaphysical subtleties' and decided the case on the broad basis that by allowing his cousin the use of the bag, and by leaving it in his house, the defendant should be taken to have assumed the risk that the consenting party would allow someone else to look inside; see also *United States v. Matlock*, supra, at 993.

[6] 569 P. 2d 1174 (1977).

[7] See *Silva v. State*, 344 So. 2d 559, 562 (1977).

disprove that the consenting party did indeed enjoy the required common authority, as with husbands and wives who are normally empowered to waive each other's rights from warrantless searches with regard to the house they occupy—the decisive criterion in such cases is not the marital status or the existence of any other legal relationship between the parties but rather whether the consenting party possessed at the relevant time the necessary common authority or joint control over the property searched;[1] and in appropriate circumstances other persons sharing the use of premises are allowed to consent to warrantless searches that implicate their cohabitants.[2] The cases are numerous and difficult to reconcile, but the general rule, as recently elaborated by the Supreme Court, appears to be that the voluntary consent of any joint occupant or user of a residence or other property allowing a search of the premises or property jointly occupied or used is valid against the co-occupant or co-user, with the result that evidence discovered in the search may be used against him at a subsequent criminal trial.[3] Most of the cases fit into this framework. Thus in one case[4] the girlfriend of the defendant was held to have authority to consent to a search of the defendant's apartment where she and the defendant has been living together and she had unrestricted access to the apartment as well as the use of it, and in another[5] the defendant's grandmother and cousin were recognised as having power to consent to a search of his living quarters since all three were found to be sharing the same apartment. Other propositions that also emerge from the cases are the following. If a child is living at the home of his parents either the head of the household or the child's mother may allow a search of his living quarters,[6] unless it is demonstrated that the child enjoys a special expectation of privacy in the area sought to be searched that must be protected from intrusion by means of third-party consent, as in *People v. Nunn*[7] where the son has locked his bedroom and adjoining kitchenette and had told his mother not to enter and not to allow anyone else to enter, the mother agreeing to this arrangement. Finally, a casual visitor has no authority to consent to a search of the house where he is staying but if he is found to be not a transient guest but 'an occupant of indefinite duration' he will be held to be endowed with those rights to the use or occupation of the premises that will allow him to give an effective consent to a warrantless search the fruits of which can then be adduced in evidence against the owner or lessor.[8]

Another category of cases deals with the waiver of Fourth Amendment rights in the employment and contractual contexts. Whether an employer or employee may validly consent to a warrantless search of the other's property is

[1] Ibid.; see also *United States v. Wilson*, 447 F. 2d 1 (1971).

[2] 68 *Am. Jur.* 2d, at 703–4.

[3] See *United States v. Matlock*, 94 S.Ct. 988, 992 (1974).

[4] *United States v. Wilson*, 447 F. 2d 1 (1971).

[5] *People v. Smith*, 243 N.W. 2d 677 (1976).

[6] *Commonwealth v. Reiland*, 359 A. 2d 811 (1976); see also La Fave, 'Search and Seizure: "The Course of True Law . . . Has Not . . . Run Smooth"', 1966 *U. Ill. L.F.* 255, 318.

[7] 304 N.E. 2d 81 (1973).

[8] *United States v. Turbyfill*, 525 F. 2d 57 (1975).

a question that depends upon all the facts of the particular case, even though the mere existence of the relationship between employer and employee will not normally, without more, suffice to support a third-party consent since it will usually show neither the possession of adequate authority over nor the existence of some other sufficient relationship to the premises or other property sought to be searched. Thus in *United States v. Blok*[1] the question was whether police officers could search without a warrant a desk assigned exclusively to an employee in her absence if permission was obtained from her employer. The search was held to be illegal in the absence of a warrant, the employer's consent being incapable of making it reasonable. Similarly, in the converse situation, it was held in one case[2] that a secretary's consent to a warrantless search could not waive the constitutional rights of her employers, and in another[3] the fact that a dentist, as an employer, had given his receptionist the limited right of allowing patients into his office was not regarded as sufficient to confer upon her authority to consent to a warrantless police entry and search since her rights did not amount to 'joint access or control for most purposes' over the area in issue. But if the employee is in effective control or in charge of the property searched his consent may well be valid against the employer, as in *United States v. Phifer*[4] where a pilot had consented to a search of an airplane owned by the defendant; since the pilot was at the time in operational control of the plane his consent made the warrantless search constitutional and the evidence obtained admissible against the defendant. Similarly, in *United States v. House*,[5] it was held that since a taxpayer's accountant was authorised, without any specific limitation, to deal with revenue agents in connection with his client's affairs, he also had authority to permit revenue agents to examine the taxpayer's records; thus any search of the records was consensual and therefore not in violation of the defendant's Fourth Amendment rights.

Another group of cases deals with the rights of landlords and other persons with a 'superior' or 'antecedent' proprietary interest. That a landlord or owner of rented or leased premises has no authority solely on the basis of his interest to consent to a search of the premises occupied by the tenant or lessee has been forcefully affirmed by the Supreme Court in *Chapman v. United States*[6] where it was held that a search of a tenant's premises without either a warrant or the tenant's consent, but with the consent of the landlord, could not be justified on the basis of the landlord's common law rights to enter and inspect the premises; any other holding, it was observed, would leave tenants' homes secure only in the discretion of landlords. Similar reasoning was employed in *Stoner v. California*[7] where the Supreme Court disallowed a search of the defendant's hotel room that had been authorised by the hotel

[1] 188 F. 2d 1019, 1021 (1951).
[2] *People v. Smith*, 204 N.W. 2d 308 (1973).
[3] *People v. Polito*, 355 N.E. 2d 725 (1976).
[4] 400 F. Supp. 719 (1975).
[5] 524 F. 2d 1035 (1975).
[6] 365 U.S. 610 (1961).
[7] 376 U.S. 483 (1964).

clerk. It was the defendant's constitutional right which was at stake here, the Court noted, and not the hotel clerk's or the hotel's. 'It was a right, therefore, which only the (defendant) could waive by word or deed, either directly or through an agent.' But if the facts indicate that the landlord has retained or been given coequal rights of access to and use of the property as the lessee, or that he has a significant personal interest in a prompt inspection of the property, his consent will be held sufficient for the validation of a warrantless search that implicates the defendant, as in *United States v. Botsch*[1] where the landlord not only possessed a key to the building but had also been expressly authorised by the accused to use it for the purpose of accepting deliveries flowing from the fraudulent scheme under investigation; on the facts the consenting party and the defendant did not occupy a mere landlord-tenant relationship, as in *Chapman*, but the landlord had been made an unwitting accomplice in the tenant's crime; he therefore had a vital interest in co-operating with the police so that he could exculpate himself.[2] It should finally be noted that the landlord's consent is normally sufficient to allow police officers to enter and search 'common areas', areas,[3] that is, over which the landlord has 'equal access and control'[4] with his tenants.

(j) Conclusion

It can be seen that in terms of theory the Supreme Court has taken the view that a search can normally only be reasonable if it is performed under a properly issued warrant but that there are exceptional cases, perhaps 'jealously and carefully drawn'[5] in theory but rather broad in practice,[6] when a search without a warrant is constitutionally permissible. These exceptional

[1] 364 F. 2d 542 (1966).

[2] Cf. 'Note', supra, 210 n. 6.

[3] *United States v. Kelly*, 551 F. 2d 760 (1977).

[4] *United States v. Heisman*, 503 F. 2d 1284, 1288 (1974); see also *United States v. Matlock*, 94 S.Ct. 988, 993 (1974), 'joint access or control for most purposes', and *United States v. Sferas*, 210 F. 2d 69, 74 (1954), 'equal rights to the use or occupation of premises'. It is by reference to such and similar phrases that most courts deal with situations of bailment and the like. If a person is found to have given another equal rights of access to or control over property for most purposes, or if he has given another 'complete and unrestricted freedom' over such property, then the owner or the person primarily entitled will be held to have accepted the risk that the bailee or the person given such extensive or concurrent powers of control may consent to a search (see *Corngold v. United States*, 367 F. 2d 1, 7 (1966); also *United States v. Eldridge*, 302 F. 2d 463 (1962)). Equally clearly mere surrender of custody of a package to an airline does not 'forfeit (the defendant's) right to privacy' and therefore an airline employee cannot consent to a warrantless search of the package (*Corngold v. United States*, supra, at 7).

[5] *Jones v. United States*, 357 U.S. 493, 499 (1958); see also *United States v. United States District Court*, 407 U.S. 297 (1972); *Katz v. United States*, 389 U.S. 347 (1967); *Coolidge v. New Hampshire*, 403 U.S. 443 (1971).

[6] See Weinreb, 'Generalities of the Fourth Amendment', 42 *U. Chi. L. Rev.* 47 (1974); Landynski, 'The Supreme Court's Search for Fourth Amendment Standards: The Warrantless Search', 45 *Conn. B. J.* 2, 21 (1971); Taylor, *Two Studies in Constitutional Interpretation* (1969).

cases seem to fall into three broad classes,[1] consent searches, custodial inspections and certain other routine searches, and searches when there are circumstances of urgency, for instance actual or possible danger to police officers or the risk of loss or destruction of evidence, which are thought to outweigh the normally applicable considerations demanding that intrusions should be judicially authorised, or some other 'fast-developing situation'[2] making recourse to a neutral magistrate either unnecessarily hazardous or gratuitously expensive in terms of other social interests.[3] Clearly no single explanation can bring together all the exceptions to the warrant requirement. Consent searches are explainable in terms of the doctrine of waiver of constitutional rights. As to custodial inspections, their reasonableness in the absence of a warrant seems to proceed on a theory that since the car or the individual to be searched is already in offical custody the privacy interest that is violated by the search is weaker than in the ordinary case, all the more so since the search will in such cases be made not in order to discover evidence of crime but automatically and as a matter of administrative routine, which in turn means that it will not be necessary for the inspecting officers to engage in difficult determinations about whether the particular object of the search is a legitimate target.[4] More or less the same reasons apply to searches of persons and effects crossing the international border[5] and to certain other types of administrative inspection.[6] But the most important exceptions to the warrant requirement are those where a warrant will not be insisted upon because of circumstances of necessity, that is where insistence on the usual process of antecedent justification runs contrary to 'the legitimate needs of law enforcement officers to protect (themselves and others) and preserve evidence from destruction'.[7] There has been broad agreement on the existence of three types of such 'emergency' searches, those incident to arrest, those of moving vehicles, and those under *Terry v. Ohio*[8] where, as will be seen below, a

[1] See Amsterdam, 'Perspectives on the Fourth Amendment', 58 *Minn. L. Rev.* 349, 358–60 (1974).

[2] Amsterdam, supra, at 359.

[3] *Arkansas v. Sanders*, 99 S.Ct. 2586, 2591 (1979).

[4] *Cooper v. California*, 386 U.S. 58 (1967) and *United States v. Edwards*, 415 U.S. 800 (1974) do not fit readily into any of the broad categories delineated here. Both are based partly on custodial considerations, but these are not the true reason for their holdings, because both involved searches for criminal evidence. The most likely explanation of *Cooper* is either that it deals with a narrow type of case, where items are held as criminal evidence prior to forfeiture proceedings, or that it allows the search of a car in police custody where the custody of the car is closely related to the reason for the suspect's arrest. *Edwards*, allowing the search of persons in custody and the search and seizure of their effects, is of course much more important. It must be viewed either as ancillary to the doctrine allowing searches incident to arrest or, more properly, as having brought into existence a new category of reasonable warrantless searches, namely searches and seizures conducted at the place of detention which could have taken place at the time and place of arrest.

[5] See *United States v. Ramsey*, 431 U.S. 606 (1977).

[6] See *United States v. Biswell*, 406 U.S. 311 (1972); *Colonnade Catering Corp. v. United States*, 397 U.S. 72 (1970); see generally Amsterdam, supra.

[7] *United States v. United States District Court*, 407 U.S. 297, 318 (1972).

[8] 392 U.S. 1 (1968).

police officer is empowered in certain cases to stop an individual reasonably suspected of criminal involvement and subject him if necessary to a limited search for weapons even though there is neither a warrant nor probable cause supporting an arrest.

Equally, as we have seen, it has been particularly difficult to delineate the scope of the incident-to-arrest and automobile exceptions. This is partly due to different perceptions concerning on the one hand the legitimate needs of law enforcement and on the other the proper sphere of protected privacy that must be assured the individual; partly to (ultimately) different views concerning the proper relationship between the two sections of the Amendment (whatever the invariable terminology about the primacy of the warrant requirement in which judicial holdings are now cast) and the comparative efficacy of the warrant process as contrasted with other methods as means of safeguarding the constitutional immunity from unreasonable searches; and partly to different views concerning the fundamental thrust of the Amendment itself and the proper direction of constitutional adjudication in attempted enforcement of search and seizure law, mainly whether under the various exceptions courts should proceed on an ad hoc basis and only by reference to whether a particular situation *actually* falls within an acknowledged exception—in the sense that the exigencies of the situation specifically justify what the officers have done—or whether they should translate the various reasons necessitating the recognition of the exceptions in the first place into *broad regulatory rules* which are easily intelligible to those who will administer them, namely the police, and which will be more or less automatically applicable given initial satisfaction of their prerequisites, instead of having to depend on the results of a subsequent minute judicial investigation of every turn in what may have been a fast-developing confrontation demanding quick action.[1]

Some of these strains can be seen when one studies the tension over the whole area of the exceptions to the warrant requirement between two lines of thought that often find themselves in conflict, that which holds that an exception can only be made if circumstances are present which mean that the burden of obtaining a warrant would be likely to frustrate the governmental purpose behind the search in question[2] and that which is ready to dispense with the warrant process if privacy has already, by the time of the challenged intrusion, been violated to an extent that makes insistence on the warrant requirement a needless formality.[3] These strains can be seen in judicial

[1] Some of the fundamental issues, in a somewhat different context, are discussed by Amsterdam, supra.

[2] See *Camara v. Municipal Court*, 387 U.S. 523, 533 (1967).

[3] Where of course there is no expectation of privacy there is no search. But occasionally diminution or even extinction of expectations of privacy means that even though the governmental conduct in issue falls within the Fourth Amendment it is reasonable despite the absence of a warrant. A good example of this is the 'plain view' doctrine. As it was put by Stevens J. in *Payton v. New York*, 100 S.Ct. 1371, 1380 (1980), '(t)he seizure of property in plain view involves no invasion of privacy and is presumptively reasonable, assuming that there is probable cause to associate

attitudes with regard to the automobile exception and searches incident to arrest. If the search of 'moving' vehicles is justified by reference to considerations of urgency which make it impracticable to secure a warrant without a serious danger of the destruction of evidence the exception should not apply where the particular car is not mobile and a warrant can therefore be obtained.[1] But if the preferable basis for the automobile exception is that normal expectations of privacy are substantially weaker in the case of vehicles than with regard to premises, whether homes or offices,[2] then normal constitutional safeguards will not be applied with the same emphasis, which in this context would mean that constitutional reasonableness need not depend on the presence of a warrant. Occasionally the two rationales—the actual necessity presented because of mobility and the reduced expectation of privacy—are uneasily combined, as with one version of the automobile exception which allows the police to search a vehicle they have stopped on the road but not a vehicle that prior to the seizure was parked on or near private premises even though in neither case was an *immediate* search *strictly* necessary.[3] A similar uneasy compromise can be seen with regard to the incident-to-arrest exception. This exception is traditionally justified by the need to seize weapons which the suspect may use against the arresting officer and evidence which would otherwise be destroyed. It should not therefore apply when it was practicable to obtain a warrant, or when neither of the dangers giving rise to its recognition in the first place exists. But if one of the reasons behind this exception is not only the actual danger to the arresting officer or the evidence but also that the arrest represents a significant invasion of privacy that causes the temporary abatement of other expectations of privacy (particularly with regard to one's immediate possessions and even over the whole of one's house) as well then searches of premises incident to arrest will be allowed. *Chimel*,[4] by demanding that a search on arrest should be confined to the area within the immediate control of the arrestee and be conditioned in its extent and intensity by the actual dangers to the officer's safety and the integrity of seizable evidence, marks a significant repudiation of the 'abatement of privacy' rationale in favour of the 'actual exigency' one. Sharply opposed in tone is *Robinson*[5] and the unqualified authority it seems to confer to search the person of the arrestee, wholly outside any limitations that might be derived from the twin needs to seize evidence and disarm the arrestee. By holding that a valid arrest justified a full search of the person

---

the property with criminal activity'. See also *G. M. Leasing Corp. v. United States*, 429 U.S. 338, 354.

[1] See the dissent of Harlan J. in *Chambers v. Maroney*, 399 U.S. 42 (1970).

[2] See *South Dakota v. Opperman*, 428 U.S. 364, 368 (1976); *Cardwell v. Lewis*, 417 U.S. 583, 590 (1974); *Cady v. Dombrowski*, 413 U.S. 433, 441–2 (1973).

[3] See *Texas v. White*, 423 U.S. 67 (1975); 'Note, Warrantless Searches and Seizures of Automobiles', 87 *Harv. L. Rev.* 835, 841–2 (1974); see also *Arkansas v. Sanders*, 99 S.Ct. 2586, 2594 n. 14 (1979).

[4] 395 U.S. 752 (1969).

[5] 414 U.S. 218 (1973).

irrespective of the actual circumstances of the case 'because the privacy interest protected by (the) constitutional guarantee is legitimately abated by the fact of arrest',[1] and by refusing to distinguish between the privacy interests violated by the arrest and the ensuing search respectively, the Supreme Court has sanctioned with regard to a search of the person what it refused to contemplate in the case of premises—on the one hand assimilation of conceptually distinct 'aspects of privacy',[2] and on the other adoption of a categorical approach to the interpretation of an exception to the warrant requirement that professes fidelity, not to the allegedly cardinal principle that where any exception is formulated or applied its scope should be no greater than what is required 'to accommodate the exigencies of the particular situation',[3] but to the idea that Fourth Amendment doctrines are best channelled by general predetermined rules over a given area of police work rather than by a refined ex post facto analysis of each step in every confrontation between State and citizen.[4]

[1] Ibid., at 237–8, per Powell J. concurring.
[2] See Weinreb, supra, 216 n. 6.
[3] *Chambers v. Maroney*, 399 U.S. 42, 61 (1970), per Harlan, J. dissenting.
[4] See generally Amsterdam, supra.

5. *Camara* and *Terry* Flexible Interpretation of the Fourth Amendment

In recent years the Supreme Court has devoted much time to a consideration of the constitutionality of various official practices falling short of what one might refer to as traditional searches and seizures, that is quests for criminal evidence and arrests. In the course of this consideration certain important principles have emerged, and these, in turn, have had an impact far beyond their particular contexts. The two main categories of such exceptional cases are, first, those on administrative inspections and, secondly, those where the Supreme Court has dealt with police powers to stop individuals and question them briefly for investigative purposes and if necessary frisk them for weapons.

(a) Administrative inspections

We have already seen that administrative inspections (which can be defined as entries into and examinations of premises for the purpose of ascertaining the existence or non-existence of conditions dangerous to health, safety or otherwise relevant to the public interest)[1] are 'searches', and that they may be undertaken on satisfaction of a standard less stringent than traditional probable cause. A fuller analysis must be attempted here. There is no denying the importance of the problem. Laws and ordinances authorising officials to enter homes and business premises in order to inspect them and determine their condition, and imposing sanctions for refusing entry to the inspection officers concerned, exist in great number and variety, are prolifereting at an ever-increasing speed, and it is therefore vital to know how they can be enforced consistently with constitutional safeguards of individual privacy.[2] Given that administrative inspections are searches within the Fourth Amendment, how should they be evaluated? In particular, should they be assessed in terms of the reasonableness clause, or in the same way as quests for criminal evidence, where, as is now well established, the constitutionality of a search depends upon whether it was conducted under the authority of a valid warrant? And if the latter is chosen, how should the requirements of the warrant clause, mainly the

[1] A.L.I., *A Model Code of Pre-Arraignment Procedure* 152 (Proposed Official Draft, 1975).

[2] See 3 W. La Fave, *Search and Seizure* 176–275 (1978); J. Landynski, *Search and Seizure in the Supreme Court* 245–62 (1966); 'Comment', 44 *Minn. L. Rev.* 513 (1960); 'Note', 77 *Yale L.J.* 521 (1968); 'Comment', 28 *U. Chi. L. Rev.* 664, 668 (1961); La Fave, 'Administrative Searches and the Fourth Amendment: The *Camara* and *See* Cases', 1967 *Sup. Ct. Rev.* 1.

probable cause standard, be interpreted in the context of routine regulatory inspections of private premises?

The Supreme Court first dealt with the consistutional status of administrative searches in *Frank v. Maryland.*[1] Here a divided Court sustained the constitutionality of a warrantless inspection procedure and upheld a homeowner's conviction for refusing to allow a warrantless examination of his home by a health inspector who demanded entry under a municipal health ordinance in order to locate a suspected public nuisance. Justice Frankfurter, in a confusing opinion, drew a distinction between '(t)wo protections emerg(ing) from the broad constitutional proscription of official invasion'. The first was 'the right to be secure from intrusion into personal privacy'; the second was 'self-protection', the right to resist unauthorised entry which had as its design the securing of incriminating information. Historical evidence, in his view, made it clear that 'it was on the issue of the right to be secure from searches for evidence to be used in criminal prosecutions or for forfeitures that the great battle for fundamental liberty was fought', and even though applications of the Fourth Amendment and the extent to which the right of privacy was protected by the Due Process Clause were 'not (to be) restricted within these historic bounds', protection for the right to privacy could not be invoked here. The basic reason was because 'the important interests safeguarded by the Fourteenth Amendment' were touched 'at most upon the periphery' by the warrantless inspection in issue; the interest in self-protection was not involved, since the inspection had not aimed at the discovery of evidence of crime, and the interest in privacy was adequately protected by a number of safeguards designed to make the least possible demand on the individual occupant and to cause only 'the slightest restriction on his claims of privacy', mainly that valid grounds for suspicion of the existence of the nuisance had to exist before an inspection could lawfully take place, that inspection had to be made during day time, and that the inspector had no power to force entry, only a fine being imposed for resistance. Further, 'the justification of social need' urged in support of warrantless administrative inspections was compelling; time and experience had taught that the power to inspect private premises either as a matter of systematic area-by-area search or, as in the instant case, in response to a specific problem was of 'indispensable importance to the maintenance of community health', and this power 'would be greatly hobbled' by insistence on the traditional safeguards necessary in the case of searches for criminal evidence. It could not therefore be said that the carefully circumscribed municipal ordinance before the Court deprived the defendant of due process of law. In other words, warrantless administrative searches aiming at the enforcement of 'civil' municipal regulations were not constitutionally unreasonable, at least so long as the type of inspection authorised by the particular ordinance did not impose heavy or unwarranted burdens on personal privacy. Much confusion surrounds the precise doctrinal basis of *Frank,*[2] but whatever its ambiguities

[1] 359 U.S. 360 (1959).

[2] See 44 *Minn. L. Rev.* 513, 515–16 (1960). It is thus not clear whether *Frank* was

this decision was generally taken as carving out 'an additional exception to the rule that warrantless searches are unreasonable under the Fourth Amendment'.[1]

Almost immediately *Frank* was subjected to much criticism,[2] principally on the ground that it was not easy to justify a doctrine which in effect accorded greater protection to the privacy of lawbreakers than to that enjoyed by citizens generally.[3] Eight years later the view that administrative inspections need not be authorised by warrants was rejected in *Camara v. Municipal Court*[4] where *Frank* was expressly overruled. The basis of the Court's *Camara* opinion was rejection of the *Frank* distinction between administrative searches and searches for criminal evidence, and adoption (in this context too) of the principle underlying many recent developments, namely that with the exception of certain carefully defined classes of cases a warrantless search of private property is unreasonable and unconstitutional. As regards Justice Frankfurter's main argument in *Frank*, the *Camara* majority could not agree that the Fourth Amendment interests at stake in inspection cases were merely 'peripheral', for it was surely anomalous to say that the individual and his private property should be fully protected only when the individual was suspected of criminal behaviour. All official power to enter homes threatened individual privacy and security, and should therefore be properly controlled. But the interest in self-protection, regarded as inapplicable by the *Frank* majority, was also involved in such cases, Justice White, delivering the Court's opinion, observed. Like most regulatory laws, fire, health and housing codes were invariably enforced by criminal processes, in many cities discovery of a violation led to a criminal complaint, and, as the instant case demonstrated, refusal to permit an inspection was itself normally a crime, punishable by fine or even by imprisonment. Since, then, administrative inspections endangered

---

decided on the basis that the Fourth Amendment was not violated by the warrantless inspection, or whether it was decided under the aegis of the due process clause of the Fourteenth Amendment. One could argue that, on the basis of Frankfurter, J.'s own judicial philosophy, the due process clause only requires state officers to respect those safeguards that are basic and essential to the concept of a free society, and that only 'the core of the Fourth Amendment' (*Wolf v. Colorado*, 338 U.S. 25, 27–8 (1949)) is basic to a free society, not all its specialised doctrines. It would appear that in *Frank* Frankfurter, J., assumed that the protections from unreasonable searches and seizures (as opposed to possible methods of enforcing them, for instance the exclusionary rule) were substantially 'incorporated' in the Fourteenth Amendment. *Frank*, in other words, holds that the power of warrantless inspection in issue there violated neither the Fourth nor the Fourteenth Amendments. It should also be noted that even though *Frank* does not expressly discuss the issue of whether administrative inspections are searches it assumes that what was at stake was conduct within the Fourth Amendment, namely a 'search'.

[1] *Camara v. Municipal Court*, 387 U.S. 523, 529 (1967).

[2] Landynski, supra; 'Comment', 44 *Minn. L. Rev.* 513 (1960).

[3] Barrett, 'Personal Rights, Property Rights, and the Fourth Amendment', 1960 *Sup. Ct. Rev.* 46, 70–1; see also *District of Columbia v. Little*, 178 F. 2d 13 (1949).

[4] 387 U.S. 523 (1967).

important individual interests protected by the Fourth Amendment, how could it be said that the protections provided by the warrant procedure were not needed? Indeed the desirability of a warrant could be shown from a study of the usual consequences of its absence. Under a warrantless system when the inspector demanded entry the occupant had no way of knowing whether enforcement of the municipal code involved required inspection of his premises, no way of knowing the lawful limits of the inspector's power to search, and no way of knowing whether the inspector himself was acting under proper authority. In other words, the practical effect of warrantless procedures was 'to leave the occupant subject to the discretion of the official in the field'. This was precisely the discretion to invade private property which in other areas the Supreme Court had consistently circumscribed by the requirement that both the need to search and the limits of any authorised intrusion should be reviewed by a neutral and disinterested magistrate, and it was no different in the case of administrative inspections. Here too 'broad statutory safeguards (were) no substitute for individualised review'. On the basis of this analysis the Supreme Court concluded, first that administrative searches of the kind at issue in *Camara* were 'significant intrusions' upon the interests protected by the Fourth Amendment', and secondly that such searches when conducted outside the warrant process lacked those essential and traditional safeguards which the Amendment guaranteed to the individual. In the absence of exigent or other exceptional circumstances administrative inspections should therefore only be conducted under the authority of warrants.

But because of the nature of the municipal programmes under consideration these conclusions, the *Camara* Court noted, could only be 'the beginning, not the end', of its inquiry. In terms of traditional theory the requirement of probable cause would clearly mean that a warrant for entry and inspection should only be issued on possession and production of evidence making it reasonable to believe that a *particular* building constituted a hazard to health or safety or that it offended the minimum standards of the code being enforced. But this standard, as the Court appreciated, would make the effective enforcement of much essential regulatory legislation impossible since it would obviously not allow the issuing of warrants based solely on factors such as the passage of time since the last inspection or the condition of the area as a whole. The *Frank* majority had translated its recognition of the unique character of the problems presented by typical inspection programmes into a holding that administrative inspections did not have to be preceded by warrants but should only be evaluated in terms of overall reasonableness. What 'accommodation between public need and individual rights'[1] would the *Camara* majority arrive at? How would insistence on the warrant process be reconciled with the recognition of the undeniable importance of efficaciously enforcing, mainly by routine periodic inspection, the many municipal ordinances? The Court's answer was to create 'a new species of

[1] 387 U.S. at 534.

probable cause'[1] based on the broad constitutional mandate of reasonableness and involving a balanced weighing of the need for the search against the seriousness of the anticipated invasion of privacy. According to *Camara* probable cause for an administrative search or inspection exists if reasonable legislative or administrative standards based upon factors such as the condition of the area, the passage of time, or the nature of the building have been satisfied 'with respect to a particular dwelling';[2] and no knowledge of or information about the condition of the particular dwelling is required. Thus what the magistrate is apparently required to do is first to evaluate the general reasonableness of the criteria set out in the particular municipal programme being enforced and then to decide whether a particular building or dwelling comes within 'the approved criteria'.[3] Justice White did not think that the flexibility with which the concept of probable cause was being endowed would result in a reduction of essential Fourth Amendment protection. The ultimate standard was that of reasonableness. If a valid public interest justified the intrusion contemplated, then there was 'probable cause to issue a suitably restricted search warrant'.[4]

There is no denying the doctrinal importance of *Camara's* elaboration of a new type of probable cause explicitly based on a balancing of the competing public and private interests at stake.[5] For some the concept of a flexible probable cause that does not demand the same amount of evidence in all cases but instead allows variation in the required quantum, depending both on the governmental interest allegedly justifying the official intrusion and on the threat the particular practice poses for individual privacy, is not only 'defensible'[6] but also 'an extremely important and meaningful concept'.[7] Only a variable standard, on this view, can give full recognition to conflicting public and private interests and in so doing fulfil 'the historic purpose behind the constitutional right to be free from *unreasonable* governmental invasions of privacy'.[8] For others a dilution of probable cause, even in a 'special' area, is attended by serious dangers. Three points are made here. First, there is convincing historical evidence that what worried

[1] 'Note', 77 *Yale L.J.* 521, 525 (1968).

[2] 387 U.S. at 538. The lower standard of probable cause for area administrative inspections was first put forward by Douglas, J. in his *Frank* dissent (359 U.S. at 383).

[3] 'Note', 81 *Harv. L. Rev.* 182, 185 (1967).

[4] 387 U.S. at 539. Three additional points can be made here. First, it appears that the relevant warrants must be issued by (judicial) magistrates, and not by the agency itself, even though in the case of some businesses administrative warrants might be legitimate. Secondly, it appears that in an area-wide search a separate warrant must be acquired for each building. Thus the Court referred at one point to 'the Fourth Amendment's requirement that a warrant (should) specify the property to be searched' (387 U.S. at 539); but apparently warrants may be sought 'en masse for an entire area' (81 *Harv. L. Rev.* at 185). Thirdly, 'as a practical matter', warrants are normally sought only after entry is refused (387 U.S. at 540).

[5] La Fave, 'Administrative Searches and the Fourth Amendment: The *Camara* and *See* Cases', 1967 *Sup. Ct. Rev.* 1, 13.

[6] 'Note', 77 *Yale L.J.* 521, 526.

[7] 3 W. La Fave, *Search and Seizure* 190 (1978).

[8] *Camara v. Municipal Court*, 387 U.S. at 539.

the Framers the most was the general warrant and not the warrantless search; this is why precise limits were placed on its issuance, the requirement that a warrant could only be issued on 'a showing of particularised probable cause'[1] being one of the means adopted to curb oppressive uses of the warrant power; and, while it is true that one of the main lines of development in Fourth Amendment law is that the demand for reasonableness can normally only be satisfied by the presence of a valid warrant, this does not mean that the requirements of the warrant clause should be diluted in a strained (and ultimately unnecessary) effort to force all official intrusions that are significant enough to amount to 'searches' into the confines of the warrant process.[2] Secondly, since the basis and content of 'probable cause' for administrative inspection warrants are to be found in the notion of reasonableness, and since in determining whether a proposed inspection is reasonable 'the need for the inspection must be weighed in terms of the reasonable goals of code enforcement',[3] why impose the warrant requirement at all?[4] In this connection it is interesting to observe that the 'persuasive factors'[5] referred to by the *Camara* Court as supporting 'the reasonableness of area code-enforcement inspections' and as necessitating the modification of traditional 'probable cause' are identical to the ones given by the *Frank* majority for exempting administrative inspections from the warrant requirement. These are: long judicial and public acceptance of such programmes; the great public interest in health and safety which demands that all dangerous conditions be prevented or abated and which cannot be effectuated by techniques other than periodic area-wide inspections; and the fact that administrative inspections, being neither personal in nature nor aimed at the discovery of evidence of crime, involve 'a relatively limited invasion of the urban citizen's privacy'.[6] On the basis of these factors the *Camara* opinion *first* upholds the reasonableness of area inspections and *then* concludes that probable cause exists if particular premises have been shown to come within the designated 'reasonable standards', which, it must not be forgotten, will vary according to the particular code that is being enforced and the condition of the area. A particular inspection in other words can take place because it is reasonable. Why then not acknowledge this in theory as well as in practice and simply determine the legality of particular administrative programmes by reference to overall reasonableness? Why go through the exercise of obtaining warrants? 'Why the ceremony, the delay, the expense, the abuse of the search warrant?'[7] And if it is contended, as Justice White did in *Camara*, that the inspection warrant still serves important functions, mainly to inform the occupant of the inspector's lawful authority and to advise him of

[1] *Marshall v. Barlow's Inc.*, 436 U.S. 307, 328 (1978), per Stevens, J., dissenting.
[2] Ibid.
[3] *Camara v. Municipal Court*, 387 U.S. at 536.
[4] See the dissent of Clark, J., in *See v. Seattle*, 387 U.S. 541, 554 (1967).
[5] 387 U.S. at 537.
[6] Ibid.
[7] *See v. Seattle*, 387 U.S. 541, 554 (1967), per Clark, J. dissenting.

the lawful limits of the inspection, it can be argued that the inspection warrant adds little to the protections normally embodied in the authorising statute, and that in any case any 'slight additional benefit'[1] that the warrant process may provide is insufficient to justify either dilution of traditional probable cause or the issuance of a 'new-fangled warrant'.[2] The third, related, point in opposition to *Camara* is that what the abandonment of traditional notions of probable cause does is to allow the issuance *as a matter of course* (and not after independent and meaningful scrutiny by disinterested magistrates) of inspection warrants. Such warrants therefore, Justice Clark warned in dissent in *Camara*, 'will be printed up in pads of a thousand or more—with space for the street number to be inserted—and issued by magistrates as a matter of course';[3] and apparently what happens in practice is that magistrates only scrutinise requests for inspection to see if they are statutorily authorised. For some this not only results in warrants which are unfaithful to the clear language of the warrant clause, but also degrades the magistrates issuing them and brings disrepute both upon the practice itself and upon the judicial process. But despite the strength of these objections it is now firmly established that administrative inspections to detect compliance with regulatory statutes must be authorised by warrants.

What about administrative inspections of business premises? It has been suggested that places of business are different from private homes, that different standards of reasonableness should therefore be applied to them, and that searches of commercial premises should not be unreasonable simply because they were not authorised by warrants. But the Supreme Court has not agreed. It has taken note of the historical origins of the Fourth Amendment, particularly the fact that '(the) offensiveness engendered (by the general warrant) was acutely felt by the merchants and businessmen'[4] whose premises and products were inspected for compliance with parliamentary revenue measures, and has observed that '(a)gainst this background it is untenable (to argue) that the ban on warrantless searches was not intended to shield places of business as well as of residence'.[5] It has therefore been held that the warrant clause of the Fourth Amendment protects commercial buildings as well as private homes.[6] But it is not only historical arguments that have prompted this reading. In *See v. Seattle*,[7] decided the same day as *Camara*, the Court expressed the view that '(t)he businessman, like the occupant of a residence, has a constitutional right to go about his business free from unreasonable official entries upon his private commercial property' and that this right is placed in jeopardy 'if the decision to enter and inspect for violation of regulatory laws can be made

[1] *Marshall v. Barlow's Inc.*, 436 U.S. 307, 332 (1978), per Stevens, J. dissenting.
[2] *See v. Seattle*, 387 U.S. 541, 547 (1967), per Clark, J. dissenting.
[3] Ibid., at 554.
[4] *Marshall v. Barlow's Inc.*, 436 U.S. 307, 311 (1978).
[5] Ibid., at 312.
[6] *See v. Seattle*, 387 U.S. 541 (1967).
[7] 387 U.S. 541 (1967).

and enforced by the inspector in the field without official authority evidenced by a warrant'. Unless therefore some recognised exception to the warrant requirement applies inspections of commercial and business premises can only be conducted under the authority of warrants. But Justice White, who again delivered the Court's opinion in *See*, did not doubt that business premises might reasonably be inspected in many more situations than private homes,[1] and also observed that the question of whether to require a warrant had to depend 'in part upon whether the burden of obtaining a warrant (was) likely to frustrate the governmental purpose behind the search'.[2] The door was thus left open for the validation of certain warrantless administrative searches of business premises in 'special situations'[3] where the public interest would be frustrated if the inspectors were required to obtain warrants. Such an exception was recognised a few years later in *Colonnade Catering Corp. v. United States*[4] and *United States v. Biswell*[5] in cases of 'pervasively regulated business(es)'[6] and for 'closely regulated' industries 'long subject to close supervision and inspection'.[7] Two considerations were instrumental in the elaboration of this exception. First, in certain cases, the sale of liquor and the trade in firearms for instance, particularly 'large interests are at stake',[8] and warrantless inspection appears to be a crucial part of the typical regulatory scheme; this is principally because if inspection is to be effective in terms of enforcement and serve as a credible deterrent, unannounced (and frequent) inspections are essential; since therefore insistence on a warrant would frustrate inspection and make proper enforcement impossible, inspections without warrant must be deemed reasonable official conduct under the Fourth Amendment. Secondly, warrantless inspections in the context of the enforcement of closely controlled businesses pose only limited threats to justifiable expectations of privacy. After all, the Supreme Court has observed,[9] not only do certain industries have such a history of governmental oversight that no reasonable expectation of privacy can exist over the stock of such an enterprise, but also when a businessman or entrepreneur embarks upon such a business he voluntarily chooses to subject himself to a full arsenal of governmental regulation; '(t)he businessman in a regulated industry in effect consents to the restrictions placed upon him'.[10]

Both in *See v. Seattle* and in *United States v. Biswell* it was made clear that warrantless inspections of the business premises or the stock of closely regulated industries of the type involved in *Colonnade* and *Biswell* were the exception to the general requirement of an authorising warrant; but before

[1] *See*, supra, 387 U.S. at 546.
[2] *Camara*, supra, 387 U.S. at 533.
[3] *Colonnade Catering Corp. v. United States*, 410 F. 2d 197, 200 (1969).
[4] 397 U.S. 72 (1970).
[5] 406 U.S. 311 (1972).
[6] Ibid., at 316.
[7] *Colonnade Catering Corp. v. United States*, 397 U.S. at 74.
[8] *United States v. Biswell*, 406 U.S. at 315.
[9] *Marshall v. Barlow's Inc.*, 436 U.S. 307, 313 (1978).
[10] *Almeida-Sanchez v. United States*, 413 U.S. 266, 271 (1973).

long lower courts, upholding as a matter of course warrantless searches of 'regulated'[1] businesses, expanded the exception of the 'closely regulated industry' until it came close to swallowing the rule itself. This trend has now been checked by the important case of *Marshall v. Barlow's, Inc.*[2] Here an inspector without a warrant attempted to conduct a routine inspection of an electrical and plumbing business under a congressional act. The Supreme Court held that the relevant legislative provision, insofar as it purported to authorise inspections without a warrant, was invalid. The Court's opinion, again delivered by Justice White, made three main points. First, it repeated that, in general, warrantless administrative inspections of business premises are unreasonable. Secondly, it reaffirmed that the 'closely regulated industry' was the exception, and not the rule; the business in issue here did not fall within the narrow *Colonnade-Biswell* category. Nor, finally, could the Court agree with the government's argument that requiring warrants would impose serious burdens on the inspection system or the courts, or that the relevant statute would become unenforceable; after all probable cause in the criminal law sense was not required, and since inspection warrants could be issued ex parte the element of surprise would not necessarily be lost even if in practice the government only applied for a warrant once the inspector was refused entry; no necessity had therefore been shown for exempting administrative inspections of the type before the Court from the generally applicable warrant requirement. But even after *Barlow*'s resounding reaffirmation of the primacy of the warrant requirement in the business context it is not at all clear how many other statutory inspection schemes will be affected. The Court's decision was expressly limited to 'the facts and law' involved in the administrative programme before them, and it was emphasised that the constitutionality of other warrantless regulatory schemes would depend not only on the degree of governmental regulation of the particular business or industry in issue but also on 'the specific enforcement needs and privacy guarantees of each statute'.[3] This of course is the standard of reasonableness based on a balancing of competing governmental and individual interests, on the one hand the public interest in the adequate enforcement of 'civil' regulatory codes and on the other the interest of the individual in the privacy and security of both his home and business.

A difficult question is whether warrantless inspections may be conducted in the framework of welfare programmes, particularly those that provide for the conferment of certain governmental benefits.[4] Should they be treated in the same way as the administrative inspections discussed above, or do they fall into a separate category? This difficult and 'provocative'[5] question arose

[1] See *United States ex rel. Terraciano v. Montanye*, 493 F. 2d 682, 684 (1974); see also Rothstein and Rothstein, 'Administrative Searches and Seizures: What Happened to *Camara* and *See*?', 50 *Wash L. Rev.* 341, 382 (1975).

[2] 436 U.S. 307 (1978), noted in 92 *Harv. L. Rev.* 210 (1978).

[3] 436 U.S. at 321.

[4] 3 W. La Fave, *Search and Seizure* 238 (1978).

[5] Ibid., at 239.

in *Wyman v. James*,[1] but its treatment by the Supreme Court has attracted much criticism. This case, as has been seen, involved a caseworker's visit to the home of a recipient of welfare assistance (in this particular case aid to families with dependent children). The recipient refused to consent to the home visit, upon which her assistance was terminated. The Supreme Court held that the recipient of welfare assistance could not withhold her consent to a warrantless home visit without risking termination of the benefits. The majority's standard was that of overall reasonableness. A number of factors, in Justice Blackmun's view, indicated that the proposed warrantless home visit was not unreasonable. The main ones were: the home visit was in aid of an important public interest; the focus throughout was on the dependent child whose needs were paramount, and it was not proper to subordinate these needs to the mother's alleged rights; the governmental agency involved was providing public funds, and it was not unreasonable that the State should have at its command 'a gentle means, of limited extent and of practical and considerate application', of ensuring that the aid it dispensed would not be wasted; the home visit was 'rehabilitative' in orientation, and did not have as its purpose the obtaining of information as to criminal activity; it was most unlikely that the necessary information could be obtained otherwise than through home visits; a number of regulations minimised the intrusiveness of the visit; and the warrant procedure would not be easy to transfer to the welfare context and might have adverse consequences upon the homeowner herself. *Frank* and *Camara* were distinguishable, the Court asserted, because even though in both '(t)he community welfare aspects' were highly important, 'each case arose in a criminal context where a genuine search was denied and prosecution followed', unlike *James* where the homeowner was not being prosecuted for her refusal to permit the home visit, the only consequence of her refusal being that the payment of benefits had ceased. *Wyman v. James* has been criticised on a number of grounds.[2] First, *James* appears to resuscitate, to some extent at least, the distinction between 'civil' and 'criminal' searches that had been rejected in *Camara*. Secondly, the basis on which *Camara* and *See* were distinguished is not convincing; it should surely make no difference that the result of a refusal to consent to an inspection is not the initiation of criminal proceedings but the termination of what may be essential welfare benefits, all the more so since it is now clear that constitutional safeguards apply as much to the withdrawal of public assistance as to any other adverse consequence.[3] Finally, as has been seen, one of the main reasons for the decision in *James* was the majority's perception of certain difficulties that would be involved in attempted applications of the warrant requirement to home visits. But *Camara* indicates both that probable cause standards can be made to vary with the particular programme in issue and that warrants can be tailored to accommodate conflicting public and private interests in different fact

[1] 400 U.S. 309 (1971).
[2] La Fave, supra, 229 n. 4, at 240–5; 'Note', 85 *Harv. L. Rev.* 258 (1971).
[3] See *Goldberg v. Kelly*, 397 U.S. 254 (1970).

situations. In the same way, it has been argued, that there can be administrative inspection warrants there should also be 'welfare visit warrant(s)'.[1] On this view if the particular agency is administering or has formulated a coherent and reasonable policy, and if the relevant legislative or administrative standards have been found to be satisfied with regard to a proposed welfare visit (and the request for the visit is refused), a welfare visit warrant authorising the inspection can be issued.

There is little doubt that *Wyman v. James* is unsatisfactory, both in the unconvincing way it attempted to distinguish *Camara* and in its impressionistic survey of overall reasonableness. This is not to say that it is impossible to develop principled arguments on the basis of a careful weighing of the interest of the public against that of the individual[2] why welfare visits undertaken in pursuance of reasonable regulatory schemes should not be regarded as falling within a category of official intrusions which are reasonable within the first clause of the Fourth Amendment.[3] In any case, *Wyman v. James* establishes that for the time being welfare visits are exempt from the warrant requirement.

(b) Terry v. Ohio

The seminal case of *Terry v. Ohio* has already been mentioned at a number of points, mainly in connection with its inclusion of all official seizures within the Fourth Amendment and with regard to its holding that certain limited police intrusions subject to Fourth Amendment safeguards can be justified on evidence less than that necessary to justify an arrest, i.e. less than what is demanded by the traditional requirement of probable cause. Its importance is such that both its principal determinations and its implications in terms of Fourth Amendment theory deserve further treatment.[4]

Before *Terry v. Ohio* it was questionable whether seizures and searches of the person could take place in the absence of sufficient grounds for an arrest (that would then justify an accompanying search).[5] The assumption on the part of many was that seizures of persons could only be justified if based on probable cause. 'The term "arrest" was synonymous with those seizures governed by the Fourth Amendment. While warrants were not required in all circumstances, the requirement of probable cause, as elaborated in

[1] La Fave, supra, at 244.

[2] See *United States v. Martinez-Fuerte*, 428 U.S. 543, 555 (1976).

[3] See the reasoning of Stevens, J. dissenting, in *Marshall v. Barlow's Inc.*, 436 U.S. 307, 329 (1978).

[4] See 3 La Fave, *Search and Seizure* 1–175 (1978) (hereinafter referred to as La Fave); La Fave, ' "Street Encounters" and the Constitution: *Terry, Sibron, Peters,* and Beyond', 67 *Mich. L. Rev.* 39 (1968); A.L.I., *A Model Code of Pre-Arraignment Procedure* 5–12, 262–88 (1975), hereinafter referred to as *Model Code*.

[5] See La Fave, at 2–7; Remington, 'The Law Relating to "On the Street" Detention, Questioning and Frisking of Suspected Persons and Police Arrest Privileges in General', 51 *J. Crim. L., C. & P.S.* 386 (1960); Leagre, 'The Fourth Amendment and the Law of Arrest', 54 *J. Crim. L., C. & P.S.* 393 (1963).

numerous precedents, was treated as absolute'.[1] In other words, the Fourth Amendment's guarantee against unreasonable seizures of persons was analysed in terms of the traditional categories of arrest, probable cause for arrest (always required) and warrants based on such probable cause (not always required), and there was no suggestion that official seizures of persons could be constitutional if based on anything less than probable cause. 'The standard of probable cause thus represented the accumulated wisdom of precedent and experience as to the minimum justification necessary to make the kind of intrusion involved in an arrest (a term that was synonymous with those seizures governed by the Fourth Amendment) "reasonable".'[2] This strict position was supported by two types of argument. First, both history and the traditional structure of the Fourth Amendment were invoked. On this view the requirement of probable cause was the principal means whereby oppressive practices, whether of general warrants or of arresting on mere suspicion, were controlled; only this draws a meaningful line between an officer's mere suspicion or hunch and the presence of facts within his knowledge that would satisfy a reasonable man of the seized person's complicity in criminal activity; and since after all a magistrate could not authorise a seizure of the person otherwise than on the basis of probable cause, why should the police acting without judicial authorisation be given greater power?[3] It has therefore been contended that recognition of a variety of police activity which does not depend solely upon the voluntary co-operation of the citizen and yet stops short of an arrest based upon probable cause *deviates* sharply from what should be seen as the central principle of the Fourth Amendment, namely that there is a *severe* requirement of *specific* justification for *any* intrusion upon protected personal security, *encourages* substantial (and ultimately arbitrary) interference with personal liberty and security by police officers who cannot be expected to remain unbiased in what they see as the war against crime, and thus *results* in the unmistakeable dilution of traditionally accepted constitutional guarantees.[4] The second supporting argument for the strict position is that police authority to stop and seize (and if necessary to subject to limited searches) without probable cause is attended by considerable dangers of abuse. Thus, this power can be used not for legitimate investigative purposes but to harass unpopular minorities or other persons for whom the police feel hostility, and there is little doubt, as much experience shows, that stop and frisk procedures are often resorted to not in order to disarm dangerous persons but so that the police can circumvent traditional constitutional safeguards by pretending to look for weapons when in fact they are searching for narcotics and the like without either a warrant or probable cause.[5] As against these objections to any power to detain otherwise than on probable cause two considerations have been

[1] *Dunaway v. New York*, 99 S.Ct. 2248, 2254 (1979).
[2] Ibid.
[3] *Terry v. Ohio*, 392 U.S. 1, 35 (1968), per Douglas, J. dissenting.
[4] Ibid.
[5] *Model Code*, at 273.

emphasised: first that the relevant right is not that one should never be seized without probable cause, but that one is only entitled to be free from unreasonable governmental intrusion; that what the Constitution forbids is only *unreasonable* searches and seizures, not searches and seizures unsupported by probable cause; and that the constitutionally protected right to personal security does not forbid strictly limited investigatory stops necessitated by the prevention or detection of crime. The second argument for some relaxation of traditional doctrines is that in dealing with rapidly unfolding and often dangerous situations, particularly on city streets, police officers desperately need 'an escalating set of flexible responses, graduated in relation to the amount of information they possess'.[1] A police officer may thus observe a person whom he suspects to be carrying a dangerous weapon and to be about to embark upon criminal activity; or he observes a person whom he reasonably suspects either to be committing or to have just committed a crime; or he comes across a person who corresponds in some way to the description of the perpetrator of a crime which occurred some time in the past. Does the Fourth Amendment require a policeman who lacks the precise level of information necessary to establish probable cause to arrest simply to shrug his shoulders and allow a crime to occur or a criminal to escape?[2]

The conflicting arguments concerning the constitutionality of what have come to be known as stop and frisk procedures were first addressed by the Supreme Court in *Terry v. Ohio.*[3] The facts were simple. An experienced police officer observed for some time the unusual conduct of the petitioner and two other men; their behaviour, individually and repeatedly looking into a store window and then conferring together, led him to suspect that the men might be 'casing' the store for a 'stickup' and that they might have guns; the officer followed them, approached them, identified himself, and asked for their names. When the men only 'mumbled' something in response the officer grabbed the defendant, spun him around to face the other two, and 'patted' down his clothing. This frisk led to the discovery of a pistol and to Terry's subsequent conviction on a charge of carrying a concealed weapon. It was held that the search was a reasonable one under the Fourth Amendment and that the pistol seized from the defendant had therefore been properly introduced in evidence. After holding that the Fourth Amendment was applicable on the ground that the officer's seizure of the defendant and the subsequent protective frisk clearly amounted to a 'seizure' and a 'search' respectively, Chief Justice Warren made two principal points. If the case before them had involved police conduct subject to the Warrant Clause of the Amendment one would have had to ascertain whether probable cause existed to justify the search and seizure which had taken place. But that was not the case. What the Court was dealing with here was 'an entire rubric of police conduct—necessarily swift action predicated upon the on-the-spot observation of the officer on the beat—which historically has

[1] *Terry v. Ohio*, 392 U.S. 1, 10 (1968), per Warren, C.J.
[2] *Adams v. Williams*, 407 U.S. 143, 145 (1972); see also *Model Code*, at 270.
[3] 392 U.S. 1 (1968).

not been, and as a practical matter could not be, subjected to the warrant procedure'. 'Instead', the conduct in issue had to be tested by 'the Fourth Amendment's general proscription against unreasonable searches and seizures'. Secondly, in determining whether the seizure and search were unreasonable the Court's inquiry was a dual one—was the officer's action 'justified at its inception', and was it 'reasonably related in scope' to the circumstances which justified the interference in the first place? On the basis of the governing standard of reasonableness the Court developed the general principle that, in cases where the officer had reason to believe that he was dealing with an armed and dangerous individual, 'there must be a *narrowly drawn* authority to permit a *reasonable* search for *weapons* for the protection of the police officer', regardless of whether the officer had at the relevant time probable cause to arrest the individual for a crime. The officer did not have to be absolutely certain that the individual was armed; the issue was whether 'a reasonably prudent man' in the circumstances would be warranted in the belief that his safety or that of others was in danger; and in determining whether an officer had acted reasonably in such circumstances weight was to be given not to his inchoate and unparticularised suspicion but to 'the specific reasonable inferences' which he would be entitled to draw 'from the facts in (the) light of his experience'. Applying this set of principles to the facts of the instant case the Court had little difficulty in concluding that the challenged search and seizure were reasonable (and thus constitutional) both at their inception and as conducted. At the time of the stop (the seizure) and the frisk (the search for weapons) the officer had reasonable grounds to believe that the defendant was armed and dangerous and that it was necessary for the protection 'of himself and others' that 'swift measures' be taken 'to discover the true facts and neutralise the threat of harm if it materialised'. Further, the search was carefully restricted to what was appropriate for the discovery of the particular items, weapons, which were (properly) sought. Each case of course, Chief Justice Warren observed, would depend on its own facts. But *where* a police officer observed conduct which led him reasonably to conclude that criminal activity might be afoot and that the persons with whom he was dealing might be 'armed and presently dangerous', *where* in the course of investigating this behaviour he identified himself and made reasonable inquiries, and *where* nothing in the initial stages of the encounter served to dispel his reasonable fear for his own or other persons' safety, he was entitled 'to conduct a carefully limited search of the outer clothing of such persons in an attempt to discover weapons which might be used to assault him'.

The Supreme Court, it will be seen, limited its ruling to the challenged *search*, namely the protective frisk, and refused to deal with the issue of the constitutional propriety of *investigative seizures* upon less than probable cause; only the police officer's invasion of the defendant's personal security by means of the limited search for weapons was therefore *expressly* held to be constitutional, and nothing was said about any other steps which were (in *Terry*) or might be (generally) taken to investigate suspicious behaviour.[1]

[1] See 392 U.S. at 23 and at 79 n.16.

This was convincingly criticised by Justice Harlan who thought that the constitutional status of the forcible stop (as distinct from the consequent search for weapons) and the basic issue of an officer's right to 'seize' a person for purposes of investigation should have been addressed directly.[1] This is because, as he persuasively demonstrates, the right to disarm by conducting a limited frisk must logically follow from an initial right to effect a forcible stop for purposes of investigation. On this reasoning any person, including a policeman, is at *liberty* to avoid a person he considers dangerous. But if and when a policeman has a *right* to disarm such a person 'he must first have a *right* not to avoid him but to be in his presence'. Further, this *right* (to be in one's presence, or to make a forcible stop) must be more than the usual *liberty* to address questions to other persons, for normally the person addressed has an equal right to ignore his interrogator, refuse to submit to any protective frisk and walk away, which is certainly not the case in *Terry* or in similar situations where the right to conduct a frisk is upheld. It follows that the right to conduct a frisk depends upon the presence of grounds justifying official insistence on an encounter. This in turn means that the constitutional reasonableness of a forcible stop to investigate must be assessed before the evaluation of the ensuing search, if any. Justice Harlan's distinction in *Terry v. Ohio* between the propriety of the forcible stop and the permissibility of the (subsequent) adoption of any suitable measures for the protection of the officer or of others was clearly drawn in *Adams v. Williams.*[2] Here, while a police officer was on duty in a high crime area, a person known to him came to his car and informed him that a man seated in a nearby car was carrying narcotics and had a gun at his waist. The officer approached the car to investigate the informer's report, tapped on the window and asked the defendant to open the door. The suspect rolled down the window instead, and at that point the officer reached into the car and removed from the defendant's waistband a loaded revolver which had not been visible from outside. The defendant was arrested for unlawful possession of the revolver, and a subsequent search brought to light heroin. The Supreme Court affirmed his conviction of illegal possession both of weapons and of heroin. Justice Rehnquist, delivering the Court's opinion, *first* upheld as reasonable the police officer's forcible *stop* of the suspect, rejecting the argument that reasonable cause for a stop and frisk could only be based on the officer's personal observation and not on information supplied by another person; here the informer's tip carried enough indicia of reliability to justify the officer's forcible stop of the defendant. *Secondly*, since *Terry* had held that a policeman making a reasonable investigatory stop should not be denied the opportunity to protect himself from attack by a hostile suspect, and since in this case too the officer was both entitled to make a forcible stop and had reason to believe that the suspect was armed and dangerous, his action in reaching to the spot where the gun was thought to be hidden constituted a limited intrusion designed to ensure his safety, and was reasonable.

[1] 392 U.S. at 32–3 (concurring opinion).
[2] 407 U.S. 143 (1972).

A number of questions arise from a consideration of *Terry v. Ohio*, some of them practical, others theoretical. As to the former, the following issues are particularly important:

(i) For what purposes and in what categories or types of case can the authority to stop and detain for investigative reasons be invoked? *Terry* involved the prevention of crime, but stop-and-frisk power has also been recognised where the relevant governmental interest is that of detection of crime, and not of prevention,[1] it being convincingly argued[2] that where a crime has or may have been committed and a suspect is about to disappear it would be both irrational and hardly conducive to proper respect for the law to prevent the police from effecting brief investigatory stops 'in order to determine (the) identity (of a suspicious individual) or to maintain the status quo momentarily while obtaining more information'.[3] For this reason it has been proposed[4] that the police should be allowed to make a forcible stop as a prelude to further investigation whenever there is reasonable suspicion that the person to be stopped '*has* just committed, *is* committing, or *is about* to commit' an offence. In all these three cases there is need for more or less *immediate* action in connection with the suspected involvement of the person stopped (himself) in criminal activity; the stop takes place in the approximate vicinity of the offence and is roughly contemporaneous with it (or immediately precedes it); and the reason for recognising stop and frisk powers here is so that the officer will not be put to the invidious dilemma either of having to make an illegal arrest (since there is insufficient evidence for probable cause) or of remaining inactive in the face of unfolding criminality. But the Model Code of Pre-Arraignment Procedure proposes that the authority to stop for investigatory purposes should also be recognised in two additional cases, first where a police officer detains a potential witness,[5] and secondly where a suspect is stopped on the basis of his alleged commission of an offence which took place some time in the past, and which, unlike the cases in the first category, has not just occurred nor is occurring now.[6] As to the 'witnesses' category, the Code proposes that an officer coming upon the scene of a recently committed crime may stop (and briefly question) a person whom he finds near the place of the offence and who, he reasonably believes, has knowledge that would materially aid in the investigation; but the legality of the stop is based upon any action taken being 'reasonably necessary to obtain or verify the identification of such person or to obtain an account of (the) crime'.[7] The final category aims to provide for the case where the officer has reasonable cause to believe that a crime was committed some time in the past and now comes across a person who seems to fit the description of the person suspected of committing the

[1] La Fave, at 19–22.
[2] *Model Code*, at 270–2.
[3] *Adams v. Williams*, 407 U.S. 143, 146 (1972).
[4] *Model Code*, at 5–6, 9–10.
[5] Ibid., at 6.
[6] Ibid., at 6.
[7] *Model Code* § 110.2(1)(b).

offence. A stop can take place so that the identity of the person stopped can be checked and a decision made whether to arrest him; but the stop will still only be upheld where it was reasonably necessary for the purpose of obtaining identification, so that if verification of identity could have been achieved through less intrusive means the stop will be held to be unconstitutional.[1] The actual holding of *Terry v. Ohio* is of course much more limited than the categories put forward by the Model Code, and the Supreme Court has not yet extended its authority in the directions indicated. But statements in *Terry*,[2] as well as in *Adams v. Williams*,[3] make it probable that brief investigatory stops are consistent with the Fourth Amendment if they were effected on the basis of facts and permissible inferences therefrom making investigation necessary or reasonable, *and* if they can be regarded as part of 'an effort to prevent or investigate a crime',[4] whether by attempting to determine the identity or intentions of suspicious individuals or by seeking to maintain the status quo momentarily while more information is obtained.

(ii) Can the stop and frisk power be asserted in connection with every offence or is it necessary either that the offence should be a 'serious' one or that it should be of a particular type? It has been argued[5] strongly that *Terry* should not be extended to possessory offences, like the possession of narcotics, but should be confined to 'the serious cases of imminent danger or of harm recently perpetrated to persons or property', the reason being that in the case of possessory offences '(t)here is too much danger that, instead of the stop being the object and the protective frisk an incident thereto, the reverse will be true'.[6] On this view the purpose of *Terry v. Ohio* was to free police officers from the rigidity of a rule that would prevent their taking any action in the absence of probable cause, 'no matter how grave the problem or impelling the need for swift action';[7] its authority should therefore be confined to serious cases, namely those where there is a demonstrable need for immediate action, and should not be used to sanction resort to stop and frisk powers in areas where there are no similar circumstances of urgency and where moreover the possibilities of abuse would almost certainly outweigh any social benefit that would be derived from extension of the rationale of *Terry* to cover all criminal investigations. A similar approach was adopted by the American Law Institute in their proposed Model Code. As the Code's draftsmen saw it, there was little doubt that 'at least in some cases' there was a need for recognition of an authority allowing a brief period of on-the-spot detention. Equally there was no question about the

[1] *Model Code*, at 10.

[2] 392 U.S. 1 at 22, per Warren, C.J. and at 34, per Harlan, J. concurring.

[3] 407 U.S. 143 (1972). It is not clear whether in *Adams v. Williams* the officer was *primarily* motivated by the need to prevent a crime or was engaged in crime detection; see La Fave, at 20–1.

[4] *Terry v. Ohio*, 392 U.S. 1, 34 (1968), per Harlan, J. concurring.

[5] See the dissent of Friendly, J. in the Court of Appeals in *Adams v. Williams*, 436 F. 2d 30, at 38–9 (1971).

[6] Ibid.

[7] Ibid.

obvious danger of abuse of any broad power to stop and subject to a limited 'weapons' search. What was necessary was to achieve a balance both satisfying the legitimate demands of law enforcement and minimising the social costs and attendant dangers. The Code's solution was that forcible investigatory stops could only be used in situations where the crimes in issue involved danger of forcible injury to persons or of loss or damage to property, since these were the crimes normally causing 'public alarm' and in the case of which the stop was likely to be particularly useful from the point of view of law enforcement.[1] The Code's formulation is intended to exclude not only relatively uncontroversial minor crimes, such as disorderly conduct, gaming and the like, but also major offences not involving immediate danger to persons or property, principally narcotics offences, both because in the case of the latter the frisk is likely to be seriously abused and because the view was taken that the utility of stops and frisks as bona fide aids in the investigation of narcotics offences was questionable.[2] But even the proponents of the view that *Terry* should be limited to serious offences, and that narcotics offences should be removed from its scope, have acknowledged that 'it is not easy to articulate offence-category limitations as a matter of Fourth Amendment interpretation'[3] and that *Adams v. Williams* seems to point the other way.[4] But the issue is still very much an open one.

(iii) Assuming the legality of a forcible stop, when is a further intrusion, normally a limited search, a frisk, permissible, and what is its legitimate scope? The general principles here are, first that the authority to search only arises where there is reasonable apprehension that the person stopped is 'armed and presently dangerous', and secondly that the *only* reason for a protective search is the *discovery of a weapon* which might be used to assault the officer (or others).[5] As to the first principle, it is clear that the general frisking of all persons legitimately stopped is not authorised by *Terry v. Ohio* and that the officer can only conduct the limited search for weapons if 'he (is) able to point to *particular* facts from which he inferred that the individual (stopped) was armed and dangerous',[6] if, in other words, '(t)here (is) something about the particular person or his circumstances which leads to the belief that a frisk is warranted'.[7] *Terry* was such a case because it was reasonable to suppose that the person stopped and frisked presented an immediate danger to the safety of the officer; a different conclusion was reached in *Sibron v. New York*,[8] decided on the same day as *Terry*, since

[1] See *Model Code* § 110.2(1)(a)(i), and at 276–8.

[2] Ibid., at 278.

[3] La Fave, at 26.

[4] Brennan, J., in his dissent in *Adams v. Williams*, quoted extensively from Friendly, J.'s dissent in the court below, whereas Rehnquist, J. in his majority opinion did not mention the point at all. But, as the *Model Code* points out (at 269 n.18), since the informer's tip in *Adams* referred to the gun, this case too involved (at least some) 'danger of forcible injury'.

[5] *Terry v. Ohio*, 392 U.S. 1, 32–3 (1968).

[6] *Sibron v. New York*, 392 U.S. 40, 64 (1968).

[7] *Model Code*, at 278.

[8] 392 U.S. 40 (1968).

there no facts had been observed from which it could be deduced that a suspect who was searched was armed and dangerous; a search bringing to light heroin was therefore declared unconstitutional. But even though routine frisking in association with all permissible stops is not sanctioned by *Terry*, *where* the reason for the stop is the *danger* that the suspect is thought to present either to the officer or to others it would appear that an *automatic* search for weapons will *invariably* be upheld. 'There is no reason why an officer, rightfully but forcibly confronting a person suspected of a serious crime, should have to ask one question and take the risk that the answer might be a bullet.'[1] This is illustrated by one interpretation of *Terry* itself. When the officer stopped Terry he did so because of his reasonable apprehension that a violent crime was being planned; and when the officer asked Terry his name, and no satisfactory reply was offered, a forcible frisk (upheld as constitutional) was conducted without further investigation. One can of course say that these facts gave rise to a reasonable suspicion that the suspect was carrying a weapon and that he presented an immediate danger; alternatively, and perhaps more realistically, one could say that once a forced encounter became justified because of the officer's reasonable suspicion that criminal activity involving violence was afoot '(the) right to take suitable measures for his own safety followed *automatically*'.[2] One can therefore draw a distinction between cases where the reason for the stop is 'an articulable suspicion of violence'[3] and where the right to frisk is immediate and automatic, and cases where the investigatory stop is not connected with reasonable fear for the safety of either the officer or of others, for instance where a crime not involving violence is being investigated, and where a frisk can only be upheld if *other* circumstances (in addition to the reason justifying the stop) give rise to reasonable apprehension of danger. But whatever the best way of organising the cases, the general principle remains that every police intrusion in addition to a mere stop must be capable of its own 'specialised justification', even though in the case of efforts to prevent or investigate crimes of violence this may be derivative, i.e. in effect dependent upon the legality of the stop. Occasionally however certain 'standard' police practices that strike the courts as necessary in the interests of police safety are upheld even though a seizure or interference over and above the initial intrusion represented by the stop or detention cannot *itself* be justified by means of specific facts and permissible inferences therefrom. One such case was *Pennsylvania v. Mimms.*[4] Here, after police officers stopped a car for being operated with an expired licence plate, one of the officers asked the driver (the defendant) to step out of the car and produce his licence and registration; when the defendant got out a large bulge under his jacket was noticed; the officers then frisked him and found a loaded revolver. The Supreme Court divided its opinion in three parts. First, there was no question about the propriety of

[1] *Terry v. Ohio*, 392 U.S. 1, 33 (1968), per Harlan, J. concurring.
[2] Ibid., at 34.
[3] Ibid., at 33.
[4] 434 U.S. 106 (1977).

the initial restriction of the defendant's freedom of movement, which meant that the intrusion resulting from the request to stop the vehicle was constitutional; secondly, under the standard of *Terry v. Ohio*, namely whether the facts available to the officer at the moment of the seizure or the search warranted a reasonable man in the belief that the action taken was appropriate, the officer was justified in making the search he did once the bulge in the defendant's jacket was observed; and thirdly, the order to get out of the car (accepted by the Court as a 'seizure') issued after the defendant was lawfully detained was 'reasonable and thus permissible' under the Fourth Amendment. This last conclusion was premised upon two considerations, first the nature of the governmental interest invoked by the State—the safety of police officers in circumstances such as the ones before the Court—which was both legitimate and weighty, and secondly the fact that the intrusion into the driver's personal liberty occasioned by the order to get out of the car was minimal, particularly when balanced against the State's legitimate concern for its officer's safety. This is not an easy case to fit into *Terry*'s conceptual framework. *Terry* can be said to stand for two things: first, *every* official intrusion must be capable of *specific* justification in terms of facts reasonably warranting *that* intrusion, and secondly, the nature and scope of an intrusion must be related to and limited by the reason justifying the exertion of official authority in the first place (or by further circumstances becoming apparent during the initial stop). This would mean that the order in *Mimms* to get out of the car, a distinct intrusion, should have been justified by reference to its own facts, namely by facts reasonably warranting *that* intrusion. But the *Mimms* majority abandons *Terry*'s principle that an intrusion can *only* be justified on the basis of and after an *individualised* inquiry into the *particular* facts of each situation 'in favour of a general rule',[1] namely that when a motor vehicle has been lawfully detained the police may also order the driver to get out, and also departs from *Terry*'s (apparent) requirement that in the absence of additional circumstances manifesting themselves in the course of the initial forcible encounter the nature and extent of the intrusion be limited by reference to the reason for the stop, since in the instant case, unlike *Terry* where there was an obvious connection between what supported the initial forcible encounter (the officer's suspicion that an armed robbery was being planned) and the challenged intrusion (the frisk for weapons), there was simply no relation between the circumstance justifying the interference in the first place (the expired licence plate) and the challenged intrusion (the order to get out of the car), which, it was accepted, was issued as a matter of course and as part of an official policy of ordering *all* drivers out of their vehicles whenever they had been stopped for traffic violations, and which it was sought to support by reference to general safety considerations. Some safety measures, in other words, can apparently be taken without the need for a prior showing of particularised danger. It remains to be seen whether *Mimms* is interpreted broadly or narrowly, but there are three possible ways of explaining it. It could first be said that *Mimms* qualifies *Terry* by holding

[1] 434 U.S. 106, 116 (1977), per Stevens, J. dissenting.

that there is a class of seizures falling in between arrests, requiring probable cause, and stop and frisk procedures, which must proceed on the basis of articulable reasons to suspect criminal activity, and that in their case '(there is) no requirement that an officer be able to explain the reasons for his actions',[1] which of course means that he need not have *any* reasons; secondly, it might be argued that what *Mimms* does is to decide on the basis of a weighing of the public and individual interests at stake that the danger to the officer's safety associated with *every* stop of a vehicle for a traffic violation is such that *in this area* there is need for the adoption of a standard more lenient than that permitted by *Terry*[2]—namely that once there is a traffic stop the police can automatically take the safety measure of ordering the driver to get out of the car; a final interpretation of *Mimms* is that it regards the order to *get out* of the car as de minimis, namely as imposing no imposition on the driver in addition to that represented by the order to *stop* the car; since the police have already lawfully decided that the driver should be briefly detained 'the only question is whether he shall spend that period sitting in the driver's seat of his car or standing alongside it';[3] in the circumstances, that is, the order to get out of the car is not so much a separate intrusion requiring distinct justification as a minor inconvenience that should receive automatic validation.

(iv) The final question relates to the permissible scope of the ensuing search once the initiation of a frisk has been held to be permissible on account of the perceived dangers of the situation. A protective frisk, it is well established, must be limited to what is necessary for the purpose of ensuring protection from concealed weapons. Normally this means that there should first be a pat-down, a touching of the outer clothing of the suspect; when the officer feels the presence of an object which he reasonably believes to be a weapon he may seize it and examine it. This is exactly what happened in *Terry v. Ohio* where the officer first patted down the outside of the suspect's clothing and only searched further when he felt a pistol in one of the pockets of the overcoat. In contrast, in *Sibron v. New York*,[4] even assuming that there were grounds to search the defendant for weapons, the nature and scope of the search clearly exceeded the justification of removing from the suspect dangerous weapons; here there had been no attempt of 'an initial limited exploration for arms',[5] but the officer had immediately thrust his hand into the suspect's pocket and taken from it an envelope containing heroin; this, together with the officer's statements at the time of the search,[6] showed that the search was not reasonably limited in scope to the 'accomplishment of the only goal which might conceivably have justified its inception—the protection of the officer by disarming a potentially dangerous man';[7] the search was

[1] Ibid., at 122.

[2] Ibid., at 123.

[3] Ibid., at 111 (majority opinion).

[4] 392 U.S. 40 (1968).

[5] Ibid., at 65.

[6] The officer's opening statement was 'You know what I am after', and the Court had no doubt that this indicated that what he sought was narcotics.

[7] *Sibron v. New York*, 392 U.S. at 65.

therefore illegal and the heroin would be suppressed. But, even though it will *invariably* be insisted upon, it does not appear that an external patting of the suspect's outer clothing is *always* necessary before the subsequent seizure of a weapon or other evidence can be upheld.[1] Where, for instance, the officer has reasonable grounds for believing either from his own personal observation or from reliable information received from others that a weapon will be found at a precise spot, and there is a danger that the delay involved in the pat-down will expose him to serious danger, he can apparently reach to the spot where the weapon is located and seize it, as indeed happened in *Adams v. Williams.*[2] Needless to say, if the police *in the course* of a legitimate *Terry*-type search come across seizable evidence of other crime, for instance narcotics, they may seize it.

The two most important theoretical issues in connection with *Terry v. Ohio* are first whether *Terry*'s holding can be accommodated within the traditional concepts and terminology of probable cause, and secondly whether the type of balancing it sanctions should be limited to its particular subject-matter, namely stop and frisk procedures, or can be generalised into a new (and theoretically unified) approach to Fourth Amendment problems, particularly seizures of the person. On the first issue, there is little doubt that the *Terry* Court regarded the standard of probable cause as inapplicable, taking instead the view that the challenged official conduct should be evaluated in terms of the reasonableness clause, which meant that the brief on-the-spot stop and consequent limited frisk for weapons in issue could be upheld on evidence less than that required by traditional probable cause, the new standard being defined as evidence giving rise to reason to believe or leading to reasonable suspicion or reasonably warranting the belief that official action is necessary. Could probable cause have been stretched to accommodate the Court's holding? Two main points are usually made here: first, that probable cause is not a fixed and immutable standard which must always be satisfied by the same quantum of evidence, but a variable compromise for accommodating the conflicting societal and individual interests at stake; satisfaction of probable cause depends upon all the circumstances of a given situation, including the degree of imposition a particular (type of) intrusion entails for the citizen; and since a brief on-the-street detention of the type involved in *Terry* is less onerous for the citizen than a conventional arrest it should require less by way of justification, not because probable cause is inapplicable but because probable cause is satisfied.[3] After all, *Camara*[4] shows that the amount of evidence required by probable cause is often struck only by balancing the governmental interest allegedly served by the search against the degree of imposition upon personal security which the search or seizure entails. The police conduct in question in *Terry v. Ohio*, in other words, can and should be subjected to the standard of probable cause, but the meaning of the latter in this context can only be determined by resort to the

[1] But see La Fave, at 124–5.

[2] 407 U.S. 143 (1972).

[3] La Fave, at 12–14.

[4] 387 U.S. 523 (1967). *Camara* was referred to in *Terry v. Ohio*.

governing criterion of reasonableness. The second argument has a different starting point, namely the similarity in the standards governing arrests on the one hand and stops and similar temporary detentions on the other. As to the legality of the former, the Supreme Court has often stated that probable cause for an arrest exists where the facts and circumstances within the arresting officers' knowledge and of which they have reasonably trustworthy information are sufficient to warrant a man of reasonable caution in the belief that an offence *has been or is being committed*;[1] and terms such as 'probable cause' and 'reasonable grounds' have long been regarded as substantially equivalent in meaning.[2] But the authority to stop and if necessary frisk too, as has been seen, cannot be exercised routinely, but only arises when the officer has reason to believe either that the person he is dealing with is armed and dangerous, or that there is some other good reason warranting temporary detention and further investigation. One view is that there is no difference between 'reasonable suspicion', the *Terry* standard, and 'probable cause', the standard for arrests,[3] and that the two are conceptually identical. But this ignores two points. First, probable cause in the case of arrest means reasonable grounds to believe that the person to be arrested *has committed* or *is committing* an offence, and cannot reach the situation where a crime is '*about to be* committed', the issue in *Terry*;[4] this means that probable cause for arrest, at least as traditionally understood, cannot accomplish the related tasks of 'crime prevention and deterrence of would-be criminals',[5] precisely the purpose of *Terry*. Secondly, the Court in *Terry v. Ohio* regarded an arrest as a *specific* kind of official intrusion, namely the taking of a person into custody pending prosecution for a crime; the investigative stop and the protective search for weapons on the other hand are wholly different types of intrusion from that represented by the typical arrest for a crime, since the former, unlike the latter, are not part of 'the initial stage of a criminal prosecution',[6] but only limited measures to ensure the safety of officers or to accomplish other tasks necessitating temporary restrictions on personal liberty; since therefore arrests are inherently different from investigative stops and protective frisks as regards both the interests

[1] See *Wong Sun v. United States*, 371 U.S. 471 (1963); *Ker v. California*, 374 U.S. 23 (1963); *Beck v. Ohio*, 379 U.S. 89 (1964).

[2] See *Draper v. United States*, 358 U.S. 307 (1959).

[3] This was apparently the view Black, J., expressed during argument in *Terry v. Ohio* (see 36 U.S.L. W. 3249 (1967)); see also Landynski, 'The Supreme Court's Search for Fourth Amendment Standards: The Problem of "Stop-and-Frisk",' 45 *Conn. B.J.* 146, 183 (1971).

[4] But Douglas, J., in *Terry v. Ohio*, 392 U.S. at 35 and 39, sought to remedy this by suggesting that there could be probable cause to believe that 'a crime was about to be committed' or that a criminal venture was 'about to be launched'. But there are many difficulties with this, as Landynski, supra, n. 3, at 169, shows. With what offence is the arrested person who has yet to commit a crime to be charged? Or is the 'arrest' simply a device to keep him from committing the crime he had intended—'in short, a form of preventive detention'? (see Landynaski, supra, at 169).

[5] Douglas, J.'s dissent in *Terry v. Ohio*, 392 U.S. at 35 n.1.

[6] *Terry v. Ohio,* 392 U.S. at 26.

sought to be vindicated and the resulting invasions of personal security,[1] it is hardly illogical that different standards of legality should apply to the two categories of official action, particularly since 'a perfectly reasonable apprehension of danger may arise long before the officer is possessed of adequate information to justify taking a person into custody'.[2] An alternative formulation both to the total assimilation of probable cause and reasonable suspicion and to their sharp differentiation is that even though arrests and temporary on-the-spot detentions are different, the intrusion involved in conducting a 'stop and frisk' still requires 'some kind of a showing of probable cause',[3] namely that the officer should have probable cause (or reasonable grounds) at the time of the interference to believe that the person he was confronting was armed and dangerous. What the Supreme Court has therefore done in *Terry v. Ohio* and *Adams v. Williams* is to indicate that while the validity of an ordinary arrest depends upon probable cause to believe that a person has committed or is committing an offence the validity of the type of intrusion represented by stop and frisk practices depends upon 'a different kind of "probable cause" ',[4] namely probable cause to believe that a person is armed and dangerous. But it is questionable whether the arguments for applying probable cause standards to the distinctive class of seizures dealt with in *Terry v. Ohio* and its progeny are either convincing or necessary. Traditional theory assumes, and has proceeded on the basis, that probable cause to arrest requires not only a *certain* level of information[5] *but also* satisfaction of certain 'requirements of reliability and particularity',[6] and these safeguards could well be fatally compromised by efforts to bring limited seizures falling far short of technical arrests within the same standard. The three-step *Terry* approach, to regard probable causes as inapplicable, to refer limited investigatory seizures of the type in issue to the general proscription against unreasonable searches and seizures, and *then* to develop as a precondition to legitimacy of such official action a standard of 'reasonable suspicion' on the basis of factors not unlike those which in the context of arrests have crystallised into the requirement of probable cause,[7] seems much more sensible.

[1] Ibid.

[2] Ibid., at 26–7.

[3] 'Annotation, Law Enforcement Officer's Authority, Under Federal Constitution, to "Stop and Frisk" a Person', 32 L. Ed. 2d 942, 946.

[4] Ibid.

[5] *Adams v. Williams*, 407 U.S. 143, 145 (1972).

[6] *Wong Sun v. United States*, 371 U.S. 471 (1963).

[7] See Armentano, 'The Standards for Probable Cause Under the Fourth Amendment', 44 *Conn. B.J.* 137, 165 (1970); Landynski, supra, 243 n. 3, at 181. The term 'reasonable suspicion', not used as such in *Terry v. Ohio*, does not mean that the standard is 'a subjective or intuitive' one (see *Model Code*, at 283). There is general agreement that what is required is 'an objective standard, somewhat less exigent than the arrest standard' (*Model Code*, at 283). Adoption of 'reasonable suspicion' makes two points, first that there must be *reasonable* grounds for the suspicion, and secondly that as the imposition in a stop is less onerous than in an arrest 'so the requisite likelihood of involvement in crime justifying a stop is lower than in the case of an arrest' (*Model Code*, at 282).

The related issue is whether the balancing exercise engaged in by the *Terry* and *Camara* Court can be used over the whole field of seizures of the person. One extreme approach is that what both *Terry* and *Camara* establish, whether generally or in connection with determinations under the proscription of unreasonable searches and seizures, is that 'the key principle of the Fourth Amendment is reasonableness—the balancing of competing interests',[1] and that this must be conducted on an ad hoc basis, the quantum of evidence needed to justify a particular intrusion depending on all the circumstances of each situation.[2] But this cannot be maintained, not only because of the undeniable fact that a theoretically uniform standard of justification, probable cause, applies to the principal category of seizures under the Fourth Amendment, that of arrests, 'without (any further) need to "balance" the interests and circumstances involved in particular situations',[3] but also in view of the need to have workable and more or less simple and categorical rules guiding both (initial) offical action and (subsequent) judicial evaluation. A good illustration of judicial unwillingness to embark on ad hoc balancing *either* over the whole field of seizures of the person *or* of *all* seizures that do not amount to technical arrests is *Dunaway v. New York*.[4] Here the defendant was suspected of a serious crime but there was insufficient information to obtain a warrant for his arrest; he was none the less 'picked up' and taken into custody, and even though he was not told that he was under arrest, it was clear that he would have been physically restrained if he had attempted to leave; at the police station he was questioned, and eventually made statements and drew sketches that implicated him in the crime. The state court upheld the conduct of the police on the ground that law-enforcement officials, even though lacking probable cause, may detain an individual upon reasonable suspicion for questioning for a reasonable period of time under carefully controlled conditions. The Supreme Court reversed, on the ground that the treatment of the suspect, whether or not technically an arrest, was in important respects indistinguishable from a traditional arrest, and therefore had to be supported by probable cause; 'detention for custodial interrogation—regardless of its label—intrudes so severely on interests protected by the Fourth Amendment as necessarily to trigger the traditional safeguards against illegal arrest'.[5] The approach of *Terry*, Justice Brennan observed, was inapplicable because that case dealt with 'a *special* category of Fourth Amendment "seizures" so substantially less intrusive than arrests that the *general rule* requiring probable cause to make Fourth Amendment "seizures" reasonable could be replaced by a balancing test'; *Terry*, in other words, involved 'an exception' to the general rule requiring probable cause and its scope was 'narrow', only sanctioning the standard of 'reasonable suspicion' where the challenged intrusions were 'limited', 'brief', and

[1] *Dunaway v. New York*, 99 S.Ct. 2248, 2260 (1979), per White, J. concurring.

[2] See Barrett, 'Personal Rights, Property Rights and the Fourth Amendment', 1960 *Sup. Ct. Rev.* 46, 63; see also Amsterdam, 'Perspectives on the Fourth Amendment', 58 *Minn. L. Rev.* 349, 393–4 (1974).

[3] *Dunaway v. New York*, 99 S.Ct. 2248, 2254 (1979).

[4] 99 S.Ct. 2248 (1979).

[5] Ibid., at 2258.

'narrowly circumscribed'; but where a seizure was seriously intrusive it could not come within the *Terry* exception and could only be justified if based on probable cause.[1]

Dunaway suggests that there are *only* two categories of 'seizures', arrests and similarly severe intrusions on the one hand, supportable only by probable cause, and the limited and 'narrowly defined intrusions involved in *Terry* and its progeny', justifiable by reference to reasonable suspicion or an articulable reason to suspect criminal activity. These two categories are the outgrowth of centuries of precedent and represent the distillation of much experience, and no further balancing is justified, particularly since essential constitutional protections 'could all too easily disappear in the consideration and balancing of the multifarious circumstances presented by different cases',[2] especially when that balancing must be done in the first instance by police officers. But a distinction must still be made between balancing *at large* and balancing *within* the various rubrics of official conduct demarcated by the cases. *Dunaway*'s emphatic disapproval of 'a multifactor balancing test'[3] of reasonableness, whether covering all seizures or only those not amounting to arrests, does not mean that balancing or weighing cannot be engaged in *within* the established categories, particularly the one delineated by *Terry*, as the only way of determining whether the applicable requirement of reasonable suspicion has been reached. It has thus been suggested that '(i)n striking the balance in a case involving *an investigative stop* at least four factors are pertinent',[4] the gravity of the offence suspected, the probability of the suspect's implication, the extent of the intrusion, and the need for immediate action. For since, it has been suggested,[5] the *Terry* test is what is 'reasonable', 'the lesser the seriousness and immediacy of the crime, the lesser the intrusion justified and the greater must be the likelihood of the suspect's involvement'; if the suspected crime is enormous, for instance placing a bomb, it may be legitimate to stop all in the immediate vicinity; but if the suspected misconduct does not endanger life or personal safety, particularly if the only purpose of a stop is to investigate 'a minor peccadillo', a *Terry*-type interference is only legitimate if it proceeds on the basis of highly substantial grounds for suspicion and even then would only warrant 'the most moderate intrusion'.[6]

Contrary to *Dunaway*'s suggestion that there are two only types of standard for the justification of seizures within the Fourth Amendment, the 'long prevailing standards'[7] of probable cause for arrests and 'reasonable suspicion'[8] for minor intrusions, such as brief investigative stops of the kind

[1] Ibid., at 2256.
[2] Ibid., at 2257.
[3] Ibid.
[4] *United States v. Garcia*, 450 F. Supp. 1020 (1978).
[5] Ibid.
[6] Ibid., at 1023.
[7] *Dunaway v. New York*, 99 S.Ct. 2248, 2254 (1979).
[8] See above, 244 n. 7. 'Articulable reasonable suspicion' is a term that is often used (see *Dunaway v. New York*, 99 S.Ct. 2248 (1979)).

involved in *Terry*, *Pennsylvania v. Mimms*[1] and other cases[2] support the position that there is a class of seizures which require no *separate* justification, no inquiry, that is, into the existence or adequacy of any reasons prompting the *particular* intrusion. An effort was made to explain *Mimms* above. The other cases seem to owe a lot to the authorities on administrative inspections, and appear to proceed on the principle that, even though official intrusions must be justified with particularity and only after an individualised inquiry into the circumstances of *each* case, in certain limited contexts routine (and minor) interferences unsupported by any distinct or articulable reason for suspicion, such as brief investigative stops at fixed checkpoints to check vehicles for illegal aliens,[3] may be upheld, but only if (a) the indiscriminate official practice is supported by compelling governmental interests unlikely to be fulfilled in a less drastic manner, (b) the resulting invasion of privacy is minimal, and (c) the particular scheme under which the routine intrusion takes place contains guarantees and safeguards that extend protection from discrimination and harassment comparable to that allegedly represented by the normally applicable Fourth Amendment principle that each and every 'seizure' must be subjected to, and satisfy, the requirement of individualised justifaction.[4]

On the basis of *Terry, Dunaway* and *Mimms* the following scheme, correlating the required degree of justification to the type and intrusiveness of particular police activities, can be put forward.[5] 1. In the case of an arrest and situations in substance indistinguishable from it there must be probable cause to believe that the person apprehended has committed or is committing a crime. 2. As regards the narrowly defined and strictly limited intrusions falling within the category demarcated by *Terry v. Ohio* and *Adams v. Williams*, such as forcible stops, temporary detentions and protective frisks when necessary, what is required is that there should be reasonable grounds to believe or suspect either that a particular person is armed and dangerous or that there is some other adequate reason warranting brief investigation. 3. In a few strictly limited instances the demand for particularised justification of every instance of official behaviour impinging on Fourth Amendment rights is abandoned in favour of a general rule permitting certain governmental intrusions as a matter of course and irrespective of whether there was any suspicion, reasonable or not, in the particular case; but assurances of fairness and regularity must be found both to be present and to be, in terms of protection, comparable to individualised procedures. 4. When an officer, whether in the course of an investigation or otherwise, has not, either by means of physical force or by other show of authority, restrained the liberty of a citizen, no 'seizure' within the Fourth Amendment has taken place. There is

[1] 434 U.S. 106 (1977).

[2] See *United States v. Martinez-Fuerte*, 428 U.S. 543 (1976), and compare with *Delaware v. Prouse*, 99 S.Ct. 1391 (1979).

[3] See *United States v. Martinez-Fuerte*, 428 U.S. 543 (1976).

[4] See *Pennsylvania v. Mimms*, 434 U.S. 106, 121 (1977), per Stevens, J., dissenting.

[5] For a different 'table', see *People v. De Bour*, 352 N.E. 2d 562 (1976).

then no need for any justification of what the officer has done, for instance addressing questions or requesting information.[1]

(c) Border searches

Border searches form a category of their own. It is now well established that border searches are 'reasonable' by the single fact that the person or item in question has entered the country from the outside,[2] and there has never been any additional requirement either that they should be accompanied by warrants or that they must proceed on the basis of probable cause.[3] This doctrine has a long history, and the main arguments given in its support are 'the long standing right of the sovereign to protect itself by stopping and examining persons and property crossing into (the) country'[4] and the need to exclude illegal articles from the country.[5] A border search must generally take place *when* one is attempting to enter the country[6] whether by air, sea or land, and must be conducted *at* the border itself or its functional equivalents.[7] Only recently the Supreme Court has emphasised that the border-search exception is absolute and that the mode of entry is irrelevant. It was therefore held[8] that international mail may be searched at the border as a matter of course, and that it makes no difference whether the envelopes were mailed or carried. 'The critical fact is that the envelopes cross the border and enter th(e) country, not that they are brought in by one mode of transportation rather than another.'[9]

Two important and difficult issues merit special attention, first the legality of searches, seizures and lesser intrusions not at the point of the international border but only in its general vicinity and at some distance from it, and

[1] But see *People v. De Bour*, 352 N.E. 2d 562 (1976), where even the 'minimal intrusion of approaching to request information' is only permitted where 'there is some objective credible reason for that interference'; see La Fave, 55–7.

[2] See *Carroll v. United States*, 267 U.S. 132, 153–4 (1925); *United States v. Thirty-Seven Photographs*, 402 U.S. 363, 376 (1971); *United States v. Ramsey*, 431 U.S. 606 (1977).

[3] *United States v. Ramsey*, 431 U.S. 606, 619 (1977).

[4] Ibid., at 616.

[5] *United States v. Thirty-Seven Photographs*, 402 U.S. 363, 376 (1971).

[6] Occasionally an extended border search may be justified; see *Alexander v. United States*, 363 F. 2d 379 (1966). Under *Alexander* a search away from the border may still be upheld if the circumstances, including the time and distance that elapsed as well as the manner and extent of the surveillance, are such as to convince the fact-finder with reasonable certainty that any contraband that may be found in the vehicle at the time of the search was aboard the vehicle *at the time of entry*. The *Alexander* search, it has been well put, is 'merely a deferred assertion by the customs agent of his right to search any vehicle crossing the border' ('Note', 74 *Column. L. Rev.* 53, 58–9 (1974)).

[7] See *Almeida-Sanchez v. United States*, 93 S.Ct. 2535 (1973). Functional equivalents of border searches are searches at an established station near the border and searches of the passengers of airplanes arriving at an 'internal' airport after a non-stop flight from a foreign country.

[8] *United States v. Ramsey*, 431 U.S. 606 (1977).

[9] Ibid., at 620.

secondly the permissibility of particularly intrusive border searches, mainly strip and body cavity searches, at the time of entry.

As to the first issue the following types of situation, corresponding to certain official practices, can by distinguished. There are first searches of vehicles and persons by roving patrols. These were dealt with in *Almeida-Sanchez v. United States*[1] where roving patrol units routinely stopped *and searched* vehicles in areas near the border as part of a programme to find aliens who had illegally entered the country. The Supreme Court held that warrantless searches of vehicles made without either probable cause or consent on a highway about twenty miles from the Mexican border were contrary to the Fourth Amendment. Such searches could not be justified on the basis of any special rules applicable to automobile searches, as probable cause was lacking; they could not be justified by analogy with administrative inspections, as the officers had neither a warrant nor reason to believe that the petitioners had crossed the border or committed any offence; and they were not border searches; they were therefore unconstitutional. The second category consists of cases where roving patrols *stop* vehicles near the border. Here, unlike *Almeida-Sanchez*, the border patrol does not claim authority to search cars but only to question their occupants about their citizenship and immigration status. In *United States v. Brignoni-Ponce*[2] such practices too were declared to be inconsistent with the Fourth Amendment. The Fourth Amendment, the Supreme Court declared, did not allow a roving patrol to stop, either *at their discretion* or solely on the basis of Mexican ancestry, a vehicle near (but not at) the border and question its occupants about citizenship and immigration. There was of course no denying either the magnitude of the problems posed by illegal immigration or that mere stops unaccompanied by further detention involved only a relatively modest intrusion. But still to approve of *random* roving-patrol stops would vest the government with broad and unlimited *discretion* to stop vehicles in border areas, and this would subject their residents to indiscriminate official interference with their rights to privacy and freedom of movement. This was not 'reasonable' within the Fourth Amendment. But because of the important governmental interest in combating the illegal entry of aliens at the border, the minimal intrusion of a brief stop, and the absence of practical alternatives for policing the border, an officer, whose observations led him reasonably to suspect that a particular vehicle might contain aliens who were illegally in the country, could stop the car briefly, question the driver and passengers about their citizenship and immigration status, and ask them to explain suspicious circumstances; but further detention or search had to be based on consent or probable cause. The effect of *Brignoni-Ponce* therefore is that except at the border and its functional equivalents officers on roving patrol may stop vehicles only if they are aware of specific articulable facts, together with any rational inferences from them, that 'reasonably warrant suspicion' that the vehicles contain aliens who may be illegally in the country.

The facts of *Almeida-Sanchez* did not require the Court to decide whether

[1] 93 S.Ct. 2535 (1973).
[2] 422 U.S. 873 (1975).

its disapproval of searches by roving patrols near the border, and its requirement of probable cause for vehicular searches not at the point of the border, also applied to searches of automobiles at fixed traffic checkpoints. Two reasons were suggested by the government in *United States v. Ortiz*[1] for distinguishing *Almeida-Sanchez* and for dispensing with probable cause for searches at traffic checkpoints. First, fixed checkpoints curb what would otherwise be unbridled discretion because '(the) officer's discretion in deciding which cars to search is limited by the location of the checkpoint', unlike the officers on roving patrol in *Almeida-Sanchez* who were theoretically free to stop and search any car within one hundred miles of the border. Secondly, the circumstances surrounding a checkpoint stop and search are far less intrusive than those attending roving-patrol investigations. 'Roving patrols often operate at night on seldom-travelled roads, and their approach may frighten motorists. At traffic checkpoints the motorist can see that other vehicles are being stopped, he can see visible signs of the officers' authority, and he is much less likely to be frightened or annoyed by the intrusion.'[2] These differences, Justice Powell observed in *Ortiz*, were not without *some* constitutional significance, but still they made no difference when what was involved was a *search*. 'The greater regularity attending the stop does not mitigate the invasion of privacy that a search entails. Nor do checkpoint procedures significantly reduce the likelihood of embarrassment.' It was therefore held that the admitted differences between roving patrols and traffic checkpoints did not justify in the case of the latter an abandonment of the safeguards required in *Almeida-Sanchez* and that *searches* of private vehicles at traffic checkpoints removed from the border and its functional equivalents can only take place on the basis of either probable cause or consent.[3]

What about the use of fixed checkpoints to stop (but not search) cars and question their occupants in the absence of any suspicion that they contain illegal aliens? The constitutionality of such routine checkpoint *stops* by border patrol agents was considered in *United States v. Martinez-Fuerte*[4] where the challenged practice involved slowing all oncoming traffic to a virtual, if not a complete, halt at a highway roadblock, and referring vehicles chosen at the discretion of border patrol agents to an area for secondary inspection. It was acknowledged that the governmental interest involved was the same as that furthered by roving patrol stops outlawed in *United States v. Brignoni-Ponce*, but the Supreme Court none the less sustained the constitutionality of the border patrol's checkpoint operations. The crucial distinction was the lesser intrusion upon the motorists' Fourth Amendment rights. The objective intrusion — the stop, the questioning and the visual inspection — Justice Powell observed, also existed in roving-patrol stops. But checkpoint stops should be viewed in a different light because 'the subjective intrusion — the generating of concern or even fright on the part of lawful travellers — (was) appreciably less

[1] 422 U.S. 891 (1975).
[2] Ibid., at 894–5.
[3] *United States v. Ortiz*, 422 U.S. 891, 897 (1975).
[4] 428 U.S. 543 (1976).

in the case of a checkpoint stop'.[1] *Stops* for brief questioning routinely conducted at permanent checkpoints are therefore consistent with the Fourth Amendment and need not be authorised by warrant or be supported either by probable cause or by individualised suspicion. But any further detention, namely detention going beyond a mere stop, must be based on consent or probable cause.[2]

The second problem raised by border searches concerns their permissible intrusiveness. For it is well known that narcotics are often hidden in the intimate clothing of those attempting to smuggle them into the country, or even concealed in their private parts. In what circumstances can a traveller be forced to strip, and when can a search become even more intrusive, for instance by involving an examination of the rectum, the vagina or even the stomach? The broad principle governing the intrusiveness of border searches is that they must be reasonable. For even though border searches are unique, in that the mere fact that a person is crossing the border is sufficient cause for a search, the Fourth Amendment, protecting 'personal privacy and dignity against *unwarranted* intrusion by the State',[3] still applies, and this means that 'every search must be examined in the light of the Amendment's requirement that it must not be "unreasonable" '.[4] The many cases fall into three categories. First there are searches not involving either a requirement that the suspect strip or a body cavity probe. Such searches, however intense, can take place simply on the basis of a mere crossing of the border and not even mere suspicion is required.[5] Secondly there are strip searches, where a person is required to remove his clothing. A strip search, it has repeatedly been held, can only be undertaken on the basis of real, and not mere, suspicion directed specifically at the person required to strip.[6] 'Real suspicion' in this context has been defined as '*subjective* suspicion supported by *objective, articulable* facts that would *reasonably* lead an experienced, prudent customs official to suspect that a particular person seeking to cross (the) border is concealing something on his body'[7] for the purpose of transporting it into the country contrary to law. Finally there are cases where the search goes beyond a requirement that the suspect undress and where there is 'an intrusion beyond the body's surface',[8] for instance a probe of body cavities such as the rectum or the vagina. It is not always easy to tell where a strip search ends and a body cavity search begins,[9] but if a search has been

[1] Ibid., at 558.

[2] Surprisingly, not only the 'stops' at the permanent checkpoints but also 'referrals' to secondary inspection areas for further questioning were upheld as constitutional in *Martinez-Fuerte*, 428 U.S. at 563, even in the absence of any individualised suspicion and indeed even if such referrals were made largely on the basis of apparent Mexican ancestry. The intrusion again was sufficiently minimal, Powell, J. observed, so that 'no particularised reason need exist to justify it'. See Brennan, J.'s dissent at 568.

[3] *Henderson v. United States*, 390 F. 2d 805, 807 (1967).

[4] Ibid.

[5] See 'Note', 74 *Colum. L. Rev.* 53, 73 (1974).

[6] *United States v. Holtz*, 479 F. 2d 89 (1973).

[7] *United States v. Guadalupe-Garza*, 421 F. 2d 876, 879 (1970).

[8] *Rivas v. United States*, 368 F. 2d 703, 710 (1966).

[9] Inspection of the vagina presents particular difficulty; see *Henderson v. United*

held to fall into the latter category a mere 'real suspicion', as defined above, is not enough and what is required is a 'clear indication'[1] that the suspected evidence will be found. This standard cannot readily be defined, but 'a clear indication' that a serach beyond the body's surface is justified cannot rest on the mere chance that suspected evidence may be discovered. 'There *must exist facts* creating a clear indication, or plain suggestion, of the smuggling.'[2] The test was found to be satisfied in *Rivas v. United States.*[3] Here customs officers conducted a strip search of the defendant, but he refused to spread the cheeks of his buttocks to permit observation of his rectum. Later officers restrained him while a doctor conducted a rectal examination. A packet of narcotics was found. The search was upheld because of the presence of the required 'clear indication' or 'plain suggestion'. A different result was reached in *Henderson v. United States.*[4] On the basis of a custom officer's erroneous recollection that she had been searched on a previous occasion when dangerous drugs were discovered the defendant was stopped at the border, taken to the customs office, and subjected to a body cavity search. A quantity of heroin was discovered in her vagina. The evidence was suppressed because the officer's recollection constituted at most a mere suspicion that the defendant was carrying narcotics and did not amount to the clear indication necessary to authorise a search of her vagina.

(d) Airport searches

Airport searches[5] present considerable interest because they afford an excellent example of the emergence of a special (contemporary) problem thought to present Fourth Amendment problems and of strained judicial efforts to solve it by reference to doctrines developed in other (and very different) contexts. As a result of the many hijackings of the late 1960s and early 1970s many anti-hijackings programmes were put into operation and are now universally used; these, centring on the development and implementation of techniques for the effective surveillance and search of air passengers, take many forms, but the essential components of the standard anti-hijacking system currently employed are the following. The passenger places his carry-on luggage on a table, where it is searched, either manually or by means of X-ray machines; the passenger then proceeds through a magnetometer, a device that is activated by metal on the person of the would-

---

States, 390 F. 2d 805 (1967); *Morales v. United States*, 406 F. 2d 1298 (1969); *United States v. Holtz*, 479 F. 2d 89 (1973).

[1] *Rivas v. United States*, 368 F. 2d 703, 710 (1966).

[2] Ibid. The *Rivas* requirement is based upon the language of *Schmerber v. California*, 384 U.S. 757 (1966).

[3] 368 F. 2d 703 (1966).

[4] 390 F. 2d 805 (1967).

[5] 3 W. La Fave, *Search and Seizure* 327–64 (1978); see also 'Note, The Constitutionality of Airport Searches', 72 *Mich. L. Rev.* 128 (1973); 'Note, Airport Searches: Fourth Amendment Anomalies'. 48 *N.Y.U.L. Rev.* 1043 (1973); Abramovsky, 'The Constitutionality of the Anti-Hijacking Security System', 22 *Buff. L. Rev.* 123 (1972).

be passenger; if the device is activated, further investigation is made; in some cases the follow-up investigation is made by means of a portable magnetometer which is run up and down the passenger's body to discover the location of the metal that initially activated the magnetometer; where a portable magnetometer is either not available or not used passengers are sometimes asked to remove all metal objects from their body and to proceed again through the magnetometer; if doubt still remains a frisk of the passenger is finally conducted; in other cases a frisk takes place not as a last resort but as soon as the magnetometer is activated.

Two things are clear. First, the usual airport screening procedure as set out above comes within and must therefore conform with the Fourth Amendment because its main components, the search of the carry-on luggage, the use of the magnetometer and the frisk, are 'searches' within the Amendment. Clearly physical searches of persons and effects, whether by opening carry-on luggage or by frisking passengers for weapons, are 'searches' in the fullest sense. But, as has been seen, even examination by the magnetometer, whether one is asked to walk through it or whether a portable device is applied to the passenger's body, amounts to a search 'in that it searches for and discloses metal items within areas most intimate to the person where there is a normal expectation of privacy'.[1] Nor have courts shown any inclination to accept the argument that the Fourth Amendment does not apply to airport searches because the passenger does not have an expectation of privacy either with respect to his person or with regard to his carry-on luggage (and this principally because such searches are now commonplace). In the same way that the government cannot avoid the restrictions of the Fourth Amendment by notifying the public that all telephone lines will in future be tapped or that all homes will now be liable to warrantless entries 'airport searches are not outside the Amendment simply because they are being conducted at all airports'.[2] In every case the individual's reasonable expectation of privacy can only be regarded as no longer applicable on some ground independent of the frequency of the challenged intrusion itself. Nor does the magnitude of the threatened danger justify abandonment of constitutional safeguards. 'The exigencies of skyjacking and bombing, however real and dire, should not (convert) an airport and its environs (into) an enclave where the Fourth Amendment has taken its leave.'[3] The second thing one notices from a study of the many cases is that courts, when confronted with challenges to the legality of airport searches, experience great difficulty, which is not surprising in view of the fact that neither component of the usual airport search—the use of the magnetometer or the semi-automatic frisk—seems to fit readily

[1] *United States v. Epperson*, 454 F. 2d 769, 770 (1972).

[2] *United States v. Davis*, 482 F. 2d 893 (1973).

[3] *United States v. Legato*, 480 F. 2d 408, 414 (1973), per Goldberg, J. concurring. Nor is the Fourth Amendment rendered inapplicable because airport searches are conducted by private entities and not governmental authorities. Courts have taken note of the fact that the government's participation in the development and implementation of airport search programmes has been of such significance as to bring any search conducted in pursuance thereof within the reach of the Fourth Amendment (see *United States v. Davis*, 482 F. 2d 893 (1973)).

within any of the traditional exceptions to the warrant requirement. Yet, as courts have candidly acknowledged, such searches seem, especially in view of the necessity for and the overwhelming public acceptance of anti-hijacking systems, to be reasonable;[1] and there is little doubt that currently used airport procedures have had considerable success in reducing the number of successful hijackings and hijacking attempts. Courts have therefore made valiant efforts to uphold the basic constitutionality of airport security procedures. At the same time the compelling governmental interest in preventing incidents of air piracy, principally by detecting weapons before they are brought on airplanes, does not mean that all invasions of privacy can be excused if only undertaken in pursuance of airport security systems,[2] particularly since, as some courts have noticed, 'most of these airport searches find narcotics and not bombs', which in turn has caused them to pause in the rush towards a wholesale relaxation of the Fourth Amendment under the aegis of safety.[3]

As a general matter the invariable judicial attitude has been to test airport searches and security procedures by the Fourth Amendment's general proscription against unreasonable searches and seizures since an airport search as a practical matter cannot be subjected to the warrant requirement;[4] the ultimate standard by reference to which the constitutional propriety of warrantless airport searches is to be evaluated is that of reasonableness; and 'the reasonableness of a search depends upon the facts and circumstances and the total atmosphere of each case'.[5] Within the broad rubric of overall reasonableness two types of approach have in the main been followed by American tribunals for testing the constitutionality of airport searches, that developed in the context of *Terry v. Ohio*[6] and the one deriving from the Supreme Court's treatment of administrative inspections.[7] The early cases

[1] *United States v. Albarado*, 495 F. 2d 799 (1974).

[2] Ibid.

[3] See *United States v. Legato*, 480 F. 2d 408, 414 (1973), per Goldberg, J. concurring.

[4] See *United States v. Cyzewski*, 484 F. 2d 509 (1973); *United States v. Albarado*, 495 F. 2d 799 (1974).

[5] *United States v. Albarado*, 495 F. 2d 799 (1974).

[6] 392 U.S. 1 (1968).

[7] *Camara v. Municipal Court*, 387 U.S. 523 (1967). Some would apply the rationale of the border search cases to anti-hijacking searches. Thus in *United States v. Skipwith*, 482 F. 2d 1272 (1973) it was held that 'the standards for initiating a search of a person at the boarding gate should be no more stringent than those applied in border crossing situations'. This is unconvincing, because border search procedures are used to search people before they enter the country and do not extend to those who travel within. (But it should be noted that the *Skipwith* court did not *mechanically* transfer the broad power to search people and effects at the border to internal airports. Instead, it weighed a number of factors, principally the need to prevent air piracy, the acknowledged efficacy of airport security procedures and the fact that airport searches (not unlike border ones) are considerably less offensive than searches conducted elsewhere, and concluded that *because* of all these considerations it was reasonable to allow searches of 'those who actually present themselves for boarding on an air carrier, like those seeking entrance into the country' on the basis of 'mere or unsupported suspicion'. This reasoning is similar to that employed by those courts which have applied to airport searches the standards developed in the context

relied on *Terry v. Ohio*. An important fact to remember is that, although all passengers today are subjected to examination by the magnetometer and a search of their hand-luggage, when first adopted the anti-hijacking system involved no mandatory procedure for screening all passengers but rather the administration of a series of screening techniques, starting with the use of the behavioural profile and continuing with the magnetometer; only when a passenger was designated a 'selectee' by these (consecutive) 'screening' techniques, first by fitting the profile, then by activating the magnetometer and finally by failing to satisfy the authorities that he was not carrying a weapon on board, was he required to submit his carry-on luggage and his person to a more intrusive search. On the basis of *Terry v. Ohio* constitutional evaluation of the early anti-hijacking (behavioural profile—magnetometer-interrogation—frisk) system proceeded as follows: What *Terry* demands is that in certain areas where the warrant requirement cannot apply the reasonableness of official action must be measured by balancing the *need* to search against the *invasion* which the search entails; more specifically, two questions have to be asked, first whether the facts available to the officer at the moment of the search or seizure would justify a man of reasonable caution in the belief that the action taken was appropriate, and secondly whether the intrusion entailed by the search was confined to what was necessary to ensure not only the safety of the investigating officer but also the safety of others, whether, in short, the scope of the search was consistent with the purpose for which it was initiated. It is this type of balancing, according to many cases,[1] that must also be conducted in the context of airport searches. Courts must first determine what objective evidence was available to the officer that the particular passenger was armed and dangerous, and then decide whether the action he took, for instance a frisk, was justified both in its initiation and in its scope. Statistical evidence shows that there is a certain degree of probability that any person attempting to board a plane may have a weapon. If now a passenger satisfies the psychological profile, activates the magnetometer and does not dispel the apprehensions of the authorities the risk that he is armed increases considerably, justifiable and articulable suspicion focuses on him, and a frisk for weapons becomes permissible.[2] It should be noted that, strictly speaking, this type of analysis only sanctions a *limited* pat-down or frisk for weapons *after* satisfaction of the earlier steps of the screening procedure,

---

of administrative searches). Another theory that has not attracted much support is that passengers consent to airport searches. The reason for this is that 'consent' can only amount to a waiver of Fourth Amendment rights if '(it) was, in fact, freely and voluntarily given' (*Bumper v. North Carolina*, 391 U.S. 543, 548 (1968)); and '(c)ompelling the defendant to choose between exercising Fourth Amendment rights and his right to travel constitutes coercion' (*United States v. Kroll*, 481 F. 2d 884 (1973)). But in a special situation the facts may support a finding of express consent, as in *United States v. Legato*, 480 F. 2d 408 (1973), but *Legato*, it must be noted, did not arise in the course of a normal airport search.

[1] See *United States v. Lopez*, 328 F. Supp. 1077 (1971); *United States v. Bell*, 464 F. 2d 667 (1972); *United States v. Albarado*, 495 F. 2d 799 (1974).

[2] See *United States v. Lopez*, supra.

mainly activation of the magnetometer; it can justify neither general use of the magnetometer, routine frisks or automatic searches of carry-on luggage, nor general searches after activation of the magnetometer. The first point raises the question of the applicability of *Terry v. Ohio* to indiscriminate and routine examinations of persons, whether by magnetometer or by frisks, and of effects, and will be discussed shortly. As to the second matter, many cases emphasise both the *limited* nature of the frisk and that it should only be used as *a last resort*, only when 'no lesser readily available means presently exists for determining what unexplained metal object remains on the passenger's person'.[1] This strict approach means, first that before a passenger who has activated the magnetometer before boarding an airplane can be frisked other less intrusive means, such as questioning, for discovering the location and identity of the activating metal must be exhausted, and secondly that, even when initiated, a frisk must be strictly limited by the objective of discovering weapons. It was therefore held in *United States v. Albarado*[2] that a frisk of the defendant immediately after he activated the magnetometer, rather than requesting him to remove metal objects from his person and walk through the device a second time, was unlawful in that the overall search was not as limited in its obtrusiveness as it might (and should) have been; and the principle that an airport search can only be constitutionally reasonable if it is as limited as possible in order to fulfil its function, that of discovering weapons and other dangerous substances that might cause harm when in the air, means that when the officer is looking for the item which activated the magnetometer he is not allowed to open a container which, as he knows, cannot contain the offending metal.[3] Similar reasoning prohibits a search of luggage *deposited* in the aircraft. It has been argued that such searches can be justified by the overwhelming public interest in effective protection against the threats posed by air piracy, but it has been held that special airport investigations can only come within *Terry v. Ohio* (in its airport version) if they continue until the officer satisfies himself that 'no harm would come from the *passengers* boarding the plane'[4] and go *no* further. It was therefore held in *United States v. Palazzo*[5] that the search of the defendants' checked luggage which was no longer under their control could not be justified under airport search standards; and since there were no exigent circumstances justifying an immediate warrantless search there had been a violation of Fourth Amendment rights.

What about general use of the magnetometer and automatic searches of carry-on luggage? The problem here is that all are subjected to these, unlike the frisk which under most airport security procedures is only administered to those who either by activating the magnetometer or by manifesting other suspicious signs have exhibited the degree of danger considered sufficient to

[1] *United States v. Albarado*, 495 F. 2d 799 (1974); see also *United States v. Epperson*, 454 F. 2d at 772.

[2] 495 F. 2d 799 (1974).

[3] Ibid.; see also *United States v. Kroll*, 481 F. 2d 884 (1973).

[4] *United States v. Cyzewski*, 484 F. 2d 509 (1973).

[5] 488 F. 2d 942 (1974). Compare *Palazzo* with *Cyzewski*, supra, where a different result was reached upon 'dubious' grounds (La Fave, supra, at 357 n.97).

bring *Terry v. Ohio* into operation. Some have still attempted to apply *Terry*, as follows. There is a degree of probability that any person boarding a plane has a weapon; this by itself would not justify official action in other contexts, particularly if it is as intrusive as a thorough search of private belongings or a frisk; but in the airport security context there are two differences. First, the governmental interest at stake, that of preventing air piracy, is of overwhelming importance and comfortably outweighs the governmental interest in *Terry*, that of disarming a criminal and preventing criminal activity that may be afoot; secondly, airport searches, whether applications of the magnetometer, automatic frisks or inspections of carry-on luggage, are inherently less objectionable and offensive than comparable intrusions in other contexts, not only because at airports individuals are searched as a result of 'their membership in a morally neutral class' and therefore 'have less cause to feel insulted',[1] but also because '(airport) searches are made under supervision and not far from the scrutiny of the travelling public'.[2] There is therefore no need for individualised suspicion before there can be a search whether of the person or of effects. On this view of *Terry*, determination of what is reasonable must be based on 'a weighing of the harm against the need'.[3] When the object of the search is simply the detection of past crime probable cause is required; when criminal activity is threatened, as in *Terry* itself, a lower standard prevails; and '(w)hen the risk is the jeopardy to hundreds of human lives and millions of dollars of property inherent in the pirating or blowing up of a large airplane, the danger *alone* meets the test of reasonableness, so long as the search is conducted in good faith for the purpose of preventing hijacking or like damage and with reasonable scope'.[4] But applications of *Terry* to validate currently used airport security procedures, especially routine searches of persons by the magnetometer and the compulsory search of all hand luggage and other carry-on items, *solely* on the basis of either statistical probability or the magnitude of the feared danger do not carry much conviction. The reason why has been explained persuasively in *United States v. Davis*.[5] If the Supreme Court made one thing clear in the 'stop-and-frisk' cases it is that the officer's right to conduct a frisk depends upon his possession of specific and articulable facts sufficient to satisfy a reasonably prudent person that the *particular* individual is armed and dangerous. 'To justify a stop-and-frisk (or other restraint) the government must focus on *each* person and demonstrate that as to *that* individual there is *specific* cause to fear the justifying harm'.[6] Airport

[1] 'Note, Border Searches and the Fourth Amendment', 77 *Yale L.J.* 1007, 1014 (1968).

[2] *United States v. Skipwith*, 482 F. 2d 1272 (1973).

[3] *United States v. Bell*, 464 F. 2d 667 (1972), per Friendly, J. concurring.

[4] Ibid. Mansfield, J., also concurring in *Bell*, supra, disagreed with Friendly, J.'s position. He did not share the view that airplane hijacking, however grave the threat it posed, justified 'a broad and intrusive search of all passengers', limited only by 'the good faith of those conducting the search' and 'regardless of the absence of grounds for suspecting that *the passengers searched* are potential hijackers'.

[5] 482 F. 2d 893 (1973).

[6] Ibid., at 906.

screening procedures cannot meet this standard because, with the exception of the frisk *when* conducted as a last resort, that is after satisfaction of a number of other steps increasing the probability of danger *as to the particular individual*, they are indiscriminate, not directed against any particular person as such but rather against the general introduction of weapons or explosives into a restricted area.

If *Terry's* authorisation of limited intrusions cannot be separated from the requirement that there should be specific facts establishing reasonable cause to believe that the individual who is stopped and searched is committing or is about to commit an offence and is armed and dangerous, how should airport searches be evaluated? According to *Davis*[1] and other cases, the appropriate standards for the constitutional assessment of airport security programmes are to be derived from the Supreme Court cases dealing with administrative inspections. The essence of these decisions, it will be remembered, is that searches conducted in furtherance of a valid administrative purpose rather than as part of a criminal investigation to secure evidence of crime may be permissible even though not supported by a showing of probable cause directed to the particular place or person to be searched. Similarly, screening searches of airline passengers are conducted as part of a general regulatory scheme in furtherance of a valid (and compelling) administrative purpose, namely to prevent the carrying of weapons or explosives aboard aircraft and in this way prevent hijackings. 'The *essential* purpose of the scheme is not to detect weapons or explosives or to apprehend those who carry them, but to deter persons carrying such material from seeking to board at all.'[2] Airport searches of course, like other administrative inspections, must be 'reasonable', and constitutional reasonableness can only be determined by balancing the need to search against the invasion which the search entails. As to the former, there can be no question that the need to prevent hijacking is grave and urgent. Equally, even though administrative searches must be as limited in their intrusiveness as is consistent with satisfaction of the governmental need that justifies them in the first place, a pre-boarding screening of all passengers and a search of carry-on luggage sufficient in scope to detect the presence of weapons or explosives appear to be necessary to meet the need of preventing incidents of air piracy, mainly because there is as yet no satisfactory method of confining the search to those who are potential hijackers.[3] It appears therefore that airport security procedures have in general been upheld by reference to a combination of the *Terry* rationale and the doctrines derivable from the cases on administrative inspections—the general use of the magnetometer and the automatic search of hand luggage are constitutional

[1] 482 F. 2d 893 (1973).

[2] Ibid., at 908.

[3] There is no need to obtain a warrant for this type of administrative search. The basic reason why a warrant was ordered in *Camara*, 387 U.S. at 532, according to *Davis*, supra, was that if no warrant was required premises would be searched at the discretion of the official in the field. But this would not be the case with regard to the general and indiscriminate airport procedures required by current regulations. Further, the practical effect of a warrant requirement in the context of airport searches would be 'to frustrate the governmental purpose' at stake.

because they are an essential component of a valid regulatory scheme necessitated by compelling policy considerations, and the limited frisk conducted as the last step of a process of gradual investigation is permissible under *Terry v. Ohio* because by the time it is undertaken justifiable suspicion supported by objective indications of danger has focused on the particular individual. But whatever the precise theory one thing is undeniable. Because of the gravity of the problem the airport is 'a critical zone in which special fourth amendment considerations apply'.[1]

[1] *United States v. Moreno*, 475 F. 2d 44 (1973).

6. The Common Law of Search and Seizure

The common law of search and seizure, much like our treatment of the Fourth Amendment, can be discussed in terms of three broad categories. First, has a search or seizure taken place? Secondly, if it has, is it lawful? And thirdly, what may be seized during an otherwise lawful search? The first question, in striking contrast to American experience, has not been regarded as particularly troublesome;[1] the third has long been shrouded in obscurity and unclear thought;[2] and traditionally, as was also the case with most decisions on the Fourth Amendment before the doctrinal revolution of 1967,[3] it is the second question that has commanded the most attention. The broad principle here is that which derives from *Entick v. Carrington*,[4] namely that every invasion of private property, however slight, is a trespass and that no person has the right to enter and search except by consent or in accordance with some lawful authorisation. It follows that every search of private property by a police officer is unlawful unless it is capable of justification by reference to some recognised and accepted legal ground.[5] In the case of searches, as we shall see, the necessary element of legality will derive either from a warrant issued under a statute or from a statutory authorisation to conduct searches without warrant or from some common law doctrine, for

[1] See now *Malone v. M.P.C.* (No. 2), (1979) 2 All E.R. 620.

[2] See *R. v. Waterfield*, (1964) 1 Q.B. 164; *Ghani v. Jones*, (1970) 1 Q.B. 693; *Elias v. Pasmore*, (1934) 2 K.B. 164; *Chic Fashions (West Wales) Ltd. v. Jones*, (1968) 2 Q.B. 299.

[3] See *Katz v. United States*, 389 U.S. 347 (1967).

[4] (1765) 19 State Tr. 1029.

[5] What has been said about *searches* also applies to *entries*. A constable has no general right of entry into private property for the purpose of investigating crime, questioning persons and the like. It is fundamental doctrine that there is no right to enter private property except by consent or on the basis of some applicable legal ground, and this applies to police officers as well as to private persons (see *Morris v. Beardmore*, (1980) 2 All E.R. 753). Broadly speaking, a constable may validly enter private property under the provisions of a particular statute conferring the right to enter without warrant (but statutes will be strictly construed and normally a right of entry will not be read into a statute by implication but must be given expressly: *Morris v. Beardmore*, supra); or in order to effect an arrest (see particularly s. 2(6) of the Criminal Law Act 1967); or under a search warrant validly issued under a statute; or under the common law (for instance the doctrine associated with *Thomas v. Sawkins*, (1935) 2 K.B. 249 which allows police officers to enter premises to prevent a breach of the peace or perhaps to prevent the commission of any offence which is believed to be imminent or likely to be committed (per Lord Hewart, C.J. in *Thomas v. Sawkins*, ibid., at 255)). Various statutes also authorise the issuing of warrants of entry: see the Food and Drug Act 1955, s. 100(2)–(4); the Control of Pollution Act 1974, s. 91, etc.

instance the accepted principle that the police have the power to engage in certain types of warrantless search incidental to a valid arrest.

(a) What are 'searches' and 'seizures'?

We have seen that the right to be free from illegal searches has been interpreted by the American Supreme Court to mean the right not to have one's reasonable expectations of privacy invaded by governmental intrusions not authorised by properly drawn warrants. A search within the meaning of the Fourth Amendment, in other words, is not a physical invasion of some protected space but any governmental violation that significantly encroaches upon a person's reasonable expectations of privacy, whatever the form it takes. English law has not gone the same way, has refused to extrapolate from the law of search and seizure rights or notions of privacy, however limited, and has continued to insist on the presence of a physical invasion of private property before legal protection in the form of a warrant can be extended. The law of search and seizure, in other words, only applies when there has been a trespass, namely a physical intrusion into a protected space. In *Malone v. Commissioner of Police (No. 2)*,[1] the plaintiff, an antique dealer, was tried on a number of offences of handling stolen property. During the trial the prosecution counsel stated that the plaintiff's telephone had been tapped on behalf of the police on the authority of a warrant issued by the Secretary of State. Police practice regarding telephone tapping (i.e. the interception, monitoring and recording of private telephone conversations) was to obtain a warrant to tap from the Home Secretary; the warrant was sent to the Post Office and the Post Office then made a recording of conversations on the line being tapped and forwarded that recording to the police. The plaintiff issued a writ against the police claiming, among other things, that the tapping of his telephone without his consent was unlawful, partly on the ground that he had rights of property, privacy and confidentiality with regard to telephone conversations on his telephone lines which the challenged tapping had infringed. Sir Robert Megarry, V-C, dismissed the plaintiff's claim because no rights belonging to him had been infringed. In other words, the police were entitled to have a telephone tapped by methods which did not involve any trespass or other breach of the law. The plaintiff had relied first on early search and seizure precedents and secondly on more recent American developments such as *Katz v. United States*.[2] The learned judge rejected both types of argument. First, he did not think that the plaintiff could derive assistance from the general warrant cases such as *Entick v. Carrington*[3] or from any other English search and seizure cases. It was true that many statutes authorised searches under search warrants for many different purposes; and there was admittedly no statute which in terms authorised the tapping of telephones, with or without a warrant. Nevertheless, any conclusion that the tapping of telephones was therefore illegal was 'plainly

[1] (1979) 2 All E.R. 620.
[2] 389 U.S. 347 (1967).
[3] (1765) 19 St. Tr. 1030.

superficial in the extreme'. The reason why a search of premises which was not authorised by law was illegal was that it involved the tort of trespass to those premises: and any trespass, whether to land or goods or the person, made without legal authority was prima facie illegal. Telephone tapping by the Post Office, on the other hand, involved no act of trespass. The subscriber would speak into his telephone, and the process of tapping appeared to be carried out by Post Office officials making recordings, with Post Office apparatus on Post Office premises, of the electrical impulses on Post Office wires provided by Post Office electricity. There was no question of there being any trespass to the plaintiff's premises for the purpose of attaching anything either to the premises themselves or to anything on them; all that had been done was done within the Post Office's own domain. Lord Camden, C.J., in *Entick v. Carrington* had said that the eye could not by the laws of England be guilty of trespass.[1] Nor, Sir Robert Megarry, V-C, added, could the ear.[2] Since there had been no trespass, existing English search and seizure precedents did not apply. But, secondly, could the plaintiff rely on some type of right to privacy like the one developed in *Katz v. United States* by the American Supreme Court? The learned judge's answer was that he could not. The reason was simple. There was in English law neither a general right of privacy nor a particular right of privacy regarding the holding of a telephone conversation without molestation, and therefore telephone tapping by the Post Office could not amount to a breach of such rights. The Fourth Amendment was regarded by Sir Robert Megarry as very 'different'. It was part of a Constitution, and therefore had special force. There was no statute in England which in any way resembled it. 'If there were such a statute here, it might indeed be that it would be construed in something like the same way.' But there was not. Though mainly based on the old English cases like *Entick v. Carrington* the Fourth Amendment went 'far beyond' anything to be found in those cases; and *Katz v. United States* was explicitly based on the Fourth Amendment. The learned judge did not therefore think that either the Fourth Amendment or *Katz* and similar cases gave 'any real assistance' when one was considering the law of England. In the result, since it was a common law principle that everything was permitted except that which was expressly forbidden, telephone tapping carried on without a trespass by the Post Office was not unlawful. It followed that telephone tapping involving no breach of the law did not require any statutory or common law power to justify it.[3]

To sum up, in English law protection from illegal searches and seizures can only be invoked when there has been a trespass; a 'search' is defined narrowly, as a trespassory intrusion into premises or other protected places; and practices such as telephone tapping, other types of electronic eavesdropping, and the like can lawfully be carried on so long as there is neither a trespass nor any other legal infraction. In similar fashion 'seizures' in English law refer to

[1] Ibid., at 1006. [2] (1979) 2 All E.R. 620 at 640.

[3] For a description of existing practice (mainly regulation by a system of warrants issued by the Home Secretary), see the Government's *White Paper* issued in April 1980 on the *Interception of Communications in Great Britain* (Cmnd. 5012) and the *Report* of the Royal Commission on Criminal Procedure (Cmnd. 8092), at paras. 3.53–3.60. For recommendations concerning reform, see *Report,* supra.

the seizure of tangible objects. Conversations cannot therefore be seized because there is no right of property in words, as distinct from any copyright in them.[1]

(b) Seizures of the person

In contrast to America, where all restraints on liberty and intrusions upon security, be they searches or arrests, are dealt with under the Fourth Amendment, at common law arrests and searches are treated separately. But in the result the rules for arrest in England and the principal Commonwealth jurisdictions are not dissimilar, at least in terms of doctrinal basis and concepts, to those observed under the Fourth Amendment.[2] Under both the Amendment and the common law an arrest is normally the prelude to the setting in motion of the process of prosecution[3] and can broadly be defined as the involuntary seizure of a person that not only involves deprivation of liberty but which also represents an intentional exercise of an authority to arrest and has been attended by certain formalities, principally notification of the reasons for the arrest;[4] in both cases arrests may be made with or without warrant;[5] and arrests must normally be made on the basis of reasonable grounds to believe that the person placed under restraint has committed a criminal offence.[6]

Is there a distinction between arrest and (lawful) detention?[7] In other words, do the police have authority to detain a person for questioning when they have no right to arrest him because they do not as yet have the requisite level of suspicion furnishing reasonable cause to believe that he has committed an offence? We have seen what the American position is. Arrest must be supported by probable cause. But the police also have the power to stop a person whom they reasonably suspect either of being armed and dangerous or of being involved in unfolding criminal activity and to question

[1] See *Malone v. M.P.C.* (No. 2), (1979) 2 All E.R. 620 at 631 and 640.

[2] See Karlen, *Anglo-American Criminal Justice* 107–14 (1967).

[3] This is basically Blackstone's definition. 'Arrest is the apprehending or restraining of one's person in order to be forthcoming to answer an alleged or suspected crime': 4 Bl. Comm. 289. Others take a wider approach, and simply define an arrest as the deprivation of one's liberty to go where he pleases. See *Spicer v. Holt* (1977) A.C. 987, 1000, per Viscount Dilhorne, and Halsbury's *Laws of England* (4th ed.) vol. 2, at 73, para. 9. See also *R. v. Brown* (1977) R.T.R. 160; *R. v. Inwood* (1973) 1 W.L.R. 647, 652–3, per Stephenson, L.J.; and Lidstone (1978) *Crim. L. R.* 332.

[4] See *Christie v. Leachinsky* (1947) A.C. 573; *R. v. Brown* (1977) R.T.R. 160; (1976) 64 Cr. App. R. 231; see also Zander (1977) *N.L.J.* 352, 379; Telling (1978) *Crim. L. R.* 320; Clarke and Feldam (1979) *Crim. L. R.* 702.

[5] See generally L. Leigh, *Police Powers in England and Wales* 60–103 (1975).

[6] Karlen, supra, at 108–11.

[7] Ibid., at 114–21; see also Williams, 'Police Detention and Arrest Privileges under Foreign Law—England', *J. Crim. L., C. & P.S.* 413 (1960); Remington, 'The Law Relating to "On-The-Street" Detention, Questioning and Frisking of Suspected Persons and Police Arrest Privileges in General', 51 *J. Crim. L., C. & P.S.* 386 (1960); Foot, 'The Fourth Amendment: Obstacle or Necessity in the Law of Arrest?', 51 *J. Crim. L., C. & P.S.* 402 (1960); Leagre, 'The Fourth Amendment and the Law of Arrest', 54 *J. Crim. L., C. & P.S.* 393 (1963).

him briefly in order either to decide whether to arrest him or to obtain an account of his movements and suspicious activity. *Terry*[1] and its progeny only authorise brief investigative stops. Detention for custodial interrogation is different. It intrudes so severely on interests protected by the Fourth Amendment, and so closely resembles an arrest, that it must be subjected to the normal safeguards for arrests, principally the standard of probable cause.[2]

What about the common law? The traditional view is that there is no police power to detain any person for questioning, or to restrain his liberty in any other way, otherwise than by the process of arrest. 'In law', as it has been put in an Irish case,[3] 'there can be no half-way house between the liberty of the subject, unfettered by restraint, and an arrest.' Police officers may of course ask questions of any person, seek his co-operation and ask him to accompany them to the police station so that he can 'help them with their inquiries'. But if a person is approached and asked questions by a police officer he is free to refuse to answer them, and if a person under suspicion, but who has not yet been arrested, agrees to go to the police station so that he can be questioned, he is free to change his mind and leave.[4] In other words, three principles represent the traditional common law position. There is no form of *lawful* restraint or detention short of or other than arrest; the expression and vocabulary of 'detention' have no legal meaning or justification in law; and this means that in law detention (in the sense of either restraint on liberty, whether on the street or elsewhere, or nonvoluntary confinement at a police station) amounts to arrest so that if the police have taken a person into custody or restricted his liberty in any other way they must be prepared either to justify their action as an arrest or to pay damages for trespass or false imprisonment.[5] Traditional common law formulations, it will be seen, do not draw a distinction between two types of situation which, as American experience shows, are very different. The first is the *Terry* situation, where the police see someone behaving suspiciously and wish to stop him so that they can ask him a question or two and resolve the ambiguities in the situation. The second is where the police wish not to stop an individual in the street for brief questioning but to take him for interrogation to the police station, where he is less likely to be distracted and where he can be held while the police

[1] *Terry v. Ohio*, 392 U.S. 1 (1968).

[2] *Dunaway v. New York*, 442 U.S. 200 (1979).

[3] *Dunne v. Clinton* (1930) I.R. 366.

[4] See Zander (1977) *N.L.J.* 352, 379; Ashworth (1976) *Crim. L.R.* 594; Lanham (1974) *Crim. L.R.* 288. A significant case here is *Rice v. Connolly* (1966) 2 All E.R. 649 holding that when a police officer asks a question the citizen has no legal duty to answer. In other words, the police officer has no power to require answers. This seems a strong authority on the question of the existence of a power to detain, for, as Zander ((1977) *N.L.J.* 379, 380) puts it, 'if the police have no power to require answers to questions they equally have no right to detain someone for the purpose of asking questions'.

[5] See Lanham, supra; Zander, supra; Lord Devlin, *The Criminal Prosecution in England* 68 (1960); *Dunne v. Clinton* (1930) I.R. 366.

check his answers and make further inquiries.[1] In terms of policy, almost unanswerable arguments can be made that brief-on-the-street questioning and any form of custodial confinement must be distinguished sharply, but orthodox doctrine draws no distinction between them or between any other types of case except that between unrestrained liberty and arrest. As the Home Office itself has put it, '*(a)ny form* of restraint by a police officer—or indeed by anyone—is in law an imprisonment and if the police officer has acted wrongfully an action for false imprisonment will lie'.[2]

But recently there have been hints that the orthodox position no longer commands unquestioning allegiance, or at any rate that it is not insisted upon with the same uncompromising rigour.[3] The cases are confusing and uninformative. In *Kenlin v. Gardiner*[4] police officers attempted to restrain two boys who they thought were acting suspiciously. One officer tried to stop one of the boys from running away by taking hold of his arm. The boy struck back. It was held that the officer was not entitled to take hold of the boy because the attempt to restrain the boys had been done not as an integral step in the process of arresting them but in order to secure an opportunity, by detaining them, to question them so as to decide, in the light of the answers, whether to arrest them or not. This was not justifiable, and it followed that there had been a technical assault by the officers, which in turn meant that the boys were not guilty of assaulting the officers in the execution of their duty. *Kenlin v. Gardiner* appears to say clearly that police officers possess no common law power to detain for questioning, and that they must either arrest a person for an alleged offence or allow him to go away. But *Donnelly v. Jackman*[5] adopts a very different tone. A police officer approached the defendant who was walking along a pavement with a view to making inquiries about an offence which the officer believed he might have committed. The defendant ignored the officer's requests that he should stop. The officer tapped him on the shoulder, but the defendant only tapped him back. When it became clear that the defendant was not going to stop the officer touched him on the shoulder with the intention of stopping him (but without any intention to arrest him). The defendant then struck the officer with some force, and the question was whether the officer was at the time acting in the execution of his duty. The court's starting point was that it was 'part of the obligations and duties of a police constable to take all steps which appear(ed) to him necessary for keeping the peace, for preventing crime or for protecting property from criminal injury'[6] and its conclusion was that at the material time the officer was acting in the course of his duty and that nothing which he had done had brought him outside its ambit. What about *Kenlin v. Gardiner* and the argument that a police officer has no right to stop a person otherwise

[1] See Karlen, supra, at 114; *Dunaway v. New York*, 442 U.S. 200 (1979); Ashworth, supra, at 595.

[2] In a memorandum submitted to the Royal Commission on Police Powers in 1929 (Cmnd. 3297 at para. 148).

[3] See Zander (1977) *N.L.J.* 352, 379; Lanham (1974) *Crim. L.R.* 288.

[4] (1967) 2 Q.B. 510.

[5] (1970) 1 All E.R. 987.

[6] *Rice v. Connolly* (1966) 2 Q.B. 414, 419.

than by arrest? *Kenlin v. Gardiner* was 'vastly different', the court thought, 'because there the officers had taken hold' of the boys and 'had in fact detained' them.[1] In contrast, what had happened in the case before them was '(a) trivial interference with a citizen's liberty' which did not amount to a course of conduct sufficient to bring the officer outside the course of his duties. *Donnelly v. Jackman* is a difficult case to interpret, and there are a number of possible explanations, none of them very satisfactory.[2] One is that even though what had happened may have been a technical assault it was 'a minimal matter'[3] which was not enough to bring the officer outside the scope of his duty. Another possibility is that, whatever the best explanation of *Kenlin v. Gardiner*, *Donnelly v. Jackman* allows the police in a proper case to stop a suspect for questioning,[4] or at least to take minimal measures with a view to stopping him. These measures must not include physical detention, so that if the defendant in *Donnelly v. Jackman* had insisted on going on the police would have had either to arrest him or to let him walk away. Another possible interpretation, but one which is not easy to square with the facts, is that the police officer had only tapped the defendant on the shoulder in order to attract his attention so that he could put some questions to him.[5] This is either not unlawful or at any rate not sufficiently unlawful to bring such conduct outside the scope of police duties.

Another confusing case that shows the difficulties English courts are facing in dealing with cases of arrest and other restraints on liberty is *R. v. Brown*.[6] Two constables decided to stop a car so that they could speak to the driver about his speed. The defendant first refused to stop, but then stopped his car, got out and ran away. One of the constables followed him and brought him down with a tackle. He was then taken to the police car where he was ordered to take a breathalyzer test. Eventually a test was administered and proved positive, and the defendant was convicted on a charge of driving contrary to the Road Traffic Act. His argument was that he had been arrested when he was seized on the pavement (in which case the subsequent procedure would have been illegal) instead of at a later stage and in accordance with the necessary formalities under the Act (in which case alone would the statutory requirements have been complied with). The issue therefore concerned *the*

[1] (1970) 1 All E.R. at 989.

[2] See generally Lanham (1974) *Crim. L.R.* 288; Evans (1970) 33 *M.L.R.* 438.

[3] (1970) 1 All E.R. at 989; see Smith and Hogan, *Criminal Law* (4th ed.) 363 (1978). This seems also to be the view of *Pounder v. Police* (1971) N.Z.L.R. 1808.

[4] See Evans, supra, n. 2.

[5] Talbot J., at (1970) 1 All E.R. at 988, says that the officer touched the appellant 'with the intention of stopping him'. But in the next sentence he says that the finding of the lower court was that the officer had touched the appellant 'solely for the purpose of speaking to him', and this is repeated later, at 989, where the learned judge said that the officer 'went up to the appellant and wanted to speak to him'. This is the interpretation also supported by Smith and Hogan, supra, n. 3; see also Zander (1977) *N.L.J.* 379.

[6] (1976) 64 Cr. App. R. 231; (1977) R.T.R. 160. There is a lot of literature on this case; see Zander (1977) *N.L.J.* 352, 379; Smith (1977) *Crim. L.R.* 293; Lidstone (1978) *Crim. L.R.* 332; Telling (1978) *Crim. L.R.* 320; Clarke and Feldam (1979) *Crim. L.R.* 702.

time he was placed under arrest. The court, allowing the conviction to stand, held that the defendant was not under arrest when he was taken from the pavement where he had been seized to the police van. While every arrest involved a deprivation of liberty, not every deprivation of liberty involved an arrest. Arrest could only be effected in the exercise of an asserted authority, which was not the case here. What in fact had happened was that the officers had reacted to what they regarded as suspicious conduct by detaining the defendant for as long as might be necessary to confirm their general suspicions or to show them to be unfounded. 'In the first event they could then arrest him upon a specific charge; in the second event they would be bound to release him. *In either case, they may* have rendered themselves liable to pay damages for trespass and false imprisonment.'[1] This would appear to suggest that detention falling short of an arrest is unlawful; that any restraints on liberty before a suspect is arrested are also unlawful; and that unlawful detention cannot be excused by its outcome, for instance by the detainee being charged soon thereafter with an offence. But another report of the same case supports the diametrically opposite conclusion, that there is some type of power to restrain or detain otherwise than by way of arrest,[2] and indeed the cautious 'may' might suggest that a civil action for damages will not automatically follow any and all interferences with liberty that do not amount to lawful arrests.[3]

There are some other cases containing suggestions that tend to support the view that some forms of detention short of arrest may be lawful,[4] but these are clearly insufficient to disturb the established position to the contrary.[5] Particularly clear is the position when there has been not some minor restraint of or interference with a person on the street but detention or confinement at the police station. As it was recently emphasised by Lawton L.J. in *R. v.*

[1] (1976) 64 Cr. App. R. 231, 235.

[2] This is the version of the Criminal Appeal Reports. The Road Traffic Reports are very different. Shaw, L.J. is reported as saying: 'In the first event they could then arrest him as a specific charge; in the second event they would be bound to release him, having perhaps rendered themselves liable to pay damages for trespass and false imprisonment as in *Dunne v. Clinton*'. This, in its contrast between the two situations, clearly implies that involuntary detention is retrospectively validated (see also *Elias v. Pasmore* (1934) 2 K.B. 164) if the officers finally arrest the detainee. In other words, this version of *Brown* comes close to giving the police power to detain (briefly) for purposes of questioning. It was strongly criticised by Zander, supra, at 382. As Clarke and Feldam, supra, have pointed out, the actual transcript of the case seems to bear out the Road Traffic Reports, but what seems to have happened is that the court may have realised the implications of its decision and corrected it before publication in the Criminal Appeal Reports (for another example of this, see *Ghani v. Jones* (1970) 1 Q.B. 693; see also Jackson (1970) *C.L.J.* 1, 3). The Criminal Appeal Reports version is therefore preferable, all the more so because the authority the court cited in support of the Road Traffic Reports formulation, *Dunne v. Clinton*, seems to be quite inconsistent with it (see Clarke and Feldam, supra, at 705).

[3] Clarke and Feldam, supra, at 705.

[4] See *Squires v. Botwright* (1972) R.T.R. 462; see Lanham (1974) *Crim. L.R.* 288, 292; Zander, supra, at 380–1.

[5] The cases are analysed by Zander.

Lemsatef,[1] 'it must be clearly understood that . . . police officers (do not) have any right to detain somebody for the purposes of getting (him) to help with their inquiries. Police officers either arrest for an offence or they do not arrest at all', in which case the person 'helping the police with their inquiries' can simply walk away.

Overall therefore, and despite *Donnelly v. Jackman* and some other aberrant dicta, the common law recognises no power apart from arrest either to restrain an individual on the street or to detain him for questioning. There is no legally[2] recognised intermediate state between unfettered liberty and arrest,[3] and therefore any form of restraint must be justifiable as an arrest,[4] with the possible exception of certain very minor forms of compulsion falling well short of detention which are either not unlawful or at least do not have the result of taking the police outside the course of their duty.[5]

[1] (1977) 1 W.L.R. 812, 816; see also *R. v. Inwood* (1973) 2 All E.R. 645.

[2] Reality does not exactly correspond with the legal position. As it was well put by Ashworth (1976) *Crim. L.R.* 594, 595, 'the ominous phrase "helping the police with their inquiries" connotes far less voluntariness than its almost Samaritan terminology suggests'.

[3] Leigh, *Police Powers in England and Wales* 35 (1975).

[4] See Lord Devlin, *The Criminal Prosecution in England* 68 (1960).

[5] See Lanham (1974) *Crim. L.R.* 288, 296, and Evans, 33 *M.L.R.* 438, 440. But, as Lanham puts it, surely correctly, it is not easy to reconcile on a principled basis *Donnelly v. Jackman* with *Kenlin v. Gardiner*. The issue, surely, is whether there has been illegal conduct on the part of the police, not whether what was involved was 'detention' (*Kenlin*) or 'touching' (*Donnelly*). Of course it is perfectly clear that there are many instances where actions that would otherwise amount to assaults or other civil wrongs can legally be justified without invoking the rules of arrest (see Lanham, 'Arrest, Detention and Compulsion' (1974) *Crim. L.R.* 288). One of the most prominent examples is s.3(1) of the Criminal Law Act 1967, which provides that 'a person may use such *force* as is reasonable in the circumstances in the prevention of crime, or in effecting or assisting in the lawful arrest of offenders or suspected offenders or of persons unlawfully at large'. The first part is particularly important, in that it apparently allows the police to restrain an individual whom they reasonably believe to be about to commit a crime. This preventive function of the police was analysed in *Albert v. Lavin* (*The Times*, December 4, 1980) where the Divisional Court said that it was clear law that a police officer, reasonably believing that a breach of the peace was about to take place, was entitled to take such steps as were necessary to prevent it, including the use of reasonable force; if now those steps included physical restraint it was not an unlawful detention but a reasonable use of force. It was a question of fact and degree when a restraint had continued for so long that there must be either a release or an arrest. On the facts before the court that point had not been reached. Obviously, the court also said, where a constable was restraining someone to prevent a breach of the peace he must release (or arrest) him as soon as the restrained person no longer presented a danger to the peace. 'Restraint' or 'detention' in other words is justifiable if it constitutes a step taken to prevent a breach of the peace. The distinction between this type of case on the one hand and *Kenlin v. Gardiner* (1967) 2 Q.B. 510 and the other cases establishing that there is no right to detain otherwise than by arrest on the other corresponds to the distinction between, at the one end, investigation of past criminal behaviour and, at the other, preventing future breaches of the law. The line between the two is not always very clear. And it may not be a very long time before similar principles are developed allowing temporary restraint and detention on investigatory rather than preventive grounds. After all, *Terry v. Ohio* (392 U.S. 1 (1968)) itself is more of a

(c) Patterns of statutory search

At common law the basic principle is that a person's home is inviolable. As it was put in *Semayne's Case*,[1] 'the house of everyone is to him as his castle and fortress, as well for his defence against injury and violence, as for his repose'.[2] The only exception to the inviolability (from official search) of the private home at common law is the issuing of warrants for stolen goods.[3] In no other case was a constable allowed to enter and search a man's house. Obviously this principle has been considerably modified by statute.[4] 'The integrity and privacy of a man's home and of his place of business' are of course still recognised as 'important human right(s)',[5] but the compelling interest in effective law enforcement and the achievement of other policy objectives has resulted in the enactment of numerous statutes conferring extensive powers of search and seizure.

Two broad kinds of statutory authority to issue warrants of entry and search can be distinguished.[6] The first is general, applicable to all categories of offences; the other is specific, confined to one type of offence. The former

prevention than an investigation case (even though, as we have seen, the Supreme Court took great pains to address not the issue of 'seizure' but that of the 'frisk for weapons' (see 392 U.S. at 23)); now *Terry* is recognised as acknowledging the permissibility of the power to stop otherwise than by way of arrest in a variety of contexts, both investigative and preventive (see A.L.I., *Model Code of Pre-Arraignment Procedure*, Section 110.2 (1975)).

[1] (1604) 5 Co. Rep. 91a at 91b.

[2] This same sentiment was given classic exposition by William Pitt: 'The poorest man may in his cottage bid defiance to all the forces of the Crown. It may be frail—its roof may shake—the wind may blow through it—the storm may enter—the rain may enter—but the King of England cannot enter—all his force dares not cross the threshold of the ruined tenement'. But even at the early time of *Semayne's Case*, as Dickson J. has reminded us in *Eccles v. Bourque*, (1975) 1 *W. W.R.* 609 at 611, it was recognised that 'the interest of a private individual in the security of his house must yield to the public interest, when the public at large has an interest in the process to be executed'. The criminal was not immune from arrest in his own home nor in the house of one of his friends. For these reasons a clear limitation was put on the 'castle' concept; as the Court in *Semayne's Case* put it, '(i)n all cases when the King is party, the sheriff (if the doors be not open) may break the party's house, either to arrest him, or to do other execution of the K's process, if otherwise he cannot enter. But before he breaks it, he ought to signify the cause of his coming, and to make request to open doors'. See *Eccles v. Bourque*, supra.

[3] See *Chic Fashions (West Wales) Ltd. v. Jones*, (1968) 2 Q.B. 299 at 307.

[4] Ibid., at 308.

[5] *Inland Revenue Comrs. v. Rossminster Ltd.*, (1980) 1 All E.R. 80 at 82, per Lord Wilberforce. In *Morris v. Beardmore*, (1980) 2 All E.R. 753 at 763 Lord Scarman characterised the right of privacy in the home as 'fundamental'. His Lordship acknowledged that this adjective had 'an unfamiliar ring in the ears of common lawyers', but he justified his characterisation on two grounds. First, it was apt to describe the importance attached by the common law to the privacy of the home (*Entick v. Carrington*, (1765) 19 State Tr. 1029 at 1066); secondly, the right enjoyed the protection of the European Convention for the Protection of Human Rights and Fundamental Freedoms which the United Kingdom had ratified.

[6] See generally Thomas, 'The Law of Search and Seizure: Further Ground for Rationalisation', (1967) *Crim. L.R.* 3; Leigh, *Police Powers in England and Wales* 175–96 (1975).

is illustrated by a number of comprehensive Commonwealth 'warrant' statutes. Good examples are section 10 of the Commonwealth Crimes Act 1914–1973 (Australia),[1] section 198 of the Summary Proceedings Act 1957 (New Zealand)[2] and section 443(1) of the Criminal Code, 1970 revision (Canada).[3] The basic pattern of all these is the same. If a magistrate is satisfied by information on oath that there is reasonable ground for believing or suspecting that there is in any place

(a) anything upon or with respect to which any offence (against the particular jurisdiction) has been, or is suspected (on reasonable grounds) to have been, committed; or
(b) anything which there is reasonable ground to believe will be evidence as to the commission of any such offence; or
(c) anything which there is reasonable ground to believe is intended to be used for the purpose of committing any such offence,

then he (the magistrate) may issue a warrant authorising a person named in it (invariably a police officer) to search the place in question for any such thing and to seize and carry it before the appropriate judicial authority. This is a general power to issue search warrants in connection with all types of offences (at times only if they are of a particular degree of seriousness).[4] Briefly, if there are reasonable grounds to believe that certain things (whether stolen goods, criminal instrumentalities or other evidentiary items) affording evidence as to the commission of a particular offence against the law of the jurisdiction in question are located and can be found on certain premises, and these grounds are shown to the magistrate, he may issue a warrant in connection with the offence alleged authorising the requested seizure.

The second type of authority to issue search warrants is the authority that is conferred by a particular statute for a particular offence. Examples abound both in England and the Commonwealth. The important point to notice is that this limited statutory authority is the only type that exists in English law. The implication of the absence of a comprehensive code for the issuance of search warrants is that in situations not covered by the existing statutory provisions no warrant can be issued. Thus, since a search warrant can only be issued under express statutory authority, and since no statute authorises a magistrate to issue a search warrant in the case of murder, in England a search warrant cannot be issued 'to dig for the body, (nor) to look for the axe, the gun, or the poison dregs'.[5] The only legitimate way police officers can enter premises to look for a murder weapon or some other evidence of an offence not dealt with by a statute is to obtain the consent of the householder.

[1] This is analysed extensively in *R. v. Tillett, ex parte Newton*, (1969) 14 F.L.R. 101.

[2] For an extended analysis, see *Medical Aid Trust v. Taylor*, (1975) 1 N.Z.L.R. 728.

[3] *R.S.C.* 1970, c. C-34; see *Re Purdy and The Queen*, (1972) 28 D.L.R. (3d) 720.

[4] Under the New Zealand provision the offence must be one 'punishable by imprisonment'.

[5] *Ghani v. Jones*, (1970) 1 Q.B. 693 at 705, per Lord Denning M.R,; but see now *Ghani v. Jones*, supra, and *Wershof v. M.P.C.* (1978) 3 All E.R. 540.

The only other way is if they commit trespass, which they apparently often do.[1] '(T)hat justices may order the forcible entry of private premises for the seizure of pirated music . . . but cannot issue a warrant to search premises where the disjecta membra of a human being, suspected of being feloniously murdered, may be concealed'[2] has attracted universal criticism, but nothing has yet been done to change it.

For this same reason it is almost impossible to give an adequate summary of the English law of search and seizure. Instead of a coherent framework based on the one hand on a comprehensive statutory authority to issue search warrants in the case of all offences and on the other on clear judicial principles demarcating the limits of accepted powers of search and providing guidance both to police officers searching for evidence of crime and to citizens who may wish to resist unauthorised invasions of their homes and offices and the illegal seizure of their property, English law consists of a mass of separate and widely differing statutory provisions, punctuated by serious gaps, such as murder, and supplemented by confusing judicial decisions, some of which will be studied shortly, which usually raise more problems than they solve.[3]

The various statutes which authorise the issuing of search warrants have many differences and similarities. The main similarity relates to the usual procedure leading to the issuing of a search warrant. Thus the typical statute requires the police officer seeking a warrant to put evidence before the magistrate, usually in the form of a written complaint or information, which provides reasonable grounds to believe that evidence of the particular kind is on certain premises. The magistrate may then issue a search warrant authorising a police officer to enter the premises in question and seize the evidence believed to be there. This will be discussed in greater detail later. But there are also many differences, some of them important, between the various statutory provisions authorising the issuing of search warrants. There are, first, differences in terminology. Some of them authorise the issuing of warrants if there are reasonable grounds or reasonable cause *to believe* that the search will uncover particular items; others only say that the magistrate should be satisfied that there are reasonable grounds of *suspicion or for suspecting* that an offence has been committed or that relevant evidence will be found.[4] Some have expressed the view that suspicion and belief are different, and that suspicion denotes a lesser standard than that demanded by belief.[5] But most cases draw no distinction between the two formulations, as the common phrase 'reasonable grounds' or 'reasonable cause' would indeed suggest. More on this is said below. Other differences relate to various aspects of execution.[6] Thus, some Acts expressly allow the seizure not only of what is

[1] *Ghani v. Jones*, supra.

[2] Note, 'Police Entry and Search', 88 *J.P.* 362, 387 (1924).

[3] See Thomas, supra, 269 n. 6; Leigh, supra.

[4] Compare s.26 of the Theft Act 1968, 'reasonable cause to believe', with s.23(3) of the Misuse of Drugs Act 1971, 'reasonable ground for suspecting'. 'Suspect' is by far the most usual term.

[5] *S.S. Publishing Ltd. v. Sullivan*, (1968) N.Z.L.R. 663 at 666–7.

[6] Under the common law it appears that there could be a forcible execution of a search warrant only if admittance was demanded and refused (see *Launock v. Brown*,

specified in the warrant but of other things as well;[1] others only allow the seizure of those articles mentioned in the warrant,[2] even though here too common law powers may operate to expand the category of seizable items. In some cases the execution of the warrant must take place within a certain period from its issue, as will the Obscene Publications Act 1959,[3] where the police officers can only enter and search the specified premises within 14 days from the date of the judicial authorisation, and in others the authorised search can only take place during a particular time of day, as where the officers must conduct the search during business hours;[4] in many other cases statutes contain no restriction on when warrants may be executed. Other Acts authorise not only the search of premises but also the search of persons found on them at the material time; others do not expressly confer this power, though it may exist; and in some cases the executing constables may remove persons found on the scene.[5] Finally an even more important difference relates to the issuing authority. The general rule of course is that it is a magistrate, that is a justice of the peace, who has the right to issue search warrants and before whom the necessary information and any other supporting evidence must be brought. In some cases normal procedural safeguards are strengthened by the requirement that warrants can only be issued by a high court judge,[6] and under the controversial Taxes Management Act 1970, discussed below, no warrant to enter and search can be issued except by a circuit judge.[7] But in some special cases the necessary authorisation may be given not by a neutral magistrate or other judicial officer but by a police officer. These cases fall into two categories, cases where an emergency exists and speedy action must be taken in order to avert serious harm, and other cases where no similar justification of urgency can be

---

(1819) 2 B. & Ald. 592). In most modern enactments the constable is authorised to enter 'if need be, by force'. But even in the absence of this phrase something similar may be implied since the power to enter premises appears to include the power to do all that is necessary to enter provided that unnecessary force is not used (see B. Harris, *Warrants of Search and Entry* 9 (1973)).

[1] e.g., Theft Act 1968, s.26(3).

[2] e.g., Forgery Act 1913, s.16(1).

[3] S.3.

[4] e.g., Pawnbrokers Act 1872, s.36. The Canadian Criminal Code contains an important provision with regard to the time of execution of search warrants. S.444 provides that a warrant issued under s.443 (the comprehensive section) must be executed by day *unless* the justice *by the warrant* authorises execution of it by night. In *R. v. Plummer* (1929), 52 C.C.C. 288 it was held that a search warrant that authorised a search 'at any time' was valid. If the warrant had made no mention of time the peace officer, the Court said, could have executed it only during daytime. 'Special authorisation was necessary to enable him to execute it at night', and while it was usual in such a warrant to fix the time as between certain hours, what the magistrate had done in this case was equally effective. It appears that common law warrants could only be executed during the day (2 Hale P.C. 113, 117) but such warrants are no longer used. Any limitation about time must therefore be sought in the authorising statute.

[5] For many examples, see Thomas, supra, 269 n. 6, at 5–6.

[6] See Incitement to Disaffection Act 1934, s.2; Public Order Act 1936, s.2(5).

[7] See *Inland Revenue Comrs. v. Rossminster Ltd.* (1980) 1 All E.R. 80.

invoked. The first is illustrated by the Explosives Act 1875[1] and the Official Secrets Act 1911[2] both of which, in cases where immediate action is necessary, allow a police superintendent or officer of superior rank to issue a written order giving a constable the same authority of entry and search as that which might be conferred under the same section by the warrant of a magistrate. The second and more controversial case is the Theft Act 1968[3] which allows a police officer not below the rank of superintendent to give a constable written authority to search premises for stolen goods if the premises in question are (or have recently been) occupied by a person convicted within the preceding five years of handling stolen goods. There is no requirement, as with the Explosives and the Official Secrets Acts, that there should be circumstances of urgency necessitating immediate action, and it has persuasively been argued[4] that this type of provision, which penalises the person with a previous conviction, should be repealed in favour of the usual requirement that no search warrant should be issued except with the approval of a neutral judicial officer.[5]

There is another pattern of statutory search, radically different from what we have been discussing so far, namely search under the warrant of a magistrate. This is the power conferred upon the police in a number of cases *to stop and search* a person or a vehicle if there are reasonable grounds to believe that a particular offence has been or is being committed. Some of these statutory powers of stop and search are given by local legislation; others are conferred under general Acts of Parliament, sometimes in connection with offences which cannot be regarded as very serious.[6] The most significant of the 'local' provisions is section 66 of the Metropolitan Police Act 1839 which empowers the police to stop, search and detain any vessel, boat, cart or carriage in or upon which there is reason to suspect that anything stolen or unlawfully obtained may be found, and also any person reasonably suspected of having or conveying such a thing. Of the 'general' statutory stop and search powers the one most often used is section 23(2) of the Misuse of Drugs Act 1971 giving the police the power to search without warrant any person if they have reasonable ground to suspect that he is in possession of a drug in

[1] S.73.

[2] S.9(2).

[3] S.26(2).

[4] Thomas, supra, 269 n. 6, at 10.

[5] In some jurisdictions there are statutory provisions allowing the issuing of general warrants and writs of assistance (obviously unconstitutional in the United States), which are in effect blanket search warrants not limited to any particular time or place. In Canada such general warrants are used in the enforcement of certain federal Acts (Excise Act, Customs Act, Food and Drugs Act, and Narcotic Control Act); see Trasewick, 'Search Warrants and Writs of Assistance', (1962) 5 Crim. L.Q. 341, and the Ouimet Report (1969). For statutory provisions in various Australian jurisdictions providing for general warrants, see Police Offences Act, 1953–73, s.67 (South Australia), Police Offences Act, 1953, s.60 (Tasmania), and the (federal) Customs and Excise Acts (Customs Act 1901–74, ss. 198–201; Excise Act 1901–74, ss. 88–9). On the position under Commonwealth law, see Cooper, 'Search, Seize and Question under Federal Revenue Laws', (1971) 45 *A.L.J.* 342.

[6] Thomas, supra, 269 n. 6, at 11–18.

contravention of the Act. Under this provision a constable may search that person, and detain him for the purpose of searching him; search any vehicle or vessel in which the constable suspects that the drug may be found, and for that purpose require the person in control of the vehicle to stop it; and seize and detain anything found in the course of the search which appears to him to be evidence of an offence against the Act.[1] Such stop and search powers, it must be noticed, are very different from the 'stop' and 'frisk' powers dealt with in *Terry v. Ohio.*[2] Under *Terry* the police only have power to stop an individual who is reasonably suspected of committing or of being about to commit a crime; they then may proceed to a frisk, *not* a search, *if* they have a reasonable apprehension that he is armed and dangerous. The only search the police have the power to conduct under *Terry* is a limited search for weapons; any further search can only take place after an arrest has been effected, and as an incident thereto. In contrast, under the stop and search provisions in England and other Commonwealth jurisdictions, when the police have the requisite reasonable suspicion they may proceed to a full search before the arrest. What is meant by 'reasonable grounds' for suspicion in the case of statutory powers to stop and search? There has been almost nothing by way of analysis of what this phrase means, but it is sensible to assume that it bears a meaning similar to the *Terry* standard. On this basis 'reasonable grounds to suspect' means that before the statutory power can be exercised there must be facts and circumstances which the officer either observed himself or which came to his attention in other ways and which, together with any permissible inferences therefrom, make the stop and search reasonable; the officer, in other words, must be able to justify the search not by reference to intuition, hunch or subjective suspicion but in terms of objective facts in the light of which his action appears reasonable. Should the level of suspicion be lower than it is for an arrest? Under *Terry*, it is clear, the standard of reasonable suspicion is less demanding than it is for a full arrest, but this is because the imposition represented by the stop it authorises is considerably less intrusive than it is in the case of an arrest. But if the action the officers can take is to conduct a full search, as is the position in England,

[1] See Home Office Report, *Advisory Committee on Drug Dependence, Powers of Arrest and Search in Relation to Drug Offences* (1970) (hereinafter referred to as *Report*). Another set of important provisions is that contained in the Firearms Act 1968, sections 47(3) and 49(1) and (2). Such 'stop, search and detain' powers also exist in Commonwealth jurisdictions. Examples are s.16 of the A.C.T. Police Ordinance 1927–75 and s.23 of the Northern Territory Police and Police Offences Ordinance 1923–74. Both these provide that 'any member (of the Police Force) may stop, search and detain (a) any cart, carriage or vehicle in or upon which there is reason to suspect anything stolen or unlawfully obtained may be found, and (b) any person who is reasonably suspected of having, or conveying in any manner, anything stolen or unlawfully obtained.' Such powers, it may be noticed, have some similarity with the power to conduct warrantless searches of vehicles recognised in *Carroll v. United States*, 267 U.S. 132 (1925), but under *Carroll* the power only applies if the car is capable of being removed before a warrant can be procured (but see *Chambers v. Maroney*, 399 U.S. 42) and there is *probable cause* to believe that the vehicle contains seizable items.

[2] 392 U.S. 1 (1968).

it can be argued that the required standard of suspicion is or should be the same for statutory search as it is for a full arrest, in which case 'stop and search' provisions should be abolished as they confer no power on the police which they do not already possess by virtue of the accepted police powers to arrest and then search, all the more so since in England the usual test for an arrest is *reasonable suspicion* of the commission of an offence. On this analysis[1] powers such as the ones conferred by section 66 of the Metropolitan Police Act 1839 and similar legislation are illusory and unnecessary, dating from a time when it was not clear how far the police could search arrested persons; since it is now generally accepted that there is a right to search arrested persons either immediately upon arrest or later in custody the police do not have to detain and search since they can arrest and search. Two comments can be made about this line of reasoning. It is now clear, particularly with reference to section 66 of the Metropolitan Act 1839, that the power to stop and search (for stolen goods) arises not when there are reasonable grounds to suspect that the person in possession is himself involved either in the theft or in subsequent illegal conduct with regard to the goods but when there are reasonable grounds to suspect that goods are stolen and that they can be found on a particular person.[2] The section can thus be satisfied if there are grounds for suspecting that the goods in question have been stolen or unlawfully obtained by *anyone* and it is irrelevant that no suspicion attaches to the person in possession.[3] The second point to make is that it is *generally* assumed, particularly by the police, that statutory powers of search can be resorted to on grounds which are insufficient to justify an arrest; on this view under stop and search provisions the suspicion that the officer should entertain need not be as specific but can be of 'a much more general nature'[4] than in the case of arrest; but if this is true it is a very difficult matter to know how much wider is the power to search on reasonable suspicion than the seemingly similarly formulated power to arrest on reasonable suspicion. What in fact happens, particularly with regard to powers of statutory search for drugs, is that searches take place on mere suspicion, occasionally on a random basis, and often on the basis of factors like dress, hair style and personal appearance.[5]

Not surprisingly, statutory powers of search without warrant are open to grave abuse, especially with regard to the enforcement of drugs legislation, and various proposals for reform have been made.[6] One suggestion is that stop and search provisions should be repealed and replaced by normal powers of arrest and consequential search, whether on the spot or at the police station. This change, it has been persuasively argued,[7] will have two

[1] Williams, 'Statutory Powers of Search and Arrest on the Ground of Unlawful Possession' (1960) *Crim. L.R.* 598, 606.

[2] *Sargent v. West* (1964) *Crim. L.R.* 412; *The Times*, 27 February, 1964.

[3] Thomas, supra, at 15.

[4] See Thomas, supra, at 16.

[5] See *Report*, supra.

[6] See *Report*, supra, particularly the minority views of Mr Schofield, Professor Williams and Baroness Wootton, at 37–40, 42–3.

[7] **Ibid.**

advantages. First it will lead to a considerable simplification and rationalisation of the law. Generally it is thought sufficient that the police have power to arrest on reasonable suspicion, with consequential powers of search, and there is no evidence that these powers are inadequate, even in connection with drug offences. Secondly it will both clarify and (suitably) restrict police powers. The law of arrest, requiring that reasonable suspicion should focus on the particular person who is arrested, is well settled. But when statutory powers of search are given it is very unclear, as we have seen, when these can legitimately be exercised, i.e. what level of suspicion must be found to be present before a search not accompanying an arrest can be made, and in practice this lack of clarity leads to much abuse and harassment. Another suggestion is that even if statutory powers of search are not repealed they should be curtailed by a suitable definition of 'reasonable grounds' for suspicion, 'with a view to imposing some additional safeguards'.[1] It has therefore been proposed that even though it may not be possible to formulate a legal definition of 'reasonable grounds' in positive terms it is possible to frame some kind of 'negative' definition, that is by excluding certain factors, such as dress, unconventional appearance, the fact that the person was found in a locality where drugs were frequently possessed or that he was found in a public place at night or in the early morning, from being considered in assessing the existence of 'reasonable grounds' for suspicion. This type of proposal, it should be noticed, would not wholly exclude the 'selected' factors from consideration, but it would not allow them to be sufficient in themselves, whether alone or in conjunction with each other, to establish the necessary reasonable grounds, requiring them instead to be used only as secondary factors, supporting other more acceptable grounds of suspicion.[2] A third technique for reducing the possibilities of abuse inherent in powers of search under legislation relating to drug offences is that any search that is conducted should not involve the inspection of underclothes or of the naked body.[3] But after an arrest has been effected the search may be as intrusive as is necessary. But all these proposals for curtailing statutory powers of search have until now been rejected.[4]

Another type of proposal is that far from being repealed or curtailed 'stop, search and detain powers' should be extended, principally on the ground that it is anomalous that such powers should exist only with regard to particular locations or in connection with certain categories of offences.[5] It has

[1] Ibid., at 42.

[2] Ibid., at 43.

[3] Ibid., at 38–9.

[4] See the majority's recommendations, at 54–5. But it was agreed, and recommended for adoption by the police, that 'particular modes of dress or hair style should never by themselves or together constitute reasonable grounds to stop and search' (paragraph 127).

[5] See Thomas, 'The Law of Search and Seizure', (1967) *Crim. L.R.* 3, 16–18; Australian Law Reform Commission, *Report No. 2 Criminal Investigation*, para. 204; *Home Office Evidence to the Royal Commission on Criminal Procedure, Memorandum No. III*, 28–30; and *Written Evidence of the Commissioner of Police of the Metropolis* (placed before the Royal Commission on Criminal Procedure), Part I, 8–9.

therefore been recommended that the power to stop and search persons and vehicles without warrant should be extended to situations where there are reasonable grounds to suspect that there may be found (i) an offensive weapon or (ii) something which is the fruit of a serious crime, the means by which it was committed, or material evidence to prove its commission.[1] This second type of proposal stands a much better chance of adoption than suggestions for abolition or curtailment; but in this case surely the notion of 'reasonable grounds to suspect' must receive some attention and analysis.[2]

(d) Search warrants

'There is no mystery about the word "warrant"'.[3] A search warrant is simply an order, a document, issued by a competent official under legal power, invariably statutory, authorising the doing of acts, usually to enter and search premises and to seize any of the things specified in it, which would otherwise be illegal. Search warrants, as we have seen, can only be issued under the authority of a legislative enactment,[4] common law warrants to search for stolen goods being the only exception to this now fundamental principle;[5]

[1] Australian Law Reform Commission, supra; a more limited suggestion would extend stop and search powers not over the whole range but only to persons reasonably suspected of carrying offensive weapons in a public place (see *Home Office Evidence*, supra, at 28–30, and *Written Evidence of the Commissioner of Police*, supra, at 8–9).

[2] The very basis of suggestions for extension of the law is that the standard of suspicion or belief that must exist before stop and search powers can be used is lower than that required for arrest (see Thomas, supra, at 17).

[3] *Inland Revenue Comrs. v. Rossminster Ltd.* (1980) 1 All E.R. 80 at 84, per Lord Wilberforce.

[4] A neat illustration of this principle is *Re Laporte and R.* (1972) 29 D.L.R. (3d) 651. Here the police, suspecting that the accused had been the perpetrator of a bank robbery in which the robber had been wounded by police gunfire in making his escape, obtained a search warrant authorising them to search his body for bullets by means of a surgical operation to be performed by doctors at the hospital where the accused was held. On the application of the accused to quash the search warrant, it was held that the application should be granted and the warrant quashed. Hugessen J. of the Quebec Court of Queen's Bench held that there was no jurisdiction arising either from the Criminal Code or elsewhere for a justice to issue a warrant to search the interior of a living human body. Nor could such a warrant come within s.443 of the Criminal Code authorising the issuance of warrants to search a 'building, receptacle or place' since a human body was not within any of these terms. In contrast, in Scotland warrants to take a blood sample from the suspect and impressions of his bite marks have been granted: see *H.M. Advocate v. Milford*, (1973) S.L.T. 12 and *Hay v. H.M. Advocate*, (1968) J.C. 40.

[5] Apparently, equity is of a different disposition. Recent cases have accepted the existence of an equitable order, similar in many respects to a common law search warrant. This order, known as the Anton Piller order, is an order on the defendant in personam asking him to permit the plaintiff to enter his premises and inspect documents. The difference between a search warrant and an Anton Piller order is that the former simply authorises an entry and a search irrespective of the defendant's attitude or wishes whereas the latter asks the defendant to allow the plaintiff and his solicitors to enter and inspect the documents in question; but if permission to enter is not given the defendants will in all probability be guilty of

and since statutory powers to search premises and seize property represent derogations from common law rights concerning the inviolability of home and private property the 'grave and extraordinary power'[1] to issue warrants should only be exercised when the statutory requirements for its exercise as laid down in the particular provision are clearly fulfilled. Further, since courts must look critically at legislation impairing the rights of citizens, statutory provisions conferring the power to issue warrants must be construed strictly, a construction should be placed on ambiguous or obscure words that is least restrictive of individual rights that would otherwise enjoy the protection of the common law, and any doubt in interpretation must be resolved in favour of the citizen.[2] But if the statutory words are unambiguous and plain, common law judges have no authority either to refuse to implement them or to frustrate their operation by the unwarranted discovery of non-existent ambiguities.[3] But even though everything depends on the precise construction of the particular statutory enactment the following broad comments about search warrants can be made.

---

contempt of court. Even though therefore in terms of theory '(t)he order is an order on the defendant in personam to permit inspection' (*Anton Piller K.G. v. Manufacturing Processes* (1976) 1 All E.R. 779 at 784, per Ormrod, L.J.) in practice disobedience by the defendant will make him vulnerable to considerable peril. For this reason an Anton Piller order should only be made ex parte 'where it is essential that the plaintiff should have inspection so that justice can be done between the parties', for instance when, if the defendants were forewarned, there is a grave danger that vital evidence will be destroyed, or that papers will be lost, hidden or taken beyond the jurisdiction (see *Anton Piller K.G. v. Manufacturing Processes* (1976) 1 All E.R. at 783, per Lord Denning, M.R.) and where the inspection will do no real harm to the defendant or his case. For the principles governing the issuing of these orders, see *Anton Piller K.G. v. Manufacturing Processes* (1976) 1 All E.R. 779; *E.M.I. Ltd v. Sarwar and Haidar* (1977) F.S.R. 146; *Rank Film Distributors Ltd. v. Video Information Centre* (1980) 2 All E.R. 273.

[1] *Re Worrall* (1965) 2 C.C.C. 1 at 9, per Roach J.A.

[2] *Inland Revenue Comrs v. Rossminster Ltd.* (1980) 1 All E.R. 80 at 82, per Lord Wilberforce. A good example is *King v. The Queen* (1969) 1 A.C. 304. The principle that this case stands for is that if a statute makes it possible to grant powers to the executing officer in addition to the powers of entry and search these powers must be spelled out in the warrant; otherwise the constable will be restricted to the powers which are expressly granted. In *King v. R.*, supra, a Jamaican statute allowed a justice in granting a search warrant to authorise the executing officer not only to enter and search premises but also to search persons as well. But the warrant actually issued did not in terms authorise the search of any person, and the Privy Council held that the search of a person was illegal as it was justified neither by the warrant nor by the statute (since there had been no 'express authorisation' in the warrant, supra, at 311). In *King v. R.*, supra, it was also held that the warrant was defective because it did not comply with the statutory provision which stated that the warrant should be executed by a constable 'named' in the warrant. No constable had been 'named' in the warrant, and this too in their Lordships' opinion invalidated the warrant since 'the word "named" (was) to be taken literally' and not be given some 'wider meaning' (ibid., at 312).

[3] Ibid., at 90, per Lord Diplock.

(i) Issuance

The basic principles here are first that the judicial officer authorised to issue search warrants is charged with a judicial function, and secondly that he cannot issue a search warrant unless it has been demonstrated to him that the foundation of his authority, usually reasonable ground to believe or suspect, exists.[1] Examples abound. In *Bowden v. Box*[2] the statute provided that a justice could grant a warrant if 'satisfied' by information on oath that there was reasonable ground for belief as to certain matters. Edwards J. held that it was impossible to construe this enactment as providing authority to a justice to issue a warrant upon the oath alone of a constable or any other person that there was reasonable ground. 'So to hold would be to hold that the justice may discharge the judicial duty cast upon him by acting, parrot-like, upon the bald assertion of the informant.' It was instead necessary both that the justice should exercise his own judgment on materials adduced before him and that the judicial discretion should be exercised properly—which in turn has been interpreted to mean that the grant of the requested warrant should proceed on proper grounds which should themselves appear in the complaint brought before the justice. In other words, reasonable ground for belief or suspicion is a prerequisite to the issue of a search warrant under statutory provisions authorising magistrates to issue warrants when 'satisfied' that there is reasonable ground to believe or suspect, the grounds or facts on which belief is founded or from which suspicion arises must appear in the complaint or information and be sworn to, and it is on these sworn facts alone that the magistrate 'in the exercise of a judicial and not a merely ministerial function'[3] must be satisfied.[4] As the matter was succinctly put by a Canadian judge,[5] the duty of a reviewing court is 'to examine not into whether the justice was in fact satisfied but into whether he should have been satisfied' on the basis of the information put before him. These principles have also been applied to enactments which require not that the justice should be 'satisfied' but that the reasonable grounds for suspicion should 'appear' before him,[6] and also to statutory provisions which call for information that there was reasonable cause to suspect,[7] or that a 'credible person' should show 'reasonable cause to suspect'[8], or that a 'credible person' whom the justice believes should only state 'that he believes' certain facts.[9] Here too courts invariably demand that there should be reasonable cause to believe or suspect before a warrant can be issued and that this reasonable cause should be made

[1] N. Reaburn, 'The Law of Search Warrants', (1970) 9 *W.A.L. Rev.* 242.

[2] (1916) G.L.R. (N.Z.) 443.

[3] *Mitchell v. New Plymouth Club (Inc.)* (1958) N.Z.L.R. 1070.

[4] See *Bowden v. Box* (1916) G.L.R. 443; *Mitchell v. New Plymouth Club (Inc.)* (1958) N.Z.L.R. 1070; *Seven Seas Publishing Pty. Ltd v. Sullivan* (1968) N.Z.L.R. 663.

[5] *R. v. Solloway & Mills* (1930) 3 D.L.R. 770 at 774, per Riddell J.A.

[6] *T.V.W. Ltd v. Robinson* (1964) W.A.R. 33.

[7] *Bridgeman v. Macalister* (1898) 8 Q.L.J. 151.

[8] *Feather v. Rogers* (1909) 9 S.R. (N.S.W.) 192.

[9] See Reaburn, supra, n. 1, at 249, explaining the 'imprecise' statements in *Feather v. Rogers* (1909) 9 S.R. (N.S.W.) 192.

to appear objectively, which means that the grounds on which the suspicion is based must be stated in the complaint. As the matter was succinctly put by Griffith C. J., in *Bridgeman v. Macalister,*[1] before a justice can issue a warrant 'it must be proved *to him* that there *is* reasonable cause for suspecting . . . The reasonable ground for suspicion *is* the foundation of his authority'. Clear evidence that courts will do their utmost to frustrate subjectively formulated grants of power is provided by *Palethorpe v. Nebbia*[2] where the statutory provision under consideration conferred judicial authority to issue search warrants when there had been '(a) complaint on oath . . . by any person that *he* reasonably suspects'. It was again held that the discretion to issue warrants belonged to the justice, not the informant; that the discretion should therefore only be exercised on the basis of proper materials; that 'reasonably suspects' meant 'suspects on reasonable grounds'; and that these 'reasonable grounds' should be communicated to the justice by their suitable formulation in the complaint.

As to the content of the concepts of 'reasonable grounds to believe', 'reasonable grounds for suspicion', 'reasonable cause' to believe or suspect and the like, it cannot be assumed that they all demand the same level of evidence and sometimes, as we have seen, 'reasonable grounds *to believe*' is taken to require 'something more'[3] than the usual English concept of reasonable grounds or cause *to suspect*. But on most occasions the emphasis is not on 'belief' or 'suspicion' and any possible differences between them but on the requirement that the necessary state of mind should be *reasonable*, based on 'reasonable cause' or 'reasonable grounds'. In this sense 'reasonable cause' does not appear to be different from the operative concept under the Fourth Amendment where, it will be remembered, the applicable standard is that of 'probable cause'. The position, drawing from hints in the cases and from American authorities, can therefore be set out as follows.[4] Reasonable cause to believe or suspect cannot normally be based on the unsupported (or uncorroborated) allegation or 'bare suggestion'[5] of a complainant; nor at the same time should it be equated with final proof or even a prima facie case. A prima facie case, it is now clear, is 'a much stiffer test than the reasonable suspicion'[6] which is the foundation of many statutory powers of issuing warrants, suspicion arising at or near the starting-point of an investigation of which the obtaining of prima facie proof is the end.[7] When such proof has been obtained the police case is complete, it is ready for trial and can pass on to its next stage. But if before that point arrest and search were forbidden the police would be unduly hampered. There is another distinction between reasonable cause and prima facie proof, again noticed in American cases.

[1] (1898) 8 Q.L.J. 151, 152.

[2] (1937) Q.W.N. 33.

[3] Karlan, *Anglo-American Criminal Justice* 108 (1967); see *S.S. Publishing Ltd. v. Sullivan* (1968) N.Z.L.R. 663, 666–7.

[4] See J. L. Lambert, 'Reasonable Cause to Arrest', (1973) *P.L.* 285.

[5] 4 *Coke Inst.*, 177; 5 *Burn's Justice of the Peace* 1179 (1869).

[6] *Shaaban & Ors. v. Chong Fook Kam & Anor.* (1969) 2 M.L.J. 219 at 221, per Lord Devlin.

[7] Ibid.

Prima facie proof, properly understood, consists of admissible evidence. In contrast, suspicion, even of the type that can justify the issuing of a search warrant, can take into account matters that could not be put in evidence at all.[1] On the positive side, reasonable cause, like probable cause, seems to refer to some substantial basis in fact giving rise to and in turn supporting a belief as to the existence of certain facts, in the case of a search that particular items providing evidence of the commission of a specific offence are located and can be found in a given place. English and Commonwealth tribunals, it is thought, would have no disagreement with the *Carroll* definition[2] followed by most American courts, namely that probable cause supporting the issuance of a search warrant exists if the facts and circumstances either within the direct knowledge of the police officers or of which they have reliable information are such as to warrant a man of reasonable caution in the belief that seizable items will be found on particular premises.[3]

(ii) Information

Since the justice can only exercise his discretion on the basis of the complaint or information that is put before him, and since a search warrant based on a defective complaint will be held to be invalid, what should this contain? First, the complaint should set forth the reasonable grounds relied on as showing the required suspicion or belief. This follows from what has been said above about the duty of a judicial officer authorised to issue warrants. Since it is not enough that the justice should be satisfied, but what is required is that 'he must be satisfied on reasonable grounds', which should then be capable of being subjected to judicial review, 'the grounds of belief (should be) set out in

[1] Ibid.

[2] 267 U.S. 132.

[3] It is very difficult to find cases discussing the question (which has caused so much trouble to American courts) whether particular facts and circumstances warranted the issuing of a warrant, in other words whether there was reasonable cause. One case is *Wyatt v. White* (1860) 5 H. & N. 371. Here the complainant laid an information before a magistrate that he had seen certain sacks with his mark upon them in the plaintiff's possession. It was held that the magistrate had correctly issued a warrant for stolen goods. Another case is *Jones v. German* (1897) 1 Q.B. 374, to be discussed shortly, but as Leigh (*Police Powers in England and Wales* 175 (1975)) correctly points out, this case is 'a weak authority on the question of what standards a justice ought to employ', its main subject-matter being the contents of the information. For an interesting parliamentary debate on proper standards of suspicion for the issuing of search warrants in the case of drug offences, see the case of Lady Diana Cooper 760 H.C. Deb. Col. 826ff. Here the police obtained a warrant to search for drugs on the basis of an anonymous telephone call. It was accepted that the police had made a serious mistake in acting upon an anonymous telephone call, and an undertaking was given that anonymous information would be treated with special care, and that there should normally be an attempt to find corroborative evidence supporting the anonymous tip. In the Diana Cooper case the police accepted that 'insufficient steps were taken' to check the reliability of the information on the basis of which the warrant was issued, and for this they apologised. What runs through this discussion (760 H.C. Deb. Col. 826ff.) is that invariably magistrates act upon the word of police officers. This, as Mr Norman St. John-Stevas said, tends to convert 'the intervention of a magistrate (into) a pure formality'.

the information' and 'be such as would satisfy a reasonable man';[1] if no such grounds are shown the justice cannot be taken to have been satisfied on reasonable grounds and the warrant will be quashed. Secondly, the information must identify the offence in connection with which the evidence is sought. It is sufficient but not necessary to use the actual words of the statute under which the warrant is sought, and while minor deviations in form from the correct statutory wording will be excused, a substantial deficiency may result in the complaint disclosing no sufficient grounds for the issuance of a search warrant, in this way making the ensuing search illegal. Thus to allege simply in the complaint put before the magistrate that the sought items will provide evidence that 'an offence' has been committed is not enough;[2] but the requirement of adequate particularisation has been held to be satisfied despite a failure to give the number of the relevant section of the Criminal Code creating the particular offence when there was only one section dealing with such an offence and as a result of the way in which it had been described there could be no difficulty in identifying the crime involved.[3] Further, it is not necessary to allege in the complaint that an offence has *actually taken place* provided that what is stated is that *there is reasonable cause* to believe or suspect that an offence has been committed. In *Jones v. German*[4] the information was to the effect that the claimant had reasonable cause to suspect and did suspect that his goods had been stolen by the defendant. Was the search warrant invalid because there was no allegation of the actual commission of a felony? Both Lord Russell C.J. and the Court of Appeal said no, expressing the view that it was enough if it could be gathered by reasonable implication from the complaint that the informant entertained reasonable grounds for suspecting that a larceny had been committed. Thirdly, the information should contain adequate reference to the goods which it is proposed to search for and seize. But this is best dealt with when we discuss the contents of the warrant itself. Finally the complaint should clearly describe the place that the officers wish to enter and search.

Should the information be in writing?[5] Obviously this must depend on the precise wording and intent of the particular statutory provision. But should the usual phrase 'information on oath' be understood to mean a written information? In one case[6] it was held that the 'complaint on oath' referred to in a Victoria statute had to be in writing. In other cases courts expressed the view that it is not necessary that the complaint or information should be in writing but that it can also consist of sworn oral evidence.[7] But all agree that

[1] *Re Bell Telephone Company of Canada* (1947), 89 C.C.C. 196, 198.

[2] *R. v. Munn*, No. 1 (1938), 71 C.C.C. 139, 141. Nor, obviously, is it enough if the information alleges a statement of facts which does not disclose an offence. In *Re Mackenzie and The Queen*, 10 C.C.C. (2d) 193 the information referred to a suspected 'gaming house' and not a 'common gaming house' (the expression in the Code). The absence of the word 'common' was held to be fatal since gaming per se was not an offence.

[3] *R. v. Plummer* (1929), 52 C.C.C. 288.

[4] (1896) 2 Q.B. 418; affirmed on appeal, (1897) 1 Q.B. 374.

[5] See *The Queen v. Tillett, ex parte Newton*, (1969) 14 F.L.R. 101, 109.

[6] *Montague v. Ah Shen* (1907) V.L.R. 458.

[7] See *Mitchell v. New Plymouth Club (Inc.)* (1958) N.Z.L.R. 1070.

it is desirable that there should be a written record of what takes place before the magistrate.[1]

(iii) Contents of the warrant

The first thing to notice is that there is no presumption of regularity in connection with search warrants.[2] This means that jurisdiction must appear on the face of a warrant, or otherwise it is a nullity and not merely voidable.[3] A search warrant therefore must disclose on its face that the justice satisfied himself on the material issue, namely whether reasonable grounds justifying the proposed invasion of privacy existed, and if the warrant does not do this, particularly if it shows that the magistrate addressed his mind to the wrong question, it will be struck down.[4] Specificity requirements, already touched upon in connection with what must be contained in the information, are equally if not more important when one is dealing with the contents of the search warrant itself. As regards the offence alleged it is well established that this should be clearly specified. 'To avoid search warrants becoming an instrument of abuse it has long been understood that if a search warrant fails adequately to describe the offence . . . it will be invalid.' A warrant, in other words, must be issued not only in respect of *an offence* but also in respect of a *particular offence*, for only in this way will (a) the officer executing it know what articles he may seize and (b) the owner of the premises be able to understand, and if necessary obtain legal advice about, the permissible limits of the search.[5] If the warrant specifies no offence at all it will be illegal even if the evidence placed before the magistrate had referred to, and perhaps established, a particular offence. In *The Queen v. Tillett, ex parte Newton*[6] a warrant authorised police officers to enter certain premises and 'to seize such books, papers, documents or other things which you may find in and at the same premises'. Whether this authority was completely unlimited as to what might be seized or was to be construed by reference to the recital where reference was made to reasonable grounds for a belief that certain books, documents and other things would afford evidence as to the commission of an offence against the Commonwealth Crimes Act, the warrant was held to be too general. A warrant, Fox J. stated, could not authorise either the seizure of things in general or the seizure of things which were related to offences generally. '(A) warrant should refer to a particular offence and authorise seizure by reference to that offence.' It had been argued that in reality there was no distinction between reference to a particular offence, and reference to none, or to offences in general, because, as far as the search was concerned, those executing the warrant would have to search as widely in the one case as in the others, but this argument was rejected by his Honour because it was not correct as a matter of fact. '(A) search must have a purpose and what may be searched as relevant to one purpose may, or may not, be as

[1] *The Queen v. Tillett, ex parte Newton*, (1969) 14 F.L.R. 101, 109.
[2] *The Queen v. Tillett, ex parte Newton*, (1969) 14 F.L.R. 101, 106–7.
[3] *Caundle v. Seymour* (1841) 10 L.J.M.C. 130.
[4] *The Queen v. Tillett, ex parte Newton* (1969) 14 F.L.R. 101, 106–8.
[5] *Auckland Medical Aid Trust v. Taylor* (1975) N.Z.L.R. 728, 736–7.
[6] (1969) 14 F.L.R. 101.

extensive as that which has to be searched as relevant to another purpose.'[1] Nor is it enough that a search warrant refers to a type of offence, however accurately. What is generally required is that a warrant should expressly be issued in connection with a particular offence, in the sense of a particular instance of the offence mentioned in the warrant. The reason is that if the warrant contains no particulars or information indicating the offence with sufficient specificity to enable the officers executing it and the person with regard to whose premises it is issued to know what the offence is the warrant will in effect be a general one. In *Auckland Medical Aid Trust v. Taylor*,[2] even though much of the evidence placed before the magistrate related to the termination of the pregnancy of a girl on a specific occasion, the warrant that was issued empowered the police to search the defendant's premises for written records of interviews (of women seeking abortions by counsellors and medical practitioners) and for other medical and clerical records and to seize anything which there was reasonable ground to believe would be evidence as to the commission of 'the offence of abortion'. The New Zealand Court of Appeal did not wish to suggest that a warrant had to set out with precision as much detail as would be required in a charge sheet, and also agreed that whether the particulars given were adequate was a question that in many cases would depend on the individual crime. For instance, if a search warrant was issued in respect of 'the theft of clothing from warehouse X' that would be adequate. But in the case before the Court it was impossible to say that the description in the warrant '(would) convey to anyone that it was issued in respect of a *particular* instance of illegal termination of pregnancy'.[3] The description of the offence was not therefore sufficiently specific and this made the warrant general and illegal.

But naturally even the requirement that the offence in respect of which the warrant is issued should be specified in it must give way before the express words of a statute. This was dramatically demonstrated by the decision of the House of Lords in *Inland Revenue Commissioners v. Rossminster Ltd.*[4] An officer of the Board of Inland Revenue, acting under the provisions of the Taxes Management Act 1970,[5] laid an information on oath before a circuit

[1] Ibid., at 113.

[2] (1975) 1 N.Z.L.R. 728.

[3] Ibid., at 737.

[4] (1980) 1 All E.R. 80.

[5] The relevant provision, s.20C, was inserted in the Taxes Management Act 1970 by the Finance Act 1976, s.57 and Sch. 6. Section 20C is effectively divided into two parts. The first part, s.20C(1), confers the power to issue warrants authorising entry and search. It provides that 'if the appropriate judicial authority is satisfied on information on oath given by an officer of the Board that—(a) there is reasonable ground for suspecting that an offence involving any form of fraud in connection with, or in relation to, tax has been committed and that evidence of it is to be found on premises specified in the information; and (b) in applying under this section, the officer acts with the approval of the Board given in relation to the particular case, the authority may issue a warrant in writing authorising an officer of the Board to enter the premises, if necessary by force, at any time within 14 days from the time of issue of the warrant, and search them'. As Viscount Dilhorne put it, '(t)he issue of a warrant only authorises entry and search. It does not authorise seizure and removal of anything' (at 85). It is the second part, s.20C(3), which gives the power to seize and

judge alleging that there was reasonable ground for suspecting that an offence involving a tax fraud had been committed and that incriminating documents would be found on the premises, both private and business, belonging to the respondents and specified in the information. The judge issued the requested search warrants. The warrants did not specify that any particular offence was suspected but simply stated, in the words of the relevant sections, that there was 'reasonable ground for suspecting that an offence involving fraud in connection with or in relation to tax has been committed and that evidence of it is to be found on the premises described (therein)', and authorised officers of the Revenue to enter those premises, search them and seize and remove 'any things whatsoever found there which (they had) reasonable cause to believe (might) be required as evidence for the purpose of proceedings in respect of such an offence'. In executing the warrants the officers entered the specified premises and seized and removed numerous files, papers and documents of all kinds. The Court of Appeal thought that the challenged search warrants were illegal. Lord Denning M. R.[1] thought that to be valid under the Act a warrant had to specify the offence suspected, Browne L.J.[2] held that a warrant should specify at least the general nature of the offence or offences suspected, and in Goff L.J.'s view[3] a warrant should state on its face that it related to a criminal offence or offences involving a tax fraud. But the House of Lords disagreed and overruled the decision of the Court of Appeal. Their Lordships held that on the true construction of the relevant section of the 1970 Act *all* that was required to be specified in a warrant to search issued under its provisions was the address of the premises to be searched and the name of the officer authorised to carry out the search, and although the circuit judge issuing the warrant was himself required to be satisfied that there was reasonable ground for suspecting that a tax fraud had been committed and that evidence of it was to be found on the premises to be searched, the fact that the judge was so satisfied was not required to be stated in the warrant. The warrants therefore did not have to specify the offence or offences suspected, and were valid because they satisfied the statutory requirements.

To what extent should a search warrant contain a description of the items to be seized? This again depends on the precise wording of the particular enactment,[4] but the following comments can be made. Here too the general

---

remove, in the following terms: 'On entering the premises with a warrant under this section, the officer may seize and remove any things whatsoever found there which he has reasonable cause to believe may be required as evidence for the purposes of proceedings in respect of such an offence as is mentioned in subsection (1) above . . .'. As Lord Wilberforce put it, s.20C(3) confers an independent statutory power of seizure.

[1] (1979) 3 All E.R. 385 at 403.

[2] (1979) 3 All E.R. 385 at 405.

[3] (1979) 3 All E.R. 385 at 408.

[4] In many enactments there is no requirement that the warrant should specify what is to be seized. Instead, the officer is authorised to enter and seize *any* items which he believes to be relevant to the particular offence on the basis of which the warrant was issued (e.g., s.3 of the Obscene Publications Act 1959). In such cases, as Thomas has

principle is that in describing the objects sought the warrant must contain enough information to enable the officers entrusted with its execution to ascertain with reasonable ease and accuracy the items to be seized.[1] For it is only if an adequate description of the items to be seized is given that the police officer will know what he is authorised to take away and the citizen will be able to protect the rest of his possessions.[2] But no complete description of the goods is necessary, and the magistrate does not appear to be under a duty to do more than 'to define in a reasonable way the nature of the articles which may be seized under the warrant'.[3] Indeed on occasion warrants are upheld despite the absence of any specification of the items to be searched for and seized. In *Jones v. German*[4] the information on the basis of which the warrant was issued stated that the informant reasonably suspected that a certain person had 'certain property belonging to him'. In other words, it was alleged that a larceny had been committed but the informant was not able to say what had been stolen. It was held that the warrant was not a general warrant and therefore bad simply because it did not specify the goods in issue. Lord Russell C.J. could not find it anywhere laid down that a search warrant had to specify the goods and thought that there might be many cases where it would be impossible for the person laying the information to do so. It is not clear how much authority *Jones v. German* possesses. But it should be noticed[5] first that this case involved a common law warrant which means that during its execution the complainant would accompany the officer to help him identify any of his goods to be found among the possessions of the suspect and secondly that both the information and the warrant referred to larceny and stolen goods, which narrowed the purpose of the search considerably.

---

pointed out at (1967) *Crim. L.R.* 3, 6, the warrant is an authority to enter and search the premises and seize any items providing evidence of the offence in question.

[1] *R. v. Trottier* (1966) 4 C.C.C. 321.

[2] This principle has been affirmed and applied in many Canadian cases. The most important of these is *Shumiatcher v. A-G. of Saskatchewan*, 129 C.C.C. 267. Here the warrant referred to 'certain letters, copies of letters, cancelled cheques, files, agreements, statutory declarations and drafts of same, various other documents, and typewriters pertaining to the following charges' against the defendant. The warrant was quashed because the description of the documents to be seized effectively left it to the discretion of the executing officers as to what should be seized. It also appears that in Canada specificity and particularity requirements, as regards both the items to be seized and other matters, are interpreted more strictly when the premises to be searched belong to an innocent third party. The basic case is *Re United Distillers Ltd.*, 88 C.C.C. 338, (1947) 3 D.L.R. 900. In quashing a search warrant Farris C.J. said (at 341): 'It would seem to me that where the premises which are to be searched are not the premises of those accused of committing the crime, no Magistrate could or should be satisfied unless the information should definitely show the nature of the documents to be searched for and how such documents will likely afford evidence as to the commission of the offence *and* a belief based on reasonable grounds that the owner of the premises to be searched is concealing or is likely to conceal such evidence so that it will not be available in the prosecution of the charge.'

[3] *Auckland Medical Aid Trust v. Taylor* (1975) N.Z.L.R. 728 at 742, per Richmond J.

[4] (1896) 2 Q.B. 418.

[5] Reaburn, supra, 279 n. 1, at 256.

Another type of case is where the warrant authorises the search and seizure not of a *particular* item but of a *class* of items, for instance documents of a certain type. Here it is established that it is not necessary that there should be 'something in the nature of an itemisation or specific description of particular documents or things'.[1] A good example is *Seven Seas Publishing Pty Ltd. v. Sullivan*[2] where a warrant had been issued for indecent documents. The application for the search warrant stated that the police officer concerned had reasonable cause to believe that indecent documents were kept at the premises of the plaintiff company. The main grounds stated in support of this belief were that the police had specific information with regard to two books and that the plaintiff company was known to have in its possession books of a like nature. The warrant authorised a search for and the seizure of 'indecent documents, to wit, magazines and books', and this was upheld. The learned judge thought it was impossible in cases like the one before him to describe documents individually or in other than generic terms; a general description was therefore sufficient even though the result of this was to give a discretion to the officer executing a warrant for indecent literature to seize documents and books that *seemed to him* to be indecent; but naturally his decisions as to the indecency of the documents seized would be subject to judicial review. Another example is *The Queen v. Tillett, ex parte Newton,*[3] already discussed in connection with the specification of the offence. The constable had been authorised to seize 'such books, papers, documents or other things'. The warrant was held to be bad because it had failed to specify the offence on the basis of which the seizure would be effected. But a separate contention that the warrant was also defective because it did not sufficiently specify the documents or things to be seized was rejected, the learned judge taking the view that an itemisation of particular documents or things falling within generic classes was unnecessary. The important consideration for him was that the warrant should not be a general one, and in the case before him this could be achieved by the appropriate specification of the offence. In some cases, in other words, the danger of fatal generality is met by the adequate description of the offence and by the giving of some indication of its circumstances. In others objectionable generality may be adequately narrowed by 'a sufficiently precise description of the articles (to be seized) notwithstanding that the offence involved (is) described in a general way'.[4] In the ultimate analysis what is called for is 'a sufficient measure of particularisation'[5] in the warrant enabling both the officer executing it and the person on whose premises it is to be executed (who may not be the suspect) to know 'just what are the metes and bounds of the search and seizure contemplated'.[6] The fuller the description of the offence the less particular the specification of what is to be seized may afford to be, and vice versa.[7]

[1] *The Queen v. Tillett, ex parte Newton* (1969) 14 F.L.R. 101, 114.

[2] (1968) N.Z.L.R. 663.

[3] (1969) 14 F.L.R. 101.

[4] *Auckland Medical Aid Trust v. Taylor* (1975) 1 N.Z.L.R. 728, 742.

[5] Ibid., at 749.

[6] Ibid.

[7] Our discussion of the contents of the typical search warrant and of specificity

(e) Powers of search and seizure

Police powers of search and seizure can be analysed under three headings: (i) when the articles in question are obtained under the 'authority' of a search warrant; (ii) when there has been an arrest, and the police conduct an incidental search; and (iii) when there is neither an arrest nor a search warrant but the police still seek to seize and take away property which they believe to be connected with criminal activity.

(i) Search and seizure 'under' search warrants

What is the scope of a search and what may be seized under a search warrant? Obviously the officer is entitled to look for and seize the items specified in it. To what extent can he seize items not so specified?[1] Here there has been a progressive development widening further and further the category of items that may be seized under a search warrant. This development can be represented in the form of five stages.[2]

---

requirements makes it possible to sharpen our definition of a search warrant advanced earlier. A search warrant is a judicial order authorising a police officer to go upon premises *in order* to obtain particular items reasonably believed to afford evidence of a specific offence; and as to the items sought there must be reasonable grounds for believing *that they* will be of assistance in establishing the commission of an offence, *and that* they will be found at the premises sought to be searched: *Wiens et al v. The Queen* (1973) 6 W.W.R. 757. A search warrant cannot be utilised to allow an officer to go onto premises and there search for any evidence of crime. As the matter was put by McRuer, C.J. in *Re Bell Telephone Company of Canada* (1947), 89 C.C.C. 196 at 200, 'the fundamental thing is that the purpose of the search warrant is to secure *things that will in themselves* be relevant to a case to be proved, not to secure an opportunity of making observations *in respect of the use of things* and *thereby* obtain evidence.'

[1] Occasionally there is statutory provision about this matter. This is the case with Canada. It has been seen above that the comprehensive provision under which search warrants are issued is s.443 of the Criminal Code. Section 445 provides that '(e)very person who executes a warrant issued under section 443 may seize, in addition to the things mentioned in the warrant, anything that on reasonable grounds he believes has been obtained by or has been used in the commission of an offence, and carry it before the justice who issued the warrant or some other justice for the same territorial division'. If therefore a search warrant is issued under s.443 to search for goods in connection with offence A and goods with regard to offence B are discovered these too may be seized and taken before the magistrate. It should also be noted that it makes no difference what kind of offence is the one in connection with which the unauthorised items have been seized. S.445 refers simply to 'an offence'; this might therefore be any offence under the Code, whether it is one for which a search warrant can only be issued under the general section (s.443) or one for which a special warrant can issue, or any other offence, whether under some other federal statute or even under a provincial one. But s.445, it should also be observed, is expressly confined to discoveries made during the execution of warrants issued under s.443. Where a search warrant has been issued under a statutory authority other than s.443(1), s.445 does not apply. What the situation is in these other cases is very unclear; but Canadian courts are likely to follow the lead of the English Court of Appeal in *Chic Fashions (West Wales) Ltd. v. Jones* (1968) 2 Q.B. 299: see *R. v. Nimbus News*, 11 C.R.N.S. 315 at 320.

[2] It was sketched out in masterly fashion by Lord Denning M.R. in *Chic Fashions*

(a) The earliest answer of the common law was the most restrictive. The constable executing a search warrant could seize only those goods which were mentioned in it. If the goods seized were not the ones described in the warrant, the seizure was illegal, even though he may have reasonably believed that the goods he had taken were the ones whose seizure was authorised.[1]

(b) At the beginning of the nineteenth century this strict doctrine was relaxed by the elaboration of a defence for the constable taking unauthorised goods in cases where he had reasonably believed that the goods he was seizing were included in the warrant. The fact that his belief turned out to be mistaken was irrelevant and did not make him a trespasser as to those goods. The case generally regarded as establishing this proposition is *Price v. Messenger*.[2] A warrant was issued authorising an officer to search for and seize a quantity of sugar which had been stolen from a ship. The constable entered the shop of Price and took away some sugar which turned out not to have been stolen. It was argued for the plaintiff that 'the warrant was to seize stolen sugar, and the officers were bound at their peril to seize stolen sugar or none at all'. This was rejected. The question, the court said, was 'whether the constable (had) acted in obedience to the warrant' since '(t)he public interest required that officers who really act(ed) in obedience to the warrant of a magistrate should be protected'. It was therefore held that the constable was not liable for the sugar he had taken, presumably because he had entertained at the time a bona fide (and reasonable) belief that its seizure had been authorised by the warrant.

(c) The interpretation of the next major case, *Crozier v. Cundey*,[3] is not free from difficulty, but one plausible explanation of it is that it allows the seizure of goods not mentioned in the warrant even if the officer knows this, provided however that the goods seized are likely to provide evidence of the *identity* of the articles mentioned in the warrant. In this case a search warrant authorised a constable to enter the plaintiff's house and to search for and seize some cotton copps belonging to Cundey. Before they were stolen the cotton copps had been contained in two packing cases but the warrant said nothing about them. The constable seized not only the cotton and the packing cases but also a tin pan and a sieve. It was held that the plaintiff had no action in respect of the seizure of the packing cases since they were likely to furnish evidence of the identity of the cotton copps, but that the constable had no such justification with regard to the tin pan and the sieve because these articles could not 'from their nature' be regarded as 'likely to furnish evidence of the identity of the articles stolen and mentioned in the warrant'. A more expansive interpretation of *Crozier v. Cundey* is that a constable may seize and take away not only the specific goods mentioned in the warrant but also other goods and items not mentioned in it which are likely, i.e. reasonably

---

(West Wales) Ltd. v. Jones (1968) 2 Q.B. 299 (hereinafter referred to as *Chic Fashions*).

[1] *Chic Fashions*, supra, at 309.

[2] (1800) 2 Bos. & P. 158.

[3] (1827) 6 B. & C. 232; 9 Dow. & Ry. K.B. 224; 5 L.J.O.S.M.C. 50.

believed to be likely, to furnish evidence of the *commission of the offence* on the basis of which the warrant was issued.[1]

(d) This last interpretation, that goods may be seized not only if they prove or furnish evidence of the identity of the specified goods but also when they show in other ways the guilt of the occupier on the charge in respect of which the warrant was issued, was adopted in the difficult case of *Pringle v. Bremner and Stirling*.[2] Here a warrant authorised a constable to search for pieces of wood and a fuse used in causing an explosion. During the search letters were found and seized which implicated the plaintiff in the sending of threatening letters, and which in turn threw light on who had caused the explosion. Their Lordships thought that even if a search was improper originally it would subsequently be *excused* if it brought to light evidence which could be used to substantiate the charge against the defendant (or plaintiff in this case) for which the warrant was issued.[3] Lord Chelmsford's judgment is very confusing. At the very least it allows the seizure of evidence discovered by chance during an otherwise legitimate search which implicates, i.e. provides evidence against, the defendant with regard to the offence the officers were then investigating. A broader interpretation would allow the seizure of evidence demonstrating the involvement of the occupier in *any* offence. What is more, it may be that *Pringle v. Bremner and Stirling* does not even insist that the discovery of the unspecified evidence should be accidental before it can lawfully be seized, as Lord Chelmsford would apparently still be prepared to legalise retrospectively a search that made no attempt to remain faithful to the authorising warrant but openly extended beyond in an effort to discover incriminating evidence. This part of *Pringle* no longer enjoys authority, as it is now clear that the legality of a search or seizure must be decided on as of the time it takes place and cannot be made to depend on what it uncovers.[4] In this light, and bearing in mind its uncertain decisional status, *Pringle* should only be regarded as authorising a seizure of goods not mentioned in the warrant if these have been discovered accidentally and if they provide evidence of the complicity of the occupier in the offence which is under investigation.[5]

[1] This is supported by the headnote of 6 B. & C. 232.

[2] (1867) 5 Macph. H.L. 55.

[3] Ibid., at 60.

[4] See *Chic Fashions* (1968) 2 Q.B. at 312.

[5] This is how *Pringle* was interpreted by Lord Denning, M.R. in *Chic Fashions*, supra, at 311. But in *Ghani v. Jones* (1970) 1 Q.B. 693 at 706 Lord Denning, M.R. read *Pringle* as authorising the seizure of items showing the occupier to be implicated in any crime; and this clearly comes out of Lord Chelmsford's judgment, supra, at 60 (The problem here is that the documents seized in *Pringle* provided evidence both of the offence of causing an explosion, the offence under investigation, and of the distinct offence of sending a menacing letter). Nor is it clear to what extent the discovery should have been accidental. Lord Denning, M.R. in *Ghani v. Jones*, supra, at 706, implies that the *Pringle* principle comes into operation if the officers 'come upon' other goods 'in the course of th(e) search', which would suggest that the discovery of the goods should be accidental. This interpretation finds some support in the speech of Lord Colonsay, supra, at 61. But *Pringle* is not a clear authority for anything because it does not proclaim the seizure lawful or unlawful but only says that it is excused 'by the result of the search'.

(e) In modern times the category of items that can lawfully be seized by the police despite the lack of any authorisation in the warrant has been extended considerably, well beyond those items which were taken because they were mistakenly but in good faith and reasonably regarded as being covered by the warrant, or those which enjoy some meaningful connection with the offence for which the warrant was issued, either by assisting in the identification of the specified goods or by otherwise demonstrating the occupier's guilt with regard to the offence under investigation. This considerable modern enlargement was accomplished in two stages. In the first the Court of Appeal eliminated the requirement that a seizure of unspecified articles could only be legal if there was a relationship between the seized articles and the offence for which the warrant was issued. In the second English courts, again following the lead of the Court of Appeal and building on the implications of the first development, have effectively eliminated the requirement of a search warrant itself, by allowing the seizure of evidence not under an implied grant of power theoretically derivable from the warrant but under a new doctrine allowing in certain circumstances the warrantless seizure of evidence of crime. In *Chic Fashions v. Jones*[1] the police entered the premises of a company under a warrant authorising them to search for stolen clothes made by a named company. They did not find any of the goods specified in the warrant but found and seized clothes of other makes which they thought were stolen. It was subsequently accepted by the police that the items seized had not been stolen, and it was conceded by the plaintiffs that in seizing the items the police believed upon reasonable grounds that they were stolen goods which would form material evidence on a criminal charge. On these facts the Court of Appeal held that the unauthorised seizure was lawful. Lord Denning M.R. observed that the cases contained 'no broad statement of principle'; the time had now come to state it. In his opinion, 'when a constable enters a house by virtue of a search warrant for stolen goods, he may seize not only the goods which he reasonably believes to be covered by the warrant, but also any other goods which he believes on reasonable grounds to have been stolen and to be material evidence on a charge of stealing or receiving against the person in possession of them or anyone associated with him'. For himself Salmon L.J. was not prepared to go as far as Lord Denning. He inclined instead to the view that if a police officer found property which he reasonably believed to be stolen in the possession of a person whom he had no reasonable ground to believe to be criminally implicated he would have no common law right to seize the property.[2] But the Court had no doubt in declaring the challenged seizure to be lawful even though the officers knew at the time that the seized items were outside the ambit of the authorising warrant.

In addition to the problem of whether the occupier or possessor should himself be suspected of criminal involvement before the expanded police power of seizure would arise there were two other uncertainties with *Chic Fashions*. First, was its effect to be limited to cases of stolen goods, or could it

[1] (1968) 2 Q.B. 299.

[2] Diplock, L.J. reserved his views on this question.

be extended to other types of offences[1], as had been the case with *Pringle v. Bremner* and *Stirling*? And if it could be extended beyond, could it authorise the seizure of evidence incriminating the occupier not on a similar offence to that forming the basis of the warrant but on a totally different one? Secondly, and more important, was the right conferred by *Chic Fashions* an extension of the authority of the warrant, in other words 'an implied extension of the powers'[2] it gave the police, or was it perhaps the development of new doctrine sanctioning the warrantless seizure of evidentiary items?[3] This second question is dealt with shortly; but at the time *Chic Fashions* was decided it was generally assumed that it had brought about no new rubric of the law of search and seizure but merely an expansion, though a considerable one, of the powers vested in those charged with the execution of search warrants, and this principally because traditional theory had long assumed that there were only two legitimate types of seizure in English law, that exercisable under the authority, actual or implied, of search warrants and that which could be effected as an incident of a valid arrest.

As regards the first matter, in view of recent developments[4] the position is as follows. The principles that can be derived from *Chic Fashions* are not confined to cases of stolen goods. These principles are as follows. When police officers enter a man's house under the authority of a search warrant they are entitled to take away not only the goods specified in the warrent but also any other items they have come across which they reasonably believe to be material evidence of the crime for which they have entered; if in the course of their search they come across (i.e. accidentally find) other goods or evidentiary items which show him (i.e. the occupier) to be implicated in some other crime, they may also seize them and detain them for as long as is necessary. Finally it may be that if in the course of a lawful search under a warrant the police come upon unspecified property which shows some other person to be implicated in an offence, whether the one forming the basis of the warrant or some different offence, they may take this property as well, provided they act reasonably and retain the property no longer than is necessary; but here there is much doubt, and it may be that when the property implicates a third person it should only be seized if it shows him to be involved in the offence under investigation.[5]

(ii) Search and seizure on arrest

The main category of warrantless searches is the incident-to-arrest one. It is universally regarded as settled that a police officer arresting a suspect may at the time of the arrest and as incidental to it seize and take certain items from

[1] See N. Reaburn, 'The Law of Search Warrants' (1970), 9 *W.A.L. Rev.* 242 at 245.

[2] *Frank Truman Export Ltd. v. M.P.C.* (1977) 3 All E.R. 431 at 438.

[3] See the formulations of Diplock and Salmon L.JJ., in *Chic Fashions* (1968) 2 Q.B. 299 at 314 and at 320–1; see also Australian Law Reform Commission, *Report No. 2 Criminal Investigation*, para. 189.

[4] See *Garfinkel v. M.P.C.* (1972) *Crim. L.R.* 44; *The Times*, 4 September 1971; *Frank Truman Export Ltd. v. M.P.C.* (1977) 3 All E.R. 431; *Malone v. M.P.C.* (1979) 1 All E.R. 256. See also 11 Halsbury's *Laws of England* (4th ed.) para. 126.

[5] See *Ghani v. Jones* (1970) 1 Q.B. 693 at 706, per Lord Denning, M.R.

his person or his possession.[1] It is further established that this principle applies irrespective of whether the arrest was made with or without a warrant and irrespective of the nature of the offence, whether it was a felony or merely a misdemeanour.[2] Nor is it questioned that this common law right of search is based both upon considerations of safety, that police officers should be entitled to disarm dangerous criminals at the time of arrest, and upon 'the interests of justice, in order that evidence of crime might not be destroyed or lost'.[3] But despite numerous unproblematic formulations considerable confusion surrounds this category of searches. The main issues that should be discussed are: (a) When does the authority to conduct a search incident to arrest exist? (b) What are its permissible limits, both in terms of what may be searched and in terms of what may be seized? These two issues are closely connected, but it is useful to consider them separately.[4]

The first issue is itself subdivided into a number of subsidiary questions. What is the precise connection between the authority to search incident to arrest and the arrest itself? Even more importantly, is this police authority a 'right' that derives from the arrest or is it a type of police power or right that derives from all the circumstances of the particular case? In what types or categories of cases or offences can it be invoked? On the first question English law seems to assume that the right to search on arrest only arises if there has *actually* been an arrest, i.e. it is *upon* a *lawful* arrest that the right to conduct a search of the person and take and detain certain items of property arises.[5]

[1] *Barnett & Grant v. Campell* (1902) 21 N.Z.L.R. 484 at 491; see also two important Canadian cases recognising this right, *R. v. Brezack* (1950) 2 D.L.R. 265, and *Re Laporte and R.* (1972) 29 D.L.R. (3d) 651. This is also the position in Scotland: see *Adair v. McGarry*, (1933) J.C. 72. The right to search an arrested person has been recognised quite generally even though no express power to conduct such searches is given by the comprehensive statutes governing search warrants and the like (see Adams, *Criminal Law and Practice in New Zealand* 490 (1971)).

[2] *Dillon v. O'Brien* (1887) 16 Cox C.C. 245. The distinction between felonies and misdemeanours was abolished in England in 1967: Criminal Law Act 1967, s.1.

[3] *Clarke v. Bailey* (1933) 33 S.R. (N.S.W.) 303; *Dillon v. O'Brien and Davis* (1887) 16 Cox C.C. 245 at 249.

[4] In what follows we shall attempt a unified treatment of arrest-based searches of the person and of premises. This may be too ambitious because English cases seem to regard the two as rather different. In any case the materials are scanty and incapable of supporting a generalised statement. But since both are based on (apparently) similar considerations (concerning safety and the preservation of evidence), and since they both flow from or at least depend on the legality of the preceding arrest, they can be subjected to the same type of analysis.

[5] In Scotland too it has been held that the right to search on arrest presupposes an arrest (see *Adair v. McGarry*, (1933) J.C. 72 at 89, and *McGovern v. H.M. Advocate*, (1950) J.C. 33 at 36, where the Lord Justice-General said that 'it is clear that no police officer has any right to search any person whom he does not apprehend'). But Scottish cases have recognised an exception to this in cases of emergency. A good example is *Bell v. Hogg*, (1967) J.C. 49. Here hand rubbings were taken from men suspected of the theft of some copper wire. At the time the suspects had not been arrested or charged. It was held that in view of the urgent need to preserve evidence of the substance he had observed on their hands the police officer was justified in taking the hand-rubbings even though the suspects had not yet been arrested. *McGovern v. H.M. Advocate*, supra, was distinguished on the ground that that case had involved no urgency.

This is confirmed by weighty New Zealand authority. In *Barnett and Grant v. Campbell*[1] a warrant had been issued under the Gaming Act 1881 authorising the police to search premises, arrest persons found on them and seize, among other things, instruments of gaming. But the documents seized were not instruments of gaming, and at no point was an arrest made. The seizure therefore was not justified by the warrant. But in the Supreme Court Williams J. held that the seizure of the documents on the basis of which the charge was proferred was justified on the ground that *the power* to make an arrest (which had not been exercised) had brought into operation the common law authority to seize evidence of the offence in the defendant's (i.e. the person who could be arrested) possession. In other words, it was 'the existence of the *authority* to arrest, not the *actual* arrest' which justified the seizure of the evidentiary material in issue. Williams J.'s decision was reversed by the Court of Appeal on the ground that the authority to seize evidence arose not from the power to arrest but from 'the actual arrest'. The right to conduct a personal search, the Court pointed out, was 'dependent not upon the right to arrest, but the fact of arrest'. It was therefore essential that at the material time the person searched should be 'in custodia legis'.[2] Had Grant been arrested the papers could have legitimately been seized under the common law authority vested in a constable effecting an arrest, the seized papers being at the time in the possession and control of Grant and constituting admittedly relevant evidence on a charge of gaming. But some Australian dicta support the thesis that an arrest may justify a seizure of incriminating evidence even if the seizure preceded in point of time the arrest. Thus in *Field v. Sullivan*[3] the Full Court of Victoria upheld as lawful a seizure of goods believed to be stolen despite the fact that it had been made before the actual arrest since 'the (challenged) seizure was sufficiently close to the arrest to be fairly regarded as incidental to, and part of, the same operation as the arrest'. And in *McFarlane v. Sharp*[4] the New Zealand Court of Appeal, while not prepared to distinguish *Barnett and Grant v. Campbell*, expressly left open the question whether in some cases a subsequent arrest may not legitimise a prior seizure, at least where the two are so closely connected in time that they may fairly be regarded as 'notionally contemporaneous',[5] as part of one 'continuous transaction'.

On the second question some have taken the view that the right to search as an incident of an arrest arises whenever there is an arrest. This was the view of Horridge J. in *Elias v. Pasmore,*[6] and many other statements can be found in the cases supporting it. But the authorities support neither the existence of a general right to conduct searches of the person on arrest nor

[1] (1902) 21 N.Z.L.R. 484.

[2] Ibid., at 492–3.

[3] (1923) V.L.R. 70.

[4] (1972) N.Z.L.R. 838 at 842; see J. A. Smillie, '*McFarlane v. Sharp*: Affirmation or Extension of Police Powers of Search and Seizure?' (1975) 6 *N.Z.U.L. Rev.* 271, 282–3.

[5] (1972) N.Z.L.R. at 842.

[6] (1934) 2 K.B. 164 at 169; see Stephens, 'Search and Seizure of Chattels' (1970) *Crim. L.R.* 74, 78–9.

even the automatic exercise of the right even in those areas where it is normally acknowledged to exist. In *Bessell v. Wilson*[1] a man was arrested for failing to appear in person to answer a summons arising out of his prior conviction for an infringement under the Copyright of Designs Act 1843; he was then imprisoned and searched. Lord Campbell C.J., expressing strong disapproval of the search to which the plaintiff had been subjected, made two points. First, his disapproval did not mean that 'there was no right in anyone to search a prisoner at any time'; this was not so, it often being 'the duty of an officer to search a prisoner'; thus, if a man was taken in the commission of a felony he could be searched to see whether the stolen articles were in his possession or whether he had any instruments of violence about him which it was necessary to take away from him. But there was 'no right in a case of this kind (i.e. the kind before the court) to inflict the indignity to which the plaintiff had been subjected', it being absurd to suggest that the plaintiff might have on his person an instrument which he might use to injure either himself or some other person. There are cases, in other words, where there is no right to search a person on his arrest. To put it differently, even if there is a general power or right to search on arrest, this right or power cannot be invoked or exercised in all cases. How should the distinction between permissible and impermissible exercises of the power to search incident to arrest be drawn? The correct answer appears to be that the right to search, even though dependent on the fact of a lawful arrest, attaches not 'because of the nature of the offence but because of the extrinsic circumstances',[2] i.e. all the facts and circumstances of a given situation. Only if the *actual* circumstances of a *particular* case warrant a search of the defendant upon his lawful arrest is a consequential or incidental search justified. Indeed some cases take the view that the right to search the person on arrest is 'a very limited' one.[3] Clarification is only possible if one goes back to first principle.

The power to search incident to arrest is intended to serve certain purposes;[4] these are, first to remove articles from the arrested person which he might use to escape, injure himself or others, or to commit any further crime, and secondly to take away from him evidence relevant to the crime on which he has been arrested and which he might destroy; and if on the facts of a case these dangers do not exist there is no right to conduct a search. How is

[1] (1853) 20 L.T. (O.S.) 233.

[2] Stephens, supra, at 78.

[3] *R. v. Naylor* (1979) *Crim. L.R.* 532. In a case where a woman police constable was seeking to remove jewellery from the prisoner, Judge Skinner said that on arrest police officers have the right '(to) search for and remove objects which they reasonably suspect to be connected with a criminal offence committed by the accused' and also '(to) search for and remove any object with which a prisoner might do herself or others injury', or with which an escape could be attempted (the learned judge would apparently allow a search for items connected with any criminal offence reasonably thought to be on the person of the arrestee, not only for those objects which are thought to be material to the offence for which the arrest has been made; see also Halsbury's *Laws of England*, 4th ed., vol. 11 (1976), para. 121, and *Lindley v. Rutter*, (1980) 3 W.L.R. 660, 665.

[4] See *Lindley v. Rutter* (1980) 3 W.L.R. 660.

one to decide whether these dangers exist? One should have regard both to the possibility, as indicated by the perceived facts, that the particular prisoner might use a weapon, destroy evidence or commit a crime while in custody, and to experience and common sense. Ultimately particular measures must be justified by the circumstances of the particular case. But this does not mean that the circumstances in which people are taken into custody cannot be broadly categorised; and experience may show, as it surely does, that certain measures, including searches, are prima facie reasonable and necessary in particular categories and with regard to particular offences; this experience may be given the form of, and passed on as, standing instructions; but it is always possible that the special circumstances of a particular case will justify a departure from any standard procedures that may have been adopted, whether this takes the form of the omission of what would normally be done or the taking of additional measures not generally permissible. This approach—emphasising that no 'general rule'[1] can be applied to such cases, that there is no universal right to search prisoners on arrest, but that the adoption of any particular measures whether on arrest or incarceration must always be capable of justification with reference to all the circumstances of the particular case—has now been explicitly adopted by the Divisional Court in *Lindley v. Rutter.*[2] Here the appellant was seen by a police officer staggering in the street. The officer rightly concluded that she was drunk. She was arrested. At the police station she continued to scream and swear, and was placed in a cell. The constable then, acting in accordance with standing orders which applied to any female person arrested and placed in a cell, attempted to search her and remove her brassiere for her own protection. She resisted, and was charged with and convicted of assaulting the constable in the execution of her duty. The Divisional Court quashed her conviction on the ground that the constable had exceeded her duty. The principle, the Divisional Court said, was that a police constable could search an arrested person and remove articles from his person only where he considered it necessary to prevent him from escaping, injuring himself or others, committing some further mischief or disposing of evidence. What measures could reasonably be taken in this connection depended upon the likelihood that the particular prisoner presented one or more of the dangers it was the constable's duty to neutralise. This in turn would involve him in considering the prisoner's known or apparent disposition. What could not be justified was the taking of particular measures without regard to the circumstances of the particular case. Here there was no justification for what had been done. It was inherently unlikely that the possession of the brassiere could lead to accidental injury, and there was no evidence that young female drunks in general were liable to injure themselves with their brassieres or that the appellant had shown a peculiar disposition to do so.[3] In terms of principle,

[1] *Leigh v. Cole* (1853) 6 Cox C.C. 329 at 332.

[2] (1980) 3 W.L.R. 660.

[3] The cases normally draw no distinction between a search incident to arrest and a custodial search, a distinction, as we have seen, which has, by and large, been drawn in America. On this basis a search incident to arrest is a search that is

therefore, an arrested person can only be searched if the police have reasonable grounds to believe that he has on his person either articles which he can use to injure either himself or others or evidence in connection with the offence for which he is arrested. This means that if the crime on the basis of which the accused has been arrested is one on which there can be no evidence a search of the person incident to arrest can only be conducted if there is reason to believe that unless the arrestee is deprived of certain items he could cause harm.

The second broad issue relates to the permissible *limits* of the authority to search on arrest. Here again two subsidiary questions arise. To begin with, is the authority to *search* on arrest confined to the person of the arrestee or does it extend beyond, and if so how far beyond? Secondly, what items are subject to *seizure*? The first question deals with the legitimate scope of a *search* incident to arrest. The second deals with the ambit of permissible *seizure*. As will be seen, it is the failure of English courts to distinguish between search and seizure that has long bedevilled efforts to clarify this notoriously difficult branch of the law.

On the first question the most usual formulation is that when a constable arrests a person he may take and detain (certain types of) property found 'in

---

conducted either contemporaneously with or immediately after the arrest (as indeed is stated in *Barnett and Grant v. Campbell* (1902) 21 N.Z.L.R. 484 at 491–2 where it was said that a constable may '*at the time* of such arrest, and as incidental to it, seize and take possession of articles in (his) possession'); in contrast a custodial search is one that, broadly speaking, is conducted after the defendant has been taken to the police station and been charged. At this point (since any evidentiary items will already have been removed at the time of arrest) the purposes of the search are to prevent the prisoner from causing harm to himself or others and to frustrate any escape plans he might have. (Of course the police may wish to search the prisoner again and more thoroughly for 'evidence' of the offence for which he has been arrested). The matter of custodial search is covered by legislation in many jurisdictions: see for instance s.353A(1) of the Crimes Act 1900 (New South Wales), s.236 of the Criminal Code (W.A.), and s.5(1) of the Criminal Process (Identification and Search Procedures) Act 1976 (Tas). In all these it is provided that where 'a person is in lawful custody upon a charge of committing any offence' it should be lawful for the police to search him, principally for the purpose of removing from his person or clothing a weapon or any other article capable of being used to inflict injury or to assist him in escaping from custody. Two things must be noticed. First, these provisions operate when the prisoner is in custody, i.e. which, in those cases where the arrest has not taken place at the police station, may be some time after the arrest; secondly, even in such jurisdictions which expressly provide for custodial searches, the common law right to search on arrest is of course still recognised (for a consideration of these problems, see *Clarke v. Bailey* (1933) 33 S.R. (N.S.W.) 303). But English cases (see *Lindley v. Rutter*, supra) draw no distinction between searches on arrest and custodial searches; they instead recognise, and seek to regulate, the right to conduct searches of arrested persons and of persons taken into custody by the same type of provision; and something similar has been suggested by the A.L.I. in their *Model Code of Pre-Arraignment Procedure* §§ 230.3 (1975) where searches and seizures incidental to arrest may be conducted by the officer making the arrest and the authorised officials at the police station or other police building to which the arrested individual is brought.

his possession'[1] or, more fully, that the incidental search following a lawful arrest may only be for (seizable) articles 'in the possession or under the control'[2] of the arrested person.[3] But what is meant by 'possession' and 'control' in this connection? Do these terms bear the same restrictive connotations as in current American jurisprudence following *Chimel v. California*,[4] or do they have a wider meaning? There are a number of possibilities. The first is to define 'possession' and 'control' as in *Chimel* and only allow the incidental search to cover the area within the arrestee's 'immediate control', the area that is from which he could obtain either a weapon for use against the arresting officers or easily disposable evidence for destruction. The second view is that the arresting officers may search not only the area within the arrestee's immediate control but also his entire house or premises, provided in this second case that he is arrested *at* the house or premises and that the search is *for* 'material evidence in relation to the crime for which he is arrested or for which they enter',[5] which of course means that the offence must be one involving material evidence (and perhaps that it should also be reasonable to believe that the search will unearth such

[1] *Dillon v. O'Brien and Davis* (1887) 16 Cox C.C. 245 at 249.

[2] *Barnett and Grant v. Campbell* (1902) 21 N.Z.L.R. 484 at 491.

[3] Another difficult question relates to the permissible intrusiveness of a search of the *person* of the arrestee. In other words, assuming that the circumstances justify in the abstract a search of the person (for instance on the ground that it is likely that the arrested person is carrying with him fruits of the crime), how intrusive can the search be? There are two interesting Canadian cases. In *R. v. Brezack* (1950) 2 D.L.R. 265, the Ontario Court of Appeal maintained a conviction for assault against a person who had bitten a police officer while the latter was searching the inside of his mouth for narcotic capsules which were thought to be hidden there. Robertson, C.J.O., speaking for the Court said (at 101) that 'the attempt to search the inside of (the) appellant's mouth was a justifiable incident of that arrest'. In *Re Laporte and R.* (1972) 29 D.L.R. (3d) 651, discussed earlier, it was held that the common law right to search a prisoner at the time of arrest could not justify a surgical intrusion months after the arrest for the purpose of securing evidence. The learned judge did not find it necessary to decide whether the right to search the person on arrest included minor medical procedures such as the taking of a blood sample or examination by X-rays. Scottish authorities establish that the right to conduct a personal search incidental to an arrest extends to examining the accused for any incriminating natural or artificial marks upon the person (for instance a birth mark that may help in identification, or bloodstains and the like), to taking fingerprints and presumably scrapings from under the fingernails, and to placing the accused in an identification line-up (see *Adair v. McGarry*, 1933 J.C. 72). It also appears that a search of the person on arrest includes the right to take a blood sample (see *H.M. Advocate v. Milford*, 1973 S.L.T. 12 at 13). It could also be said that recent cases (see particularly *Lindley v. Rutter*, supra) exemplify another principle that figures extensively in American search and seizure cases, namely that the more intrusive or offensive the police conduct used to obtain the evidence the more persuasive the justification should also be that is adduced in support. There were degrees of affront, said the Divisional Court in *Lindley v. Rutter*; going through someone's pockets was less of an affront than a body search; and in every case the police should have 'good reason' for acting as they did.

[4] 395 U.S. 752 (1969).

[5] *Ghani v. Jones* (1970) 1 Q.B. 693 at 706, per Lord Denning M.R.

evidence). A third and even wider view is that when a person has been arrested a search of his house or premises is permissible even if the arrest did not take place there but somewhere else, provided that the goods which the police are searching for are goods 'which they reasonably believe to be material evidence in relation to the crime for which he is arrested'.[1] An even more extreme version of this third possibility would allow the police to search a man's premises when he was arrested at a different location even if there is no relationship at all between the crime on the basis of which the arrest was effected and the subsequent search of the premises, when the subsequent search that is is clearly and unashamedly a general search or fishing expedition. This extreme version was rejected in *Jeffrey v. Black*,[2] but it is not at all clear whether English law favours the second or third possibility. In *Jeffrey v. Black* the defendant was arrested at a place other than his house for the theft of a sandwich. The police then searched his house and found cannabis. It was held that this search was illegal on the ground that a police officer who arrested a suspect for an offence *at one place* had no authority without a search warrant or the suspect's consent to search his house *at another place when* the contents of the house on their face bore no relation to the offence for which the arrest was made or the evidence required to support it. But Lord Widgery C.J. thought that if the police officers had 'any sort of reason' for thinking that the defendant's theft of the sandwhich required an inspection of his premises, 'they might very well have made that inspection without further authority'.[3] This seems to suggest that if the police arrest a person in place A they can search his house in place B if there is reason to believe that 'some material evidence can be obtained by that

[1] *Jeffrey v. Black* (1978) 1 All E.R. 555 at 558, per Lord Widgery C.J. There are come confusing dicta of Lord Denning M.R. in *Dallison v. Caffery* (1965) 1 Q.B. 348 which may support this position. He said (at 367) that when a constable has taken into custody a person reasonably suspected of felony 'he can do what is reasonable to investigate the matter', including taking the person suspected to his house to see whether any of the stolen property was there, since it might otherwise 'be removed and valuable evidence lost'. A more limited explanation of these dicta is that Lord Denning was discussing a case where the suspect consented to going home and to having his premises searched (see Leigh, *Police Powers in England and Wales* 52 n. 3 (1975)). In Scotland the basic doctrine appears to be that it is not permissible for the police to arrest a man at a place other than his house and then to search the house without warrant. But such a search of premises will be upheld if there are circumstances of urgency justifying the police action; furthermore in Scottish cases '(u)rgency is widely interpreted in favour of the police': Renton and Brown, *Criminal Procedure According to the Law of Scotland* 36 (1972). A case in point is *H.M. Advocate v. McGuigan*, 1936 J.C. 16. A man was arrested and charged with murder and rape. Later the police visited and searched a tent where the accused lived with his mother and stepfather and took possession of a number of articles. It was held that as the matter was in the view of the police one of urgency they were entitled to act without delay and without having to obtain a warrant. Further, it appears that where a person is arrested in his house 'it is probably competent to search the house for stolen property or any evidence of guilt': Renton and Brown, supra, at 37.

[2] (1978) 1 All E.R. 555.

[3] Ibid., at 558.

search',[1] i.e. if the offence is one on which there is some evidence which might possibly be found at the arrested person's house.[2] But no clear authority or even judicial statement can be found in support of this wide view, and taking all the authorities together it seems far more likely that the physical scope of a search incident to arrest extends *at most* to the person of the arrestee and his house or other premises where the arrest is made.[3] Further, the cases on the search of the *person* incident to arrest discussed above would seem to indicate that if the offence is one on which there is no possible evidence or where all the evidence has been collected no search of the premises will be allowed, for to take a different view would be to permit general searches and fishing expeditions seeking to obtain *any* evidence that might support charges against the accused.

What about the extent and limits of permissible seizure and detention? Of course it goes without saying that what may be seized depends primarily upon the purposes of the authority to search on a lawful arrest. Since the main purpose of the incidental search is to deprive the arrested person both of weapons and any other instruments by means of which he could attempt to escape or cause harm to himself or others and of evidence relevant to the

[1] This was said by counsel to be the normal practice of the police in serious cases: see *Jeffrey v. Black* (1978) 1 All E.R. 555, at 560, per Forbes J.

[2] A passage which their Lordships considered at length in *Jeffrey v. Black* is a part of Lord Denning's judgment in *Ghani v. Jones* (1970) 1 Q.B. 693 at 706 where the Master of the Rolls said that 'where police officers enter a man's house by virtue of a warrant, *or arrest a man lawfully*, with or without a warrant' (italics added), then they may take any goods which 'they find in his possession *or in his house*' (italics added) which they reasonably believe to be 'material evidence' in connection with the crime for which the arrest is made or for which they enter. Is Lord Denning here assuming that the arrest takes place *in the house*, or is he saying that there is a power of search of the arrestee's house even if the arrest takes place elsewhere? Lord Widgery, C.J. took Lord Denning to be saying the latter thing, and he himself would apparently have allowed the search in *Jeffrey v. Black* if the police were searching for evidence of the crime for which they had arrested the defendant. The judgment of Forbes J. too is very unclear. But he seems to be denying, but not very emphatically, that the police have authority to search a man's house when they have arrested him at another place (Forbes, J. said: '*Apart* from the question' of the officers searching for something having no materiality to the accusation they were making against the accused, there was '*the other point*' that the arrest had taken place at a location other than the place searched. This suggests that he would not accept the preference of Lord Widgery, C.J. as to the wider authority the Chief Justice was prepared to vest in the police).

[3] But, it must be pointed out, no actual authority holds that this is so, and it might be argued both that permissible search and seizure should be confined to what is within the arrestee's control or possession, and that in the absence of exceptional circumstances an incidental search should not extend beyond the room in which the arrest takes place. This indeed appears to be the holding of *Dillon v. O'Brien and Davis* (1887) 16 Cox C.C. 245. Here the constables arrested the plaintiff under a warrant of arrest and proceeded to take bank-notes and other property then in the room in which the arrest took place (ibid., at 247) for the purpose of producing them in the prosecution of the plaintiff. It was held that constables were entitled upon a lawful arrest 'to take and detain property found in (the arrestee's) possession' which would form 'material evidence in his prosecution for that crime' (ibid., at 249, per Palles C.B.); see also the approach of the Supreme Court of Eire in *Jennings v. Quinn* [1968] I.R. 305 at 309.

crime for which he is arrested which he might otherwise seek to destroy it follows that on arrest the police may certainly seize and detain items which constitute evidence of the offence for which the arrest was made and articles which the accused could use as weapons or as means of escape. What if the police during an otherwise legitimate incidental search come across evidence that incriminates either the arrested person on some crime other than the one on the basis of which the arrest was effected or some third person? As regards the first matter Lord Denning, M.R., in *Ghani v. Jones*[1] expressed the view that if in the course of a lawful search following an arrest the police come across some other evidence which shows the arrestee to be implicated in some other crime, this evidence too may be seized. The second and more difficult point is whether evidence implicating a third person is also subject to seizure. One view, apparently supported by *Elias v. Pasmore*,[2] is that following an arrest the police may seize any property they find in the course of an otherwise legitimate incidental search which constitutes evidence 'of a crime committed by *anyone*'. Lord Denning in *Ghani v. Jones*[3] did not agree with this, because he thought that the words 'by anyone' went too far, and was in favour of confining the *Elias* principle to cases where the incriminating evidence that is found during an incidental search implicates the third person in the offence for which the arrestee himself is apprehended. If therefore the incriminating evidence the police come across does not relate *in any way* to the offence on the basis of which the arrest was effected but only relates to the involvement of another person in a different offence is should not be seized. A different holding, his Lordship thought, would be 'a flat contradiction of *Entick v. Carrington*' in that it would permit police officers to conduct searches 'simply' to see if a person *may have committed* some crime or other.[4] But, it is respectfully suggested, the reason his Lordship gives for disagreeing with what has here been referred to as the *Elias* view is unconvincing. It is of course correct that the common law does not permit general searches or fishing expeditions that are unsupported by probable cause or reasonable suspicion but only seek to see if some incriminatory evidence of some offence can be uncovered. To allow this would indeed be to do away with one of the themes emerging from *Entick v. Carrington*.[5] But the fears that Lord Denning expresses are best answered not by putting an arbitary limitation on what may be seized, but by insisting on two different requirements which alone can ensure that general searches and indiscriminate seizures are not allowed: first that a search is valid or invalid at its inception and that an unlawful search cannot be validated by what it uncovers, and secondly that only things or other evidence affording evidence of crime *inadvertently* discovered *in the course* of an otherwise lawful search should be subject to seizure. In other words, what English law needs but has yet to develop is something akin to the American 'plain view' doctrine,[6] namely that when the police in the course

[1] (1970) 1 Q.B. 693 at 706.
[2] (1934) 2 K.B. 164.
[3] (1970) 1 Q.B. 693 at 706.
[4] Ibid.
[5] (1765) 19 State Tr. 1029.
[6] See *Coolidge v. New Hampshire*, 403 U.S. 443 (1971).

of a bona fide and appropriately circumscribed search come across incriminatory items, irrespective of whether these relate to the involvement of the arrestee in some different offence or the involvement of some third person in an offence (whether the one on the basis of which the arrest has been effected or some other totally different offence), they may seize them.[1] The reason for this is simply that a different view would allow the destruction of otherwise relevant evidence, or at the very least impose upon the police 'an unnecessarily cumbersome and time-consuming procedure',[2] that is to have to go to a magistrate in order to obtain a warrant even though the evidence they wish to take away has already been discovered and is before them. Of course in many cases of searches incident to arrest the only evidence that will be discovered either on the person or in the vicinity of the arrestee is evidence of his own involvement in the offence for which he has been arrested. But this is not always so, particularly if the authority to search following a lawful arrest extends not only to the area within the arrestee's immediate control but also to the whole of his house. If then the police are not allowed to seize evidence in 'plain view' concerning the commission of an offence by some third person who is not present at the scene (and therefore cannot be arrested), the police must either go away to obtain a search warrant, which will possibly allow the destruction or disappearance of the evidence, or remain near by until the warrant is obtained in case the person implicated by

[1] The 'plain view' doctrine seems to be recognised in Scotland. Two cases can be contrasted, *H.M. Advocate v. Turnbull*, 1951 J.C. 96 and *H.M. Advocate v. Hepper*, 1958 J.C. 39. In the former a warrant had been obtained to search an accountant's office for documents relating to a particular client. Many files were removed; some of these related to the client mentioned in the charges, but the great number related to other clients, each file being clearly marked with the name of the client to whom it related. Furthermore, the documents contained in these files were not examined at the time of the search but were passed to the Inland Revenue authorities for investigation. Lord Guthrie held that the seizure of the documents not specified in the warrant was unlawful. As the learned judge put it, '(w)hen a warrant was granted to search an accused's premises for certain articles tending to implicate him in one crime, it could not be used as authority to ransack the whole premises to find other articles which might implicate him in the same crime, much less articles which might implicate him in other crimes not charged'. In this case, '(t)here was no question of the police having stumbled unexpectedly on evidence of a plainly incriminating character'; rather, 'they had deliberately and without authority searched for and seized documents which would require careful examination before their incriminating nature could be revealed'. This was illegal. In *H.M. Advocate v. Hepper*, supra, the police searched the house of a person with his consent. In the course of the search the police seized and removed an attaché case which was unconnected with the matter under investigation but was connected with the charge of theft subsequently preferred. Lord Guthrie held that the attaché case had been properly seized and removed. Here, unlike *Turnbull*, supra, the police had 'accidentally stumbled upon evidence of a plainly incriminating character'. The seizure was lawful since the object (which at the very least was of 'a very suspicious character') might otherwise have disappeared. In Scotland therefore, much like America, the 'plain view' doctrine validates the seizure of incriminating evidence *if* this was discovered *inadvertently in the course* of an otherwise *legitimate* intrusion, and *if* it was either of a plainly incriminating character or of a very suspicious character.

[2] Smillie, supra, 294 n. 4, at 281.

the fortuitously discovered evidence returns (in which case he may be arrested and the evidence itself seized), a procedure that is not only cumbersome but also unnecessary in view of the fact that the damning evidence has already been discovered and the magistrate will automatically issue a warrant for its seizure. It may of course be true that limitations on what may be seized in practice narrow the scope of the evidentiary quest itself. But so will many other totally arbitrary limitations on seizability, like the overruled *Gouled* doctrine forbidding the seizure of 'mere evidence', which nobody would seriously put forward as ways of remaining faithful to *Entick v. Carrington*. It is thought instead that the *proper way* to ensure that searches incident to arrest do not degenerate into fishing expeditions is, first to insist that they should remain tied to their original rationale, that of disarming suspects of dangerous instruments and of taking from them evidence relevant to the offence on which the particular arrest was effected, and secondly to allow into evidence *only* those incriminatory items discovered *inadvertently* during a legitimate and properly limited search. Given these conditions it would be arbitrary and contrary to common sense to confine the category of seizable items either to those that relate to the offence on the basis of which the arrest took place or to those somehow connected with the criminal complicity of the arrestee himself. Seizable items, it is suggested, are all items that afford evidence of crime provided they were found *inadvertently* by the police *in the course* of an otherwise *legitimate* search.[1]

[1] Difficult problems are also raised when an arrested person or prisoner has been searched and money has been taken from him. The general principle is that the police have no right to seize money found on a prisoner where there is no ground for believing that it was connected with the offence charged. Such money should be returned immediately to him (*Welch v. Gilmour and Blackstone* (1955) 111 C.C.C. 221). This principle was expressed succinctly in *R. v. O'Donnell* (1835) 7 Car & P. 138, as follows: 'Generally speaking, it is not right that a man's money should be taken away from him, unless it is connected in some way with the property stolen. If it is connected with the robbery, it is quite proper that it should be taken. But unless it is, it is not a fair thing to take away his money, which he might use for his defence'. But if there is a connection between the money seized and the offence under investigation there is a police power to retain it. This principle is illustrated by *Malone v. M.P.C.* (1979) 1 All E.R. 256. This case deals with a seizure of money when the police were acting under a search warrant, but its holding would also apply in the case of a seizure incident to an arrest. In *Malone* the plaintiff was suspected of receiving and handling stolen goods. The police searched his house and seized, among other things, numerous English and foreign banknotes. The plaintiff was charged with handling stolen goods. No charges were made in respect of the banknotes. The plaintiff claimed that he required the money to pay the legal fees for his trial; the police conceded that the banknotes were not the subject of charges against the plaintiff and had not been made an exhibit at the committal proceedings but argued, among other things, that they had reason to believe that the banknotes were to be used for the purchase of stolen property and were thus material evidence in connection with the offences for which the plaintiff had been charged. The Court of Appeal accepted that the police had no power to retain property seized from an accused person if it was not stolen or the subject of any charges unless the retention was justified on ascertainable grounds. However, where the property was a reasonably necessary and valuable part of the evidence material to the charges against the accused it was in the public interest, having regard to the

(iii) Power of seizure without arrest or search warrant

Is there a power to seize evidence of crime when the seizure cannot be justified either under a search warrant or on the basis of the authority to search incident to a lawful arrest? Until recently it was widely believed that no such power existed, and that evidence of crime could only be seized if the search had proceeded either on the basis of a search warrant or following a lawful arrest. This principle is illustrated by the decision of the New Zealand Court of Appeal in *Barnett and Grant v. Campbell*[1] that has already been discussed. It was assumed there that since the seizure could not be justified under the search warrant it would only be held to be valid if it was found to be incidental to a lawful arrest, which it was not because no arrst had taken place. In other words, a seizure of evidence of crime must either be authorised by a search warrant or be made on the basis of an arrest, as described in the previous section. To put it even more simply, a seizure cannot be legal if there is neither a search warrant nor an arrest.

It is not easy to fit the difficult and much-discussed case of *Elias v. Pasmore*[2] into this doctrinal framework. Here police officers, armed with a warrant for the *arrest* of a man called Hannington, entered a house of which Elias was the tenant. Hannington was in the house and was arrested. The police had no search warrant; but they conducted a search of Elias' premises and seized and took away a number of seditious papers which implicated not only Hannington, the arrested person, but Elias as well. The police prosecuted first Hannington and then Elias, and both were convicted. Some of the seized documents, but not all, were used at the trial of Elias, who subsequently contended that their seizure was illegal and brought an action for their return and for damages for their detention. Horridge J. rejected this claim on the ground that '(t)he interests of the state must excuse the seizure of documents, which seizure would otherwise be unlawful, if it appears in fact that such documents were evidence of a crime committed by anyone'.

---

unpredictability of the course of a criminal trial and the risk to the administration of justice if the property were not available as evidence, for the police to retain the property until the trial, and that public interest prevailed over the right of the individual not to be deprived of his property. In the instant case because the banknotes were part of the evidence material to the charges against the plaintiff and because it could not be predicted with sufficient certainty that there would be no circumstances under which it would be necessary to adduce the banknotes in evidence at the plaintiff's trial, the police were entitled to retain them until the trial. Another difficult and as yet unresolved problem relates to the apparently common practice of searching *prisoners* and taking away from them all articles, including money, for safekeeping. Is this practice lawful? There are dicta both ways (see Leigh, *Police Powers in England and Wales* 52 (1975); see aso *Leigh v. Cole* (1853), 6 Cox C.C. 329; *Gottschalk v. Hutton*, 66 D.L.R. 499, (1922) 1 W.W.R. 59; *R. v. McDonald* (1933) 1 D.L.R. 46; *Yakimishyn v. Bileski* (1946) 3 D.L.R. 390; *Welch v. Gilmour* and *Blackstone* (1955), 111 C.C.C. 221).

[1] (1902) 21 N.Z.L.R. 484.

[2] (1934) 2 K.B. 164; see Wade, 'Police Search' (1934) 50 *L.Q.R.* 354. Here only the relevant facts of *Elias v. Pasmore* will be given. It should be noted that in fact the documents that were seized fell into a number of categories. The seizure of some was not 'excused', and damages for their unlawful seizure were awarded.

Since these documents 'were capable of being and were used as evidence in (Elias') trial', their seizure, though 'improper at the time', was subsequently 'excused' and became 'justified'. Not only is Horridge J.'s reasoning shrouded in obscurity, but it is also very unclear whether his judgment retains any authority. Three possible interpretations of *Elias v. Pasmore* can be offered. The first is that this case was wrongly decided on the simple ground that a seizure must be justifiable at the outset, that is when it takes place, and irrespective of whether the case eventually goes to trial or whether the seized items are used in criminal proceedings. Since the initial seizure of the documents was, on Horridge J.'s own admission, wrongful, it remained unlawful. A search or seizure, as Lord Denning, M.R., has put it,[1] cannot be made lawful or unlawful according to what happens afterwards. The second possible interpretation is that *Elias v. Pasmore* rests on an extensive view of the powers of the police to search and seize on arrest.[2] But this is not borne out by Horridge J.'s judgment even though the learned judge took a broad view of the right to search following an arrest. In his view the right to search the arrestee included the power to seize and detain property found in his possession which constituted material evidence against him with regard to the crime for which he had been arrested; it also included the power to seize property found in his possession which constituted evidence on the prosecution of *any* offence; but the authority to search and seize on arrest could not encompass the seizure of 'property found on premises occupied by persons other than the person of whom the arrest was made'. The challenged seizure in *Elias v. Pasmore* therefore was not held valid as incident to a valid arrest. The third explanation, admittedly not formulated with any coherence by Horridge J., is that the police may seize any evidence of crime they come across during an otherwise lawful search. On this interpretation the seizure of the documents was lawful from the beginning because *at the time* the police were engaged in a lawful intrusion, the arrest of Hannington. When so engaged they came across evidence implicating a third person, the occupier of the premises, in criminal activity. This chance discovery gave them the right to seize the evidence because otherwise it might have disappeared. But this version of events cannot stand up to scrutiny because it is relatively clear from the facts that the police did not simply stumble upon the evidence when legitimately attempting to arrest Hannington. Almost certainly they searched Elias' premises, and it was during *this* search rather than Hannington's apprehension that the documents were found and seized. It can not be argued that there is no right at common law to search premises not in the possession of the person arrested just because he happens to be on the premises at the time of his arrest; to put it differently, the authority to conduct a search incidental to an arrest extends to the premises of the arrestee if the arrest takes place there but not to the premises of some third party simply because the arrestee was there at the time of his arrest; since therefore the incriminating documents in *Elias v. Pasmore* were taken not in

[1] See *Chic Fashions v. Jones*, supra.
[2] Leigh, *Police Powers in England and Wales* 186 (1975).

the course of an otherwise lawful intrusion but during an impermissible exercise of police power their seizure was illegal.

Further doubt was thrown on *Elias v. Pasmore* by *R. v. Waterfield and Lynn.*[1] Here two police officers, having been informed that a car was involved in a serious offence, were keeping watch on the car which was at the time in a public car park. The two defendants entered the car intending to remove it. Neither was arrested but the constables attempted to prevent them from taking the car away. When one of the police officers stood in the path of the car he was assaulted by the defendants who were than charged with assaulting a police officer in the execution of his duty. They were convicted, but the Court of Criminal Appeal quashed their conviction on the ground that the constables had no power to detain the car and were therefore in excess of their duty when the alleged assault took place. The court seemed to accept that a duty rested upon the police to preserve for use in court evidence of a crime, but the execution of that duty did not in its view authorise them to prevent removal of the car in the circumstances of the case before them. But Ashworth J., delivering the court's opinion, acknowledged that there might be other instances involving the attempted warrantless seizure of evidence when there had been no arrest that would be more troublesome. What if a police officer was attempting to prevent the removal of an article which had been used in the course of a crime, for instance an axe used by a murderer? Such cases, the learned judge said, could be dealt with if and when they arose. But the court did go on to certify that a point of law of general public importance was involved, namely whether at common law a constable, in the absence of an arrest, has the power or duty to detain as prospective evidence property found in a public place which he has reasonable grounds to believe to be material evidence with regard to the commission of an offence. But no appeal was taken to the House of Lords. *R. v. Waterfield* and *Elias v. Pasmore* are not easy to reconcile. One possible distinction is to say that *Elias v. Pasmore* allows, or rather retrospectively legalises, the seizure of items *actually used in a trial*, as opposed to the seizure of property that never becomes an exhibit, as was the case with *Waterfield*. But this distinction is 'absurd in practice and repugnant in theory',[2] principally because it runs counter to the cardinal principle that a search must be good or bad when it starts and that it is not to be given retrospective legality either by what it turns up or by how what is discovered is used. A more plausible view is that *Waterfield* and *Elias v. Pasmore* are incompatible,[3] and that *Waterfield* affirms, though not unequivocally, the traditional principle that property cannot lawfully be seized without either a search warrant or an arrest. In other words, in the absence of a search warrant evidence of crime can only be

[1] (1964) 1 Q.B. 164. The facts of *Waterfield* are not very clear (see Smith and Hogan, *Criminal Law* (4th ed.) 363 (1978)). Why exactly was the police officer's conduct unlawful if he only stood in front of the car? Was he guilty of obstructing the highway? See P.J. Fitzgerald, 'The Arrest of a Motor-Car' (1965) *Crim. L. R.* 23.

[2] Thomas, 'The Law of Search and Seizure: Further Ground for Rationalisation', (1967) *Crim. L.R.* 3 at 5.

[3] Ibid.

seized if found either on the person of the arrestee or in his possession.

There is little doubt that the absence of a common law power to seize evidence of crime otherwise than under the authority of a warrant or on the basis of an arrest leads to serious problems. Many examples can be suggested. One is the case of the murderer's axe referred to by Ashworth J. in *Waterfield*. What if there is no arrest? Are the police expected to walk away, or should they simply take it, irrespective of whether the seizure is illegal? Or, again, the police enter premises in pursuance of some statutory power and there find goods or other items that constitute material evidence of a criminal offence. Why should they not seize the *inadvertently discovered* items in order to preserve them as evidence?[1] If they go away to obtain a warrant the evidence may disappear by the time they get back. If they stay on or near the premises to keep watch until the warrant is obtained, they again risk the destruction of the evidence, particularly if there are persons in the house at the time, and in any case it is not clear why one should insist on this inconvenient, cumbersome and unnecessary procedure, especially as it is obvious that in almost all instances of the discovery of such evidence the requested warrant will be given as a matter of course.[2] Equally clearly, so complex is this area and so important and neatly balanced the conflicting personal and societal interests involved—on the one hand the interest of the individual that his privacy and possessions should not be invaded except for the most compelling reasons and on the other the interest of society at large in detecting and apprehending criminals—that the necessary modifications to traditionally accepted common law principles forbidding the warrantless seizure of incriminating evidentiary items except from arrested persons are best effected by comprehensive and well-considered legislation.[3] But in *Chic Fashions v. Jones* and *Ghani v. Jones* the Court of Appeal took the initiative. In *Chic Fashions v. Jones*,[4] it will be remembered, the Court of Appeal allowed the seizure of goods reasonably believed to be evidence of crime committed by the person in possession or the occupier where the premises had been entered and searched by the police under a search warrant. One possible view is that this case only deals with what may be seized under search warrants, and says nothing about what may be seized when there is neither a search warrant nor the arrest of the person in possession or control. But another view is that the search warrant was only relevant in so far as it allowed the officers to gain access to the premises lawfully, and that the true effect of *Chic Fashions* is to create 'a new class of permissible warrantless seizures'.[5] Whatever the best interpretation of *Chic Fashions*, in *Ghani v. Jones*,[6] in a sweeping decision, the Court of Appeal expressly recognised the existence of a power to seize evidence of serious crime in the absence of either an arrest or a

[1] See the hypothetical case discussed by Salmon L.J. in *Chic Fashions v. Jones* (1968) 2 Q.B. 299 at 320.

[2] See Smillie, supra, 294 n. 4, 280–5.

[3] See *McFarlane v. Sharp* (1972) N.Z.L.R. 838 at 844.

[4] (1968) 2 Q.B. 299.

[5] See Australian Law Reform Commission, *Report No. 2 Criminal Investigation*, para. 193.

[6] (1970) 1 Q.B. 693.

search warrant. In *Ghani v. Jones* police officers inquiring into the disappearance of a Pakistani woman searched without a warrant the house of her father-in-law. The police asked for his passport and for the passports of his wife and daughter. Some time later the father-in-law asked for the return of the passports and certain other documents that had also been handed over as they wished to visit Pakistan. The police refused because they suspected that the Pakistani woman had been murdered and because they believed that in the event of charges being brought some of the documents handed over would be 'of evidential value' and others 'certainly of potential evidential value'. The passport holders brought actions claiming their return. The Court of Appeal held that the police officers were not entitled to hold on to the passports and other documents, and made an order for their return. But Lord Denning, M.R., with whom the other members of the Court agreed, recognised, or more properly brought into existence, a common law power to seize without warrant and detain property reasonably suspected of being evidence of a serious offence even when there had been no arrest. But certain requirements had to be present before this power could be exercised. These were set out by his Lordship in quasi-legislative fashion.

> First: The police officers must have reasonable grounds for believing that a serious offence has been committed.
>
> Second: The police officers must have reasonable grounds for believing that the article in question is either the fruit of the crime . . . or is the instrument by which the crime was committed . . . or is material evidence to prove the commission of the crime. . . .
>
> Third: The police officers must have reasonable grounds to believe that the person in possession of it has himself committed the crime, or is implicated in it, or is accessary to it, or at any rate his refusal (to hand it over) must be quite unreasonable.
>
> Fourth: The police must not keep the article, nor prevent its removal, for any longer than is reasonably necessary to complete their investigations or preserve it for evidence. . . .
>
> Finally: The lawfulness of the conduct of the police must be judged at that time, and not by what happens afterwards.

In the light of these criteria the police officers were not entitled to hold on to the passport and the other documents. They might have reasonable grounds for believing that the woman had been murdered. But they had not shown reasonable grounds for believing that the passports and letters were 'material evidence to prove the commission of the murder'. Nor had they shown reasonable grounds for believing that the plaintiffs were 'in any way implicated in a crime, or accessary to it'. And in any case the police had held the documents long enough. They would therefore be ordered to return them.

Three types of critical comment with regard to *Ghani v. Jones* have been made. First, some have expressed the fear that the new principles endanger private property and privacy, and needlessly extend police powers.[1] Secondly, as we have seen, even if it is accepted that the traditional rules do not satisfy the legitimate demands of law enforcement, it is questionable whether essential law reform in this area should be left in the hands of the judges. Legislation is much preferable, both because detailed provision can be made on all aspects of the problem, as opposed to the enunciation of imprecisely worded general guidelines, and because it is only by means of comprehensive legislative regulation that the conferment of new powers can be accompanied by the elaboration of much needed safeguards.[2] Finally, even if judicial intervention had become necessary as a result on the one hand of growing problems for law enforcement and on the other of continuing legislative inactivity, the *Ghani v. Jones* guidelines are full of serious uncertainties.[3] The most obvious are the following: The new police power to seize evidentiary matter in the absence of both search warrant and arrest is said to apply only to serious offences, but no guidance is given as to which offences are serious. Lord Denning said that the offence must be 'so serious that it is of the first importance that the offenders should be caught and brought to justice', but this does not clarify matters. Is the new power confined to offences like murder, the subject-matter of *Ghani v. Jones*, and robbery, also touched upon by Lord Denning, or does it embrace all arrestable offences, or does it have some intermediate meaning?[4] Secondly, what does it mean that the article can still be seized even if the person in possession is not himself suspected of complicity in the offence under investigation *if* his refusal to give it up is *unreasonable*?[5] What are the criteria of reason in this context? Does reasonableness depend on all the circumstances of the particular case, or will some rough guidelines be applied, and if so what are they? Is it for the police to demonstrate unreasonableness or is the correct principle that once they have shown that there were reasonable grounds for suspecting that the article in question constituted evidence of a serious crime the burden shifts to the person in possession who must then convince the court that his refusal to hand it over was reasonable? Thirdly, is the new power recognised by *Ghani v. Jones* only a power of seizure or does it also include the power of search, and perhaps entry, as well? The two alternatives are the following. The limited interpretation of Lord Denning's guidelines is that they only apply where the police officers were at the time of the challenged seizure lawfully on the premises or any other place where the evidence was found. It is not necessary that the police should have got there in any particular manner, whether under the authority of a search warrant or in order to arrest someone or in

[1] S.A. de Smith, *Constitutional and Administrative Law* 460 (1971).

[2] Leigh, supra, 305 n. 2, at 196.

[3] Leigh, supra, 193–6; Smillie, '*McFarlane v. Sharp*: Affirmation or Extension of Police Powers of Search and Seizure?' (1975) 6 *N.Z.U.L.* Rev. 271.

[4] See now *Frank Truman Export Ltd. v. M.P.C.* (1977) 3 All E.R. 431; *Wershof v. M.P.C.* (1978) 3 All E.R. 540.

[5] The words 'or at any rate his refusal must be quite unreasonable' did not appear when *Ghani v. Jones* was first reported (see *The Times*, 30 October, 1969) and appear to have been added by Lord Denning when he revised his judgment for publication in the law reports (see R.M. Jackson (1970) *C.L.J.* 1, 3).

pursuance of some statutory provision conferring a power of entry. It is enough if the police were on the premises at the time the seizure was made *lawfully*, which of course means that they must be able to justify their presence on some specific and recognised legal ground, for instance consent or entry to make an arrest or a search warrant. What if the police suspect on reasonable grounds that there is an evidentiary item on private premises that otherwise falls within the Denning guidelines but the householder refuses to permit the police to enter and there are grounds neither for an arrest within the premises nor for a search warrant? On this first interpretation the evidentiary item is beyond police powers of seizure. This first version of *Ghani v. Jones* in other words is quite similar to the American 'plain view' doctrine, in that it only allows the police to seize an incriminating piece of evidence they *inadvertently* come across in the course of an *otherwise legitimate intrusion*, and does not apply where the police are in reality looking for the item in question. The second and broader interpretation of *Ghani v. Jones* would not only allow the police to seize evidentiary items inadvertently discovered during a lawful intrusion but also enable them to use their reasonable suspicion that such an item could be found on the premises as *a reason for* entering and searching as well. The power conferred by *Ghani v. Jones* in other words is not only a power to seize and detain; it is also a power to search. It is not at all clear which is the better interpretation. Both Lord Denning in *Ghani v. Jones* and Diplock and Salmon L.JJ. in *Chic Fashions* seem to demand that the police should have been on the premises at the relevant time *lawfully*, but in this context, i.e. where there is neither a search warrant nor a prior arrest, it is not clear whether reasonable suspicion that the goods are on private premises can confer the necessary element of legality.[1]

Ghani v. Jones has been applied in England a number of times even though one cannot say with any confidence what reception Lord Denning's guidelines may one day receive in the House of Lords. The most important of these cases is *Garfinkel v. Metropolitan Police Commissioner*.[2] On the authority of a search warrant granted under the Explosive Substances Acts police officers searched premises occupied by one of the plaintiffs. No explosive substances were found but the police found and removed a large number of documents which afforded evidence of other crimes such as conspiracy to pervert the course of justice. Ackner J., applying *Ghani v. Jones,* held that the seizure of the documents was valid. Where, according to the learned judge, police officers entered a man's house by virtue of a warrant and in the course of their search found goods which showed him to be implicated in some crime

[1] This second interpretation receives some support from Lord Denning's remarks about the great train robbery. When in hiding, the robbers had apparently used a saucer belonging to a farmer. The police took the saucer and examined it. Lord Denning said: 'Could the farmer have said to them: "No, it is mine. You shall not have it?" Clearly not.' As Hartley and Griffith point out (*Government and Law* 151 (1975)), if the police have the right *to take* the saucer it would be absurd if the farmer could have prevented them from going on to his land to get it. In other words, *Ghani v. Jones* confers not only a power of seizure but related powers of entry and search as well.

[2] (1972) *Crim. L.R.* 44; *The Times*, 4 September 1971.

other than that to which the warrant was directed they could seize and remove them provided they acted reasonably and detained them no longer than necessary. *Ghani v. Jones* has also been applied in two more recent cases, both of which, interestingly, turned in part on the meaning to be given to Lord Denning's third requirement, namely that the police officers can take away the article in issue when they have reasonable grounds to believe that the person in possession is involved in the crime, or at any rate when his refusal to hand it over is 'quite unreasonable'. The first, *Frank Truman Export Ltd. v. Metropolitan Police Commissioner,*[1] represents a novel and potentially far-reaching extension of Lord Denning's guidelines into the area of privileged communications. Police officers entered the premises of a solicitor's office pursuant to a search warrant issued under the Forgery Act 1913, and with the apparent authority of the solicitor removed a large number of documents. Not all the documents that were removed had been specified in the warrant, but the seizure of the unauthorised papers was also approved even though these were held to have been privileged. The police, Swanwick J. held, were not acting unreasonably in seizing and retaining the unspecified privileged documents because (a) the solicitor had given them permission to take all the bundles of documents for searching and sorting, (b) at the time when they took them away they were investigating a crime, an alleged conspiracy, and had already charged a number of people, and (c) they had reasonable grounds for believing that the items taken would be material evidence to prove the commission of a crime, namely the alleged conspiracy. The police had therefore acted reasonably, and in these circumstances, 'on the balance of public policy', were entitled to retain the documents seized and use them as evidence in the prosecution of the alleged crime. The learned judge acknowledged that the solicitor was not himself implicated in any crime, and indeed that he was not refusing to give up the documents. But these features of the case did not make *Ghani v. Jones* inapplicable. Lord Denning, Swanwick J. observed, was neither drafting a statute nor considering every situation, but only setting forth certain guidelines on the basis of which the conflicting requirements of public policy, that the individual should have adequate protection and that crime should be suppressed and wrongdoers apprehended, were to be balanced. For the learned judge the seizure of evidence of crime when there had been neither an authorising warrant nor a valid arrest was 'one of the balance of public policy and of discretion', and 'on balance' the police would be held to be entitled to retain the documents. The two important features of *Frank Truman Export* are the following: first, in the application of Lord Denning's guidelines there seems to be a shift from the requirement that the person in possession should be either implicated in crime or clearly unreasonable in refusing to give the documents or in trying to get them back to the rather less exacting criterion that the police, taking all circumstances into account, should only be found to be acting reasonably; secondly the question of privilege is insufficiently noticed.[2] Can privilege be destroyed by otherwise validly exercisable powers

[1] (1977) 3 All E.R. 431.

[2] See (1978) 41 *M.L.R.* 72; (1978) *P.L.* 238.

of search and seizure, particularly by seizure in accordance with the principles of *Chic Fashions* and *Ghani v. Jones*? Conversely, if privilege does not lose its relevance even though what was taken is material evidence, should it have the effect of making the seizure of the privileged matter unlawful,[1] or should it only be taken into account as one factor in the balancing of the conflicting interests, that is as an additional consideration in support of the view that the seizure was illegal? In any case, since the privilege belongs not to the lawyer but to the client, and since it is the client alone who can waive it, should a solicitor be able to frustrate it simply by giving up privileged documents? And can the claims of privilege be defeated when a solicitor hands privileged documents to the police either 'through a misunderstanding or mere inadvertence',[2] as appears to have happened in *Frank Truman*? Indeed at the end of his judgment Swanwick J., emphasising that the documents in issue had been handed over, suggested that any sorting of papers in a solicitor's office should whenever possible take place in the office itself 'and be so conducted that documents which are clearly both privileged and inadmissible . . . can be eliminated at once'. Does this mean that if the solicitor had not handed over the documents they could not have been seized by the police?[3] This is doubtful. As it is, *Frank Truman* not only applies *Ghani v. Jones* in a rather relaxed manner but also allows the seizure or at least the retention of privileged documents which would not normally be admissible in evidence. The second case, *Wershof v. Commissioner of Police*,[4] is less controversial, involving a more or less straightforward application of Lord Denning's guidelines. A police officer suspected that a ring in a jewellers' shop had been stolen. He wished to seize it so that it could be used as evidence in any subsequent prosecution of the thief. The plaintiff, a young solicitor who was the son of the principal of the jewellery firm, told the police officer that he was not prepared to give up the ring without a receipt and on a number of occasions asked for a receipt. The police officer refused to give him one. After more argument the police officer arrested the plaintiff for wilfully obstructing him in the execution of his duty. It was held that the police officer had not been acting in the execution of his duty at the relevant time. His refusal to give the plaintiff a receipt was *unreasonable*, and the plaintiff's refusal to hand it over without a receipt was therefore 'entirely *reasonable*'. The third requirement of Lord Denning in *Ghani v. Jones* had not been satisfied, and it followed that the police officer had no right in law to

[1] One view is that it is a condition of the legality of a seizure that the material to be seized should be admissible; that privileged documents in a solicitor's office are not admissible; and that therefore such privileged documents cannot be seized (see J.C. Smith, (1977) *Crim. L.R.* 477 at 478).

[2] (1978) 41 *M.L.R.* 72 at 76. Apparently the solicitor thought that the privilege was overridden by the warrant; it cannot therefore be said that he freely waived it (see J.C. Smith, (1977) *Crim. L.R.* 477 at 478 and *The Times*, 22 December, 1976).

[3] As J.C. Smith, supra, points out, it would be odd to say that privileged documents should not be taken away from a solicitor's office but then to say that any privileged documents which are carried away should become admissible; see also (1978) 41 *M.L.R.* 72.

[4] (1978) 3 All E.R. 540.

seize the ring and was not at the time acting in the execution of his duty.

In other parts of the Commonwealth the status and authority of *Ghani v. Jones* are subjects of great uncertainty. In some jurisdictions the law as stated by Lord Denning has been accepted without qualification;[1] elsewhere there are old authorities holding that a seizure in the absence of either a search warrant or an arrest is unlawful;[2] and in New Zealand courts have explicitly refused to follow Lord Denning's lead and recognise the existence of a power to seize evidentiary matter when there is no search warrant and no one has as yet been arrested or charged.[3] In *McFarlane v, Sharp*[4] the police obtained warrants authorising the search of McFarlane's house and car for evidence of a robbery he was suspected of having committed. The search revealed nothing that could assist the police in their investigation of the robbery, but while engaged in the search the officers found and took possession of certain documents relating to another offence, bookmaking. The plaintiff was not under arrest when the documents were seized. The New Zealand Court of Appeal was faced with a clear conflict between *Barnett and Grant v. Campbell*,[5] establishing the proposition that evidence cannot be seized if there has been neither an authorising warrant nor an arrest before the seizure, and *Ghani v. Jones*, allowing the seizure and detention of evidence if Lord Denning's requirements are met, which presumably they were in *McFarlane v. Sharp*. The Court took the view that *Barnett and Grant v. Campbell* was a long-standing decision which should not be overruled by the judiciary and that it was for the legislature to overrule or amend it. Since the seizure of the documents had been neither authorised by search warrant nor preceded by an actual arrest it was unlawful. But at the end of its judgment the Court indicated that the extent of police powers of seizure and more particularly the restrictive principles derivable from *Barnett and Grant v. Campbell* should be reconsidered by the legislature.[6] It was of course necessary to protect the citizen against the possibility that police officers, putting forward some plausible pretext for obtaining a search warrant, would use the opportunity thereby given not to look for the authorised evidence but rather to engage in fishing expeditions, 'having a look' in the hope of uncovering evidence of some crime of which as yet there was no suspicion against the occupier. But as against this 'real' danger there was the possibility of the type of case where *in the course* of a bona fide search the police discovered cogent evidence of participation by the occupier in some more serious crime, for instance armed robbery. Why should the police, simply

[1] See *G. H. Photography Pty Ltd. v. McGarrigle* (1974) 2 N.S.W.L.R. 635.

[2] See *Levine v. O'Keefe* (1930) V.L.R. 70. This is still the clearest authority supporting the orthodox position. Mann J., at 72, said: '(T)here are two ways in which the seizure of goods . . . can be justified. One is by showing that they were seized being in the possession of a person at the time of his arrest . . . The other way in which such a seizure can be justified is under a search warrant lawfully issued'.

[3] See generally Bridge, 'Search and Seizure: An Antipodean View of *Ghani v. Jones*' (1974) *Crim. L.R.* 218.

[4] (1972) N.Z.L.R. 64 (S.C.), (1972) N.Z.L.R. 836 (C.A.); see Smillie, supra, 309 n. 3.

[5] (1902) 21 N.Z.L.R. 484.

[6] (1972) N.Z.L.R. 838 at 844.

because the occupier was not present and therefore could not be arrested, be prohibited from taking the material into their custody?[1] The Court was clearly of the view that the police should be allowed to seize such matter; but the whole question of seizability in the absence of arrest and search warrant deserved careful legislative consideration.

(f) Reform

It is obvious that the common law of search and seizure, particularly in England, cries out for drastic reform, either by way of wholesale codification or by the effectuation of changes that are particularly urgently needed. The whole subject deserves long and careful study, much empirical research about the true needs of law enforcement, and the submission of comprehensive and detailed proposals, of a kind that is beyond the range of legitimate judicial intervention. Here a few broad comments and tentative suggestions will be made. Essential rationalisation, it is thought, must proceed on three distinct fronts. There must first be the enactment of a comprehensive statute, perhaps on the lines of section 10 of the Australian Federal Crimes Act 1914–1950, allowing the issuing of warrants irrespective of type of offence. A suitable model might be something like this: If a judicial officer is satisfied by information on oath that there is reasonable cause to believe that a criminal offence has been committed and that a search of a particular place or specified premises will disclose either:

(a) stolen goods, contraband, the fruits of crime, or other things unlawfully possessed; or
(b) weapons or other things used as instrumentalities of crime; or
(c) any other evidence concerning the commission of a criminal offence, except for that which is privileged and otherwise inadmissible;

then he may issue a search warrant authorising a named police officer to enter and search the place or premises in question and to seize the things specified in it. An even simpler provision, but one which most would find too general, would allow a magistrate, when the necessary facts and circumstances demonstrating the presence of reasonable cause have been shown to exist, to issue a warrant to enter premises or any other place and 'to search for and seize any property that constitutes evidence of a criminal offence' in violation of the law.[2] It may also be advisable at this point to make two things clear. First, the scope of a search under the authority of a search warrant must be such as is authorised by the warrant and is reasonably necessary to discover the things specified in it, and upon discovery of the things so specified the search must proceed no further; but, secondly, if in the course of such a search, i.e. a search remaining within the authorisation of the warrant, the officer discovers things not specified in it which are reasonably believed to provide evidence of an offence these too may be seized.

Secondly, there should be clarification of currently recognised powers of

[1] Ibid.
[2] See the Omnibus Crime Control and Safe Streets Act of 1968 (United States).

search without warrant. The most important of these is the power to conduct searches incidental to arrest. With regard to the power to search the person incidentally to a valid arrest the position, as recently clarified, appears more or less satisfactory. Broadly, an officer who is making a valid arrest may, without a search warrant, conduct a search of the arrested individual, for two basic purposes: first, to effect the arrest without danger to himself, the arrested individual, or others; and secondly, to obtain and seize criminal instrumentalities, fruits of crime and any other things possessed or used in connection with the offence for which the individual is arrested and to obtain and seize any other evidence of the same offence.[1] But great confusion surrounds the right to conduct a search of premises incidental to an arrest made in them. Any sensible regulation with regard to this problem must have two aims, on the one hand to prevent the destruction of relevant evidence while not on the other allowing the police to engage either in fishing expeditions or in unnecessarily broad invasions of privacy. As American experience indicates, many different types of regulation can be suggested. One model could be formulated as follows.[2] If when an individual is arrested on *his* premises the arresting officers have reasonable grounds for believing that a search of the premises will uncover seizable items (as defined previously) in connection with the offence for which the arrest is made then the officers may search the premises (and only the premises) and seize not only the things for which the search is made but also any other items providing evidence of any offence that are discovered in the course of the search. A more restrictive formulation would authorise a search of premises incidental to arrest only when the officers have reasonable grounds for believing not only that seizable items connected with the offence for which the arrest is made will be found there but also that such evidence will (or is likely to) be destroyed or removed unless it is immediately seized. These formulations attempt on the one hand to steer clear of the excessively severe ruling in *Chimel v. California* and on the other to forbid routine searches of premises whenever a person is arrested there. Under both a search of premises will only be authorised as an incident of an arrest, first if the arrest is of the individual in apparent occupation of the premises in question, and secondly if there is reason to believe that a search of the premises will bring to light evidentiary items in connection with the offence for which the individual has been arrested. The second formulation is narrower in that it effectively imposes a duty on police officers to obtain a warrant whenever practicable, only allowing them to act without one in circumstances of urgency.

A third matter that demands urgent elucidation (or recognition if it does not exist) is the existence and extent of (the currently disputed) police power

[1] This formulation means that if on the facts of a particular case a personal search incident to an arrest cannot serve one or both of these purposes, either because the arrested individual is demonstrably neither dangerous nor in possession of a weapon or because the offence in issue involves no evidence other than that already in the officer's possession on the basis of which the arrest has been effected, then the search should either not take place at all or be suitably limited in scope.

[2] I have derived much assistance from the A.L.I.'s *Model Code of Pre-Arraignment Procedure* § 230.5 (1975).

to seize criminal evidence when there has been neither an arrest nor a search warrant authorising its seizure. Above, we identified arguments on both sides. If there is no power to seize evidence of crime in the absence of arrest and of search warrant much evidence will be destroyed. On the other hand the broader the power of seizure the greater the temptation that is put in the way of the police to engage in fishing expeditions in the hope of discovering evidence of criminal activities. But this danger, it is thought, is best met not by artificially restricting the category of what may be seized or by making it unnecessarily difficult for the police to apprehend those who break the law but *first* by refusing to uphold the legality of unauthorised seizures unless there is a convincing showing on the part of the police that these were not the purpose of their investigation but accidental discoveries, inadvertently made, in the course of an otherwise lawful intrusion, and *secondly* by adequately penalising police illegality, both by the more determined administration of existing sanctions, civil and criminal, and by the development of new and more effective remedies. In the light of these considerations it is thought that the police should be able to take seizable items, namely items reasonably thought to provide evidence of the commission of a criminal offence, if these are inadvertently discovered in the course of an otherwise lawful intrusion, whether this is an arrest, a search under a warrant or any other entry.[1]

A final matter that must urgently be dealt with is that of the power to interfere with personal liberty otherwise than by arrest.[2] There is a strong case for giving the police additional powers in this area not only because strict insistence on the traditional doctrine that there is no half-way house between arrest and full liberty would seriously handicap the police in their detection of crime, but also because it is clear that existing police practices do not observe common law orthodoxy.[3] And it is vitally important that police practices which undoubtedly take place (and will always take place whatever the strict legal position to the contrary) should be controlled by being recognised and made subject to clearly defined limits.[4] As has already been indicated, there are two issues that merit attention. First, should the police, in the absence of sufficient grounds for an arrest, be given the power to stop and question a person as to his identity and reason for being at a particular place or for

[1] For a similar approach, see Smillie, supra, 309 n. 3, at 281.

[2] See generally Ashworth, (1976) *Crim. L.R.* 594; Australian Law Reform Commission, *Report No.2, Criminal Investigation* (1975), hereinafter referred to as *A.L.R.C.;* Thomson Committee, *Criminal Procedure in Scotland*, Cmnd. 6218 (1975), referred to as Thomson; A.L.I., *Model Code of Pre-Arraignment Procedure* (1975), referred to as *Model Code;* see also Williams, 'Police Detention and Arrest Privileges under Foreign Law—England', 51 *J. Crim. L., C. & P.S.* 413 (1960); Remington, 'The Law Relating to "On the Street" Detention, Questioning and Frisking of Suspected Persons and Police Arrest Privileges in General', 51 *J. Crim. L., C. & P.S.* 386, 391 (1960); Foote, 'The Fourth Amendment: Obstacle or Necessity in the Law of Arrest?', 51 *J. Crim. L., C. & P.S.* 402 (1960); Karlen, *Anglo-American Criminal Justice* 114–21 (1967). See also the *Report* of the Royal Commission on Criminal Procedure (Cmnd. 8092), paras. 3.75–3.113.

[3] The existence of stop and search powers, mainly the Firearms Act 1968, sections 47(3), 49(1) and (2), make the problem less pressing than it might otherwise have been.

[4] See Ashworth, supra, n. 2, at 595; *A.L.R.C.* para. 80.

behaving in a particular manner if the conduct of this person has aroused reasonable suspicion? There is little doubt that a limited power of on-the-street detention in order to put some questions or ask for an explanation of suspicious behaviour is necessary not only for preventive but also for investigative purposes. There are a number of possible models for adoption. One, proposed in Australia, is that police officers should have the power to require that a person whose identity is unknown to the officer in question and who is reasonably believed to be able to assist him in his inquiries in connection with an offence (which has been, may have been or may be committed) should give his name and address. The proposed power extends only to questions about name and address. It does not allow questions to be put, or require them to be answered, as to where a person has been, where he is going, what he is doing and the like. These questions need only be answered at the police station.[1] Another, more comprehensive, proposal is that a police officer should have the power to stop and question a person who is observed in circumstances giving rise to a reasonable suspicion that he has just committed, is committing or is about to commit a crime of a certain degree of seriousness. The purposes of this power are to enable the officer to obtain or verify either the identification of the person who is stopped or an account of his presence or conduct or both, and to determine whether to arrest him; but the stop should in no circumstances last for more than twenty minutes.[2] Whatever the proposal that is adopted,[3] there will be the dangers of abuse and harassment that have also been confronted in America in the wake of *Terry v. Ohio*. In the last analysis, the only possible safeguards are a vigilant judiciary and the development and adoption of suitable procedures for superintending the work of the police. The second issue is whether the police should be given the power to detain an individual at the police station for questioning without having to arrest him. This is a considerably more controversial matter. The main objections to custodial detention for questioning are first that it is not demonstrably demanded by compelling policy arguments, as with on-the-street detention, and secondly that it is open to considerably greater danger of abuse, more particularly that it deprives the suspect of safeguards which have been thought important enough to be incorporated in the law of arrest. The arguments that have been urged in its favour are that the suspect may be innocent and that detention without arrest or charge will give him the chance to persuade the police of his innocence and thus obtain his release without publicity or stigma, that detention will enable the police to isolate the detainee while they continue their inquiries elsewhere, and that it will also enable them to obtain the suspect's fingerprints, to question him and to search him without his consent.[4] A number of recent proposals accept that there should be a power of police custodial detention

[1] *A.L.R.C.*, 79–81.

[2] *Model Code*, section 110.2. There is also power to stop and question witnesses (paragraph (b)) and suspects sought for certain previously committed felonies (paragraph (c)).

[3] The Thomson proposal is rather different: see 3.13–3.20.

[4] See Williams, supra; Thomson, 3.22–3.27; *A.L.R.C.* 87–98.

and investigation before arrest, and proceed to define the conditions in which it may take place and its limits.[1] But others[2] are not convinced that so drastic a power, even for a relatively short period of time, is justified; they argue that the conferment of such a power will seriously threaten civil liberty and that there is no evidence that the present regime, namely that there is no power to subject to custodial detention otherwise than by arrest, unduly hampers the task of the police; and they would therefore not disturb traditional doctrine as regards detention at the police station.[3]

[1] Both Thomson and the *A.L.R.C.* accept that there should be this power; the main difference between the two proposals is the duration of permissible detention; under Thomson the detainee should be charged or released within six hours; under the *A.L.R.C.* proposals detention should not exceed four hours (see Ashworth, supra, at 596–9).

[2] See Foote, supra.

[3] Recently comprehensive proposals for reform of the law of search and seizure were put forward by the Royal Commission on Criminal Procedure (*Report*, Cmnd. 8092). Its main recommendations are the following:

1 *Police power to stop and search*
The Commission proposed that a single uniform power to stop and search should be created, replacing the hotch-potch of laws currently in force. The proposal was that a police officer should have the power to stop, and if necessary search, any person in a public place whom he, on reasonable grounds, suspected of conveying stolen goods, or of being in possession of anything whose possession in a public place was of itself a criminal offence. The Commission also recommended that a similar power should exist to stop and search vehicles for the same purposes (*Report*, paras. 3.11–3.33).

2 *Search of premises on arrest*
The Commission thought that 'the criterion' for searches of premises on arrest should be similar to that for searches of the person on arrest and indeed for any other lawful search, that is 'suspicion on reasonable grounds that there are in the premises (or in a vehicle) occupied by or under the control of the arrested person articles material to the offence for which the person has been arrested or a similar offence' (see *Report*, paras. 3.119–3.122).

3 *Searching for evidence*
Should the police be able to apply for warrants to search for *evidence* of crime? The Commission was worried that allowing such searches could lead to fishing expeditions. It nevertheless thought that there would be 'exceptional circumstances' when a compulsory power should be available—but only 'as a last resort'—to enable the police to get access to evidence in respect of 'grave offences'. The following conditions would have to be satisfied before *an order* for the production of evidence would be granted: other methods of investigation had been tried and failed; the nature of the items sought was specified with some precision; there were reasonable grounds for believing that the items would be found on the particular premises; and there were reasonable grounds for believing that the evidence would be of substantial, not merely incidental, value. The order, if the court were satisfied of the above conditions, would operate to require the person to whom it was addressed to provide or to allow the police to inspect or have access to the items specified in the order. In two cases—either when an order for the production of evidence had been made and disobeyed, or when there was reason to believe that the delay involved in the standard procedure would lead to the destruction or disappearance of the evidence—a search warrant for seizing the evidence in issue could be obtained (see *Report*, paras. 3.40–3.43).

7. Enforcement

Rights to freedom from illegal searches and seizures must obviously be enforced. Without effective remedies the rights themselves are illusory and 'no more than rhetoric'.[1] This means that the disregard of the right to be secure from unlawful searches must be attended by unwelcome consequences for those responsible. These consequences fall into two broad categories, first what may be called conventional ones and secondly the exclusionary rule, namely the rule that makes inadmissible the evidence that has been obtained in violation of the constitutional or common law norms concerning searches and seizures.

(a) Traditional remedies and sanctions

The conventional consequences fall into three distinct categories. First there are penal sanctions. Thus the circumstances surrounding an illegal search may support a charge of assault, theft or other offence against the police officer concerned; but it is not often that an illegal search will result in the bringing of criminal charges against police officers, and there are very few instances in the reports of the conviction on criminal charges of police officers responsible for an illegality in the obtaining of evidence. Secondly, there are possible disciplinary proceedings and other internal sanctions calculated to punish officers for disobeying the rules. Not surprisingly, the main disadvantages of internal police review systems are that police officers cannot normally be trusted to investigate adequately complaints against each other and that even if complaints from citizens are upheld the disciplinary measures that are usually taken do not inspire the public with confidence. The most prominent conventional method of enforcing rights to be free from unconstitutional and illegal searches is the tort remedy,[2] namely a civil action for damages, brought by the victim of the illegal search or seizure and calculated to give him compensation or redress for the wrong that has been done, whether this is trespass to goods, trespass to land, conversion, assault or any other. Usually the action for damages is brought against the searching officer,[3] but the common law provides actions against certain other persons

[1] Australian Law Reform Commission, *Report No. 2, Criminal Investigation* (1975), para. 287.

[2] See generally Foote, 'Tort Remedies for Police Violations of Individual Rights', 39 *Minn. L. Rev.* 493 (1955); 'Comment, The Tort Alternative to the Exclusionary Rule in Search and Seizure', 63 *J. Crim. L., C. & P.S.* 256 (1972) (hereinafter referred to as Comment).

[3] *Entick v. Carrington*, 19 How St. Tr. 1030.

as well,[1] principally against one who procures the issuance of a warrant maliciously and without probable cause,[2] against a magistrate who has acted without jurisdiction in issuing a warrant,[3] and against any other persons assisting in the execution of an illegal search.[4] As regards the liability of police officers, where a search warrant is issued by a magistrate having authority to issue it, and is regular upon its face, it constitutes a defence for the officer who has executed it even though it may later turn out to be invalid, provided the officer has executed it in the way he has been directed and in an orderly fashion.[5] 'It is incomprehensible,' said Lord Kenyon, 'to say that a person shall be considered a trespasser who acts under the process of the court.'[6] But where the warrant appears on its face to be invalid, or the magistrate who 'issued' it did so without jurisdiction, the executing officer is not acting under the process of the court and is liable.[7]

What is the measure of damages that the common law tort remedy will give the aggrieved party? Since the main purpose of the trespass action is to provide compensation for the injury, loss or damage that results from the wrong, if the illegal search has caused substantial damage to property the measure of damages will be such as to cover the loss or injury suffered by the plaintiff. Occasionally this will be substantial.[8] But even if there is no material harm to the plaintiff's property there may be an award of compensatory damages to cover injury to reputation and feelings, mental and emotional distress, disturbance of family life, and the like.[9] Further, if there has been oppressive or arbitrary use of power by government officials there may be an award of exemplary damages.[10] In such cases the award of damages must reflect the gravity of the defendant's offence, i.e. the illegal search.

In an important development—and in a clear attempt to provide more effective civil remedies under the Fourth Amendment to victims of unconstitutional searches and seizures—the Supreme Court held in *Bivens v.*

[1] See *Wolf v. Colorado,* 338 U.S. 25, 30 n.1 (1949), and the many authorities given there by Frankfurter, J.

[2] As regards the liability of the person who swore the complaint and provided the information on the basis of which the search warrant was obtained it is established that an action will not lie for inducing a magistrate to issue a search warrant if the applicant was acting bona fide and therefore without malice (see *Hope v. Evered,* (1886) 17 Q.B.D. 338, and Carter, *The Law Relating to Search Warrants* 85–9 (1939)).

[3] On the liability of the magistrate, see Carter, supra, at 89–91. The terminology in many of the cases is confusing, but the basic test is whether the magistrate was acting within or without jurisdiction. In the latter case, as Griffith, C. J. put it in *Bridgeman v. Macalister*, (1898) 8 Q.L.J. 151 at 152, a justice is no longer a judicial officer and therefore 'cannot any more than any other person authorize another to enter the premises of a stranger'. If therefore the ground for the exercise of a statutory power is wanting (as opposed to the presence of a defect that does not deprive of jurisdiction) the issuing 'magistrate' is 'liable to an action by the person affected by his act' (at 153).

[4] See *Wolf v. Colorado*, supra, n.1.

[5] See *Knisley v. Ham*, 136 P. 427 (1913); *Moore v. Kilmer*, 90 P. 2d 892 (1939).

[6] *Belk v. Broadbent*, 3 T.R. 183, 185.

[7] 68 *Am. Jur.* 2d § 123.

[8] As in *Entick v. Carrington*, supra.

[9] See Comment, supra, 319 n. 2, at 260, and the authorities there cited.

[10] See *Rookes v. Barnard* (1964) A.C. 1129, 1226.

Six Unknown Fed. Narcotics Agents[1] that a violation of the Fourth Amendment by a federal agent acting under colour of federal authority gives rise to a cause of action for damages against the offending official in a federal court despite the absence of any statute conferring such a right. But if Congress provides an alternative remedy for the violation of Fourth Amendment rights which is either declared 'to be a substitute for recovery directly under the Constitution'[2] or which, at the very least, is viewed as 'equally effective'[3] to the *Bivens* action, the latter will become unnecessary and will apparently no longer be implied from the Constitution itself.

An important American provision that may afford a cause of action in the event of an illegal search and seizure is 42 U.S.C. § 1983 (42 U.S.C.S. § 1983) which provides that any person who under colour of state law (or of the law of a Territory) subjects a citizen of the United States to the deprivation of any of the rights secured by the Constitution will be liable to the injured party in an action calculated to secure redress for him. This provision derives from §1 of the Civil Rights Act of 1871, itself enacted to enforce the provisions of the Fourteenth Amendment, and its purpose appears to be to provide a federal right in federal courts for the violation of constitutional rights because it was feared that state laws guaranteeing adequate protection might either not exist or not be enforced. In other words, the purpose of the civil rights legislation presently embodied in 42 U.S.C.S. § 1983 is to interpose the federal courts between the States and the people as guardians of the people's federal rights, a purpose that is achieved by protecting the people from unconstitutional action effected under colour of state law, whether this action is executive, legislative or judicial.[4] The terms of § 1983 indicate that two elements must be proved before there can be recovery. It must be proved first that the plaintiff has been deprived by the defendant of a right secured by 'the Constitution and laws' of the United States, whether it is the rights guaranteed by the Fourth Amendment or any other, and secondly that the defendant was acting 'under colour of law'. This last phrase, the Supreme Court has held, bears the same meaning as the 'state action' doctrine of the Fourteenth Amendment, namely the requirement that constitutional rights only become applicable when there has been state action, that is some manifestation of state power.[5] Action taken 'under colour' of state law was found to be present in *Monroe v. Pape*,[6] the case that first sanctioned

[1] 403 U.S. 388 (1971).

[2] *Carlson v. Green*, 64 L. Ed. 2d 15, 23–4, per Brennan, J.

[3] *Bivens* appears to require only that the alternative should be 'equally effective' (see *Bivens*, 403 U.S. 388, 397 and *Carlson v. Green*, supra, at 29, per Powell, J. concurring), but Brennan, J. in *Carlson v. Green*, supra, appears to shift to a requirement that there should be an explicit declaration of substitution.

[4] See *Monroe v. Pape*, 365 U.S. 167 (1961); *Mitchum v. Foster*, 407 U.S. 225 (1972); District of *Columbia v. Carter*, 409 U.S. 418 (1973). The purpose of this provision, when it was first adopted in 1871, was to deal with the activities of the Ku Klux Klan.

[5] *Monroe v. Pape*, 365 U.S. 167 (1961); *Adickes v. S. H. Kress & Co.*, 398 U.S. 144 (1970).

[6] 365 U.S. 167 (1961).

extensive interpretation of the reach of 42 U.S.C.S. § 1983, where it was held that a cause of action under 42 U.S.C.S. § 1983 was stated by a complaint, filed by a married couple and their children against Chicago police officers, alleging that the officers broke into the plaintiffs' home, searched it without warrant and arrested and detained the husband, also without warrant and without arraignment. The 'under colour' of law provision of the statute, the Supreme Court held, applied not only to unconstitutional action authorised by the State but also to unconstitutional actions taken without state authority. All that was necessary was that the act complained of should be the result of '(a) misuse of power, possessed by virtue of state law and made possible only because the wrongdoer (was) clothed with the authority of state law'.[1] But purely private conduct does not come within the provision.[2]

Section 1983 provides a private right of action against any '*person*' acting under colour of state law who causes a deprivation of constitutional rights. Natural persons are of course included.[3] What about state instrumentalities? *Monroe v. Pape*[4] had held that the word 'person' did not include municipal corporations, but this part of *Monroe* has now been overruled by *Monell v. New York City Dept. of Social Services.*[5] Local government bodies (and local government officials sued in their official capacities) can therefore be sued directly under § 1983 for redress, including monetary relief, in those situations where the action that is alleged to be unconstitutional implements or executes a policy statement, ordinance, regulation, or decision officially adopted or promulgated by those whose edicts or acts may fairly be said to represent official policy. Additionally, local government bodies, like any other 'person' under § 1983, may be sued for constitutional deprivations effected in pursuance of governmental 'custom' even though such custom has not received formal approval by passing through official decision making channels.[6] On the other hand, a local government body cannot be held liable *solely* because it employs a tortfeasor—in other words, local government authorities cannot be held liable under § 1983 on a respondeat superior basis. To put it even more simply, liability cannot be imposed directly on a municipality or other local organ on the basis of the existence of the employer-employee relationship with the tortfeasor but only when the relevant authority *itself causes* the injury.[7]

What is the type of liability recognised by § 1983? It will be noticed that, in terms, § 1983 'creates a species of tort liability that on its face admits of no

[1] *United States v. Classic*, 313 U.S. 299, 326 (1941), quoted with approval in *Monroe v. Pape*, supra, at 184.

[2] *District of Columbia v. Carter,* 409 U.S. 418 (1973).

[3] Since the statute deals only with those deprivations of rights that are accomplished under the colour of the law of 'any State or Territory' actions of the federal government and its officers (with the exception of the territories) are facially exempt from its proscriptions (see *District of Columbia v. Carter*, 409 U.S. 418, 424).

[4] 365 U.S. 167, 187.

[5] 436 U.S. 658 (1978).

[6] *Adickes v. S.H. Kress & Co.*, 398 U.S. 144, 167–8 (1970).

[7] *Monell v. New York City Dept. of Soc. Serv.*, 436 U.S. 658, 692–5.

immunities'.[1] Its language is absolute and unqualified, and no mention is made of any privileges, immunities or defences that may be asserted. But § 1983 has not been read in so sweeping a fashion. Despite its expansive language and the absence of any express incorporation of immunities and defences recognised by the common law, the Supreme Court has found on a number of occasions that 'a tradition of immunity was so firmly rooted in the common law and was supported by such strong policy reasons'[2] that 'Congress would have specifically so provided had it wished to abolish the doctrine'.[3] In addition, the Supreme Court has noted that 'the public interest requires decisions and action to enforce laws for the protection of the public'[4] and that unless some immunities are extended public officials may decide to take no action at all rather than risk some error and the automatic initiation of proceedings.[5] In other words, by granting certain immunities to government officials 'the Court has attempted to ensure that public decisions will not be dominated by fear of liability for actions that may turn out to be unconstitutional'.[6] On the basis of such considerations the Supreme Court has recognised, first *absolute* immunity from actions under § 1983 for state legislators, judges, and prosecutors in their role as advocates for the State, and secondly a *qualified* immunity that protects certain officials who in good faith have implemented policies or taken other types of action they reasonably thought to be constitutional.[7] This second type of immunity provides a 'good faith and probable cause'[8] defence to actions under § 1983, and has the result of only authorising liability either when government officials acted with malicious intent or when they 'knew or should have known that their conduct violated the constitutional norm'.[9] This limited immunity extends to police officers,[10] state executive officers,[11] local school board members,[12] the superintendent of a state hospital,[13] and prison officals,[14] so that all these officials will only be held liable under § 1983 if at the relevant time they knew or *should* have known that their conduct violated the constitutional right in issue. But this qualified immunity does not extend to governmental organs, such as municipal corporations, brought within the orbit of § 1983 by *Monell v. New York City Dept. of Social Services.*[15] It was therefore held in *Owen v.*

[1] *Imbler v. Pachtman*, 424 U.S. 409, 417 (1976).
[2] *Owen v. City of Independence*, 63 L. Ed. 673, 685.
[3] *Pierson v. Ray*, 386 U.S. 547 ,555 (1967).
[4] *Scheuer v. Rhodes*, 416 U.S. 232, 241 (1974).
[5] *Owen v. City of Independence*, 63 L. Ed. 2d 673, 703, per Powell, J. dissenting.
[6] Ibid.
[7] See *Owen v. City of Independence*, supra, and the many authorities reviewed there.
[8] See *Pierson v. Ray*, 386 U.S. 547, 555–7 (1967).
[9] *Procunier v. Navarette*, 434 U.S. 555, 562 (1978).
[10] *Pierson v. Ray*, supra, at 555–8.
[11] *Scheuer v. Rhodes*, 416 U.S. 232 (1974).
[12] *Wood v. Strickland*, 420 U.S. 308 (1975).
[13] *O'Connor v. Donaldson*, 422 U.S. 563, 576–7 (1975).
[14] *Procunier v. Navarette*, 434 U.S. 555 (1978).
[15] 436 U.S. 658 (1978).

City of Independence[1] that municipalities sued under 42 U.S.C.S. § 1983 for the violation of federally protected rights are not entitled to qualified immunity from liability by asserting the good faith of their officials. As a result of this decision the position is as follows: Where there is abuse of governmental authority, as defined previously, the victim of the constitutional deprivation will be compensated for his injury; the offending official, so long as he conducts himself in good faith, may go about his business secure in the knowledge that a qualified immunity will protect him from personal liability for damages; and the public, represented by the municipal entity or other government organ, will be forced to bear only the costs of injury inflicted by the execution of governmental policy or custom, whether 'made' by its lawmakers or by those whose acts may fairly be said to represent official policy.[2]

If one thing is clear, it is that conventional sanctions and remedies have failed and are demonstrably inadequate either to deter police illegality or to compensate the victims of unlawful searches and seizures.[3] This is due to a number of reasons.[4] To begin with, the current tort system does not provide *a defendant* from whom adequate damages can be sought. As a result of the usually applicable doctrine of sovereign immunity which prevents the plaintiff from bringing an action against the police force itself or other governmental body employing the police officer, liability for the trespass or other actionable wrong an illegal search entails is almost always restricted to the particular officer conducting the search, and it is unlikely either that he will be able to pay substantial damages where these are warranted or that a jury or judge will be eager to award damages in favour of a criminal (where, as often happens, an illegal search has brought to light incriminating evidence). A second difficulty relates to the problems associated with *the use* of the trespass action to provide redress for unlawful searches and seizures. There are many uncertainties and inadequacies, due no doubt to the fact that the common law action was not specifically developed, and is not therefore suited, for instances of unlawful governmental conduct, but only for ordinary civil wrongs. For example, is some defence available to a police officer conducting an unlawful search in cases where he entertained a bona fide belief that the action he was taking was necessary in the interests of law enforcement? As we have seen, he is apparently protected when he was acting under a warrant that was valid on its face. What about warrantless searches? Does perhaps a similar principle apply to the one followed in actions under section 1983 where the officer is protected if he can show both good faith and

[1] 63 L. Ed. 2d 673.

[2] Ibid., at 697, per Brennan, J.

[3] See Australian Law Reform Commission, *Report No. 2, Criminal Investigation* (1975), para. 287–302; 'Comment, The Tort Alternative to the Exclusionary Rule in Search and Seizure', 63 *J. Crim. L., C. & P.S.* 256 (1972) (hereinafter referred to as Comment); *Mapp v. Ohio*, 367 U.S. 643 (1961). But apparently in Canada the tort remedy is working well (see Oaks, 'Studying the Exclusionary Rule in Search and Seizure', 37 *U. Chi L. Rev.* 665, 701–6 (1970)).

[4] These are set out in Comment, supra, n. 3, at 259–62.

probable cause?[1] And if liability is established, there are serious problems, as we have seen, with the measure of damages, particularly where there is no tangible damage to property. A final source of difficulty relates to the problems that *the victim* of an unlawful search faces. Litigation is expensive, in many jurisdictions bringing a civil action for trespass or similar wrongs involves considerable delay, and in many cases it is likely both that the plaintiff will find it difficult to secure proper legal representation and that he is unlikely to receive much sympathy from the court, particularly where his case is dealt with by a jury, since the victim of an illegal search is more often than not a person who either has been convicted or at least is obviously guilty of crime.[2] For all these reasons traditional sanctions and remedies have proved singularly ineffective either in deterring objectionable police practices or in redressing in an adequate manner the grievances of those subjected to illegal searches and seizures.[3] This has led to the development of the exclusionary doctrine.[4]

(b) The exclusion of illegally obtained evidence

(i) General considerations

The problem of whether illegally obtained evidence should be excluded in attempted enforcement of rights of security from unlawful searches and seizures has long bedevilled courts and academic commentators alike. This is principally for two reasons: first the great number and variety of police improprieties relied on as a reason for excluding incriminating evidence, and secondly the compelling policy arguments advanced with equal conviction by the proponents and opponents of the various suggested solutions. Thus, as regards the former, relevant and damning evidence may have been obtained

[1] See *Pierson v. Ray*, 386 U.S. 547, 555 (1967).

[2] See *Massantonio v. People*, 235 P. 1019, 1020–1 (1925).

[3] As will be seen below, there have been influential suggestions that the tort remedy should be rationalized. See particularly Oaks, supra, 324 n. 3; 'Comment', supra; and *Bivens v. Six Unknown Fed. Narcotics Agents*, 403 U.S. 388 (1971), per Burger, C.J. dissenting.

[4] Other ways of challenging the legality of warrants are occasionally followed. In many jurisdictions, principally Canada, prerogative writs are often used. There are also many cases where it is sought to recover wrongfully seized articles by application to a judge (who may be trying the case) to order their return; see Stephens, 'Search and Seizure of Chattels' (1970) *Crim. L.R.* 74, 148; see also *R. ex. rel. Webb v. MacKenzie*, 21 C.R.N.S. 284 (1973); *Re Purdy & R.*, (1972) 28 D.L.R. (3d) 720; *R. v. Black*, 24 C.R.N.S. 203 (1973). These Canadian authorities establish the proposition that even though the police obtained property or articles illegally they can hold on to them if they are required as evidence in a prosecution (for as long as is necessary, that is until the proceedings are completed). As the matter was put by Disbery J. in *R. ex. rel. Webb v. MacKenzie*, supra, when things are seized illegally there arises a conflict between on the one hand the right of the individual to possess and enjoy his property subject only to its being lawfully seized and on the other the interest of the community as a whole in relevant evidence being available for use in criminal proceedings. The interest of the community in the administration of justice, Disbery J. concluded, 'takes priority over the matter of the temporary loss by an individual of the enjoyment of the possession of the seized articles while they are required by Her Majesty's courts'.

by means of a flagrant violation of the suspect's rights, as by a knowingly illegal search, or even by the use of force, or perhaps by way of some other positive infraction of the law, even though this may not have been wilful; at the other extreme conclusive evidence of guilt in a serious case may have been obtained by means of conduct which was only technically illegal or improper, as where a search warrant contains a minor mistake due to oversight; or, again, the police may have resorted to a violation of the law in a case of great urgency.[1]

As regards arguments of policy, essentially similar ones have been advanced in all the jurisdictions we have considered. The rule admitting all relevant evidence, however obtained, is supported as follows.[2] To begin with, rules of evidence are, or should be, only designed to enable courts to reach correct determinations of specifically defined disputed issues; illegally obtained evidence is as reliable and as probative as evidence lawfully obtained; and since the court needs all reliable evidence material to the only issue before it, which is the guilt or innocence of the particular accused, the way in which probative evidence currently before the court was obtained is immaterial to *this* issue and should therefore be disregarded. Secondly exclusion of relevant and incriminating evidence cannot be justified in terms of protecting rights;[3] suppression is not a remedy in the strict sense,[4] the only defendants who benefit from application of exclusionary doctrines are those who are by definition guilty, and as a result of viewing exclusion of evidence as effectively the only response to resort to illegality in the obtaining of evidence is that both the crime and the police officer's disregard of the law will go unpunished; '(t)wo wrongs go unpunished, at the expense of society'.[5] Thirdly, in answer

[1] See *Hogan v. The Queen*, (1975) 48 D.L.R. (3d) 427, at 441, per Laskin J. dissenting. An important distinction not sufficiently explained either in the Commonwealth cases or in the literature is between illegal means or acts used as vehicles through which the evidence has been obtained and other acts not so causatively connected with the obtaining of the evidence; see *Hogan*, supra, and compare with *Police v. Hall* (1976) 2 N.Z.L.R. 678, discussed by Orchard, 'A Commentary on *Hall v. Police*', (1976) *N.Z.L.J.* 434 and Polyviou (1977) *A.S.C.L.* 270.

[2] See 8 Wigmore, *Evidence* § 2183 et seq (McNaughton rev. 1961); see also *People v. Defore*, 242 N.Y. 13, 19–25 (1926), per Cardozo, J., and *Eleuteri v. Richman*, 141 A. 2d 46, 48–52 (1958), per Weintraub, C.J.

[3] But see Ashworth, 'Excluding Evidence as Protecting Rights', (1977) *Crim. L.R.* 723.

[4] See *Stone v. Powell*, 428 U.S. 465, 484 (1976), per Powell, J.; see also *Linkletter v. Walker*, 381 U.S. 618, 637 (1965).

[5] 8 Wigmore, supra, § 2184, and *Eleuteri v. Richman*, supra, at 50. This argument is not as compelling as it sounds, for clearly exclusion of evidence does not necessarily mean that the offending police officer is to go unpunished. Suppression (whether general or selective) of illegally obtained evidence is (in theory) or can (in practice) be supplemented by a variety of other remedies or sanctions, criminal or civil. But resort to the exclusionary rule is normally prompted by the realisation that other remedies have failed, and therefore adoption of exclusionary doctrines is often seen as the only effective response to illegal police methods in the obtaining of evidence—in which case the argument that suppression results in two wrongs escaping punishment becomes stronger.

to the argument that the exclusion of evidence can be justified as the only effective deterrent to those wishing to flout the law,[1] it is contended first that there is no evidence that the exclusionary rule has any such effect, and secondly that more effective alternatives can be devised for ensuring official observance of procedural safeguards.[2] In turn, three main arguments are given in support of excluding illegally obtained evidence.[3] It is first said that government officers should not stoop to 'dirty business',[4] that it is imperative that the law must be observed scrupulously, and that the activities of law enforcement agencies must be closely supervised and controlled by the courts; and if illegal or improper means have been used to obtain evidence those responsible must be disciplined by the suppression of what they have obtained. A second argument is that if illegally obtained evidence is regularly admitted courts will in practice find themselves participating in, and in effect condoning, lawless police activities; out of regard for their dignity as agencies of justice and custodians of liberty, courts, it is said, should not 'have a hand' in the objectionable activities of law enforcement officers.[5] Finally, it is argued that if the suspect's rights and any other relevant safeguards of a fair system of criminal procedure are to remain meaningful they must be enforced, and if courts are to prove equal to their duty they must be willing to aid in their enforcement; rights to be secure from illegal searches and seizures cannot be enforced otherwise than by exclusion of the fruits of illegal police behaviour; and since, as is commonly accepted, civil and criminal remedies against the offending officer are undoubtedly ineffective, even though the deterrent effects of the exclusionary rule cannot be demonstrated statistically, no other alternative exists if police lawlessness is to be discouraged and if important personal rights are to be vindicated.[6] More will be said about the contending arguments when we discuss the American exclusionary rule.

Very broadly, three solutions to the problem of improperly obtained real evidence are possible. The first is that if the evidence that the prosecution proposes to adduce before the court is relevant and of the required probative value it cannot be excluded on the ground that it was obtained irregularly. If evidence is relevant it must be admitted. The diametrically opposed answer is to exclude all evidence that has not been obtained in accordance with legal procedures. Illegally obtained evidence is inadmissible. The third solution is an intermediate one. On this view no dogmatic answer is possible. In some cases illegally obtained evidence should be admitted and in others it should be excluded, the decisive criterion being that of an assessment in each case of the needs of two competing requirements of public policy, first the public need to

[1] See *Terry v. Ohio*, 392 U.S. 1, 12 (1968); also, see Douglas and Murphy, JJ., dissenting, in *Wolf v. Colorado*, 338 U.S., at 40 and 42 (1949).

[2] Much more on 'deterrence' and the 'alternatives' to the exclusionary rule is set out when the American doctrine of suppression is discussed. See below, at 346–8, 355–60.

[3] See *People v. Cahan*, 282 P. 2d 905, 907, 909–14 (1955), and *Mapp v. Ohio*, 367 U.S. 643 (1961).

[4] See *Olmstead v. United States*, 277 U.S. 438, 470 (1928), per Holmes J, dissenting.

[5] *People v. Cahan*, 282 P. 2d 905, 912 (1955), per Traynor, J.

[6] Ibid., at 911–13.

secure the conviction of those who commit criminal offences and secondly the public interest that the citizen should be protected from illegal or irregular action on the part of the State, if need be by the exclusion of improperly secured evidence.

(ii) Inclusionary models—Canada and England

The strict inclusionary model is exemplified by the attitude of the Canadian Supreme Court. Here all relevant evidence, however obtained, is admissible, subject only to a discretion to exclude evidence that is 'gravely prejudicial' to the accused, of 'trifling' probative force and of 'tenuous admissibility';[1] it is only the admission of such evidence that will result in unfairness to the accused and with which courts must concern themselves; and any illegalities or improprieties attending the obtaining of incriminating evidence are res inter alios acta, to be dealt with in separate civil, criminal or internal disciplinary proceedings.[2]

The English position, in terms of principle, is quite similar to the Canadian one. But it deserves extensive treatment because of important recent developments. Until recently English law presented a rather strange appearance. Its two noticeable features were the following. To begin with, its unmistakable starting point appeared to be uncompromising insistence that the only test of admissibility was relevance to the matters in issue, i.e. guilt or innocence, and that therefore courts were not concerned with how relevant evidence was obtained.[3] Yet such reiteration of orthodoxy was, starting with *Kuruma*[4] and particularly in more recent cases, followed by the imprecise delineation of a broadly based doctrine of discretionary exclusion of real evidence on the ground of unfairness to the accused. One possible view is that by 'fairness' to the accused one meant the exclusion of evidence whose prejudicial effect outweighed its true testimonial value, but this did not appear to be the most plausible explanation of the wide dicta of Lord Goddard in *Kuruma*,[5] of Lord Parker in *Callis v. Gunn*,[6] of Lord Widgery in

[1] *R. v. Wray*, (1970) 11 D.L.R. (3d), at 689–690, per Martland, J.

[2] See *Hogan v. The Queen*, (1975) 48 D.L.R. (3d) 427.

[3] 'It matters not how you get it; if you steal it even, it would be admissible', per Crompton, J. in *R. v. Leatham* (1861) 8 Cox C.C. 498 at 501; *Kuruma Son of Kaniu v. R.* (1955) A.C. 197 at 203.

[4] (1955) A.C. 197 at 203.

[5] Lord Goddard, C.J., although he had earlier said that if evidence is admissible 'the court is not concerned with how the evidence was obtained', nevertheless went on to say: 'No doubt in a criminal case the judge always has a discretion to disallow evidence if the strict rules of admissibility would operate unfairly against the accused. This was emphasised in the case before this Board of *Noor Mohamed v. Regem*, and in the recent case in the House of Lords of *Harris v. Director of Public Prosecutions*. If, for instance, some admission or some piece of evidence, e.g., a document, had been obtained from a defendant by a trick, no doubt the judge might properly rule it out'.

[6] (1964) 1 Q.B. 495 at 501 ('a judge has a discretion to disallow evidence . . . if admissibility would operate unfairly against an accused . . . (and) in considering (this) . . . one would certainly consider whether it had been obtained in an oppressive manner, by force or against the wishes of an accused person.')

Jeffrey v. Black[1] and of Lord Hodson in *King v. R.*[2] which clearly seemed to envisage the existence of a judicial power to disallow evidence because of the oppressive or morally objectionable manner in which it had been obtained. But if the concept of 'unfairness' extended beyond the conduct of the trial and was not confined to the exclusion of evidence that might adversely affect the trustworthiness of the judicial process, particularly if it encompassed the manner in which evidence had been obtained, what was its meaning, how should it be limited, and how was the existence of a broad discretion to exclude to be reconciled with the orthodox position, equally vehemently asserted, that all relevant evidence was admissible? The second noticeable feature of English law was that even though the cases seemed to accept the existence of a general discretion to exclude in the interests of fairness its exercise has never actually been approved by the Court of Appeal[3] except for the non-cases of *Payne*[4] and *Court*[5] where medical evidence was excluded on the ground that the defendant had only submitted to an examination as a result of a representation that the doctor would not examine him for the purpose of seeing whether he was fit to drive.[6] But if unfairness to the accused is the central test, why should evidence procured as a result of such a misrepresentation, or even a trick, be excluded in a purported exercise of the discretion, whereas evidence obtained by the most flagrantly illegal searches, as in *Kuruma* and *Jeffrey v. Black*, would be routinely admitted? Some thought that the concept of 'trick' (which had also been referred to by Lord Goddard in *Kuruma* as a ground for excluding relevant evidence) was a

[1] (1978) Q.B. 490 at 498, when it was suggested that if the police had behaved in a manner that was 'morally reprehensible' the discretion could be exercised.

[2] (1969) 1 A.C. 304 at 319, where it was suggested that the discretion to exclude could be exercised if the evidence had been obtained 'by conduct of which the Crown ought not to take advantage'. This phrase, Stephen and Aickin, JJ. observed in *Bunning v. Cross*, 19 A.L.R. 641 at 660, 'savours more of the *Ireland* approach than of *Kuruma*'.

[3] It must be borne in mind that an exercise of the discretion by a trial judge in favour of an accused is not appealable, and it appears that in certain unreported cases at first instance illegally obtained evidence has been excluded in the exercise of the judicial discretion. See, from a different context not affected by *Sang* (1979) 2 All E.R. 1222, *R. v. Allen* (1977) *Crim. L.R.* 163 for an illustration of the exercise of the discretion to exclude *statements* obtained by depriving the suspect of legal advice (cf. *R. v. Elliott* (1977) *Crim. L.R.* 551 and *R. v. Lemsatef* (1977) 1 W.L.R. 812 (C.A.)).

[4] (1963) 1 All E.R. 848. [5] *R. v. Court (1962) Crim. L.R. 687.*

[6] Apparently in neither case was there either a police trap or a conscious lie. There had rather been a change of policy after the medical examinations but before the cases came to trial. It is interesting to note that neither in *Payne* nor apparently in *Court* was there any reference either to *Kuruma* (and its canvassing of an exclusionary discretion in the interests of fairness) or indeed to the concept of 'fairness' itself. It was in later cases (particularly *King v. R.* (1969) 1 A.C. 304) that the result of *Payne* became associated with the *Kuruma* principle allowing exclusion in the interests of fairness. The only reason given in *Payne* (1963) 1 All E.R. 848, at 849, is that 'if the accused realised that the doctor would give evidence . . . he might refuse to subject himself to examination'. This sounds like a sui generis rule (savouring perhaps of the privilege against self-incrimination), and this is how the case was viewed in *R. v. Sang*.

'dubious'[1] reason for exclusion since much crime nowadays can only be solved by resort to underhand stratagems and methods, and others not surprisingly found it strange that evidence obtained by a trick or misrepresentation without illegality was more likely to be excluded than 'evidence obtained in breach of a positive rule of law'.[2]

The whole problem of improperly obtained evidence came up for consideration before the House of Lords in *R. v. Sang.*[3] This was a case of entrapment, but their Lordships' judgments, ranging well beyond the particular situation before them, addressed themselves to the wider issues of improperly obtained evidence. The question before the House of Lords in *Sang* was the following: 'Does a trial judge have a discretion to refuse to allow evidence, being evidence other than evidence of admission, to be given in any circumstances in which such evidence is relevant and of more than minimal probative value?' But those who hoped that the House of Lords would at last resolve the antinomies and tensions inherent in the cases and judicial pronouncements regarding improperly obtained evidence and discretionary exclusion on the basis of fairness will surely have been disappointed as their Lordships' endeavours have left the law in as great a state of confusion and uncertainty as before. Only one point has been put beyond doubt. It was agreed that as an integral part of his function of ensuring that the accused has a fair trial according to law the judge always has a discretion to disallow evidence when its probative value is outweighed by its prejudicial effect. If therefore the prosecution proposes to introduce prejudicial evidence of uncertain and tenuous probative worth, the judge will exclude it in order to prevent the accused from being unjustly convicted. But this is not a rule about searches and seizures, but a general rule of evidence. It applies to any evidence, however obtained, whether in consequence of an illegal search or a legal one or in any other way.

Obviously the important question for the law of search and seizure is whether the judicial discretion to exclude is limited to evidence which is likely to have a prejudicial effect out of proportion to its evidential value or can extend to other types of evidence not so vitiated. Lord Diplock, who delivered the leading speech, expressed the view that '(s)ave with regard to admissions and confessions and generally with regard to evidence obtained from the accused after commission of the offence, (a trial judge) has no discretion to refuse to admit relevant admissible evidence on the ground that it was obtained by improper or unfair means'. In terms of formulation none of their Lordships disagreed with Lord Diplock's answer (which had indeed been suggested by Viscount Dilhorne in the course of argument), but Lord Salmon only expressed concurrence with it on the understanding that it did not conflict with what appeared to be his general thesis that the judge's duty to ensure that the accused has a fair trial could not be confined to any closed category of cases;[4] Lord Fraser, even though in express agreement with the

[1] *The People v. O'Brien*, (1965) I.R. 142, at 160.

[2] Heydon, 'Current Trends in Evidence', 8 *Syd. L.R.* 305, 324 (1977).

[3] (1979) 2 All E. R. 1222.

[4] See ibid., at 1237, where he grouped together under the same heading of the

Diplock-Dilhorne formula, would in all probability interpret its pivotal element, the possibility of the discretionary exclusion in certain cases of evidence other than confessions or admissions 'obtained from the accused', differently;[1] and Lord Scarman's position is even less clear, both apparently agreeing with Lord Diplock's *interpretation* of their Lordships' answer to the certified question and yet at the same time taking a rather broader and more expansive attitude towards the exclusionary discretion.[2] But whatever the differences between their Lordships' approaches, since three of them would almost certainly agree with Lord Diplock's interpretation of his own principle, this seems to be the ratio of *R. v. Sang* and the nearest thing we have to a statement of the English position. This restricts the discretion to the exclusion of 'evidence tantamount to a self-incriminatory admission' obtained from the defendant after the commission of the offence by means which would justify a judge in excluding a confession having a similar self-incriminatory effect, namely cases where 'the accused has been induced to produce voluntarily' incriminatory evidence by unfair means. The reason for this, according to Lord Diplock, is the need to protect the principle that no person should be required to betray himself, nemo debet prodere se ipsum. On this basis he was apparently prepared to uphold *R. v. Barker*,[3] where *existing* incriminating documents obtained from the defendant by a promise were excluded, and *R. v. Payne*.[4] For this same reason Lord Diplock would

---

requirements of 'justice' a number of disparate things, including the inadmissibility of confessions, the recent case of *Wong Kam-ming v. The Queen* (1979) 1 All E.R. 939 on the voir dire, etc.

[1] Lord Fraser's speech is not always easy to follow. At one point he states that 'the principle of fairness to the accused' applied by Lord Guthrie in *H.M. Advocate v. Turnbull*, 1951 J.C. 96 (that tainted methods of obtaining important evidence may render 'a fair trial' impossible) is the same as that put forth by Lord Widgery, C.J. in *Jeffrey v. Black* (1978) 1 All E.R. 555 at 559, and that it was this same principle 'that seems to have been recognised by Lord Goddard, C.J.' in *Kuruma*; nor is he willing to reject the broad dicta of earlier cases. But later he expresses agreement with the more restrictive interpretation adopted by the rest of their Lordships (but still refers to the discretion as applicable to the obtaining of evidence from the accused or from premises occupied by him).

[2] The learned editors of Phipson on *Evidence* point out (3rd supplement to 12th ed., 1980) that, even though Lord Scarman at times used language that was wider than that employed by Lords Diplock and Dilhorne, he would agree with them as to a restrictive interpretation of the agreed formula, i.e. that only evidence tantamount to admissions obtained from the defendant by means that would compromise the rule against self-incrimination should be within the exclusionary discretion.

[3] (1941) 2 K.B. 381. In *Barker*, it must be emphasised, it was held that the excluded documents were inadmissible as a matter of law, not of discretion. But the basis on which Lord Diplock would uphold *Barker* is by no means certain as his Lordship's treatment of this case is not very clear; but the general tenor of his judgment is that the inadmissibility of the *Barker* evidence and the exclusion of the *Payne* evidence are related in that both are 'analogous' to excluded confessions (he also says that *Payne* 'would appear to fall into this category', i.e. the one exemplified by *Barker*). Surely *Barker* must be viewed in one of two ways, either as having established a sui generis rule (placing documents of the kind considered in that case on the same footing as an inadmissible confession) or as having been wrongly decided.

[4] (1963) 1 All E.R. 848.

not accept the existence of a discretion to exclude evidence discovered as a result of illegal searches, the phrase 'evidence obtained from the accused' being restrictively interpreted by him as evidence which the accused had been induced or persuaded to produce (apparently) voluntarily.

The current position with regard to illegally obtained real evidence can therefore be set out as follows. The basic principle is that all relevant evidence is admissible, however it was obtained. But there is an exception The trial judge has a discretion to exclude where the defendant has been tricked or misled or otherwise induced by unfair or improper means to reveal or produce evidence against himself. In other words, if the means used to induce the accused to hand over or provide evidence against himself are objectionable in that their use would result in the suppression, as a matter of law or discretion, of a confession obtained in reliance thereupon, their employment in the area of other evidence would similarly justify a judge in excluding the evidence so obtained. But this exception does not extend to cases of search and seizure, namely cases where the evidence was secured as a result of an illegal search of either the accused or his premises, or to other instances of the obtaining of evidence otherwise than by the co-operative participation of the accused, either because in such cases there is no analogy with the established doctrine of the exclusion of confessions or because the privilege against self-incrimination would not be endangered by the admission into evidence of incriminatory items unearthed by illegal searches and seizures as opposed to evidence voluntarily produced by a misled or tricked defendant.[1]

Is the Diplock principle, and its distinction between evidence obtained in consequence of illegal searches and seizures, that is admissible, and evidence which the accused is unfairly induced to provide against himself, which may be suppressed in the exercise of a judicial discretion calculated to preserve the privilege against self-incrimination, satisfactory? To begin with, it is not at all clear what *types of evidence* are envisaged by the *Sang* 'self-incrimination' rule. If one were here dealing with the traditional privilege against self-incrimination one would be likely to have in mind testimonial disclosures, not any other type of evidence, even though its provision may have involved co-operative participation by the suspect.[2] But by definition this cannot be so in the context of improperly obtained real evidence. Thus the provision of

[1] One possibility might be to say that the ratio of *Sang* is that, as regards the issue(s) considered by their Lordships, it was *held* that there is no discretion to exclude except on the basis of insufficient probative value, and that the Diplock phrase '(s)ave with regard . . . to evidence obtained from the accused . . .' means that this issue was not settled in *Sang* but has been reserved for future consideration. But this is contradicted, first by the rest of that phrase ('(s)ave with regard to admissions and confessions and *generally* with regard to evidence obtained . . .') that clearly implies that all three types of evidence referred to are subject to judicial exclusion, secondly by the unequivocal statement of Lord Diplock (at 1230c) that there is discretion to exclude evidence voluntarily produced by the accused, and thirdly by their Lordships' evident determination to give guidance to judges and practitioners over the whole area of illegally obtained (real) evidence. This is how *R. v. Sang* has been regarded by the Court of Appeal (*R. v. Trump*, *The Times*, 28 December, 1979).

[2] 8 Wigmore, *Evidence* § 2263 (McNaughton rev. 1961); see *Schmerber v. California*, 384 U.S. 757 (1966).

fingerprints, medical evidence, documents, as in *Barker*, and indeed apparently any other type of evidence can come within the newly fashioned rule, provided that the challenged evidence is, presumably in its impact, 'tantamount to a confession',[1] itself not an easy concept to define. But can it reach perfectly reliable items of real evidence neither previously part of the body nor constituting the accused's make up that a suspect has been induced *to hand over* as a result of some police trick or misrepresentation? The answer to this is very uncertain. The phrase 'obtained from the defendant' is also ambiguous in certain other respects. First, does it envisage any *provision* of evidence by the defendant which he would not otherwise have handed over to the police, or should the production of the challenged evidence be 'voluntary',[2] as Lord Diplock would seem to demand, in which case a threat of force by the police in consequence of which the defendant hands over incriminating evidence would be outside the field of the possible applicability of the exclusionary discretion, a strange result given the fact that it is compulsion that normally triggers the operation of the privilege against self-incrimination? To put it somewhat differently, it is not easy to know from a reading of *Sang* what are the improper or unfair means inducing the defendant to turn over the incriminating evidence that could result in the activation of the exclusionary discretion. Are they those, and only those, that would cause a resulting confession to be excluded, whether as a matter of law or of discretion, as Lord Diplock again seems at one point to suggest,[3] or does his principle concentrate upon different types of inducement, such as tricks and the like, which cause the accused, *apparently voluntarily*, to co-operate in his own incrimination? In any case, what considerations should judges take into account in deciding what police means and methods are 'unfair'?[4] Does the notion of 'unfairness' relate only to the position of the accused or should it also encompass considerations regarding the seriousness of the offence and the urgency of the case?' Secondly, since the *Sang* rule is apparently not limited to fingerprint evidence, the results of medical examination and the like, what does the phrase 'from the defendant' mean? Does it denote that the evidentiary item should have been on the person of the accused or does it not matter if it was elsewhere so long as it was within his control? The only thing that is clear is that if *Barker* is regarded as an example of the new *Sang* rule, rather than as a sui generis category relating to documents produced as a result of inadmissible inducements, it will not be easy to draw principled lines either between types of evidence or between types of location of the incriminating item prior to discovery. Finally, is the Diplock rule one that applies automatically whenever there has been a trick or the use of other improper means, in which case a new peremptory rule analogous to the one relating to confessions will have come into existence and which cannot be what their Lordships had in mind (since after all the new rule is presented as

[1] *R. v. Sang*, at 1230, per Lord Diplock.

[2] Ibid. See also Lord Fraser's judgment, at 1241, where *Payne* is described as a case where the accused was induced 'to permit' (and 'cooperate' in) the process that led to the discovery of the evidence.

[3] *R. v. Sang*, at 1230.

[4] Ibid, at 1230–1.

one of 'discretion'), or is the power to exclude one that does not have to be resorted to in some cases involving the use of improper means eliciting from the accused damning evidence even though it may be in others, in which case no information about the criteria of its applicability is given? A different criticism of the distinction between evidence equivalent to self-incriminatory admissions which the defendant has been induced to provide by unfair means, that might justify the operation of the exclusionary discretion, and evidence obtained in other ways, e.g. by illegal searches and seizures, where there is apparently no room for any exclusion in the interests of fairness, is that it does not appear to find support in or to correspond to any of the rationales usually canvassed as bases for the suppression of improperly obtained real evidence. Thus it is not intended to advance the cause of deterring police impropriety, it does not fit in comfortably with any theory regarding the undesirability of courts appearing to participate in 'dirty business' by seemingly sanctioning investigatory irregularities, and it cannot be thought of as a distinction brought in to give better effect to the rights of suspects, as it surely cannot be argued that the right to be free from illegal searches is inferior either to the traditional privilege against self-incrimination, on the highly debatable assumption that this is involved in the situations envisaged in *Sang*, or to the allegedly analogous rule concocted by their Lordships in their attempt to explain *Barker* and *Payne*. Any theory that admits without reservation the evidence in *Jeffrey v. Black* while holding inadmissible real evidence that the defendant was tricked or misled into producing himself is in need of compelling justification, and their Lordships' convoluted speeches in *Sang* provide none.

What then is the theoretical basis for *Sang*? This is sketched out by Lords Diplock and Scarman, and can be referred to as the 'fair trial' doctrine. On this theory the role of the judge is confined to the forensic process; he controls neither the police nor the prosecuting authority, neither the right to prosecute nor the prosecution's right to lead admissible evidence in support of its case being subject to judicial control; the judge's duty is 'to see that the accused has a fair trial according to law'. But what does 'fair' mean in this context? This relates to the process of trial, Lord Scarman says, and three principles are given by him as constituting this concept. 'No man is to be compelled to incriminate himself . . . No man is to be convicted save on the probative effect of legally admissible evidence. No admission or confession is to be received in evidence unless voluntary.' If legally admissible evidence is tendered which endangers these principles, which is what in Lord Scarman's view happened in *Payne*, the judge may exercise his discretion to exclude it, thus ensuring that 'the accused has the benefit of principles which exist in the law to secure him a fair trial'. But this theory is open to serious difficulties. If the judge is only in charge of the trial and is not concerned with the behaviour of the police or of the prosecution, except in so far as such behaviour may affect the conduct of the trial, it is difficult to see why a rule analogous to the privilege against self-incrimination and calculated to exclude evidentiary items of unquestioned probative value which the accused was unfairly induced to provide *before the trial* should be assigned a different status in terms of its effect on the trial from other rules also intended to protect suspects and control the police, for instance the rule prohibiting illegal searches and seizures, and it is surely no good declaring by definitional fiat that the right not to be compelled to incriminate oneself as opposed to other safeguards is part of the concept of a fair trial. For what should not be forgotten is that there is no single privilege against self-incrimination, but 'many things in as many settings'.[1] There is thus the defendant's right not to take the stand during his own trial, the witness's right in any judicial proceeding to refuse to answer questions tending to incriminate him, and the suspect's immunity from compulsory self-incrimination at the *pre-trial* stage, and it is only the first two that could plausibly be said to form part of the trial process, not the defendant's privilege not to incriminate himself at the investigatory stage. In both the case where the suspect at the pre-trial stage has been misled into providing evidence against himself by means of a misrepresentation or trick, as in *Barker* and *Payne*, and in the one where the incriminating evidence has come to light as a result of an illegal search or some other illegality not involving the co-operative participation of the defendant, where there is apparently no judicial power to suppress either for the sake of some notion of fairness to the accused or in the interests of a fair trial, the evidence has been obtained before the trial; the two situations cannot be distinguished; and it is difficult to avoid the conclusion that if the role of the judge is only to conduct a fair trial and not to exercise disciplinary powers over the police or the prosecution as regards the way in which relevant evidence has been obtained by them all sufficiently probative evidence should be allowed in. Strangely, Lord Diplock's definition of '(a) fair trial according the law' is more restrictive than Lord Scarman's in that it is only said to encompass the related principles that the case against the accused should be proved beyond all reasonable doubt and that information likely to have a prejudicial influence out of proportion to its true probative value should be excluded, presumably for fear that the accuracy of the judicial process will thereby be impaired. On this approach, '(h)owever much the judge may dislike the way in which a particular piece of evidence was obtained before proceedings were commenced, if it is admissible evidence probative of the accused's guilt it is no part of his judicial function to exclude it for this reason'.[2] But adoption of this principle should surely have led to the position that with the exception of confessions and admissions all probative evidence obtained before the trial should be admissible, something that is not reflected either in the Diplock distinction or in their Lordships' approval of *Payne* and *Barker*.

In any case the effective result of *Sang* if one regards the Diplock interpretation of their Lordships' agreed answer as the nearest thing to a ratio[3] is the establishment of a new hybrid rule of dubious parentage, partly

[1] Wigmore, supra, at § 2251.

[2] *R. v. Sang*, supra, at 1230, per Lord Diplock.

[3] See now *R. v. Trump (The Times*, 28 December 1979) where the Court of Appeal expressed the view that the House of Lords in *Sang* had recognised a limited exception (to admissibility) in cases analogous to improperly obtained admissions, quoting from

based on the privilege against self-incrimination and partly analogous to the rule concerning confessions, that allows the exercise of an exclusionary discretion in the interests of a fair trial in cases where the accused was unfairly induced to provide real evidence against himself. Conceptually, it is either as if the rule prohibiting the reception of objectionable confessions has been expanded to include not only statements but also real evidence obtained by means of apparent infractions of the principle that no man should be made to betray himself or as if there has been recognition of a new type of pre-trial privilege that confers on the accused immunity from the admission into evidence of non-testimonial items which he was unfairly induced to provide against himself. This rule, a generalised type of *Barker* and *Payne*, is difficult to justify in terms of either principle, policy or prior authority, runs contrary to the principle announced by Lord Diplock that courts are not concerned with how real evidence was obtained, will be exceedingly difficult to apply with anything approaching either consistency or coherence, and will, it is confidently predicted, be short-lived. Before long English law is bound to go the Canadian way.

(iii) Intermediate models

What has been called the intermediate position is best exemplified by the Scottish rule.[1] This avowedly strives to reconcile two highly important interests which are liable to come into conflict, first the public interest that the individual should be protected from unlawful and unfair treatment at the hands of public authorities, and secondly the interest of the State that relevant evidence of crime necessary to secure the conviction of those who

---

Lord Scarman that if the accused had been misled or tricked into providing evidence against himself the privilege against self-incrimination was likely to be endangered; so in such cases the evidence might be excluded; and in *Trump* it was indeed held that the evidence provided by the appellant, a specimen of blood, should be treated as being *subject to* the judicial discretion to exclude since it had been provided as a result of a threat; but since the officer had acted in good faith the evidence should not be excluded. An interesting analogy can be drawn between *Sang* and the principle of *Boyd*. *Boyd*, it will be remembered, exemplifies the principle that if the defendant is forced to hand a document on pain that if he does not its contents will be taken to be as alleged by the government the privilege is violated because even though what is handed over is preexisting real evidence the defendant is contemporaneously forced to affirm that the document he hands over is what was demanded of him. In similar fashion, *Sang* regards as falling within the policy of the privilege against self-incriminating certain situations where real evidence was obtained from the defendant by means which would justify the exclusion of oral communications having a similar self-incriminating effect. In other words, *Boyd* and *Sang* are similar in that they emphasize not the character of what is compelled but its effect and in that they depart from the strict theory that the privilege (or its policy) can only be violated when the compelled act *itself* constitutes an incriminating *communication*, the mere act of *production* not amounting to such communication. (The American Supreme Court, as we have seen, is now returning to the strict position: see *Fisher v. United States*, 425 U.S. 391 (1976) and *Andresen v. Maryland*, 427 U.S. 463 (1976)).

[1] See *Lawrie v. Muir*, (1950) S.C. (J)19; *McGovern v. H.M. Advocate*, (1950) S.C. (J) 33.

violate the law must as a general rule not be withheld from judicial tribunals. This intermediate approach, that is now also followed in Ireland[1] and Australia,[2] does not regard the issue of illegally obtained evidence either from the narrow evidentiary angle or from the essentially undefined perspective of broadly formulated theories based on alleged unfairness to the accused. As originally developed by Scottish courts and as recently elaborated by the High Court of Australia,[3] it begins with strong emphasis on the related requirements of public policy that the law should be observed in the investigation of crime, that it is undesirable that curial approval or encouragement should (appear to) be given to the unlawful conduct of those who are entrusted with the enforcement of the law, and that the liberty of the individual should not be completely subordinated to the executive, but then goes on to declare that it is not appropriate that merely accidental or trivial illegalities should lead to the inadmissibility of resulting incriminating evidence when these involve neither overt defiance of the law nor intentional disregard of the rights of suspects and when therefore the reception of the evidence thus obtained would not compromise the position of the court 'as a tribunal whose concern is in upholding the law'.[4] 'Convictions obtained by the aid of unlawful or unfair acts may be obtained at too high a price',[5] but at the same time 'exclusion of a vital piece of evidence from the knowledge of a jury because of some technical flaw in the conduct of the police would be an outrage upon common sense and a defiance of elementary justice'.[6]

What decisional yardsticks have emerged for giving effect to these weighty but conflicting public interests? Scottish law formulates the initial rule that even though 'an irregularity in the obtaining of evidence does not necessarily render that evidence inadmissible'[7] '(i)rregularities require to be excused'[8] before improperly obtained evidence can be allowed in; and whether any particular irregularity ought to be disregarded depends upon the nature of the irregularity (mainly on whether it was deliberate or accidental, serious or trivial) and upon any other circumstances under which it was committed (in particular whether there were pressing circumstances of urgency or emergency in effect making an illegality necessary if important evidence was to be preserved, the seriousness of the offence being investigated, and whether it should have been easy to secure the same evidence by complying with the

[1] *The People v. O'Brien*, (1965) I.R. 142.

[2] See *R. v. Ireland*(1970) A.L.R. 727, at 735, as explained and amplified in *Bunning v. Cross* (1978) 19 A.L.R. 641, particularly at 658–9.

[3] *Bunning v. Cross*, supra. Here it was recognised that the law in Australia differed markedly from that in England, but it was decided that the principles established in *Ireland's* case should be followed. The principal judgment in *Bunning v. Cross* was delivered by Stephen and Aickin JJ., and Barwick C.J. 'entirely' agreed with their observations regarding the principles to be followed in exercising the judicial discretion to exclude.

[4] *Bunning v. Cross*, supra, at 661.

[5] *R. v. Ireland*, (1970) A.L.R. 727, at 735.

[6] *Lawrie v. Muir*, (1950) S.C.(J) 19, at 26.

[7] *H.M. Advocate v. M'Guigan* (1936) S.C.(J) 16.

[8] *Lawrie v. Muir*, (1950) S.C.(J) 19.

law).[1] Irish and Australian courts would not disagree with this, but seem to start with no particular presumption, whether that improperly obtained evidence should be excluded unless sufficient justification for discretionary admission is adduced by the State or that such evidence should be admitted unless the accused persuades the court to exercise its discretion in his favour. Thus the answer of Kingsmill Moore J. in *O'Brien* was that in every case a determination had to be made by the trial judge as to 'whether the public interest is best served by the admission or by the exclusion of evidence of facts'[2] ascertained as a result of illegal actions, and Stephen and Aickin JJ. in *Bunning v. Cross* thought that in all cases of evidence having been obtained by police impropriety a discretion to admit or exclude had to be exercised 'by reference to large matters of public policy'[3] and so as to achieve a balanced result in the light of all the conflicting considerations at stake. The factors formulated by the Irish Supreme Court and by the Australian High Court on the basis of which the balancing of conflicting interests should proceed are similar to the considerations canvassed by Scottish courts. They are: the nature and extent of the illegality; whether the nature of the illegality affects the cogency of the evidence so obtained; the ease with which the law could have been complied with; the nature of the offence charged; the existence of circumstances of urgency or emergency; and whether the police were operating under narrowly defined constraints demarcated by a carefully formulated and detailed statutory scheme or under more general grants of power. All these things have to be placed on 'the discretionary scales',[4] and even though there may be much uncertainty in practice, a balancing of conflicting interests in each case is regarded as the 'only rational way of resolving the problems involved'.[5]

It is interesting to note that in a number of recent Commonwealth proposals for legislative action in this area the solution that has found the most favour is something not dissimilar to the Scottish-Irish-Australian intermediate solution. Thus, the Draft Evidence Code of the Law Reform Commission of Canada,[6] proceeding on the basis that 'courts must be able to protect the integrity of the adjudicative process' and despite the improbability of rules of evidence proving effective in controlling police behaviour, first proposes that evidence should be excluded if it was obtained under such

[1] Ibid; see also *Fairley v. Fishmongers of London*, (1951) S.C.(J) 14; *Hay v. H.M. Advocate*, 1968 J.C. 40; *Bell v. Hogg*, (1967) J.C. 49. Even though there are many formulations of the Scottish rule the predominant one is that what Scottish courts use is an *inclusionary discretion*.

[2] (1965) I.R. 142, at 160. Later in his judgment Kingsmill Moore, J. formulated the rule somewhat differently, namely that 'the presiding judge has a discretion to exclude evidence of facts ascertained by illegal means where it appears to him that public policy, based on a balancing of public interests, requires such exclusion'.

[3] 19 A.L.R. 641, 660. It is the requirements of public policy rather than considerations of fairness to the accused that should determine the exercise of the judicial discretion, the High Court in *Bunning v. Cross* emphasised (at 659 and 660).

[4] *Bunning v. Cross,* supra, at 663.

[5] Sheriff I.D. MacPhail, 'Research Paper on the Law of Evidence of Scotland' (presented to the Scottish Law Commission, April 1979), para 21.06.

[6] See s. 15(1) and (2).

circumstances that 'it's use in the proceedings would tend to bring the administration of justice into disrepute', and then sets out certain guidelines to facilitate the judicial task; the judicial discretion should thus be exercised on the basis of 'all the circumstances surrounding the proceedings and the manner in which the evidence was obtained', including 'the extent to which human dignity and social values were breached', 'the seriousness of the case', 'the importance of the evidence', and the more traditional criteria of the existence of an emergency and of whether the challenged police action was wilful or accidental. The Australian Law Reform Commission[1] similarly recommends adoption of a statutory scheme combining exclusion of illegally obtained evidence with discretionary admission in the event of the court being satisfied that admission would 'specifically and substantially benefit the public interest without unduly prejudicing the rights and freedoms of any person'. The matters that a court may consider in deciding whether it can be so satisfied *include* the seriousness of the offence being investigated, the urgency of detecting the offender and the urgency or need to preserve the relevant evidence; the nature and seriousness of the police contravention or failure; and the extent to which the improperly obtained evidence might have lawfully been obtained.[2] Both these sets of proposals are vague, imprecise and confusing, and, if adopted, will certainly lead to much litigation, considerable uncertainty, and perhaps the development of a body of law characterised not so much by beneficial results in terms of a proper performance of police functions and the protection of suspects' rights as by minute distinctions of fact and subjective judicial perceptions. In terms of phraseology they do not seem preferable to the classic statement of Lord Cooper in *Lawrie v. Muir* or the principles put forward by Kingsmill Moore J. in *O'Brien* and by Stephen and Aickin JJ. in *Bunning v. Cross* Their sole advantage is that if enacted these proposals would represent not some contentious judicial formula awkwardly engrafted onto the law of evidence and neither fairly referable to traditional legal considerations nor clearly mandated by weighty arguments of public policy but rather a legislative attempt at reconciling conceptually incommensurable but in terms of importance compelling public interests, that of ensuring accurate trials and that of not appearing to condone the improper conduct of those whose task it is to enforce the law.[3]

But not all reformers would abandon common law doctrines.[4] Another solution that many favour would be to adhere to the traditional common law rule of admissibility, but also to supplement it by the development of a new remedy sounding in damages, the purposes of which will be both to give adequate compensation to the victims of illegal searches and to 'penalise' the police for failing to observe the law.[5]

[1] See *Report No. 2 Criminal Investigation* (1975), paras. 288–298.

[2] This proposal has been included in the Criminal Investigation Bill 1977.

[3] The rationale of 'judicial integrity' is discussed below, at 346–8.

[4] See the English Criminal Law Revision Committee, *11th Report, Evidence (General)* (Cmnd. 4991, 1972), para. 68. But the *Report* did not question the general statement of Lord Hodson in *King v. R.*, supra.

[5] See below, at 377–9.

(iv) The American exclusionary rule

In stark contrast both to the traditional common law doctrine of admissibility and to intermediate models sometimes excluding and sometimes admitting illegally obtained evidence is the strict American exclusionary rule which demands the suppression of all evidence secured in violation of the Fourth Amendment.[1] Our treatment of it can be divided into three parts, first its development and objectives, secondly its scope and administration, and thirdly its future.

(a) *Development and objectives.* The attitude of early American cases and judicial pronouncements was to admit all relevant evidence even though it may have been obtained illegally.[2] As it was put in one case,[3] if there was an illegal search the officer conducting it would be responsible for the wrong done. But this was 'no good reason for excluding the (items) seized, as evidence, if they were pertinent to the issue' before the court. When items were offered in evidence 'the court can take no notice how they were obtained, whether lawfully or unlawfully'. This is a clear statement of the orthodox common law position, that the admissibility of evidence depends solely on its relevance and is not affected by the illegality or impropriety of the means by which it was acquired. But before long the Supreme Court began the development of a federal doctrine of exclusion demanding the suppression of evidence obtained by illegal search and seizure. The first hints of this new doctrine can be found in *Boyd v. United States*[4] where, it will be remembered, the Court held first that a violation of the Fourth as well as of the Fifth Amendment was involved in the situation before them and secondly that the 'admission in evidence' of the relevant matter thereby obtained was itself unconstitutional.[5] The Fifth Amendment on this view requires the suppression of evidence obtained in violation of the Fourth . But this part of *Boyd*, that the product of an illegal search must be excluded either under the Fourth Amendment or under the Fifth or as a result of the combined operation of the two, appeared to be decisively repudiated by the Supreme Court in *Adams v. New York*[6] in 1904. The Court said that the weight of authority as well as reason supported the position that courts would not stop to inquire as to the means by which evidence was obtained and that any inquiry as to its admissibility should be limited to its relevance; cited Greenleaf who had written that unlawfully obtained evidence was admissible provided it was pertinent to the issue before the court with approval; and referred, again with full approval, to earlier state cases propounding the

[1] The best analysis of the exclusionary rule is by La Fave, *Search and Seizure* (1978); see also Oaks, 'Studying the Exclusionary Rule in Search and Seizure', 37 *U. Chi. L. Rev.* 665 (1970); Wright, 'Must the Criminal Go Free if the Constable Blunders?', 50 *Tex. L. Rev.* 736 (1972); Paulsen, 'The Exclusionary Rule and Misconduct by the Police', 52 *J. Crim. L., C. & P.S.* 255 (1961).

[2] See 8 Wigmore, *Evidence* § 2183–2184a (McNaughton rev. 1961).

[3] *Commonweath v. Dana*, 43 Mass. (2 Met.) 329 (1841).

[4] 116 U.S. 616 (1885).

[5] 116 U.S. at 638.

[6] 192 U.S. 585 (1904).

orthodox common law doctrine of admissibility premised exclusively on relevance. The *Adams* opinion is so clear a statement of traditional theories of admissibility that one would have been justified in thinking that it had finally rejected heretical theories of exclusion based on illegality and once more restored common law orthodoxy. But only ten years later the Supreme Court in *Weeks v. United States*,[1] a federal case, held that illegally seized documents and contraband lottery tickets were inadmissible. The main ground both for the decision and for the adoption of the exclusionary doctrine was that any other holding would be a negation of the Fourth Amendment. If letters and other items could be illegally seized and still be used in evidence against a citizen, Justice Day said, the protection of the Fourth Amendment, declaring his right to be secure against such searches and seizures, would be 'of no value', and, so far as those thus placed were concerned, 'might as well be stricken from the Constitution'. The rationale of *Weeks* appears to be not so much deterrence as the notion of judicial duty. As Justice Day put it, it was the courts which were charged with the task of supporting the Constitution and to which all people had a right to appeal for the maintenance of fundamental rights; therefore it was important that unlawful searches and seizures should find no support in judicial decisions; for '(t)o sanction such (unlawful) proceedings would be to affirm by judicial decision a manifest neglect if not an open defiance of the prohibitions of the Constitution, intended for the protection of the people against such unauthorised action'.

The exclusionary doctrine of *Weeks* is confined to federal prosecutions. The States are not bound by the Fourth Amendment as such, which only applies to the federal government, but are of course subject to the Fourteenth Amendment's due process clause. This, as currently interpreted, protects, and therefore makes applicable to the States, those values that are basic to a free society.[2] One of the most significant of these values is 'the security of one's privacy against arbitrary intrusion by the police'.[3] The safeguards of the Fourth Amendment are therefore part of the Fourteenth Amendment's 'concept of ordered liberty' and as such are enforceable against the States through the Due Process Clause.[4] Does it also follow that the exclusionary rule is similarly applicable to the States through the due process clause? This raises the question whether the *Weeks* exclusionary rule is a doctrine of constitutional dimensions, deriving from the Fourth Amendment itself or from some other basic constitutional provision, or is only a rule of evidence adopted by some judicial tribunals for the more effective implementation of constitutional rights of privacy.[5] If it is the former, the exclusionary rule is a doctrine that is required by the Constitution and which, like the Fourth

[1] 232 U.S. 383 (1914). The Supreme Court feebly distinguished *Adams* on the ground that there the point was 'collateral', but this is not convincing (see 8 Wigmore, *Evidence* § 2184a).

[2] See *Palko v. Connecticut*, 302 U.S. 319, 325 (1937); *Wolf v. Colorado*, 338 U.S. 25 (1949); *Rochin v. California*, 342 U.S. 165 (1952).

[3] *Wolf v. Colorado*, 338 U.S. 25, 27–8 (1949).

[4] *Wolf v. Colorado*, 338 U.S. 25, 27–8, 31–3 (1949).

[5] 8 Wigmore, *Evidence* § 2184a (1961).

Amendment itself, must be applied to the States. But if it is only a rule of evidence it does not enjoy in terms of incorporation in the Fourteenth Amendment and enforceability against the States the exalted status which must be accorded to basic constitutional principles but is rather a judicially-fashioned expedient falling within the province of courts and legislatures alike which are therefore free if they so wish to refuse to adopt it and instead use other remedies and procedures for the adequate safeguarding of Fourth Amendment rights. The vital question of whether the *Weeks* exclusionary rule constituted a limitation upon the States as well as federal authorities first came before the Supreme Court in *Wolf v. Colorado*,[1] and was answered in the negative. Justice Frankfurter, delivering the majority opinion, had no doubt that Fourth Amendment rights were enforceable against the States because these were fundamental to a free society. Therefore if a State were affirmatively to sanction arbitrary incursions into protected privacy it would run counter to the Due Process Clause of the Fourteenth Amendment. But the exclusionary rule was of a different order. This related not to recognition of the right of privacy itself but to the ways of enforcing it: and for Justice Frankfurter issues of enforceability—how arbitrary governmental conduct should be checked, what remedies against it should be afforded and the means by which the right of privacy should be made effective—fell within the jurisdiction of the States. In other words, the exclusionary rule was not 'an essential ingredient of the right'[2] to be secure from unreasonable searches and seizures enshrined in the Fourth and Fourteenth Amendments; it was for the appropriate state organs to decide whether enforcement was best achieved by way of the adoption of suitable disciplinary measures or by overriding the usually applicable rules of evidence or by the recognition of any other remedies; and therefore in a prosecution in a state court for a state crime the Fourteenth Amendment did not forbid the admission of evidence obtained by an unlawful search and seizure.

But even during the currency of the *Wolf* doctrine it was established federal constitutional law that a defendant could not consistently with the due process clause be convicted by the use of methods which 'shock(ed) the conscience'.[3] On this view, most fully formulated by Justice Frankfurter[4], due process is incapable of exact definition but embodies values and standards felt to be basic to a free society. It is not to be measured by personal reaction or refined sensibility but 'by that whole community sense of "decency and fairness" that has been woven by common experience into the fabric of acceptable conduct'.[5] There are some types of conduct that society cannot tolerate. If a proceeding offends society's essential sense of justice, if it shocks the conscience, if it goes contrary to those standards which even hardened sensibilities would regard as basic, then it is inconsistent with the due process

[1] 338 U.S. 25 (1949).

[2] 338 U.S. at 29.

[3] See *Rochin v. California*, 342 U.S. 165, 172–3 (1952), per Frankfurter, J.

[4] See his judgments in *Wolf v. Colorado*, supra, and in *Rochin v. California*, supra.

[5] *Breithaupt v. Abram*, 352 U.S. 432, 436–8 (1957), per Clark, J.

clause and a conviction made possible only by reliance on it will not be allowed to stand.[1] This doctrine, in other words, while not demanding the exclusion of material evidence obtained in violation of the Fourth Amendment or comparable standards, forbids not only resort to deeply offensive methods of law enforcement, but also the admission of evidence obtained by methods so shocking to the conscience as to amount to due process violations. To put it somewhat differently, while the *Weeks* exclusionary rule is not as such binding on state authorities, the acknowledged right of the States to fashion their own rules of evidence for criminal trials is not without limitation, but is subject to the superior claims of due process, in this instance represented by the principle that if evidence has been obtained in a particularly offensive way then it must be suppressed. Two cases can be contrasted. In *Rochin v. California*[2] police officers broke into the defendant's home. They saw him swallowing two capsules, later shown to contain morphine. He was handcuffed and taken to a hospital where, on the instructions of the officers, a doctor forced an emetic solution through a tube into his stomach against his will. This 'stomach pumping' produced vomiting, which in turn revealed the two capsules. The Supreme Court held that the evidence so obtained was inadmissible because the method the State had used was deeply offensive, being 'close to the rack and the screw'. In *Irvine v. California*[3] police officers, attempting to obtain evidence of illegal bookmaking, had a key made to the defendant's house; two days later they entered the house illegally, installed a concealed microphone in the hall, and made a hole in the roof by means of which the wires were extended from the hall to a neighbouring garage where the officers stationed themselves; and on further occasions the police again entered surreptitiously in order to shift the microphone to a more suitable location; after much listening incriminating conversations were overheard. Should the defendant's conviction be upheld, or was it inconsistent with applicable due process standards as formulated by *Rochin*? A majority thought that the case before them was governed by *Wolf v. Colorado* and not by the principles of *Rochin v. California*. *Rochin*, Justice Jackson said, was much more than a case of an illegal search; it involved the element of coercion, represented by a physical assault upon the defendant's person to compel submission to the use of the stomach pump, an element totally lacking in *Irvine* where, despite the seriousness of the police misconduct, there had been no 'coercion, violence or brutality to the person', but only 'a trespass to property, plus eavesdropping'. *Wolf*, in other words, applied over the whole range of illegal searches and seizures whereas *Rochin* had developed a totally different doctrine for cases where there had been an element of brutality or coercion, and *Irvine* fell under *Wolf*.

Wolf v. Colorado was finally overruled in *Mapp v. Ohio*.[4] Its facts were simple. Police officers demanded to be allowed into Miss Mapp's house because they had information that a person who was wanted for questioning

[1] *Rochin v. California*, 342 U.S. 165 (1952).
[2] 342 U.S. 165 (1952).
[3] 347 U.S. 128 (1954).
[4] 367 U.S. 643 (1961).

was hiding there. She refused to admit them without a search warrant, but three hours later the officers came back, broke down the door and entered the house. She demanded to see a search warrant, the police produced a piece of paper which Miss Mapp took from them, a violent struggle took place, and eventually she was handcuffed. During the ensuing search the police found obscene books and materials for the possession of which the defendant was convicted. The state court thought that a reasonable argument might be made that the conviction should be reversed because the methods employed to obtain the evidence were such as to offend that sense of justice which *Rochin* had identified as being at the core of due process but it was nonetheless held that since the evidence had not been taken 'from (the) defendant's person by the use of brutal or offensive physical force' the books that were seized should not be suppressed. The Supreme Court, by a simple majority, overruled *Wolf v. Colorado*, declared the exclusionary rule to be applicable to the States, and held that 'all evidence obtained by searches and seizures in violation of the Constitution' was inadmissible in state courts, as much as in federal ones. For the majority, speaking through Justice Clark, since the Fourth Amendment's right of privacy had been declared to be enforceable against the States through the Due Process Clause of the Fourteenth, it should also be enforceable against them by the same sanction of exclusion as was used against the Federal Government under the *Weeks* doctrine. If it was otherwise then just as without the *Weeks* rule 'the assurance against unreasonable federal searches and seizures would be "a form of words", valueless and undeserving of mention in a perpetual charter of inestimable human liberties', so too, without the exlusionary rule, the now securely recognised constitutional freedom from state invasions of privacy would be 'ephemeral' and undeserving of '(the) Court's high regard as a freedom "implicit in the concept of ordered liberty" '. *Mapp's* effect then is twofold. It first reads the whole of search and seizure law as developed by federal courts into the Fourteenth Amendment, so that whatever constitutes a violation of the Fourth Amendment, however technical, is automatically a violation of the due process clause of the Fourteenth,[1] and secondly it applies the exclusionary rule to the States in all instances where suppression would be ordered at the federal level. As elaborated in *Mapp* and subsequent cases the exclusionary rule is of striking severity. It is applied 'inflexibly, rigidly, and mechanically',[2] and its result is the exclusion of all illegally obtained evidence, namely evidence obtained in violation of the Fourth Amendment, whatever the nature of the irregularity,[3] whether it was flagrant, as in *Irvine,*

[1] In dissent Harlan, J., joined by Frankfurter, J., attacked the majority's conclusion on the ground that *Wolf* had not held that the Fourth Amendment as such is enforceable against the States, but that only 'the principle of privacy' lying 'at the core' of the Amendment is so enforceable.

[2] *Bivens v. Six Unknwon Fed. Narcotics Agents*, 403 U.S. 388, 420 (1971), per Burger, C.J. dissenting.

[3] See *Stone v. Powell*, 428 U.S. 465, 538 (1976), per White, J. dissenting; *Bivens v. Six Unknown Fed. Narcotics Agents*, 403 U.S. 388, 419 (1971), per Burger, C.J. dissenting.

or at worst a minor and technical one, as in *Coolidge v. New Hampshire*,[1] and even though the officers had strictly complied with what they reasonably thought to be the applicable law. In other words, the 'capital punishment'[2] of suppression will be inflicted on all evidence, including its 'fruits', as soon as any police error amounting to a breach of Fourth Amendment law has been shown in its acquisition.

But two important questions which may ultimately determine not only the scope of the exclusionary rule but also its future are: what is the juridical basis of the rule, and what is its main purpose and rationale? As regards the first issue, already touched upon earlier with regard to the enforceability of the *Weeks* doctrine against the States, the majority opinion in *Mapp appears* to adopt the view that the exclusion of unconstitutionally seized evidence is required by the Fourth Amendment itself, in a rather confusing sentence Justice Clark describing the exclusionary rule as a 'clear, specific, and constitutionally required—even if judicially implied—deterrent safeguard'.[3] This view regards 'the exclusionary rule (as) an essential part of'[4] the Fourth Amendment and as an integral part of the right to be secure from unreasonable searches and seizures, and this would seem to imply that exclusion is not only a way of safeguarding Fourth Amendment rights generally but also a personal constitutional right of the party aggrieved that must not be subjected to dilution simply because the principal objective of the rule may not be borne out by the available empirical evidence. Another view is that the Fourth Amendment of itself supports no exclusionary rule but that a *constitutional* basis for it may emerge as a result of the alleged interaction between the Fourth and Fifth Amendments first detected in *Boyd*. This was the view of Justice Black in *Mapp* itself. He was unwilling to derive the exclusionary rule from the Fourth Amendment since the Amendment itself contained no provision expressly forbidding the use of such evidence and he was 'extremely doubtful that such a provision could properly be inferred from nothing more than the basic command against unreasonable searches and seizures'.[5] But when the Fourth Amendment's ban against unreasonable searches and seizures was considered 'together' with the Fifth Amendment's ban against compelled self-incrimination 'a constitutional basis'[6] for the rule emerged. This position no longer commands support. *Boyd's* elaboration of a close relationship between the two Amendments has been largely discredited, the exclusionary doctrines used under the Fourth and Fifth Amendments are now known to be very different in both thrust and operation, and in any case Justice Black's view seems ultimately to depend on an expansive theory concerning the function and scope of the privilege against self-incrimination,

[1] 403 U.S. 443 (1971).

[2] *Bivens*, supra, at 419, per Burger, C.J. dissenting.

[3] 367 U.S. 643, 648.

[4] Ibid., at 656.

[5] 367 U.S. at 661–2.

[6] Ibid. Paradoxically, in a later case, Clark, J. himself, the author of the *Mapp* opinion, supported the view that it is only 'the Fourth Amendment *implemented* by the self-incrimination clause of the Fifth' that requires exclusion: *Ker v. California*, 374 U.S. 23, 30 (1963).

specifically a theory that would extend its protection well beyond the area of testimonial compulsion. This theory has now been decisively rejected.[1] A more convincing view, and the one that is currently in fashion, is that exclusion of illegally obtained evidence is not required by the Constitution but is a judicially created 'remedy' designed for the purpose of safeguarding Fourth Amendment rights generally through its deterrent effect.[2] This has two implications: First, if the exclusionary rule neither flows from nor is demanded by the Constitution but is '(a) judicially contrived doctrine',[3] it enjoys no special sanctity but can be either modified or even overruled by the Supreme Court when it thinks fit to do so, for instance when the suppression of evidence is shown to be practically ineffective in accomplishing its objectives, whatever these may be, or when other 'adequate' but less drastic measures for effectuating the Fourth Amendment have been devised by state legislatures or Congress. Secondly, if the exclusionary rule is not an inseparable part of the Fourth Amendment or of any other constitutional provision but at most a judicial remedy, it does not constitute a personal constitutional right of the victim of an unreasonable search, which in its turn is usually taken to mean that, as with most other remedial devices, its application may be restricted to those areas where its objective, whatever it may be, is best served.[4]

What about the principal purpose of the exclusionary rule as this was developed in *Mapp* and subsequently? Two main purposes have been identified. The first is that of deterrence, namely that without the exclusionary rule the constitutional guarantee of freedom from unreasonable searches will remain an 'empty promise'.[5] Exclusion, in other words, will deter future unlawful police conduct.[6] As this function of deterrence was put in a case decided before *Mapp*, '(t)he rule is calculated to prevent, not to repair. Its purpose is to deter—to compel respect for the constitutional guarantee in the only effective available way—by removing the incentive to disregard it'.[7] The second broad justification for the American exclusionary rule is that of 'judicial integrity',[8] first put forward in *Weeks*. This asserts that if law enforcement officers break the law and are allowed to use the evidence they have illegally obtained in court then judicial tribunals too will be guilty of or at the very least become accomplices in the disregard of the Constitution which they are sworn to uphold. And the reason why admission of illegally obtained evidence will result in the moral contamination of the judicial process, 'the imperative of judicial integrity'[9] justification argues, is that as

[1] See *United States v. Wade*, 388 U.S. 218 (1967); *Schmerber v. California*, 384 U.S. 757 (1966).

[2] *United States v. Calandra*, 414 U.S. 338, 348 (1974).

[3] *Stone v. Powell*, 428 U.S. 465, 501, per Burger, C.J. concurring.

[4] *United States v. Calandra*, 414 U.S. 338, 348 (1974).

[5] *Mapp v. Ohio*, 367 U.S. at 660.

[6] *United States v. Calandra*, 414 U.S. 338 (1974).

[7] *Elkins v. United States*, 364 U.S. 206, 217 (1960).

[8] For analysis, see *United States v. Peltier*, 422 U.S. 531, 536–9 (1975); *Stone v. Powell*, 428 U.S. 465, 485–6 (1976).

[9] See *Elkins v. United States*, 364 U.S. 206, 222 (1960).

the criminal justice system has developed it is 'evidentiary rulings (that) provide the context in which the judicial process of inclusion and exclusion approves some conduct as comporting with constitutional guarantees and disapproves other actions by state agents'. A ruling admitting evidence in a criminal trial is therefore viewed by this theory as having the effect of 'legitimising the conduct' which produced it, 'while an application of the exclusionary rule withholds the constitutional imprimatur'.[1] Two other justifications for the exclusionary rule occasionally referred to, based in part on elements of deterrence and judicial integrity, are, first, ensuring that the government does not profit from any dirty business it may have engaged in, and secondly, assuring the people generally that constitutional safeguards will be observed both in theory and practice. The two are closely connected, and rest on the view that courts are invested with a special responsibility to protect fundamental rights and ensure respect for the law. The first, premised on the moral incongruity of the State flouting constitutional rights and at the same time demanding that its citizens should observe the law,[2] was eloquently articulated by Justices Brandeis and Holmes in their dissents in *Olmstead v. United States*.[3] The government, Justice Holmes said, should not play 'an ignoble part'; if it did it should be prevented from gaining from its iniquities, and this could best be done if it was not allowed to use evidence obtained illegally.[4] Justice Brandeis focused on the long-term effects of the government failing to observe the law. If the government became a lawbreaker it would breed contempt for the law; it would tempt every man to become a law unto himself, and would invite anarchy. 'To declare that in the administration of the criminal law the end justifies the means—to declare that the Government may commit crimes in order to secure the conviction of a private criminal—would bring terrible retribution.'[5] It was therefore vital both that the government should respect constitutional rights (and be seen to be so doing) and that the courts should set their face against any disturbance or erosion of the rule of law. The second justification is that the exclusionary rule is the best if not the only way of *assuring* the people *generally* that constitutional provisions conferring fundamental rights will be respected.[6] Without the exclusionary rule, this justification asserts, the Fourth Amendment will be deprived of content, and ultimately *the people's trust* in their Constitution and government will be imperilled. As these last two objectives of the exclusionary rule have been put forward, in combination, by Justice Brennan, the doctrine of excluding illegally obtained evidence aims not only to deter unlawful searches and seizures but also to accomplish 'the twin goals of enabling the judiciary to avoid the taint of partnership in official lawlessness and of assuring the people—all potential victims of unlawful

[1] *Terry v. Ohio*, 392 U.S. 1, 13 (1968).
[2] *People v. Cahan*, 282 P. 2d 905, 907, 909–14 (1955).
[3] 277 U.S. 438 (1928).
[4] Ibid., at 470.
[5] Ibid., at 485.
[6] *United States v. Calandra*, 414 U.S. 338, 355 (1974), per Brennan, J. dissenting; see also *Weeks v. United States*, 232 U.S. 383, 391–2 (1914).

government conduct—that the government would not profit from its lawless behaviour, thus minimising the risk of seriously undermining popular trust in government'.[1]

But even though, as we have seen from *Weeks*, the exclusionary rule when first formulated was based not so much on considerations of deterrence as on the need to enforce constitutional safeguards in a meaningful manner and on the related arguments of judicial integrity and of respect for the law generally recent Supreme Court cases identify deterrence as the 'prime purpose'[2] of the rule, 'if (indeed) not the sole one'.[3] This currently dominant view of the objectives and aims of the exclusionary rule under the Fourth Amendment can be set out as follows. The primary and perhaps exclusive justification for the exclusionary rule is 'the deterrence of police conduct that violates Fourth Amendment rights'.[4] Also, as post-*Mapp* decisions have established,[5] the rule is not a personal constitutional right of a person subjected to an unconstitutional search but only a remedial device developed in order to serve the cause of deterring police conduct violative of the Fourth Amendment. If therefore in a particular area exclusion of evidence will not advance 'the broad deterrent purpose of the exclusionary rule',[6] or if any gain in deterrence which might accrue from extending the rule to a type of case is clearly outweighed by competing considerations concerning the impairment of compelling interests which the State also has the right to advance, then the operation of the exclusionary rule will be suitably restricted.[7] In this way, that is by shifting the basis of the exclusionary rule from an essentially normative judgment that it is better for some guilty persons to go free than for the police to behave in a forbidden fashion or for the courts to appear to be participating in dirty business to the 'pragmatic'[8] goal of deterring future police misconduct, the Burger Court has been able to restrict its operation by preventing its application in particular types of proceedings. For some this is the beginning of a major modification of the exclusionary rule, ultimately leading to its total abandonment.[9] For if deterrence is its sole purpose, and empirical evidence shows that there is no connection between exclusion and deterrence—or between deterrence and exclusion in a particular type of case, for instance minor violations—it could be strongly argued that exclusion of illegally obtained evidence should be dispensed with, either generally or for those cases where the connection between suppression and deterrence is especially tenuous.

(b) *The scope of the exclusionary rule.* Discussion of the scope of the exclusionary rule can be divided into two parts, first the types of proceedings

[1] *United States v. Calandra*, 414 U.S. at 357.
[2] *United States v. Calandra*, 414 U.S. 338, 347 (1974).
[3] *United States v. Janis*, 428 U.S. 433, 446 (1976).
[4] *Stone v. Powell*, 428 U.S. 465, 486 (1976).
[5] See mainly *United States v. Calandra*, supra, and *Stone v. Powell*, supra.
[6] *Stone v. Powell*, supra, at 486.
[7] *United States v. Calandra*, supra.
[8] *Stone v. Powell*, supra, at 484.
[9] See the dissent of Brennan, J. in *United States v. Calandra*, supra.

and circumstances in which it can or cannot be invoked, and secondly the extent of exclusion.

(i) On the first issue, even though the effect of the exclusionary rule is to exclude otherwise admissible evidence, the exclusionary rule has not been held to mean 'that illegally seized evidence is inadmissible against anyone for any purpose'.[1] Some types of proceedings and certain kinds of circumstances have been excluded from its ambit, in the sense that the exclusionary rule cannot be activated in their context even though there has been illegality in the way the evidence which it is now sought to adduce was obtained. These proceedings and sets of circumstances are now explained on the basis of the rationale of deterrence, namely that the evidence in issue can be used even though there has been illegality *because* suppression would not result in gains in deterrence that would outweigh the social cost which invocation of the rule inevitably entails for the fair administration of the criminal law (fair in the sense of the acquittal of the innocent and the conviction of the guilty).[2] The three most prominent cases of the non-applicability of the exclusionary rule even though the government seeks to introduce in evidence the product of an illegal search are the following. There is first the standing requirement, namely that standing to invoke the exclusionary rule is confined to situations where the government seeks to use such evidence to incriminate the victim of the unlawful search. One who is not the victim of the unlawful search cannot complain if illegally obtained evidence is used against him.[3] One explanation of the rule regarding standing is that certain individuals are unable to invoke the exclusionary rule not because of any arguments concerning deterrence but because the rights of individuals who have not been the victims of illegal searches and seizures have not been violated.[4] But recently the Supreme Court explained the Fourth Amendment standing requirement in terms of 'a recognition that the need for deterrence and hence the rationale for excluding the evidence are strongest where the government's unlawful conduct would result in (the) imposition of a criminal sanction on the victim of the search'.[5] Secondly, grand jury proceedings have also been held to be outside the ambit of the exclusionary rule.[6] This means that a witness summoned to appear and testify before a grand jury may not refuse to answer questions on the ground that they were based on evidence discovered as a result of an unlawful search and seizure. This, the Supreme Court said in *United State v. Calandra,*[7] was because extending the exclusionary rule to

[1] *Alderman v. United States*, 394 U.S. 165, 175 (1969); see also *United States v. Calandra*, 414 U.S. 338, 348 (1974), where Powell, J. pointed out that '(d)espite its broad deterrent purpose, the exclusionary rule has never been interpreted to proscribe the use of illegally seized evidence in *all* proceedings or against *all* persons'.

[2] *United States v. Calandra*, 414 U.S. 338 (1974); *Stone v. Powell*, 428 U.S. 465 (1976).

[3] *Alderman v. United States*, 394 U.S. 165 (1969).

[4] See the dissenting opinion of Brennan, J. in *Calandra*, supra.

[5] *United States v. Calandra*, supra, at 348, per Powell, J.

[6] *United States v. Calandra*, 414 U.S. 338 (1974).

[7] Ibid., at 351–2.

grand jury proceedings would achieve only a small and minimal advance in deterring police misconduct at the expense of substantially interfering with the role of the grand jury.

Thirdly, it seems that, at least in certain cases, illegally obtained evidence may be admitted not as part of the prosecution's evidence-in-chief but for the purpose of impeaching the defendant's inconsistent testimony. But the position is by no means free of difficulty. In *Walder v. United States*[1] the defendant, at his trial on a charge of selling narcotics, testified on direct examination that he had *never* sold or possessed narcotics. He reiterated these assertions on cross-examination. The government then questioned him about a heroin capsule unlawfully seized from his home and suppressed in another proceeding two years *earlier*, and when the defendant denied that any narcotics had been taken from him at that time the prosecution called two witnesses who testified that narcotics had indeed been discovered on the previous occasion. The Supreme Court held that under the circumstances the illegally obtained evidence in issue was admissible for the sole purpose of impeaching the defendant's testimony on direct examination. The crucial fact was that the defendant had stated on *direct* examination that he had *never* possessed any narcotics. It was one thing to say that the government could not make an affirmative use of evidence unlawfully obtained. It was quite another to say that the defendant could turn the illegal method by which evidence in the government's possession was obtained to his own advantage, in this way providing himself with a shield against contradiction of his untruths. Such an extension of the *Weeks* doctrine, Justice Frankfurter said, would be 'a perversion of the Fourth Amendment'. The *Walder* situation can be contrasted with that presented in *Agnello v. United States.*[2] Here the government, having failed to introduce the illegally obtained evidence in its case in chief, tried to smuggle it in on cross-examination by asking the accused whether he had ever seen narcotics before. After the defendant's denial the prosecution attempted to bring in some cocaine which had been illegally seized. The evidence was held to be inadmissible, on the ground that the government would not be allowed to do indirectly, during cross-examination, what it could not do directly, in its evidence-in-chief. The distinction between *Walder* and *Agnello* is that in the latter case the defendant had said nothing, whether in his direct testimony or during cross-examination, that either put his character in issue or could be interpreted as a waiver of his constitutional protection, whereas in the former the defendant had made sweeping statements that amounted not merely to a denial of the charge against him but to the giving of substantive evidence concerning his general good character which it would be unfair to prevent the prosecution from challenging. A difficult decision that casts some doubt on the traditional understanding of the *Agnello—Walder* doctrine is *Harris v. New York,*[3] involving not the Fourth Amendment but the Fifth Amendment's privilege against self-incrimination. The accused was questioned by the police

[1] 347 U.S. 62 (1954).
[2] 269 U.S. 20 (1925).
[3] 401 U.S. 222 (1971).

without being warned of his rights. The questioning was therefore illegal and the statements he had made could not be admitted at his trial on a charge of selling heroin. But after the accused had testified the statements he had made to the police were put to him and were admitted in evidence for the purpose of impeaching his credibility. A narrow majority held that the defendant's inadmissible statements could still be used to impeach his credibility even though the defendant was impeached as to testimony bearing directly on the crimes charged, in obvious contrast to *Walder* where the defendant had only been impeached as to matters collateral to the crime charged. The majority thought that this made no difference in principle. But this is not supported by *Walder*. Further, *Harris* and *Agnello* are not easy to reconcile. If *Agnello* had been followed the result in *Harris* should have been different.[1] One possibility is that *Agnello* has been overruled. Another is that *Harris* will not be followed, or that at least it will not be regarded as setting out a new general rule that radically refashions the traditional theory concerning impeachment that emerges from *Agnello* and *Walder*. What is obvious is that for the time being the question of the extent to which the defendant can safely deny guilt without making himself vulnerable to impeachment is very unclear.[2]

(ii) What is the scope of exclusion that a court will order upon proof of a violation of the Fourth Amendment? Normally there is no difficulty since there is a direct link between the violation and the challenged evidence. But occasionally the evidence that the defendant objects to is derivative or secondary in nature.[3] One of the most usual examples is where there is an illegal arrest followed by the arrestee giving a confession. Should the confession be excluded because it would not have been obtained if it had not been for the illegal arrest or can it still be used because there was no immediate causal nexus between violation and evidence? This is a difficult question. On the one hand to allow secondary evidence to be used simply because it does not enjoy a primary relationship with the unlawful conduct would be to encourage indirect methods of circumventing the law, equally if not more damaging to personal liberty and the proper administration of justice than more flagrant abuses. On the other hand to apply a 'but for' test, in other words to hold that all evidence is 'fruit of the poisonous tree'[4] and should therefore be excluded *simply because* it would not have come to light

[1] See Dershowitz and Ely, '*Harris v. New York*: Some Anxious Observations on the Candor and Logic of the Emerging Nixon Majority', 80 *Yale L.J.* 1198 (1971). The learned authors correctly point out (at 1214–15) that it should be more difficult to create exceptions to the exclusionary rule used to implement the privilege against self-incrimination than to the one developed under the Fourth. The basic reason for this is that the Fifth Amendment itself '*is*' an exclusionary rule—'and a constitutionally created one', in sharp contrast to the *Mapp* suppression doctrine. What this means of course is that *Harris* can be used to allow the type of impeachment it sanctioned in the area of the Fifth Amendment for cases of illegally obtained evidence as well.

[2] See 3 La Fave, *Search and Seizure* 703–11 (1978).

[3] The best treatment is by La Fave, supra, at 612–80.

[4] *Nardone v. United States*, 308 U.S. 338, 341 (1939), per Frankfurter, J.

but for the illegal actions of the police, is to apply the exclusionary rule in a manner that will almost certainly impose a greater burden on the legitimate demands of law enforcement than can be justified by the rule's deterrent purpose. To put it differently, there comes a point where the relationship between the illegality and the subsequently obtained evidence which the prosecution proposes to adduce is so remote and attenuated that application of the exclusionary rule, with the inevitable and serious cost it entails for the claims of law enforcement, is no longer warranted.[1] Not surprisingly, the fixing of the point at which 'the deterrent effect of the exclusionary rule no longer justifies its cost'[2] has proved a matter of great difficulty.

The approach of the Supreme Court to the problems posed by derivative evidence, as this has been sketched out in a number of cases, may be called the theory of attenuation or dissipation and can set out as follows. Evidence will not be excluded simply because it would not have come to light but for the prior Fourth Amendment violation. Equally, any evidence following and obtained in consequence of illegal conduct must be excluded *unless* the prosecution proves that the connection between the unlawful arrest or search and the secondary evidence has become 'so attenuated as to dissipate the taint'.[3] The question, the Supreme Court has said, is whether, given proof of a primary illegality, the challenged evidence 'has been come at by exploitation of that illegality or instead by means sufficiently distinguishable to be purged of the primary taint'.[4] More simply, should the challenged evidence still be regarded as the product of the primary illegality, or should it, as a result of what has happened since then, be viewed as the product of sufficiently distinguishable intervening circumstances?[5] If it cannot be so regarded the evidence will remain affected by 'the vice of primary illegality'[6] and will have to be suppressed. A good example is *Wong Sun v. United States*.[7] Two statements were in issue here. The statement of the first defendant was obtained immediately after his illegal arrest. The second defendant's statement was not given until after he had been arraigned and released. He voluntarily returned to the station a few days after his illegal arrest, and his statement was preceded by an official warning of his right to remain silent and to have counsel if he wished. The Supreme Court did not allow the first statement to be given in evidence because it could not agree

[1] See Powell, J.'s concurring opinion in *Brown v. Illinois*, 422 U.S. 590, 606 (1975).

[2] Ibid., at 609.

[3] *Nardone v. United States*, 308 U.S. 338, 341 (1939).

[4] Maguire, *Evidence of Guilt* 221 (1959), cited with approval by the Supreme Court in *Wong Sun v. United States*, 371 U.S. 471, 488 (1963).

[5] Of course it goes without saying that the exclusionary rule has no application where despite any illegality the evidence was obtained from an independent source: see *Silverthorne Lumber Co. v. United States*, 251 U.S. 385, 392; *Nardone*, supra; *Wong Sun*, supra, at 487. Occasionally the 'independent source' and 'attenuation' doctrines are not sufficiently distinguished; but they are different. The 'attenuation' or 'dissipation' doctrine only applies where the government did not learn of the evidence from an independent source.

[6] *Takahashi v. United States*, 143 F. 2d 118, 122.

[7] 371 U.S. 471 (1963).

with the government's contention that it was the product not of the illegal arrest but of 'an intervening independent act of a free will'. Under the circumstances, the defendant being immediately handcuffed and arrested, the confession had not been shown to be free from 'the primary taint of the unlawful invasion'. It was very different with the second statement. Given the fact that the second defendant had been released and had returned voluntarily several days later to make the statement, it was held that the connection between the arrest and the statement had become 'so attenuated as to dissipate the taint'.[1] The Supreme Court in *Wong Sun* did not give much guidance on how its doctrine of attenuation should be applied or on the factors that one must consider in deciding whether suppression of subsequently obtained evidence is no longer required. But it appears clearly from the Court's opinion that where the period that elapses between the illegality and the obtaining of the challenged evidence is long, itself a matter of degree, or has been punctuated by intervening circumstances which are likely to have either obliterated or at least neutralised the effects of the initial violation, for instance release after an illegal arrest and consultation with one's lawyer, then suppression of the secondary evidence is no longer appropriate, either because it cannot in this case plausibly be maintained that the police officers used their initial breach of the law as a means of securing the evidence now in issue or because it can safely be assumed that the defendant as a result of the intervening developments is no longer labouring under the disability entailed by the original official misconduct. But it is also clear from the Court's opinion that if the police broke the law *in order* to secure the challenged evidence, their calculating disregard of the Fourth Amendment, whatever the length of time separating the two events, will inevitably activate the exclusionary doctrine. Deterrence demands no less.

Particular difficulty has been caused by cases where after an illegal arrest the defendant is given an otherwise adequate warning of his rights and then makes an inculpatory statement. Is this statement admissible because it is voluntary in the traditional sense, i.e. it has not been obtained in violation of the Fifth Amendment? After *Wong Sun v. United States* a number of state courts adopted the position that the giving of the *Miranda* warnings was sufficient to break the causal connection between a violation of the Fourth Amendment and a subsequent confession so that the defendant's act in making the statements after being informed of his rights would be considered an act of free will not tainted by the vice of the previous illegality. This view has now been rejected by the Supreme Court in *Brown v. Illinois.*[2] The correct position, as it appears from *Brown*, can be set out as follows. The exclusionary rules under the Fourth and Fifth Amendments are quite different. In particular, the exclusionary doctrine, when utilised to effectuate the Fourth Amendment, serves interests and policies that are distinct from those it serves under the Fifth. The basic difference is that the Fourth Amendment is directed at all unlawful searches and seizures, and

[1] Ibid., at 491.
[2] 422 U.S. 590 (1975).

not merely those that happened to produce incriminating material or testimony. Therefore, even though exclusion of a confession made without *Miranda* warnings might be regarded as necessary (and in general sufficient) to effectuate the Fifth Amendment, it would not be enough to protect the Fourth in an adequate manner. For not only would *Miranda* warnings and the exclusion of confessions made without them fail on their own to deter violations of the Fourth Amendment but also a holding that *Miranda* warnings could by themselves bring about the required attenuation of the taint of an unconstitutional arrest, however wanton and purposeful, would clearly result in a substantial dilution of the deterrent effect of the exclusionary rule. Arrests made without warrant or without probable cause, for questioning or 'investigation', would be encouraged by the knowledge that evidence derived from them could be made admissible at trial by the simple expedient of giving *Miranda* warnings, and any incentive to avoid Fourth Amendment violations would be eviscerated by making the warnings, in effect, 'a cure-all'.[1] Instead, what is required for the causal link between the illegal arrest and any statement made subsequently to be broken is not merely that a confession should meet the Fifth Amendment standard of voluntariness but that it should be 'sufficiently an act of free will to purge the primary taint'.[2] The test therefore is not simply whether the disputed statement is a voluntary one either in the abstract or under the Fifth Amendment, but whether it is 'the product of a free will under *Wong Sun*'.[3] How is this question to be answered? The *Brown* Court was unwilling to offer precise guidance. The question is one to be answered on the facts of each case and no single fact should be regarded as dispositive. 'The workings of the human mind are too complex, and the possibilities of misconduct too diverse, to permit protection of the Fourth Amendment to turn on (any) talismanic test'.[4] The *Miranda* warnings are still an important factor to consider in determining whether the confession is obtained by means of the exploitation of an illegal arrest. But there are other important factors too. The three most significant appear to be the temporal proximity of the arrest and the confession, the presence of intervening circumstances, and, 'particularly, the purpose and flagrancy of the official misconduct'. This last criterion is especially important.[5] It thus seems that where official conduct is flagrantly abusive of Fourth Amendment rights, whether by the arrest being a pretext for the achievement of collateral objectives or by the physical circumstances of the arrest having unnecessarily intruded upon personal privacy, 'some demonstrably effective break in the chain of events leading from the illegal arrest to the statement' will be required before the taint can be deemed removed, for instance actual consultation with counsel or the defendant's presentation before a magistrate. At the opposite end of

[1] Ibid., at 602, per Blackmun, J.

[2] Ibid., quoting from *Wong Sun*, 371 U.S. at 486.

[3] Ibid., at 603.

[4] Ibid.

[5] It is developed at length by Powell, J. in his concurring opinion in *Brown*, at 610–12.

the spectrum, that is where there is only a 'technical' violation of Fourth Amendment rights, for instance where officers acting in good faith arrested an individual in reliance on a warrant that was later invalidated, it appears unlikely that a court will require more than proof that effective *Miranda* warnings were given and that the ensuing statement is voluntary in the Fifth Amendment sense.

In conclusion, it can be seen that under both *Wong Sun* and *Brown* the material issue, that of attenuation, is 'largely a matter of degree'. But the two most prominent factors that courts consider in making this determination are, first the quality of the chain—in terms of length of time, evenness and density—connecting the challenged evidence with the primary illegality, and secondly the quality of the official conduct activating the exclusionary rule in the first place. The longer the chain, the greater the dissipation of the taint, and therefore the suppression the court will order will be narrower. Conversely, the more offensive the conduct leading to the eventual securing or discovery of the evidence, the more compelling the claims of deterrence, and therefore the scope of exclusion should similarly be broader.

(c) *The future of the exclusionary rule.* Recently the future of the strict exclusionary rule has become the subject of heated debate. It still enjoys influential support. The main arguments for its retention are the following: It is first pointed out that there is no other effective remedy for the enforcement of Fourth Amendment rights, that if the exclusionary rule is repealed or substantially modified the Fourth Amendment will become largely unenforceable, and that '(i)t would be intolerable if the guarantee against unreasonable search and seizure could be violated without practical consequence'.[1] There is therefore no alternative to the rule of exclusion. The second argument focuses on the importance of having 'a practical procedure by which courts can review alleged violations of constitutional rights and articulate the meaning of those rights'.[2] The advantage of the exclusionary rule is thus said to be that 'it provides an occasion for judicial review'[3] and for the elaboration of the principles by which the Fourth Amendment is to be enforced, and it is only in this way, it is argued, that constitutional guarantees in general, and the guarantee of freedom from unconstitutional searches in particular, can acquire credibility. 'By demonstrating that society will attach serious consequences to the violation of constitutional rights, the exclusionary rule invokes and magnifies the moral and educative force of the law. Over the long term this may integrate some fourth amendment ideals into the value system or norms of behaviour of law enforcement agencies'.[4] Nor is the exclusionary rule a failure as a deterrent, its supporters argue. It is of course true that reliable statistics do not exist to allow one to say with

[1] Oaks, 'Studying the Exclusionary Rule in Search and Seizure', 37 *U. Chi. L. Rev.* 665, 756 (1970).
[2] Ibid.
[3] Ibid.
[4] Ibid. See the dissent of Brennan, J. in *United States v. Calandra*, 414 U.S. 338 (1974).

confidence whether the exclusionary rule is an effective deterrent or not, and that the available evidence is at best inconclusive. But at the same time it has been observed that since the available data do not provide any reliable 'empirical substantiation or refutation'[1] of the deterrent effect of suppressing illegally obtained evidence one is justified in resorting to common sense, which certainly suggests that at least on many occasions the exclusionary rule 'ought'[2] to deter, because why should the police engage in illegal searches if they know or suspect that the evidence they will thus obtain will not be allowed in at the trial? In this sense, as one commentator has put it,[3] an analogy can be drawn between the exclusionary rule and capital punishment. The fact that murders still occur does not prove that capital punishment does not deter murder. Similarly, what the many continuing violations of the Fourth Amendment show is simply that the exclusionary rule is no perfect deterrent, not that it does not deter at all. 'With the exclusionary rule, as with capital punishment, the occasions on which the deterrent effect has failed are easy to see' because by definition the issue of the rule's applicability only becomes relevant if there has been a violation. In contrast, '(i)t is more difficult to measure the occasions on which the deterrent has been successful', but at the very least it does not appear unreasonable for someone to rely on 'a feeling' that the exclusionary rule must have a far from negligible impact as a deterrent.[4] Indeed there are two rather important indications that the rule is not the total failure as a deterrent that its enemies allege.[5] First, police officers have long complained that the suppression of illegally obtained evidence hampers law enforcement, which would appear to suggest that the exclusionary rule does have an appreciable impact on police behaviour; secondly, there is much evidence, for instance a marked increase in the number of search warrants and the adoption of suitable working rules within police departments, that following *Mapp* police practices in the area of search and seizure have undergone a marked transformation in the direction of a more faithful compliance with the Fourth Amendment and the way it has been interpreted by the Supreme Court.

Despite some continuing approval the exclusionary rule has been much criticized in recent years, and influential calls have been made for its substantial modification. In particular, both the rationales of judicial integrity and of deterrence have been found to be insufficient as justifications for the exclusionary doctrine, at least in its present severe form. As regards the former, the Supreme Court is now taking the view that the primary meaning of judicial integrity in the context of evidentiary rules is that judicial tribunals must not *themselves* commit or encourage violations of the Constitution. But in the area of search and seizure the violation is not committed by the court but by a police officer, and it is complete by the time

[1] Oaks, supra, at 709. See generally 1 LaFave, *Search and Seizure* 22–39 (1978).

[2] Wright, 'Must the Criminal Go Free If the Constable Blunders?', 50 *Tex. L. Rev.* 736, 739 (1972).

[3] Wright, supra, at 738–40.

[4] Ibid., at 739–40.

[5] See La Fave, supra, at 26–9.

the evidence is presented for introduction at the trial. In other words, admission of illegally obtained evidence is only viewed as impairing judicial integrity if it *encourages* violations of Fourth Amendment rights, and this inquiry has lately been regarded as '*essentially* the same as the inquiry into whether exclusion would serve a deterrent purpose'.[1] The focus is thus moved to the question of deterrence. Does the exclusion of illegally obtained evidence deter violations of the Fourth Amendment? Here the usual attack against the exclusionary rule relies on three main reasons why it is ultimately ineffective as a deterrent.[2] The first is that the rule penalises not the individual police officer whose illegal conduct results in the exclusion of evidence in a criminal trial but the prosecutor whose case against a suspect is either weakened or destroyed. The suppression doctrine, Chief Justice Burger has complained,[3] vaguely assumes that law enforcement is 'a monolithic governmental enterprise', and that only through exclusion of illegally obtained evidence will '*the prosecutor* be expected to emphasise the importance of observing the constitutional demands in *his instructions to the police*'.[4] But the prosecutor who loses his case because of police misconduct is not a police official; he can rarely set in motion corrective action or administrative penalties; and in any case he does not have control or direction over police procedures or police actions that result in the exclusion of evidence. How then will a policeman be deterred by a judicial ruling on suppression of evidence 'which never affects him personally, and of which he learns, if at all, long after he has forgotten the details of the particular episode which occasioned suppression?'[5] A second argument why the rule is no deterrent is that it only applies when evidence is obtained and it is sought to have it admitted against the defendant. But much law enforcement activity is carried on without any expectation that it will lead to prosecution and conviction, and there are large areas of police activity well outside the possible range of any exclusionary doctrines.[6] The deterrent impact of the rule is therefore said to be sharply diluted. A third, and more convincing, argument against a strict exclusionary rule is that arguments of deterrence are only plausible if the police know before embarking on a particular search whether it is legal or not. This of course is often the case. But such is the complexity of the substantive law of search and seizure that in many cases the police believe that they are complying with the law when in fact they are not. Further, not only do many judicial opinions lack clarity, but also police officers will usually

[1] *United States v. Janis*, 428 U.S. 433, 458 n. 25 (1976); see also *United States v. Peltier*, 422 U.S. at 538; and *Stone v. Powell*, 428 U.S. 465, 485–6. Another strong argument against the 'judicial integrity' rationale is that 'no such rule is observed in other common law jurisdictions such as England and Canada, whose courts are otherwise regarded as models of judicial decorum and fairness': Oaks, supra, at 669.

[2] See Wright, supra, 356 n. 2, at 740–1; and see the dissenting opinion of Burger, C.J. in *Bivens v. Six Unknown Fed. Narcotics Agents*, 403 U.S. 388, 411 (1971).

[3] See his *Bivens* dissent, supra, at 416.

[4] This was stated by the dissenters in *Wolf v. Colorado*, supra, at 44.

[5] Burger, 'Who will Watch the Watchman?', 14 *Amer. U. L. Rev.* 1, 11 (1964).

[6] See *Terry v. Ohio*, 392 U.S. 1, 14 (1968); Wright, supra, at 740; and Burger, C.J.'s *Bivens* dissent, at 417–18.

react to the many situations they are confronted with not by attempting to remember what elaborate interpretations of the Fourth Amendment say they should do but by taking what action they think is necessary, which a narrow majority of judges may then declare unconstitutional because of what is at most a technicality.[1] Often, in other words, the police will do what they think will solve the immediate problem before them without worrying very much about questions of admissibility. Some of these arguments are weaker than others. They certainly do not establish that the exclusionary rule is a total failure as a deterrent, nor that it does not (or cannot) have any appreciable impact upon police practices. Thus there is no good reason either why prosecutors and police officers should be regarded as totally independent functionaries or why effective channels of communication and co-operative arrangements should not be set up between them. Nor does the inherent inapplicability of the exclusionary rule in certain areas mean that the rule should not apply elsewhere, for instance where the main purpose of the type of police action in issue is to obtain evidence of wrongdoing for subsequent use, whether in judicial or other proceedings or as a link in a chain leading to other evidence. And the difficulty of following some particularly obscure decisions does not mean that clearer judicial pronouncements should be either ignored or misunderstood.

Whatever the exact deterrent impact of the doctrine of suppression developed in *Weeks* and *Mapp*—and this as we have seen cannot be determined because of the lack of reliable empirical evidence—there is little doubt both that the effect of the exclusionary rule is a drastic one, resulting in the loss of much probative evidence and in the release of many guilty criminals, and that the cost it inevitably entails is particularly difficult to justify in cases where exclusion will advance neither judicial integrity nor deterrence, for instance where there is no question of intentional illegality or where the law officers involved had made every possible effort to comply with what they reasonably thought to be the law. This last feature of the strict American exclusionary rule—namely its inflexible, mechanical and universal application whenever there is *any* violation of the Fourth Amendment—has provoked the most adverse criticism. The strict exclusionary rule was characterised by Chief Justice Burger[2] as a pernicious doctrine because it was based on the view that all official violations of the Fourth Amendment must be treated by way of the same 'drastic judicial response', whether the misconduct in issue consisted of a deliberate and flagrant *Irvine*-type violation or of an honest and inadvertent error of judgment; this in his view was untenable; vastly dissimilar cases should not be treated as if they were the same; and society had the right to expect rationally graded responses from judges related to 'gravity and need' instead of exactly the same inflexible response to widely varying degrees of police misconduct that was the essence of the modern American doctrine of suppression. Similarly, Justice White in

[1] See Wright, supra, 740–1; Burger, C.J.'s *Bivens* dissent, supra, at 417; and *Stone v. Powell*, 428 U.S. 465, 538–42 (1976), per White, J.

[2] See his *Bivens* dissent, at 418–20, and his concurring opinion in *Stone v. Powell*, supra, at 496–502.

Stone v. Powell[1] has pointed out that when law enforcement officers acted mistakenly, but in good faith and on reasonable grounds, and yet the evidence they seized was later excluded, the exclusion could have no deterrent effect. The officers were likely to act in similar fashion in similar circumstances in the future, and the only consequence of the rule as administered was that unimpeachable and probative evidence would be kept from the trier of fact, with the inevitable result that the process of discovering the truth would be substantially impaired.

On the basis of this widespread dissatisfaction with the current model of the exclusionary rule a number of proposals have been put forward about how it should be modified. Three of the most prominent suggestions for change are the following. The first was put forward by Chief Justice Burger in *Bivens v. Six Unknown Fed. Narcotics Agents*.[2] In his view the suppression doctrine was both harmful for law enforcement and ineffective as a deterrent. It was therefore desirable that it should be abandoned *if* some 'meaningful alternative' could be developed. His recommendation was that the appropriate legislative body should develop 'an administrative or quasi-judicial remedy against the government itself to afford compensation and restitution' for persons whose Fourth Amendment rights had been violated. A statute might thus be enacted, based on the following elements: (a) a waiver of sovereign immunity as to the illegal acts of law enforcement officials committed in the performance of assigned duties; (b) the creation of a cause of action for damages sustained by any person aggrieved by conduct of governmental agents in violation of the Fourth Amendment or statutes regulating official conduct; (c) the creation of a tribunal, quasi-judicial in nature, to adjudicate upon all claims under the statute; (d) a provision that this statutory remedy was in lieu of the exclusion of evidence secured for use in criminal cases in violation of the Fourth Amendment; and (e) a provision directing that no evidence, otherwise admissible, should be excluded from any criminal proceeding because of a violation of the Fourth Amendment. As soon as such a statute was adopted, the Chief Justice concluded, the exclusionary rule should be abandoned because there would then be an effective remedy for the enforcement of the Fourth Amendment that both deterred unlawful governmental conduct and did not result in the frustration of the criminal process.[3] A different view is that the exclusionary rule should not be totally abandoned but only limited, and that this should be done now by judicial action. Its chief exponent is Justice White.[4] For him, as we have seen, the objectionable feature of absolute exclusion is that it results in the suppression of evidence in cases where there can be no realistic expectation that exclusion will contribute in the slightest to the purposes of the rule. He therefore expressed readiness to join four or more other members of the Court in significantly curtailing the reach and operation of the exclusionary rule as administered under the Fourth Amendment in federal and state criminal

[1] 428 U.S. 465, 536–42.
[2] Supra, at 422–4.
[3] For criticism of this, see La Fave, supra, at 32–4.
[4] See his opinion in *Stone v. Powell*. supra.

trials alike. His proposal was that the rule should be 'substantially modified' so that it would no longer apply in those 'many' circumstances where the evidence in issue was seized by an officer acting in the good-faith belief that his conduct complied with existing law and where there were reasonable grounds for this belief. A final proposal is that put forward by the American Law Institute.[1] This envisages a flexible approach to the exclusion of evidence because of illegality in the method by which it was obtained. It provides that a motion to suppress evidence shall be granted only if the court finds that the violation upon which it is based was 'substantial'. It then goes on to provide that 'all the circumstances' will be considered in determining whether the violation was substantial, including the following criteria: (a) the importance of the particular interest violated; (b) the extent of the deviation from lawful conduct; (c) the extent to which privacy was invaded; (d) the extent to which the violation was wilful; (e) the extent to which exclusion would tend to prevent future violations; and (f) whether, but for the violation, the things seized would have been discovered.[2]

But despite these proposals for reform and continuing dissatisfaction with its operation the exclusionary rule continues to exist in its current strict and inflexible form.

[1] See their *Model Code of Pre-Arraignment Procedure* § SS 290.2(4).

[2] For criticism of proposals aiming to restrict the exclusionary rule to 'substantial' violations, see La Fave, supra, 34–7; the dissent of Brennan, J. in *United States v. Peltier*, 422 U.S. 531 (1975); and Kaplan, 'The Limits of the Exclusionary Rule', 26 *Stan. L. Rev.* 1027, 1044–5 (1974).

8. Concluding Comments

Two things stand out from our study of Anglo-American doctrines of search and seizure. The first is their similarities. These are due partly to common historical origins, principally the 'general warrant' cases, and to the use of similar concepts and terminology that have been part of the common law tradition as early as Hale, especially the ideas that in general searches and seizures should not take place at the discretion of executive officers but only after the authorisation of independent magistrates, that such authorisation should only be given after there has been evidence of criminal complicity and of the location at the place to be searched of criminal evidence, and that executive power to search and seize should also be limited by stringent requirements of specificity regarding what is to be looked for and seized. The similarity of the two systems is also due to the similarity of the functions they must perform and of the questions and issues they must settle. Thus every system of search and seizure law must try to balance the same two interests—that of the right of the citizen not to be subjected to unjustified invasions of his privacy and security and that of the community to take adequate measures for the detection of crime and the apprehension of criminals. Further, this task must be done at the same two levels—that of substantive protection and that of enforcement. In similar fashion, as we have seen, the questions which systems of search and seizure must attempt to settle are fundamentally the same. Has there been a search? Is it legal? If it is illegal, what remedy or sanction should be made available? Nor are the common questions confined to the issues of what the law is or of how it should be enforced. Similar perplexities relating to jurisdiction and adjudication abound. In response to new problems, such as modern technological advances, should the courts develop search and seizure safeguards creatively and aggressively, or should they only engage in interstitial legal development, relying on legislation, in a common law regime, or the process of amendment, under a constitutional system? To what extent should established patterns of authority be regarded as controlling, and what measure of freedom should the judiciary enjoy either in bringing about new formulations by the synthesis of existing doctrines or with regard to the outright creation of new decisional premises with no visible support in past precedents? To what extent should 'contemporary norms'[1] or perceived social needs intrude into the process of judicial decision?

The second thing one notices is the sharp divergences between the developed jurisprudence of the Fourth Amendment on the one hand and common law doctrines on the other. These are due to two principal

[1] *Payton v. New York*, 100 S.Ct. 1371, 1382 (1980), per Stevens, J.

factors—first to the fact that the American system is constitutional and secondly to differences in the procedural forum in the context of which decisions on search and seizure are made. The first is obviously the most important. At common law the law of search and seizure must be extracted from the cacophonous multiplicity of numerous statutory provisions and from a few narrow judicial holdings, noted neither for their rigorous reasoning nor for their internal consistency and more often than not creating more difficulties than they solve. In contrast, by the adoption of the Fourth Amendment the law of search and seizure is elevated from the category of 'general' law to the status of impregnable constitutional doctrine. The two principal effects of this are first that the right that is recognised is made superior to any repugnant legislation or other official action, which will thus be declared invalid, and secondly that there is a temptation (as strict constructionists would call it) or a need (as activists would describe it) to look upon what is granted not as a specific and more or less narrow entitlement but as a fundamental and broadly based right of affirmative thrust whose scope transcends the events and experiences originally giving rise to its enactment and whose emanations are capable of reaching what most would not regard as naturally falling within the ordinary textual meaning of the conferring instrument. This attitude stands in sharp contrast to the essentially negative approach of the common law tradition premised on the theory that what is not forbidden is permitted,[1] or, to put it differently, that freedoms, including 'rights' to security and privacy, are residual, which means that the content of protected liberty can only be defined by subtracting from its totality the sum of the legal restraints to which at any particular time it is subject.[2] In this sense the right to be free from searches and seizures at common law means the right to be free from those intrusions that under the law government officials are not allowed to make, those intrusions, that is, which they are forbidden by law, whether common law or statutory, to make. In so far as the law confers upon officials the power to enter private premises or otherwise to encroach upon privacy and security the relevant rights are diminished to a commensurate extent by the power thereby given. A third effect of the admission of a right to the constitutional sanctum—perhaps only the consequence of the joint operation of the first two—is the effect it normally has on adjudication. Thus the judiciary that is entrusted with the protection of a fundamental constitutional right will often find itself engaged not in the task of interpretation, however positive or adventurous, but in nothing less than the immeasurably more difficult and unmistakably legislative tasks of the elaboration of its so-called implications over many diverse fields and the gradual building on its basis of an ultimately complex body of law, at one end premised on a few broad and general principles deriving from the constitutional text or its historical background but at the other crystallising into considerable and at times intricate detail. In particular, activities which in a common law regime will almost always be left to legislation, and which it would be unthinkable to regulate by judicial

[1] See *Malone v. M.P.C.* (No. 2) (1979) 2 All E.R. 620.

[2] S.A. Smith, *Constitutional and Administrative Law* 452 (1973).

action, whether because of the complexity of the matters in issue or because of traditional views concerning the relative jurisdictional ambits of courts and the more accountable political organs, invariably find themselves in a constitutional setting—particularly the American one—being evaluated under constitutional clauses embodying what here too used to be 'limited' and 'weak' common law rights, in this instance the constitutional provision extending protection from unreasonable searches and seizures. These features of constitutional adjudication have been noticed in our treatment of the Fourth Amendment.

The second important factor, distinct from the constitutional nature of the rules in the American jurisdiction, why the jurisprudence of the Fourth Amendment is so much more developed is the procedural forum in which issues of search and seizure law fall to be considered. At common law the question of the legality of an arrest, search or seizure typically arises either in a civil action for trespass or false imprisonment or in an action for assault or a criminal prosecution, usually depending upon whether a police officer was at the relevant time acting in the execution of his duty.[1] Not only are such actions relatively rare; they do not constitute a suitable forum for the orderly development of principles regarding the legality of searches and seizures, either because what they focus on is the availability of a tort remedy rather than the extent of a person's immunity from unlawful governmental action or because the issue of an unlawful search or other exertion of governmental authority is a matter that is regarded as subsidiary to others, for example the delineation of the officer's duty. In contrast, in America search and seizure issues invariably arise in the course of considering whether to apply the exclusionary rule. Since the exclusionary rule demands the suppression of evidence obtained in violation of the Fourth Amendment, the meaning of the constitutional guarantee presents itself and must be dealt with directly. The exclusionary rule, in other words, provides a suitable (and unified) occasion for judicial review,[2] in obvious contrast to the fragmented state of the common law. It does not of course follow that the right to be secure from unlawful search and seizure can only be developed if something akin to the exclusionary rule is adopted. But what is essential is that there should be a suitable venue that both makes available a convenient and direct procedure for the systematic review of alleged violations of the rights at stake and which provides adequate remedies and sanctions in the event of their proven disregard.

In the light of these general comments we can now turn to a final survey of the three principal issues to which the Anglo-American law of search and seizure has addressed itself.

The chief difference between Fourth Amendment law and common law doctrines relates to the concept of a 'search', or, to put it differently, to the interest that will receive protection by way of the safeguards from illegal searches and seizures. The common law remains anchored to property considerations and concepts. There is only a search if there has been a

[1] *Payton v. New York*, 100 S.Ct. 1371, 1383 (1980), per Stevens, J.

[2] Oaks, 37 *U. Chi.L.Rev.* 665, 756 (1970).

trespass. This means not that the object of the law of search and seizure is to protect property rather than privacy and security, but that rights to privacy and security will only be protected by way of the warrant requirement or any other safeguards that have been adopted or developed to shield from unlawful search and seizure if property interests have been invaded. It is of course very different in America. Under Katz protection from unlawful searches and seizures is limited neither by the trespass doctrine nor by the more generous concept of constitutionally protected areas, but extends to reasonable expectations of privacy. The results of this are that under the Fourth Amendment interests in privacy and security will receive protection even when they are independent from and unattended by interests in property; that a constitutionally cognisable interest in privacy can attach to intangibles, such as conversations; and that the individual is entitled in a proper case to receive Fourth Amendment protection even though at the material time he is not in a place traditionally viewed as private, such as his home or office, but in a public area, an area, that is, that is generally accessible to the public. How should *Katz* and its privacy analysis be interpreted and evaluated? The first point to notice is that the approach of *Katz* is geared to the protection of a particular type of privacy, that of control over information. In this sense its break with the past is perfectly understandable. As early as *Entick v. Carrington* itself the law was concerned not only with physical entry but also with the appropriation of secrets and the invasion of the individual's exclusive intellectual domain.[1] But at that time and when the Fourth Amendment was adopted, since the only kinds of invasion of security that both the common law judges of the general warrant cases and the framers of the Fourth Amendment were concerned about were physical intrusions of homes and other premises and the seizure of persons and tangible things, it is hardly surprising that it was automatically assumed that protection of property relationships was sufficient to protect privacy and security as well. Now, however, property rights and the right to privacy, again in the sense of the claim of individuals and others to determine for themselves when and to what extent restricted information about them is communicated to others, diverge significantly; interests in privacy and types of control over information generally regarded as vitally important in contemporary democratic society and which therefore most would wish to protect are embodied in legal situations and relationships other than ownership, physical possession and occupation, control, or the like; and therefore if rights to personal security and individual privacy, as early as *Boyd* declared to be the main values the Fourth Amendment is intended to preserve, are to receive meaningful protection, constitutional doctrines extending immunity from unlawful search and seizure must reach beyond property interests and physical intrusions, whether these take the form of entries into protected places or the seizure of tangible objects. At the same time any broadly-based

[1] Lord Camden referred to the individual's house being 'rifled', to 'his most valuable secrets' being taken 'out of his possession', and to the fear that 'the secret cabinets and bureaus of every subject in this kingdom will be thrown open to the search and inspection of a messenger': 19 How. St. Tr. at 1063–4.

test severed from property concepts, whether it is 'justifiable reliance on privacy' or 'reasonable expectations of privacy' or any similar one, suffers from serious defects which cannot be concealed beneath liberal rhetoric. Whatever its shortcomings, the trespass doctrine (and to a lesser extent the doctrine emerging from the judicial holdings and pronouncements with regard to constitutionally protected areas) was a clear one, indicating with much certainty to police officer and citizen alike the limits and extent both of the government's power to investigate without having to resort to the warrant process and of the citizen's right to the undisturbed enjoyment of his privacy and security. In contrast, the *Katz* criterion of 'reasonable expectations of privacy', particularly if it is viewed in an undifferentiated and holistic manner and as totally displacing less ambitious doctrines geared to property and protected areas, is set at a very high level of abstraction and consequently suffers from much ambiguity and lack of clarity. This in turn has three principal results. It produces confusing and unprincipled case law, ultimately depending on the judges' perception of the importance of the particular privacy interest at stake when weighed against the needs of law enforcement; as the particular judges' values and priorities vary, so will the scope of the Fourth Amendment expand and contract accordingly.[1] A second result of broad and amorphous tests such as legitimate expectations of privacy is that the task of law enforcement agencies becomes so much more difficult; most investigative activities impinge on the individual's and on society's collective sense of security, and therefore, on the basis of *Katz*, become candidates for judicial control through the warrant requirement; if *Katz* and its language are extended to their logical limit, much essential law enforcement activity will become impossible, and both the warrant requirement and the concept of probable cause will be stretched to breaking point; conversely, if it is sought to give a more limited and manageable meaning to the concept of expectations of privacy or the doctrine that governmental practices that encroach on security should be judicially controlled, for instance by interposing an epithet like 'significant' before governmental 'invasion' or 'encroachment' or by determining both the *applicability* and the *application* of the Fourth Amendment by the method of explicitly balancing in each case any sense of personal or societal insecurity resulting from governmental activities as against the requirements of law enforcement,[2] even greater uncertainty and confusion are likely to follow. Thirdly, it may well be that another consequence of *Katz* will be a diminution of Fourth Amendment protection, not only because expectations of privacy are vulnerable to the dangers of governmental manipulation but also because it often happens that the broader the base and expanse of a particular right, and the less precise its

[1] See Dutile, 'Some Observations on the Supreme Court's Use of Property Concepts in Resolving Fourth Amendment Problems,' 21 *Cath. U.L. Rev.* 1 (1971); 'Note, Government Access to Bank Records', 83 *Yale L.J.* 1439 (1974) (hereinafter referred to as 'Note'); 'Note, A Reconsideration of the *Katz* Expectation of Privacy Test', 76 *Mich.L.Rev.* 154 (1977).

[2] See, e.g., *South Dakota v. Opperman,* 428 U.S. 364, 377 -8 (1976), per Powell, J. concurring.

positive content, the more difficult it may prove to protect it efficaciously. 'Must not one know his right — and the extent of that right — to appreciate and enjoy it fully?'[1] As some commentators have put it, one result of the equation (which *Katz* arguably brings about) of one's right to security in the home with that when using the phone in a public telephone booth is not only a strengthening of the latter but also a considerable weakening of the former.[2]

What follows from all this is that rights to privacy and security, whether under the Fourth Amendment or elsewhere, can best be protected not by indeterminate tests based on concepts as vague and as difficult to comprehend or apply as privacy or its legitimate expectations, nor by way of the individualised resolution of search and seizure issues in terms of the ad hoc weighing of the governmental and societal interests advanced to justify a challenged intrusion against the allegedly endangered interest of the citizen in the privacy of his person, his property or the information he seeks to maintain private, but by means of a more precise analysis and the elaboration of a more limited 'framework of principle'.[3] Can *Katz* and its analysis be made to yield such a framework? There are a number of possibilities, all of which figure to some extent in cases decided after *Katz*. The usual judicial answer, following Justice Harlan's concurring opinion in *Katz*, is to subdivide the question of whether a person has a cognisable expectation of privacy into two issues, first whether a person exhibited an actual expectation of privacy and secondly whether this expectation is one which the judiciary should protect by the application of the Fourth Amendment, either because of its social importance or because of the part it plays in society's scheme of values. A similar formulation would divide the *Katz* inquiry into two questions. Has the individual claiming Fourth Amendment protection manifested as a matter of fact adequate control over the information he seeks to keep private, and secondly, assuming a positive answer to the first question, should such control over information be recognised as one that is sufficiently important to deserve protection in terms of the guarantee from unlawful search and seizure?[4] The two criteria are closely related in as much as actual control over information — particularly when the focus is not upon the particular claimant but upon those similarly situated to him, not upon the control over the information in issue actually exercised by the specific individual but upon the incidence of informational control in cases of the type before the court — is on many occasions related to current social practices and habits, themselves often referable to the success many have had in asserting a privacy interest in similar circumstances.[5] But, functionally, they are different. The first, as currently interpreted, seeks to exclude from the parameters of constitutional protection not only instances where there has been a failure to take suitable precautions to preserve privacy but also cases where the claimant has taken

[1] Dutile, supra, 365 n. 1, at 11.
[2] See T. Taylor, *Two Studies in Constitutional Interpretation* 114 (1969); 'Note', 76 *Mich. L. Rev.* 154, 175 (1977).
[3] See Dutile, supra.
[4] 'Note' supra, 365 n. 1, at 1462.
[5] Ibid.

what the court regards as an unwarranted risk, for instance where he has passed secrets or confidences to a fellow wrongdoer, as in the informer cases, or where the information he seeks to protect has been either kept or voluntarily conveyed by him to others in circumstances presenting the risk of its exposure, in which event again constitutional protection will be denied, as in *Miller*[1] and *Smith v. Maryland*.[2] In contrast, the second part of the *Katz* test is openly prescriptive—should either the control over information which the individual claims or the challenged investigative practice in question be brought within the Fourth Amendment because any other holding would endanger the basic values the Amendment seeks to protect, principally security, privacy, autonomy?[3] Not surprisingly, the presence of so pronounced a normative element makes these bifurcated versions of the *Katz-White* analysis as subject to confusion, uncertainty and variability of judicial interpretation, with all the dangers to which these can lead, as the even more general 'justifiable reliance' and 'expectations of privacy' approaches.

A more viable model is to read *Katz* more restrictively. This takes the position that the 'expectations of privacy' approach has not displaced constitutional standards relating to protected areas but only supplemented them. This view[4] can be set out as follows. What *Katz* has done is not to eliminate property considerations from Fourth Amendment adjudication, but rather to abandon the notion that constitutional protection can only be invoked when what is claimed can be expressed in terms of property concepts; the notion of constitutionally protected areas retains independent significance so that the *Katz* privacy approach and its reasonable expectations test should only be employed when Fourth Amendment protection cannot be based on traditional pre-1967 analysis geared either to property rights or to protected places; and the principal result of the continuing relevance of property criteria is that an analysis phrased in terms of privacy only becomes necessary in cases where there is neither a physical intrusion into a protected area, for instance the physical penetration of a home or office, nor the violation of a tangible property interest, such as the seizure of tangible items.[5] But where Fourth Amendment protection cannot be grounded in some traditionally accepted property interest, the *Katz-White* approach becomes necessary, and the question then becomes, first whether a congnisable privacy interest (in the sense of the retention of control over otherwise restricted information) exists, and secondly whether the governmental conduct in question has intruded upon it to an extent that should bring into operation the principle that investigative practices that significantly jeopardise individuals' (and society's) sense of security should not be permitted solely at the discretion of law-

[1] 425 U.S. 435 (1976).

[2] 99 S.Ct. 2577 (1979).

[3] See both plurality opinion of White, J. and the dissenting opinion of Harlan, J. in *United States v. White*, 401 U.S. 745 (1971).

[4] See Dutile, supra, 365 n. 1; 'Note', supra, 365 n. 1; 'Note', 76 *Mich. L. Rev.* 154, 172–5 (1977).

[5] See 'Note, Beepers, Privacy, and the Fourth Amendment', 86 *Yale L.J.* 1461, 1479 (1977).

enforcement officers. It is possible of course to say that property interests are only protected in so far as they are reflected or crystallise in expectations of privacy, but this is to abandon the relative comfort and manageability of a specific and familiar concept in favour of a large and amorphous one. Further, to proclaim the irrelevance of property and to assert that the reasonable expectations test has totally absorbed the protected areas one is to move dangerously close to the view that even as regards a traditionally protected place, such as a home or office, an expectation of privacy is only *prima facie* reasonable and that it can be displaced by certain types of evidence normally considered with regard to the attribution of legitimate expectations of privacy where a property rights analysis cannot be invoked, for instance that the complainant had not at the time exhibited a sufficiently active control over information or that he had not taken precautions to forestall observation or surveillance. In contrast, to say that the Fourth Amendment protects property as well as privacy, or at least that expectations of privacy emanating from property concepts are legitimate in the fullest sense and as such automatically entitled to Fourth Amendment protection, is not only to give traditionally protected areas the recognition they surely deserve (and greater protection than they would get under a holistic reasonable expectations of privacy approach) but also to adopt an analysis that over a large area of search and seizure law provides surer guidance to police and citizens alike, that is the guidance that derives from traditional concepts of property law, than what could possibly be extracted or manufactured from the nebulous and abstract directives of *Katz* and its progeny.[1] *Katz*, therefore, should be looked at not as totally reconstructing the boundaries of the Fourth Amendment but as extending protection in cases where none existed before.[2]

There is greater similarity between constitutional and common law doctrines when one moves from the question of whether a search or seizure has taken place to the issue of the legality of acknowledged searches and seizures. Naturally the jurisprudence of the Fourth Amendment is characterised by much greater consistency, in that it revolves round a few central ideas derivable from a single text, and comprehensiveness, in that these central ideas are formulated in a way that allows them to encompass any situation that may arise, in obvious contrast to common law patterns based on the one hand on a great multiplicity and variety of statutory schemes and on the other on a few (and not always well reasoned) judicial decisions which, at most, settle specific problems (and this, occasionally, in a very inconclusive manner) and, not surprisingly, fail to elaborate principles of 'general' applicability based on an explicit weighing of the conflicting governmental and individual interests at stake. The central criteria for adjudging the legality of admitted searches and seizures both under the Fourth Amendment and (less obviously) under the common law are the warrant requirement and the concept of probable cause. It has been investigated above in what

[1] See the analysis in *Rakas v. Illinois*, 439 U.S. 128, 143 n.12.

[2] On this general subject, see Weinreb, 'Generalities of the Fourth Amendment', 42 *U. Chi. L. Rev.* 47, 53–4 (1974).

circumstances either or both may be departed from. As regards the warrant requirement, this is based on the notion that freedom from unlawful search is best secured through prior judicial control intended both to establish whether a search is justified at all and to demarcate the limits of authorised intrusions. Is this assumption justified? It naturally depends upon the thoroughness with which judicial officers scrutinise requests for search warrants, and there is much evidence that the practical effectiveness, as a control device, of the warrant requirement is overstated.[1] Empirical studies in America suggest that arrest and search warrants are issued without serious consideration of whether probable cause exists, and in England it is apparently only very rarely that an application for a search warrant will be refused. How can practice be made to conform more closely to theory? Three points can be made. The first is that the process of advance judicial authorisation can only be made more effective by improving the quality of the lower judiciary on whom the task of issuing search warrants usually devolves and, more importantly, by asking the police themselves to adopt suitable internal regulations that provide them with guidance about when to apply for a warrant. The second point to make is that there is no surer way of subverting the warrant process than by extending it to excessive and unwarranted lengths. The most obvious result of an all-pervasive warrant system is that warrants will be issued routinely and without any investigation of the grounds on which applications are made; instead, it may well be that as a practical matter the best way of strengthening the warrant process is by using it selectively and with discrimination, in other words by confining it to those areas where unsupervised police investigative practices would be most destructive of the values underlying Anglo-American doctrines of search and seizure. Thus, it is unquestionable that it is the individual's home that must receive the greatest measure of protection under the law of search and seizure; hence the justifiability of insisting that any search or seizure carried out on an individual's premises without a warrant is unreasonable unless the police can show that it falls within one of a few narrowly defined exceptions based on the presence of 'exigent circumstances'. In contrast, the interest in privacy is not so compelling when what is in issue is not the physical entry of a home but the seizure of personalty; in other words, in the case of the seizure of certain personal items not located on private premises it may be that the interests in privacy and security can adequately be safeguarded even if the demand for prior judicial authorisation is replaced by a prompt ex post facto hearing aimed at assessing the existence of probable cause,[2] particularly if other safeguards of a more institutional nature providing protection from systematic abuse of power or discrimination are also adopted. The third point is a more general one.[3] Police search and seizure practices cannot be controlled satisfactorily through the warrant process even in those areas where a warrant is normally required. For even though the need to go before a magistrate with some evidence may well

[1] See La Fave, 'Warrantless Searches and the Supreme Court: Further Ventures Into the "Quagmire" ', 8 *Crim. L. Bull.* 9, 27–30.

[2] Ibid., at 28.

[3] See Hartley and Griffith, *Government and Law* 151–2 (1975).

discourage wholly unjustifiable applications, the fact is that the structure of the warrant procedure and the place it occupies in the overall scheme of the adversary process make it impossible for the magistrate to probe deeply into the grounds the officer has brought before him as justifying a requested search. What is vitally important is not only to maintain control of police action in *individual cases*, but also to keep a check on *general patterns* of police searches and seizures in order to make sure that police powers are not systematically abused, either in general or with regard to the harassment of vulnerable groups, such as racial minorities. This need can best be met by the development of a mechanism whereby all police searches, whether conducted under warrants or not, are recorded with sufficient detail to enable a subsequent independent authority to ascertain whether the particular action was justified or not.[1] If it is found either that a substantial number of searches turn out to be groundless or that a disproportionate number of them were of premises in the control of members of minority groups, then police guidelines should be changed.

Even more fundamental than the warrant requirement is the concept of probable cause. Here too there has been constant tension between on the one hand the claims of conceptual purity, expressed by insistence that the notion of probable cause is a constant one, always demanding a uniform amount of evidence, and on the other the need to bring within the purview of the Amendment types of investigative activity that cannot be fitted within traditional concepts of probable cause. Not unexpectedly, here too there has been a compromise between doctrinally opposed views. At least three main types of probable cause have been distinguished. The first is conventional probable cause, demanding that a search should only proceed if it can be shown that the sought items are, first, seizable by virtue of being connected with criminal activity and, secondly, to be found at the place to be searched. A second standard is the one applied in *Terry*, requiring that the facts available to the officer at the moment of the seizure (the investigative stop) or the search (the frisk) should warrant a man of reasonable caution in the belief that the action taken was appropriate.[2] In common with other seminal Fourth Amendment cases, it is possible to approach *Terry* in two fundamentally different ways. One is to read it as representing and exemplifying a broad theory towards the Fourth Amendment that views balancing of individual rights against governmental interests as both inevitable and desirable. On this view searches, seizures, and lesser intrusions are justified if in all the circumstances the action taken was appropriate. In all cases the need to search should be balanced against the invasion which the search entails, and the question is whether on the totality of the facts of a particular situation the right to personal security has been violated by an unreasonable search and seizure.[3] This reading is essentially a return to

[1] Ibid., at 152.

[2] 392 U.S. 1, 21–2 (1968).

[3] This is a view that has often been expressed by White, J.; see particularly his opinions in *Camara v. Municipal Court*, 387 U.S. 523, 534–5 (1967) (majority opinion) and in *Almeida-Sanchez v. United States*, 93 S.Ct. 2535, 2547 (1973) (dissenting opinion).

the overall reasonableness standard of *Rabinowitz*, this time not with regard to the issue of whether a warrant should have been obtained but with regard to the meaning of probable cause. On this view of *Terry* 'the governing standard under the Fourth Amendment is reasonableness',[1] and this is flexible enough to authorise searches and other intrusions that are necessary, necessity being measured either by sufficient statistical probability indicating that the particular person or place subjected to the challenged governmental action may be a legitimate target or by the compelling nature of the governmental interest at stake coupled with the unavailability of other similarly effective methods of enforcement. The other view of *Terry* is more limited. On this, the *Terry* standard represents a modified version of probable cause, not fundamentally different from it. The reason it *appears* so different is that it addresses itself to a type of situation where, unlike the typical case of a search aimed at the discovery of criminal evidence, there is no primary crime. The intrusion is made for the purpose of deterrence and self-protection, not for detection. Since the 'facts' that must be proved vary so too do the kinds of evidence that must be adduced in support.[2] But *Terry* action is only legitimate if there are reasonable grounds for believing that criminal conduct has taken or is taking place and that the person stopped and searched *is* himself dangerous. Nothing in *Terry* therefore supports dispensing with the need to point to articulable and objective facts the result of which is to focus suspicion on the particular individual. The case law, as we have seen, supports this second reading. But that the Fourth Amendment can occasionally be satisfied in the absence of individualised suspicion is shown by *Camara* and similar cases, and these represent a third type of probable cause, fundamentally different to both the *Carroll*[3] and *Terry* standards. This, on certain occasions, detects 'a constitutionally adequate equivalent of probable cause'[4] in the satisfaction of general governmental standards which are adjudged to be reasonable with respect to the type of official activity in question. This approach, it is clear, will only be resorted to in areas where the governmental interests to be advanced clearly outweigh the constitutionally protected interests of the citizen and where the other circumstances surrounding the intrusion in question are such that they substantially minimise its adverse impact.[5] In the final analysis one's approach to probable cause, its *Terry* offshoot, and its other functional equivalents will be determined not only by the *degree* of protection one wants to extend to the individual but also by the *way* one wishes to strike the elusive balance between the public interest and the individual's right to security from arbitrary official interference. Should the necessary accommodations be channelled through doctrinally confined categories, or should the balancing process be conducted in a more openended manner, for instance simply under the aegis of what the

[1] *Almeida-Sanchez v. United States*, 93 S.Ct. 2535, 2547 (1973), per White, J. dissenting.

[2] 'The Supreme Court, 1967 Term', 82 *Harv. L. Rev.* 63, 184 (1968).

[3] 267 U.S. 132 (1925).

[4] *Almeida-Sanchez v. United States*, 93 S.Ct. 2535, 2543 (1973), per Powell, J. concurring.

[5] See *United States v. Martinez-Fuerte*, 428 U.S. 543, 558.

public interest demands? We have seen what the answer of American law is. Even though there is widespread recognition that in practice degrees of probability cannot rigidly be fixed[1] and that the variables that must be fed into the applicable equation, whether that of probable cause or of reasonable suspicion or of overall reasonableness, are bound to differ widely from case to case,[2] it has been regarded as much preferable, indeed as essential, in terms not only of developing a coherent body of law but also of extending adequate protection to Fourth Amendment rights, to accommodate conflicting public and private interests not by ad hoc balancing or by returning to standards of overall reasonableness but by the recognition and principled development of a small number of settled categories and by the consequent organisation both of existing legal materials and of any new situations that may arise at a number of broadly based but yet clearly definable, distinct and separable levels. It has been regarded as particularly important that the *Camara* standard or any other test capable of satisfaction by less than the minimum quantum of individualised suspicion should be confined to certain routine situations, in particular those where the governmental need is great and the intrusion on Fourth Amendment interests limited, and where in addition there are factors that provide security from the unregulated exercise of governmental discretion.[3]

Even beyond the more systematic treatment to which basic concepts like the warrant requirement, probable cause and specificity requirements have been subjected, immeasurably greater doctrinal coherence and more orderly organisation of the materials have been achieved under the Fourth Amendment than at common law. The basic reason is that the whole of search and seizure law developed under its auspices, both that regulated by search warrants and the remainder where the legality of a search depends upon other circumstances, is held together by a few principles, which both synthesise past results and help guide future development. These principles are in truth but the distillation of the fusion between the concept of probable cause and the venerable common law doctrine that general exploratory searches are unlawful. But they have now assumed a significance of their own, divorced from the concepts to which they owe their origin. The most prominent of these connecting themes have repeatedly been identified. The first is the making of a distinction between the (initially) permissible scope of a search and what may legitimately be seized during its course, i.e. adoption of the 'plain view' doctrine. The way this has been formulated, namely that only inadvertent discoveries made in the course of an otherwise appropriately limited search may be seized, seems to reconcile in a sensible manner both the need to ensure that the police do not engage in fishing expeditions in a speculative search of evidence of crime and the legitimate demands of law enforcement, more particularly that the police should not needlessly endanger relevant evidence in order to satisfy the warrant requirement when

[1] See *United States v. Lopez*, 328 F. Supp. 1077 (1971).

[2] Player, 'Warrantless Searches and Seizures,' 5 *Geo.L.Rev.* 269, 277 (1971).

[3] See *Delaware v. Prouse*, 99 S.Ct. 1391 (1979); *United States v. Martinez-Fuerte*, 428 U.S. 543; *Pennsylvania v. Mimms*, 434 U.S. 106.

in the circumstances its observance cannot be other than a cumbersome formality. The other two principles are even more fundamental. They relate not to what can excuse a presumptively unlawful seizure but to what validates a search in the first place, and are facets of the same idea. The first is that there must be reasons justifying the initiation of any search or seizure. This normally means that every police intrusion must be justified by way of an individualised inquiry into the particular facts of the case in issue; but in certain contexts, as we have seen, minor intrusions necessitated by compelling governmental interests need not be justified with this level of particularity, provided that the governmental scheme under which the challenged intrusion took place is operated in circumstances affording an adequate measure of regularity, fairness and protection from discrimination to the individual target.[1] The second principle is the 'scope limitation' one, namely that the scope of a search should be determined by the reasons and circumstances justifying its initiation. This means that one must first determine the exact basis of an authority to search. Is it based on considerations of safety, on the need to preserve evidence, or on other governmental objectives? Once the legitimate goals of a species of permissible search are settled, the question is whether the scope of a particular search remained faithfully tied to their effectuation. If it does not there has been an excessive intrusion. At times the logical thrust of this second principle is blunted by the countervailing force of other considerations, for instance considerations of public safety or that it will be asking too much of the police to insist that they should tailor all their reactions to the particular demands of each situation and never take automatic and routine action. Good examples are the legality of a full search of the person incident to a valid arrest recognised in *Robinson*[2] and the permissibility of certain minor intrusions not strictly necessitated by the perceived facts of the situation but justified by the weight of compelling governmental concerns, as in *Mimms*.[3] Another factor, already touched upon in a number of contexts, that is influential, whether consciously or unconsciously, with both the formulation and application of these principles relates to the more effective method of safeguarding Fourth Amendment rights. Is it by an individualised inquiry into the facts of each case or by the adoption of broad rules that guide the police officer, limit his discretion and in this way afford greater protection to the right *of the people* to be free from unwarranted governmental intrusion? On one view the central teaching of Fourth Amendment jurisprudence is that each particular intrusion, however minor, must be capable of justification in terms of the specific and articulable facts surrounding it. On another view, in certain situations, determined by a definitional balancing of the governmental interest at stake as against the degree of intrusion involved, it is legitimate to formulate a general rule allowing automatic police action. On this view not only should accumulated experience and common sense be allowed to crystallise in standardised

[1] See *Pennsylvania v. Mimms,* 434 U.S. 106, at 121, per Stevens, J. dissenting; *United States v. Martinez-Fuerte*, 428 U.S. 543; *South Dakota v. Opperman*, 428 U.S. 364; *United States v. Biswell*, 406 U.S. 311.

[2] 414 U.S. 218 (1973).

[3] 434 U.S. 106.

guidelines and procedures permitting instinctive action for the protection of the officer and others, but it is from reliance on the uninstructed individual judgment of each officer in the field that the greatest threat to Fourth Amendment freedoms flows. In contrast, adoption of and obedience to carefully prescribed standard procedures provide security from harassment and discrimination, inform the citizen of his rights, and simplify the reviewing task of the judiciary.[1] The tension between these two perspectives is apparent in a number of areas. *Terry* exemplifies the former, *Robinson* and *Mimms* the latter. What is clear is that a middle course must be steered. To allow wholesale invasions of privacy simply because police regulations known to both citizen and officer so provide would be intolerable. Equally, to define either the exceptions to the warrant requirement or any other Fourth Amendment principles with minute sophistication rather than common sense clarity, and to make the applicable rules dependent on the presence or absence of numerous factors and considerations that must be resolved first by the officer in the field and then by a judge on review, is to perform a disservice not only to law enforcement but to the guarantee from arbitrary search as well.

On the basis of our survey of these principles and themes, a broad comment can be made about the process of judicial development. Some of the principles unifying the jurisprudence of the Fourth Amendment have been elaborated not by bold judicial declaration, but in a typically experimental and tentative common law fashion. A proposition or a theme is sketched out in a particular context; something similar is floated in another context; a parallel idea is canvassed in yet a third situation. On further reflection the three ideas are seen to share a common rationale, to be based on essentially the same considerations, or even perhaps to be manifestations or fragments of the same broad theme, itself arrived at, or rationalised after the event, by balancing the individual and governmental interests at stake. A judicial decision will finally recognise this, and will propound a 'new' broad principle that is now declared to be applicable over the whole of search and seizure law. A good example is again the 'plain view' doctrine.[2] This seems to be first recognised when the search is conducted under a search warrant. It is thus accepted that when the police have a warrant to search a given area for specified objects and in the course of the search come across some other incriminating article they may seize that too. It is then recognised that a similar result should also be reached when the intrusion that brings the police within plain view of an incriminating article was not authorised by a prior warrant but took place under one of the exceptions to the warrant requirement, for instance the 'hot pursuit' of a fleeing suspect. It is also accepted that an object that comes into view during an otherwise lawful arrest-based search is also subject to seizure, and that a police officer can similarly seize an inadvertently discovered incriminating item even when he

[1] See the excellent dissenting judgment of Wilkey J. in *United States v. Robinson*, 471 F.2d 1082, 1112–5 (1972).

[2] This whole development is analysed by Stewart J. in *Coolidge v. New Hampshire*, 403 U.S. 433, 465–9.

was not searching for criminal evidence but was only performing some administrative task. All these situations are finally seen to share certain important characteristics. In each the police had a good justification for being where they were when they came across the evidence. The presence of a warrant is therefore irrelevant except in so far as it makes the intrusion legitimate. And in all the discovery was inadvertent, thus satisfying those who fear that the legality of the seizure of unauthorised articles may usher in exploratory searches. The time is therefore ripe for the formulation of a 'new' doctrine, that authorising the seizure of things in 'plain view', and this is done in *Coolidge*. There is nothing exclusively 'constitutional' about this process. Indeed it has been suggested above that we may be witnessing a similar development in English law. Hints of a 'plain view' doctrine have emerged in a number of contexts, and it may not be long before search and seizure are firmly distinguished and the taking of incriminating articles accidentally discovered in the course of an otherwise legitimate search is permitted whether or not the initial entry or search had been authorised by a warrant and irrespective of whether there was any connection between the discovered item and either the person in possession or the crime under investigation. In terms of adjudication then the main difference between the common law and the body of law deriving from the Fourth Amendment lies not in the presence or absence of an inherent capacity for growth or in whether the law, whether constitutional or common law, can or should meet new needs or combat new evils, but in the much greater ability of constitutional law both to absorb currently prevalent ideas about how much security and privacy individuals should be given and to respond to new problems. Thus the Fourth Amendment, mainly because it is constitutional law but also because it is phrased so ambiguously and because it has come down with the aura of one of those guarantees that were uppermost in the minds of the framers, has in general evolved 'in (the) light of contemporary norms and conditions',[1] in short in terms of the judiciary's view of what a free and democratic society requires. The dangers in so sweeping an analysis have been noticed and discussed. In contrast, the common law has had to evolve in the very different regime of numerous different statutory schemes punctuated by sporadic decisions from contexts that are hardly conducive either to fruitful generalisation or to the development of principles that balance in a satisfactory manner the claims of liberty against the demands of law enforcement. The result is a most unsatisfactory body of law which makes it difficult for the police to do their job and on many occasions impossible for the citizen to know his 'rights'.[2]

Ultimately, the basic problem with the law of search and seizure, especially the Fourth Amendment, and the reason why neither logic nor systematic analysis can bring total coherence to it, is that the main doctrinal categories, that is the definition of a search, the warrant requirement and the concept of probable cause, interact in strange ways. In one sense they complement one another. It is only if there is a search that there will be constitutional

[1] See *Payton v. New York*, 100 S.Ct. 1371, 1382–3 (1980), per Stevens J.

[2] Hartley and Griffith, *Government and Law* 151 (1975).

protection. It is only if there is probable cause that there can be a warrant.[1] But in other ways these categories intersect in less harmonious ways. The more one expands one category the more the pressure increases on the others, and the more one tries to accommodate different types of case within one category the more one weakens central concepts traditionally regarded as essential components of the Anglo-American system of search and seizure. We have seen many examples of this. The broader the definition of a search the more difficult it will be to insist on the traditional doctrine that searches should be accompanied by warrants. Even more importantly, whether one broadens the definition of 'search' or extends the need for a warrant the greater the pressure one will bring to bear on the notion of probable cause, perhaps the most basic of search and seizure concepts. There is no easy way out. At one extreme there is the danger that insistence on traditional purity—that all searches barring extreme emergencies must be preceded by the usual type of warrant and that all searches must be based on probable cause in the sense of a uniform amount of information concerning either the location of incriminating evidence at a particular place or some other 'fact'—will result in much potentially dangerous investigative activity being totally immunised from all judicial control. At the other extreme, to cast the net too widely, to join without reservation the bandwagon of privacy, or indeed to rely too much on the Fourth Amendment, will be *either* to abandon or, worse, to trivialise the warrant requirement, revert to a *Rabinowitz* type of formula based on overall reasonableness, and convert probable cause into a malleable and frail test that will have to be stretched so thinly in order to encompass all the variables that one will have to balance—ranging from the degree of intrusion to the seriousness of the governmental interest at stake—that it will no longer afford meaningful protection: *or* to frustrate legitimate law enforcement; *or* to make inevitable much disregard of the law by the police and other official agencies. The jurisprudence of the Fourth Amendment, in its totality, seems to have survived these tensions reasonably well; and in common with so much of American constitutional law, the concepts on which it is based, as well as the main decisional rubrics by which it is currently channelled, are ultimately so vague, so easy to modify and so vulnerable to changing views, whether in society at large or among the judiciary, that the perception of fresh problems and the awareness of new needs are bound to bring new accommodations and fresh solutions.

But whatever these accommodations or solutions may be at any given time, they will always have to be enforced; and, surprisingly for systems normally priding themselves on their pragmatic orientation and their emphasis on remedies, it is in the remedial field that both American and English law have miserably failed. The remedial response to the illegal gathering of evidence has oscillated between two extremes. At the one end, a violation of search and seizure safeguards can take place with virtual impunity, there being little doubt that conventional remedies and sanctions have proved totally ineffective either in penalising police irregularities or in affording adequate

[1] But there can be special warrants: see *Camara v. Municipal Court*, 387 U.S. 523 (1967).

compensation to the victims of illegal searches. At the other, the absolute suppression doctrine observed in America has striking defects.[1] As administered, it neither protects nor compensates the victims of police illegality and does not punish either the particular offending official or the police in general but rather seeks to further the (factual) goal of deterrence and the (normative) one of preventing the contamination of the judicial process in an extraordinary manner, that is by acquitting the guilty, by doing close to nothing to protect innocent persons who are the victims of illegal but fruitless searches, and ultimately by punishing the public 'by unloosing criminal(s) in their midst'.[2] It is indeed startling that in a futile and vain effort 'to deter the police both the guilty defendant and the law-breaking officer (should) go unpunished'.[3] It is therefore thought that since the price the exclusion of improperly obtained relevant evidence exacts from society is clear, not to say overwhelming, and since on a rigorous analysis of the matter apart from sentimentalism and rhetoric its cost can be justified neither by normative considerations nor by factual arguments concerning its deterrent effect, exclusionary doctrines, whether total and absolute, as in America, or qualified and provisional, as in Scotland and Australia, should be abandoned in favour of a reinstatement of orthodox classical doctrine, namely the admission of all relevant evidence, however obtained.[4]

But another thing is equally clear. There is an urgent need for some remedy that will provide meaningful protection to the victims of illegal searches and that will discourage official misconduct by making disregard of the rules costly. Without some effective remedy protection from illegal searches and seizures will amount to very little.[5] There have been many suggestions, but the most promising appears to be the development of a tort remedy along the lines suggested by Chief Justice Burger in *Bivens*,[6] namely an action for damages based on the following features: first, the action should lie not against the particular police officer but against the police department or other governmental authority that employs him; secondly, the cause of action should arise not because there has been some ordinary tort, for instance trespass, but because there has been illegal police conduct;[7] thirdly, provision should be made for substantial damages, for instance by expressly stating that the measure of damages should be related not only to the loss or injury sustained by the aggrieved party, as normal principles of tort liability would basically have it, but also to the nature of the official misconduct in

[1] See generally 'Oaks, Studying the Exclusionary Rule in Search and Seizure', 37 *U. Chi. L. Rev.* 665 (1970).

[2] 8 Wigmore, *Evidence* § 2184, at 51–2 (McNaughton ed. 1961).

[3] Paulsen, 'The Exclusionary Rule and Misconduct by the Police', 52 *J. Crim. L., C. & P.S.* 255, 256 (1961).

[4] See the dissent of Burger, C.J. in *Bivens v. Six Unknown Fed. Narcotics Agents,* 403 U.S. 388, 411–27 (1971).

[5] See Burger C.J. in *Bivens*, supra, at 415; and Oaks, supra, at 756.

[6] At 422–4; see also 'Comment, The Tort Alternative to the Exclusionary Rule', 63 *J. Crim. L. C. & P.S.* 256 (1972).

[7] This will allow courts to develop the law of search and seizure, something they cannot easily do if they have to operate within the conceptually narrow and sterile context of the action for trespass.

issue; and fourthly, special tribunals, whose constitution would guarantee satisfactory enforcement however unworthy the particular plaintiff, should be created to adjudicate upon such claims.

But as yet no effective remedy in tort or any other meaningful sanction to provide compensation and penalise illegal searches has been developed, and it does not appear as if one will be adopted in the foreseeable future. What should be done? Should jurisdictions with exclusionary doctrines retain them until some satisfactory substitute is introduced, or should the judiciary abandon them *in order* to put pressure on legislative organs to proceed to much-needed reform? And should jurisdictions without a recognised doctrine of excluding evidence adopt some version of exclusion, however glaring its theoretical deficiencies and however severe its practical cost, as the only means both for *developing* and for *vindicating* substantive and procedural safeguards from unlawful search and seizure? The problem is complex, and answers to it will depend not only on one's perception of the merits and demerits of the exclusionary rule itself but also on one's view of the proper jurisdictional ambits of legislative and judicial organs respectively.[1]

At the moment, as matters stand—particularly in view of the total lack of any appropriate remedy to effectuate search and seizure safeguards—the realistic choice in terms of a tolerable (if not wholly supportable) doctrine of improperly obtained evidence would appear to be between the orthodoxy of the Canadian model where evidence can only be rejected because it is flawed and not because of the way it was obtained,[2] and the 'balancing of interests' approach of the Scottish, Irish and Australian courts. Both have merits and demerits. The chief advantages of the Canadian model are its evidential purity, its certainty, the fact that it does not cause the acquittal of the guilty, and the fact that judges are not burdened, in this context, with the invidious task of disciplining the police, undoubtedly an essential duty but one that equally obviously is best discharged otherwise than by manipulating and distorting the law of evidence. Its main shortcomings are that the premise on which it partly rests, namely that those whose rights have been adversely affected by illegal searches can seek appropriate remedies elsewhere, is patently false; and that in consequence a rigid policy of admissiblity, as well as occasionally encouraging the police to break the law *if* they feel that important evidence may result, poses a very real threat that the protection in theory extended by the law of search and seizure may in practice become a dead letter.[3] The basic strengths of the balancing approach of the Scottish and Australian tribunals are said to be its flexibility, its adaptability to the varied and widely differing circumstances of each case, and its awareness of the necessary part judges must *in practice* perform— given the absence of other alternatives—both in protecting and rendering meaningful 'the citizen's precious right to immunity from arbitrary and unlawful intrusion'[4] and in

[1] See *Bivens*, supra.

[2] It should be noted that the tort remedy appears to be working well in Canada; see Oaks, supra, at 701–6.

[3] Heydon, 'Current Trends in Evidence', 8 *Syd. L. Rev.* 305, 326 (1977).

[4] *Bunning v. Cross*, 19 A.L.R. 641, 659.

deterring unlawful police practices. Its principal weaknesses, apart from the fact that it will inevitably result in many guilty criminals being set free, are its pronounced subjectivity which will unavoidably lead to confusion and uncertainty, the fact that its adoption will result in judges weighing broad questions of public policy far removed from the familiar and judicially manageable task of assessing the relevance of evidence, and its likely tendency to retard the development and introduction of an efficient remedy, on the lines of the tort action set out above, that both 'penalises' the police and affords adequate compensation to victims of illegal searches without bringing about the release of obviously guilty persons, something that as much as anything brings the administration of justice into disrepute.[1]

[1] Paulsen, supra, 377 n. 3.

Table of Cases

Index